Ultimate Guide to Law Schools

Third Edition

Anne McGrath and the Staff of U.S.News & World Report

Robert Morse, Director of Data Research

Brian Kelly, Series Editor

SOURCEBOOKS, INC.®
NAPERVILLE, ILLINOIS

Table of Contents

Introduction

So you want to be a lawyer.

Are you sure?

It's no idle question, given the impact choosing law will have on your life. Before walking away from three years of income (and head-on into a $100,000-plus commitment), you'd better figure out whether the reality of legal practice jibes with your vision of what your day-to-day experience will be. Many applicants, attracted by eye-popping salaries and the drama of shows such as *Law and Order*, are "woefully uninformed about what the practice of law is like," says Deborah Post, a professor at Touro College's law school in Huntington, New York, and former co-chair of the committee on admissions for the Society of American Law Teachers. Much too often, they "stumble into the law because they don't know how to find a job," says Michael Young, former dean of the George Washington University Law School in Washington, D.C., and now president of the University of Utah. "If you love it, you'll have a great life. But do you really want to spend 10 to 14 hours a day thinking about the stuff of law? If not, it might be an acceptable living, but you won't necessarily be happy."

Indeed, several studies suggest that attorneys are among the *least* happy people. A 1990 analysis of data on 104 different occupations by researchers at Johns Hopkins University, for example, found that lawyers were 3.6 times as likely as the general working population to suffer from major depression. University of Pennsylvania psychologist Martin Seligman, in his book *Authentic Happiness*,

---

"If you love law, you'll have a great life."

---

suggests three reasons: attorneys are primed to constantly anticipate "every conceivable snare and catastrophe that might occur in any transaction"; young lawyers, in particular, often hold high-pressure jobs in which they have little voice or power to make decisions; and these days lawyering often seems more about making money and crushing opponents than offering wise counsel and finding justice.

"There's been a huge change over the last 20 years," says David Stern, an attorney and head of Equal Justice Works, a Washington, D.C. advocacy group that promotes public interest law. "It's no longer a profession—it's a business. The number one priority is profits-per-partner." That's undoubtedly a major reason for the incessant lawyer jokes you'll put up with. A 2002 survey conducted for the American Bar Association found that about 70 percent of Americans think of lawyers as "greedy and manipulative," and only 19 percent have confidence in them. (Full disclosure: of the 10 professions and institutions covered in the survey, only the media inspires less confidence.)

Obviously, these conditions don't define every lawyer's job, and some attorneys thrive on the intrigue and competition. Moreover, graduates whose motivation is a strong commitment to social justice have plenty of opportunities to find work in public service, perhaps with the government, or maybe (more lucratively) through pro bono work for a law firm. The point is simply that you need to make this choice with both eyes open.

Those who *do* end up with a fancy paycheck—the median first-year salary at large firms is now $135,000 plus bonuses— are apt to work into the wee hours, researching case law and statutes, and then drafting memos for the partners (who are doing the interesting work). Partnership, the carrot dangled seven or eight years down the line that confers a share of the firm (and even more money), comes less easily than it once did, as the ranks of young associates have swelled and as firms have created alternative salaried partnership tracks. According to John Heinz and Robert Nelson, Northwestern professors who have studied the changing career paths of Chicago attorneys for the American Bar Foundation, only 16 percent of lawyers surveyed in 1995 who had started out at a large law firm had made full partner at the firm and stayed, compared with 35 percent in 1975, for example.

And the fact is that many lawyers end up in small or solo practices, making ends meet by taking on debt collections work or acting as public defenders. When the time comes, students who had planned a career in public interest law often find they can't pay off their debts and buy groceries on a $40,000-a-year salary—and so they end up at a big firm after all.

How can you tell if you're among those who truly belong in law school—whether the "stuff of the law," in Young's words, really "lights you up"? He advises prospective attorneys to first expose themselves to legal ideas, if not by taking an undergraduate course in law, then by talking to lawyers and following newspaper coverage of legislation and the courts. Can't make it to the end of a *New York Times* article about a Supreme Court decision without yawning? Take that as a sign.

Tom Arthur, former dean and now professor at Emory University's law school, suggests that anybody considering law first answer these questions:

Am I truly interested in public issues?

You'd better be, because you'll be working on them; typically, the law is the vehicle by which society's knotty issues are resolved. "The environment went from a movement to statutes," says Arthur.

Do I *really* like to read and write?

If not, be prepared to suffer. "Cases, decisions, statutes, regulations—we read all the time," says Arthur. And write: "It's always, 'When can we have a draft?'"

Do I get stage fright?

Even if you never take part in a trial, a big part of your job will entail presenting your argument cogently and credibly to partners, clients, and opposing counsel, all of whom will be judging you—and some of whom will be hostile.

How good am I with details?

Partners don't tolerate mistakes. Nor do clients.

Miss a filing deadline, and you might be guilty of malpractice.

Can I separate my feelings from the facts?

Whatever your own personal value system is telling you, you'll have to step back and analyze every situation rationally and objectively, and then act in your client's best interest—which may not be where your heart is.

"Law is no longer a profession—it's a business. The number one priority is profits-per-partner."

Am I someone people can turn to for help?

There's a reason lawyers are called "counselors." If listening and empathizing and patiently advising confused people isn't part of your skill set, you might belong somewhere else.

Do I have good judgment?

Clients who assume you do will be trusting you—and paying you—to make the right decisions about what strategies they ought to follow and how much risk they ought to take to get the desired result.

● ● ●

Even if the answers to these questions point you directly to law school, consider testing your certainty by taking some time off. "I tell everybody to work for a couple years," says David Van Zandt, dean of the law school at Northwestern University in Illinois, which has adopted a policy of preferring work experience. "We feel much better about students after they've grown some, and are giving up a job and a salary," says Van Zandt. "I run into far too many 50-year-olds who were performance-oriented [in college] and got on the track seeing law school as a place where they could be rewarded. Then down the road they wake up and say 'Why did I get on the track so fast?'"

Once you've studied the evidence and decided law school is indeed for you, this book will help you get there. The first chapter, "Choosing the Right School," sorts through all the factors you'll

"I think anyone who applies to both Cornell and NYU hasn't got a clue what they're doing."

need to consider: reputation, curriculum, faculty, placement services, location, and cost, among others. As those who attend the country's most elite institutions will find themselves in demand for great jobs pretty much anywhere in the country, Chapter 2 takes you inside the law schools at Yale, Harvard, Stanford, Columbia, and New York University, which regularly top the annual *U.S. News* rankings. Chapter 3 describes the attributes top schools—which have their pick of hundreds, even thousands, of qualified applicants—look for beyond grades and LSAT scores in those they accept. In Chapter 4, you'll find out how to prepare for the LSAT and put together an outstanding application; Chapter 5 advises you on how to pay for it all. Finally, in Chapter 6, you'll read about getting that first job—and where the great opportunities are these days.

The tables that begin on page 73 allow you to compare law schools on a number of attributes key to your decision. Among them: which programs are the toughest and easiest to get into (page 75); which schools hand out the most generous financial aid (page 91); which ones leave their students with the heaviest and lightest debt loads (page 95); and which have the most success at placing graduates—and at producing new lawyers who can pass the bar exam on the first try (pages 103).

Finally, at the back of the book, you'll find detailed profiles of law schools accredited by the American Bar Association. The profiles, which are based on a comprehensive survey that *U.S. News* sends out to law schools each year, contain the most up-to-date information on everything from the academic credentials of students to programs of study and joint-degree options to the availability of financial aid and the sorts of jobs graduates land. Study it. And then go visit. Law schools are much less alike than you might think. Says Seattle-based admissions consultant Loretta DeLoggio: "I think anyone who applies to both Cornell and NYU hasn't got a clue what they're doing." This guide will clue you in.

Chapter One

Choosing the Right Law School

For many would-be attorneys, the process of picking a law school requires the coolest of calculations: apply to the most elite five or six schools within reach and enroll at the best one you can. All of those considerations that mattered so much in comparing undergraduate colleges—looking for the best campus culture, the place where you felt you fit in—get hardly a moment's thought. "I saw the choice as utilitarian—what doors will open for me for the rest of my life?—rather than as a question of how happy I'd be for the next three years," says Kimberly Parker, Harvard Law class of 1996 and now an attorney for the big corporate firm WilmerHale in Washington, D.C. "You just cannot overestimate the importance the prestige of the degree has for your life." She speaks not only as someone for whom doors have opened, but as an attorney who has recruited young lawyers to her firm.

It's undeniable that in a profession as pedigree-conscious and tradition-bound as law, the name on your diploma will have enormous influence on the trajectory of your career. "If you have a choice between a top 15 or a second-tier school, you're *crazy* not to go to the top school—the opportunities are so much better," says David Van Zandt, law dean at Northwestern University in Illinois. Graduates of the

---

"You just cannot overestimate the importance the prestige of the degree has for your life."

---

world-class institutions that sit atop the *U.S. News* rankings year after year (see table, page 14) are wooed by the most prestigious law firms, offered plum judicial clerkships, plucked for the most visible slots in government and public service, and granted entrée to ultraselective academic jobs. Degrees from these schools hold currency in every corner of the country, and they put alumni on a national stage: these are the people working on Supreme Court cases and merging the AOLs and Time Warners, while somebody else handles the contract dispute between the local restaurant and its supplier. Says Parker: "If you want to practice on the national level, being at a top 10 or top 20 school matters *a lot*."

Anybody following that most ambitious path thus starts off with a readymade short list: Yale, Harvard, Stanford, Columbia, New York University, Chicago, and the 15 or so other truly name-brand, national institutions. What if your aspirations or LSAT scores don't point you toward the top? The quality and stature of school you choose will still be very important to your career success and your geographic flexibility—as will an exceptional performance there.

"Recruiters won't come in the same numbers," admits Patricia Adamski, former vice dean of the law school at Hofstra University in New York and now an administrator for the university. "But the top of Hofstra's class gets offers that meet those at the middle of Harvard's." Generally, she says, students who are in the top 5 or 10 people of their class at good but not name-brand law schools, or even the top 10 percent, can expect to find themselves in demand.

Below the top ranks, other factors besides a school's overall reputation may influence your chances for success. Someone who's bent on getting a public interest job, for example, should know that many cash-strapped nonprofit agencies are especially interested in graduates of law schools that offer students lots of hands-on experience working with Legal Aid clients, for example, because the agencies just don't have the budget to train beginners. Applicants contemplating a career in politics might be wise to opt for the law school at their state university. "You've got to be elected from somewhere," says Andrew Coats, dean of the University of Oklahoma College of Law. The people you meet in a law school like Oklahoma's—your class plus the two ahead of you and the two behind you—will hold many of the state's positions of power in business, law, and government when you're running for office, and they'll probably help a fellow grad regardless of their own political leanings, says Coats. He graduated from the law school himself in 1963 and has been a district attorney for Oklahoma County, a Democratic nominee from the state for the U.S. Senate, and the mayor of Oklahoma City.

For the same reason—a strong alumni network—those who are certain that they want to settle and practice in a given area of the country might want to pick a fine regional law school in that area rather than a more highly ranked law school elsewhere. Still, most say, if you can make it in the top 20, go for it.

No matter how high you're aiming, law deans, undergraduate pre-law advisors, and independent admissions consultants agree (as does *U.S. News*) that a decision about which school is the best one for you should never hang on its position in a numerical ranking alone. Though law schools may look much the same on paper—a standard first-year courseload, upper-level electives and clinics, lots of library time—comparable schools can have vastly different characters and areas of strength. There's large and impersonal, there's small and collegial, there's merely competitive, and there's "don't leave your notes around," says Stuart Rabinowitz, former dean of Hofstra's law school and now the university's president. Some schools emphasize legal theory (in an ideal system, how should the law work?); others emphasize actual practice (how the law works in reality).

So the experts suggest a more nuanced approach to thinking about quality: find the most excellent *cluster* of schools that you can get into, and within the cluster, pick the school whose character and culture and curricular strengths suit you best. "There might be 15 to 30 schools for any one candidate," says Katharine Bartlett, dean of the law school at Duke University. And within a cluster, your career opportunities are apt to be very similar. So, says George Washington University's former law dean Michael Young, you can afford to think, "Am I interested in

things international? I might pick G.W. over Northwestern. Am I interested in policy formation through an economic perspective? Yale or Chicago." An applicant intrigued by the "countercultural view of the law" might pick Georgetown, says Young.

"Someone who is thinking of Yale, which is very small and 'all for one, one for all' might be very unhappy at Harvard, a big school of very com-

> *"If you have a choice between a top 15 or a second-tier school, you're crazy not to go to the top school."*

petitive, very motivated, Type A people," says Mark Meyerrose, a former Harvard Law admissions officer who now advises law school applicants for AdmissionsConsultants, Inc. (www.admissions consultants.com), an independent Virginia-based counseling firm that helps clients get into college and graduate school. (The vast majority of law schools in the country—though not all—have been accredited by the American Bar Association, which means that they've met standards for legal education set by the profession. In many states, a lawyer who holds a JD from a nonapproved school is not eligible to sit for the bar exam.)

The *U.S. News* rankings—which measure schools by several yardsticks, including expert opinion of their programs, test scores and grades of students, placement record, and bar passage rate—are not intended to drive a decision between numbers three and four or five. But the rankings can help you identify your cluster. ("The difference between the [school] that ranks 4th or 7th and the one that ranks 34th or 37th? Let's not kid ourselves," says Saul Levmore, law dean at the No. 7 University of Chicago.) Then, as you narrow the field in search of the right fit, a number of key questions are worth thinking about.

How big is the student body—and the typical class?

Harvard is home to some 1,700 students; Yale, to just under 600. George Washington University boasts some 1,600 full- and part-timers. Boalt Hall, the law school at the University of California–Berkeley, has a total enrollment of just under 900; Duke, about 650. Considering that all these numbers are pretty small compared to undergraduate colleges, why should you care? Because the size of the student body and the entering class affects law schools' personalities, the availability of professors outside of class, the extent to which you'll engage with your classmates, and, most likely, the breadth of the curriculum.

"You know everyone, and it didn't feel like we had to fight against each other," says Joe Lemon, a 2002 graduate of Stanford Law who went to work for a high-tech law firm in Menlo Park, California. "We formed study groups, shared notes, talked, created tests for each other." Stanford, one of the country's smaller law schools with some 550 students, has a first-year class of about 170. On the other hand, the roster of different classes offered after the first year may by necessity be much more limited at a small school. (For a peek inside Stanford, Harvard, and the other law schools at the very top of the newest *U.S. News* ranking, see Chapter 2 on page 15.)

The size of the first-year sections at the school you pick—the standard classes in civil procedure, constitutional law, torts, and criminal law—is apt to have a big impact on the quality of your experience. Many schools have focused recently on bringing section size down and on putting stu-

dents in one small seminar their first year. At Harvard, "the resources are amazing and the professors are top-notch, but it was hard to get personal attention," recalls 1996 grad Parker. Until just a few years ago, Harvard's first-year sections numbered 140 students each. Responding to criticism that the school felt too cold and impersonal, the administration has since trimmed sections to about 80, a fairly typical size among law schools. At G.W., where sections average 85 to 90 students, first-years now take at least one of their classes in a small section of 36.

At the University of Oklahoma, Dean Coats has shrunk the size of the entering class from about 225 to under 170 over the past few years, and has created four first-year sections of only 40 to 44; for instruction on legal research and writing, the class is divided into eight sections of about 20 students each. Partly as a result, the number of applicants to the school has more than doubled since 1998, and the median LSAT score and grade point average have moved higher, from 152 to 156 and from 3.28 to 3.54.

You'll also want to find out how many students will be in most of the second- and third-year classes, advises David Cohen, former dean of law at Pace University in White Plains, New York. A reasonable range would be 20 to 30, he says. A related piece of data, the student–faculty ratio, offers another clue about faculty accessibility and what the chances are that your professors will actually get to know you. At most of the top schools, the ratio is somewhere around 10 to 1 or 15 to 1. At Yale, there's a professor for every 7.4 students.

What to look for in a part-time program

Is the part-time path a route for you? "How flexible is your work schedule? Do you need to be on call or take work home with you? Law school will require every other minute of your life," warns Loretta DeLoggio, an admissions consultant based in Seattle (www.deloggio.com) who specializes in helping minority students choose a school and get in. This is because you'll have no flexibility in how long you take to earn your degree; part-time means a-little-bit-less-than-full-time for four years instead of three.

Many would-be lawyers have no choice: it's their day-job salary that will pay for night school. The advantages of a full-time program—the generally much greater availability of externships, the extensive interaction with other students outside of class through study groups and extracurricular activities—don't outweigh the need for an income. Fortunately, a number of good schools offer evening programs;

you'll find detailed information about them in the directory entries at the back of this book. As you compare programs, here are the questions you should ask:

Who are the teachers? Ideally, they'll be the same people teaching the day students. At Georgetown, which was founded in 1870 as an evening program, part-timers are taught weekday evenings by members of the regular full-time faculty, and they're held to the same academic standards.

Are admissions yardsticks different for evening students? If the LSAT scores and grade point averages of students accepted into the part-time program are significantly lower than those of the day students, you might qualify for a law school that wouldn't otherwise take you. On the other hand, the level of discourse might be lower, too.

Will you get any hands-on experience? Many clinics are impossible to hold at night because the courts are closed, but there should be experiential learning going on. Look for simulation courses that involve role-playing or clinics that don't rely on courtroom experiences. Evening students at Pace often participate in securities arbitration and disability rights clinics, for example.

Will you get the same services as full-time students? Find out whether you'll have the same access as day students to career services programs, the financial aid office, the registrar, and the school's information-technology and library resources. What about student organizations? All opportunities afforded by the school should be available.

What does the school's location offer?

You'll care about location for a couple of reasons—okay, maybe three. ("It's beautiful all the time!" says Lemon of Stanford's relentlessly sunny weather.)

For starters, educational and externship opportunities may vary considerably according to where a law

---

"If you think you want to practice in Milwaukee, you might better go to Marquette than DePaul."

---

school is situated. For example, Georgetown Law Center students, whose classes meet a mere 10-minute walk from the Supreme Court, sometimes get a chance to work on Supreme Court cases. Students at the Washington, D.C., law schools also have access to externships at a whole list of federal government agencies, while those at the University of California–Los Angeles can take courses in sports and entertainment law and find externships at television and movie studios. In Grand Forks, University of North Dakota students help Native American tribal governments develop environmental programs and offer legal assistance to the Spirit Lake Tribal Court.

Secondly, bear in mind that if you're not a candidate for a national school, your future job opportunities will certainly be shaped by where you choose to enroll. The connections students make through externships or local pro bono work often lead to the permanent offers, and a school's alumni network is apt to be much stronger in its immediate region than elsewhere. "If you think you want to practice in Milwaukee, you might better go to Marquette than DePaul," says Tom Arthur, former law dean at Emory. "If you go to

Suffolk Law School, you'll be really well placed to practice in Boston and New England, but it'll take you five or 10 years of practice to establish yourself and make the leap to San Francisco," warns admissions consultant Meyerrose.

What's the culture like?

The size of the school will tell you something about its climate, but to really get a handle on the campus culture—how intense and competitive students are, for example, or how committed to social justice or to high-paying corporate law—you're going to have to visit. Even though only a tiny fraction of law schools interview applicants, most are only too happy to entertain visitors. "We want students to figure out if this is a place that will work for them," says Hannah Arterian, dean of the College of Law at Syracuse University, which regularly hosts formal programs for prospective students that start with a group meeting with her and include breakfast, a first-year class, an introduction to the career services office, a workshop on financial planning, lunch with faculty members, and tours of the law school, Syracuse's campus, and campus housing. "Not only do prospective students get an opportunity to check out our environment, we get a chance to see how they might fit in a culture that puts a high premium on maturity and interpersonal skills," says Van Zandt of Northwestern, the only major law school that tries to interview every applicant.

Sarah Russell Vollbrecht, a native of Oklahoma and a 2003 graduate of the University of Virginia's law school, applied only to institutions ranked among the *U.S. News* top 10 in the hope that her degree would take her anywhere in the country. (It worked: she graduated into a job clerking for a judge on the U.S. Court of Appeals for the 5th Circuit in Houston, after which she planned to work for a Dallas law firm.) At the outset, she expected to enroll at the most highly ranked institution that accepted her. Once she'd visited several campuses, however, she realized that distinctions in academic excellence were small, and other qualities mattered more to her than place in the pecking order.

"Duke and UVA were very similar—their facilities were impressive, the campuses were pretty, and the students were *really* friendly; they smiled and were eager to assist me," says Vollbrecht. "At Harvard it felt like everybody was rushing to do what they needed to do. Chicago might have been a better school academically than UVA, but the students seemed a lot more serious—I studied hard at Virginia, but also made time for softball." Accepted by Duke, Chicago, New York University, and UVA, Vollbrecht narrowed her picks to Duke and UVA, then made the "easy choice." She'd lived in Virginia and qualified for in-state tuition, so UVA was the cheapest by far.

"You need to talk to students—they're verbal and critical by nature," advises David Leebron, former dean of Columbia Law School and now president of Rice University. One good reason to quiz students in person (beyond seeking the inside dope about the place) is to gauge their capabilities and interests— and, by extension, the likely capabilities and interests of the people you'd be learning with next year. "I firmly believe that what makes a law school is the student body," says Robert Berring, a professor and former interim dean at Berkeley's Boalt Hall, whose students he describes as a "politically awake and less formal" bunch. "This isn't the same as the college

decision," says Leebron, who advises applicants to consider whether their classmates would challenge and excite them. "It's about making career choices. This is the most important group of people you will know for the rest of your life."

Check into how diverse the student population is, too—not just in terms of ethnic background, but also in work experience, education, age, gender,

> ## "You need to talk to students—they're verbal and critical by nature."

and socioeconomic background. "Much of the learning happens between students, and the more perspectives you have, the richer the discussion will be," says Evan Caminker, dean and professor of law at the University of Michigan, whose methods of factoring minority status into the admissions decision won the Supreme Court's approval (for more on the Michigan decision, see page 49). "Part of being a lawyer is seeing through others' eyes. Your clients—what's motivating them? The judge— where is he coming from?" When Leebron was at Columbia, he found the school's relatively large population of Mormons and Orthodox Jews and generally rich religious mix to be a selling point: "One of my Torts students [was] a priest—what an interesting perspective!"

What are the strengths of the curriculum?

Yes, the first-year coursework will be pretty standard wherever you go, but step back and take a look at the big picture. What are the hallmarks of the schools you're considering?

Chicago is known for its academic rigor, its examination of the law through an economics filter, and its conservative viewpoint. Boalt Hall is among the most liberal schools. Yale students, who can revel in their intellectual pursuits without obsessing over grades (they either pass with honors, pass, low pass, or fail), are steeped in the theory and philosophy of the law and not in the nuts and bolts of practice. Northwestern and Duke have made a priority of transitioning students into practice by stressing teamwork and collaboration on group projects. Georgetown is noted for its large and strong program of legal clinics in which students learn by practicing with real clients. The City University of New York is devoted to public service.

As you dig more deeply into the specifics, it's important to consider the breadth and diversity of schools' second- and third-year curricula because most students who think they've settled on a practice area before they arrive change their mind. "Law school is a transforming experience—and that's true here and at the University of Baltimore night school," says Chicago's Levmore, who advises against choosing a school based solely on its areas of specialization.

On the other hand, in what is clearly an age of specialization, most law schools *do* now have areas of strength. Each year, in addition to the general ranking of law schools, *U.S. News* also ranks specialty programs based on the opinions of faculty who teach in the field; Vermont Law School regularly gets top billing for environmental law, for example, and NYU is highly ranked for international and tax law.

"It used to be that the top schools were trying to be great in everything, but now we're setting strategic priorities," says Duke's Bartlett. Her school, for example, has paid particular attention

to developing four of its programs: intellectual property, telecommunications law, health and biotech law, and international and comparative law. Syracuse boasts five "centers" (in family law; indigenous law; global law; law and business enterprise; and law, technology, and management) and has launched an institute that focuses on national security. Students who complete a concentration of coursework in one of the centers receive a certificate. The University of Pittsburgh offers several certificates, including civil litigation, environmental law, and health law; the University of Missouri–Columbia offers dispute resolution, tax, European Union studies, and electronic commercial and intellectual property law.

But take note: many schools *market* an area of specialty that isn't exactly substantive. Check what the current course offerings are. It's not unheard of for courses to appear in the catalogs that haven't been offered in years.

Investigate how much emphasis is placed on the practical skills: writing, advising clients, negotiating, arguing. Employers have complained loudly that their new hires arrive ill-prepared to practice, so now many law schools are building hands-on experience into the curriculum in the form of clinics; simulation courses that have actors or students playing the roles of opposing counsel and judge, for example; and intensive first-year classes in legal research and writing. While some schools think of the practical instruction as lesser courses and assign part-timers to teach them, ideally they'll be handled by full-time faculty members who meld the teaching of practice with theory in a child advocacy clinic, for example. Look for the student-faculty ratio to be very low. The best programs limit clinics to 8 or 10 students and teach legal research and writing in small groups of 20 or 30.

"Textbooks don't tell you what clients are like or how to be in front of a judge, but that's what you need for the real world," says one recent graduate of the CUNY School of Law who spent 30 hours a week in the Family Law Clinic, where she represented a victim of domestic violence in a custody case, filing child-support orders, writing briefs, and arguing with opposing counsel before a judge. In Georgetown's clinics, participants represent a whole range of clients, from noncitizens seeking political asylum to victims of domestic violence to tenants in disputes with landlords to children accused of crimes. Some 60 percent of students take a clinic before graduation. One of the clinics at Northwestern puts students to work in the internationally recognized Center for Wrongful Convictions, where they work on cases involving claims of innocence.

As noted before, practical experience is especially valued by public interest employers, so anyone planning on a public service career will want to consider law schools whose clinical programs reflect a commitment to it. Several that get high marks include Georgetown, NYU, CUNY, Fordham, and Northeastern. Besides strong clinics, says Equal Justice Works CEO David Stern, good public interest programs tend to have full-time counselors who help students do career planning and find pro bono work; a selection of summer public interest internship opportunities; and a structured (and sometimes mandatory) pro bono program. (The truly committed schools also have generous loan-repayment assistance programs. For more on how these plans work, see "How much will it cost?" on page 12.)

As the practice of law gets increasingly global, a growing number of students are looking for more than just a class or two in international and comparative law. Some law schools have begun to aggressively integrate discussion

> *"It used to be that the top schools were trying to be great in everything, but now we're setting strategic priorities."*

of other legal systems into courses throughout the curriculum, and a growing number make it possible for students to actually study law abroad. At Tulane, for example, students can spend anywhere from one week to a month in one of seven foreign countries, including Canada, England, France, Germany, and Greece; semester-abroad programs are also an option. Cornell students who are fluent in the language of the host country can study for a semester at one of several foreign law schools. Students at American University's law school can also take a semester abroad at several European, Canadian, or Mexican law schools or the City University of Hong Kong.

One advantage of choosing a school that is part of a university is the richness other programs can add to the law curriculum. At Penn, for example, with 12 schools on one campus, law students can study with Wharton business students in a small-business clinic and in a negotiation class; medical students and law students study together how to use the legal and medical systems to protect children's rights. The Institute for National

Profile: The politician

Chuck Larson Jr. went into politics before he went to law school, but it's his University of Iowa JD that really launched his career. Law school "has been the foundation of everything I do," says the 40-year-old Iowa native, who is U.S. ambassador to Latvia and a former member of the Iowa House and Iowa Senate.

Larson had already put aside plans for a career in business back in 1992 after a conversation with some buddies. "The economy wasn't good, and we were talking about the large part of our generation that was leaving the state because we didn't have good-paying jobs," he says. By the time the chat was over, Larson had decided not only to stay in Iowa, but to get involved in running it. He campaigned by knocking on virtually every door in his district—twice.

Shortly after winning a seat in the state House of Representatives, Larson realized that "some 40 percent of the bills that land on the governor's desk move through the Judiciary Committee," and he wanted to know how the laws would affect his constituents. So he went back to school, taking his spring semester courses in the summers so as not to miss the legislative season. "I didn't have a lot of free time," he concedes, but the hard work paid off: his understanding of the intricacies of case law and constitutionality propelled him to leadership roles on first the House and then the Senate Judiciary Committees.

Day to day, Larson tackled civil issues such as the definition of marriage ("a hot topic right now") and bankruptcy law ("it's narrow and specific and can be confusing—law school helped me put it into sharp focus"). On the criminal front, his understanding of drug laws helped when he and his colleagues drafted the nation's toughest law on methamphetamine abuse (first offense: mandatory treatment; second offense: jail).

Because of its strong alumni network in the state, the University of Iowa has been a powerful support to Larson, no small consideration when he was choosing law schools.

Many of his colleagues in government are Iowa graduates—and, perhaps most importantly, so are many of his constituents. "Obviously the ties with alums across the state work politically," he says. "Iowans like their universities. Politically, it's a mark of distinction." On the other hand, he says, Iowa is "a fairly liberal school, and I'm a Republican. Some of my [professors] have contributed to my opponents." He may not have raked in political contributions on campus, but he did save some money: choosing the flagship state university allowed Larson to leave law school "relatively debt free."

As a member of the U.S. Army National Guard's Judge Advocate General corps, Larson spent a year in Iraq, where, when he wasn't handling the legal affairs of fellow soldiers, he helped build schools and water filtration systems.

Security and Counterterrorism at Syracuse University's law school will bring together students and faculty in law, journalism, history, and public affairs to study and discuss their various perspectives on how threats to national security should be handled. And at the University of Michigan, students can take up to nine credits in graduate programs outside the law school.

At the extreme, student interest in crossdisciplinary study expresses itself in the pursuit of a joint degree, which may add an extra year or two to the educational experience but (at least theoretically) offers an edge in the ultracompetitive job market. While the most common combo degree is probably law and business, there's a whole array of possible combinations, and many schools allow students to create their own dual degrees.

At Michigan, choices include a JD/master's of science in information (for those interested in the intellectual property issues created by technology) and a JD/MS in natural resources (for anyone with a particular interest in pollution and the environment). At Duke—where fully a quarter of the law school population is enrolled in a joint-degree program—students can complete a three-year-plus-one-summer combination JD/master's degree in any of some 15 academic disciplines from English to psychology to Romance studies. They can also complete longer professional joint degrees with the divinity school, the Fuqua School of Business, and the medical school, among others.

Who's doing the teaching, and are they good?

Talking to students and sitting in on first-year classes should give you a sense of the faculty as teachers, a factor that's difficult to judge from a distance. On many campuses, there's been quite a shift since *The Paper Chase* days, toward an educational experience much friendlier to students. (The noble explanation: professors have realized that using the Socratic method to intimidate and humiliate doesn't promote learning and probably inhibits it. A more practical reason: schools are battling each other to attract the most-qualified candidates—who happen to be a more vocal and demanding bunch of consumers than previous generations.)

The result is that many deans have put a premium on good teaching and student-faculty interaction as well as a professor's legal scholarship. Vanderbilt University law profs are expected to know every student by name from the first day and to have their doors open anytime. At the University of Pennsylvania law school, which encourages informal student-professor contact, the whole faculty pretty much lunches out with students nonstop, says Dean Michael Fitts. "We all have this irrational fear that we're going to go in [to see a professor] and our question will be stupid," says Karen Tani of Penn, who remembers those fears evaporating during her first term after she and a handful of other students had lunch with each of her four professors. Pace University law school in New York has introduced a merit-based pay system in which the strength of professors' syllabi, grading methods, and student evaluations counts as 35 to 40 percent of their marks for performance, along with their records of scholarship and public service. Chicago has worked at creating an "intellectual community" by holding frequent lunchtime panel discussions by faculty and seminars at professors' homes, says Levmore.

A side effect of the reform movement has been a "huge variance in the degree to which teaching is still rigorous," says Kent Syverud, dean of the law school at Washington University in St. Louis and former president of the American Law Deans' Association. He advises prospective applicants to observe the interactions in one or two first-year classes with a critical eye. As argument and analysis are such vital legal skills, "You don't want to see a replication of Psych 101, where the professor lectures, poses rhetorical questions, and walks out," he says. It should be clear that the presentation has been carefully thought through, and that the students are engaged and involved; where the Socratic method is practiced properly, students are respectfully asked to articulate and defend their arguments and are doing the talking at least a third of the time. Rather than embarrassing the unprepared by calling on students randomly, many professors now use an "on call" system that alerts those who need to be ready ahead of time.

Will your classes be led by the great legal minds who have established the school's reputation? Or are the scholars off doing their research while attorney adjuncts do the teaching? You definitely want a faculty still active out in the field and on the cutting edge of legal scholarship; the bios and vitae posted on school websites can give you some indication of professors' accomplishments and publications. Penn's Paul Robinson is a recognized scholar on criminal law who has served on the U.S. Sentencing Commission; William Banks, head of Syracuse's counterterrorism institute, is an expert in national security law who lectures around the world and has testified before the Senate Judiciary Committee on the U.S. Patriot Act.

But you also want reassurance that the scholars are the people you'll be learning from—and that they're accessible to you outside of class, too. When you quiz current students, ask them whether "when you ask to see a professor, they say 'See you in a week and a half,'" advises Andrew Popper, a professor at American University's Washington College of Law.

How much will it cost?

Take a deep breath.

Perhaps $250,000 or $300,000 or even a lot more, counting all the income you'll give up to go to school. Graduates of the top programs, where yearly tuition now runs more than $40,000, may not have to worry so much about accumulating $100,000 in debt; they can expect to be making lots of money if they choose to. But the rest of the world will need to weigh the tradeoffs of choosing an in-state public institution (tuition and fees at Ohio State's law school run under $20,000 a year for state residents; in-state tuition and fees at the University of Georgia, just a bit over $12,000); apply for financial aid; investigate the availability of merit awards based on academic credentials or commitment to public service rather than need; and check out loan repayment assistance programs. (For a complete discussion on how to pay for law school, see Chapter 5 on page 51.)

One advantage of applying to school where your LSAT scores stand out is that you might well be a candidate for a scholarship. A growing number of schools now offer merit money in an effort to attract the most talented students possible. "It's amazing," says admissions consultant Mark Meyerrose of the explosion of merit aid. "We can't *not* do it in this competitive environment," says Hofstra's Rabinowitz. The pool of aid money at Hofstra, which includes some need-based aid but is mostly awarded based on merit, tripled from $1.1 million to

$3.3 million between 1994 and 2002; merit aid accounted for the entire increase. Quinnipiac Law School in Connecticut, which has been working hard on attracting a student body with higher LSAT and GPA numbers, gave out some $3.4 million in 2006, up from $500,000 12 years earlier. In the past six years, the 25th/75th percentile range of LSAT scores at Quinnipiac has moved from 144–151 to 157–160. Pace University law school gave out $380,000 to first-year students in 1999; a mere four years later, the pot had grown to $1.9 million.

Pace has also joined the ranks of law schools with loan repayment assistance programs. These programs, also sometimes called loan forgiveness programs, are designed to help graduates who take public interest jobs pay back their law school loans. They now exist at more than 100 schools, according to *U.S. News* surveys (for the list, see page 60). Under the typical plan, a graduate who takes a job at a nonprofit or government agency that pays less than a certain amount, say $40,000, is either granted or loaned money each year to cover part of his yearly debt payments. If you receive the funds as a loan, the debt is forgiven after a certain number of years as long as you stay in a public interest job and your income doesn't rise too high.

What kind of help will I get finding a job?

One stop on your campus tour should be the career services office, whose assistance (or lack thereof) may mean the difference between your graduating into a job or not. Does it appear to be a professionally run operation with counselors on staff—rather than just administrative assistants who schedule interviews? In addition to arranging for scores of employers to recruit on campus, the best place-ment services are constantly scheduling workshops on job-hunting strategies and various career paths, bringing attorneys to campus to speak about their work, sending students to recruitment fairs, and offering individual advice.

While you're there, ask how many graduates end up getting jobs after graduation, and how soon. "Most schools have extraordinarily detailed placement data that they'll share with you if asked," says Syverud of Wash U. You'll want to know the proportion of the class with a job offer at graduation and how many are working six months or nine months later; the directory entries at the back of this guide provide each school's most recent placement data. You'll want to know how many grads accepted clerkships, positions at different sized corporate law firms, and public interest slots. At Yale, for example, nearly half of the 2004 graduating class accepted judicial clerkships, and 8 to 10 percent of students typically go into teaching law.

Find out where graduates end up geographically, too, advises Syverud. "If your goal is to be a litigator in New York, does this school produce litigators in New York? If your goal is to practice employment law in San Francisco, does this school produce San Francisco lawyers?"

How much do graduates make? According to the most recent surveys by the National Association of Law Placement, the median starting pay for all JD full-time jobs has lately been $62,000; the figure for first-year associates ranged from $68,000 at small firms to $145,000 (plus bonus) at firms of 500 or more attorneys; for the class of 2004, median pay was only $43,000 for clerkships, $45,000 for government jobs, and $38,000 for public interest positions. It may surprise aspiring lawyers to learn that, "for all full-time jobs, half of salaries were

The latest Top 20

Each year, *U.S. News & World Report* ranks the nation's accredited law schools based on such measures of excellence as the expert opinion of deans and faculty members, expenditures per student on instruction, placement success, and how well students fare on the bar exam. To see where your schools rank, check out "America's Best Graduate Schools," available on newsstands, or go to www.usnews.com. Here is this year's Top 20. Schools whose ranks are identical are tied.

1. Yale University (CT)
2. Harvard University (MA)
    Stanford University (CA)
4. Columbia University (NY)
5. New York University
6. University of California–Berkeley
7. University of Chicago
    University of Pennsylvania
9. Northwestern University (IL)
    University of Michigan–Ann Arbor
    University of Virginia

12. Cornell University (NY)
    Duke University (NC)
14. Georgetown University (DC)
15. Vanderbilt University (TN)
16. University of California–Los Angeles
    University of Texas–Austin
18. University of Southern California
19. Washington University in St. Louis
20. George Washington University (DC)

$55,000 or less, outnumbering by a considerable margin salaries of more than $75,000."

But the actual pay packages that individuals are offered vary widely by law school and by job location. The placement office can give you the data you need, and the entries in this book provide the starting salaries reported by the class of 2006.

Finally, check out how many graduates pass the bar exam on the first try. (For a look at how the schools stack up on this measure, see page 103.) Once you've decided to go into law—and committed all that time and money—you'll want to know your odds of clearing the final hurdle.

Chapter Two

Inside America's Top Law Schools

Last year, some 1,750 people claimed a spot in the first-year law school classes at Yale, Harvard, Stanford, Columbia, and New York University—which means that, at least in terms of their career opportunities, they pretty much have it made. Are you, too, planning on gunning for the top? Here's a peek inside the elite of the elite: The top five schools on this year's *U.S. News* law school ranking.

Number 1: Yale Law School

New Haven, Connecticut

"Anarchic" isn't a word often associated with the Ivy League. But it's how students, faculty, and even a former dean describe Yale Law. And with good reason: the traditionally grueling first term is ungraded here (and subsequent courses are graded on an honors, pass, low pass or fail basis), there are virtually no course requirements past first term, and professors are free to choose what they want to teach. The current dean, Harold Koh, an international human rights expert who served as an assistant secretary of state in the Clinton administration, once took a class to a screening of *Runaway Jury*, during which he loudly enumerated the film's many procedural errors.

Such a freewheeling approach might be less successful if Yale weren't so small. With around 640 students, the school has a student–faculty ratio of about 8 to 1, and the hallways of its rambling Gothic building near the heart of campus are abuzz with chance meetings between students and professors. Even in crowded first-year courses, where enrollment tops 100, professors call on students by name without checking seating charts. The school's size and the absence of grades or class ranking breeds a collaborative spirit and a homey informality. When Yale students express interest in a subject not accounted for in the course catalog—like maritime law or 9/11-related litigation—they simply draft a faculty advisor and create their own course, or "reading group."

The anarchic spirit extends to classroom interaction, where students challenge professors constantly and debate one another on issues such as the legitimacy of the International Criminal Court and the limits of Supreme Court power. "We take a very spacious view of the law," says Anthony T. Kronman, who served as dean for 10 years. "We don't see the law as a narrow professional enterprise, but as a vantage point from which the entire world can be viewed. It's a window into the human comedy."

Classes at Yale are thus highly theoretical; this is not the place to look for a lot of attention to the nuts and bolts of practice. "You're going to have to cram for six miserable weeks for the bar exam anyway, so why waste time preparing when you're in law school?" says Kronman. A recent contracts course included a long, spirited discussion over whether Pepsi could in theory be held liable for what amounts to a joke: its ad campaign offering a Harrier Jet to customers who collected 7,000,000 Pepsi points. At other schools, "I might spend time going over statutes, talking about black-letter law," or clear-cut legal principles, says Richard Brooks, an associate professor who teaches contracts. But this high-minded approach has its limits, students say. "Sometimes we're criticizing the doctrine before we've even learned what it is," says Matt Alsdorf, class of 2004. "I'm going to have to gain a lot of experience on the job."

Given this theoretical bent, it should come as no surprise that Yale is an incubator for academics; a 2001 Yale survey found that 10 percent of the class of 1997 had jobs in academia. The law school is home to a dozen research centers and projects, including the China Law Center, which aims to help the legal reform process in that country, and the Information Society Project, which studies the effect of the Internet on law and society. Each student is required to do original research and write a major paper of about 60 to 80 pages, which they might publish in one of Yale's student-run law journals.

Yale is known as an activist school, where students often fight legal battles in the larger world and a relatively large percentage pursue public interest law, which is emphasized by professors, career counselors, and Dean Koh. More than 70 percent of the class of 2005 took first-year summer jobs in public interest work, most of them unpaid (Yale provided funding).

Roughly half of Yale Law's graduating class traditionally take judicial clerkships—and a large chunk stay with public interest work afterward. Easing their way is Yale's generous loan repayment program for graduates making less than a certain amount, recently $45,000, which covers their loan payments for up to 10 years.

While most law schools permit students to enroll in their clinics only after the first year, Yale opens clinics to students after a single term. Fourteen distinct clinical projects cover areas such as immigration, tenant eviction proceedings, child advocacy, and legislative advocacy. The international human rights law clinic matches students with lawyers working on cases in federal and U.N. courts, and with regional human rights bodies in South America and Africa. Nearly 80 percent of Yale JD students take at least one clinical course, gaining experience in all aspects of lawyering, from writing and filing briefs to negotiating with opposing counsel to representing clients in court.

A burning commitment to law is practically a prerequisite for study at a school with virtually no requirements, no class rankings, and a hardly noticeable grading system. Which is not to suggest that Yalies aren't competitive: the median LSAT score and grade point average of the 2005 entering class were 173 and 3.89. "People here live, breathe, and eat law school—there's no competing social structure like in New York. Even if you go to a bar, you're talking law school," says Alsdorf. While the freedom is a gift for most students, it can be tough at first for the undisciplined. "Students who have always been told to climb the ladder—and who climb it really well—may be a little lost," says Kate Stith, a professor and formerly the deputy dean, "when we don't tell them which ladder to climb."

Tied for Number 2: Harvard Law School

Cambridge, Massachusetts

With nearly 1,700 students, the "metropolis" is roughly the size of the law schools at Yale, Stanford, and the University of Chicago combined. The law library, with two million volumes, is the largest of its kind in the world. More than 80 full-time professors and about 100 part-time faculty teach 250-plus electives, providing depth in many areas—Islamic law, for example—that smaller schools simply can't achieve.

Harvard's platinum reputation rests largely on its biggest resource: a marquee faculty that includes defense attorney Alan Dershowitz, former U.S. Solicitor General Charles Fried, and constitutional scholar Laurence Tribe, to name just a few of the larger lights. The big names often teach first-year classes, bringing the material alive with war stories from the trenches. "A course with Alan Dershowitz is not criminal law—it's criminal law with Alan Dershowitz," says 2004 graduate John Doulamis. "I took constitutional law with Fried, and he'd argued the cases we were reading in front of the Supreme Court."

But one big downside of Harvard's size has long been its tendency to feel cold and impersonal to students. "The stereotype used to be that everybody wanted to come here because it was Harvard, but didn't much expect to like it," says Dean Elena Kagan. That perception started changing five years ago, when the school hired an outside management firm to direct a makeover. Responding to complaints that professors were inaccessible, administrators went on a hiring spree and halved the student-faculty ratio to about 11 to 1. First-year sections—the big groups of students who take the basic courses together—shrank from 140 to about 80. And first-year students are now divided into groups, or "law colleges," that aim to promote a sense of community by sponsoring social events. "We're never going to get an intense intimacy here, but we can make sense within this big city—we can have neighborhoods," says Kagan. "It's a much friendlier place now," says Doulamis.

> *"The stereotype used to be that everybody wanted to come here because it was Harvard, but didn't much expect to like it."*

Some students still see room for improvement. Small seminars for second and third years can be tough to get into, for example. "I don't have enough credits this semester because I'm on too many wait lists," is not a rare complaint. First-year sections are sometimes bundled together, forcing class size beyond 150 students. And many professors, engaged in their research, continue to be inaccessible. "One of my professors saw me as a nuisance," says one first-year student. "He had me out of his office in 10 minutes after I'd waited two weeks to see him." Kagan hopes to extend the law college system to second- and third-year students and hire 15 additional faculty to drive the student-faculty ratio down even further.

While students at some smaller law schools seem uniformly bent on changing the world, many Harvard students—who coming in 2007 had a median 3.81 undergraduate GPA and a median 173 LSAT—proudly advertise that they're here for the renowned corporate law curriculum.

The program boasts nearly 20 professors, research centers in international tax, corporate governance, and international finance, plus opportunities for interdisciplinary study through the esteemed business school. Recently, though, the school has strengthened its focus on public interest law, adding a graduation requirement of pro bono work and increasing funds for students who do low- or nonpaying public interest work during the summer. While the last dean was a corporate law specialist, Kagan is a veteran of the Clinton White House.

Though some students—especially those on the corporate law track—chafe at the pro bono requirement, Kagan says "students should feel like public service is an integral part of the legal profession." Harvard's "low-income protection plan" repays the loans of graduates making less than $38,000. Slightly higher-paid grads are eligible for partial loan repayments. The school also promotes public service through 20-plus courses with clinical components that have students doing such work as helping low-income area residents with immigration, housing, and family law issues. The clinical courses also place roughly 50 JD students each year in the office of the state Attorney General and in Boston's U.S. attorney's office.

Still, two-thirds of graduates end up taking private practice jobs—indeed, HLS attracts more than 700 private recruiters each year to its job bazaars. And students often snag a handful of offers in a single day.

Tied for Number 2: Stanford Law School

Stanford, California

"Who could resist a world-class law school in paradise?"

That's a pretty sizable boast from former dean Kathleen Sullivan. But academically topnotch Stanford is also easily one of the nation's most beautiful law schools, situated on an 8,000-acre campus that looks more like a Spanish-colonial country club than a college. Nearly every student has a bike (and knowledge of local hiking trails). Beaches and ski slopes are just an hour or two away. Indeed, Stanford is often portrayed as a land of laid back would-be lawyers brushing up on their torts while they work on their tans. (Actually, since

> "So many people have done really interesting non-law-related things before they come here to school."

it's a wireless campus, this might be easily done).

But don't buy the "Dude, where's my lawn chair?" rap. "It's considered kind of cool here not to show how intense you are or how much you care," says one second-year student. "It's not that we're not really serious. We just don't flash it around." Last year, Stanford had more than 4,000 applicants for its entering class of just over 170 students. The median LSAT range for accepted students was 160–180 and the median GPA was above a 3.87.

Those who make the cut learn quickly how much size matters at the so-called Harvard of the West. With fewer than 180 students entering each year (compared to roughly three times that at Harvard), Stanford is able to foster a level of community among students and faculty that many law schools cannot. First-year sections typically average no more than 60 students, and with an average student–teacher ratio of about 8 to 1, getting extra time with professors outside of class is easy. The entire law school is housed in one small building, and most of the faculty's office doors are routinely open. "There's a feeling that no one will be left behind," says one student who is also somewhat of an expert on graduate programs, with a master's degree in philosophy from Columbia University and a doctorate in rhetoric from the University of California–Berkeley. "The faculty have the time and the inclination to talk to students about everything from questions that come up in class to career advice to abstract ideas. I've been to a lot of schools—a lot of good schools—and that's not always the case."

Decades younger than Harvard and Yale, the law school, like the West itself, is more cutting edge than traditional. Stanford is well known for its program in technology and law, for example; in fact, one of the few criticisms of the school is that its position at the forefront of that emerging field has come at the expense of more traditional areas of study, such as constitutional law.

Not surprisingly, Stanford's proximity to Silicon Valley has made it a magnet for scholars in Internet-age intellectual property law. The faculty includes Lawrence Lessig, a leading light in cyberlaw lured from Harvard in 2000 to head up the Center for Internet and Society, which examines the many constitutional and public policy legal issues raised by the Internet. Stanford also recently established the Center for E-Commerce to explore the field of electronic commerce law. In the school's cyberlaw clinic, students guided by full-time faculty study legal issues such as ethics, free speech, and privacy as they prepare real cases for real clients.

All told, Stanford offers seven legal clinics, including one on civil rights, another on criminal prosecution, and one on Supreme Court litigation. At the Stanford Community Law Clinic, which serves needy people in East Palo Alto, students get a chance to put their learning into practice handling cases concerning such issues as housing, workers' rights, and immigration. They work alongside lawyers with years of experience fighting the system on behalf of low-income clients and are involved from start to finish on cases, often seeing them through to trial.

Students at Stanford are highly encouraged to develop a broad view of the law in several contexts, so the curriculum includes a large offering of interdisciplinary programs. The school's Center on Conflict and Negotiation, for instance, brings together students and faculty from all parts of the university to study mediation and conflict resolution theory and practice in domestic and international settings. The International Studies program is open to grad students in law, business, engineering, and the arts and sciences, and offers classes that explore the global nature of law, business, science, and politics, taught by faculty from several disciplines.

Another area of strength is the environmental law program, consistently mentioned among the top in the nation. The program relies heavily on situational case studies—much like those used in business schools—to bring disputes over

resources and regulations to life and give students a crack at solving real problems, such as how to balance business interests and conservation. In the public interest arena, where the number of course offerings rivals those in technology and intellectual property, students are trained in such areas as racial equality, voting rights, and gender law and public policy, and have access to a full-service, public interest career counseling office. Stanford offers annual fellowships to second- and third-year students pursuing public interest careers, plus summer fellowships for those who want to do nonpaying public interest work. Graduates who take low-paying public interest jobs can have as much as 100 percent of their law school loans forgiven depending on the number of years they stay in the job. (Typically, a loan is

"Who could resist a world-class law school in paradise?"

completely forgiven after 10 years.)

With so many older students in Stanford's law school population—the average age is 24—count on an often unusual mix of experiences and some lively discussion. Former investment bankers, doctors, legislators, even dancers become law students; the mix is consistently mentioned by students and faculty as one of the most valuable aspects of a Stanford education. "So many people have done really interesting non-law-related things before they come here to school," says Gabrielle Vidal, a grad of the class of 2000, which included a former Texas legislator and a coroner. "Then when they get here, they have interesting life stories to bring to the law."

Profile: The lobbyist

Kelly Farrell had reached the midpoint of her time at Harvard Law when it happened: she realized that she didn't want to be a lawyer. Farrell hadn't figured she'd end up at Harvard initially. Waitlisted, she'd made plans to attend the University of Virginia. "I was very excited about UVA, actually," she says. But when the phone call came, "my parents were like, 'Harvard calls,' so I went," heading off to Cambridge, Massachusetts, in the autumn of 1999 with great expectations and prepared for "a really amazing experience."

And yet, she says, her time at HLS "was only so-so. My roommate was the best thing to come out of my Harvard experience." The competitiveness on campus was part of the problem. It wasn't as if people were hoarding notes, she says, or sabotaging fellow classmates. But the classes were large and populated liberally with "gunners," always at the ready with an answer. The real pressure, she says, came from the high standards people imposed on themselves. "These expectations breed a little bit more anxiety. You're told that Harvard is the key to unlocking all of these great doors."

Which it did: after her identity crisis, Farrell took stock and decided to use her law degree to work in politics, an interest since her days as a political science major at Duke University. First, she snagged a summer internship at Verner Liipfert, which had just been named one of the most powerful firms in Washington in a survey of Congressmen, Hill staffers, and senior White House aides. Then, upon graduation, she accepted a job with the law firm, where she spent her days on Capitol Hill lobbying members of Congress and attending hearings that related to the public policy interests of the firm's clients, which included Lockheed Martin, Visa, and British Aerospace.

In 2002, the firm merged with a larger company—and while the merger went smoothly, Farrell says, the atmosphere changed. Then a newlywed, Farrell was much more concerned about her quality of life, which was being affected by late nights and pressure to increase billable hours. "It drains you to be working 65–70 hours a week—and my hours were even more reasonable than other associates," she says.

She went next to the United States Maritime Administration, within the Department of Transportation, where as an attorney-advisor she followed legislation and new developments pertaining to initiatives such as the Maritime Security Program. For example, she worked on legislation allowing merchant marines to enter into agreements with private vessels during times of national emergency so that they can carry cargo for the government. Then she moved into space travel; as a legislative affairs specialist at NASA headquarters in Washington, she serves as a liaison with Congress on matters having to do with the space shuttle and international space station. One notable effort in which she played a part: getting *Discovery* off the ground again after the *Columbia* accident.

Farrell took a pay cut when she moved to the government, but notes that "averaged out by hours, I'm probably making about the same as I used to." The lifestyle change, of course, is just about priceless. "I was almost stunned when I didn't have to stay until 8 or 9 at night." That extra time at home has been especially precious since the birth of Jake, her first child. What's more, she loves the work. "It's kind of a nobler purpose than representing big corporations," she says. "You do your own little part for the country."

annual tuition now over $35,000 coupled with the San Francisco Bay Area's high cost of living, a Stanford Law education runs over $50,000 a year. However, stop any Stanford student and they'll tell you the investment is well worth it: they, like graduates of the other elites, are walking away with six-figure starting salaries. And don't be surprised if the student tries to interest you in a T-shirt that says "Harvard, the Stanford of the East."

Number 4: Columbia Law School

New York, New York

Columbia is a school that prides itself on its diversity. As a former director of admissions put it, Columbia students are "people comfortable [being] uncomfortable. They want to feel that a community is there for them, and then surround themselves with people who are different." Students typically have worked in all sorts of capacities: as Peace Corps volunteers, human rights activists, physicists, performing artists, journalists, teachers, and management consultants, among other things; only about a quarter come to campus straight from college. And though the law school is medium-sized—with some 1,200 students, it's not as big as Harvard, not as small as Yale—it's one of the most cultur-

ally diverse of the elites, with a healthy percentage of minority students. It's religiously diverse, too, with substantial populations of Mormons, Muslims, Catholics, and Orthodox Jews. One attribute all do share: a strong academic record. The median LSAT score is 172 and the median GPA is 3.70.

By virtue of its location in the epicenter of international business, Columbia's areas of greatest strength traditionally have been corporate, comparative, and international law. Professors include such leaders in their fields as John Coffee, once named one of the country's 100 most influential lawyers by *The National Law Journal*; Harvey Goldschmid, who has served as a commissioner with the Securities and Exchange Commission; and Jose Alvarez and Lori Fisler Damrosch, both widely recognized experts in international law.

In recent years, the school has worked to build a reputation in public interest law and legal philosophy as well. The Center for Public Interest Law, offers counseling to students who want to pursue service careers and funds summer internships in human rights and public service organizations. Interested students are paid by Columbia to work in over 40 countries with groups such as the Human Rights and Equal Opportunity Commission in Australia, the International

Criminal Tribunals in Yugoslavia and Rwanda, and the European Court of Human Rights in France. Others go to nonprofits and government agencies that have included the U.S. Attorney's office, the United Nations, the American Civil Liberties Union, and the NAACP Legal Defense and Education Fund.

The Center for Public Interest Law also helps students fulfill their obligation of 40 hours of pro bono work before graduation. The pro bono experience, which can range from representing death row prisoners to helping children in foster care, is rewarding enough that more than half of students put in more than the 40-hour minimum.

In the upper-class years, students can enroll in one of eight clinical programs, taught by full-time faculty members, in child advocacy, law and the arts, environmental law, human rights, lawyering in the digital age, mediation, nonprofit organizations and small business, and prisoners and families. "It was definitely the best class at law school," says 2004 grad Dale Margolin, who took the child advocacy clinic and then became a clinic teaching assistant. "The highlight was when my lawyer let me handle a case that involved getting a mother out of a homeless shelter and reuniting her with all her seven children."

Though Columbia has long had a reputation for being overly competitive, students beg to differ. "Everyone's so aware of the cutthroat image that there's social pressure to act noncompetitive," says a student from Belton, Texas. Anne Ochsendorf from Elkins, West Virginia, says she found classmates friendly and actually eager to lend notes to anyone who missed a class. But that didn't surprise her as much as the closeness that often develops between students and professors. Each 1L is assigned a faculty advisor, who takes him or her out to dinner or lunch sometime during the fall. Some 130 small seminars are open to upperclassmen, all with a student-to-teacher ratio of 14 to 1. "I came from Wellesley to the big city, and I was pleased to find that professors here are very much interested in getting

> *"Even if you're not in the top of your class at Columbia, you still get a job."*

to know and support and involve students," Ochsendorf says.

Individual attention is emphasized in career counseling, too. Essentially, students are encouraged to do what they like the first summer (typically, 32 percent of 1Ls spend the summer working for a firm), and to get serious the second summer (90 percent work for firms). More than 700 interviewers come to campus each fall. "Even if you're not in the top of your class at Columbia, you still get a job," says JaMille Jackson, class of 2005. "I did 22 interviews, got 12 callbacks, and 6 offers." She accepted an offer from Morgan Lewis in Washington, D.C., for the summer of 2004.

And Columbia students land their first choice job more often than not. Many grads stay on in New York, and, while Columbia, like its peers, has a loan-forgiveness program for those who take public interest jobs, the vast majority opt for private practice. It's easy to see why: first-year associates can expect to earn a median of $125,000, plus bonus—just about what you need to survive in New York City these days.

Number 5: New York University School of Law

New York, New York

Like many would-be attorneys, Liyah Brown chose her law school with an eye on finding job opportunities, not friends. Interested in using the legal system to create social change, Brown planned to

> *"I think the thing that most impressed me when I came here is just how people were uniformly very sharp."*

immerse herself in New York University law school's renowned public interest courses and clinical programs, then move on to a job as a civil rights or poverty lawyer. What's more, she was occupied with being pregnant during her first year and commuting from Brooklyn, far from the dorm scene. So she was startled when her classmates started checking in with her. "People would email me and say, 'If there's ever a day you don't feel like coming to class, if you need an assignment, just email me, and my notes are your notes,'" says Brown, class of 2004. "I feel like there's definitely more than 10 people that I'll [stay] in touch with, professors included. And that's a nice surprise."

There's no question that NYU is highly competitive: seventy-five percent of last fall's 1Ls scored 168 or higher on their LSATs and boasted undergraduate GPAs of at least 3.6. "I think the thing that most impressed me when I came here is just how people were uniformly very sharp," says Matthew Ginsberg, who previously was an organizer for a service employees' union in Baltimore and is planning a career in labor or immigration law.

But students report that success doesn't come at the next guy's expense. "People want to do well, but they want that for each other, too," says Brown. Professors, two-thirds of whom live within a five-minute walk of campus, are generally helpful and accessible, students say. Dean Richard Revesz, an Argentinian-born environmental lawyer, answers to "Ricky." Even the school's location—in a handful of brick mansions facing historic Washington Square Park in Greenwich Village, near coffeeshops and bars where both the servers and the customers often know your name—has a small-town feel.

Perhaps the collegial atmosphere should come as no surprise—one of the strengths of the NYU curriculum is that specialty dedicated to making the world a better place: public interest law. The school supplements its wide variety of courses and clinics with a weekly speakers' series, a public interest career counseling center, and financial assistance for students interested in pursuing such jobs. The school's loan repayment assistance program covers up to 100 percent of law school debt payments for as long as 10 years after graduation for students entering public interest careers and earning less than a certain amount ($58,000 for those graduating in 2005 and beyond; the salary cap is adjusted upward in year four and year seven as careers progress, to take account of inflation). And last year, the school announced it would provide several thousand dollars to every first- and second-year student who wanted to take a nonpaying summer job in a public interest organization in the United States or abroad.

Another area of distinction here is international law. In addition to its star-studded

American faculty, NYU maintains a "global faculty" from universities abroad who visit each year to teach special classes on subjects ranging from foreign tax treaties to gender issues in Islamic law. Driven by a school-wide sense that domestic lawyers increasingly will work on global issues, professors even outside the international arena often roll non-U.S. cases into their courses; a first-year student might study an Australian case asserting aboriginal rights in a course examining sovereignty, for example.

Many students are drawn to NYU by the opportunities it provides for students to practice before they graduate. All 1Ls take a one-year, ungraded course called Lawyering in which they role-play client interviews and negotiations, for example, under the guidance of tenured or tenure-track profs. Upperclassmen may apply for admission to any of about 20 clinics in which they assist real clients in such areas as immigrant rights, child welfare, and capital defense cases. Asit Panwala, class of 1999 and now a prosecutor in the Bronx, says that focusing on the facts of actual cases in his prosecution clinic while simultaneously having class discussions of the big-picture issues was the highlight of his law school experience. "Sometimes people see the forest and they don't see the trees,"

he observes. His clinic helped him see both, he says, and "that experience put me light years ahead when I started working."

Students also gain exposure to the real world through a faculty that features lawyers often quoted in the morning papers, like Noah Feldman, the Bush Administration's senior advisor for constitutional law in postwar Iraq; Gerald Lopez,

> *"People want to do well, but they want that for each other, too."*

author of *Rebellious Lawyering*, a seminal book on progressive law practice; and Burt Neuborne, a former legal director of the ACLU.

In spite of the school's efforts to support alternative careers, most graduates pick the path of least resistance. Most accept jobs at private firms, while only a small percentage typically join public interest organizations and government agencies. Students say they have their pick of job offers. According to the career placement office, during the average school year, more than 550 employers interview on campus and the majority of graduates accept their first- or second-choice job. And, as is true at all the top schools, virtually everybody lands a job by graduation.

Chapter Three

What Law Schools Will Look For in You

The University of Chicago law school received just under 4,800 applications for 190 spots in the 2007 entering class. At the University of Pennsylvania, 5,604 people applied for about 260 slots. Georgetown fielded almost 11,490 applications last year for 383 day and 121 evening spots.

And it's not only the top 20 or 25 schools that are flooded with candidates; the competition is tougher just about everywhere. American University's Washington College of Law received about 8,400 applications last year. At Quinnipiac in Connecticut, a third-tier law school that has made improving the quality of its academic program and student body a top priority, the number of applicants rose 108 percent between 2001 and 2005.

How can you possibly stand out in such a crowd? This chapter tells you what attributes the admissions committee is looking for in a candidate and how you can best convey that you've got them. Your superior qualities are going to have to shine through in your test scores, transcript, personal statement, and letters of recommendation, because only a handful of law schools offer the

---

"The numbers matter, and anybody who says otherwise—that's ridiculous."

---

chance to impress in person. (For more detailed advice on how to tackle the application, see Chapter 4.)

Start with strong numbers

While it's not true—as many applicants fear—that your fate will hang entirely on your LSAT score, "the numbers matter, and anybody who says otherwise—that's ridiculous," says Georgetown's Cornblatt. Typically, grades and test scores serve as a kind of sorting mechanism, an efficient way for admissions staffers to mentally put applicants into one of three categories as they read through all the files: the probably admitted (unless something unexpected turns up to detract from the numbers), the probably denied (unless something unexpected turns up that makes them really appealing), and the ones who require considerable mulling over and discussion. Some schools do this analysis based on the LSAT, some do it based on the GPA, and some use both. Another option is to use an index number calculated by the Law School Admission Council (administrator of the LSAT)

that factors in LSAT score and GPA. Since schools can ask LSAC to correlate their index with the academic success of first-year law classes, the number can offer some indication of how an applicant is apt to fare during his or her first year at the school.

But contrary to popular belief about automatic acceptances and rejections, all applications generally get read—even at the very top and very bottom of the range. "In my experience, the goal of admissions is to enroll a dynamic class, and this commands a look beyond the numbers," says one person with experience both in the admissions office at an elite law school and as a private counselor. Some admissions experts believe that applications are bound to be read with even greater attention to non-numerical factors in the future. When the Supreme Court said it was legal for the University of Michigan Law School to consider race in admissions (see page 49), the justices "made clear that genuine diversity is an interest of constitutional significance—and that could include exotic languages," says Andrew Popper, a professor at American University's law school who has lots of experience reading applications himself as a member of the admissions committee. "If we're going to attempt to establish diversity, [law schools] have to really look at every file."

Indeed, some of the "probably denied" may turn out to bring unique experience to the table. One admissions dean, for example, recalls a Vietnamese applicant who spent time living under a bridge before escaping to the United States; he wouldn't have made it into law school based on numbers alone. And files of the almost-certain-to-be-admitted are typically read to be sure "they're not psycho killers," says Robert Berring, formerly interim dean at UC–Berkeley's Boalt Hall—and to check for honor code violations, for example, or whether applicants reveal themselves in their personal statement as offensively arrogant or whiny.

Some schools are much more numbers-driven than others, says Seattle-based admissions consultant Loretta DeLoggio, and one way to tell is to check the variance between the 25th percentile and the 75th percentile in LSAT and GPA scores. If the bottom of the range is just a couple of points below the top, the school may well be pushing to get its numbers higher, she says. But in general, says DeLoggio, who specializes in helping minority students choose a law school and get in, applicants "grossly misuse" the 25th–75th percentile ranges in choosing schools. It's important to remember, she says, that "the 25th percentile is not a bottom. In 200 people accepted, 50 are below it!"

On the other hand, candidates who get in with scores on the low side are sure to be exceptional in some other way. In general, "someone with a 3.0 and an average LSAT score hasn't got a chance in hell of getting admitted to a top school—I'd discourage students from wasting their money" on the application, says former University of Dayton pre-law advisor Roberta Alexander, now retired.

"We have an informal sorting mechanism based on LSAT and GPA, but every applicant gets a holistic review. We're trying to find people who will be a good fit," says Derek Meeker, former associate dean for admissions and financial aid at the University of Pennsylvania law school. At the University of Chicago, applicants are admitted, denied, or held on the first reading; those who are held might be offered the oppor-

tunity to write an additional essay or explain any puzzle in their files—really high grades and a low LSAT score, for example. "We read every single application from cover to cover," says Megan Barnett, associate dean for admissions and financial aid at Yale. The best 20 percent or so are then sent to the faculty for consideration; three faculty members read each file and rate

> *"In my experience, the goal of admissions is to enroll a dynamic class, and this commands a look beyond the numbers."*

candidates on a 2-to-4 scale. Of the pool of around 12,000 that Georgetown considers to admit maybe 2,000, some "2,500 are easy 'nos' and 800 are easy 'yeses,'" says admissions head Andrew Cornblatt. "Of the rest, I get to admit 1 in 9. That's where I earn my salary." Every file at Columbia is read by at least two people.

Show them you're a thinker

One characteristic of law students who succeed—the only kind admissions officers intend to accept—is that they're informed and incisive thinkers. So your application will be closely studied for evidence that you can measure up. "I try to gauge the intellectual ability of the student—who's analytically really good?" says Kate Stith, former deputy dean and professor at Yale. "I'm looking for the students who will come up with new ideas, the ones that aren't in the textbooks."

While the grades and test scores certainly indicate intellectual ability, the transcript tells a much more nuanced story. Anybody who still has maneuvering time ahead should know that grades

Transferring to the top

If your heart is set on a top school but your grades and LSAT scores won't get you there, consider enrolling elsewhere and taking another shot next year. "There are two ways to get into law school now," says Deborah Post, former co-chair of the Society of American Law Teachers' committee on admissions and a professor at Touro College's law school in Huntington, New York. "You've got the numbers, or you prove you can do the work: you go to a lower-tier school and transfer."

While they don't exactly advertise it, many highly competitive law schools rely on their transfer programs to fine-tune the composition of their student bodies and bring in appealing near-miss applicants after they've blossomed academically at another school. (Because the undergraduate grade point averages and LSAT scores of first-year students figure in the *U.S. News* law school rankings, taking less-credentialed applicants into the second-year class is also seen by many administrators as a way to avoid putting a school's rank at risk.)

"It's a terrific, terrific program," says Robert Berring, formerly interim dean at the University of California–Berkeley's Boalt Hall, which accepts about 30 transfer students each year. "We can take people from the top of lots of little law schools, and they're often [our] best students, with fire in their eyes."

It's also a good way to "do something for your legacy and donor kids—it's a better message than 'we don't have room,'" says Andrew Cornblatt, head of admissions at Georgetown University law school, who calls transfer programs "an underreported way to get into a top place."

That fire in the eye is what admissions committees will be looking to find—a position in the top 5 or 10 percent of your law school class, and, better yet, a spot on the law review, too. On the other hand, if you've *got* those credentials and are flourishing where you are, be sure to weigh the benefits of being at a higher-prestige institution against the likelihood that you'll give up star status.

"A transfer student might not make law review at the next school—you're giving up a very, very important credential and taking a risk," says Stuart Rabinowitz, president of Hofstra University in New York and formerly dean of its law school, which regularly loses top students to more prestigious places. Moreover, students at the very top of their classes at well-respected but not prestigious schools very often find themselves in contention for jobs on par with those offered to middling students at highly ranked schools. If you move, are you at risk of falling toward the bottom?

by themselves don't mean a whole lot: what matters is that you performed well in a curriculum of rigorous, challenging courses that required you to think, and to write. "I want to see people who are intellectually curious and ambitious, and who have taken some courses outside their typical realm," says Meeker. "Many people have studied political science or history, and this is all fine, but it's common. A polysci major might want to take some science and math." Any patterns in your undergraduate grades will also be of great interest. "Did your grades improve over time? Is there a special explanation for a particularly weak semester?" says Evan Caminker, dean and professor of law at the University of Michigan law school.

"Some students think you have to be a polysci major—forget it!" says Cheryl Ficarra, associate dean for enrollment management at Syracuse University. "English! Or any subject that shows they've done serious analytical writing and been critiqued. These students have a serious advantage." In fact, Carol Leach, an associate professor of political science and pre-law advisor at Chicago State University, analyzed data on the undergraduate majors of the entering class at American law schools several years ago and found that the highest rates of admission were among physics majors, with history, English, economics, math, and the other sciences close behind. "I tell students to pick a major they like so they'll do well, but one that's challenging," says Leach. The bottom line, she says, is that "you have to have really good grades in hard subjects."

Put it in writing

There's no doubt about it—a poorly written essay speaks volumes.

The main function of the personal statement is to give the committee some insight on what kind of person you are. But your essay will also demonstrate whether you've got that all-important legal skill: the ability to marshal your arguments on paper in an articulate and persuasive fashion. So not only do you have to give information that will put you over the top, but you also must present it in a well-organized, elegant way. "Someone could have an outstanding LSAT score and GPA, and if he's not able to write compellingly or effectively, that's a *big* problem," says admissions consultant Mark Meyerrose.

> "I'm looking for the students who will come up with new ideas, the ones that aren't in the textbooks."

You'll get partway there by choosing your topic well; for detailed advice on coming up with a theme, see page 44. Some general tips: it's far better to talk about yourself than about legal issues, or politics, or the state of the country today. If you try to take on the world in two pages, the result is bound to sound naïve or pseudo-intellectual. But don't just describe an experience or an achievement—go a step further and explore how it's influenced you. "What have you learned? Don't just say that you've worked at a camp for disabled children, tell us how that's changed you," says Ann Perry, assistant dean for admissions at the University of Chicago's law school. Beware of overdoing it. Grandiose claims will certainly spur admissions officers to carefully search for the supporting evidence.

Then you need to structure your story effectively, express yourself clearly and artfully, perhaps use a bit of humor if you've got the touch. "Your personal statement is a writing sample in the most profound sense—there's no excuse for sloppy expression," says Berring of Boalt Hall. "Use crisp, clear sentences. Many people think legal writing is complex clauses—not true!"

"Is the use of language effective? Does it paint a picture? Does it make me and my colleagues stop and listen? If you've got a great story to tell and you don't tell it until the second page, I won't see it," says AU's Andrew Popper. It probably goes without saying—or should—that every comma and period better be in the right place, too.

> *"If you take on the world in two pages, it comes across as naïve, or pseudo-intellectual."*

Make the most of your experience

Once a candidate's academic abilities have been established, the committee wants to know if she'll arrive with a perspective that will make for informed and lively debate. "I'm looking for an interesting class," says Popper. At AU's Washington College of Law, where last year some 8,400 applicants vied for 365 full-time and about 100 part-time slots, the LSAC-calculated index number assigned to each candidate gives the admissions committee a sense of his or her capabilities. Each file is read by one of the committee members, who review about 50 applications a week apiece and meet regularly to discuss them and give a thumbs-up or thumbs-down.

Many kinds of experience may make a particular candidate interesting, depending on the mix of other people applying: ethnic or religious background, socioeconomic status, undergraduate major—even geographic location. "People from the West think differently about the role of government and individual rights than people in New York City do," says Michael Young, who served as dean of George Washington University law school before moving to the presidency of the University of Utah. "People from California and Florida understand the melting pot and the importance of legal systems that work for all cultures." An applicant whose experience as a member of a minority group has been influential may want to explore that theme in the essay because most law schools value diversity for what it brings to class discussion.

One factor that has grown increasingly important in recent years is work experience. This has happened partly because the nature of the pool is changing; due to the economic downturn, the applicant pool has been rich with experienced people returning to school. "Ten years ago, 85 percent of our students came directly from college," says Lynell Cadray, dean of admission at Emory law school. This year, it was just under 40 percent.

This is also a function of a desire on the part of law deans and professors to seed their classes with wise and seasoned students attuned to the way the world operates now. "Lawyers today are part of a team, working with people whose experience is finance or human resources—it's no longer the Abe Lincoln version of law," says David Van Zandt, dean of the law school at Northwestern University, where almost everybody arrives with at least one year of work experience, and 80 percent typically have two or more. "What we're looking for is people who have had to work with a team or lead a team to get a project done. We've turned away people with very high LSATs who've had no work experience."

"Work experience adds to the level of what we can do with them here," says Cadray. "It's fun to have young, energetic students, but it's good to have balance. People interpret the legal sys-

Profile: The corporate lawyer

After five summers playing outfield for the Asheville Tourists, the Carolina Mudcats, and other minor league teams, David Feuerstein was ready for a change. He had graduated from Yale in 1995, grabbed his mitt, and begun the circuit of 14-hour bus trips to games up and down the East Coast. "That's a lot of baseball," he says. "As a minor leaguer, you make no money. And I was tired of it."

During the off-season, Feuerstein paid the bills by working as a paralegal for five months a year and discovered that he liked what he was doing. While he wasn't sure he wanted to be a lawyer, he figured that "a law degree [gives] you the most flexibility in the professional world. I knew I could do really whatever I wanted with it."

Because Feuerstein's girlfriend (now his wife) was living in New York City, he applied to the law schools at New York University, Columbia, and Yeshiva University. When he didn't get in to Columbia or NYU, he enrolled at Yeshiva's Benjamin N. Cardozo School of Law—though he worried that it didn't have the name recognition of the Ivies. "You take a risk not going to a top name law school, and I rolled the dice a little bit," Feuerstein says. "But I thought, 'I can do well. I can make the most of it.'"

As it turned out, he loved it. Taking a position and defending it to the bitter end appealed to the athlete in him. "My time away from higher intellectual challenges may have helped, too," he adds. In his third year, he was approached by the faculty to help organize a symposium on a subject one Cardozo professor had written extensively about: the similarities between law and baseball. The symposium drew the former commissioner and deputy commissioner of baseball, the president of the Florida Marlins, a sports writer from the *New York Times*, and, perhaps most importantly, the former dean of Cardozo Law School, Paul Verkuil. Later, when Feuerstein was searching for a job, it was Verkuil who introduced him to his future employer.

After graduation, Feuerstein joined Boies, Schiller, and Flexner in New York, where the majority of his clients were big corporations and the work involved such complex commercial litigations as antitrust cases and contract disputes. Many of Feuerstein's clients were sports organizations: the firm does work for the Yankees and NASCAR, for example.

Now, Feurerstein is an associate at Herrick, Feinstein, a general practice firm with offices in New York and New Jersey, where he hopes to continue combining his love of sports and the law.

---

tem differently depending on what they have done. And people who have worked tend to know how to work together, and want everyone to succeed."

While you might assume it's best to take a job in the legal field, perhaps as a paralegal, that's not necessarily the case. As Sandra Oakman, AU's late admissions director once put it, "It really doesn't matter what it is—you could be a bartender in Vail. Go out and work beside people and learn what it's like to be a single mother making $12 an hour. As a lawyer, you'll deal with all kinds of people, and wouldn't it be nice to know something about their culture?" Joe Lemon of the Stanford Law class of 2002 wrapped up his undergraduate studies at Brown in 1992 then managed a hotel for several years before applying

> *"Go out and work beside people and learn what it's like to be a single mother making $12 an hour."*

to law school. In his personal statement, he wrote about how the experience taught him to handle unexpected challenges—like the time two hours before a 200-guest wedding service when the groom had a seizure. (The wedding quickly was turned into a private affair, and the party went on as planned—except that the groom took a number of breaks to lie down.)

Remember, the point is to highlight how your background will allow you to offer something to the intellectual life at the school. "There's not one formula," says Katharine Bartlett, a former dean of the law school at Duke University, one of whose essays simply asks applicants to discuss what they might contribute that's different. A 37-year-old mom with three kids will certainly have an unusual perspective, says consultant DeLoggio. "People who have overcome eating disorders and drug addictions often want to hide these successes because they only see the failure they were before. But tomorrow's leaders need to understand a broad swath of society—not just the one in which they grew up," she says.

Demonstrate that you're a leader

One detail law schools can often glean from your work experience is whether or not you've got what it takes to motivate other people, solve problems, and make things happen. Ideally, your essay and your letters of recommendation will work together to paint you as the type of person who takes on responsibilities and produces results, either on the job if you've had one or in your activities as a student. "We want someone who's taken ownership of a group or a project, and made a difference," says Bartlett.

"It's very common for people to write 'I went to college, I studied this because I wanted to do this. I was president of this,'" says Ann Perry of Chicago. "Better to tell us what challenges you faced. You needed funding? Tell us how you worked the system. We want to see that you're capable."

Prove you've got a passion— and compassion

It's definitely in your favor to show a passionate interest in something other than your schoolwork or your work. Otherwise, you might come across as a "not very active citizen," says admissions consultant Mark Meyerrose. "What have you done? I don't want someone who has just gone to class and gone home," says Cornblatt.

But no one will be impressed by a padded résumé of activities that shows breadth without any depth. Much better to be very involved in a couple of activities—perhaps you studied the environment as an undergraduate, have taken a lead role in your local community group's battle against rapid development, and have religiously biked to work for the past two years—than to be a dabbler in a whole list of organizations. That's because admissions people recognize that those who graduate and become leaders in their field are likely to be the ones who show true commitment. Keep in mind that your letters of recommendation can be very helpful here. "It would raise flags for me if someone talks about how active on campus they've been and the recommender doesn't mention it," says Cornblatt. "It's great stuff when the application and letter both say it."

Because public service is such a major focus of the legal profession (even if many lawyers can't afford to take the jobs) many law schools are impressed by evidence of heart. "We're definitely on the lookout for compassionate students who have worked in their communities. This is a profession of counseling, being altruistic, caring," says Lynell Cadray, Emory's admissions dean. One of the more memorable personal statements that Cadray has read came from an older applicant who had served in the military; he wrote about bravery and his own experience pulling an accident victim from a burning car. "If we'd only looked at the numbers, he'd have been put on the wait list," she says. "But this is the kind of character you want in the profession."

Chapter Four

The Application

Whether you've dreamed your whole life of becoming the next Thurgood Marshall or are angling to hide out in law school until the job market recovers, one thing is for sure: you're not alone. Law schools across the country are reporting record numbers of applicants, so you'll be applying during the most intensely competitive era in history.

The fact is, it's tough to get into any school, anywhere, these days.

To stand out among the overachieving, type-A masses, you'll need to submit a virtually flawless application. The four parts of the package—your academic credentials, Law School Admission Test score, personal statement, and letters of recommendation—will demonstrate whether you're equipped (or not) with the skills you'll need to succeed in a law career: the powers of persuasion, ana-

---

It's tough to get into any school, anywhere, these days.

---

lytical and critical thinking, and a mastery of clear, precise, and direct writing.

First, understand that you're playing a numbers game. Law school admission is largely about two stats: your undergraduate grade point average and your performance on the LSAT. Chances are it's too late to do very much about the former—although any opportunity to raise your GPA even just a point or two should be taken seriously. (Note that grades are generally considered in the context of who's granting them and in what subject. In other words, a B in physics from Yale may be more impressive than an A in physics from your local public college.) Even more important, you've got to kick butt on the LSAT. Together, "the numbers account for 80 percent of the decision," estimates Roberta Alexander, who served as director of the pre-law program at the University of Dayton before retiring and was a former president of the Midwest Association of Pre-Law Advisors.

The other 20 percent? You've got to prove that you're interesting and accomplished, as well as smart. "Making a law school class is a lot like making a guest list for a dinner party," says R. Michael Cassidy, associate dean for academic affairs at Boston College Law School. "We want people who will have exciting discussions." The personal statement, handled properly, will reveal something about your character that speaks to your desirability as a dinner companion, if you will—and also your abilities as an effective and fluent writer. You've also got to get your professors, bosses, ex-bosses, or anyone else who knows you well to lend credence to the impressive picture you've painted of yourself.

The advice that follows on navigating the admissions process is gleaned from interviews with dozens of people who've either been there themselves or watch it over and over, including pre-law advisors at undergraduate colleges, law school admissions officers, and students who wish they'd handled a few things differently than they did. You still can.

Get a little guidance

If you haven't already done so, stop by your college's pre-law advising office. Though pre-law advisors, unlike high school guidance counselors, don't usually write recommendations or have any say in admissions at all, they do know a lot about the priorities of the decision makers. And sometimes, they *are* in a position to help or hurt your case: "I use pre-law advisors when we're trying to make decisions to find out about curricula and an applicant's major and colleges' grading scales," says Lynell Cadray, dean of admissions at Emory University's law school in Atlanta.

Most pre-law advisors are also professors, administrators, or career counselors with all of the multiple responsibilities of two full-time jobs. As a result, it can take some work to get a bit of face time, much less an hour-long appointment. But students who take the initiative early in their college career will find that a dedicated advisor can help them figure out which classes enhance a transcript, for example, or what major might make sense. Later on, an advisor might help you figure out which law schools are within your reach and which ones offer scholarships, and then review your personal statement before you send it off. Applicants who have been out of college for a while should feel free to tap the advising office at their alma mater—although they may be charged a fee for any services. (When you register for the LSAT, the Law School Admission Council, which administers the test, will provide you with the name and contact information of the pre-law advisor on your old campus.)

Unfortunately, many students report that overtaxed pre-law advisors are no help at all. If yours hasn't been responsive, you might consider hiring a private counselor. "Applying to law school is very much about self-assessment; this introspection really can't effectively take place unless there is another person to bounce ideas off of," argues Mark Meyerrose, a former Harvard Law School admissions officer who now works for Admissions Consultants, Inc., a Virginia-based firm that offers strategy and essay editing for applicants to college and graduate schools. "Everyone needs a critical reader." The firm's soup-to-nuts packages range from $1,795 for help with three applications to $4,995 for 15 applications (www.admissionsconsultants.com).

Indeed, while seeking the feedback of a trusted friend or professor is a fine idea, applicants appear to be increasingly willing to pay for professional guidance. Test-prep behemoth Kaplan Educational

Services has seen demand for its pre-law consulting services climb rapidly in recent years. The cost for its comprehensive admissions advice, usually given over the phone or by email, is anywhere from $599 for three hours of service to $1,599 for 10 hours; check out www.kaptest.com for more details. Test Masters, at www.testmasters180.com, will help you pick a topic for your personal statement and write an outline in one hour, for $200, and will continue to lend a hand as you hone your prose for an additional $150 per hour; full admissions counseling is also available at $200 for an initial hour and $150 for each hour after that. The 10-hour package runs $1,250.

If you're not willing or able to cough up the fees, consider contacting current law students for their insight about what qualities matter most to a school. One current 3L at the University of Pennsylvania suggests calling or emailing student organizations you may be interested in and asking a member or two how best to market yourself. Though most schools don't offer admissions interviews, deans and other faculty members also may be willing to answer questions about their school and what they value in a candidate. "I talk to every student who wants to meet with me," says David Cohen, professor and former dean at Pace University law school.

These contacts can come in handy later, after your applications are in. Randy Reliford contacted admissions officers at all of the nine law schools he applied to in late December and January of 2001–2002, and he often got put through to the dean. "I said 'I just want to talk to you about my application, to see if I can clear up any questions you might have had,'" says Reliford, who also visited schools in Philadelphia, where he's from, and met with admissions officers, faculty members, and representatives from black student organizations. "I wanted them to have a voice to put with my application, which I think has its weight just like anything else." Reliford was accepted at six of the schools he applied to and chose the University of Wisconsin Law School, whose admissions dean had mentioned to him that graduates of the flagship institution's law school don't have to take the bar exam to become credentialed in Wisconsin.

> *"I wanted them to have a voice to put with my application, which I think has its weight just like anything else."*

Watch your timing

The number one tip from pre-law advisors, paid and otherwise: it really helps to get your paperwork in early. Why? Better that your scintillating story about tutoring underprivileged inner-city kids be the first one a dean reads, rather than the 245th. "Earlier is always better," says Mark Meyerrose. "But there is a limit to that. I never push an applicant to get his application in by the beginning of, say, November, if that push will compromise quality. As long as the application is submitted by the December holidays, an applicant should be in good shape." See page 43 for more help with timing.

To help you stay on track, the Law School Admission Council, or LSAC—a nonprofit corporation of law schools that manages the admission process for its members—has streamlined the process of applying to multiple schools.

The LSAC administers the Law School Data Assembly Service, or LSDAS, which aggregates a report that just about every law school requires you use. For a fee, the group will compile a file that includes a summary of your undergraduate academic career, copies of all undergraduate, graduate, and law school transcripts, your LSAT score and writing sample from the test, and copies of your letters of recommendation. Registering for the LSDAS gives you access to electronic applications for all ABA-approved law schools. Save time by collecting and filling out all your applications at the same time.

Once a school receives your completed application, it will contact LSAC and request your LSDAS file, which will be sent once the report is complete and payment is received. You must pay for each report sent to a different law school.

LSDAS suggests that you register at least six weeks before you want your applications to go out, and for convenience, the organization strongly recommends you sign up for the service online at www.lsac.org. A mail-in registration option is also available.

Familiarize yourself with the LSAT

Ah, the dreaded Law School Admission Test—the bane of every future lawyer's existence. "I hate to say it's the key factor in admissions, but it certainly predominates," says one admissions officer at a top 20 school who asked not be identified. "When other things are weak and it is really strong, [it] will often make admissions officers forgive all the weaknesses." The converse can also be true, since most top schools are choosing among thousands of students with top grades *and* scores.

Why is the test so crucial? For one thing, it offers a quick and dirty way for admissions officers to compare applicants from diverse backgrounds and different schools—it's the one thing that a pottery major from State U. and a biochemical engineer from the Ivy League have in common. In addition, the test is widely considered to be a fairly reliable predictor of success during the first year of law school (as is college performance).

Part academic exercise and part endurance test, the LSAT is a half-day exam that tests skills as opposed to knowledge. It measures critical reading, verbal reasoning, analytical thinking, and writing abilities; there's no content involved whatsoever— no math or memorizing dates, in other words. "The LSAT is all about being able to pull apart arguments and understanding how evidence works," says Justin Serrano, general manager of graduate programs at Kaplan Test Prep and Admissions, who notes that these are exactly the talents you'll need in law school and, later, on the job.

The test is organized as five, 35-minute multiple-choice sections. Logical reasoning tests your capacity to understand, analyze, and complete arguments that are presented in short paragraph form; there are two logical reasoning sections that together account for half of your score. The problems in the analytical reasoning section measure your ability to understand relationships and draw conclusions about those relationships; there are four "games" with several questions apiece, and you will likely need to sketch diagrams in your test booklet to answer them. This is by far the most feared section of the test, say veterans; it's also the most coachable, claim test-prep experts.

Reading comprehension is similar to what you experienced on the SAT; you'll have to read four long, complex passages and answer questions about them. Finally, an experimental section tests questions for future LSATs; although it appears to be a real part of the test, it doesn't count toward your score. (Unfortunately, you won't necessarily know which section is experimental when you see it on the test.) The exam wraps up with a writing sample, which doesn't count either. You'll be given two alternatives and asked to choose a position and advocate it. Though the essay is sent to law schools along with your LSDAS report, it's generally not considered an important part of the package, and might not even merit a glance. But complete it carefully, just in case, because some application readers find the essay revealing. "The only thing you can't get editing help with is the written essay on the LSAT," says Barbara Safriet, former associate dean at Yale's law school. "I read it for writing skills."

> "The LSAT is all about being able to pull apart arguments and understanding how evidence works."

There's no penalty for wrong answers on the LSAT, so you should always take a guess, educated or not. The number of questions you answer correctly is your raw score, which is then converted to a scaled mark between 120 and 180. The average score is 150, but anything over 160 is considered competitive; anything over 170 puts you at or above the 98th percentile. An interesting fact: you can often miss a question or two and still nail a perfect 180.

The LSAT is offered four times a year: on a Saturday morning in October, December, and February, and on a Monday in June. (Alternatives are available for anyone who observes the Jewish

Sabbath.) You can register online at www.lsac.org, with a form from the LSAT/LSDAS Registration and Information Book, or over the phone. Be sure to sign up as soon as you can; with record numbers of test takers, popular testing sites can fill up early. (You may first want to check out www.kaptest.com/testsites, which rates various locations for the last five test dates, based on student evaluations of proctors, desk space, and the like.) Scores remain valid for five years, so anyone planning on working a year or two before applying to law school may want to tackle the exam during junior or senior year, when he or she is still in test-taking mode.

In fact, all applicants should take the test as early as possible in order to allow for further preparation and a retest, if necessary. February and June of the junior year—or one full year before you plan to matriculate—are increasingly the norm. "This is a big mindset change," says Heather Struck, pre-law advisor at Binghamton University in New York. "Students used to be able to study during the summer and take the test in October [of senior year]. But there's a lot more stress now, and it helps if you can take it in your junior year." Still, you can procrastinate until December, if necessary, and still have time to beat the final February 1 or March 1 application deadlines.

Prepare to beat the test

Though the LSAT tests for capabilities rather than knowledge, that doesn't mean you can't prepare for the exam. In fact, practicing is crucial so you'll know what types of questions and games to expect: with only 60 to 90 seconds allotted per question, there's no time for confusion. The more familiar you are with all aspects of the exam, the more confident you'll feel on test day—and the better you'll do.

Do you have enough self-discipline to set your own study schedule and stick to it? Alex Murray did. In the first week of September of his senior year at Tulane, Murray bought a test-prep book and began completing problems and taking timed practice tests on the weekends. "I started out just doing one section at a time without a time limit to get used to the questions and format," he recalls. "Then I would do one or two sections and time myself. I didn't start taking full, timed exams until about two or three weeks before the exam, because it's so time-consuming." The week before Murray sat for the exam, he took advantage of a free practice test at the local Kaplan Test Prep center, which was timed and scored for him. In the end, he raised his score from the "high 150s" on practice tests to an extremely competitive 169 on the real thing—which helped get him into the University of California–Los Angeles School of Law.

In addition to the shelves of good commercial test-prep booklets out there (those published by Kaplan and Peterson's, for example), LSAC (www.lsac.org) offers such "official" help as the $20 SuperPrep, which contains three previously administered LSATs, with explanations. The most recent exams are available there for $8 each, too. Applicants also can take free sample tests at websites such as www.ivyleagueadmission.com, a for-profit site run by former admissions counselors. (Print out the sample exams first in order to best approximate a real test-taking situation.)

There are less expensive online options for those who prefer to learn at their own pace, with 24-hour-a-day access to online instruction and practice tests. In fact, due to increased demand, The Princeton Review has extended its web-based offerings with a course featuring live, real-time instruction for $899, a do-it-anytime online course for $599, and an express version with three hours of lessons and two practice tests for $99.

Not everyone can do this kind of prep on his own, however. If you need additional motivation in the form of a class commitment and several hours' worth of homework a week, there are virtually endless opportunities. Many colleges and law schools offer their own test prep; the University of Arizona's

The application timeline

18 months prior to enrollment

- Contact your pre-law advisor to set up a meeting; attend any related seminars offered on your college campus.
- Research schools and come up with a target list.
- Take a practice, timed LSAT to see where you stand.
- Register for the June LSAT.
- Decide on the method of test prep that suits you best and start studying.

June before applying

- Take the June LSAT, and if you don't do as well as expected, re-register for October and start studying again.
- Start visiting campuses, if possible.

August–September

- Begin crafting the "story" that will become your personal statement, then write and rewrite it—and then

rewrite it again. Get feedback from an unbiased editor.
- Put together a résumé to submit with your application.
- Figure out whom you will ask for recommendations—and whether or not each will write you a positive letter.
- Send away for or download applications.

October–November

- Continue to perfect your personal statement and résumé.
- Make sure the people writing your letters of recommendation have enough source material to draw from and remind them about deadlines.
- Take the October LSAT, if necessary.
- Subscribe to LSDAS and request transcripts from all undergraduate and graduate schools you've attended.
- Sign up for an LSAC online account so you can obtain a

copy of your master Law School Report from LSDAS. Proofread for any errors.
- Complete and mail your applications to schools—the earlier the better.

December

- Finish up any remaining applications.
- If you have not yet taken the LSAT or want to try it again, the December test is your last shot, assuming you want to be considered for the fall entering class.

January–February

- Request that any supplemental transcripts be sent to LSDAS.
- Check in with your schools to see if they need any additional information.
- Wait for the acceptance letters to start rolling in!

law school, for example, gives a free four-day class to local students who demonstrate they can't afford a commercial one. Check with your pre-law advising center for similar opportunities in your area.

On the other end of the spectrum are intensive classes offered by companies such as Kaplan and The Princeton Review, the latter of which boasts an average seven-point gain for its students. They offer options for everyone from the ultraorganized student who plans to spend at least three months studying to the person holding down a full-time job who only has a couple of weeks to get ready. Those seeking more personalized attention can also purchase private, one-on-one tutoring.

The quality of tutors and programs can vary from region to region, so it's a good idea to research test prep offerings in your area before signing up for a particular company's course. Talk to different teachers and investigate their review materials to determine what approach they take, for instance, and consult friends and acquaintances who have prepped before you.

Make the most of your second time around

Didn't quite hit 175 this time? Think hard about whether you want to try again. The LSAC reports your LSAT scores (plus any decisions you make to cancel a score) over a five-year span, as well as an average score. You're also assigned a "score band" that ranges from roughly three points below to three points above your actual score—an attempt by the LSAC to recognize that there could be statistical errors, and to discourage schools from putting too much weight on single-point differentials. When applicants take the test

more than once, most schools look at the average score, not just the higher one, and so only a fairly significant jump is going to have any real impact.

Admissions officers suggest sitting for the LSAT again only if practice tests taken under realistic conditions suggest that you'll get a much higher score, or if circumstances the first time—a marching band outside the testing room, say, or a nasty case of mono—had an obvious impact on your performance. If you do take the exam twice and end up with a large discrepancy between your scores, you might want to write a note of explanation countering any suspicion of cheating (and clarifying why the higher grade makes sense).

Write a mind-blowing personal statement

Here is your chance to take the admissions committee beyond the cold, hard numbers and demonstrate why you'll be an asset to the class. Think of your personal statement as the interview you probably won't have—an opportunity to showcase your personality and drive and talk about your passions and events that have made you who you are. The idea is to demonstrate that your superlative record comes with humor, an ability to reflect, and a measure of gained wisdom.

First, you need to decide on a specific topic. "Students should really hone in on one thing—one activity they're involved in or one challenge that was significant," says Don Rebstock, associate dean for enrollment management and career strategy at Northwestern University School of Law in Illinois. Otherwise, there's an unappealing tendency to ramble. Rebstock suggests brainstorming for ideas by going to a bookstore and paging through a manual on hiring for questions intended to get at interviewees' characters. What is the defining moment of your life? What are your biggest strengths and weaknesses? It might be tempting to expound on the complex legal theory du jour, but an academic treatise won't help your case—it doesn't really address anything about *you*. "Let us know what type of voice you'll bring," says Ann Perry, assistant dean for admissions at the University of Chicago law school. "I don't want a résumé, and I don't want to know what kind of law you want to practice."

You needn't deal directly with the law at all, in fact, to show that you've got what it takes to be a lawyer. When he applied to New York University School of Law, Paul Millen wrote about scaling a difficult stretch of rock formations while hiking in Central China. "The story illustrated a method of problem solving that analyzed information to the degree possible, but recognized that the ultimate decision required a certain amount of courage and risk-acceptance," he explains. "I highlighted my travel experiences, demonstrated my adventuresome spirit, and, in discussing the decision-making process, exhibited an ability to work [with others], since the rest of my group consisted of Chinese, Israelis, and Europeans."

Another applicant wrote about organizing hotel workers in New Orleans. Although her LSAT scores were only so-so, Washington and Lee School of Law admired her pluck, commitment, and unique experience and came through with a generous financial aid package. A Naval officer accepted by an Ivy League law school described how confounded he'd felt as judge of a local beauty pageant when he'd tried to issue orders to the crowd of 17-year-old girls with absolutely no effect. "If he'd written about the wisdom and maturity

he'd gained in his naval command, he would only have put himself among everyone else with five years' work experience," says Seattle admissions consultant Loretta DeLoggio.

Many admissions officers recommend staying away from potentially inflammatory subjects such as politics or religion, as you can never be sure who your reader will be. Others counter that any topic is

> *"Students should really hone in on one thing—one activity they're involved in or one challenge that was significant."*

fine, as long as you're invested in it. But there are some definite no-no's: unless the story is dramatic and compelling, you'll want to avoid predictable themes such as "Why I've dreamed of becoming a lawyer since I was 4." It's also smart to steer clear of areas that are already well-covered in your application, like your LSAT score or your grades. (Consider an addendum to the application if you really feel there's more to say on these matters, say experts.)

Writing about challenges overcome is okay, but be sure to hit the right notes. "I'm often struck by people who seem to lack perspective, and who think minor hurdles overcome were extraordinary," says Sarah Zearfoss, assistant dean and director of admissions at the University of Michigan Law School in Ann Arbor. "It's fine and good to talk about hurdles," she says, but do not make a bigger claim for yourself than the situation warrants. And the last thing you want to seem to do is whine.

Whatever the topic, your personal statement should be well-organized and compelling because effective communication is so key to the practice of law. And make sure to proofread for any goofs in grammar, spelling, or punctuation. Or worse: you don't want to say you'd be a perfect fit at Yale on your Cornell essay, for instance (a more common occurrence than you might think). Inattention to detail is unacceptable in the field of law, so why should the application process be any different? Further, think long and hard about the tone of your personal statement, as nearly every admissions officer has a horror story about a mean-spirited or arrogant essay that doomed a candidate's application. It goes without saying that the work should be wholly your own.

One dean remembers a successful essay written as a recipe, but creative writers should generally err on the side of caution; law school, after all, is a pretty conservative place. "We're open to various styles, with one caveat: it can definitely be taken too far," says Monica Ingram, assistant dean for admissions at the University of Texas–Austin. "If you're not Charles Dickens before you write your statement, this is probably not the opportunity to take a foray into creative writing."

"No one with a rhyming essay has gotten in for at least the last five years," adds Megan Barnett, Yale's former dean of admissions and financial aid.

Get glowing recommendations

Now that you've presented your accomplishments, it's time to have a third party back you up. Ask people you've worked with closely to write your letters of recommendation—people who will offer enthusiastic support. You might assume that a letter from your senator or a local Pulitzer Prize-winning author will carry great weight, but if she doesn't know you from your next-door neighbor, it's unlikely she can say anything about you that will have any impact. Far better to have a teaching assistant who's observed you in class comment on

how smart you are and how enthusiastically you participate, or to ask a former boss to describe how you went the extra mile. Then make sure each letter writer has the necessary raw material as inspiration, including a copy of your résumé and personal statement and perhaps a particularly impressive paper you wrote for class or a project you've worked on with a colleague.

"The best advice I can give to students is that they keep papers and exams so they can furnish them to letter writers," says now-retired Dayton pre-law advisor Roberta Alexander, who kept all of her grade books from 35 years of teaching and used them to write letters of recommendation for students she taught as many as 15 years earlier. Some undergraduate institutions, such as the University of California–Berkeley, will keep letters of recommendation on file for a period of years for a fee and mail them out, as needed, for an additional cost.

Most law schools allow up to three letters of recommendation, though some request only one. Be sure to follow any directions for submitting the letters: some institutions request or require that they come through LSDAS. If so, log onto www.lsac.org to download the necessary form; anyone vouching for you will need to fill it out and return it to LSDAS along with a signed copy of the letter itself.

Interview, if you can

While most admissions officers will meet with candidates for informational meetings as time allows, only a handful of schools offer true admissions interviews. Pace University, for one, conducts up to 450 on- and off-campus interviews a year on a first-come, first-served basis; some schools make it a point to meet their "borderline" candidates. Such meetings are used to obtain additional information about an applicant's communication skills and recent accomplishments.

Profile: The public defender

When Brian Marsicovetere enrolled in Vermont Law School, he was pretty sure he wanted to study environmental law. The school has one of the best programs in the country. But then something happened that changed his mind. "That would have been my first criminal law class," he says.

The more cases he read, the more fascinated he became with "the idea that there are limits on the government's ability to reach into people's private lives," he says. "I became really interested in the notion of privacy and of protecting people's liberty. I just really wanted to stand up for people in relation to institutions." His professor, a former prosecutor, "did a really great job of bringing out the personal elements of the cases," he says.

Vermont gave Marsicovetere the option of taking up to 18 credits of internships, so he promptly went to work in a public defender's office. By graduation, he had argued bail hearings in trial court, won his first motion to suppress an illegal search, cross-examined a police officer—and even argued an appeal before the Vermont Supreme Court. The case involved a police officer who had gone to a house to investigate a noise complaint. When the officer arrived, the homeowner refused to let him in "to the point of using force," Marsicovetere says. It was reasonably clear that it was an unlawful search, but did the homeowner have the right to resist with force?

The early immersion in the day-to-day of trial law would make Marsicovetere an attractive job candidate: before he even began scouring the want ads, he was offered an associate position doing criminal defense with the firm of Kevin W. Griffin in White River Junction, Vermont. "I had so much experience by the time I graduated," he says. "I had this well of motions already drafted, and a whole bunch of legal research for issues that would occur in case after case. I was very much ahead of the game." He also had developed people skills. Most valuable lesson? How to ask opposing counsel for what you need without triggering a hostile response or blowing the lines of communication.

Today, the firm's name has expanded to Griffin Marsicovetere, and Wilkes. Marsicovetere spends 60 percent of his time taking on assigned public defender cases—aggravated assaults, rapes, murders, and kidnappings—and the rest devoted to a thriving private practice across the state and in New Hampshire, representing plaintiffs in civil rights lawsuits and clients in criminal cases. And he loves small-town lawyering. "You really get to see the product of your work in the community—I run into past clients all the time, walking down the street, in the diner," he says. "The fact that you see these people around town really pushes you to do a better job for them." In short, he says, he doesn't miss big-city firm life at all.

Northwestern aims to interview as many candidates as possible, giving each a numerical rating and a page-long write-up. "We really feel that law is a very interactive profession, and no employer is going to hire anyone without interviewing them first," explains Don Rebstock. "I scratch my head [wondering] why other law schools aren't doing this." Rebstock says he won't admit recent college grads until he has a sense of their maturity and how well they'll interact with people who've been in the work force for several years.

It's a good idea to seek an interview if you can, and to prepare for it as carefully as you would a job interview. Bring a résumé, dress professionally, and be ready to answer questions about your studies, the value of any work experience you've had, and your interest in the law school—what attracted you to the program, for example. Rebstock recalls applicants who looked great on paper but who stared at the ground and had nothing to say and who did not get admitted as result. He has also interviewed wait-list candidates and been so impressed by their interpersonal skills that he has offered them admission on the spot.

Escape wait-list limbo

What if you land in that twilight zone between acceptance and rejection? Though it's become increasingly difficult to get into law school off of the wait list, it does still happen. Admissions deans counsel those in wait-list limbo to stay in touch over the summer about additional grades and honors, and to periodically let law schools know that they're still interested.

One Binghamton University student who found herself on the wait lists at Georgetown, Columbia, and NYU a few years ago started making plans to attend another New York law school, but stayed in touch with the admissions directors at the other three, sending an updated transcript and an additional recommendation letter, as well as an article about her role in a national mock trial competition. She also kept in phone and email contact with her pre-law advisor, who talked to several admissions staffers on her behalf. She eventually got the nod from NYU and decided to enroll there instead.

What minority students need to know

In June 2003, the Supreme Court ruled in *Grutter v. Bollinger* that the University of Michigan Law School was justified in favorably counting an underrepresented minority applicant's race when making admissions decisions. While the case concerned Michigan—whose policies were challenged by a 49-year-old white consultant and mother of two who had been rejected by the school—every other law school sat up and took note, too.

Much like other schools, there is no formula for admission at Michigan; deans weigh race, among other myriad factors, in a complex decision-making process. As a result, sometimes students with lower-than-average scores or grades are admitted to the school because they have other important assets such as leadership, service experience, or are from underrepresented racial backgrounds.

In Michigan, the use of race in admissions is still in flux. In 2006, voters in the state passed a ballot initiative—similar to one in California—that again challenges the school's affirmative action policies. But the larger result of the 2003 *Grutter v. Bollinger* decision remains: Most schools will continue to consider minority status as one attribute among many that influence their choices—though not as an overriding factor, nor through a point system or quotas. And it certainly will not compensate for generally poor performance.

How should you handle the question of race in your application? "It's helpful to speak about race if it has meaning for you," advises Sarah Zearfoss, assistant dean and director of admissions at Michigan. "It's not necessary, but it is certainly additional information that we would consider positively in reviewing a file." Tamara Gustave, a graduate of the University of Baltimore School of Law, wrote in her personal statement about why she—a multilingual Haitian woman who was the first member of her family to graduate from college in the United States—wanted to be a lawyer. "I think that all of these qualities are positive things that added to me as a person," she explains. "I talked about the fact that my family were immigrants from Haiti, my involvement with my [undergraduate] black student union, and the fact that the law sometimes doesn't apply to everybody equally, which I saw firsthand as a black woman."

"Don't think that just marking off a box indicating your racial and ethnic identity on your application is enough," says Evangeline Mitchell, author of *The African American Pre-Law School Advice Guide: Things You Really Need to Know before Applying to Law School*. She suggests students include any race-related organizations, activities, and community service work on their résumés. If you have other topics to cover in your personal statement, she also advises submitting an additional, one- to two-page "diversity statement" that covers what race means to you, how it's shaped you, and how this may have drawn you to the law—as well as how you can contribute to the incoming class.

Chapter Five

Finding the Money

Not many pieces of paper are more expensive than a law diploma. At the priciest schools—Northwestern University Law School in Illinois and Columbia Law School in New York City, to name two—the total cost of a JD degree (including living expenses and books) now tops $150,000. How do law students cover the bills? "Loans, loans, and more loans," says one assistant director of student financial aid. Debts of $80,000 are common among law school grads—and that's not counting the load that many have taken on as undergraduates.

How can you limit the damage? Most schools award at least a little financial aid based on need, and a rapidly growing number also offer merit-based scholarships to numerically attractive candidates who would enhance the student-body profile. Uncle Sam's largesse, in the form of tax credits for the cost of higher education, can also free up some extra cash. And work-study, summer employment, or tuition reimbursement from an employer can lessen your out-of-pocket expense.

Even if you do have to borrow significant sums, you can take some comfort in the fact that education debt is still pretty cheap; through your tax deductions, Uncle Sam will chip in on the interest you do pay. And if you don't wind up with a hefty salary after graduation because you're working for a government or nonprofit agency, one of a growing number of debt-forgiveness programs can help you pay off the bills (see list, page 60). Here's what you need to know to pay for your degree.

Need-based grants might help a little—very little

As you probably recall from your undergraduate days, anyone applying for financial aid funds handed out by the federal government has to fill out the Free Application for Federal Student Aid, more commonly known as the FAFSA. That's where you'll start, but the truth is that most law schools have only a modest amount of money available for need-based grants. They assume that most students will borrow to finance their degrees and will easily be able to repay their debts once they are lawyers. Even schools with more available money generally do not meet their students' full need with grants: there simply aren't enough funds available at the graduate level to fully fund the

requirements of students no longer dependent on their parents. Apply early, generally before the end of January, if you hope to qualify for a need-based grant; some schools make their awards on a first-come, first-served basis.

You may find that your eligibility for need-based aid varies dramatically from school to school. That's because law schools, like undergraduate colleges and universities, use different formulas to calculate how big a discrepancy you've got between your resources and how much law school will cost. Under the formula used to disburse federal aid, for example, all graduate students are considered independent and supporting themselves, regardless of their age or whether they have financial help from their parents. Since most recent graduates have income levels in the $20,000s or $30,000s, schools that use the federal methodology see quite a bit of need.

But at law schools that use their own institutional formulas—such as those at Harvard, Yale, Columbia, and Syracuse University—many students are classified as dependent, which means that financial aid officers consider Mom's and Dad's resources to be available to pay the bills. Typically, a school would call you dependent if you're under age 29 or 30, say, and don't have any dependents of your own. Other schools are stricter. At Fordham, "If the parents are alive, we look at them," says Stephen Brown, assistant dean of admissions and financial aid for the law school.

Apply with an eye on the merit money

In the past decade, many law schools have boosted the amount of merit aid they award in an effort to compete for the best students; these grants are given out not on the basis of need but to reward academic performance (and to snag top candidates). The awards are usually made based on your application for admission: high LSAT scores and undergraduate grades are the predominant criteria, but schools are also looking to lure in people with interesting work and life experience, and those who would bring geographic and racial diversity to the student body. You'll have a shot at one of these scholarships if you apply to schools where your academic credentials are above average or where you stand out in some other way. At the very top law schools, where every successful applicant is a standout student, merit awards are harder to come by. (But remember: a degree from such a school is a key credential if you hope to land a job at a prestigious corporate law firm.)

More than a dozen schools now offer scholarships specifically for students who are planning careers in public interest law and have a record of community service to prove it. Boston College's Public Service Scholarships are worth two-thirds of the $36,500 tuition each year. The University of Denver offers full-tuition Chancellor's Scholarships to 12 students who have a solid record of service and aspire to practice public interest law. At some schools, law students can apply for university-wide fellowships available to graduate students. Florida State University, for instance, offers a University Fellowship that covers tuition for up to 12 credit hours a semester and pays a $15,000 stipend to cover living expenses. You may need to apply for the university-wide awards through the graduate school financial aid office rather than the law school, but your law school's financial aid counselor should know what's available.

Search for outside scholarships

Scholarships from foundations, associations, and civic organizations are not as plentiful for law students as they are for other graduate and professional students. Many outside awards are reserved for minority students, for residents of specific states, or for students concentrating in specific areas of the law. But it's well worth spending a few hours searching scholarship sites such as www.fastweb.com or www.collegenet.com to see if there's an award you might be eligible for. Also try the excellent listing of grants on Michigan State University's website at www.lib.msu.edu/harris23/grants/3subject.htm. Some examples:

- The Association of Trial Lawyers of America awards a handful of scholarships, worth $1,000 to $3,000, to students who are active ATLA student members.
- The Attorney-CPA Foundation awards 12 scholarships a year ($250 to $1,000) to law students who are also certified public accountants.
- Some state and local bar associations award scholarships. For instance, the Foundation of the State Bar of California makes awards of $2,500 to $7,500 to students at California law schools; it made 47 such awards in 2003.
- The American Bar Association Legal Opportunity Scholarship Fund offers 20 awards per year of $5,000 each to minority students.

Some law schools keep a binder of outside scholarship listings; others post listings on their websites. An undergraduate pre-law advisor may also be able to steer you to scholarship opportunities. Other possible sources of leads include state bar associations, unions, and civic groups you're

Go part-time. There's nothing easy about working full-time and then going to class four nights a week. But part-time study allows some students to foot the bill, at least in part, from cash flow and perhaps to take advantage of employer-paid tuition (see below). The best part-time programs are those where the same instructors teach both full-time and part-time students. (For more on choosing a part-time program, see page 5.)

Let your employer pay for it. Many large employers offer corporate tuition benefits for employees pursuing graduate degrees. But there's a catch: most require the courses you take to be job-related. That means paralegals and legal assistants are the most likely to qualify for corporate benefits to fund a law degree. Colleges and universities also tend to be generous with their tuition benefits for employees and sometimes spouses; some prospective law students even seek out university employment for this very reason.

Live like a student. The student expense budget law schools estimate for yearly housing, food, and personal expenses is almost laughable—$12,000 to $15,000 is typical. "Food is the number one budget buster," says Stephen Brown at Fordham. "It's very easy to grab a bagel and coffee out every day and spend $900 a year."

"The living expense choices that students make will affect how much they have to borrow," says Gina Soliz, director of financial aid at Syracuse University's College of Law. Those who manage to keep their debt to a minimum are the ones who say, "I don't need digital cable right now. I can get a roommate and live like a student."

Build up some savings. If you're looking ahead to law school in the next couple of years and can set aside some savings, take advantage of the tax benefits of a state-sponsored 529 plan. While most investors use these plans to save for a child's undergraduate expenses, they generally allow you to open an account and name yourself as the beneficiary. The primary benefit is that the earnings on your savings won't be taxed, and your state may throw in a deduction for your contributions. All 529 plans include investments that are appropriate for adults who will need to tap the money soon, such as bonds and money-market accounts.

While many of the broker-sold 529 plans impose up-front sales fees that would minimize or offset any tax benefits over just a year or two, many of the direct-sold plans, such as those offered by TIAA-CREF and Vanguard, do not. Several are paying a guaranteed 3 percent or so right now. Not a bad parking place for a year or two, especially when Uncle Sam isn't claiming any of the gains.

affiliated with, as well as honor societies, fraternities, or sororities you belonged to as an undergraduate.

Be aware that if you qualify for a need-based grant from your law school, an outside scholarship probably won't just add to your kitty; it may be used to reduce the size of your grant. At such a school, say, a $2,500 award might lighten your loan burden by $1,000 and trim a need-based grant by $1,500.

Get set to borrow

Debt is a fact of life for most law students; at many pricey private law schools, the average debt at graduation now exceeds $80,000. But low interest rates definitely help ease the sting.

Federal loans. Government-guaranteed Stafford loans made directly to students are a staple for most law students; a typical full-time student takes out the annual maximum of $20,500 per year. (Overall, you can borrow up to $138,500 in Stafford loans to finance your education, including what you've borrowed as an undergraduate.) Part of that total, up to $8,500, is often a "subsidized" loan, meaning that the federal government pays the interest while you're in school and for six months after you graduate or drop below half-time status. The rest is unsubsidized, so interest accrues while you're in school. Payments on both subsidized and unsubsidized Staffords can be deferred until after graduation.

To be eligible for a subsidized loan, your FAFSA form will have to show that you can't shoulder much of the financial burden yourself—fairly easy to do with law school costs so high. If your school participates in the Federal Direct Loan Program, you'll borrow directly from the federal government. Otherwise, you can choose your own funding source using a list of preferred lenders provided by your school. While all lenders offer Stafford loans at the same interest rate, some waive the up-front origination and guarantee fees (which can run 4 percent of the loan amount), some reduce the interest rate in repayment if you sign up for automatic payments or make a certain number of payments on time, and some do both. So it can pay to shop around. Rates on these variable-rate loans change every summer, but will not exceed a cap of 8.25 percent.

Students with high financial need—that is, the FAFSA shows that they're expected to contribute very little or nothing toward their law school education—will also qualify for a Perkins loan of up to $6,000 per year at an interest rate that's fixed at 5 percent. In addition, there are no up-front origination fees. The Perkins is a subsidized loan, so no interest accrues until nine months after you graduate or drop below half-time status.

Private loans. If the federal loan limits leave you short, private lenders stand ready to lend you as much as the full cost of your education less any financial aid. (Some law schools also have their own loan programs.) Interest rates tend to be only slightly higher than the rates on Stafford loans. However, origination and other fees can be significantly higher—running as much as 8.5 percent of the loan amount—and interest begins accruing right away. Loan programs geared specifically to law students will even lend you up to $10,000 or so on top of what you need for tuition and living expenses during the school year to help cover your costs while you study for the bar exam. Some popular programs include CitiAssist from Citibank (www.studentloan.com), Law Access Loan from Access Group Inc. (www.accessgroup.org), Law Loans from Sallie Mae (www.salliemae.com/lawloans), and LawAchiever from KeyBank (www.keybank.com/educate).

To qualify for private loans, you need a clean credit history—or a cosigner. Financial aid officers recommend that prospective students pay down their debts, close unnecessary lines of credit, and check their credit histories for errors before applying for admission. Ann Weitgenant, assistant director of financial aid at Valparaiso University Law School in Indiana, says she sometimes even counsels students to work an extra year to pay down their credit cards and car loans.

Home-equity loans. For students who own a home, a home-equity line of credit is another attractive choice. Rates are low, fees are minimal, and interest on up to $100,000 in debt is tax deductible if you itemize. If you expect to graduate into a high-paying job, home-equity debt may be a better choice than other debt because you won't qualify for tax-deductible interest on government or private student loans. Interest on regular student loans will be fully tax deductible only if your income falls below $50,000 if you're a single taxpayer and below $100,000 if you file jointly. Remember, though, that a home-equity line of credit is secured by your home, so be certain you'll be able to make the payments regardless of where your career path leads after graduation.

Find help paying the money back

At current rates, the payment on $80,000 in debt is more than $900 a month over 10 years. Those payments may be easily manageable for newly minted lawyers who land high-paying jobs in the private sector. For those who don't, there are ways to ease the burden.

Flexible repayment options. While the standard term for repaying Stafford loans is 10 years, you can stretch the term in various ways to make your payments more affordable. With an extended repayment plan, for instance, you can lengthen the loan term to up to 30 years. Another option, a graduated repayment schedule that extends over 12 to 30 years, starts you off with lower payments than the standard plan and then ratchets them up annually. Income-contingent or income-sensitive repayment plans adjust your payment each year based on your income. In the end, you'll pay more interest over longer payback periods. But you can always boost your payments as your income rises to pay down the loan more quickly than you're asked to.

Loan consolidation. You may also be able to reduce the interest you pay on Stafford loans by consolidating them when interest rates are low. That locks in current interest rates instead of allowing them to fluctuate annually. You may even be able to consolidate your undergraduate and early law school loans to take advantage of low rates while you're still in school. For more details about student loan consolidation, you may wish to visit www.loanconsolidation.ed.gov at the Department of Education's website, or www.federalconsolidation.org, a website sponsored by Access Group, Inc., a private, nonprofit lender.

Student-loan interest deduction. If your income is modest, Uncle Sam will step in to help with the interest payments. You can deduct up to $2,500 a year in student-loan interest if you earn less than $50,000 as a single taxpayer or less than $100,000 if you are married and filing jointly. (You can deduct a lesser amount with income up to $65,000 filing singly or $130,000 filing jointly.)

Note to parents: you get to take this deduction if you're legally obligated to pay back the debt and you claim the student as a dependent on your tax return.

Loan repayment assistance programs. "If you get out of here with $70,000 of debt and get a job for $30,000, it's tough to pay the debt back," says Christine Falzerano, associate director of student financial services at Pace's law school. That's why more than 70 schools, 50 employers, and a number of states now offer loan repayment assistance to lawyers who practice public interest law for a non-profit agency or who work as government prosecutors or public defenders. University of Oregon law grads earning less than $45,000 a year in a public service or public interest law job can qualify for up to $25,000 in loan-repayment assistance over five years, for instance. The university lends graduates up to $5,000 per year to make payments to the government or the bank that holds their student loans, then later forgives all or part of the debt, depending on the graduate's level of income and length of time doing public interest work. Instead of forgivable loans, a few law schools make outright grants to cover student loan debt. The University of San Diego, for one, awards grants of $2,000 to $5,000 per year for up to five years to graduates in public interest jobs.

Loan repayment programs vary dramatically from school to school. Those with meager budgets may offer help to only a handful of students, may offer relatively small loans or grants, or may cap eligibility at salaries of $35,000 or less. Institutions with ample resources, such as Harvard, Yale, Columbia, and New York University, can afford to offer loan repayment help to more graduates and to graduates with higher salaries. If you're comparing LRAPs when choosing a law school, ask how much funding is available and how many eligible students receive loans or grants. Also, be aware that you may have to repay some or all of an LRAP loan if you leave your public interest job during the course of a year, and you may cease to be eligible if your income rises over a certain amount.

Find work

While the American Bar Association recommends that first-year law students do not work during the academic year, "a lot of students feel they can handle it," says Valparaiso's Ann Weitgenant. "It lets them step away from the law for awhile." In fact, students who apply for financial aid may be awarded a work-study job to meet some of their financial need; an award of $1,500 to $2,000 a year is typical, for 10 to 15 hours of work a week. Some students manage to get work-study jobs off campus providing legal services to a nonprofit organization such as Bay Area Legal Aid and the Folsom City Attorney's Office, two of the off-campus employers in UC–Berkeley's work-study program. In that case, the employer and the school, subsidized by the federal government, jointly provide the funds paid to the student.

Research assistantships are another option at some universities. At Syracuse, for instance, law students can take a graduate assistantship position anywhere in the university. "That's probably the best deal out there," says Gina Soliz, director of financial aid at Syracuse University's College of Law. "For a little bit of work, you could get part or all of your tuition paid, plus a stipend," she says. Law students would generally have to seek out such positions by knocking on faculty doors once they arrive on campus.

Summer jobs can be a way to rack up some serious earnings, especially for second- and third-year students at good schools, where corporate law firms recruit for summer positions that can pay

Theresa Owens knew when she decided on law school that she wanted to represent children. So she researched schools with specialized programs in juvenile law and settled on Whittier in Costa Mesa, CA. She was swayed by Whittier's financial package and the fact that she would be eligible for summer stipends of $3,000 if she chose to do public interest work in the community. (Having grown up in New Jersey and having attended the University of Massachusetts–Amherst, Owens didn't mind the prospect of some balmy Southern California weather, either.)

Along with 20 other entering students, Owens enrolled in Whittier's children's law program, which includes courses in family law, juvenile trial advocacy, and juvenile justice in addition to the standard courses. She also took a special writing class with a focus on the research and briefs likely to be encountered in juvenile law. Monthly colloquia brought judges, doctors, and child psychologists to campus to shed light on such topics as signs of child abuse, hurdles of the adoption process, and how to interview children in court. To fulfill one of the program's requirements, she worked for one semester at the school's clinic for underprivileged families, delving into the details of domestic violence cases and restraining orders, and helping the grandparents of abandoned children file for guardianship. As the first editor-in-chief of the program's newly launched *Children and Family Law Journal*, she commissioned and published articles by legal scholars on subjects that ranged from juvenile delinquency to reproductive issues such as surrogacy and custody of eggs.

As they honed their skills, Owens and her colleagues were sent into juvenile detention centers in Los Angeles to assist on civil rights cases. She recalls a talk with one child offender who was HIV positive, and was having trouble getting medication because "it wasn't the sort of thing you'd want to tell any of the staff there about." Then there were the allegations of sexual abuse of children by juvenile hall staffers. To practice questioning young witnesses, Owens and her classmates took turns playing frightened four-year-olds in mock trials.

After graduation, Owens worked frequently with the foster care system as a court-appointed lawyer helping parents get their children back. Usually, the children had been removed from their parents due to abuse or neglect, or maybe because the home was overrun with rats or roaches. In those cases, particularly if it seemed as if the parents were doing their best, she felt as if the family were in a Catch-22. "The public financial benefits don't kick in until you have your children back with you," she says. But, understandably, "the state won't return your children until you have a home with electricity, water"—and no rodents. "You look for the cases that can bring you some joy," she says, "because a lot of them are very frustrating and very hard."

Eventually, Owens hopes to represent young people accused of juvenile offenses. Meantime, her career has taken her to California's Administrative Office of the Courts in San Francisco, where she analyzed the effectiveness of state laws and procedures for placing abused and neglected children, and to New Jersey's Office of the Public Defender in Newark, where she defends parents fighting to retain custody of their kids.

$1,500 to $2,500 a week. Many students at Fordham, for instance, have summer earnings in the $32,000 range, says Stephen Brown. On the other hand, students interested in public service often pursue volunteer work, clerkships, or other public interest work that doesn't pay much at all. A job at a public interest agency may in fact pay nothing, but some law schools come up with at least some money.

Take advantage of a hand from Uncle Sam

If your income is modest, the federal government will help foot the bill for your law degree by giving you a tax credit or tax deduction for educational expenses. Most law students will want to take advantage of the Lifetime Learning tax credit, worth $2,000 a year (20 percent of the first $10,000 you spend in tuition and fees each year) You qualify for the full credit if your income is under a certain threshold ($47,000 for single filers in 2007; $94,000 for people married and filing jointly). You qualify for a partial credit if you make somewhat more (up to $57,000 for singles in 2007 and $114,000 on joint returns). A tax credit reduces your tax bill dollar for dollar.

Full-time students aren't likely to exceed those thresholds. But if you do—perhaps as a part-time student—you may still qualify for a tax deduction for your educational expenses. In 2007, students could take a deduction for up to $4,000 in tuition and fees if their incomes don't exceed $65,000 filing singly or $130,000 filing jointly. That's worth up to $1,000 to a taxpayer in the 25 percent tax bracket. With income up to $80,000 filing singly or $160,000 filling jointly, you can deduct up to $2,000 in tuition and fees. Note: you can't take both the credit and the deduction.

While a law degree is obviously a major financial investment, chances are good you'll graduate knowing you've significantly boosted your earning power over your lifetime. Then you can move on to bigger worries—like passing the bar exam.

Law schools that help with the payments

According to the latest survey by Equal Justice Works, a Washington, D.C.–based organization that promotes public interest law, more than 70 American law schools (below) now offer or are developing loan repayment assistance programs (LRAPs). These plans, which help graduates who take public interest jobs repay their student loans, can differ dramatically, and some schools can only afford to fund a few students each year. It's important to research the particulars by calling a school's admissions or financial aid office, or by consulting "Financing the Future: Equal Justice Works 2004 Report on Loan Repayment Assistance and Public Interest Scholarship Programs" (available at www.equaljusticeworks.org).

American Univ. Washington College of Law (DC)

Boston College Law School

Boston University School of Law

Brooklyn Law School (NY)

Case Western Reserve Univ. School of Law (OH)

Catholic U. of America–Columbus Sch. of Law (DC)

Columbia University School of Law (NY)

Cornell University Law School (NY)

Creighton University School of Law (NE)

Duke University School of Law (NC)

Emory University School of Law (GA)

Fordham University School of Law (NY)

Franklin Pierce Law Center (NH)

George Washington University Law School (DC)

Georgetown University Law Center (DC)

Golden Gate University School of Law (CA)

Harvard Law School (MA)

Hofstra University School of Law (NY)

Lewis & Clark Coll., Northwestern Sch. of Law (OR)

Loyola Law School, Los Angeles

Loyola University, Chicago School of Law

Loyola University, New Orleans School of Law

Marquette University Law School (WI)

New York Law School

New York University School of Law

Northeastern University School of Law (MA)

Northwestern University School of Law (IL)

Ohio State Univ. Michael E. Moritz College of Law

Pace University School of Law (NY)

Penn. State Univ., The Dickinson School of Law

Pepperdine University School of Law (CA)

Regent University School of Law (VA)

Rutgers University School of Law–Camden (NJ)

Rutgers University School of Law–Newark (NJ)

Santa Clara University School of Law (CA)

Seattle University School of Law

Seton Hall University School of Law (NJ)

Southwestern University School of Law (CA)

Stanford University Law School (CA)

St. Thomas University School of Law (FL)

Suffolk University Law School (MA)

Temple Univ. James E. Beasley School of Law (PA)

Touro College: Jacob D. Fuchsberg Law Center (NY)

Tulane University School of Law (LA)

University of California–Berkeley School of Law

University of California–Davis School of Law

University of California–Hastings College of Law

Univ of Cal.–Los Angeles (UCLA) School of Law

University of Chicago Law School

University of Georgia School of Law

University of Iowa College of Law

University of Maine School of Law

University of Maryland School of Law

University of Michigan Law School

University of Notre Dame Law School (IN)

University of Oregon School of Law

Univ of the Pacific, McGeorge School of Law (CA)

University of Pennsylvania Law School

University of San Diego School of Law

University of San Francisco School of Law

University of Southern California Law School

University of Utah College of Law

University of Virginia School of Law

Valparaiso University School of Law (IN)

Vanderbilt University Law School (TN)

Vermont Law School

Wake Forest University School of Law (NC)

Washington and Lee University School of Law (VA)

Washington University School of Law

Whittier Law School (CA)

Widener University School of Law (DE)

College of William and Mary School of Law (VA)

Willamette University College of Law (OR)

Yale Law School (CT)

Yeshiva University (Cardozo) (NY)

In addition, the following four Minnesota law schools contribute funds to LRAP Minnesota, their state program. Students who are eligible for funding apply to the state.

Hamline University School of Law

University of Minnesota Law School

University of St. Thomas School of Law

William Mitchell College of Law

Chapter Six

Getting Your First Job

The past few years were tough even at prestigious law firms, many of which have handed out pink slips by the dozen. Other firms cut back their summer associate programs, which put rising third-year law students into jobs that traditionally lead to permanent offers, and have employed fewer newly-minted JDs as well.

Alas, the good not-so-old days when law students were wooed by multiple firms with fancy dinners and promises of even fancier bonuses are over, at least for the moment.

"Two or three years ago, people had to work hard *not* to get a job," says a hiring partner at one top firm. "Now it's a different story." Today's third-year students will compete for fewer positions and will certainly not receive as many

---

"Two or three years ago, people had to work hard not to get a job. Now it's a different story."

---

offers as they would have in previous years; some students with subpar grades might not get any offers.

But don't tear up your law school applications just yet. Even though work has been harder to come by lately, there are still opportunities to be had. And students entering law school now may find the picture much rosier by the time they're out job hunting. Indeed, many schools report the same number of recruiters showing up on campus this year as last, and experts in both career counseling offices and law firms say that with the economy on the rebound there is reason to be optimistic. Even firms that have cut back in recent years, such as Holland & Knight and Shearman & Sterling, say that the hiring picture is decidedly brighter these days.

And new JDs, by and large, do pretty well—though how well clearly depends on the type of work you're interested in. The median starting salary for 2006 graduates was $62,000, taking into account everyone from young lawyers in public interest law, where the figure is only $40,000, to those in private practice, where median base salary is $95,000. (Starting salaries at firms in big cities such as Boston, Chicago, and Los Angeles can reach $135,000–$145,000.)

To land that first job in a competitive market, you'll need impeccable credentials, and will probably have to take more initiative and be more flexible about what and where you end up practicing than young law grads of several years ago. The more prepared you are, the easier the job hunt will be. And believe it or not, the groundwork will begin almost the first day of school. That's because grades and summer work experiences play a major role in where grads end up.

Where will the jobs be?

The type of law you choose to practice clearly will have an impact on how much money you make. It may also determine how much in demand your services will be—and where. The larger the metropolis, the more specialized the law tends to be, and certain cities dominate certain practice areas. Students who specialize in corporate law may find that the best opportunities are in New York, for example, while technology centers Austin and San Francisco are still hot for intellectual property lawyers.

It's tough to predict how the employment picture might change between now, as you apply to law school, and your first round of job interviews. Consistently busy practice areas, in good times and bad, include family law and criminal law; divorce is constant, and fewer jobs and a stressed economy often equal more murders, thefts, and the like. As you look ahead for growth areas in law, here are some current winners to keep an eye on.

Litigation. It takes more than bad economic news to dampen the demand for litigators, the attorneys who argue cases in court. Litigation is the nation's favorite method for settling disputes;

most clients—corporate and otherwise—sue whenever they perceive a wrong that needs to be addressed no matter what the economy happens to be doing, says Jackie Burt, former assistant dean of career services at the Benjamin N. Cardozo School of Law at Yeshiva University in New York. And each suit filed means an equal amount of work for the other side.

Young lawyers with visions of yelling, "Objection, your honor!" often gain experience in state, district, or city attorneys' offices doing legal research and preparing briefs (and may, in fact, end up settling most of their cases out of court). Starting salaries are much lower for attorneys at small- and medium-sized firms, which often represent plaintiffs on a contingency basis, than for those who work in the litigation departments of big-time firms.

Intellectual property. The prospects for IP specialists are excellent over the long term because rapid innovations in science and technology continue to drive the economy. Career opportunities can be found in patent, trademark, and copyright law, as people create new gadgets, literary works, computer programs, and logos—all of which need to be protected.

"IP continues to be a growing practice area," says Sheron Hindley-Smith, former executive director of Robert Half Legal, a legal staffing firm in Menlo Park, California. "Patent prosecution is especially hot." This is particularly true in the science and technology fields, which depend so heavily on being first in research and development. As companies strive to guard their patents on new drugs, software, and the like—not to mention their brand names—law students who fully understand the technical nature of the breakthroughs as well as the applicable law will find themselves at a premium and commanding top starting salaries. A science or engineering background is widely considered essential; patent attorneys also have to pass the patent bar exam, administered and required by the Patent and Trademark office.

> *"IP continues to be a growing practice area. Patent prosecution is especially hot."*

In IP, "you are always dealing with something complex and new," says one recent graduate of the University of Texas–Austin School of Law, who signed on with a Houston-based firm, "You are jumping from new technology to new technology." Interested graduates can work in-house for a corporation, at a firm, for a university, or for the government.

Bankruptcy. Whenever the economy sours, the demand for bankruptcy lawyers jumps. (Think Enron.) "There are some huge bankruptcies out there, and they get very complicated and very complex, and they need a lot of attorneys," says Michael Schiumo, former assistant dean for career planning at Fordham University School of Law in New York City. They can also take decades to sort out. (Think Enron.) In addition, companies fail and people lose their shirts even in the brightest of boom times.

Trust and estate. This field is expanding as the first wave of baby boomers is hitting 60. "People want to make sure their kids get their hard-earned money," says Eric Janson, an adjunct professor at Vermont Law School in South Royalton who also

Is a clerkship right for you?

Each year, roughly 10 percent of law school grads opt to spend a year or two working with a judge in one of the nation's many courts. The median wage is just $46,450, but the payoff is far greater: a judicial clerkship is a great way to see many different aspects of the law as it unfolds—as well as have an impact on it yourself. The experience also provides a lifelong résumé boost and, often, a lifelong advisor.

Jerry Noblin Jr., for one, viewed his clerkship with Chief Judge Robin Cauthron of the U.S. District Court for the Western District of Oklahoma as the best possible way to prepare for a career as a trial lawyer—to "learn how to run a trial, without having a real client's case on the line," and to "be involved in myriad cases with all kinds of causes of action, both civil and criminal, which is something that a firm simply could not offer."

There is a range of clerkship opportunities at every court level—federal, state, and even local—and your experience will vary with each. For example, if you work for a trial court, you'll likely be involved in every stage of a hearing, from writing jury voir dire questions and instructions to helping your judge write and edit his or her decision before it's published. The court of appeals is a more studious exercise; you'll hear oral arguments from attorneys and then help research and prepare decisions on the legal issues. Debra Strauss, author of *Behind the Bench: The Guide to Judicial Clerkships* and administrator of www.judicialclerkships.com, a site that helps students navigate the application process, suggests seeking the court that's right for you in terms of your future goals. "Federal clerkships are considered more prestigious than state, but it's great to work in the state court system if you know you want to practice law in that state, because you get to know all the attorneys and court procedures intimately," she explains. "Moreover, the highest court in a state can be just as prestigious as a federal clerkship."

Competition for all such positions is stiff. Top grades at a good school and solid writing skills are important, though some judges will pass over Ivy Leaguers in favor of in-state students who have a demonstrated interest in local legal issues. Pursuing activities such as law review and moot court can help you stand out. Strauss also suggests doing a judicial externship, like the one she oversees at the Pace University School of Law: The Federal Judicial Extern Honors Program, a yearlong course that includes a lengthy research and writing project (in which students use motion papers from federal court to write a decision, which can later serve as a writing sample for a clerkship application), places students with federal district or court of appeals judges where they act as junior clerks, of sorts.

All clerkship candidates should be proactive about the process. This includes researching what type of court you're interested in, where, as well as which judge, specifically, you'd like to work for. The recommended deadline for federal clerkship applications is now fall of the third year of law school, though that varies by court and individual judge; the cutoff date for state clerkships can be even earlier, from the spring or summer of second year on.

If you're successful, a clerkship can pay off in many ways—most ideally, in close mentorship from a judge. The post can also open doors later in your career, as firms, government agencies, and non-profits alike actively recruit former law clerks for their varied experiences and close exposure to the court system. In addition, it's seen as an essential credential if you hope to teach. One last potential advantage: federal positions can lead to the mother of all clerkships—working for one of the nine U.S. Supreme Court justices, who typically choose clerks who have worked for peers in the U.S. Court of Appeals. Those interested should focus on working for one of the federal "feeder judges" who have sent numerous staff members to the Supreme Court in the past.

has his own private practice and specializes in estate planning, wills, trusts, and probate administration. T&E lawyers, who may create living wills, plan for the eventual dispersal of billion-dollar fortunes, and arrange the transfer of long-held family businesses from one generation to the next, are needed at firms of all sizes, which handle estates of all sizes.

Employment. "Whether you are hiring or firing, a company needs lawyers," says Susan Guindi, assistant dean for career services at the University of Michigan's law school. Employment attorneys can work in-house or for a company's outside counsel, as well as for unions and government agencies. In the process, they may deal with a range of issues, including labor relations; age, race, or sex discrimination; and workplace health and safety.

Tax. Although there will almost certainly never be a sexy television show about tax attorneys, don't rule out entering this field. "Tax is always solid," says Merv Loya, former assistant dean at the University of Oregon's law school in Eugene, who notes that companies and individuals need attorneys in good and bad economic cycles who enjoy digging into financial documents and interpreting the tax code; the president's tax initiative will also heat up demand. But often, Loya adds, students need a master's degree in tax law to set them apart.

• • •

Shortly after you arrive on campus, you'll want to start getting to know the people in the career counseling office; the men and women who run on-campus recruiting programs have close contacts in the field, know the experiences of all those who've come seeking employment before, and can offer the most specific, well-tailored advice on how to make your particular career goals a reality, no matter what area of law you're interested in. Stop by early and often to get help formulating your long-term plan and attend career-oriented seminars from day one on.

Make the most of the summer

It used to be that finding a substantive legal job after the first year of law school was optional, but that is no longer the case, say many career counselors. "We recommend doing anything law-related during your first summer, even if you have to do something unrelated part-time—like word processing, waiting tables, or slinging lattes at Starbucks—in order to finance some sort of volunteer gig in the legal community," says Skip Horne, former assistant dean for career services at the Santa Clara University School of Law. "The key is to get experience, and not wait until your second or third year when it will get harder and harder to overcome that initial 'I don't have any legal experience' hump."

Finding a law firm job that first summer is going to be difficult, but this is an excellent time to take advantage of opportunities in the nonprofit sector. Many law schools offer scholarships that help support students who want to do low- or non-paying public interest work for a summer. The Equal Justice America fellowship, for example, is an award for first- and second-year students who work at organizations that provide civil legal services for the poor. It's offered at more than 50 schools, including Brooklyn Law School, the University of Virginia School of Law, and Stanford. Working for a judge or doing research for a professor is another common first-year choice, as is a study-abroad program. The University of Wisconsin's law school, for one, has partnered with Thammasat University Faculty of Law in Bangkok so students can study the Thai legal system firsthand while working in international law firms.

For those interested in going into private practice—that is, the vast majority of law school students—the employment process starts in the fall of the second year of law school, with interviews for summer associate positions. These eight-week jobs allow students to get firm experience for great pay, often with the promise of future employment.

However, be forewarned: such programs are no longer the schmooze-fests recent grads may have described, where getting to know the other young associates and partners over expense-account lunches at hip restaurants and outings to baseball games or sold-out rock concerts took precedence over real work. Many firms are now working their "summers" considerably harder than in the past and evaluating them more closely. "It used to be that summer associates really had to screw up badly in order to not get an offer," says Gihan Fernando, assistant dean for career services at Georgetown University Law Center. "In past years, behaviors of all kinds were tolerated and not much work was accomplished. Now there's much more of a sense that you should put your best foot forward." Georgetown, for one, provides an intensive, one-day seminar to help prepare students for the experience, complete with panels of hiring partners and 3Ls and discussions about firm life, etiquette, and the kinds of basic research and writing assignments summer associates will be expected to handle.

No matter what you do on the job, try not to follow in the footsteps of one law student who, as a 2003 summer associate at Skadden, Arps in New York, mistakenly sent the following email, meant for a friend, to 40 people at the firm, including 20 partners: "I'm busy doing jack shit. Went to a nice 2hr sushi lunch today at Sushi Zen. Nice place. Spent the rest of the day typing emails and bullshitting with people. Unfortunately, I actually have work to do—I'm on some corp finance deal, under the global head of corp finance, which means I should really peruse these materials and not be a fuckup." The email slowly made its way around the firm, the city, and the rest of the country, and became a classic lesson in what not to do for summer associates everywhere, for all time. (Neither the student nor the firm will comment on what happened as a result.)

Finally, take heart: for those who maintain the appropriate level of decorum and impress associates and partners alike with their research, writing, and communication skills, many benefits remain—including the free food. "I worked really, really hard, but I gained like seven pounds," says one recent summer associate at a top New York firm. She also gained a full-time job offer.

Get recruited

So how do you obtain such plum summer positions? Most students go through on-campus recruiting, which brings in employers to interview job candidates who are either prescreened using their résumés or selected in a lottery. The employers then call back those they're interested in hiring for a second interview at the office. This occurs in the fall, mostly, though there is some overflow in the spring. While recruiting schedules and procedures differ from school to school (meaning it's wise to check with your career center for details about how the process operates), it's true at most institutions that on-campus recruiting has become ever more competitive, as firms have limited the number of campuses they visit and offered fewer interview slots at those they do. Still, on-campus recruiting has rebounded along with the economy.

Needless to say, the better your law school performance is, the better your chances. Often, top firms will only interview students whose GPA falls above a certain cutoff—though they do adjust that cutoff based on the name and reputation of a

"The key is to get experience, and not wait until your second or third year."

school. For example, a firm may only meet candidates with a 3.7 or higher at a second-tier institution, while those at top 20 schools simply need a 3.3; grades may not matter at all for candidates from Harvard or Yale. Hiring partners say having substantial legal experience in summer positions, as noted, also helps people stand out, as does participation in clinics, which signals that you'll bring a toolbox of practical skills to the job—not just theory learned in class.

After academics, motivation and initiative matter most of all. You can no longer rely on the on-campus interview process to find a job—be prepared to do some independent outreach, too, even if it means cold calling or sending your résumé and a cover letter out to several hundred firms across the country.

"I was extraordinarily aggressive and shameless—I sent out hundreds of letters and got rejected by so many great places," recalls Alex Wellen, a graduate of Temple University's law school in Philadelphia and the author of *Barman: Ping-Pong, Pathos, & Passing the Bar*, his account of coming out of law school into the work world. Wellen says he was "crazy about Temple," but

Like many young college grads, Stephen Sincavage applied to law school for lack of a better idea. "I never had any grand plans that I wanted to go to law school or anything like that," he says. "But...I kind of realized that I wasn't sick of school, and I knew a couple of people who'd gone to law school," he says. In fact, he'd heard some horror stories of cutthroat law schools where students hoarded notes and ripped pages out of library books to thwart the competition. "There were exceptions," says Sincavage, "but generally when I talked to other people, they'd say, 'law school was hell.'" He knew that *that* wasn't the kind of experience he wanted.

And he figured he knew how to avoid it. Sincavage had so enjoyed being an undergraduate at the University of Virginia that the decision about where to go was easy: he'd stay in Charlottesville. "It's very social," he says. That sense of community was the key to his happy law school experience, Sincavage adds. The first week on campus, his class of 300 was divided into first-year sections

of 30 each. If someone missed a class, other students would share notes and outlines. Regular softball games "gave everybody a focus and a reason to be together." It helped that the school's grading system centered around a B mean, notes Sincavage. "That meant that, for the most part, unless you were really brilliant on an exam—or you were really just out to lunch—you were more than likely to get a B," he adds. "I don't know how you get by in an atmosphere where everyone's out for themselves."

Sincavage began to zero in on his career path during his second summer when he clerked for a circuit judge in Loudoun County, Virginia, one of the fastest-growing counties in the country. His time there made him realize he liked the courtroom experience and gave him a pretty good idea of the sort of work he *didn't* want to do—domestic relations, for example. "The rancor, the hatred—that just didn't seem like something that I'd be up for," he says. The work a friend was doing in a prosecutor's office seemed a lot

more appealing. So after graduating in 1993, he clerked for the Loudon County Circuit Court and, in 1997, went to work for the county prosecutor's office. It didn't hurt that he'd graduated from a "fairly local university known to be prestigious," had grown up in the county, and had spent time as a law clerk becoming known to the legal community around the old courthouse that still dominates the center of downtown Leesburg, Virginia, where the Loudoun County prosecutor's offices are located.

His office overlooking the green, campus-like lawn of the old Leesburg courthouse is as sociable a place as his alma mater; the county prosecutors share the fascinating cases and the not-so-scintillating work alike. "You're not just the traffic guy, or the white collar crime guy, or the drug guy," he says. Sincavage does tend to get a fair number of drug cases—he often carries a pager so narcotics officers can reach him 24 hours a day—but also handles everything from juvenile cases to embezzlement and identity fraud. Some days he spends in traffic court—often

that, in his experience, aiming for a top firm out
of a non–Top 20 law school (Temple is currently
No. 59) was "harder at every fricking step of the
way—it was harder to get an interview, harder to
get a callback, harder to get an offer." His deter-
mination paid off, however, and he eventually
landed a job at a prestigious New York firm.

Networking is key, say many career counselors—and it should start your first year of law
school. Try getting involved with a range of
organizations on campus and attending local bar
association and alumni events, for instance, so
you can get out into the real world and interact
with practicing attorneys. You never know who'll
be able to lend a hand in the future, and the
experience in creating and maintaining contacts
will likely help you in your future practice, as
well. (One of Wellen's strategies was to identify
and contact all of the Temple alumni working in
midsize to large New York practices.)

No matter what happens, you should bear in
mind that your first job is just that—you can
always move on. Indeed, even while the hiring of
first-year associates was down across the board,
there's been an increase in the lateral hiring of
those who have at least several years of experience.

Consider public interest law

Ironically, low-paying public interest jobs can be
even more difficult to land than glamorous firm
positions. Just 5.4 percent of graduates find positions in the field, which encompasses nonprofit
groups such as legal aid organizations and public
defender offices, as well as national, state, and
local government agencies. Experts attribute this
not to a lack of interest, but to a dearth of entry-
level openings and graduates' huge debt loads,
which make a miniscule paycheck impractical. At
the same time, more JDs seem to be competing for
these posts than in past years, perhaps because of
the difficult firm market. "If anything, the public
sector has tended to stay fairly constant," says Skip
Horne. "So with similar numbers of opportunities
but more students interested in them, the competition is more fierce."

Demonstrated interest and experience in the
public domain are essential when you're looking for
nonprofit or government jobs; organizations and
agencies with extremely tight budgets simply can't
afford to train rank beginners. Committed students
can increase their chances of finding employment
by making their own opportunities. For example,

volunteering at a local nonprofit organization may eventually turn into a full-time position.

There are quite a few fellowship openings, as well, offered through individual law schools and a range of private organizations, including the Skadden Fellowship Foundation, an arm of Skadden, Arps in New York (www.skadden fellowship.org). Such programs aim to make help-

---

"I was extraordinarily aggressive and shameless—I sent out hundreds of letters and got rejected by so many great places."

---

ing others—which usually pays around $46,000, to start—a financial feasibility. For example, Equal Justice Works, a public interest advocacy group in Washington, D.C., offers fellowships for recent law graduates and experienced attorneys inter-

ested in giving back. Fellows receive up to $37,500, as well as generous student loan repayment assistance and work for such organizations as the National Housing Law Project in Oakland, California, Health Law Advocates in Boston, Alliance for Children's Rights in Los Angeles, and the Legal Assistance Foundation of Metropolitan Chicago. Get more information at www.equal justiceworks.org.

Though the post-JD job market may be tougher than in the recent past, graduates who are determined and well prepared are clearly finding jobs. Since those are attributes that every good lawyer needs, anyway, they'll serve you well even in a new age of competing offers.

The U.S. News
Insider's Index

How Do
the Schools
Stack Up?

What are the hardest and easiest law schools to get into?

How much competition are you facing? Here we rank schools from most to least selective based on a formula that takes into account their acceptance rates (the proportion of applicants who make the cut into the full-time program), and students' LSAT scores and grades. The 25th–75th percentile LSAT and grade-point-average ranges show you where 50 percent of enrollees fall, but remember: that means if 200 people make up the class, 50 of them fall below the bottom of the range.

Most to least selective

School	Acceptance rate	Undergraduate grade point average (25th–75th percentile)	LSAT score (25th–75th percentile)
Yale University (CT)	7%	3.77-3.97	170-177
Harvard University (MA)	12%	3.75-3.95	170-175
Stanford University (CA)	9%	3.74-3.95	167-172
University of California–Berkeley	12%	3.64-3.90	163-170
University of Pennsylvania	16%	3.52-3.86	166-171
University of Virginia	24%	3.51-3.87	167-171
Columbia University (NY)	16%	3.56-3.81	169-174
George Washington University (DC)	20%	3.40-3.86	163-168
Duke University (NC)	27%	3.61-3.82	167-170
New York University	23%	3.54-3.86	169-173
Northwestern University (IL)	18%	3.40-3.80	166-172
University of California–Los Angeles	18%	3.54-3.85	163-169
Vanderbilt University (TN)	25%	3.54-3.83	164-168
Georgetown University (DC)	23%	3.44-3.82	167-171
University of Chicago	16%	3.49-3.83	169-173
Cornell University (NY)	22%	3.54-3.78	166-168
University of Michigan–Ann Arbor	21%	3.49-3.79	167-170
Boston University	27%	3.51-3.81	164-166
Brigham Young University (Clark) (UT)	29%	3.51-3.85	162-167
Fordham University (NY)	24%	3.41-3.74	163-167
Southern Methodist University (TX)	23%	3.28-3.84	157-165
College of William and Mary (VA)	27%	3.44-3.82	159-166
University of Colorado–Boulder	25%	3.33-3.83	160-165
University of Notre Dame (IN)	19%	3.40-3.76	164-167
University of Southern California (Gould)	19%	3.46-3.72	165-167
Washington and Lee University (VA)	24%	3.25-3.81	161-167
George Mason University (VA)	22%	3.11-3.86	159-166
University of Georgia	25%	3.42-3.86	159-165
University of Maryland	16%	3.47-3.84	160-166
University of Texas–Austin	24%	3.38-3.80	163-168
Washington University in St. Louis	26%	3.30-3.70	163-167
Boston College	20%	3.44-3.78	162-165
University of Alabama	29%	3.31-3.84	160-165
University of Illinois–Urbana-Champaign	30%	3.18-3.80	160-167
University of Washington	23%	3.47-3.82	159-165
University of Minnesota–Twin Cities	25%	3.28-3.78	163-167
University of North Carolina–Chapel Hill	19%	3.45-3.80	157-164
Ohio State University (Moritz)	29%	3.34-3.81	158-164
University of California (Hastings)	27%	3.36-3.74	160-165

What are the hardest and easiest law schools to get into?

Most to least selective

School	Acceptance rate	Undergraduate grade point average (25th-75th percentile)	LSAT score (25th-75th percentile)
Illinois Institute of Technology (Chicago-Kent)	33%	3.20-3.77	157-164
Yeshiva University (Cardozo) (NY)	27%	3.30-3.70	162-166
Loyola University Chicago	26%	3.35-3.75	159-163
University of California–Davis	29%	3.38-3.75	159-165
University of Cincinnati	35%	3.39-3.87	157-162
University of Florida (Levin)	34%	3.44-3.83	156-162
University of Iowa	35%	3.41-3.86	159-163
University of Houston	29%	3.30-3.79	158-163
University of Kentucky	36%	3.36-3.79	156-162
University of Wisconsin–Madison	30%	3.32-3.74	157-163
Baylor University (Umphrey) (TX)	30%	3.38-3.78	157-162
St. John's University (NY)	34%	3.19-3.74	157-162
Tulane University (LA)	36%	3.37-3.75	158-163
University of Connecticut	14%	3.24-3.64	160-164
University of Tennessee–Knoxville	29%	3.35-3.82	157-162
Florida State University	24%	3.30-3.77	158-162
Wake Forest University (NC)	35%	3.17-3.68	159-166
Arizona State University (O'Connor)	24%	3.30-3.81	156-162
Brooklyn Law School (NY)	29%	3.17-3.63	162-165
Emory University (GA)	26%	3.28-3.62	162-166
University of Toledo (OH)	27%	3.10-3.74	156-161
University of Utah (Quinney)	37%	3.31-3.77	156-162
Pepperdine University (CA)	32%	3.42-3.73	158-162
University of Arizona (Rogers)	31%	3.23-3.73	157-164
Lewis and Clark College (Northwestern) (OR)	37%	3.15-3.73	157-163
Loyola Marymount University (CA)	30%	3.22-3.65	159-163
Temple University (Beasley) (PA)	41%	3.27-3.65	160-164
American University (Washington) (DC)	23%	3.14-3.59	161-163
Indiana University–Bloomington	39%	3.03-3.67	158-165
Rutgers–Camden (NJ)	22%	3.09-3.65	160-162
University of Missouri–Columbia	36%	3.26-3.80	156-161
DePaul University (IL)	35%	3.10-3.66	159-162
University of Akron (OH)	32%	3.16-3.76	156-160
University of Richmond (Williams) (VA)	35%	3.23-3.66	158-162
Villanova University (PA)	43%	3.14-3.63	160-163
Georgia State University	18%	3.11-3.62	158-162
Indiana University–Indianapolis	35%	3.36-3.78	151-158
Northeastern University (MA)	36%	3.14-3.61	156-162
Seton Hall University (NJ)	43%	3.22-3.65	157-162
University of Denver (Sturm)	33%	3.15-3.66	155-160
University of Nevada–Las Vegas (Boyd)	23%	3.20-3.66	156-161
University of Mississippi	31%	3.28-3.79	152-157
Michigan State University	42%	3.21-3.64	155-161
Pennsylvania State University (Dickinson)	33%	3.02-3.69	156-159
Seattle University	28%	3.17-3.62	155-161
University of Arkansas–Fayetteville	30%	3.17-3.70	151-159
University of Hawaii (Richardson)	19%	3.09-3.62	155-160
University of Louisville (Brandeis) (KY)	38%	3.17-3.73	155-159
University of Nebraska–Lincoln	37%	3.50-3.82	153-159
University of Oklahoma	38%	3.35-3.78	154-160
University of Oregon	41%	3.27-3.68	156-160
University of Pittsburgh	37%	3.11-3.65	158-161

What are the hardest and easiest law schools to get into?

Most to least selective

School	Acceptance rate	Undergraduate grade point average (25th–75th percentile)	LSAT score (25th–75th percentile)
University of South Carolina	31%	3.04-3.69	156-161
Case Western Reserve University (OH)	35%	3.17-3.60	156-160
Hofstra University (NY)	42%	3.11-3.69	154-159
University of San Diego	32%	3.10-3.53	160-164
Quinnipiac University (CT)	28%	3.01-3.62	157-160
Rutgers–Newark (NJ)	30%	3.08-3.55	155-161
University of Kansas	37%	3.09-3.77	155-160
University of San Francisco	38%	3.02-3.56	156-161
University of the Pacific (McGeorge) (CA)	40%	3.13-3.60	155-159
Catholic University of America (Columbus) (DC)	34%	3.08-3.57	156-160
Chapman University (CA)	32%	3.10-3.61	154-159
Marquette University (WI)	46%	3.20-3.65	155-159
Mercer University (GA)	32%	3.20-3.69	155-158
Santa Clara University (CA)	51%	3.16-3.59	156-161
Stetson University (FL)	31%	3.48-3.71	153-157
University of Miami (FL)	51%	3.21-3.63	155-160
Louisiana State University–Baton Rouge	37%	3.16-3.70	155-159
St. Louis University	52%	3.24-3.74	154-159
Texas Tech University	43%	3.34-3.75	151-157
University at Buffalo–SUNY	39%	3.19-3.65	154-159
University of St. Thomas (MN)	49%	3.16-3.63	154-161
Wayne State University (MI)	52%	3.29-3.69	152-158
University of New Mexico	22%	3.09-3.72	152-159
Hamline University (MN)	49%	3.22-3.70	152-158
University of Memphis (Humphreys)	34%	3.03-3.64	154-158
Creighton University (NE)	45%	3.23-3.68	151-156
West Virginia University	37%	3.18-3.75	150-156
Cleveland State University (Cleveland-Marshall)	36%	3.14-3.65	153-157
University of Maine	47%	3.06-3.69	154-159
University of Montana	42%	3.12-3.75	151-158
Pace University (NY)	37%	3.13-3.59	153-157
Samford University (Cumberland) (AL)	40%	3.07-3.52	155-159
Florida International University	25%	2.97-3.58	153-157
Northern Illinois University	37%	3.09-3.66	150-157
Southwestern Law School (CA)	33%	3.06-3.58	153-157
University of Idaho	44%	3.03-3.64	151-159
University of Wyoming	28%	3.18-3.63	150-156
Northern Kentucky University (Chase)	43%	3.07-3.56	153-156
University of Baltimore	41%	3.00-3.57	153-157
Drake University (IA)	51%	3.11-3.72	153-158
New York Law School	47%	3.08-3.57	153-157
Ohio Northern University (Pettit)	30%	3.10-3.70	148-156
Suffolk University (MA)	50%	3.03-3.49	154-158
University of Arkansas–Little Rock (Bowen)	26%	2.94-3.68	151-156
Valparaiso University (IN)	27%	3.23-3.67	150-154
William Mitchell College of Law (MN)	51%	3.15-3.63	151-157
Gonzaga University (WA)	45%	3.06-3.54	153-157
Duquesne University (PA)	53%	3.28-3.65	151-155
Willamette University (Collins) (OR)	45%	2.85-3.52	153-158
University of Missouri–Kansas City	50%	3.03-3.64	152-156
Southern Illinois University–Carbondale	52%	2.90-3.60	151-156
University of South Dakota	49%	3.21-3.75	150-156

What are the hardest and easiest law schools to get into?

Most to least selective

School	Acceptance rate	Undergraduate grade point average (25th–75th percentile)	LSAT I Verbal (25th–75th percentile)
Syracuse University (NY)	50%	3.09-3.59	152-156
Vermont Law School	59%	2.95-3.54	151-158
Washburn University (KS)	52%	3.06-3.69	150-156
Campbell University (Wiggins) (NC)	36%	2.94-3.55	151-157
Albany Law School-Union University (NY)	45%	2.92-3.48	152-157
South Texas College of Law	51%	2.99-3.52	150-155
Loyola University New Orleans	67%	3.09-3.56	149-155
Roger Williams University (RI)	57%	2.90-3.50	151-155
Capital University (OH)	51%	2.94-3.54	151-156
Howard University (DC)	23%	2.90-3.50	149-155
John Marshall Law School (IL)	49%	2.85-3.42	151-156
Regent University (VA)	53%	2.95-3.66	150-156
Texas Wesleyan University	46%	2.89-3.40	152-156
California Western School of Law	55%	3.00-3.53	150-156
University of Dayton (OH)	51%	2.96-3.50	149-154
University of North Dakota	28%	3.02-3.73	147-154
University of Tulsa (OK)	51%	2.95-3.50	151-155
CUNY–Queens College	25%	2.92-3.47	151-156
Franklin Pierce Law Center (NH)	50%	3.00-3.50	150-155
New England School of Law (MA)	58%	3.02-3.52	150-153
Western New England College (MA)	71%	2.80-3.38	150-156
Nova Southeastern University (Broad) (FL)	47%	3.00-3.53	147-151
Widener University (DE)	51%	2.88-3.46	150-154
St. Mary's University (TX)	51%	2.80-3.41	149-156
Florida Coastal School of Law	55%	2.81-3.47	149-154
Mississippi College	52%	2.88-3.50	148-153
Ave Maria School of Law (MI)	51%	2.93-3.47	147-155
Golden Gate University (CA)	63%	2.82-3.37	150-154
Touro College (Fuchsberg) (NY)	43%	2.81-3.32	150-153
University of the District of Columbia (Clarke)	19%	2.70-3.40	148-153
Whittier Law School (CA)	62%	2.56-3.19	149-153
Thomas Jefferson School of Law (CA)	45%	2.75-3.23	148-151
University of Detroit Mercy	47%	2.95-3.36	146-154
Appalachian School of Law (VA)	38%	2.75-3.32	147-153
Barry University (FL)	55%	2.70-3.30	148-152
Oklahoma City University	57%	2.87-3.40	147-152
St. Thomas University (FL)	46%	2.75-3.43	147-151
North Carolina Central University	22%	2.88-3.45	143-151
Texas Southern University (Marshall)	36%	2.83-3.29	146-151
Thomas M. Cooley Law School (MI)	74%	2.75-3.35	145-154
Southern University (LA)	37%	2.52-3.26	143-149

As you compare schools, you'll want to pay attention to the total enrollment, the size of first-year sections, the availability of small classes, and the student-faculty ratio. All will have an impact on the schools' personalities, the availability of professors outside of class, the extent to which you engage with your classmates, and the breadth of the curriculum. Schools are ranked here by total enrollment.

School	Total full- and part-time enrollment	Full-time enrollment	Part-time enrollment	Size of first-year class	Typical first-year section size	Public or private	Student to faculty ratio	% classes under 25	% classes 25–100	% classes over 100	Number of course offerings after first year
Thomas M. Cooley Law School (MI)	3,664	535	3,129	1,808	57	Private	24.3	64%	31%	5%	247
Georgetown University (DC)	1,990	1,605	385	581	112	Private	13.2	49%	46%	5%	354
Harvard University (MA)	1,734	1,734	N/A	559	80	Private	10.3	46%	48%	5%	N/A
George Washington University (DC)	1,662	1,412	250	508	108	Private	14.9	61%	35%	4%	200
Suffolk University (MA)	1,625	1,021	604	534	85	Private	16.5	60%	35%	5%	280
New York Law School	1,572	1,165	407	552	106	Private	22.9	55%	34%	11%	219
Fordham University (NY)	1,509	1,191	318	495	80	Private	14.6	43%	51%	6%	237
Brooklyn Law School (NY)	1,496	1,186	310	493	51	Private	19.9	59%	34%	7%	169
American University (Washington) (DC)	1,479	1,246	233	496	95	Private	13.8	52%	48%	0%	316
New York University	1,424	1,424	N/A	447	112	Private	10.4	44%	46%	10%	276
Florida Coastal School of Law	1,395	1,231	164	572	75	Private	19.7	52%	48%	0%	203
John Marshall Law School (IL)	1,384	1,067	317	454	70	Private	17.9	64%	35%	0%	230
Widener University (DE)	1,376	879	497	519	62	Private	13.7	75%	25%	0%	216
Loyola Marymount University (CA)	1,294	1,003	291	416	87	Private	15.8	59%	36%	5%	141
University of Texas–Austin	1,291	1,291	N/A	415	109	Public	14.2	66%	29%	5%	160
University of Florida (Levin)	1,290	1,290	N/A	371	100	Public	15.7	37%	55%	8%	145
University of Miami (FL)	1,268	1,252	16	492	100	Private	19.1	41%	49%	10%	130
South Texas College of Law	1,252	936	316	661	95	Private	20.4	60%	40%	0%	120
Columbia University (NY)	1,236	1,236	N/A	372	108	Private	9.5	45%	45%	10%	228
University of California (Hastings)	1,215	1,215	N/A	403	83	Public	16.2	62%	37%	1%	153
University of Virginia	1,175	1,175	N/A	361	69	Public	13.3	56%	39%	6%	230
University of Michigan–Ann Arbor	1,148	1,148	N/A	355	93	Public	12.7	40%	56%	4%	135
Hofstra University (NY)	1,142	870	272	360	104	Private	15.5	61%	31%	7%	147
University of Denver (Sturm)	1,134	855	279	380	90	Private	18.7	71%	29%	0%	161
New England School of Law (MA)	1,101	715	386	369	135	Private	23.2	53%	43%	4%	191
University of Baltimore	1,082	657	425	384	73	Public	18.9	69%	30%	1%	124
Yeshiva University (Cardozo) (NY)	1,075	948	127	343	49	Private	16.2	40%	51%	9%	137
Seattle University	1,071	845	226	317	86	Private	14.4	55%	42%	3%	161
Seton Hall University (NJ)	1,064	722	342	364	70	Private	15.4	51%	49%	0%	137
University of San Diego	1,048	768	280	357	90	Private	14.0	65%	33%	1%	136
University of California–Los Angeles	1,025	1,025	N/A	323	80	Public	12.9	43%	51%	6%	161
University of the Pacific (McGeorge) (CA)	1,014	615	399	345	74	Private	13.5	51%	48%	1%	133
Michigan State University	1,006	696	310	389	63	Private	19.4	54%	43%	3%	153
Stetson University (FL)	994	765	229	340	67	Private	17.9	57%	43%	0%	118
DePaul University (IL)	993	745	248	310	84	Private	13.6	72%	27%	0%	145
Southern Methodist University (TX)	987	562	425	278	97	Private	14.7	52%	47%	1%	117
Illinois Institute of Technology (Chicago-Kent)	975	751	224	316	50	Private	11.5	73%	25%	2%	135
Southwestern Law School (CA)	972	698	274	353	73	Private	16.3	52%	48%	0%	136
St. Louis University	968	750	218	326	85	Private	17.6	60%	35%	6%	105

What are the largest and smallest law schools?

School	Total full- and part-time enrollment	Full-time enrollment	Part-time enrollment	Size of first-year class	Typical first-year section size	Public or private	Student to faculty ratio	% classes under 25	% classes 25-100	% classes over 100	Number of course offerings after first year
Temple University (Beasley) (PA)	968	754	214	312	60	Public	12.8	68%	32%	0%	185
University of Houston	955	785	170	293	80	Public	13.9	58%	42%	0%	215
Indiana University–Indianapolis	952	647	305	384	97	Public	17.0	41%	56%	2%	126
Nova Southeastern University (Broad) (FL)	946	770	176	385	51	Private	14.1	67%	33%	0%	115
Santa Clara University (CA)	945	728	217	321	78	Private	15.9	69%	31%	0%	186
St. John's University (NY)	914	748	166	319	85	Private	16.4	58%	41%	1%	116
Catholic University of America (Columbus) (DC)	902	607	295	298	48	Private	13.6	70%	30%	0%	139
Loyola University Chicago	865	621	244	274	62	Private	14.5	70%	30%	1%	155
University of California–Berkeley	864	864	N/A	268	90	Public	12.3	68%	28%	4%	209
Loyola University New Orleans	858	700	158	323	82	Private	17.5	33%	65%	2%	85
California Western School of Law	847	755	92	338	80	Private	17.7	61%	36%	3%	94
University of Wisconsin–Madison	842	807	35	280	71	Public	13.4	61%	38%	2%	154
Boston University	834	815	19	277	89	Private	12.3	54%	42%	3%	172
University of Maryland	831	678	153	290	69	Public	11.4	75%	24%	0%	193
Rutgers–Newark (NJ)	818	558	260	262	60	Public	14.8	47%	50%	3%	101
Washington University in St. Louis	810	801	9	221	89	Private	11.6	64%	32%	5%	122
University of Minnesota–Twin Cities	793	793	N/A	259	106	Public	12.1	60%	38%	2%	193
Rutgers–Camden (NJ)	790	561	229	232	52	Public	14.1	60%	38%	1%	109
George Mason University (VA)	788	503	285	267	90	Public	16.7	77%	22%	0%	168
Boston College	783	778	5	270	84	Private	12.6	65%	32%	2%	120
University of Pennsylvania	782	782	N/A	258	83	Private	12.1	45%	50%	5%	157
Thomas Jefferson School of Law (CA)	777	581	196	219	98	Private	14.9	63%	36%	2%	107
Northwestern University (IL)	771	771	N/A	238	62	Private	10.4	53%	47%	0%	200
Pace University (NY)	765	533	232	262	54	Private	14.2	79%	21%	1%	144
Florida State University	764	764	N/A	192	66	Public	13.7	54%	43%	2%	124
St. Mary's University (TX)	762	699	63	324	87	Private	22.1	51%	49%	0%	112
Texas Wesleyan University	757	443	314	366	79	Private	20.8	66%	32%	1%	87
Tulane University (LA)	752	752	N/A	244	74	Private	15.4	46%	51%	3%	160
University at Buffalo–SUNY	751	746	5	246	83	Public	15.6	69%	31%	0%	208
University of Detroit Mercy	751	591	160	274	61	Private	16.8	52%	48%	0%	98
Touro College (Fuchsberg) (NY)	747	513	234	287	69	Private	15.7	63%	35%	2%	72
Villanova University (PA)	727	727	N/A	252	101	Private	16.0	63%	35%	2%	118
Lewis and Clark College (Northwestern) (OR)	725	537	188	218	74	Private	10.6	54%	46%	1%	122
Marquette University (WI)	718	530	188	223	89	Private	17.5	55%	45%	0%	127
University of Pittsburgh	714	714	N/A	242	82	Public	15.3	62%	36%	2%	189
University of San Francisco	712	556	156	248	92	Private	19.1	59%	41%	0%	93
Emory University (GA)	709	709	N/A	255	70	Private	10.8	64%	35%	1%	97
Cleveland State University (Cleveland-Marshall)	706	503	203	217	59	Public	13.0	65%	35%	0%	73
Case Western Reserve University (OH)	702	678	24	262	80	Private	13.7	63%	36%	1%	154
Hamline University (MN)	700	489	211	221	60	Private	14.6	56%	44%	0%	141
University of North Carolina–Chapel Hill	699	699	N/A	242	77	Public	15.7	43%	53%	3%	110
Barry University (FL)	692	536	156	332	82	Private	20.7	60%	39%	1%	138
Texas Tech University	692	692	N/A	240	56	Public	15.4	48%	48%	4%	90
Golden Gate University (CA)	688	538	150	272	89	Private	18.9	73%	27%	0%	122
Albany Law School-Union University (NY)	684	662	22	247	80	Private	14.7	63%	33%	4%	118
Duquesne University (PA)	679	470	209	247	90	Private	18.2	45%	54%	1%	82
Capital University (OH)	675	459	216	243	85	Private	16.2	65%	35%	0%	168
Ohio State University (Moritz)	669	669	N/A	199	74	Public	12.6	58%	40%	2%	109
University of South Carolina	667	665	2	215	75	Public	14.3	51%	48%	1%	118
Syracuse University (NY)	666	659	7	219	62	Private	12.7	77%	23%	0%	144
Georgia State University	665	473	192	212	70	Public	12.8	59%	41%	N/A	114

What are the largest and smallest law schools?

School	Total full- and part-time enrollment	Full-time enrollment	Part-time enrollment	Size of first-year class	Typical first-year section size	Public or private	Student to faculty ratio	% classes under 25	% classes 25–100	% classes over 100	Number of course offerings after first year
University of Connecticut	663	484	179	216	71	Public	11.0	71%	29%	0%	151
Pennsylvania State University (Dickinson)	655	573	82	229	56	Public	11.5	77%	23%	0%	126
University of Georgia	642	642	N/A	218	77	Public	14.8	57%	42%	1%	127
Pepperdine University (CA)	633	633	N/A	224	75	Private	16.9	65%	31%	4%	108
University of Iowa	633	633	N/A	211	80	Public	13.0	56%	44%	0%	73
St. Thomas University (FL)	625	625	N/A	226	60	Private	18.0	71%	29%	0%	97
Northeastern University (MA)	624	624	N/A	200	67	Private	16.9	44%	56%	0%	84
Duke University (NC)	620	583	37	207	69	Private	13.9	61%	35%	4%	168
Indiana University–Bloomington	620	619	1	212	73	Public	11.4	65%	34%	1%	137
College of William and Mary (VA)	617	617	N/A	216	72	Public	14.8	62%	35%	3%	116
Wayne State University (MI)	615	481	134	152	86	Public	14.2	57%	39%	4%	80
University of Chicago	607	607	N/A	190	96	Private	10.3	26%	71%	3%	159
North Carolina Central University	604	478	126	234	63	Public	17.6	66%	32%	2%	72
Vanderbilt University (TN)	601	601	N/A	193	95	Private	12.9	51%	45%	3%	133
Oklahoma City University	598	501	97	218	58	Private	18.2	63%	37%	0%	85
University of Southern California (Gould)	598	598	N/A	194	70	Private	12.7	58%	34%	8%	93
Arizona State University (O'Connor)	595	595	N/A	162	50	Public	9.4	50%	49%	2%	128
Whittier Law School (CA)	592	372	220	201	82	Private	13.9	75%	25%	0%	123
Charleston School of Law (SC)	591	394	197	206	65	Private	19.8	48%	52%	0%	62
University of Illinois–Urbana-Champaign	587	587	N/A	169	66	Public	12.4	63%	37%	0%	145
Yale University (CT)	587	586	1	189	60	Private	7.4	50%	45%	5%	145
Roger Williams University (RI)	586	556	30	195	70	Private	18.3	50%	48%	2%	105
Cornell University (NY)	583	583	N/A	196	93	Private	11.2	62%	32%	6%	116
Louisiana State University–Baton Rouge	583	570	13	200	67	Public	16.2	59%	40%	2%	79
Texas Southern University (Marshall)	583	583	N/A	193	65	Public	14.5	57%	43%	0%	123
Western New England College (MA)	579	397	182	209	50	Private	13.8	60%	40%	0%	90
University of California–Davis	577	577	N/A	200	65	Public	12.4	50%	39%	11%	84
Florida A&M University	570	357	213	210	60	Public	19.2	51%	49%	0%	52
Gonzaga University (WA)	565	549	16	206	75	Private	14.8	49%	51%	0%	90
University of Notre Dame (IN)	564	563	1	176	99	Private	14.7	58%	42%	1%	113
Vermont Law School	555	555	N/A	194	70	Private	11.6	59%	41%	0%	123
Chapman University (CA)	545	474	71	190	65	Private	12.6	58%	42%	0%	95
Northern Kentucky University (Chase)	543	304	239	205	94	Public	17.1	43%	56%	1%	60
University of Toledo (OH)	543	348	195	221	64	Public	15.1	71%	29%	0%	87
Valparaiso University (IN)	542	486	56	225	65	Private	15.8	67%	32%	1%	110
Stanford University (CA)	538	538	N/A	170	60	Private	8.3	75%	24%	1%	168
Mississippi College	537	528	9	197	98	Private	18.9	54%	46%	0%	66
University of Colorado–Boulder	530	530	N/A	175	87	Public	12.2	66%	34%	0%	101
University of Akron (OH)	529	308	221	175	58	Public	13.3	69%	30%	1%	97
University of Oregon	528	528	N/A	178	61	Public	17.6	58%	41%	2%	124
University of Washington	528	528	N/A	182	60	Public	10.2	62%	38%	0%	122
University of Mississippi	517	517	N/A	173	58	Public	15.8	49%	46%	6%	82
University of Alabama	515	492	23	186	57	Public	9.8	68%	31%	1%	105
University of Tulsa (OK)	511	452	59	157	50	Private	13.5	71%	29%	0%	146
University of Oklahoma	510	510	N/A	173	38	Public	11.9	43%	57%	0%	99
Samford University (Cumberland) (AL)	495	495	N/A	158	56	Private	17.6	47%	53%	0%	96
University of Missouri–Kansas City	493	467	26	179	56	Public	12.8	67%	33%	0%	113
University of Kansas	491	491	N/A	157	61	Public	12.1	69%	30%	1%	99
Southern University (LA)	488	377	111	185	45	Public	13.0	44%	56%	0%	37
University of Richmond (Williams) (VA)	487	486	1	160	55	Private	15.6	69%	31%	0%	90
Atlanta's John Marshall Law School	474	302	172	181	45	Private	13.1	46%	54%	0%	39

What are the largest and smallest law schools?

School	Total full- and part-time enrollment	Full-time enrollment	Part-time enrollment	Size of first-year class	Typical first-year section size	Public or private	Student to faculty ratio	% classes under 25	% classes 25-100	% classes over 100	Number of course offerings after first year
Creighton University (NE)	469	451	18	174	78	Private	18.1	70%	29%	1%	85
University of Tennessee–Knoxville	469	469	N/A	171	55	Public	13.1	72%	28%	0%	126
University of St. Thomas (MN)	467	467	N/A	165	83	Private	16.8	73%	27%	0%	71
University of Nevada–Las Vegas (Boyd)	463	341	122	153	55	Public	14.0	76%	24%	0%	82
Wake Forest University (NC)	462	452	10	156	40	Private	10.3	50%	50%	0%	96
Regent University (VA)	459	437	22	153	80	Private	20.0	69%	31%	0%	82
Brigham Young University (Clark) (UT)	457	457	N/A	145	104	Private	18.9	44%	55%	1%	100
University of Missouri–Columbia	455	449	6	147	75	Public	17.2	60%	40%	0%	111
University of Arizona (Rogers)	453	453	N/A	158	79	Public	11.7	76%	23%	1%	131
Florida International University	450	307	143	195	65	Public	15.0	80%	20%	0%	57
Mercer University (GA)	448	448	N/A	145	72	Private	13.3	73%	27%	1%	105
Washburn University (KS)	445	445	N/A	161	71	Public	13.8	55%	45%	0%	92
West Virginia University	443	443	N/A	136	70	Public	13.8	49%	50%	1%	66
University of Arkansas–Little Rock (Bowen)	442	292	150	163	87	Public	14.3	72%	28%	N/A	79
Howard University (DC)	428	428	N/A	149	50	Private	18.7	39%	61%	0%	108
University of Kentucky	426	426	N/A	125	62	Public	15.0	31%	69%	0%	50
University of Dayton (OH)	424	424	N/A	177	80	Private	14.5	69%	30%	1%	74
Drake University (IA)	421	414	7	155	72	Private	12.9	56%	44%	0%	112
University of Memphis (Humphreys)	417	395	22	148	75	Public	17.7	54%	46%	0%	69
CUNY–Queens College	412	412	N/A	149	80	Public	13.0	51%	47%	1%	61
Baylor University (Umphrey) (TX)	411	411	N/A	161	57	Private	16.6	52%	47%	1%	85
University of Louisville (Brandeis) (KY)	410	323	87	172	51	Public	14.4	47%	53%	0%	64
University of Arkansas–Fayetteville	407	407	N/A	141	75	Public	13.8	79%	21%	1%	93
Franklin Pierce Law Center (NH)	400	400	N/A	135	71	Private	14.4	71%	29%	0%	93
University of Nebraska–Lincoln	398	397	1	137	70	Public	12.5	68%	32%	0%	75
University of Utah (Quinney)	397	397	N/A	122	37	Public	9.9	67%	33%	0%	114
Washington and Lee University (VA)	395	395	N/A	115	49	Private	10.6	61%	39%	0%	76
Willamette University (Collins) (OR)	395	395	N/A	156	79	Private	14.1	62%	38%	0%	102
Quinnipiac University (CT)	388	235	153	129	30	Private	10.4	81%	19%	0%	104
Western State University (CA)	388	259	129	150	65	Private	15.6	61%	39%	0%	50
University of Cincinnati	356	356	N/A	118	54	Public	9.6	64%	36%	0%	112
Southern Illinois University–Carbondale	354	352	2	133	60	Public	11.7	69%	31%	0%	82
University of New Mexico	347	347	N/A	108	57	Public	10.0	71%	29%	0%	110
Appalachian School of Law (VA)	339	339	N/A	126	158	Private	21.0	46%	31%	23%	39
Campbell University (Wiggins) (NC)	339	339	N/A	128	80	Private	16.5	51%	42%	7%	67
William Mitchell College of Law (MN)	336	233	103	338	80	Private	22.5	51%	50%	0%	127
Ave Maria School of Law (MI)	332	331	1	130	65	Private	15.7	59%	41%	0%	70
Northern Illinois University	326	310	16	113	52	Public	18.6	49%	51%	0%	55
Ohio Northern University (Pettit)	311	311	N/A	116	60	Private	12.2	70%	30%	0%	77
University of La Verne (CA)	310	205	105	136	50	Private	16.8	61%	39%	0%	43
University of Idaho	308	308	N/A	105	52	Public	16.0	63%	36%	2%	65
Faulkner University (Jones) (AL)	291	228	63	138	75	Private	10.0	78%	22%	0%	48
University of Hawaii (Richardson)	272	257	15	86	93	Public	8.5	74%	26%	0%	83
University of Maine	254	254	N/A	89	96	Public	15.3	65%	35%	0%	74
University of Montana	252	252	N/A	84	43	Public	14.3	N/A	N/A	N/A	N/A
University of North Dakota	249	249	N/A	80	78	Public	17.7	69%	31%	0%	58
University of the District of Columbia (Clarke)	237	237	N/A	93	95	Public	10.5	48%	52%	0%	38
University of Wyoming	228	228	N/A	75	75	Public	11.4	73%	27%	N/A	58
University of South Dakota	222	222	N/A	66	72	Public	16.2	55%	45%	N/A	46
Phoenix School of Law	194	103	91	91	27	Private	16.8	76%	24%	0%	3

If you're looking for a law school culture that features students from a wealth of backgrounds, the *U.S. News* diversity index can point you to institutions with both a significant proportion of minority students and a mix of different ethnic groups. The closer the index number is to 1.0, the more likely you are to interact with people of a different ethnicity than you.

School	Diversity index	American Indian	Asian	Black	Hispanic	White	International	Men	Women	Minority faculty	Male faculty	Female faculty
Texas Southern University (Marshall)	0.67	0.5%	7.9%	47.2%	23.2%	21.3%	0.0%	49.9%	50.1%	75.4%	62.3%	37.7%
Florida A&M University	0.65	0.9%	3.7%	46.5%	16.5%	31.8%	0.7%	43.2%	56.8%	72.4%	55.2%	44.8%
University of New Mexico	0.60	9.8%	2.3%	3.2%	29.4%	55.3%	0.0%	48.7%	51.3%	37.5%	60.4%	39.6%
Florida International University	0.59	0.7%	1.8%	7.8%	41.6%	46.9%	1.3%	55.8%	44.2%	56.3%	56.3%	43.8%
University of the District of Columbia (Clarke)	0.59	1.3%	4.2%	27.4%	9.3%	54.9%	3.0%	39.7%	60.3%	57.6%	54.5%	45.5%
St. Thomas University (FL)	0.58	0.0%	3.8%	8.5%	31.4%	53.9%	2.4%	53.3%	46.7%	19.7%	60.7%	39.3%
North Carolina Central University	0.57	1.0%	3.5%	41.7%	3.5%	48.5%	1.8%	40.6%	59.4%	57.8%	37.8%	62.2%
Rutgers–Newark (NJ)	0.57	0.2%	12.0%	13.3%	11.7%	61.2%	1.5%	56.5%	43.5%	12.7%	69.8%	30.2%
Santa Clara University (CA)	0.57	0.3%	27.4%	4.4%	8.8%	58.6%	0.4%	54.1%	45.9%	21.1%	53.9%	46.1%
University of Southern California (Gould)	0.57	0.7%	16.9%	9.0%	11.4%	59.5%	2.5%	52.7%	47.3%	21.7%	63.8%	36.2%
Loyola Marymount University (CA)	0.56	0.4%	24.0%	3.7%	10.7%	59.9%	1.3%	50.8%	49.2%	18.8%	67.0%	33.0%
Northwestern University (IL)	0.56	0.9%	18.3%	8.2%	8.7%	59.9%	4.0%	53.7%	46.3%	19.5%	75.4%	24.6%
University of San Francisco	0.56	1.0%	19.4%	6.7%	10.3%	61.2%	1.4%	48.2%	51.8%	25.0%	66.4%	33.6%
University of Hawaii (Richardson)	0.54	1.1%	56.3%	2.2%	3.3%	34.9%	2.2%	57.0%	43.0%	40.6%	69.6%	30.4%
University of Maryland	0.54	0.8%	12.8%	13.6%	8.1%	63.4%	1.3%	44.9%	55.1%	13.2%	58.1%	41.9%
Southwestern Law School (CA)	0.53	0.7%	16.3%	5.1%	12.4%	64.7%	0.7%	48.8%	51.2%	17.9%	69.5%	30.5%
Stanford University (CA)	0.53	1.7%	13.4%	8.6%	9.7%	65.2%	1.5%	54.3%	45.7%	N/A	N/A	N/A
Southern University (LA)	0.52	0.0%	0.4%	54.1%	1.8%	43.6%	0.0%	48.0%	52.0%	71.2%	61.0%	39.0%
University of California–Davis	0.52	0.5%	24.3%	2.3%	8.5%	63.1%	1.4%	45.2%	54.8%	28.6%	59.7%	40.3%
American University (Washington) (DC)	0.51	1.4%	10.5%	7.8%	12.4%	67.2%	0.7%	46.4%	53.6%	15.1%	61.7%	38.3%
St. Mary's University (TX)	0.51	1.2%	5.2%	3.5%	24.3%	65.6%	0.1%	54.5%	45.5%	14.5%	65.2%	34.8%
University of California–Los Angeles	0.51	1.3%	19.4%	3.6%	9.0%	65.9%	0.9%	50.9%	49.1%	11.9%	73.8%	26.2%
Columbia University (NY)	0.50	0.6%	14.1%	8.0%	6.1%	62.0%	9.1%	55.6%	44.4%	9.7%	70.5%	29.5%
CUNY–Queens College	0.50	0.2%	15.5%	7.0%	8.3%	66.3%	2.7%	35.0%	65.0%	39.7%	42.3%	57.7%
Harvard University (MA)	0.50	0.8%	10.8%	11.5%	6.9%	65.8%	4.2%	53.5%	46.5%	11.8%	80.0%	20.0%
University of California–Berkeley	0.50	1.4%	17.4%	4.3%	8.9%	68.1%	0.0%	45.1%	54.9%	8.6%	68.0%	32.0%
University of California (Hastings)	0.50	0.5%	23.7%	3.2%	6.6%	65.0%	1.5%	47.0%	53.0%	19.5%	63.3%	36.7%
University of La Verne (CA)	0.50	0.3%	13.5%	2.9%	15.5%	66.5%	1.3%	58.4%	41.6%	13.9%	69.4%	30.6%
Whittier Law School (CA)	0.50	0.5%	19.9%	2.4%	10.3%	66.2%	0.7%	47.5%	52.5%	.0%	.0%	.0%
Thomas Jefferson School of Law (CA)	0.49	0.9%	9.5%	7.3%	13.4%	68.9%	0.0%	52.5%	47.5%	12.5%	62.5%	37.5%
Western State University (CA)	0.49	0.5%	16.8%	4.1%	9.8%	67.3%	1.5%	51.0%	49.0%	23.5%	61.8%	38.2%
University of Nevada–Las Vegas (Boyd)	0.47	2.2%	11.9%	5.2%	9.5%	70.8%	0.4%	52.3%	47.7%	23.5%	70.6%	29.4%
University of Texas–Austin	0.47	0.5%	6.7%	6.3%	16.4%	70.1%	0.0%	60.0%	40.0%	9.4%	71.7%	28.3%
Yale University (CT)	0.47	0.3%	13.3%	7.7%	7.2%	67.6%	3.9%	52.1%	47.9%	9.9%	75.4%	24.6%
Emory University (GA)	0.46	0.3%	9.9%	9.2%	8.2%	69.0%	3.5%	52.8%	47.2%	22.2%	61.6%	38.4%
University of Michigan–Ann Arbor	0.46	2.3%	13.2%	6.3%	5.7%	68.6%	4.0%	56.2%	43.8%	9.5%	68.6%	31.4%
University of San Diego	0.46	0.8%	17.0%	3.2%	8.2%	70.4%	0.4%	57.2%	42.8%	9.4%	77.8%	22.2%
Brooklyn Law School (NY)	0.45	0.2%	15.1%	6.2%	6.0%	71.7%	0.7%	52.2%	47.8%	7.8%	62.9%	37.1%
California Western School of Law	0.45	0.8%	13.7%	2.8%	10.6%	71.2%	0.8%	47.7%	52.3%	11.9%	69.5%	30.5%

What are the most and least diverse law schools?

School	Diversity index	American Indian	Asian	Black	Hispanic	White	International	Men	Women	Minority faculty	Male faculty	Female faculty
University of Arizona (Rogers)	0.45	5.7%	8.4%	2.6%	10.6%	72.0%	0.7%	48.6%	51.4%	12.6%	68.5%	31.5%
University of Houston	0.45	0.7%	11.1%	6.3%	9.4%	72.5%	0.0%	58.1%	41.9%	10.9%	74.3%	25.7%
University of Illinois–Urbana-Champaign	0.45	0.3%	11.8%	8.0%	5.8%	68.1%	6.0%	59.6%	40.4%	12.4%	69.9%	30.1%
Arizona State University (O'Connor)	0.44	5.5%	3.9%	3.5%	13.4%	71.9%	1.7%	56.8%	43.2%	12.8%	75.5%	24.5%
Golden Gate University (CA)	0.44	0.7%	18.0%	2.8%	6.1%	71.5%	0.9%	44.5%	55.5%	16.7%	59.4%	40.6%
Northeastern University (MA)	0.44	1.0%	9.9%	6.4%	9.5%	73.2%	0.0%	41.3%	58.7%	17.5%	52.4%	47.6%
University of Chicago	0.43	0.3%	11.4%	6.6%	7.6%	72.2%	2.0%	55.4%	44.6%	8.8%	78.4%	21.6%
University of Pennsylvania	0.43	0.4%	9.1%	7.4%	7.9%	71.6%	3.6%	54.0%	46.0%	12.8%	73.7%	26.3%
University of the Pacific (McGeorge) (CA)	0.43	1.1%	12.7%	3.4%	8.7%	74.2%	0.0%	52.3%	47.7%	18.2%	67.3%	32.7%
George Washington University (DC)	0.42	0.8%	9.9%	7.5%	7.1%	74.2%	0.4%	56.9%	43.1%	10.6%	67.2%	32.8%
Loyola University New Orleans	0.42	1.0%	4.7%	11.4%	7.7%	74.7%	0.5%	47.9%	52.1%	16.7%	71.7%	28.3%
Nova Southeastern University (Broad) (FL)	0.42	0.2%	3.4%	5.1%	16.9%	72.0%	2.4%	48.0%	52.0%	17.9%	58.9%	41.1%
Seattle University	0.42	1.4%	15.0%	3.3%	5.6%	73.5%	1.2%	48.2%	51.8%	20.0%	63.8%	36.2%
University of Wisconsin–Madison	0.42	2.6%	7.2%	7.4%	7.8%	74.0%	1.0%	53.1%	46.9%	19.0%	53.3%	46.7%
Fordham University (NY)	0.41	0.5%	8.0%	5.6%	9.5%	74.3%	2.1%	53.1%	46.9%	12.3%	63.9%	36.1%
Georgetown University (DC)	0.41	0.3%	9.6%	9.3%	4.7%	73.4%	2.8%	57.2%	42.8%	5.7%	74.2%	25.8%
South Texas College of Law	0.41	1.0%	11.3%	3.8%	8.5%	75.2%	0.3%	55.0%	45.0%	10.9%	68.1%	31.9%
Atlanta's John Marshall Law School	0.40	0.6%	3.6%	15.8%	4.4%	75.1%	0.4%	49.8%	50.2%	14.6%	48.8%	51.2%
Chapman University (CA)	0.40	0.4%	15.2%	1.7%	6.6%	75.2%	0.9%	54.5%	45.5%	5.1%	71.4%	28.6%
Hofstra University (NY)	0.40	0.2%	7.0%	8.8%	7.8%	75.5%	0.8%	52.6%	47.4%	17.1%	68.3%	31.7%
Ohio State University (Moritz)	0.40	0.9%	9.3%	9.0%	4.0%	75.0%	1.8%	57.4%	42.6%	20.6%	66.7%	33.3%
Pennsylvania State University (Dickinson)	0.40	0.2%	7.0%	8.9%	6.9%	74.4%	2.7%	55.9%	44.1%	7.5%	50.9%	49.1%
University of Arkansas–Fayetteville	0.40	2.5%	3.2%	16.2%	2.2%	75.9%	0.0%	60.9%	39.1%	7.0%	71.9%	28.1%
Boston College	0.39	0.4%	11.1%	4.5%	7.0%	75.0%	2.0%	55.4%	44.6%	12.5%	63.2%	36.8%
New York Law School	0.39	0.2%	9.1%	5.9%	7.8%	77.1%	0.0%	48.0%	52.0%	10.1%	65.2%	34.8%
New York University	0.39	0.0%	10.7%	7.1%	4.8%	73.8%	3.6%	53.0%	47.0%	6.3%	73.5%	26.5%
Southern Methodist University (TX)	0.39	0.5%	9.9%	4.0%	8.3%	77.0%	0.3%	54.6%	45.4%	10.3%	72.2%	27.8%
St. John's University (NY)	0.39	0.1%	9.6%	5.6%	7.3%	76.3%	1.1%	52.4%	47.6%	10.7%	66.4%	33.6%
University of Miami (FL)	0.39	0.2%	4.7%	5.8%	11.8%	72.9%	4.7%	56.5%	43.5%	18.3%	70.4%	29.6%
University of Oklahoma	0.39	9.8%	3.3%	5.7%	3.7%	77.1%	0.4%	56.3%	43.7%	16.3%	75.5%	24.5%
Cornell University (NY)	0.38	1.4%	9.8%	5.1%	5.1%	73.8%	4.8%	49.6%	50.4%	11.7%	68.6%	31.4%
DePaul University (IL)	0.38	0.4%	5.5%	6.7%	9.6%	76.5%	1.2%	49.8%	50.2%	N/A	N/A	N/A
University of Colorado–Boulder	0.38	2.3%	8.3%	3.8%	7.9%	77.2%	0.6%	52.1%	47.9%	14.5%	60.0%	40.0%
University of Notre Dame (IN)	0.38	1.4%	7.1%	4.3%	9.2%	77.3%	0.7%	62.4%	37.6%	8.7%	62.0%	38.0%
Temple University (Beasley) (PA)	0.37	0.8%	9.8%	7.5%	3.0%	77.4%	1.4%	53.0%	47.0%	16.9%	66.8%	33.2%
Texas Wesleyan University	0.37	1.8%	6.2%	4.8%	8.9%	78.3%	0.0%	52.4%	47.6%	13.3%	63.3%	36.7%
Thomas M. Cooley Law School (MI)	0.37	0.3%	5.2%	10.1%	5.0%	75.1%	4.3%	53.0%	47.0%	9.1%	65.8%	34.2%
Touro College (Fuchsberg) (NY)	0.37	0.7%	7.1%	9.4%	4.1%	77.2%	1.5%	52.7%	47.3%	10.2%	64.4%	35.6%
University of Washington	0.37	2.3%	12.1%	2.5%	4.2%	76.5%	2.5%	40.9%	59.1%	10.8%	53.8%	46.2%
Northern Illinois University	0.36	0.0%	6.4%	8.3%	6.4%	78.8%	0.0%	50.0%	50.0%	25.9%	77.8%	22.2%
Texas Tech University	0.36	0.7%	3.6%	3.8%	12.9%	79.0%	0.0%	57.1%	42.9%	20.8%	67.9%	32.1%
University of Florida (Levin)	0.36	0.4%	4.7%	6.0%	9.5%	78.1%	1.3%	53.3%	46.7%	12.2%	65.3%	34.7%
University of North Carolina–Chapel Hill	0.36	2.0%	6.6%	7.2%	5.3%	79.0%	0.0%	48.2%	51.8%	17.8%	61.4%	38.6%
Florida Coastal School of Law	0.35	1.7%	5.9%	6.7%	5.9%	79.7%	0.0%	52.2%	47.8%	12.7%	53.2%	46.8%
Yeshiva University (Cardozo) (NY)	0.35	0.3%	9.6%	3.4%	6.2%	77.8%	2.7%	51.2%	48.8%	5.6%	68.3%	31.7%
Boston University	0.34	0.4%	12.1%	3.5%	3.1%	77.5%	3.5%	50.5%	49.5%	8.9%	73.3%	26.7%
Georgia State University	0.34	0.5%	5.7%	11.7%	2.1%	80.0%	0.0%	52.0%	48.0%	14.6%	63.5%	36.5%
Illinois Institute of Technology (Chicago-Kent)	0.34	0.2%	8.1%	5.7%	5.2%	78.8%	1.9%	51.8%	48.2%	7.7%	70.0%	30.0%
Rutgers–Camden (NJ)	0.34	0.3%	7.2%	5.7%	6.5%	80.0%	0.4%	58.7%	41.3%	3.8%	68.8%	31.3%
Stetson University (FL)	0.34	0.6%	2.7%	6.5%	9.6%	79.8%	0.8%	47.0%	53.0%	12.5%	67.5%	32.5%
University of Arkansas–Little Rock (Bowen)	0.34	1.4%	2.0%	12.9%	3.4%	78.5%	1.8%	52.3%	47.7%	12.0%	63.0%	37.0%

What are the most and least diverse law schools?

School	Diversity index	American Indian	Asian	Black	Hispanic	White	International	Men	Women	Minority faculty	Male faculty	Female faculty
John Marshall Law School (IL)	0.33	1.2%	6.6%	5.3%	5.5%	80.0%	1.4%	57.3%	42.7%	7.9%	73.2%	26.8%
Lewis and Clark College (Northwestern) (OR)	0.33	1.9%	8.7%	2.2%	6.1%	79.4%	1.7%	52.3%	47.7%	5.1%	59.3%	40.7%
Phoenix School of Law	0.33	2.1%	2.1%	3.1%	11.9%	80.9%	0.0%	49.0%	51.0%	28.6%	57.1%	42.9%
Syracuse University (NY)	0.33	1.1%	10.2%	4.4%	3.2%	78.4%	2.9%	54.7%	45.3%	19.5%	72.0%	28.0%
University of Georgia	0.33	0.0%	4.2%	13.7%	1.7%	79.8%	0.6%	53.6%	46.4%	N/A	N/A	N/A
Washington University in St. Louis	0.33	0.6%	8.9%	6.5%	1.5%	75.9%	6.5%	54.6%	45.4%	8.1%	71.0%	29.0%
Barry University (FL)	0.32	0.7%	3.8%	4.9%	8.5%	82.1%	0.0%	53.0%	47.0%	9.7%	64.5%	35.5%
Catholic University of America (Columbus) (DC)	0.32	0.7%	7.9%	4.9%	5.0%	81.4%	0.2%	51.8%	48.2%	9.2%	65.8%	34.2%
Duke University (NC)	0.32	0.2%	5.8%	8.2%	3.1%	78.2%	4.5%	55.6%	44.4%	7.1%	70.5%	29.5%
Indiana University–Bloomington	0.32	0.3%	4.7%	8.1%	5.2%	81.8%	0.0%	61.1%	38.9%	6.1%	65.2%	34.8%
Loyola University Chicago	0.32	0.7%	6.9%	5.5%	4.6%	81.2%	1.0%	48.1%	51.9%	7.8%	54.5%	45.5%
University of Connecticut	0.32	0.5%	5.9%	5.4%	6.5%	81.3%	0.5%	52.2%	47.8%	9.9%	74.7%	25.3%
University of Iowa	0.32	0.8%	7.7%	4.1%	5.1%	80.7%	1.6%	55.0%	45.0%	N/A	N/A	N/A
University of Oregon	0.32	1.7%	9.3%	2.8%	4.0%	81.1%	1.1%	57.8%	42.2%	11.9%	64.2%	35.8%
Wayne State University (MI)	0.32	0.3%	4.4%	9.8%	3.7%	80.5%	1.3%	51.5%	48.5%	6.4%	70.0%	30.0%
George Mason University (VA)	0.31	0.4%	8.0%	3.7%	5.1%	81.1%	1.8%	59.9%	40.1%	6.7%	77.0%	23.0%
University of Cincinnati	0.31	0.3%	6.5%	7.0%	3.7%	82.6%	0.0%	54.5%	45.5%	10.1%	69.7%	30.3%
Ave Maria School of Law (MI)	0.30	0.6%	7.2%	2.4%	6.6%	81.3%	1.8%	65.1%	34.9%	2.5%	77.5%	22.5%
Brigham Young University (Clark) (UT)	0.30	1.8%	7.2%	1.3%	6.8%	82.1%	0.9%	65.9%	34.1%	7.4%	74.1%	25.9%
Florida State University	0.30	0.5%	3.7%	5.4%	7.3%	81.2%	2.0%	60.5%	39.5%	10.2%	65.9%	34.1%
Franklin Pierce Law Center (NH)	0.30	0.5%	8.0%	3.5%	4.0%	77.0%	7.0%	65.5%	34.5%	5.8%	65.4%	34.6%
Howard University (DC)	0.30	1.6%	4.4%	76.4%	2.3%	7.2%	7.9%	40.9%	59.1%	71.4%	63.5%	36.5%
Pepperdine University (CA)	0.30	0.8%	8.5%	3.5%	4.1%	83.1%	0.0%	49.8%	50.2%	12.3%	76.6%	23.4%
University of Denver (Sturm)	0.30	2.6%	4.5%	3.2%	6.3%	83.2%	0.2%	54.8%	45.2%	14.4%	72.2%	27.8%
University of Memphis (Humphreys)	0.30	0.5%	2.2%	13.4%	1.2%	82.5%	0.2%	56.4%	43.6%	11.4%	63.6%	36.4%
Vanderbilt University (TN)	0.30	0.8%	4.7%	8.3%	2.7%	81.2%	2.3%	54.2%	45.8%	14.4%	60.6%	39.4%
College of William and Mary (VA)	0.29	0.5%	4.4%	10.5%	1.3%	82.7%	0.6%	51.1%	48.9%	12.7%	67.6%	32.4%
Mercer University (GA)	0.29	0.4%	2.9%	10.7%	2.5%	83.5%	0.0%	57.1%	42.9%	6.6%	72.1%	27.9%
Oklahoma City University	0.29	5.5%	2.8%	2.8%	4.8%	83.9%	0.0%	59.4%	40.6%	10.1%	68.1%	31.9%
Tulane University (LA)	0.29	1.2%	3.5%	6.9%	4.4%	81.9%	2.1%	59.7%	40.3%	6.3%	77.2%	22.8%
University at Buffalo–SUNY	0.29	0.4%	6.8%	4.8%	4.1%	83.9%	0.0%	51.3%	40.7%	10.5%	67.3%	32.7%
University of Detroit Mercy	0.29	0.1%	3.2%	9.5%	1.3%	70.3%	15.6%	54.2%	45.8%	7.1%	73.2%	26.8%
University of Kansas	0.29	3.7%	5.7%	2.6%	3.7%	80.0%	4.3%	62.1%	37.9%	11.4%	64.3%	35.7%
University of Virginia	0.29	0.9%	6.6%	6.8%	2.1%	82.8%	0.8%	60.6%	39.4%	6.0%	79.5%	20.5%
Villanova University (PA)	0.29	0.6%	8.3%	4.0%	3.6%	82.7%	1.0%	55.3%	44.7%	10.7%	68.0%	32.0%
University of Baltimore	0.28	0.3%	5.5%	8.2%	1.5%	84.0%	0.5%	47.6%	52.4%	15.7%	66.4%	33.6%
University of Dayton (OH)	0.28	0.7%	4.5%	6.1%	4.2%	84.4%	0.0%	56.8%	43.2%	10.9%	56.5%	43.5%
University of Minnesota–Twin Cities	0.28	1.1%	8.7%	2.3%	3.4%	82.6%	1.9%	58.3%	41.7%	5.2%	57.0%	43.0%
University of Tennessee–Knoxville	0.28	0.6%	2.1%	11.5%	1.7%	83.8%	0.2%	51.6%	48.4%	6.3%	63.5%	36.5%
Washington and Lee University (VA)	0.28	1.3%	7.8%	4.3%	1.8%	82.5%	2.3%	61.8%	38.2%	9.6%	72.6%	27.4%
Pace University (NY)	0.27	0.0%	8.9%	2.7%	3.4%	84.1%	0.9%	41.0%	59.0%	6.8%	53.4%	46.6%
Quinnipiac University (CT)	0.27	0.8%	7.5%	3.1%	3.6%	85.1%	0.0%	49.0%	51.0%	6.8%	63.0%	37.0%
University of St. Thomas (MN)	0.27	0.6%	5.6%	4.7%	4.1%	85.0%	0.0%	54.6%	45.4%	9.2%	61.5%	38.5%
Albany Law School-Union University (NY)	0.26	0.1%	7.3%	2.9%	3.7%	84.4%	1.6%	54.5%	45.5%	12.7%	63.1%	36.9%
Case Western Reserve University (OH)	0.26	0.1%	8.8%	4.3%	1.0%	82.3%	3.4%	58.0%	42.0%	8.7%	66.9%	33.1%
Seton Hall University (NJ)	0.26	0.2%	6.7%	2.7%	4.5%	83.8%	2.1%	56.5%	43.5%	10.9%	67.9%	32.1%
Suffolk University (MA)	0.26	0.6%	6.8%	2.8%	3.9%	83.9%	2.0%	50.8%	49.2%	N/A	N/A	N/A
University of Idaho	0.26	1.3%	5.8%	0.6%	6.5%	83.8%	1.9%	55.2%	44.8%	2.8%	75.0%	25.0%
University of Missouri–Columbia	0.26	1.5%	4.4%	5.5%	2.9%	85.7%	0.0%	61.8%	38.2%	11.5%	67.3%	32.7%
University of Pittsburgh	0.26	0.0%	7.1%	5.0%	2.5%	85.3%	0.0%	56.7%	43.3%	7.5%	70.1%	29.9%
Cleveland State University (Cleveland-Marshall)	0.25	0.4%	3.3%	7.1%	2.8%	85.6%	0.8%	53.4%	46.6%	8.9%	65.8%	34.2%

What are the most and least diverse law schools?

School	Diversity index	American Indian	Asian	Black	Hispanic	White	International	Men	Women	Minority faculty	Male faculty	Female faculty
Indiana University–Indianapolis	0.25	0.4%	3.3%	6.0%	3.3%	82.7%	4.4%	52.0%	48.0%	6.4%	66.0%	34.0%
Michigan State University	0.25	1.3%	4.2%	4.4%	3.0%	81.3%	5.9%	57.8%	42.2%	11.4%	65.8%	34.2%
Regent University (VA)	0.25	2.4%	3.7%	5.9%	1.5%	85.2%	1.3%	50.5%	49.5%	7.7%	80.8%	19.2%
University of Mississippi	0.25	0.8%	1.5%	11.4%	0.6%	85.3%	0.4%	55.5%	44.5%	11.9%	64.3%	35.7%
University of Richmond (Williams) (VA)	0.25	0.6%	4.7%	8.0%	0.4%	86.2%	0.0%	50.7%	49.3%	6.7%	70.4%	29.6%
University of South Carolina	0.25	0.3%	2.1%	8.4%	2.7%	85.5%	1.0%	57.4%	42.6%	8.5%	70.7%	29.3%
Hamline University (MN)	0.24	0.7%	5.1%	2.7%	4.3%	86.0%	1.1%	48.0%	52.0%	6.7%	58.7%	41.3%
St. Louis University	0.24	0.6%	4.5%	5.9%	2.3%	86.0%	0.7%	51.7%	48.3%	6.0%	65.5%	34.5%
University of Alabama	0.24	0.6%	2.7%	8.2%	1.9%	86.6%	0.0%	60.6%	39.4%	8.6%	76.2%	23.8%
Washburn University (KS)	0.24	1.8%	2.5%	3.8%	4.7%	87.2%	0.0%	59.8%	40.2%	11.4%	69.6%	30.4%
Widener University (DE)	0.24	0.5%	5.9%	4.5%	2.3%	86.3%	0.5%	56.3%	43.7%	6.9%	61.4%	38.6%
Willamette University (Collins) (OR)	0.24	1.0%	7.1%	1.5%	3.3%	87.1%	0.0%	54.4%	45.6%	10.4%	71.6%	28.4%
University of Akron (OH)	0.23	0.2%	4.2%	6.2%	2.1%	86.6%	0.8%	56.5%	43.5%	5.4%	64.9%	35.1%
University of North Dakota	0.23	4.4%	3.6%	1.2%	3.2%	85.9%	1.6%	53.0%	47.0%	16.0%	64.0%	36.0%
University of Tulsa (OK)	0.23	6.5%	1.2%	2.2%	2.7%	86.9%	0.6%	62.2%	37.8%	9.9%	62.0%	38.0%
Valparaiso University (IN)	0.23	0.2%	1.8%	5.7%	5.0%	86.7%	0.6%	54.4%	45.6%	9.3%	57.4%	42.6%
Drake University (IA)	0.22	0.5%	2.6%	6.2%	2.6%	88.1%	0.0%	54.4%	45.6%	11.3%	64.2%	35.8%
Marquette University (WI)	0.22	1.0%	3.2%	3.3%	4.0%	87.9%	0.6%	56.4%	43.6%	7.9%	58.4%	41.6%
Roger Williams University (RI)	0.22	0.7%	3.9%	3.1%	4.3%	87.5%	0.5%	52.2%	47.8%	8.9%	71.1%	28.9%
Vermont Law School	0.22	1.3%	2.7%	5.0%	2.7%	87.2%	1.1%	49.7%	50.3%	7.3%	63.6%	36.4%
Wake Forest University (NC)	0.22	0.0%	2.8%	7.6%	1.7%	87.7%	0.2%	58.7%	41.3%	6.2%	66.2%	33.8%
Baylor University (Umphrey) (TX)	0.21	0.2%	5.4%	1.0%	5.1%	88.3%	0.0%	60.3%	39.7%	4.0%	82.0%	18.0%
Capital University (OH)	0.21	0.6%	2.1%	7.7%	1.3%	88.0%	0.3%	56.0%	44.0%	10.3%	75.9%	24.1%
West Virginia University	0.21	0.2%	2.9%	7.9%	0.7%	87.8%	0.5%	56.0%	44.0%	4.5%	65.9%	34.1%
Ohio Northern University (Pettit)	0.20	0.3%	3.2%	6.1%	1.3%	89.1%	0.0%	53.1%	46.9%	13.3%	66.7%	33.3%
Samford University (Cumberland) (AL)	0.20	0.8%	1.2%	7.3%	1.4%	89.3%	0.0%	54.3%	45.7%	8.2%	73.5%	26.5%
Faulkner University (Jones) (AL)	0.19	1.0%	1.4%	6.9%	1.0%	89.7%	0.0%	55.3%	44.7%	14.3%	71.4%	28.6%
Louisiana State University–Baton Rouge	0.19	1.0%	0.5%	4.6%	3.8%	90.1%	0.0%	52.3%	47.7%	9.0%	87.2%	12.8%
University of Nebraska–Lincoln	0.19	0.8%	2.8%	3.0%	3.8%	89.4%	0.3%	52.8%	47.2%	3.3%	68.3%	31.7%
University of Utah (Quinney)	0.19	0.5%	4.0%	1.0%	4.5%	89.4%	0.5%	60.2%	39.8%	14.0%	64.0%	36.0%
Western New England College (MA)	0.19	0.3%	3.1%	3.1%	3.3%	88.3%	1.9%	56.0%	44.0%	4.6%	64.6%	35.4%
Creighton University (NE)	0.18	0.2%	3.8%	2.3%	3.2%	90.0%	0.4%	59.1%	40.9%	N/A	N/A	N/A
New England School of Law (MA)	0.18	0.5%	5.0%	1.5%	2.5%	89.2%	1.3%	45.2%	54.8%	8.3%	62.4%	37.6%
Northern Kentucky University (Chase)	0.18	0.6%	2.0%	4.8%	2.0%	90.6%	0.0%	56.0%	44.0%	9.1%	72.7%	27.3%
University of Missouri–Kansas City	0.18	0.6%	2.6%	3.9%	2.6%	89.7%	0.6%	58.8%	41.2%	5.6%	73.2%	26.8%
Mississippi College	0.17	0.2%	0.9%	7.1%	1.1%	90.7%	0.0%	58.5%	41.5%	11.5%	69.0%	31.0%
Southern Illinois University–Carbondale	0.17	0.0%	3.1%	4.0%	2.0%	91.0%	0.0%	62.7%	37.3%	5.1%	61.5%	38.5%
University of Kentucky	0.17	0.2%	1.6%	5.9%	1.4%	90.1%	0.7%	57.3%	42.7%	5.7%	71.7%	28.3%
University of Louisville (Brandeis) (KY)	0.17	0.0%	2.4%	5.1%	1.7%	90.5%	0.2%	53.9%	46.1%	10.0%	66.7%	33.3%
Gonzaga University (WA)	0.16	1.4%	4.1%	0.7%	2.5%	91.2%	0.2%	57.7%	42.3%	4.7%	64.1%	35.9%
University of Toledo (OH)	0.16	0.4%	3.1%	2.0%	3.1%	90.4%	0.9%	61.1%	38.9%	3.3%	67.2%	32.8%
University of Wyoming	0.16	0.4%	3.5%	1.3%	3.1%	89.9%	1.8%	52.6%	47.4%	12.5%	62.5%	37.5%
Campbell University (Wiggins) (NC)	0.14	0.6%	1.5%	2.9%	2.4%	92.6%	0.0%	54.3%	45.7%	7.5%	85.0%	15.0%
Duquesne University (PA)	0.14	0.3%	1.2%	4.9%	1.0%	92.6%	0.0%	49.8%	50.2%	3.8%	75.0%	25.0%
William Mitchell College of Law (MN)	0.14	0.9%	3.0%	3.0%	0.6%	92.0%	0.6%	51.8%	48.2%	21.1%	59.9%	40.1%
University of Montana	0.13	6.0%	0.4%	0.0%	0.8%	92.9%	0.0%	49.2%	50.8%	12.5%	69.6%	30.4%
Charleston School of Law (SC)	0.11	0.3%	1.2%	4.1%	0.2%	94.2%	0.0%	58.4%	41.6%	25.0%	72.7%	27.3%
Appalachian School of Law (VA)	0.10	0.0%	1.5%	1.2%	2.7%	94.7%	0.0%	64.9%	35.1%	15.0%	50.0%	50.0%
University of South Dakota	0.07	1.8%	0.0%	0.5%	1.4%	96.4%	0.0%	55.4%	44.6%	N/A	N/A	N/A
University of Maine	0.03	0.0%	1.2%	0.4%	N/A	98.0%	0.4%	54.3%	45.7%	1.8%	64.9%	35.1%

Who's the priciest? Who's the cheapest?

The total cost of a JD degree can easily top $150,000 at the most expensive schools, once you factor in living expenses. (And that's not counting lost income, since you won't be working full-time while you're in school.) Private law schools are listed here by tuition and fees for the 2007-2008 academic year, with the most expensive on top. Public institutions follow, sorted by in-state tuition so you can easily see what you might save by sticking close to home.

Private Schools

School	Total tuition and fees	Room and board	Books	Other expenses
Yale University (CT)	$43,750	$15,100	$1,000	N/A
Columbia University (NY)	$43,470	$15,035	$1,263	$3,300
Northwestern University (IL)	$42,942	$12,376	$1,418	$7,680
Cornell University (NY)	$42,683	$10,300	$850	$6,200
University of Southern California (Gould)	$42,640	$13,146	$1,664	$3,856
University of Pennsylvania	$41,960	$11,695	$1,150	$4,855
New York Law School	$41,950	$15,750	$1,000	$4,035
Syracuse University (NY)	$41,694	$11,270	$1,250	$4,296
New York University	$40,890	$19,731	$1,050	$2,789
Duke University (NC)	$40,748	$9,180	$1,140	$6,309
Stanford University (CA)	$39,916	$16,218	$1,640	$2,842
Vanderbilt University (TN)	$39,838	$12,056	$1,574	$6,988
Brooklyn Law School (NY)	$39,625	$15,725	$1,100	$3,741
Yeshiva University (Cardozo) (NY)	$39,470	$18,900	$1,200	$5,580
Fordham University (NY)	$39,450	N/A	N/A	N/A
Georgetown University (DC)	$39,390	$14,600	$970	$4,640
Harvard University (MA)	$39,325	$17,497	$1,075	$4,503
University of Chicago	$39,198	$13,466	$1,654	$7,186
St. John's University (NY)	$38,400	$13,670	$1,400	$4,140
George Washington University (DC)	$38,198	$12,900	$1,100	$6,500
Washington University in St. Louis	$38,189	$11,000	$2,000	$6,600
Emory University (GA)	$38,176	$16,516	$2,250	$3,046
Seton Hall University (NJ)	$38,040	$12,150	$1,000	$4,140
University of San Diego	$37,704	$11,268	$956	$6,372
Hofstra University (NY)	$37,600	$11,116	$1,400	$3,160
Albany Law School-Union University (NY)	$37,550	$9,650	$1,100	$6,300
Pace University (NY)	$37,430	$16,780	$1,120	$5,170
American University (Washington) (DC)	$37,190	$13,635	$1,015	$5,407
Boston University	$36,806	$11,305	$1,254	$4,500
Tulane University (LA)	$36,670	$11,690	$1,500	$5,530
Boston College	$36,590	$12,785	$1,000	$4,605
Northeastern University (MA)	$36,564	$15,300	$1,200	$1,825
Quinnipiac University (CT)	$36,240	$8,919	$1,200	$7,597
Suffolk University (MA)	$36,068	$11,503	$900	$1,711
Loyola Marymount University (CA)	$36,058	$13,500	$1,000	$5,720
University of Notre Dame (IN)	$35,950	$7,650	$1,300	$6,450
Pepperdine University (CA)	$35,520	$15,110	$800	$4,700
Case Western Reserve University (OH)	$35,220	$14,120	$1,275	$1,240
University of Miami (FL)	$34,652	$10,673	$1,088	$7,491

Who's the priciest? Who's the cheapest?

Private Schools

School	Total tuition and fees	Room and board	Books	Other expenses
Southern Methodist University (TX)	$34,576	$14,400	$1,900	$2,700
Catholic University of America (Columbus) (DC)	$34,505	$14,600	$1,500	$7,724
University of the Pacific (McGeorge) (CA)	$34,474	$12,062	$950	$6,359
California Western School of Law	$34,300	$10,800	$1,088	$8,194
Chapman University (CA)	$34,250	$13,752	$1,500	$5,868
Touro College (Fuchsberg) (NY)	$33,920	$17,151	$1,874	$3,981
Illinois Institute of Technology (Chicago-Kent)	$33,879	$14,247	$1,000	$3,780
University of San Francisco	$33,870	$13,500	$950	$4,660
Washington and Lee University (VA)	$33,685	$8,470	$1,500	$5,725
Southwestern Law School (CA)	$33,410	$14,220	$1,250	$5,580
Loyola University Chicago	$33,300	$13,200	$1,200	$5,300
Baylor University (Umphrey) (TX)	$33,294	$9,936	$1,839	$5,148
DePaul University (IL)	$33,110	$21,604	$1,300	N/A
Golden Gate University (CA)	$32,940	$13,500	$1,200	$6,615
University of Denver (Sturm)	$32,752	$9,585	$1,698	$4,550
University of La Verne (CA)	$32,370	$16,833	$1,386	$3,618
Ave Maria School of Law (MI)	$32,302	$12,618	$900	$6,170
Mercer University (GA)	$32,292	$7,200	$1,000	$6,000
Thomas Jefferson School of Law (CA)	$31,770	N/A	N/A	N/A
St. Louis University	$31,750	$11,988	$1,300	$5,589
Whittier Law School (CA)	$31,750	$10,800	$1,158	$5,756
Vermont Law School	$31,514	$9,720	$1,000	$7,568
Wake Forest University (NC)	$31,500	$8,810	$800	$6,440
John Marshall Law School (IL)	$31,460	$22,970	$2,060	$6,562
Valparaiso University (IN)	$31,208	$7,300	$1,200	$2,610
Western New England College (MA)	$31,048	$12,456	$1,386	$5,867
Villanova University (PA)	$30,890	$14,400	$1,200	$3,674
Widener University (DE)	$30,870	$8,930	$1,200	$5,185
Franklin Pierce Law Center (NH)	$30,780	$9,450	$1,250	$4,850
Charleston School of Law (SC)	$30,598	$7,700	$1,020	$4,300
Loyola University New Orleans	$30,456	$12,600	$1,500	$5,150
Michigan State University	$30,124	$9,962	$1,292	$1,640
University of Richmond (Williams) (VA)	$30,010	$9,360	$1,200	$3,710
Seattle University	$29,938	$10,575	$1,258	$4,486
Western State University (CA)	$29,770	$14,018	$1,500	$7,299
Marquette University (WI)	$29,410	$10,130	$1,162	$5,314
Gonzaga University (WA)	$29,397	$8,775	$1,000	$4,600
Barry University (FL)	$29,300	$12,600	$1,600	$6,300
Stetson University (FL)	$29,240	$8,212	$1,200	$4,847
Nova Southeastern University (Broad) (FL)	$29,180	$13,950	$2,325	$4,698
William Mitchell College of Law (MN)	$29,020	$13,550	$1,550	$800
Lewis and Clark College (Northwestern) (OR)	$28,984	$10,395	$1,000	$4,950
Florida Coastal School of Law	$28,870	$8,820	$1,200	$8,100
University of St. Thomas (MN)	$28,832	N/A	N/A	N/A
Hamline University (MN)	$28,682	$14,353	$1,200	N/A
Phoenix School of Law	$28,640	N/A	N/A	N/A
University of Detroit Mercy	$28,500	$11,166	$1,800	$5,590
New England School of Law (MA)	$28,020	$10,905	$1,200	$4,500
Samford University (Cumberland) (AL)	$27,892	$13,300	$1,550	$4,850
St. Thomas University (FL)	$27,840	$13,000	$1,250	$5,595
Drake University (IA)	$27,756	$7,125	$1,125	$3,900

Who's the priciest? Who's the cheapest?

Private Schools

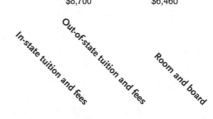

School	Total tuition and fees	Room and board	Books	Other expenses
Willamette University (Collins) (OR)	$27,495	$15,986	$0	$0
Duquesne University (PA)	$27,230	$8,054	$1,254	$1,750
Regent University (VA)	$26,862	$6,752	$1,509	$8,231
Campbell University (Wiggins) (NC)	$26,800	$8,922	$1,400	$2,500
University of Tulsa (OK)	$26,528	$5,850	$1,500	$5,869
Ohio Northern University (Pettit)	$26,350	$8,865	$1,200	$2,250
Creighton University (NE)	$25,850	$12,500	$1,350	$2,680
Thomas M. Cooley Law School (MI)	$25,436	$6,860	$800	$3,500
Appalachian School of Law (VA)	$24,000	$12,620	$900	$1,400
Mississippi College	$23,720	$9,000	$900	$7,300
South Texas College of Law	$23,610	$9,000	$1,700	$6,000
St. Mary's University (TX)	$23,440	$7,730	$1,300	$5,482
Texas Wesleyan University	$23,250	$10,521	$1,740	$2,034
Faulkner University (Jones) (AL)	$22,000	$12,000	$2,400	$4,500
Howard University (DC)	$20,445	$14,722	$1,486	$4,176
Brigham Young University (Clark) (UT)	$8,700	$6,460	$1,760	$3,888

Public Schools

School	In-state tuition and fees	Out-of-state tuition and fees	Room and board	Books	Other expenses
North Carolina Central University	$5,709	$17,569	$17,180	$2,000	$556
Southern University (LA)	$6,611	$11,211	$9,059	$2,081	$1,693
University of the District of Columbia (Clarke)	$7,350	$14,700	N/A	N/A	N/A
Florida A&M University	$7,567	$26,828	$10,450	$1,000	$6,000
University of Wyoming	$8,491	$17,977	$9,237	$1,200	$2,200
University of North Dakota	$8,774	$18,909	$8,250	$900	$4,500
University of Mississippi	$8,930	$18,550	$10,218	$1,300	$3,340
University of Montana	$8,973	$20,239	$10,500	$1,100	$127
University of South Dakota	$8,991	$17,606	$6,526	$1,400	$4,530
University of Nebraska–Lincoln	$9,018	$20,935	$7,454	$1,286	$3,180
Georgia State University	$9,530	$27,916	$9,000	$1,500	$4,474
West Virginia University	$9,856	$22,432	$8,700	$1,225	$2,790
University of Idaho	$10,200	$20,280	$8,486	$1,430	$3,666
University of Arkansas–Little Rock (Bowen)	$10,201	$20,524	$7,454	$1,250	$3,508
University of Nevada–Las Vegas (Boyd)	$10,502	$20,302	$13,110	$900	$250
University of New Mexico	$10,561	$24,467	$7,858	$1,040	$4,702
CUNY–Queens College	$10,562	$16,462	$5,311	$938	$7,057
Florida State University	$10,770	$30,782	$11,000	$1,200	$5,500
University of Florida (Levin)	$10,809	$30,174	N/A	N/A	N/A
University of Alabama	$11,190	$22,170	$8,950	$1,300	$4,704
University of Memphis (Humphreys)	$11,412	$30,598	$7,885	$1,500	$4,056
University of Tennessee–Knoxville	$11,502	$27,762	$8,996	$1,514	$3,334
Texas Southern University (Marshall)	$11,528	$15,278	$7,000	$1,900	$3,600
University of Utah (Quinney)	$11,896	$26,256	$8,964	$1,916	$4,432
University of Georgia	$12,058	$29,054	$5,600	$1,200	$5,900
Northern Kentucky University (Chase)	$12,168	$26,544	$9,278	$1,000	$0

Who's the priciest? Who's the cheapest?

Public Schools

School	In-state tuition and fees	Out-of-state tuition and fees	Room and board	Books	Other expenses
Louisiana State University–Baton Rouge	$12,190	$21,286	$11,354	$2,000	$3,162
Southern Illinois University–Carbondale	$12,265	$29,185	$8,800	$1,150	$2,435
University of Louisville (Brandeis) (KY)	$12,610	$25,956	$6,618	$1,000	$8,780
University of North Carolina–Chapel Hill	$13,004	$25,422	$12,330	$1,000	$3,970
Northern Illinois University	$13,036	$23,620	$8,568	$1,500	$2,536
University of Kansas	$13,384	$24,085	$9,088	$900	$4,698
Texas Tech University	$13,654	$20,759	$7,680	$1,000	$4,310
University of Hawaii (Richardson)	$13,656	$24,480	$12,125	$1,179	$1,693
University of Missouri–Kansas City	$13,681	$26,188	$8,630	$3,900	$7,070
University of Wisconsin–Madison	$13,708	$32,774	$7,910	$2,100	$4,510
University of Kentucky	$13,998	$24,804	$10,500	$900	$3,102
Arizona State University (O'Connor)	$14,628	$26,320	$10,530	$2,180	$6,490
University at Buffalo–SUNY	$14,633	$21,433	$9,581	$1,534	$3,329
Indiana University–Indianapolis	$14,638	$31,993	$11,296	$1,700	$8,928
University of Missouri–Columbia	$14,854	$28,336	$8,100	$1,460	$5,432
University of Oklahoma	$15,025	$24,953	$9,906	$1,110	$4,538
University of Toledo (OH)	$15,666	$25,910	$7,859	$1,750	$4,321
Temple University (Beasley) (PA)	$15,800	$27,078	$11,162	$1,500	$6,546
University of Iowa	$16,341	$32,589	$9,270	$2,300	$4,120
Cleveland State University (Cleveland-Marshall)	$16,478	$22,608	$10,630	$1,300	$4,332
University of Akron (OH)	$16,497	$26,089	$13,320	$1,082	N/A
George Mason University (VA)	$16,716	$28,532	$15,000	$990	$5,144
University of South Carolina	$16,936	$33,622	$10,985	$900	$3,875
University of Houston	$17,192	$24,632	$8,964	$1,100	$5,472
University of Connecticut	$17,520	$36,960	$10,930	$1,100	$5,170
University of Arizona (Rogers)	$17,768	$28,574	$11,840	$816	$5,050
University of Washington	$17,847	$26,231	$11,742	$1,176	$3,708
Indiana University–Bloomington	$17,912	$34,486	$8,732	$1,558	$4,498
University of Maine	$18,210	$28,290	$8,270	$952	$3,310
College of William and Mary (VA)	$18,336	$28,536	$8,134	$1,250	$1,350
University of Colorado–Boulder	$18,594	$31,278	$7,465	$1,567	$3,888
University of Cincinnati	$18,982	$33,102	$9,765	$1,227	$4,386
Ohio State University (Moritz)	$19,246	$33,946	$7,490	$3,500	$6,880
University of Oregon	$19,596	$24,396	$7,848	$1,050	$2,556
University of Maryland	$20,535	$31,814	$15,480	$1,725	$7,193
University of Baltimore	$20,597	$32,754	$12,124	$1,376	$3,698
University of Texas–Austin	$20,632	$35,130	$8,896	$1,000	$3,740
Rutgers–Newark (NJ)	$21,302	$30,307	$10,683	$1,285	$1,980
Wayne State University (MI)	$21,328	$23,305	$12,696	$1,060	$8,424
Rutgers–Camden (NJ)	$21,488	$30,492	$10,683	$1,285	$1,795
University of Pittsburgh	$22,106	$30,362	$14,910	$1,500	$690
University of Minnesota–Twin Cities	$22,505	$32,005	N/A	N/A	N/A
University of California (Hastings)	$24,120	$35,345	$14,040	$1,150	$4,103
University of California–Davis	$25,489	$37,734	$11,279	$987	$3,637
University of Illinois–Urbana-Champaign	$26,056	$36,056	$10,412	$1,750	$2,740
University of California–Los Angeles	$26,855	$37,648	$13,002	$1,836	$4,887
University of California–Berkeley	$26,896	$39,141	$15,104	$1,495	$4,908
Pennsylvania State University (Dickinson)	$29,674	$29,674	$9,378	$1,200	$7,456
University of Virginia	$33,500	$38,500	$15,309	$1,800	$591
University of Michigan–Ann Arbor	$38,949	$41,949	$10,100	$1,035	$3,865

What schools award the most and the least financial aid?

Compared to what you're going to need, you may be surprised at how little you get: Law schools assume that their students can afford to borrow to pay the bills because they'll easily make enough after graduation to manage the loan payments. However, students whose LSAT scores and undergraduate grades put them near the top of a law school's applicant pool may find a generous merit award on the table.

Private Schools

School	Median grant	% of students receiving grants	Grants range (25th–75th percentile)	Grants of full tuition	Grants of more than full tuition
Loyola Marymount University (CA)	$26,900	25%	$12,500-$34,219	0%	10%
Wake Forest University (NC)	$22,125	40%	$10,000-$29,500	13%	2%
Michigan State University	$20,968	37%	$13,978-$27,956	18%	0%
Ave Maria School of Law (MI)	$20,000	69%	$10,000-$27,100	25%	0%
Hamline University (MN)	$20,000	50%	$10,700-$26,786	19%	1%
Mercer University (GA)	$20,000	28%	$8,000-$28,600	7%	6%
Northwestern University (IL)	$20,000	32%	$15,000-$30,000	1%	1%
St. John's University (NY)	$20,000	42%	$9,000-$35,100	13%	2%
Yale University (CT)	$19,850	50%	$11,450-$25,600	0%	0%
Chapman University (CA)	$19,222	44%	$8,008-$28,832	5%	3%
Albany Law School-Union University (NY)	$18,000	35%	$15,000-$22,000	2%	0%
Samford University (Cumberland) (AL)	$18,000	36%	$2,000-$26,190	12%	5%
University of San Diego	$18,000	44%	$12,000-$26,200	2%	2%
Seton Hall University (NJ)	$17,500	42%	$8,750-$26,250	9%	0%
Stetson University (FL)	$17,479	21%	$5,000-$28,660	5%	6%
Western New England College (MA)	$17,000	54%	$8,000-$19,000	2%	0%
Harvard University (MA)	$16,705	41%	$9,530-$24,030	1%	0%
Stanford University (CA)	$16,613	41%	$10,828-$24,840	1%	1%
California Western School of Law	$16,140	34%	$10,000-$29,080	6%	2%
Emory University (GA)	$16,000	35%	$8,700-$20,000	2%	2%
University of Miami (FL)	$16,000	35%	$9,866-$20,000	1%	1%
Brooklyn Law School (NY)	$15,860	71%	$11,239-$23,401	0%	0%
Boston University	$15,000	57%	$10,000-$20,000	0%	3%
Illinois Institute of Technology (Chicago-Kent)	$15,000	56%	$5,000-$20,000	7%	3%
New York University	$15,000	33%	$10,000-$38,980	9%	0%
Nova Southeastern University (Broad) (FL)	$15,000	10%	$2,000-$26,800	3%	0%
Ohio Northern University (Pettit)	$15,000	50%	$10,000-$20,000	2%	0%
Vanderbilt University (TN)	$15,000	69%	$10,000-$18,000	0%	2%
Washington University in St. Louis	$15,000	56%	$8,000-$22,000	1%	3%
Georgetown University (DC)	$14,550	32%	$8,425-$21,600	2%	0%
Valparaiso University (IN)	$14,125	21%	$7,063-$21,187	5%	2%
University of Pennsylvania	$14,080	33%	$10,000-$19,665	2%	0%
Loyola University New Orleans	$14,000	45%	$4,000-$20,000	2%	0%
Oklahoma City University	$14,000	30%	$8,000-$20,255	0%	2%
University of La Verne (CA)	$14,000	58%	$6,000-$19,000	0%	0%
Hofstra University (NY)	$13,540	50%	$7,500-$21,149	7%	0%
Cornell University (NY)	$13,000	38%	$7,800-$20,000	0%	0%
St. Louis University	$13,000	44%	$8,875-$18,000	5%	0%
University of Notre Dame (IN)	$13,000	67%	$10,000-$18,000	0%	0%
Boston College	$12,500	57%	$7,500-$17,000	0%	0%

What schools award the most and the least financial aid?

Private Schools

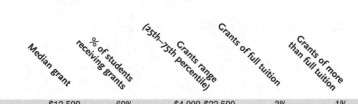

School	Median grant	% of students receiving grants	Grants range (25th–75th percentile)	Grants of full tuition	Grants of more than full tuition
Yeshiva University (Cardozo) (NY)	$12,500	60%	$4,000-$22,500	3%	1%
DePaul University (IL)	$12,000	60%	$8,000-$15,000	0%	0%
Pace University (NY)	$12,000	51%	$7,500-$20,000	1%	0%
Quinnipiac University (CT)	$12,000	89%	$5,000-$20,000	6%	0%
Thomas Jefferson School of Law (CA)	$12,000	45%	$5,000-$20,000	4%	0%
Whittier Law School (CA)	$12,000	53%	$5,000-$24,057	4%	5%
Willamette University (Collins) (OR)	$12,000	54%	$8,000-$16,000	0%	0%
Washington and Lee University (VA)	$11,500	66%	$8,000-$16,000	0%	0%
Appalachian School of Law (VA)	$11,250	28%	$6,544-$19,900	9%	0%
Capital University (OH)	$11,000	58%	$8,000-$13,500	0%	0%
Case Western Reserve University (OH)	$11,000	46%	$9,000-$16,000	0%	0%
Drake University (IA)	$11,000	61%	$6,000-$16,000	6%	4%
George Washington University (DC)	$11,000	47%	$10,000-$14,000	0%	0%
Roger Williams University (RI)	$11,000	43%	$5,000-$21,406	10%	0%
St. Thomas University (FL)	$11,000	29%	$6,150-$19,000	0%	0%
University of Dayton (OH)	$11,000	62%	$8,000-$12,000	0%	0%
University of Chicago	$10,800	55%	$7,200-$18,000	0%	0%
University of the Pacific (McGeorge) (CA)	$10,500	45%	$7,500-$15,000	1%	0%
American University (Washington) (DC)	$10,000	23%	$6,500-$14,000	2%	1%
Catholic University of America (Columbus) (DC)	$10,000	29%	$7,000-$14,500	0%	0%
Columbia University (NY)	$10,000	44%	$5,000-$17,000	2%	2%
Duke University (NC)	$10,000	79%	$5,200-$14,000	3%	0%
Gonzaga University (WA)	$10,000	67%	$7,000-$12,000	0%	0%
Howard University (DC)	$10,000	56%	$5,000-$15,000	3%	6%
Loyola University Chicago	$10,000	72%	$7,000-$16,000	1%	0%
Santa Clara University (CA)	$10,000	40%	$7,000-$16,000	1%	0%
Southwestern Law School (CA)	$10,000	29%	$8,000-$17,625	0%	1%
Tulane University (LA)	$10,000	66%	$6,000-$17,500	1%	0%
University of Denver (Sturm)	$10,000	41%	$3,100-$15,500	2%	0%
University of Southern California (Gould)	$10,000	58%	$5,000-$15,000	3%	1%
University of St. Thomas (MN)	$10,000	70%	$5,000-$24,154	21%	0%
Villanova University (PA)	$10,000	20%	$5,000-$15,000	1%	0%
Western State University (CA)	$10,000	53%	$5,444-$18,320	5%	0%
University of San Francisco	$9,633	30%	$3,500-$16,641	0%	0%
Fordham University (NY)	$9,600	34%	$5,000-$14,100	0%	0%
Lewis and Clark College (Northwestern) (OR)	$9,000	47%	$7,000-$12,000	4%	0%
Phoenix School of Law	$8,995	37%	$5,000-$13,065	1%	0%
New York Law School	$8,750	32%	$4,500-$12,000	0%	0%
Duquesne University (PA)	$8,564	37%	$2,570-$25,125	12%	0%
Northeastern University (MA)	$8,500	84%	$3,600-$9,500	1%	0%
Southern Methodist University (TX)	$8,500	92%	$1,000-$16,000	0%	4%
Creighton University (NE)	$8,000	38%	$6,000-$12,402	3%	0%
University of Tulsa (OK)	$8,000	35%	$3,778-$15,855	4%	0%
Thomas M. Cooley Law School (MI)	$7,872	86%	$6,488-$13,840	5%	0%
Syracuse University (NY)	$7,600	72%	$4,700-$15,070	0%	1%
Charleston School of Law (SC)	$7,500	40%	$5,000-$10,000	0%	0%
Faulkner University (Jones) (AL)	$7,500	26%	$3,750-$11,250	4%	0%
Golden Gate University (CA)	$7,500	43%	$6,000-$15,000	5%	0%
Texas Wesleyan University	$7,500	37%	$2,500-$10,000	1%	0%
University of Richmond (Williams) (VA)	$7,500	51%	$4,000-$8,500	0%	0%
Mississippi College	$7,333	28%	$100-$19,850	3%	4%
Widener University (DE)	$7,170	32%	$2,000-$14,000	1%	0%

What schools award the most and the least financial aid?

Private Schools

School	Median grant	% of students receiving grants	Grants range (25th–75th percentile)	Grants of full tuition	Grants of more than full tuition
Seattle University	$7,000	56%	$4,000-$9,000	0%	0%
Campbell University (Wiggins) (NC)	$6,600	52%	$2,500-$12,500	0%	0%
Marquette University (WI)	$6,500	44%	$3,000-$10,500	3%	0%
Suffolk University (MA)	$6,500	49%	$4,000-$14,189	0%	0%
University of Detroit Mercy	$6,270	15%	$3,563-$13,664	0%	0%
John Marshall Law School (IL)	$6,000	38%	$4,000-$8,000	0%	0%
Pepperdine University (CA)	$6,000	76%	$1,750-$16,750	0%	4%
Regent University (VA)	$6,000	78%	$2,000-$8,960	7%	0%
Vermont Law School	$6,000	52%	$3,000-$8,000	N/A	N/A
Barry University (FL)	$5,000	66%	$3,000-$8,000	0%	0%
Florida Coastal School of Law	$5,000	48%	$5,000-$10,000	0%	0%
William Mitchell College of Law (MN)	$5,000	43%	$2,000-$20,610	1%	0%
Touro College (Fuchsberg) (NY)	$3,628	64%	$1,500-$7,128	0%	0%
Franklin Pierce Law Center (NH)	$3,500	65%	$1,800-$7,500	1%	0%
Baylor University (Umphrey) (TX)	$3,000	91%	$3,000-$21,645	14%	6%
New England School of Law (MA)	$3,000	46%	$2,500-$6,300	5%	0%
Brigham Young University (Clark) (UT)	$2,500	43%	$1,500-$4,100	4%	0%
South Texas College of Law	$2,040	34%	$1,368-$2,650	0%	0%
St. Mary's University (TX)	$1,432	44%	$336-$4,195	0%	1%
Atlanta's John Marshall Law School	N/A	0%	N/A	0%	0%

Public Schools

School	Median grant	% of students receiving grants	Grants range (25th–75th percentile)	Grants of full tuition	Grants of more than full tuition
University of Virginia	$14,000	60%	$10,000-$16,500	0%	1%
University of Toledo (OH)	$13,426	59%	$10,244-$15,426	21%	19%
University of Iowa	$13,374	36%	$6,500-$13,500	19%	2%
University of Wisconsin–Madison	$13,000	24%	$6,000-$22,163	0%	7%
University of Akron (OH)	$12,738	55%	$5,000-$17,182	20%	9%
Northern Kentucky University (Chase)	$11,112	38%	$4,000-$11,112	20%	0%
University of Illinois–Urbana-Champaign	$10,000	68%	$5,000-$15,000	11%	0%
University of Pittsburgh	$10,000	53%	$8,000-$12,000	1%	1%
University of New Mexico	$9,565	24%	$3,500-$9,565	11%	3%
Georgia State University	$9,350	15%	$1,000-$9,530	8%	0%
University of Connecticut	$9,000	73%	$5,000-$9,000	0%	5%
Northern Illinois University	$8,910	22%	$4,455-$11,610	4%	12%
University of Michigan–Ann Arbor	$8,800	56%	$5,800-$13,680	1%	3%
University of California–Los Angeles	$8,760	61%	$3,500-$12,500	0%	3%
University of California–Berkeley	$8,300	69%	$5,800-$10,000	1%	2%
University of California–Davis	$8,300	69%	$6,158-$8,400	0%	1%
University of Minnesota–Twin Cities	$8,000	59%	$5,000-$12,000	1%	3%
University of Nebraska–Lincoln	$8,000	41%	$6,000-$10,000	0%	11%
University of South Carolina	$7,992	32%	$1,800-$15,124	1%	0%
Indiana University–Bloomington	$7,484	74%	$4,000-$11,000	1%	7%
University of Arizona (Rogers)	$7,000	79%	$4,000-$10,037	1%	9%
University of Alabama	$6,603	45%	$3,000-$10,936	9%	9%
University of Cincinnati	$6,500	71%	$3,600-$10,000	3%	0%
University of Hawaii (Richardson)	$6,444	40%	$4,470-$6,444	2%	0%
University of Texas–Austin	$6,416	90%	$3,208-$9,624	0%	2%

What schools award the most and the least financial aid?

Public Schools

School	Median grant	% of students receiving grants	Grants range (25th–75th percentile)	Grants of full tuition	Grants of more than full tuition
University of Idaho	$6,030	46%	$2,000-$10,200	6%	2%
Southern Illinois University–Carbondale	$6,000	53%	$4,000-$8,000	0%	11%
Temple University (Beasley) (PA)	$6,000	44%	$2,500-$10,000	3%	0%
University of Arkansas–Fayetteville	$6,000	39%	$3,000-$8,000	0%	4%
University of Washington	$6,000	45%	$4,125-$9,000	0%	1%
University of North Dakota	$5,780	34%	$875-$6,762	4%	15%
University of California (Hastings)	$5,500	75%	$5,000-$7,000	0%	0%
University at Buffalo–SUNY	$5,340	72%	$5,340-$5,340	13%	1%
Indiana University–Indianapolis	$5,010	47%	$3,265-$10,300	0%	1%
Arizona State University (O'Connor)	$5,000	48%	$2,250-$10,000	2%	6%
College of William and Mary (VA)	$5,000	23%	$3,000-$6,000	0%	0%
Florida International University	$5,000	30%	$5,000-$5,000	0%	4%
George Mason University (VA)	$5,000	13%	$3,000-$10,000	0%	1%
University of Kentucky	$5,000	56%	$1,000-$10,800	0%	3%
University of Louisville (Brandeis) (KY)	$5,000	34%	$3,000-$6,500	0%	0%
University of Maryland	$5,000	67%	$3,000-$11,000	5%	0%
University of Missouri–Kansas City	$5,000	39%	$2,063-$12,912	2%	3%
University of Nevada–Las Vegas (Boyd)	$5,000	49%	$1,000-$8,900	17%	0%
University of Tennessee–Knoxville	$5,000	46%	$3,000-$9,142	4%	4%
Washburn University (KS)	$5,000	39%	$1,225-$13,000	0%	4%
Pennsylvania State University (Dickinson)	$4,800	39%	$2,900-$7,500	0%	0%
University of Mississippi	$4,750	39%	$1,400-$9,300	0%	5%
Rutgers–Camden (NJ)	$4,500	39%	$1,000-$7,000	0%	1%
Ohio State University (Moritz)	$4,302	84%	$2,000-$6,500	1%	4%
Rutgers–Newark (NJ)	$4,000	46%	$2,500-$6,000	3%	1%
University of Missouri–Columbia	$4,000	40%	$2,650-$5,000	0%	2%
University of Oregon	$4,000	63%	$2,000-$5,425	0%	1%
University of the District of Columbia (Clarke)	$4,000	70%	$2,750-$6,500	0%	0%
Wayne State University (MI)	$4,000	67%	$2,500-$9,000	5%	3%
University of Memphis (Humphreys)	$3,850	28%	$2,713-$5,000	4%	0%
Cleveland State University (Cleveland-Marshall)	$3,840	35%	$3,840-$13,124	8%	1%
University of Arkansas–Little Rock (Bowen)	$3,500	34%	$2,000-$10,398	7%	1%
North Carolina Central University	$3,464	27%	$1,732-$6,550	5%	5%
Texas Tech University	$3,400	75%	$2,000-$7,000	6%	7%
Texas Southern University (Marshall)	$3,000	43%	$1,500-$3,500	0%	0%
University of Baltimore	$3,000	11%	$3,000-$4,000	0%	3%
University of Houston	$3,000	75%	$2,000-$5,000	0%	1%
Louisiana State University–Baton Rouge	$2,981	51%	$1,500-$8,042	0%	6%
University of Colorado–Boulder	$2,500	36%	$1,000-$7,500	3%	2%
University of Oklahoma	$2,500	63%	$1,000-$6,000	0%	1%
University of Maine	$2,300	50%	$800-$5,000	2%	0%
CUNY–Queens College	$2,290	42%	$1,145-$3,435	5%	0%
University of North Carolina–Chapel Hill	$2,200	82%	$700-$5,450	0%	3%
University of Florida (Levin)	$2,100	17%	$1,000-$4,200	1%	0%
Florida State University	$2,000	33%	$1,500-$4,000	1%	0%
University of Georgia	$2,000	49%	$1,000-$3,000	1%	0%
University of Utah (Quinney)	$2,000	40%	$1,375-$4,850	0%	1%
University of Kansas	$1,700	73%	$1,700-$5,300	4%	5%
West Virginia University	$1,600	36%	$1,000-$3,000	1%	3%
Southern University (LA)	$1,567	42%	$784-$2,351	0%	4%
University of Wyoming	$1,500	75%	$1,000-$2,500	2%	2%
University of South Dakota	$1,196	33%	$598-$1,794	1%	1%

Whose graduates have the most debt? The least?

How much should you expect to borrow? Debts of $70,000 to $80,000 are common for law school grads—and that's not counting any college loans. This table shows the average amount of debt incurred by borrowers in the class of 2007, as well as the proportion of the class that took out loans.

School	Average amount of law school debt	% of grads with debt
Northwestern University (IL)	$126,398	74%
University of Chicago	$121,782	82%
New York University	$117,636	81%
Columbia University (NY)	$113,540	81%
Catholic University of America (Columbus) (DC)	$112,589	88%
Golden Gate University (CA)	$112,477	96%
Pepperdine University (CA)	$111,173	88%
Vermont Law School	$108,666	88%
Duke University (NC)	$108,596	86%
Villanova University (PA)	$108,084	81%
Georgetown University (DC)	$108,074	81%
John Marshall Law School (IL)	$108,022	91%
University of Southern California (Gould)	$107,609	83%
University of the Pacific (McGeorge) (CA)	$106,729	90%
Stetson University (FL)	$105,900	86%
New York Law School	$105,793	90%
Harvard University (MA)	$105,494	85%
Southwestern Law School (CA)	$105,029	87%
DePaul University (IL)	$104,715	85%
George Washington University (DC)	$104,468	89%
California Western School of Law	$104,338	86%
American University (Washington) (DC)	$104,062	88%
Tulane University (LA)	$102,095	80%
Cornell University (NY)	$102,000	81%
Loyola Marymount University (CA)	$101,800	81%
Stanford University (CA)	$101,379	82%
Hofstra University (NY)	$100,915	79%
Vanderbilt University (TN)	$100,891	84%
University of Pennsylvania	$100,701	89%
Fordham University (NY)	$100,554	82%
Yeshiva University (Cardozo) (NY)	$100,298	81%
Washington University in St. Louis	$100,220	78%
University of San Francisco	$100,140	91%
Syracuse University (NY)	$99,886	91%
Barry University (FL)	$99,832	91%
Roger Williams University (RI)	$99,573	90%
Illinois Institute of Technology (Chicago-Kent)	$98,981	89%
Whittier Law School (CA)	$98,385	78%
Santa Clara University (CA)	$98,307	76%
Franklin Pierce Law Center (NH)	$97,592	89%
Oklahoma City University	$96,522	90%
Chapman University (CA)	$94,397	71%
Suffolk University (MA)	$94,360	88%
Lewis and Clark College (Northwestern) (OR)	$94,341	92%
Emory University (GA)	$94,326	79%
Samford University (Cumberland) (AL)	$94,263	85%

Whose graduates have the most debt? The least?

School	Average amount of law school debt	% of grads with debt
Nova Southeastern University (Broad) (FL)	$93,948	86%
Northeastern University (MA)	$93,775	93%
St. John's University (NY)	$93,619	80%
University of San Diego	$93,403	98%
St. Thomas University (FL)	$93,000	83%
Brooklyn Law School (NY)	$92,447	79%
Thomas Jefferson School of Law (CA)	$92,397	96%
Washington and Lee University (VA)	$92,280	82%
Florida Coastal School of Law	$91,861	90%
Creighton University (NE)	$91,517	78%
Seton Hall University (NJ)	$91,500	88%
University of California–Los Angeles	$91,435	84%
University of Denver (Sturm)	$91,062	85%
Charleston School of Law (SC)	$91,015	74%
University of Michigan–Ann Arbor	$91,000	95%
Loyola University Chicago	$90,518	84%
Willamette University (Collins) (OR)	$90,196	95%
Regent University (VA)	$90,193	83%
University of Miami (FL)	$90,109	88%
St. Louis University	$89,682	90%
Pennsylvania State University (Dickinson)	$89,529	85%
Campbell University (Wiggins) (NC)	$89,500	94%
Boston University	$89,198	84%
Western State University (CA)	$89,151	92%
Touro College (Fuchsberg) (NY)	$88,249	83%
University of Notre Dame (IN)	$87,849	85%
Widener University (DE)	$87,629	82%
Gonzaga University (WA)	$87,458	94%
Hamline University (MN)	$86,882	91%
University of Virginia	$86,600	83%
University of Detroit Mercy	$86,431	61%
New England School of Law (MA)	$86,346	88%
Seattle University	$86,253	91%
Albany Law School-Union University (NY)	$85,839	87%
Yale University (CT)	$85,789	93%
Ohio Northern University (Pettit)	$85,570	90%
Thomas M. Cooley Law School (MI)	$85,450	90%
University of Richmond (Williams) (VA)	$84,714	88%
Loyola University New Orleans	$84,155	87%
St. Mary's University (TX)	$84,124	86%
University of Tulsa (OK)	$84,115	65%
Case Western Reserve University (OH)	$83,730	87%
University of Dayton (OH)	$83,575	88%
Baylor University (Umphrey) (TX)	$83,338	87%
Wake Forest University (NC)	$83,265	82%
University of California (Hastings)	$83,000	88%
University of Minnesota–Twin Cities	$82,981	75%
Western New England College (MA)	$82,793	75%
Indiana University–Bloomington	$82,400	92%
Marquette University (WI)	$81,722	87%
Drake University (IA)	$81,702	91%
Boston College	$80,497	90%
Valparaiso University (IN)	$80,424	100%
Ave Maria School of Law (MI)	$79,211	86%
Appalachian School of Law (VA)	$78,315	84%
Pace University (NY)	$78,000	88%

Whose graduates have the most debt? The least?

School	Average amount of law school debt	% of grads with debt
Mississippi College	$77,716	84%
Quinnipiac University (CT)	$77,288	83%
Mercer University (GA)	$76,293	81%
Southern Methodist University (TX)	$75,831	78%
Duquesne University (PA)	$75,760	91%
University of St. Thomas (MN)	$75,312	86%
University of California–Berkeley	$74,802	70%
Capital University (OH)	$74,598	90%
William Mitchell College of Law (MN)	$74,555	92%
University of the District of Columbia (Clarke)	$74,536	89%
University of Missouri–Kansas City	$73,343	100%
Temple University (Beasley) (PA)	$72,529	82%
University of Connecticut	$72,421	86%
South Texas College of Law	$72,381	88%
University of Pittsburgh	$71,787	79%
Michigan State University	$71,762	86%
University of Oregon	$71,136	91%
Rutgers–Camden (NJ)	$71,113	89%
University of Iowa	$69,375	86%
University of Illinois–Urbana-Champaign	$68,688	80%
College of William and Mary (VA)	$68,270	82%
University of Oklahoma	$68,208	69%
Cleveland State University (Cleveland-Marshall)	$66,118	93%
University of Toledo (OH)	$65,654	89%
University of South Carolina	$65,585	85%
University of Washington	$65,507	79%
University of Wisconsin–Madison	$65,082	85%
Rutgers–Newark (NJ)	$64,775	81%
Indiana University–Indianapolis	$64,571	65%
University of Maryland	$63,621	76%
George Mason University (VA)	$62,589	80%
University of Houston	$62,584	80%
University of Colorado–Boulder	$62,485	89%
Faulkner University (Jones) (AL)	$62,400	86%
University of Texas–Austin	$62,399	84%
University of California–Davis	$62,077	91%
University of Arizona (Rogers)	$61,912	89%
Northern Kentucky University (Chase)	$61,857	63%
Washburn University (KS)	$61,200	99%
University of La Verne (CA)	$60,875	85%
University of Missouri–Columbia	$60,858	92%
Wayne State University (MI)	$60,228	81%
Louisiana State University–Baton Rouge	$59,218	80%
Atlanta's John Marshall Law School	$59,204	76%
Arizona State University (O'Connor)	$58,964	87%
University of Akron (OH)	$57,669	92%
University of Georgia	$57,545	75%
University of Kentucky	$57,400	74%
CUNY–Queens College	$57,262	77%
Texas Wesleyan University	$57,231	66%
University of Louisville (Brandeis) (KY)	$57,165	78%
University of North Carolina–Chapel Hill	$56,740	80%
Florida State University	$56,270	84%
University of Idaho	$55,326	95%
University of Memphis (Humphreys)	$55,250	83%
University at Buffalo–SUNY	$54,294	88%

Whose graduates have the most debt? The least?

School	Average amount of law school debt	% of grads with debt
University of Cincinnati	$53,982	89%
University of Florida (Levin)	$53,949	82%
University of Utah (Quinney)	$53,839	87%
University of Tennessee–Knoxville	$53,767	87%
Ohio State University (Moritz)	$53,525	96%
University of North Dakota	$53,367	93%
Georgia State University	$52,245	71%
Southern Illinois University–Carbondale	$52,167	91%
University of Hawaii (Richardson)	$51,702	66%
Texas Tech University	$50,716	90%
University of Arkansas–Fayetteville	$50,031	81%
University of Arkansas–Little Rock (Bowen)	$49,730	83%
University of Nevada–Las Vegas (Boyd)	$49,186	78%
University of Maine	$48,965	87%
Northern Illinois University	$48,472	85%
University of Mississippi	$48,400	72%
West Virginia University	$46,094	84%
University of South Dakota	$46,014	99%
University of Nebraska–Lincoln	$44,985	84%
Brigham Young University (Clark) (UT)	$44,128	86%
University of Kansas	$40,690	78%
University of Wyoming	$39,033	85%
University of Alabama	$37,611	69%
University of New Mexico	$34,558	91%
University of Baltimore	$33,928	92%
Howard University (DC)	$24,705	98%
Texas Southern University (Marshall)	$20,000	98%
North Carolina Central University	$19,886	96%
Florida A&M University	$18,500	84%
Florida International University	$17,774	76%
Southern University (LA)	$16,793	100%

Whose students are the most and least likely to drop out?

If the schools you're considering have a seemingly high attrition rate, you'll want to investigate why. The reasons students leave run the gamut, of course, from an inhospitable culture and dissatisfaction with the program to personal or family problems or a lack of money. The dropout rates shown here are for students who discontinued their law school education in the 2006-2007 academic year.

School	% not returning after 1st year	% not returning after 2nd year
Western State University (CA)	39%	18%
California Western School of Law	30%	5%
Ave Maria School of Law (MI)	28%	10%
Florida A&M University	28%	2%
Golden Gate University (CA)	28%	3%
University of the District of Columbia (Clarke)	25%	9%
Capital University (OH)	23%	2%
St. Thomas University (FL)	23%	4%
University of La Verne (CA)	23%	4%
Willamette University (Collins) (OR)	23%	11%
Texas Southern University (Marshall)	22%	2%
Campbell University (Wiggins) (NC)	21%	0%
Touro College (Fuchsberg) (NY)	21%	3%
University of Akron (OH)	21%	3%
Ohio Northern University (Pettit)	20%	0%
Valparaiso University (IN)	19%	1%
Florida International University	18%	0%
New England School of Law (MA)	16%	2%
Oklahoma City University	16%	6%
Pace University (NY)	16%	3%
Southern Illinois University–Carbondale	16%	2%
St. Mary's University (TX)	16%	9%
University of San Francisco	16%	1%
Whittier Law School (CA)	16%	3%
Widener University (DE)	16%	1%
Santa Clara University (CA)	15%	1%
Syracuse University (NY)	15%	2%
University of Louisville (Brandeis) (KY)	15%	2%
University of Maine	15%	N/A
Franklin Pierce Law Center (NH)	14%	1%
New York Law School	14%	2%
Thomas M. Cooley Law School (MI)	14%	9%
University of Baltimore	14%	2%
University of Detroit Mercy	14%	3%
University of Toledo (OH)	14%	3%
Western New England College (MA)	14%	3%
Cleveland State University (Cleveland-Marshall)	13%	2%
Loyola Marymount University (CA)	13%	0%
University of Miami (FL)	13%	1%
University of Nebraska–Lincoln	13%	0%
Appalachian School of Law (VA)	12%	4%
Catholic University of America (Columbus) (DC)	12%	1%
Georgia State University	12%	0%
Gonzaga University (WA)	12%	1%

Whose students are the most and least likely to drop out?

School	% not returning after 1st year	% not returning after 2nd year
Mississippi College	12%	1%
North Carolina Central University	12%	1%
Seton Hall University (NJ)	12%	1%
Southern University (LA)	12%	1%
Texas Wesleyan University	12%	0%
University of Nevada–Las Vegas (Boyd)	12%	3%
Baylor University (Umphrey) (TX)	11%	0%
Creighton University (NE)	11%	0%
DePaul University (IL)	11%	0%
Florida Coastal School of Law	11%	4%
George Mason University (VA)	11%	1%
Indiana University–Bloomington	11%	0%
Nova Southeastern University (Broad) (FL)	11%	1%
Pennsylvania State University (Dickinson)	11%	0%
Thomas Jefferson School of Law (CA)	11%	25%
University of Arkansas–Little Rock (Bowen)	11%	7%
University of San Diego	11%	2%
Washburn University (KS)	11%	1%
CUNY–Queens College	10%	8%
West Virginia University	10%	1%
American University (Washington) (DC)	9%	0%
Chapman University (CA)	9%	6%
Loyola University New Orleans	9%	1%
Mercer University (GA)	9%	0%
Northern Illinois University	9%	2%
Roger Williams University (RI)	9%	1%
St. Louis University	9%	1%
University of Memphis (Humphreys)	9%	9%
University of the Pacific (McGeorge) (CA)	9%	9%
Wayne State University (MI)	9%	1%
Arizona State University (O'Connor)	8%	6%
George Washington University (DC)	8%	2%
Southwestern Law School (CA)	8%	11%
University of Cincinnati	8%	0%
University of Idaho	8%	0%
Yeshiva University (Cardozo) (NY)	8%	2%
Albany Law School-Union University (NY)	7%	4%
Boston College	7%	0%
Drake University (IA)	7%	0%
John Marshall Law School (IL)	7%	1%
Lewis and Clark College (Northwestern) (OR)	7%	3%
Michigan State University	7%	6%
Regent University (VA)	7%	9%
Samford University (Cumberland) (AL)	7%	1%
Temple University (Beasley) (PA)	7%	1%
Tulane University (LA)	7%	1%
University of California–Davis	7%	0%
University of Maryland	7%	0%
University of Oklahoma	7%	1%
Vermont Law School	7%	1%
Hofstra University (NY)	6%	0%
Quinnipiac University (CT)	6%	3%
Rutgers–Newark (NJ)	6%	3%
Seattle University	6%	3%
South Texas College of Law	6%	1%
University of Illinois–Urbana-Champaign	6%	1%

Whose students are the most and least likely to drop out?

School	% not returning after 1st year	% not returning after 2nd year
University of Minnesota–Twin Cities	6%	1%
University of Oregon	6%	3%
University of Pittsburgh	6%	N/A
University of Richmond (Williams) (VA)	6%	0%
University of St. Thomas (MN)	6%	1%
University of Tennessee–Knoxville	6%	0%
Villanova University (PA)	6%	1%
Brooklyn Law School (NY)	5%	0%
Florida State University	5%	0%
Louisiana State University–Baton Rouge	5%	0%
Marquette University (WI)	5%	1%
University of Arkansas–Fayetteville	5%	1%
University of Mississippi	5%	0%
University of Missouri–Kansas City	5%	1%
University of New Mexico	5%	0%
University of North Dakota	5%	5%
University of Notre Dame (IN)	5%	0%
University of Tulsa (OK)	5%	11%
University of Wyoming	5%	0%
Boston University	4%	1%
Cornell University (NY)	4%	2%
Duquesne University (PA)	4%	1%
Hamline University (MN)	4%	2%
Howard University (DC)	4%	1%
Illinois Institute of Technology (Chicago-Kent)	4%	1%
Northern Kentucky University (Chase)	4%	3%
Pepperdine University (CA)	4%	N/A
Suffolk University (MA)	4%	0%
University of Alabama	4%	2%
University of California (Hastings)	4%	6%
University of Connecticut	4%	1%
University of Missouri–Columbia	4%	0%
University of North Carolina–Chapel Hill	4%	0%
University of Southern California (Gould)	4%	0%
Vanderbilt University (TN)	4%	1%
Barry University (FL)	3%	1%
Northeastern University (MA)	3%	3%
St. John's University (NY)	3%	6%
Texas Tech University	3%	0%
University of Dayton (OH)	3%	1%
University of Denver (Sturm)	3%	7%
University of Florida (Levin)	3%	0%
University of Iowa	3%	4%
University of Washington	3%	0%
Washington University in St. Louis	3%	1%
Emory University (GA)	2%	6%
Indiana University–Indianapolis	2%	4%
Loyola University Chicago	2%	8%
Northwestern University (IL)	2%	3%
University of Hawaii (Richardson)	2%	3%
University of Kansas	2%	0%
University of Kentucky	2%	1%
University of Texas–Austin	2%	3%
University of Utah (Quinney)	2%	N/A
William Mitchell College of Law (MN)	2%	0%
Yale University (CT)	2%	1%

Whose students are the most and least likely to drop out?

School	% not returning after 1st year	% not returning after 2nd year
Atlanta's John Marshall Law School	1%	0%
Brigham Young University (Clark) (UT)	1%	2%
Case Western Reserve University (OH)	1%	15%
College of William and Mary (VA)	1%	7%
Fordham University (NY)	1%	4%
Georgetown University (DC)	1%	1%
Stetson University (FL)	1%	0%
University at Buffalo–SUNY	1%	11%
University of California–Berkeley	1%	2%
University of Chicago	1%	0%
University of Colorado–Boulder	1%	1%
University of Georgia	1%	0%
University of South Dakota	1%	N/A
University of Virginia	1%	2%
Wake Forest University (NC)	1%	1%
Columbia University (NY)	0%	2%
Duke University (NC)	0%	2%
Harvard University (MA)	0%	1%
New York University	0%	1%
Ohio State University (Moritz)	0%	4%
Rutgers–Camden (NJ)	0%	N/A
Southern Methodist University (TX)	N/A	N/A
Stanford University (CA)	0%	1%
University of Arizona (Rogers)	0%	7%
University of California–Los Angeles	0%	0%
University of Houston	0%	3%
University of Michigan–Ann Arbor	0%	0%
University of Montana	N/A	N/A
University of Pennsylvania	0%	0%
University of South Carolina	0%	1%
University of Wisconsin–Madison	0%	4%
Washington and Lee University (VA)	0%	11%

What schools have the best first-time bar passage rate?

How well do the schools you're considering prepare students for the bar exam? To judge, you'll need to know not only how many grads pass on their first try, but also how that compares with the overall pass rate of everybody taking the test in the same state. Schools appear under the state in which most 2006 grads sat for the bar and are then organized by their individual passage rates.

State	State's overall bar passage rate	School	School's pass rate
Alabama	79%	University of Alabama	97%
Alabama	79%	Samford University (Cumberland) (AL)	90%
Arizona	75%	University of Arizona (Rogers)	87%
Arizona	75%	Arizona State University (O'Connor)	79%
Arkansas	82%	University of Arkansas–Little Rock (Bowen)	86%
Arkansas	82%	University of Arkansas–Fayetteville	83%
California	65%	Stanford University (CA)	89%
California	65%	University of California–Los Angeles	86%
California	65%	University of California–Berkeley	85%
California	65%	University of Southern California (Gould)	85%
California	65%	Pepperdine University (CA)	83%
California	65%	University of California (Hastings)	82%
California	65%	Santa Clara University (CA)	77%
California	65%	University of California–Davis	76%
California	65%	University of San Diego	76%
California	65%	Loyola Marymount University (CA)	75%
California	65%	University of San Francisco	73%
California	65%	University of the Pacific (McGeorge) (CA)	73%
California	65%	California Western School of Law	68%
California	65%	Southwestern Law School (CA)	64%
California	65%	Chapman University (CA)	61%
California	65%	Golden Gate University (CA)	60%
California	65%	Whittier Law School (CA)	56%
California	65%	Thomas Jefferson School of Law (CA)	55%
Colorado	76%	University of Colorado–Boulder	91%
Colorado	76%	University of Denver (Sturm)	66%
Connecticut	83%	University of Connecticut	87%
Connecticut	83%	Quinnipiac University (CT)	83%
Florida	74%	Florida State University	88%
Florida	74%	University of Miami (FL)	85%
Florida	74%	Florida International University	83%
Florida	74%	Stetson University (FL)	82%
Florida	74%	University of Florida (Levin)	78%
Florida	74%	Florida Coastal School of Law	74%
Florida	74%	Barry University (FL)	71%
Florida	74%	Nova Southeastern University (Broad) (FL)	69%
Florida	74%	St. Thomas University (FL)	65%
Georgia	85%	Emory University (GA)	95%
Georgia	86%	Georgia State University	93%
Georgia	85%	University of Georgia	91%
Georgia	85%	Mercer University (GA)	88%
Hawaii	77%	University of Hawaii (Richardson)	82%
Idaho	85%	University of Idaho	88%
Illinois	87%	University of Chicago	98%
Illinois	87%	Northwestern University (IL)	95%

What schools have the best first-time bar passage rate?

State	State's overall bar passage rate	School	School's pass rate
Illinois	87%	Washington University in St. Louis	93%
Illinois	87%	Illinois Institute of Technology (Chicago-Kent)	90%
Illinois	87%	Loyola University Chicago	90%
Illinois	87%	University of Notre Dame (IN)	90%
Illinois	87%	University of Illinois–Urbana-Champaign	89%
Illinois	87%	DePaul University (IL)	87%
Illinois	87%	John Marshall Law School (IL)	87%
Illinois	87%	Southern Illinois University–Carbondale	86%
Illinois	87%	Northern Illinois University	84%
Indiana	83%	Indiana University–Bloomington	86%
Indiana	83%	Indiana University–Indianapolis	85%
Indiana	83%	Valparaiso University (IN)	83%
Iowa	87%	Drake University (IA)	91%
Iowa	87%	University of Iowa	90%
Kansas	90%	University of Kansas	92%
Kansas	90%	Washburn University (KS)	89%
Kentucky	83%	University of Kentucky	90%
Kentucky	83%	University of Louisville (Brandeis) (KY)	85%
Kentucky	83%	Northern Kentucky University (Chase)	81%
Louisiana	75%	Louisiana State University–Baton Rouge	89%
Louisiana	75%	Tulane University (LA)	83%
Louisiana	75%	Loyola University New Orleans	80%
Louisiana	75%	Southern University (LA)	63%
Maine	83%	University of Maine	86%
Maryland	77%	University of Maryland	88%
Maryland	77%	American University (Washington) (DC)	81%
Maryland	77%	Catholic University of America (Columbus) (DC)	80%
Maryland	77%	University of Baltimore	75%
Maryland	77%	University of the District of Columbia (Clarke)	54%
Massachusetts	86%	Franklin Pierce Law Center (NH)	96%
Massachusetts	86%	Boston College	95%
Massachusetts	86%	Boston University	95%
Massachusetts	86%	Northeastern University (MA)	88%
Massachusetts	86%	Roger Williams University (RI)	85%
Massachusetts	86%	Suffolk University (MA)	82%
Massachusetts	86%	New England School of Law (MA)	80%
Massachusetts	86%	Western New England College (MA)	75%
Michigan	89%	Ave Maria School of Law (MI)	96%
Michigan	89%	Michigan State University	94%
Michigan	89%	University of Detroit Mercy	92%
Michigan	89%	Wayne State University (MI)	92%
Michigan	89%	Thomas M. Cooley Law School (MI)	80%
Minnesota	91%	University of Minnesota–Twin Cities	96%
Minnesota	91%	University of St. Thomas (MN)	91%
Minnesota	91%	William Mitchell College of Law (MN)	91%
Minnesota	91%	Hamline University (MN)	86%
Mississippi	88%	University of Mississippi	92%
Mississippi	88%	Mississippi College	83%
Missouri	86%	University of Missouri–Columbia	91%
Missouri	86%	University of Missouri–Kansas City	88%
Missouri	86%	St. Louis University	86%
Montana	92%	University of Montana	95%
Nebraska	83%	University of Nebraska–Lincoln	87%
Nebraska	83%	Creighton University (NE)	75%
Nevada	72%	University of Nevada–Las Vegas (Boyd)	77%
New Jersey	79%	Seton Hall University (NJ)	85%

What schools have the best first-time bar passage rate?

State	State's overall bar passage rate	School	School's pass rate
New Jersey	79%	Rutgers–Newark (NJ)	80%
New Jersey	79%	Rutgers–Camden (NJ)	79%
New Mexico	88%	University of New Mexico	92%
New York	77%	Duke University (NC)	97%
New York	77%	Harvard University (MA)	97%
New York	77%	Columbia University (NY)	96%
New York	77%	New York University	95%
New York	77%	University of Michigan–Ann Arbor	95%
New York	77%	George Washington University (DC)	94%
New York	77%	University of Pennsylvania	94%
New York	77%	Cornell University (NY)	92%
New York	77%	Georgetown University (DC)	91%
New York	77%	Yale University (CT)	91%
New York	77%	Fordham University (NY)	89%
New York	77%	St. John's University (NY)	89%
New York	77%	Yeshiva University (Cardozo) (NY)	89%
New York	77%	Albany Law School-Union University (NY)	86%
New York	77%	Brooklyn Law School (NY)	85%
New York	77%	New York Law School	81%
New York	77%	Pace University (NY)	81%
New York	77%	University at Buffalo–SUNY	81%
New York	77%	Syracuse University (NY)	80%
New York	77%	Touro College (Fuchsberg) (NY)	78%
New York	77%	CUNY–Queens College	76%
New York	77%	Hofstra University (NY)	74%
New York	77%	Howard University (DC)	62%
North Carolina	74%	Campbell University (Wiggins) (NC)	97%
North Carolina	74%	Wake Forest University (NC)	88%
North Carolina	74%	University of North Carolina–Chapel Hill	87%
North Carolina	74%	North Carolina Central University	82%
North Dakota	80%	University of North Dakota	76%
Ohio	84%	University of Cincinnati	92%
Ohio	84%	University of Toledo (OH)	91%
Ohio	84%	University of Akron (OH)	85%
Ohio	84%	Capital University (OH)	84%
Ohio	84%	Ohio State University (Moritz)	84%
Ohio	84%	Case Western Reserve University (OH)	83%
Ohio	84%	Cleveland State University (Cleveland-Marshall)	82%
Ohio	84%	Ohio Northern University (Pettit)	81%
Ohio	84%	University of Dayton (OH)	78%
Oklahoma	92%	University of Oklahoma	96%
Oklahoma	92%	Oklahoma City University	90%
Oklahoma	92%	University of Tulsa (OK)	88%
Oregon	82%	Lewis and Clark College (Northwestern) (OR)	86%
Oregon	82%	University of Oregon	85%
Oregon	82%	Willamette University (Collins) (OR)	84%
Pennsylvania	83%	Temple University (Beasley) (PA)	90%
Pennsylvania	83%	University of Pittsburgh	90%
Pennsylvania	83%	Duquesne University (PA)	88%
Pennsylvania	83%	Pennsylvania State University (Dickinson)	87%
Pennsylvania	83%	Villanova University (PA)	86%
Pennsylvania	83%	Widener University (DE)	77%
South Carolina	81%	University of South Carolina	88%
South Dakota	87%	University of South Dakota	84%
Tennessee	78%	Vanderbilt University (TN)	98%
Tennessee	78%	University of Tennessee–Knoxville	92%

What schools have the best first-time bar passage rate?

State	State's overall bar passage rate	School	School's pass rate
Tennessee	78%	University of Memphis (Humphreys)	91%
Texas	82%	Baylor University (Umphrey) (TX)	99%
Texas	82%	Southern Methodist University (TX)	90%
Texas	82%	University of Houston	89%
Texas	82%	University of Texas–Austin	89%
Texas	82%	Texas Tech University	87%
Texas	82%	Texas Wesleyan University	86%
Texas	82%	St. Mary's University (TX)	83%
Texas	82%	South Texas College of Law	82%
Texas	82%	Texas Southern University (Marshall)	56%
Utah	87%	Brigham Young University (Clark) (UT)	96%
Utah	87%	University of Utah (Quinney)	86%
Vermont	77%	Vermont Law School	72%
Virginia	74%	University of Virginia	91%
Virginia	74%	College of William and Mary (VA)	87%
Virginia	74%	University of Richmond (Williams) (VA)	85%
Virginia	74%	George Mason University (VA)	84%
Virginia	74%	Washington and Lee University (VA)	79%
Virginia	74%	Regent University (VA)	74%
Virginia	74%	Appalachian School of Law (VA)	47%
Washington	82%	University of Washington	88%
Washington	82%	Gonzaga University (WA)	84%
Washington	82%	Seattle University	82%
West Virginia	66%	West Virginia University	66%
Wisconsin	89%	Marquette University (WI)	100%
Wisconsin	89%	University of Wisconsin–Madison	100%
Wyoming	62%	University of Wyoming	78%

Whose graduates are the most and least likely to land a job?

Even with the economy still limping along, many law schools in 2006 could boast that virtually the entire class had accepted a job offer by the time they'd been given their diplomas. (The schools that didn't provide information about how many graduates were immediately working appear at the end of the list, so that prospective students can see the proportion of students who were employed nine months out.)

School	% employed at graduation	% employed at 9 months
Columbia University (NY)	99%	99%
University of California–Berkeley	99%	99%
Stanford University (CA)	98%	99%
Cornell University (NY)	97%	99%
University of Michigan–Ann Arbor	97%	99%
University of Virginia	97%	100%
Boston University	96%	99%
Emory University (GA)	96%	98%
Harvard University (MA)	96%	98%
New York University	96%	99%
Northwestern University (IL)	96%	99%
University of Chicago	96%	99%
University of Utah (Quinney)	96%	99%
Yale University (CT)	96%	100%
Georgetown University (DC)	95%	98%
George Washington University (DC)	95%	97%
University of California–Los Angeles	95%	98%
University of Pennsylvania	95%	98%
University of Baltimore	94%	95%
George Mason University (VA)	93%	98%
Duke University (NC)	92%	98%
University of Texas–Austin	92%	97%
Vanderbilt University (TN)	91%	98%
Seton Hall University (NJ)	90%	98%
University of Southern California (Gould)	90%	96%
University of Colorado–Boulder	89%	97%
Howard University (DC)	88%	94%
Indiana University–Bloomington	88%	98%
University of Georgia	88%	98%
University of Washington	88%	97%
University of Minnesota–Twin Cities	87%	98%
Ohio State University (Moritz)	86%	95%
American University (Washington) (DC)	85%	96%
University of Alabama	84%	97%
University of Notre Dame (IN)	84%	97%
Washington University in St. Louis	84%	99%
Boston College	83%	98%
DePaul University (IL)	83%	90%
College of William and Mary (VA)	82%	96%
Florida State University	82%	95%
Fordham University (NY)	82%	95%
Indiana University–Indianapolis	82%	96%
Rutgers–Newark (NJ)	82%	95%
University of Oklahoma	82%	96%

School	% employed at graduation	% employed at 9 months
University of Iowa	80%	93%
University of Maryland	80%	94%
Southern University (LA)	79%	84%
University of Arizona (Rogers)	79%	95%
University of California–Davis	79%	87%
University of Nebraska–Lincoln	79%	94%
Tulane University (LA)	78%	96%
University of Florida (Levin)	78%	97%
University of Illinois–Urbana-Champaign	78%	93%
University of Kentucky	78%	99%
University of Houston	77%	96%
Southwestern Law School (CA)	76%	85%
Brigham Young University (Clark) (UT)	75%	91%
University of Akron (OH)	75%	92%
Yeshiva University (Cardozo) (NY)	75%	95%
Louisiana State University–Baton Rouge	74%	94%
University at Buffalo–SUNY	74%	93%
University of Connecticut	74%	96%
University of Pittsburgh	74%	94%
University of Tennessee–Knoxville	74%	95%
Washington and Lee University (VA)	74%	92%
Creighton University (NE)	73%	97%
University of Cincinnati	73%	96%
University of Richmond (Williams) (VA)	73%	95%
University of Wisconsin–Madison	73%	97%
Illinois Institute of Technology (Chicago-Kent)	72%	91%
Rutgers–Camden (NJ)	72%	92%
Santa Clara University (CA)	72%	93%
University of Miami (FL)	72%	91%
University of Toledo (OH)	72%	92%
Case Western Reserve University (OH)	71%	97%
St. Louis University	71%	93%
Wake Forest University (NC)	71%	95%
Catholic University of America (Columbus) (DC)	70%	94%
Southern Methodist University (TX)	70%	95%
Baylor University (Umphrey) (TX)	68%	96%
University of California (Hastings)	68%	93%
West Virginia University	68%	95%
Brooklyn Law School (NY)	67%	97%
Loyola Marymount University (CA)	67%	97%
Seattle University	67%	99%
Temple University (Beasley) (PA)	67%	94%
University of Denver (Sturm)	67%	96%
Franklin Pierce Law Center (NH)	66%	96%

Whose graduates are the most and least likely to land a job?

School	% employed at graduation	% employed at 9 months
Samford University (Cumberland) (AL)	66%	90%
St. John's University (NY)	66%	89%
University of Kansas	66%	95%
University of Hawaii (Richardson)	64%	94%
University of South Carolina	64%	94%
Villanova University (PA)	64%	94%
Campbell University (Wiggins) (NC)	63%	94%
Cleveland State University (Cleveland-Marshall)	63%	93%
Loyola University New Orleans	63%	95%
Marquette University (WI)	63%	96%
Syracuse University (NY)	63%	93%
University of North Carolina–Chapel Hill	63%	89%
University of Oregon	63%	90%
Mercer University (GA)	62%	94%
University of New Mexico	61%	99%
University of Mississippi	60%	88%
University of Louisville (Brandeis) (KY)	59%	94%
University of South Dakota	59%	93%

School	% employed at graduation	% employed at 9 months
Suffolk University (MA)	57%	91%
University of Tulsa (OK)	56%	91%
Northern Illinois University	55%	90%
Northern Kentucky University (Chase)	55%	89%
University of Missouri–Columbia	55%	99%
Loyola University Chicago	54%	89%
Texas Wesleyan University	54%	83%
Widener University (DE)	53%	83%
Chapman University (CA)	51%	95%
Mississippi College	45%	87%
Regent University (VA)	41%	83%
Texas Tech University	41%	92%
Valparaiso University (IN)	39%	88%
CUNY–Queens College	37%	88%
University of Memphis (Humphreys)	36%	89%
New England School of Law (MA)	31%	76%
Florida International University	21%	84%

School	% employed at 9 months
Georgia State University	98%
Stetson University (FL)	98%
Albany Law School-Union University (NY)	97%
Ohio Northern University (Pettit)	96%
Drake University (IA)	95%
Pepperdine University (CA)	95%
University of St. Thomas (MN)	95%
Northeastern University (MA)	94%
Quinnipiac University (CT)	94%
University of Montana	94%
University of the Pacific (McGeorge) (CA)	94%
Washburn University (KS)	94%
Arizona State University (O'Connor)	93%
Gonzaga University (WA)	93%
Hofstra University (NY)	93%
University of Idaho	93%
University of San Francisco	93%
Hamline University (MN)	92%
Lewis and Clark College (Northwestern) (OR)	92%
Pennsylvania State University (Dickinson)	92%
University of Maine	92%
University of Nevada–Las Vegas (Boyd)	92%
University of North Dakota	92%
Whittier Law School (CA)	92%
Michigan State University	91%
University of Missouri–Kansas City	91%
Vermont Law School	91%
New York Law School	90%
William Mitchell College of Law (MN)	90%
University of Arkansas–Fayetteville	89%

School	% employed at 9 months
Florida Coastal School of Law	88%
John Marshall Law School (IL)	88%
Pace University (NY)	88%
Texas Southern University (Marshall)	88%
University of Arkansas–Little Rock (Bowen)	88%
University of Dayton (OH)	88%
University of San Diego	88%
Wayne State University (MI)	88%
Willamette University (Collins) (OR)	88%
University of Wyoming	87%
Duquesne University (PA)	86%
University of Detroit Mercy	86%
Nova Southeastern University (Broad) (FL)	85%
Southern Illinois University–Carbondale	85%
California Western School of Law	84%
Oklahoma City University	84%
Roger Williams University (RI)	84%
St. Thomas University (FL)	83%
Capital University (OH)	82%
St. Mary's University (TX)	82%
North Carolina Central University	81%
Barry University (FL)	80%
Thomas Jefferson School of Law (CA)	80%
Golden Gate University (CA)	78%
South Texas College of Law	78%
Western New England College (MA)	76%
Touro College (Fuchsberg) (NY)	74%
Ave Maria School of Law (MI)	73%
Thomas M. Cooley Law School (MI)	73%

Whose graduates earn the most? The least?

According to the most recent surveys by the National Association for Law Placement, the median salary for first-year associates at law firms ranges from $68,000 in small firms to $145,000 at firms with 500 lawyers or more. But, as this table of median starting salaries for the class of 2006 shows, many make considerably more—or, if they go into the public sector, considerably less.

School	Private sector starting salary (median)	Private sector starting salary (25th–75th percentile)	Public sector starting salary (median)
Columbia University (NY)	$145,000	$145,000-$145,000	$55,000
Cornell University (NY)	$145,000	$135,000-$145,000	$46,000
Fordham University (NY)	$145,000	$125,000-$145,000	$47,733
New York University	$145,000	$135,000-$145,000	$54,272
University of Pennsylvania	$145,000	$135,000-$145,000	$50,000
University of Virginia	$145,000	$115,000-$160,000	$55,000
Yale University (CT)	$145,000	$135,000-$145,000	$52,737
Boston College	$135,000	$125,000-$135,000	$47,018
Boston University	$135,000	$95,000-$135,000	$46,500
Duke University (NC)	$135,000	$115,000-$145,000	$50,000
Georgetown University (DC)	$135,000	$135,000-$145,000	$50,000
George Washington University (DC)	$135,000	$115,000-$135,000	$52,000
Harvard University (MA)	$135,000	$135,000-$145,000	$51,000
Howard University (DC)	$135,000	$100,000-$145,000	$49,185
Northwestern University (IL)	$135,000	$135,000-$135,000	$55,000
Stanford University (CA)	$135,000	$135,000-$145,000	$54,272
University of California–Berkeley	$135,000	$135,000-$135,000	$50,000
University of California–Los Angeles	$135,000	$100,000-$135,000	$56,896
University of Chicago	$135,000	$120,000-$135,000	$53,000
University of Michigan–Ann Arbor	$135,000	$135,000-$145,000	$55,706
University of Southern California (Gould)	$135,000	$135,000-$135,000	$55,000
University of Texas–Austin	$135,000	$100,000-$135,000	$50,000
George Mason University (VA)	$128,750	$75,000-$135,000	$53,000
University of Illinois–Urbana-Champaign	$125,000	$77,500-$135,000	$50,000
University of California (Hastings)	$120,000	$76,500-$135,000	$52,000
College of William and Mary (VA)	$115,000	$80,000-$135,000	$50,000
Emory University (GA)	$115,000	$75,000-$125,000	$48,000
Rutgers–Newark (NJ)	$115,000	$90,000-$145,000	$39,000
Tulane University (LA)	$115,000	$85,000-$145,000	$49,000
Vanderbilt University (TN)	$115,000	$100,000-$135,000	$43,115
Santa Clara University (CA)	$110,000	$70,000-$135,000	$52,000
University of Notre Dame (IN)	$110,000	$90,000-$125,000	$51,972
University of Wisconsin–Madison	$105,000	$72,000-$125,000	$46,000
Brooklyn Law School (NY)	$104,000	$65,000-$145,000	$50,000
University of California–Davis	$103,500	$78,500-$135,000	$50,000
University of Miami (FL)	$103,500	$83,500-$125,000	$40,000
Loyola University Chicago	$100,000	$70,000-$135,000	$45,000
Rutgers–Camden (NJ)	$100,000	$60,001-$115,000	$38,040
University of Georgia	$100,000	$70,000-$115,000	$50,500

Whose graduates earn the most? The least?

School	Private sector starting salary (median)	Private sector starting salary (25th-75th percentile)	Public sector starting salary (median)
University of Minnesota–Twin Cities	$100,000	$65,000-$110,000	$47,000
University of North Carolina–Chapel Hill	$100,000	$70,000-$115,000	$45,218
Villanova University (PA)	$100,000	$65,000-$120,000	$47,000
Washington and Lee University (VA)	$100,000	$70,000-$125,000	$46,725
Washington University in St. Louis	$100,000	$83,000-$130,000	$50,000
Franklin Pierce Law Center (NH)	$95,000	$60,000-$125,000	$48,500
Ohio State University (Moritz)	$95,000	$63,000-$105,000	$45,000
University of Iowa	$95,000	$60,000-$115,000	$39,500
University of San Francisco	$95,000	$70,000-$135,000	$45,000
Brigham Young University (Clark) (UT)	$92,500	$70,000-$110,000	$46,440
New York Law School	$92,500	$65,000-$145,000	$45,000
Southern University (LA)	$92,500	$70,000-$135,000	$42,000
Case Western Reserve University (OH)	$91,000	$70,000-$110,000	$45,000
Lewis and Clark College (Northwestern) (OR)	$90,000	$57,000-$95,000	$42,533
Pepperdine University (CA)	$90,000	$65,000-$135,000	$57,600
University of Arizona (Rogers)	$90,000	$65,000-$110,000	$49,900
University of Cincinnati	$90,000	$65,000-$100,000	$43,000
University of Washington	$90,000	$65,000-$101,000	$44,500
Yeshiva University (Cardozo) (NY)	$90,000	$65,000-$145,000	$50,000
American University (Washington) (DC)	$87,500	$60,000-$135,000	$48,000
Northeastern University (MA)	$87,500	$52,250-$135,000	$45,000
Hofstra University (NY)	$86,000	$70,000-$160,000	$49,000
Indiana University–Bloomington	$85,000	$60,000-$110,000	$50,000
Southern Methodist University (TX)	$85,000	$65,000-$135,000	$47,500
Texas Southern University (Marshall)	$85,000	$65,000-$105,000	$41,018
University of Alabama	$85,000	$45,000-$95,000	$54,000
University of Maryland	$85,000	$50,000-$110,000	$40,000
Arizona State University (O'Connor)	$80,000	$65,000-$100,000	$56,000
Catholic University of America (Columbus) (DC)	$80,000	$60,000-$125,000	$53,000
Loyola Marymount University (CA)	$80,000	$67,650-$125,000	$58,000
St. John's University (NY)	$80,000	$60,000-$145,000	$49,000
Temple University (Beasley) (PA)	$80,000	$57,000-$120,000	$47,000
University of Colorado–Boulder	$80,000	$52,000-$105,000	$45,000
University of Florida (Levin)	$80,000	$60,000-$100,000	$39,000
University of Houston	$80,000	$60,000-$135,000	$45,000
South Texas College of Law	$79,000	$70,000-$135,000	$46,125
Texas Tech University	$77,000	$36,000-$101,000	$41,000
Wake Forest University (NC)	$77,000	$58,000-$115,000	$40,000
Baylor University (Umphrey) (TX)	$75,000	$60,000-$90,000	$49,000
Illinois Institute of Technology (Chicago-Kent)	$75,000	$55,000-$135,000	$50,500
Southwestern Law School (CA)	$75,000	$65,000-$87,500	$60,000
Stetson University (FL)	$75,000	$65,000-$90,000	$41,000
University at Buffalo–SUNY	$75,000	$50,000-$83,000	$49,432
University of Nevada–Las Vegas (Boyd)	$75,000	$60,000-$90,000	$55,000
University of Pittsburgh	$75,000	$53,500-$120,000	$40,000
University of Connecticut	$74,000	$73,000-$125,000	$47,500
University of Hawaii (Richardson)	$72,500	$63,500-$74,500	$47,052
Chapman University (CA)	$70,000	$62,500-$75,000	$58,000
Creighton University (NE)	$70,000	$50,000-$78,000	$50,600
Georgia State University	$70,000	$55,500-$115,000	$48,070
John Marshall Law School (IL)	$70,000	$51,250-$90,000	$48,796
Seton Hall University (NJ)	$70,000	$55,000-$105,000	$38,038

Whose graduates earn the most? The least?

School	Private sector starting salary (median)	Private sector starting salary (25th–75th percentile)	Public sector starting salary (median)
Suffolk University (MA)	$70,000	$52,000-$125,000	$45,000
University of Richmond (Williams) (VA)	$70,000	$55,000-$95,000	$49,000
University of San Diego	$70,000	$57,000-$91,000	$55,000
University of the Pacific (McGeorge) (CA)	$70,000	$60,000-$80,000	$52,000
Whittier Law School (CA)	$70,000	$65,000-$83,000	$59,000
Florida State University	$68,000	$56,000-$80,000	$40,000
University of South Carolina	$68,000	$52,000-$80,000	$40,000
University of Utah (Quinney)	$68,000	$50,750-$108,500	$43,000
Seattle University	$67,500	$45,000-$90,000	$45,000
St. Mary's University (TX)	$67,500	$45,000-$75,000	$41,334
University of Mississippi	$66,500	$45,000-$81,000	$47,034
University of Akron (OH)	$65,824	$46,253-$87,912	$58,280
California Western School of Law	$65,000	$60,000-$70,000	$54,900
Capital University (OH)	$65,000	$50,000-$85,000	$42,000
CUNY–Queens College	$65,000	$51,003-$80,000	$51,125
DePaul University (IL)	$65,000	$50,000-$86,000	$47,650
Golden Gate University (CA)	$65,000	$52,000-$75,000	$59,700
Louisiana State University–Baton Rouge	$65,000	N/A	$39,000
Mississippi College	$65,000	$60,000-$85,000	$50,000
Pace University (NY)	$65,000	$54,000-$95,000	$54,548
St. Louis University	$65,000	$52,000-$90,000	$42,000
Syracuse University (NY)	$65,000	$45,000-$85,000	$42,000
University of Baltimore	$65,000	$50,625-$95,000	$42,223
University of Denver (Sturm)	$65,000	$52,000-$95,000	$46,000
University of Oklahoma	$65,000	$52,000-$88,000	$40,000
William Mitchell College of Law (MN)	$63,611	$50,000-$100,000	$51,000
Pennsylvania State University (Dickinson)	$63,000	$50,000-$100,000	$41,000
Samford University (Cumberland) (AL)	$62,500	$50,000-$82,500	$40,000
Touro College (Fuchsberg) (NY)	$62,500	$48,000-$75,500	$50,000
University of Detroit Mercy	$62,500	$55,000-$100,000	$45,000
University of La Verne (CA)	$62,421	N/A	N/A
Texas Wesleyan University	$62,000	$48,000-$80,000	$50,000
University of Oregon	$62,000	$48,000-$89,000	$46,000
University of the District of Columbia (Clarke)	$61,876	$41,600-$70,000	$47,174
University of Tennessee–Knoxville	$61,500	$55,000-$85,000	$42,750
Atlanta's John Marshall Law School	$60,000	$36,400-$80,000	$28,000
Cleveland State University (Cleveland-Marshall)	$60,000	$50,000-$90,000	$48,500
Duquesne University (PA)	$60,000	$50,000-$80,000	$39,000
Florida International University	$60,000	$55,000-$92,000	$40,000
Indiana University–Indianapolis	$60,000	$45,000-$90,000	$43,250
Mercer University (GA)	$60,000	$52,000-$85,000	$39,669
Michigan State University	$60,000	$48,000-$87,000	$42,000
Ohio Northern University (Pettit)	$60,000	$42,000-$73,500	$45,000
Quinnipiac University (CT)	$60,000	$47,500-$78,000	$42,500
St. Thomas University (FL)	$60,000	$40,000-$70,000	$39,000
University of Maine	$60,000	$48,000-$68,000	$39,900
Wayne State University (MI)	$60,000	$50,000-$90,000	$48,000
Widener University (DE)	$60,000	$50,000-$68,600	$38,750
Ave Maria School of Law (MI)	$58,000	$48,100-$90,000	$52,000
University of Nebraska–Lincoln	$57,900	$43,125-$76,250	$40,000
Valparaiso University (IN)	$57,000	$47,500-$70,000	$45,000
University of Kansas	$56,500	$48,000-$90,000	$48,500

Whose graduates earn the most? The least?

School	Private sector starting salary (median)	Private sector starting salary (25th–75th percentile)	Public sector starting salary (median)
University of Dayton (OH)	$55,892	$45,000-$60,000	$40,000
Northern Illinois University	$55,023	$42,000-$60,000	$43,427
Albany Law School-Union University (NY)	$55,000	$47,000-$72,000	$48,500
Campbell University (Wiggins) (NC)	$55,000	$48,000-$75,000	N/A
Gonzaga University (WA)	$55,000	$45,000-$68,500	$49,000
Nova Southeastern University (Broad) (FL)	$55,000	$50,000-$75,000	$40,000
Roger Williams University (RI)	$55,000	$45,000-$70,000	$46,000
University of Kentucky	$55,000	$40,000-$83,000	$37,250
University of Louisville (Brandeis) (KY)	$55,000	$45,000-$83,000	$36,500
University of Memphis (Humphreys)	$55,000	$40,000-$72,000	$45,000
University of Missouri–Columbia	$55,000	$45,000-$75,000	$38,250
Drake University (IA)	$54,250	$43,300-$66,875	$43,250
Hamline University (MN)	$54,000	$46,000-$90,000	$42,000
Marquette University (WI)	$54,000	$45,000-$84,000	$47,000
Thomas Jefferson School of Law (CA)	$54,000	$40,000-$65,000	$49,500
Western State University (CA)	$54,000	$40,000-$75,000	$68,000
University of New Mexico	$53,000	$36,000-$72,000	$40,000
West Virginia University	$52,500	$35,400-$106,000	$39,000
University of Arkansas–Little Rock (Bowen)	$52,200	$45,000-$58,000	$42,000
Northern Kentucky University (Chase)	$52,000	$40,000-$63,000	$39,250
University of St. Thomas (MN)	$52,000	$48,000-$61,000	$42,000
Thomas M. Cooley Law School (MI)	$51,000	$40,000-$67,000	$43,000
Washburn University (KS)	$51,000	$44,000-$65,000	$42,036
Barry University (FL)	$50,000	$45,000-$55,000	$40,000
New England School of Law (MA)	$50,000	$40,000-$70,000	$47,000
Oklahoma City University	$50,000	$40,000-$70,000	$45,000
Regent University (VA)	$50,000	$40,000-$65,000	$44,000
University of Arkansas–Fayetteville	$50,000	$44,500-$62,000	$42,000
University of Missouri–Kansas City	$50,000	$43,000-$73,000	$40,000
University of Toledo (OH)	$50,000	$40,000-$60,000	$47,500
Vermont Law School	$50,000	$39,500-$70,000	$40,000
Western New England College (MA)	$50,000	$40,000-$60,000	$38,250
Willamette University (Collins) (OR)	$50,000	$43,200-$60,000	$40,000
Florida Coastal School of Law	$48,500	$39,000-$55,000	$40,000
University of Wyoming	$47,250	$43,250-$57,000	$46,000
University of Tulsa (OK)	$46,500	$40,000-$54,000	$46,900
Southern Illinois University–Carbondale	$46,250	$38,000-$61,000	$36,500
University of Montana	$45,000	$41,500-$50,000	$43,716
University of South Dakota	$44,500	$38,700-$50,000	$39,450
University of Idaho	$44,000	$40,000-$50,000	N/A
University of North Dakota	$42,500	$37,000-$45,000	$43,000
Appalachian School of Law (VA)	$41,600	$36,000-$62,000	$41,730

You can tell a great deal about a law school by looking at where its newly minted JDs go to work. Harvard, whose corporate law program is one of its great strengths, launched 60 percent of its 2004 graduating class into law firms, for example. Yale sent 43 percent to judicial clerkships and 8 percent into government and public service. Schools are sorted by the percentage of graduates who took jobs at law firms.

School	% employed by law firms	% employed in business and industry	% employed in government	% employed in public interest jobs	% employed in judicial clerkships	% employed in academia	% employed in law school's state	% employed in foreign countries
Texas Tech University	86%	1%	8%	3%	2%	0%	96%	0%
Cornell University (NY)	82%	4%	2%	2%	9%	1%	58%	1%
Columbia University (NY)	80%	3%	2%	6%	9%	1%	69%	4%
University of Pennsylvania	80%	5%	1%	2%	13%	0%	21%	1%
University of Chicago	76%	3%	6%	1%	14%	1%	34%	1%
University of La Verne (CA)	75%	14%	11%	0%	0%	0%	96%	0%
Wayne State University (MI)	75%	13%	4%	3%	3%	2%	94%	0%
Northwestern University (IL)	74%	8%	3%	2%	11%	1%	50%	2%
University of Michigan–Ann Arbor	73%	4%	4%	6%	13%	2%	9%	2%
Georgetown University (DC)	71%	4%	8%	4%	10%	1%	32%	2%
Texas Southern University (Marshall)	71%	13%	10%	1%	1%	2%	74%	1%
University of Virginia	71%	4%	5%	4%	16%	1%	13%	2%
Vanderbilt University (TN)	71%	8%	7%	3%	10%	0%	23%	1%
Atlanta's John Marshall Law School	70%	14%	11%	3%	0%	3%	86%	0%
Emory University (GA)	70%	7%	5%	7%	11%	0%	49%	0%
Mercer University (GA)	70%	4%	14%	4%	5%	4%	68%	1%
University of Miami (FL)	70%	7%	13%	5%	4%	1%	62%	0%
Campbell University (Wiggins) (NC)	69%	9%	12%	5%	5%	0%	86%	0%
Fordham University (NY)	69%	8%	8%	7%	4%	1%	78%	1%
New York University	69%	2%	3%	13%	12%	0%	66%	2%
Southern Methodist University (TX)	69%	16%	7%	1%	5%	2%	89%	1%
University of Alabama	69%	7%	9%	4%	8%	1%	70%	0%
Wake Forest University (NC)	69%	4%	11%	3%	11%	0%	52%	0%
University of California (Hastings)	68%	8%	8%	10%	3%	2%	88%	2%
University of Southern California (Gould)	68%	10%	8%	4%	8%	3%	87%	0%
Samford University (Cumberland) (AL)	67%	9%	14%	3%	7%	0%	55%	0%
University of California–Berkeley	67%	3%	5%	11%	14%	0%	67%	2%
University of Texas–Austin	67%	9%	9%	1%	11%	2%	72%	1%
Duke University (NC)	66%	6%	6%	3%	19%	0%	13%	2%
Harvard University (MA)	66%	4%	2%	5%	23%	0%	11%	2%
Stanford University (CA)	66%	2%	2%	2%	27%	1%	46%	2%
Boston College	65%	6%	9%	5%	14%	1%	51%	1%
Marquette University (WI)	65%	14%	9%	5%	5%	2%	73%	0%
University of Notre Dame (IN)	65%	6%	13%	6%	10%	2%	10%	1%
University of San Francisco	65%	11%	13%	8%	1%	0%	97%	0%
University of Tennessee–Knoxville	65%	7%	12%	4%	11%	1%	72%	0%
University of California–Los Angeles	64%	9%	8%	6%	11%	1%	78%	1%
University of Illinois–Urbana-Champaign	64%	13%	10%	2%	7%	3%	70%	0%
University of Tulsa (OK)	64%	17%	12%	3%	1%	2%	51%	0%

Where do graduates work?

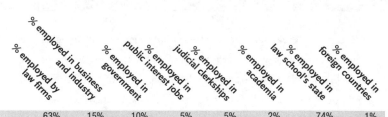

School	% employed by law firms	% employed in business and industry	% employed in government	% employed in public interest jobs	% employed in judicial clerkships	% employed in academia	% employed in law school's state	% employed in foreign countries
California Western School of Law	63%	15%	10%	5%	5%	2%	74%	1%
George Washington University (DC)	63%	9%	11%	4%	11%	0%	45%	0%
South Texas College of Law	63%	16%	11%	2%	3%	1%	95%	1%
University of California–Davis	63%	14%	6%	11%	3%	1%	90%	0%
Georgia State University	62%	12%	14%	6%	4%	2%	88%	0%
Loyola University New Orleans	62%	12%	9%	6%	11%	0%	63%	0%
St. Louis University	62%	16%	12%	6%	3%	1%	67%	1%
Washington University in St. Louis	62%	6%	17%	5%	10%	0%	26%	2%
Baylor University (Umphrey) (TX)	61%	14%	16%	1%	7%	1%	86%	0%
Boston University	61%	8%	6%	3%	9%	1%	37%	1%
Mississippi College	61%	13%	11%	5%	8%	2%	75%	0%
North Carolina Central University	61%	8%	16%	7%	5%	3%	86%	0%
Southern Illinois University–Carbondale	61%	9%	20%	9%	1%	0%	77%	0%
University of Dayton (OH)	61%	15%	2%	11%	6%	3%	52%	0%
Louisiana State University–Baton Rouge	60%	7%	14%	2%	14%	1%	80%	0%
Ohio Northern University (Pettit)	60%	15%	17%	3%	3%	2%	35%	0%
Oklahoma City University	60%	19%	14%	4%	0%	3%	65%	0%
Touro College (Fuchsberg) (NY)	60%	15%	16%	5%	3%	1%	84%	0%
University of Arkansas–Fayetteville	60%	14%	12%	8%	5%	1%	72%	0%
University of San Diego	60%	17%	13%	5%	2%	2%	81%	0%
Yeshiva University (Cardozo) (NY)	60%	17%	14%	5%	3%	1%	82%	1%
Drake University (IA)	59%	17%	9%	5%	9%	1%	68%	1%
Loyola Marymount University (CA)	59%	21%	8%	8%	3%	2%	92%	2%
University of Detroit Mercy	59%	24%	7%	3%	4%	1%	73%	18%
Villanova University (PA)	59%	14%	8%	4%	13%	2%	59%	1%
Franklin Pierce Law Center (NH)	58%	14%	12%	4%	9%	1%	21%	2%
Nova Southeastern University (Broad) (FL)	58%	15%	16%	7%	3%	1%	86%	1%
St. John's University (NY)	58%	14%	20%	3%	4%	1%	89%	0%
University of Georgia	58%	6%	6%	9%	19%	1%	79%	N/A
University of Iowa	58%	14%	10%	9%	5%	5%	29%	0%
University of Mississippi	58%	6%	11%	4%	18%	2%	64%	1%
University of North Carolina–Chapel Hill	58%	5%	11%	9%	13%	2%	58%	1%
University of Oklahoma	58%	18%	16%	5%	3%	0%	73%	0%
University of Utah (Quinney)	58%	11%	13%	3%	14%	0%	75%	1%
Arizona State University (O'Connor)	57%	11%	15%	5%	8%	2%	77%	0%
Brigham Young University (Clark) (UT)	57%	17%	11%	1%	13%	1%	43%	1%
DePaul University (IL)	57%	21%	12%	4%	3%	2%	87%	1%
Pepperdine University (CA)	57%	18%	15%	2%	5%	2%	77%	2%
Southwestern Law School (CA)	57%	14%	13%	1%	4%	2%	93%	1%
University of Arkansas–Little Rock (Bowen)	57%	12%	15%	2%	8%	2%	83%	0%
University of Houston	57%	26%	8%	3%	5%	1%	89%	1%
University of Missouri–Kansas City	57%	25%	8%	3%	6%	1%	76%	1%
University of Pittsburgh	57%	17%	7%	6%	11%	2%	63%	1%
Brooklyn Law School (NY)	56%	19%	15%	4%	5%	0%	90%	1%
Hofstra University (NY)	56%	22%	11%	3%	5%	2%	71%	0%
Illinois Institute of Technology (Chicago-Kent)	56%	18%	14%	3%	5%	1%	88%	0%
St. Mary's University (TX)	56%	15%	11%	1%	4%	1%	93%	N/A
University of Cincinnati	56%	16%	9%	5%	8%	4%	76%	0%
University of Florida (Levin)	56%	13%	16%	9%	4%	1%	83%	0%
University of Louisville (Brandeis) (KY)	56%	15%	8%	12%	8%	1%	83%	0%
University of Memphis (Humphreys)	56%	21%	5%	4%	10%	4%	87%	N/A

Where do graduates work?

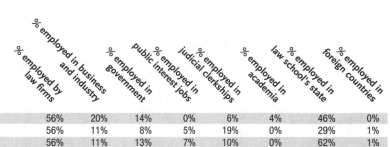

School	% employed by law firms	% employed in business and industry	% employed in government	% employed in public interest jobs	% employed in judicial clerkships	% employed in academia	% employed in law school's state	% employed in foreign countries
Valparaiso University (IN)	56%	20%	14%	0%	6%	4%	46%	0%
Washington and Lee University (VA)	56%	11%	8%	5%	19%	0%	29%	1%
Willamette University (Collins) (OR)	56%	11%	13%	7%	10%	0%	62%	1%
Chapman University (CA)	55%	21%	7%	2%	2%	9%	91%	0%
Duquesne University (PA)	55%	23%	8%	4%	8%	2%	86%	0%
Tulane University (LA)	55%	12%	13%	7%	9%	1%	23%	1%
University of Wisconsin–Madison	55%	12%	17%	7%	7%	2%	47%	1%
Western State University (CA)	55%	21%	13%	2%	0%	5%	95%	N/A
Faulkner University (Jones) (AL)	54%	6%	28%	2%	10%	0%	94%	0%
John Marshall Law School (IL)	54%	24%	18%	1%	2%	1%	87%	1%
Loyola University Chicago	54%	23%	16%	1%	6%	0%	87%	0%
University at Buffalo–SUNY	54%	11%	14%	11%	6%	2%	73%	2%
University of Washington	54%	7%	14%	6%	16%	2%	72%	4%
College of William and Mary (VA)	53%	11%	15%	5%	16%	1%	31%	1%
Golden Gate University (CA)	53%	25%	12%	3%	2%	5%	92%	0%
Indiana University–Bloomington	53%	19%	11%	5%	9%	3%	37%	0%
Northern Kentucky University (Chase)	53%	21%	10%	9%	4%	3%	46%	0%
St. Thomas University (FL)	53%	21%	13%	8%	2%	1%	87%	0%
University of Nebraska–Lincoln	53%	16%	13%	8%	6%	4%	65%	3%
University of Wyoming	53%	5%	15%	3%	20%	3%	58%	0%
New York Law School	52%	18%	11%	4%	5%	2%	77%	1%
Santa Clara University (CA)	52%	27%	9%	3%	1%	1%	92%	1%
Stetson University (FL)	52%	13%	21%	7%	5%	2%	89%	0%
University of Missouri–Columbia	52%	5%	20%	8%	13%	0%	87%	0%
University of South Carolina	52%	5%	10%	6%	25%	2%	79%	0%
University of Toledo (OH)	52%	15%	15%	6%	4%	3%	66%	1%
Albany Law School-Union University (NY)	51%	17%	18%	3%	9%	1%	86%	0%
Northern Illinois University	51%	14%	25%	9%	1%	0%	88%	0%
Pace University (NY)	51%	27%	15%	2%	3%	1%	61%	0%
University of Kansas	51%	18%	15%	4%	9%	3%	44%	1%
University of Kentucky	51%	11%	10%	9%	18%	1%	81%	0%
University of Minnesota–Twin Cities	51%	15%	6%	7%	19%	2%	59%	2%
West Virginia University	51%	14%	7%	5%	19%	5%	69%	0%
Case Western Reserve University (OH)	50%	20%	12%	9%	6%	2%	43%	2%
Indiana University–Indianapolis	50%	22%	22%	2%	2%	2%	83%	1%
Pennsylvania State University (Dickinson)	50%	14%	12%	3%	14%	2%	57%	0%
Thomas Jefferson School of Law (CA)	50%	24%	11%	6%	2%	3%	65%	2%
University of Connecticut	50%	16%	12%	6%	13%	3%	55%	0%
University of New Mexico	50%	6%	17%	12%	9%	5%	79%	1%
American University (Washington) (DC)	49%	18%	13%	7%	11%	2%	51%	2%
Quinnipiac University (CT)	49%	20%	14%	5%	5%	3%	67%	0%
Temple University (Beasley) (PA)	49%	19%	11%	6%	12%	2%	73%	1%
Washburn University (KS)	49%	18%	15%	10%	6%	2%	57%	0%
Whittier Law School (CA)	49%	30%	9%	8%	1%	2%	90%	3%
Florida Coastal School of Law	48%	15%	17%	12%	5%	1%	75%	0%
Gonzaga University (WA)	48%	13%	20%	6%	12%	1%	48%	0%
Howard University (DC)	48%	16%	14%	7%	13%	2%	32%	3%
Ohio State University (Moritz)	48%	18%	15%	6%	7%	4%	59%	1%
Roger Williams University (RI)	48%	18%	8%	9%	12%	3%	37%	0%
Thomas M. Cooley Law School (MI)	48%	20%	17%	5%	7%	2%	34%	1%
University of Montana	48%	5%	6%	9%	32%	0%	76%	N/A

Where do graduates work?

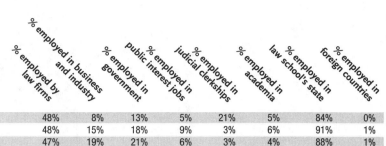

School	% employed by law firms	% employed in business and industry	% employed in government	% employed in public interest jobs	% employed in judicial clerkships	% employed in academia	% employed in law school's state	% employed in foreign countries
University of Nevada–Las Vegas (Boyd)	48%	8%	13%	5%	21%	5%	84%	0%
University of the Pacific (McGeorge) (CA)	48%	15%	18%	9%	3%	6%	91%	1%
Capital University (OH)	47%	19%	21%	6%	3%	4%	88%	1%
Cleveland State University (Cleveland-Marshall)	47%	29%	14%	5%	5%	1%	85%	1%
Creighton University (NE)	47%	23%	15%	5%	9%	1%	47%	1%
Lewis and Clark College (Northwestern) (OR)	47%	17%	16%	12%	7%	1%	67%	0%
Michigan State University	47%	18%	14%	5%	5%	2%	54%	3%
University of Idaho	47%	9%	9%	8%	24%	3%	61%	1%
University of Oregon	47%	11%	15%	13%	12%	1%	56%	0%
Suffolk University (MA)	46%	23%	13%	2%	10%	2%	85%	0%
Syracuse University (NY)	46%	16%	16%	4%	15%	3%	37%	1%
University of Denver (Sturm)	46%	12%	17%	4%	9%	1%	80%	0%
New England School of Law (MA)	45%	20%	17%	5%	11%	2%	63%	0%
Rutgers–Newark (NJ)	45%	14%	7%	3%	28%	2%	63%	1%
Southern University (LA)	45%	9%	26%	3%	12%	3%	73%	0%
William Mitchell College of Law (MN)	45%	25%	10%	5%	11%	1%	86%	0%
Appalachian School of Law (VA)	44%	15%	22%	7%	8%	0%	29%	0%
Florida State University	44%	7%	31%	9%	7%	1%	85%	0%
Regent University (VA)	44%	14%	23%	6%	6%	6%	38%	0%
University of North Dakota	44%	4%	13%	8%	31%	0%	50%	0%
Barry University (FL)	43%	8%	24%	16%	1%	2%	91%	0%
Seattle University	43%	30%	15%	7%	3%	2%	85%	2%
University of Colorado–Boulder	43%	9%	18%	3%	19%	1%	79%	1%
Western New England College (MA)	43%	26%	18%	4%	7%	2%	39%	2%
Yale University (CT)	43%	4%	2%	7%	43%	3%	9%	3%
Texas Wesleyan University	42%	26%	12%	4%	2%	1%	95%	0%
George Mason University (VA)	41%	14%	25%	5%	12%	3%	38%	3%
Rutgers–Camden (NJ)	41%	8%	6%	2%	40%	0%	61%	1%
University of Akron (OH)	41%	30%	16%	4%	7%	2%	85%	0%
University of Arizona (Rogers)	41%	13%	16%	3%	23%	4%	62%	3%
Ave Maria School of Law (MI)	40%	24%	14%	3%	17%	2%	25%	0%
Northeastern University (MA)	40%	18%	10%	16%	14%	1%	62%	2%
University of Maryland	40%	10%	15%	5%	25%	5%	71%	1%
Seton Hall University (NJ)	39%	16%	7%	1%	33%	1%	70%	0%
University of Richmond (Williams) (VA)	38%	13%	22%	4%	22%	1%	62%	1%
Widener University (DE)	38%	22%	16%	3%	19%	1%	14%	0%
University of Maine	37%	25%	12%	8%	13%	4%	64%	1%
Catholic University of America (Columbus) (DC)	36%	20%	26%	5%	14%	0%	48%	1%
Hamline University (MN)	36%	24%	15%	5%	13%	3%	73%	1%
University of Baltimore	36%	18%	14%	5%	23%	3%	71%	0%
University of Hawaii (Richardson)	36%	10%	15%	11%	24%	3%	82%	2%
University of St. Thomas (MN)	36%	23%	9%	14%	16%	2%	83%	1%
Florida International University	34%	9%	17%	4%	3%	0%	87%	1%
Vermont Law School	33%	17%	13%	18%	16%	3%	20%	1%
Florida A&M University	32%	13%	6%	30%	2%	4%	96%	0%
University of South Dakota	28%	17%	16%	14%	21%	4%	46%	1%
CUNY–Queens College	21%	15%	14%	28%	17%	5%	74%	4%
University of the District of Columbia (Clarke)	9%	27%	25%	18%	14%	5%	62%	0%

The U.S.News & World Report

Ultimate Law School Directory

How to use the directory

In the following pages, you'll find exhaustive profiles of the country's American Bar Association–accredited law schools, based on a survey that *U.S. News* conducts each year. The directory is organized by state, and schools are presented alphabetically within each state. The online version of the directory at www.usnews.com allows you to do a customized search of our database. Want to know which law schools specialize in tax law and are located within 100 miles of your home? Enter those criteria and pull up a list.

The vital statistics shown in each directory entry are explained below. The data were collected from the schools during late 2007 and early 2008. If a law school did not supply the data requested, you'll see a N/A, for "not available." If a school did not return the full *U.S. News* questionnaire, it appears at the end of the directory on page 504 with limited information, gathered by calling the schools and consulting their websites.

Addresses and Essential Stats

In addition to the law school's address and the year the school was founded, you'll find key facts and figures here.

Website: Use the website to research the law school's programs.

Tuition: Figures cited for tuition are for the 2007–2008 academic year.

Enrollment: The number represents full-time students during the 2007–2008 academic year.

***U.S. News* ranking:** A school's overall rank, shown in the lower-right-hand corner of the gray box, indicates where it sits among its peers in the 2009 ranking of law schools published by *U.S. News* at www.usnews.com and in its annual guide "America's Best Graduate Schools." Law schools among the top 100 are ranked numerically. Other schools are grouped in tiers. The school's ranking in various specialty areas (clinical training, dispute resolution, environmental law, healthcare law, intellectual property law, international law, tax law, and trial advocacy) is presented as well.

GPA and LSAT: The Law School Admission Test scores and grade point averages shown are for the Fall 2007 entering class and represent the range within which half of the students scored. In other words, 25 percent of students scored at or below the lower end of the range, and 25 percent scored at or above the upper end of the range.

Acceptance rate: The percentage of applicants accepted is provided for the full-time class entering in Fall 2007.

Admissions

Use the admissions phone number or the admissions email address to request information or an application. Many law schools also allow you to complete and submit an application online.

Application deadline: The application deadline for Fall 2009 admission is reported. Some schools allow students to enter at times other than the fall term; those entry points are also listed.

Applicants and acceptees: The admissions statistics provided—numbers of applicants and people accepted, and their credentials—are for the fall 2007 entering class. If the law school has a part-time option, the admissions data is presented for both full-time and part-time programs.

Financial Aid

Call the financial aid office with questions or requests for applications. Note that the deadlines for a school's financial aid form may not be the same as deadlines to apply for federal and state aid.

Tuition and other expenses: The tuition figures are for the 2007–2008 academic year. For public schools, we list both in-state and out-of-state tuition and the estimated cost of books and other miscellaneous living expenses. Whether or not the university offers student housing for law students is also noted.

Financial aid profile: The data on financial aid packages are for the 2006–2007 academic year. Grants are awarded by the university to full- or part-time students who either show need or have excellent academic records. We also list here the average amount of law-school debt borrowers in the Class of 2007 graduated with, and the proportion of students who took out at least one loan.

Academic Programs

Calendar: We tell you whether the school operates on a traditional semester schedule or a quarter system.

Joint degrees awarded: Many law students pursue a second degree in another university department to marry their interests or gain an edge in the job market. One common joint degree, the JD/MBA, combines law and business. Some people get a JD and master's or PhD degree in any of a number of arts or humanities or science disciplines. Other degree combos include the JD/MD (medicine) and the JD/MPH (public health).

Curricular offerings: What are the classes like? This section provides information on the size of both first-year and upper-level classes as well as the breadth of the curriculum during the 2006–2007 academic year. (If the school has a part-time program, its data is broken out.) If first-year students have the opportunity to take a class other than Legal Writing in a small section, that fact is noted. While the first-year curriculum is standard at most schools, the offerings in the second and third year vary widely. The number of course titles refers only to classroom courses offered, not to clinical or field placement offerings. Class-size figures include full- and part-time programs and exclude seminars.

Areas of specialization: A school listed any of the following: appellate advocacy, clinical training, dispute resolution, environmental law, healthcare law, intellectual property law, international law, tax law, and trial advocacy.

Faculty profile: Here, you'll find the total number of full-time tenured or tenure-track faculty (not including professors on leave or on sabbatical) plus part-time faculty during 2007–2008, as well as a breakdown. Part-timers include adjuncts, permanent part-time, and emeritus part-time. The student/faculty ratio (for Fall 2007) gives some indication of how accessible professors are likely to be.

Special programs: The text describing special programs was written by the schools. *U.S. News* edited this text for style but did not verify the information.

Student Body

What will your classmates be like? This section supplies the breakdown of full-time and part-time students, the male and female enrollments, and the ethnic makeup of the student body. All figures are for the 2007–2008 academic year. Note that students who did not identify themselves as members of any demographic group are classified by schools as "White" and that numbers may not add up to 100 percent because of rounding.

Attrition rates: The attrition rates indicate the percentage of students who chose not to come back to the law school during the 2006–2007 academic year. Students who transferred or left for health or financial reasons are included in the count. The percentage of full- and part-time students who left the law school during the 2006–2007 academic year is broken down by gender and by their year in school.

Library resources: In this section, you'll find key stats about the size of the library's collection at the end of the 2006–2007 academic year. Titles are those items that have their own bibliographic record. Subscriptions refers to active subscriptions, regardless of format, for which the library maintains an active record. Total volumes includes any printed, typewritten, mimeographed, or processed work including microforms that are contained in a single binding. The total number of seats includes carrel and non-carrel seats.

Information technology: How many wired network connections are available to students? Is there a wireless network? How many users can access the wireless network at the same time? Are students required to lease or own a computer? These questions are answered in this section.

Employment and Salaries

This section provides data on the employment status of the 2006 graduating class both at the time of their graduation and nine months later. (Some schools did not know the status or location of all graduates, so the data may not be a complete reflection of the graduating class.) Salary information is provided for graduates working in the private sector, which includes law firms and any for-profit company. We also list the median salary and the 25th–75th percentile salary range. Salary figures are also listed for the public service sector, which includes government, judicial clerkships, academic posts, and non-profit jobs.

Occupational breakdown by type: The employment data listed here includes both part-time and full-time jobs. Graduates working in the government are employed by federal, state, or local entities. Public interest work includes Legal Aid groups and other non-profits. The unknown category includes graduates who reported to the school that they were employed but did not note the type of employment.

Employment location: We show the percentage of 2006 employed graduates who are employed in the same state as the law school, the percentage whose jobs are located outside of the United States, and the number of states in which the remaining graduates work. We also show the percentage employed in each of the following geographic areas: New England (Connecticut, Maine, Massachusetts, New Hampshire, Rhode Island, Vermont); Middle Atlantic (New York, New Jersey, and Pennsylvania); East North Central (Illinois, Indiana, Michigan, Ohio, and Wisconsin); South Atlantic (Delaware, District of Columbia, Florida, Georgia, Maryland, North Carolina, South Carolina, Virginia, and West Virginia); East South Central (Alabama, Kentucky, Mississippi, and Tennessee); West South Central (Arkansas,

Louisiana, Oklahoma, and Texas); Mountain (Arizona, Colorado, Idaho, Montana, Nevada, New Mexico, Utah, and Wyoming); and Pacific (Alaska, California, Hawaii, Oregon, and Washington).

Bar Passage Rates

Bar passage statistics are based on 2006 graduates taking either the Summer 2006 or Winter 2007 bar exams. Schools reported the bar passage rates and state in which the largest number of their 2006 graduates took the bar exam. So that you can see how a school's graduates fared compared to all first-time test-takers in the state, we also show the state's overall pass rates.

Albany Law School–Union University

■ 80 New Scotland Avenue, Albany, NY, 12208-3494
■ http://www.albanylaw.edu
■ Private
■ Year founded: 1851
■ 2007-2008 tuition: full-time: $37,550; part-time: $28,200
■ Enrollment 2007-08 academic year: full-time: 662; part-time: 22
■ U.S. News 2009 law specialty ranking: N/A

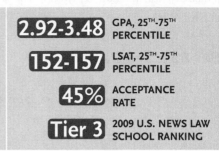

2.92-3.48 GPA, 25TH-75TH PERCENTILE

152-157 LSAT, 25TH-75TH PERCENTILE

45% ACCEPTANCE RATE

Tier 3 2009 U.S. NEWS LAW SCHOOL RANKING

ADMISSIONS
Admissions phone number: **(518) 445-2326**
Admissions email address: **admissions@albanylaw.edu**
Application website: **N/A**
Application deadline for Fall 2009 admission: **03/01**

Admissions statistics:
Number of applicants for Fall 2007: **2,065**
Number of acceptances: **932**
Number enrolled: **246**
Acceptance rate: **45%**
GPA, 25th-75th percentile, entering class Fall 2007: **2.92-3.48**
LSAT, 25th-75th percentile, entering class Fall 2007: **152-157**

FINANCIAL AID
Financial aid phone number: **(518) 445-2357**
Financial aid application deadline: **N/A**
Tuition 2007-2008 academic year: full-time: **$37,550**; part-time: **$28,200**
Room and board: **$9,650**; books: **$1,100**; miscellaneous expenses: **$6,300**
Total of room/board/books/miscellaneous expenses: **$17,050**
University does not offer graduate student housing for which law students are eligible.

Financial aid profile
Percent of students that received grants for the 2006-2007 academic year: full-time: **35%**; part-time **50%**
Median grant amount: full-time: **$18,000**; part-time: **$13,500**
The average law-school debt of those in the Class of 2007 who borrowed: **$85,839**. Proportion who borrowed: **87%**

ACADEMIC PROGRAMS
Calendar: **semester**
Joint degrees awarded: **J.D./M.B.A.; J.D./M.P.A.; J.D./M.R.P.; J.D./M.P.P.; J.D./M.S.W.; J.D./M.S. Bioethics**

Typical first-year section size: Full-time: **80**
Is there typically a "small section" of the first year class, other than Legal Writing, taught by full-time faculty?: Full-time: **yes**
Number of course titles, beyond the first year curriculum, offered last year: **118**
Percentages of upper division course sections, excluding seminars, with an enrollment of:
Under 25: **63%**   25 to 49: **16%**
50 to 74: **15%**   75 to 99: **2%**
100+: **4%**
Areas of specialization: appellate advocacy, clinical training, dispute resolution, environmental law, healthcare law, intellectual property law, international law, tax law, trial advocacy

Fall 2007 faculty profile
Total teaching faculty: **157**. Full-time: **51%**; **51%** men, **49%** women, **18%** minorities. Part-time: **49%**; **75%** men, **25%** women, **8%** minorities
Student-to-faculty ratio: **14.7**

SPECIAL PROGRAMS (as provided by law school):
The Law Clinic and Justice Center and the Government Law Center offer students the chance to participate in representing clients in five in-house clinics and more than 140 placements. Students can spend a semester working in a government agency in Albany, NY, or in Washington, DC, through the semester in government program, a joint project of the Justice Center and the Government Law Center.

STUDENT BODY
Fall 2007 full-time enrollment: 662
Men: **55%**   Women: **45%**
African-American: **2.7%**   American Indian: **0.2%**
Asian-American: **7.6%**   Mexican-American: **0.9%**
Puerto Rican: **0.6%**   Other Hisp-Amer: **2.1%**
White: **80.5%**   International: **1.5%**
Unknown: **3.9%**

Fall 2007 part-time enrollment: 22

Men: 41%	Women: 59%
African-American: 9.1%	American Indian: 0.0%
Asian-American: 0.0%	Mexican-American: 0.0%
Puerto Rican: 4.5%	Other Hisp-Amer: 0.0%
White: 77.3%	International: 4.5%
Unknown: 4.5%	

Attrition rates for 2006-2007 full-time students
Percent of students discontinuing law school:

Men: 4%	Women: 4%
First-year students: 7%	Second-year students: 4%
Third-year students: 1%	

LIBRARY RESOURCES

Total volumes: 683,237
Total seats available for library users: 472

INFORMATION TECHNOLOGY

Number of wired network connections available to students: 1142 total (in the law library, excluding computer labs: 128; in classrooms: 973; in computer labs: 2; elsewhere in the law school: 39)
Law school has a wireless network.
Students are not required to own a computer.

EMPLOYMENT AND SALARIES

Proportion of 2006 graduates employed at graduation: N/A
Employed 9 months later, as of February 15, 2007: 97%
Salaries in the private sector (law firms, business, industry): $47,000–$72,000 (25th-75th percentile)
Median salary in the private sector: $55,000
Percentage in the private sector who reported salary information: 73%

Median salary in public service (government, judicial clerkships, academic posts, non-profits): $48,500

Percentage of 2006 graduates in:

Law firms: 51%	Government: 18%
Bus./industry: 17%	Judicial clerkship: 9%
Public interest: 3%	Unknown: 1%
Academia: 1%	

2006 graduates employed in-state: 86%
2006 graduates employed in foreign countries: 0%
Number of states where graduates are employed: 16
Percentage of 2006 graduates working in: New England: 3%, Middle Atlantic: 91%, East North Central: 0%, West North Central: 1%, South Atlantic: 4%, East South Central: 0%, West South Central: 0%, Mountain: 0%, Pacific: 0%, Unknown: 1%

BAR PASSAGE RATES

Based on 2006 graduates taking Summer 2006 or Winter 2007 exams. Most of the school's first-time test takers took the bar in New York.

86%
School's bar passage rate for first-time test takers

77%
Statewide bar passage rate for first-time test takers

American University (Washington)

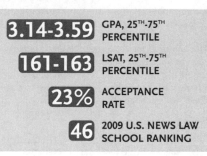

- 4801 Massachusetts Avenue NW, Washington, DC, 20016-8192
- http://www.wcl.american.edu
- Private
- Year founded: 1896
- 2007-2008 tuition: full-time: $37,190; part-time: $26,066
- Enrollment 2007-08 academic year: full-time: 1,246; part-time: 233
- U.S. News 2009 law specialty ranking: clinical training: 2, intellectual property law: 21, international law: 5, trial advocacy: 9

3.14-3.59 GPA, 25TH-75TH PERCENTILE

161-163 LSAT, 25TH-75TH PERCENTILE

23% ACCEPTANCE RATE

46 2009 U.S. NEWS LAW SCHOOL RANKING

ADMISSIONS

Admissions phone number: **(202) 274-4101**
Admissions email address: **wcladmit@wcl.american.edu**
Application website: **http://www.wcl.american.edu/admiss/**
Application deadline for Fall 2009 admission: **03/02**

Admissions statistics:
Number of applicants for Fall 2007: **7,401**
Number of acceptances: **1,685**
Number enrolled: **394**
Acceptance rate: **23%**
GPA, 25th-75th percentile, entering class Fall 2007: **3.14-3.59**
LSAT, 25th-75th percentile, entering class Fall 2007: **161-163**

Part-time program:
Number of applicants for Fall 2007: **1,000**
Number of acceptances: **214**
Number enrolled: **104**
Acceptance rate: **21%**
GPA, 25th-75th percentile, entering class Fall 2007: **3.10-3.62**
LSAT, 25th-75th percentile, entering class Fall 2007: **159-161**

FINANCIAL AID

Financial aid phone number: **(202) 274-4040**
Financial aid application deadline: **03/01**
Tuition 2007-2008 academic year: full-time: **$37,190**; part-time: **$26,066**
Room and board: **$13,635**; books: **$1,015**; miscellaneous expenses: **$5,407**
Total of room/board/books/miscellaneous expenses: **$20,057**
University offers graduate student housing for which law students are eligible.

Financial aid profile
Percent of students that received grants for the 2006-2007 academic year: full-time: **23%**; part-time **6%**

Median grant amount: full-time: **$10,000**; part-time: **$2,310**
The average law-school debt of those in the Class of 2007 who borrowed: **$104,062**. Proportion who borrowed: **88%**

ACADEMIC PROGRAMS

Calendar: **semester**
Joint degrees awarded: **J.D./M.A.; J.D./M.B.A.; J.D./M.S.**
Typical first-year section size: Full-time: **95**; Part-time: **89**
Is there typically a "small section" of the first year class, other than Legal Writing, taught by full-time faculty?: Full-time: **yes**; Part-time: **no**
Number of course titles, beyond the first year curriculum, offered last year: **316**
Percentages of upper division course sections, excluding seminars, with an enrollment of:

Under 25: **52%**	25 to 49: **26%**
50 to 74: **14%**	75 to 99: **8%**
100+: **0%**	

Areas of specialization: appellate advocacy, clinical training, dispute resolution, environmental law, healthcare law, intellectual property law, international law, tax law, trial advocacy

Fall 2007 faculty profile
Total teaching faculty: **298**. Full-time: **33%**; **55%** men, **45%** women, **22%** minorities. Part-time: **67%**; **65%** men, **35%** women, **12%** minorities
Student-to-faculty ratio: **13.8**

SPECIAL PROGRAMS *(as provided by law school):*
Clinics: community/economic development, criminal, disability, domestic violence, tax, intellectual property, human rights. Centers include: environment, international law, law and government, gender, innocence project. Study in Chile, U.K./France/Switzerland, Turkey, Canada, Mexico, Spain, China, Finland, Netherlands. Externships in government, public interest groups. J.D./M.B.A., J.D./M.A.

STUDENT BODY

Fall 2007 full-time enrollment: 1,246

Men: 46%   Women: 54%
African-American: 7.5%   American Indian: 1.1%
Asian-American: 11.0%   Mexican-American: 2.2%
Puerto Rican: 0.6%   Other Hisp-Amer: 10.1%
White: 62.0%   International: 0.9%
Unknown: 4.6%

Fall 2007 part-time enrollment: 233

Men: 51%   Women: 49%
African-American: 9.0%   American Indian: 2.6%
Asian-American: 8.2%   Mexican-American: 1.7%
Puerto Rican: 1.7%   Other Hisp-Amer: 6.0%
White: 64.8%   International: 0.0%
Unknown: 6.0%

Attrition rates for 2006-2007 full-time students
Percent of students discontinuing law school:
Men: 4%   Women: 2%
First-year students: 9%   Second-year students: 0%
Third-year students: N/A

LIBRARY RESOURCES

Total volumes: 592,065
Total seats available for library users: 644

INFORMATION TECHNOLOGY

Number of wired network connections available to students: 2,614 total (in the law library, excluding computer labs: 412; in classrooms: 2,004; in computer labs: 78; elsewhere in the law school: 120)
Law school has a wireless network.
Students are not required to own a computer.

EMPLOYMENT AND SALARIES

Proportion of 2006 graduates employed at graduation: 85%

Employed 9 months later, as of February 15, 2007: 96%
Salaries in the private sector (law firms, business, industry): $60,000–$135,000 (25th-75th percentile)
Median salary in the private sector: $87,500
Percentage in the private sector who reported salary information: 89%
Median salary in public service (government, judicial clerkships, academic posts, non-profits): $48,000

Percentage of 2006 graduates in:
Law firms: 49%   Government: 13%
Bus./industry: 18%   Judicial clerkship: 11%
Public interest: 7%   Unknown: 0%
Academia: 2%

2006 graduates employed in-state: 51%
2006 graduates employed in foreign countries: 2%
Number of states where graduates are employed: 24
Percentage of 2006 graduates working in: New England: 3%, Middle Atlantic: 11%, East North Central: 3%, West North Central: 1%, South Atlantic: 76%, East South Central: 0%, West South Central: 1%, Mountain: 1%, Pacific: 3%, Unknown: 0%

BAR PASSAGE RATES

Based on 2006 graduates taking Summer 2006 or Winter 2007 exams. Most of the school's first-time test takers took the bar in Maryland.

81%
School's bar passage rate for first-time test takers

77%
Statewide bar passage rate for first-time test takers

Appalachian School of Law

■ PO Box 2825, Grundy, VA, 24614-2825
■ http://www.asl.edu
■ Private
■ Year founded: 1994
■ 2007-2008 tuition: full-time: $24,000; part-time: N/A
■ Enrollment 2007-08 academic year: full-time: 339
■ U.S. News 2009 law specialty ranking: N/A

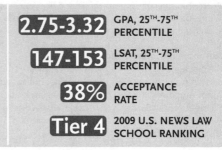

2.75-3.32 GPA, 25TH-75TH PERCENTILE

147-153 LSAT, 25TH-75TH PERCENTILE

38% ACCEPTANCE RATE

Tier 4 2009 U.S. NEWS LAW SCHOOL RANKING

ADMISSIONS

Admissions phone number: **(800) 895-7411**
Admissions email address: **aslinfo@asl.edu**
Application website:
   http://www.asl.edu/admissions/onlineApp.php
Application deadline for Fall 2009 admission: **rolling**

Admissions statistics:
Number of applicants for Fall 2007: **1,578**
Number of acceptances: **599**
Number enrolled: **127**
Acceptance rate: **38%**
GPA, 25th-75th percentile, entering class Fall 2007: **2.75-3.32**
LSAT, 25th-75th percentile, entering class Fall 2007: **147-153**

FINANCIAL AID

Financial aid phone number: **(800) 895-7411**
Financial aid application deadline: **N/A**
Tuition 2007-2008 academic year: full-time: **$24,000**; part-time: **N/A**
Room and board: **$12,620**; books: **$900**; miscellaneous expenses: **$1,400**
Total of room/board/books/miscellaneous expenses: **$14,920**
University does not offer graduate student housing for which law students are eligible.

Financial aid profile
Percent of students that received grants for the 2006-2007 academic year: full-time: **28%**
Median grant amount: full-time: **$11,250**
The average law-school debt of those in the Class of 2007 who borrowed: **$78,315**. Proportion who borrowed: **84%**

ACADEMIC PROGRAMS

Calendar: **semester**
Joint degrees awarded: **N/A**
Typical first-year section size: Full-time: **158**
Is there typically a "small section" of the first year class, other than Legal Writing, taught by full-time faculty?:
   Full-time: **yes**
Number of course titles, beyond the first year curriculum, offered last year: **39**
Percentages of upper division course sections, excluding seminars, with an enrollment of:
   Under 25: **46%**   25 to 49: **18%**
   50 to 74: **5%**   75 to 99: **8%**
   100+: **23%**
Areas of specialization: appellate advocacy, dispute resolution, environmental law, healthcare law, intellectual property law, tax law, trial advocacy

Fall 2007 faculty profile
Total teaching faculty: **20**. Full-time: **75%**; **53%** men, **47%** women, **20%** minorities. Part-time: **25%**; **40%** men, **60%** women, **N/A** minorities
Student-to-faculty ratio: **21.0**

SPECIAL PROGRAMS *(as provided by law school):*

Externships (required) for all rising second-year students; community service required (all students). Certificate: Lawyer as a Problem Solver (optional).

STUDENT BODY

Fall 2007 full-time enrollment: **339**
Men: **65%**   Women: **35%**
African-American: **1.2%**   American Indian: **0.0%**
Asian-American: **1.5%**   Mexican-American: **0.3%**
Puerto Rican: **0.6%**   Other Hisp-Amer: **1.8%**
White: **80.8%**   International: **0.0%**
Unknown: **13.9%**

Attrition rates for 2006-2007 full-time students
Percent of students discontinuing law school:
Men: **7%**   Women: **4%**
First-year students: **12%**   Second-year students: **4%**
Third-year students: **N/A**

LIBRARY RESOURCES

Total volumes: 208,654
Total seats available for library users: 232

INFORMATION TECHNOLOGY

Number of wired network connections available to students: 730 total (in the law library, excluding computer labs: 213; in classrooms: 379; in computer labs: 50; elsewhere in the law school: 88)
Law school has a wireless network.
Students are not required to own a computer.

EMPLOYMENT AND SALARIES

Proportion of 2006 graduates employed at graduation: N/A
Employed 9 months later, as of February 15, 2007: 69%
Salaries in the private sector (law firms, business, industry): $36,000–$62,000 (25th-75th percentile)
Median salary in the private sector: $41,600
Percentage in the private sector who reported salary information: 59%
Median salary in public service (government, judicial clerkships, academic posts, non-profits): $41,730

Percentage of 2006 graduates in:

Law firms: 44%	Government: 22%
Bus./industry: 15%	Judicial clerkship: 8%
Public interest: 7%	Unknown: 4%
Academia: 0%	

2006 graduates employed in-state: 29%
2006 graduates employed in foreign countries: 0%
Number of states where graduates are employed: 19
Percentage of 2006 graduates working in: New England: 3%, Middle Atlantic: 5%, East North Central: 2%, West North Central: N/A, South Atlantic: 67%, East South Central: 16%, West South Central: 3%, Mountain: 3%, Pacific: 2%, Unknown: 0%

BAR PASSAGE RATES

Based on 2006 graduates taking Summer 2006 or Winter 2007 exams. Most of the school's first-time test takers took the bar in Virginia.

47%
School's bar passage rate for first-time test takers

74%
Statewide bar passage rate for first-time test takers

Arizona State University (O'Connor)

- 1100 S. McAllister Avenue, Tempe, AZ, 85287-7906
- http://www.law.asu.edu
- Public
- Year founded: 1967
- 2007-2008 tuition: In-state: full-time: $14,628; part-time: N/A; Out-of-state: full time: $26,320
- Enrollment 2007-08 academic year: full-time: 595
- U.S. News 2009 law specialty ranking: N/A

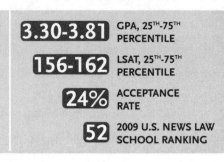

3.30-3.81 GPA, 25TH-75TH PERCENTILE

156-162 LSAT, 25TH-75TH PERCENTILE

24% ACCEPTANCE RATE

52 2009 U.S. NEWS LAW SCHOOL RANKING

ADMISSIONS

Admissions phone number: (480) 965-1474
Admissions email address: law.admissions@asu.edu
Application website:
https://www4.lsac.org/lsacd_on_the_web/login/openfirst.aspx?ID=KE934007A1489MO
Application deadline for Fall 2009 admission: 02/01

Admissions statistics:

Number of applicants for Fall 2007: 3,082
Number of acceptances: 731
Number enrolled: 159
Acceptance rate: 24%
GPA, 25th-75th percentile, entering class Fall 2007: 3.30-3.81
LSAT, 25th-75th percentile, entering class Fall 2007: 156-162

FINANCIAL AID

Financial aid phone number: (480) 965-1474
Financial aid application deadline: 03/15
Tuition 2007-2008 academic year: In-state: full-time: $14,628; part-time: N/A; Out-of-state: full-time: $26,320
Room and board: $10,530; books: $2,180; miscellaneous expenses: $6,490
Total of room/board/books/miscellaneous expenses: $19,200
University offers graduate student housing for which law students are eligible.

Financial aid profile

Percent of students that received grants for the 2006-2007 academic year: full-time: 48%
Median grant amount: full-time: $5,000
The average law-school debt of those in the Class of 2007 who borrowed: $58,964. Proportion who borrowed: 87%

ACADEMIC PROGRAMS

Calendar: semester
Joint degrees awarded: J.D./M.B.A.; J.D./M.D. (Mayo Clinic); J.D./Ph.D. Psychology; J.D./Ph.D. Justice and
Social Inquiry; J.D./M.H.S.M.
Typical first-year section size: Full-time: 50
Is there typically a "small section" of the first year class, other than Legal Writing, taught by full-time faculty?: Full-time: yes
Number of course titles, beyond the first year curriculum, offered last year: 128
Percentages of upper division course sections, excluding seminars, with an enrollment of:

Under 25: 50%		25 to 49: 35%
50 to 74: 9%		75 to 99: 5%
100+: 2%		

Areas of specialization: appellate advocacy, clinical training, dispute resolution, environmental law, healthcare law, intellectual property law, international law, tax law, trial advocacy

Fall 2007 faculty profile

Total teaching faculty: 94. Full-time: 61%; 68% men, 32% women, 18% minorities. Part-time: 39%; 86% men, 14% women, 5% minorities
Student-to-faculty ratio: 9.4

SPECIAL PROGRAMS (as provided by law school):

The Center for the Study of Law, Science and Technology is the most comprehensive in the country. The Indian legal program is nationally renowned. Joint degrees include J.D./M.D.(Mayo Medical School) and J.D./Ph.D. in Psychology. The college has two LL.M.s: Biotechnology and Genomics; and Tribal Policy, Law, and Government. The Master of Legal Studies familiarizes nonlawyers with the law.

STUDENT BODY

Fall 2007 full-time enrollment: 595

Men: 57%	Women: 43%
African-American: 3.5%	American Indian: 5.5%
Asian-American: 3.9%	Mexican-American: 4.4%
Puerto Rican: 0.5%	Other Hisp-Amer: 8.6%
White: 61.7%	International: 1.7%
Unknown: 10.3%	

Attrition rates for 2006-2007 full-time students
Percent of students discontinuing law school:
Men: **5%**   Women: **5%**
First-year students: **8%**   Second-year students: **6%**
Third-year students: **0%**

LIBRARY RESOURCES
Total volumes: **418,114**
Total seats available for library users: **544**

INFORMATION TECHNOLOGY
Number of wired network connections available to students: **186** total (in the law library, excluding computer labs: **170**; in classrooms: **10**; in computer labs: **3**; elsewhere in the law school: **3**)
Law school has a wireless network.
Students are not required to own a computer.

EMPLOYMENT AND SALARIES
Proportion of 2006 graduates employed at graduation: **N/A**
Employed 9 months later, as of February 15, 2007: **93%**
Salaries in the private sector (law firms, business, industry): **$65,000–$100,000** (25th-75th percentile)
Median salary in the private sector: **$80,000**
Percentage in the private sector who reported salary information: **68%**
Median salary in public service (government, judicial clerkships, academic posts, non-profits): **$56,000**

Percentage of 2006 graduates in:
Law firms: **57%**   Government: **15%**
Bus./industry: **11%**   Judicial clerkship: **8%**
Public interest: **5%**   Unknown: **2%**
Academia: **2%**

2006 graduates employed in-state: **77%**
2006 graduates employed in foreign countries: **0%**
Number of states where graduates are employed: **15**
Percentage of 2006 graduates working in: New England: **0%**, Middle Atlantic: **1%**, East North Central: **2%**, West North Central: **1%**, South Atlantic: **5%**, East South Central: **0%**, West South Central: **3%**, Mountain: **80%**, Pacific: **7%**, Unknown: **0%**

BAR PASSAGE RATES
Based on 2006 graduates taking Summer 2006 or Winter 2007 exams. Most of the school's first-time test takers took the bar in Arizona.

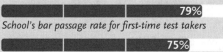

79%
School's bar passage rate for first-time test takers

75%
Statewide bar passage rate for first-time test takers

Atlanta's John Marshall Law School

■ 1422 W. Peachtree Street, NW, Atlanta, GA, 30309
■ http://www.johnmarshall.edu
■ Private
■ **Year founded:** 1933
■ **2007-2008 tuition:** full-time: $930/credit hour; part-time: $930/credit hour
■ **Enrollment 2007-08 academic year:** full-time: 302; part-time: 172
■ **U.S. News 2009 law specialty ranking:** N/A

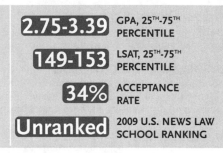

2.75-3.39 GPA, 25ᵀᴴ-75ᵀᴴ PERCENTILE

149-153 LSAT, 25ᵀᴴ-75ᵀᴴ PERCENTILE

34% ACCEPTANCE RATE

Unranked 2009 U.S. NEWS LAW SCHOOL RANKING

ADMISSIONS
Admissions phone number: **(404) 872-3593**
Admissions email address: **admissions@johnmarshall.edu**
Application website: **http://www.johnmarshall.edu**
Application deadline for Fall 2009 admission: **rolling**

Admissions statistics:
Number of applicants for Fall 2007: **1,470**
Number of acceptances: **503**
Number enrolled: **136**
Acceptance rate: **34%**
GPA, 25th-75th percentile, entering class Fall 2007: **2.75-3.39**
LSAT, 25th-75th percentile, entering class Fall 2007: **149-153**

Part-time program:
Number of applicants for Fall 2007: **315**
Number of acceptances: **98**
Number enrolled: **49**
Acceptance rate: **31%**
GPA, 25th-75th percentile, entering class Fall 2007: **2.48-3.36**
LSAT, 25th-75th percentile, entering class Fall 2007: **149-153**

FINANCIAL AID
Financial aid phone number: **(404) 872-3593**
Financial aid application deadline: **N/A**
Tuition 2007-2008 academic year: full-time: **$930/credit hour**; part-time: **$930/credit hour**
Room and board: **$8,400**; books: **$1,816**; miscellaneous expenses: **$5,674**
Total of room/board/books/miscellaneous expenses: **$15,890**
University does not offer graduate student housing for which law students are eligible.

Financial aid profile
Percent of students that received grants for the 2006-2007 academic year: full-time: **0%**

Median grant amount: full-time: **N/A**
The average law-school debt of those in the Class of 2007 who borrowed: **$59,204**. Proportion who borrowed: **76%**

ACADEMIC PROGRAMS
Calendar: **semester**
Joint degrees awarded: **N/A**
Typical first-year section size: Full-time: **45**; Part-time: **39**
Is there typically a "small section" of the first year class, other than Legal Writing, taught by full-time faculty?: Full-time: **no**; Part-time: **no**
Number of course titles, beyond the first year curriculum, offered last year: **39**
Percentages of upper division course sections, excluding seminars, with an enrollment of:
Under 25: **46%**   25 to 49: **43%**
50 to 74: **10%**   75 to 99: **0%**
100+: **0%**
Areas of specialization: appellate advocacy, dispute resolution, environmental law, healthcare law, intellectual property law, international law, tax law, trial advocacy

Fall 2007 faculty profile
Total teaching faculty: **41**. Full-time: **63%**; **35%** men, **65%** women, **19%** minorities. Part-time: **37%**; **73%** men, **27%** women, **7%** minorities
Student-to-faculty ratio: **13.1**

SPECIAL PROGRAMS *(as provided by law school):*
Through the externship program, students who have completed 59 hours may be eligible to practice law under the supervision of a licensed attorney in a government, public service, or not-for-profit organization. Full-time students may and part-time students must register for elective classes in the summer semester. The Career Development Office also assists students in obtaining internships.

STUDENT BODY
Fall 2007 full-time enrollment: 302
Men: **50%**   Women: **50%**
African-American: **12.6%**   American Indian: **0.7%**

Asian-American: 3.6% Mexican-American: 0.0%
Puerto Rican: 2.0% Other Hisp-Amer: 2.6%
White: 70.9% International: 0.7%
Unknown: 7.0%

Fall 2007 part-time enrollment: 172

Men: 49% Women: 51%
African-American: 21.5% American Indian: 0.6%
Asian-American: 3.5% Mexican-American: 0.0%
Puerto Rican: 2.3% Other Hisp-Amer: 1.7%
White: 65.7% International: 0.0%
Unknown: 4.7%

Attrition rates for 2006-2007 full-time students
Percent of students discontinuing law school:
Men: 1% Women: N/A
First-year students: 1% Second-year students: N/A
Third-year students: N/A

LIBRARY RESOURCES
Total volumes: 242,928
Total seats available for library users: 212

INFORMATION TECHNOLOGY
Number of wired network connections available to students: 177 total (in the law library, excluding computer labs: 94; in classrooms: 55; in computer labs: 24; elsewhere in the law school: 4)
Law school has a wireless network.
Students are not required to own a computer.

EMPLOYMENT AND SALARIES
Proportion of 2006 graduates employed at graduation: N/A
Employed 9 months later, as of February 15, 2007: N/A

Salaries in the private sector (law firms, business, industry): $36,400–$80,000 (25th-75th percentile)
Median salary in the private sector: $60,000
Percentage in the private sector who reported salary information: 70%
Median salary in public service (government, judicial clerkships, academic posts, non-profits): $28,000

Percentage of 2006 graduates in:
Law firms: 70% Government: 11%
Bus./industry: 14% Judicial clerkship: 0%
Public interest: 3% Unknown: 0%
Academia: 3%

2006 graduates employed in-state: 86%
2006 graduates employed in foreign countries: 0%
Number of states where graduates are employed: 5
Percentage of 2006 graduates working in: New England: 0%, Middle Atlantic: 0%, East North Central: 0%, West North Central: 0%, South Atlantic: 89%, East South Central: 5%, West South Central: 2%, Mountain: 2%, Pacific: 0%, Unknown: 3%

BAR PASSAGE RATES
Based on 2006 graduates taking Summer 2006 or Winter 2007 exams. Most of the school's first-time test takers took the bar in Georgia.

N/A

School's bar passage rate for first-time test takers

N/A

Statewide bar passage rate for first-time test takers

Ave Maria School of Law

- 3475 Plymouth Road, Ann Arbor, MI, 48105-2550
- http://www.avemarialaw.edu
- Private
- Year founded: 2000
- 2007-2008 tuition: full-time: $32,302; part-time: N/A
- Enrollment 2007-08 academic year: full-time: 331; part-time: 1
- U.S. News 2009 law specialty ranking: N/A

2.93-3.47 GPA, 25ᵀᴴ-75ᵀᴴ PERCENTILE

147-155 LSAT, 25ᵀᴴ-75ᵀᴴ PERCENTILE

51% ACCEPTANCE RATE

Tier 4 2009 U.S. NEWS LAW SCHOOL RANKING

ADMISSIONS

Admissions phone number: **(734) 827-8063**
Admissions email address: **info@avemarialaw.edu**
Application website: **http://www.avemarialaw.edu/apply**
Application deadline for Fall 2009 admission: **04/01**

Admissions statistics:
Number of applicants for Fall 2007: **1,542**
Number of acceptances: **786**
Number enrolled: **127**
Acceptance rate: **51%**
GPA, 25th-75th percentile, entering class Fall 2007: **2.93-3.47**
LSAT, 25th-75th percentile, entering class Fall 2007: **147-155**

FINANCIAL AID

Financial aid phone number: **(734) 827-8051**
Financial aid application deadline: **06/01**
Tuition 2007-2008 academic year: full-time: **$32,302**; part-time: **N/A**
Room and board: **$12,618**; books: **$900**; miscellaneous expenses: **$6,170**
Total of room/board/books/miscellaneous expenses: **$19,688**
University does not offer graduate student housing for which law students are eligible.

Financial aid profile
Percent of students that received grants for the 2006-2007 academic year: full-time: **69%**
Median grant amount: full-time: **$20,000**
The average law-school debt of those in the Class of 2007 who borrowed: **$79,211**. Proportion who borrowed: **86%**

ACADEMIC PROGRAMS

Calendar: **semester**
Joint degrees awarded: **N/A**
Typical first-year section size: Full-time: **65**
Is there typically a "small section" of the first year class, other than Legal Writing, taught by full-time faculty?:

Full-time: **no**
Number of course titles, beyond the first year curriculum, offered last year: **70**
Percentages of upper division course sections, excluding seminars, with an enrollment of:
Under 25: **59%**   25 to 49: **26%**
50 to 74: **10%**   75 to 99: **5%**
100+: **0%**
Areas of specialization: appellate advocacy, clinical training, dispute resolution, environmental law, healthcare law, intellectual property law, international law, tax law, trial advocacy

Fall 2007 faculty profile
Total teaching faculty: **40**. Full-time: **63%**; **72%** men, **28%** women, **4%** minorities. Part-time: **38%**; **87%** men, **13%** women, **0%** minorities
Student-to-faculty ratio: **15.7**

SPECIAL PROGRAMS *(as provided by law school):*

The Ave Maria curriculum provides students with a rigorous intellectual experience that prepares graduates for the study of law in all jurisdictions.

STUDENT BODY

Fall 2007 full-time enrollment: 331

Men: **65%**	Women: **35%**
African-American: **2.4%**	American Indian: **0.6%**
Asian-American: **7.3%**	Mexican-American: **2.1%**
Puerto Rican: **0.9%**	Other Hisp-Amer: **3.6%**
White: **81.3%**	International: **1.8%**
Unknown: **0.0%**	

Fall 2007 part-time enrollment: 1

Men: **0%**	Women: **100%**
African-American: **0.0%**	American Indian: **0.0%**
Asian-American: **0.0%**	Mexican-American: **0.0%**
Puerto Rican: **0.0%**	Other Hisp-Amer: **0.0%**
White: **100.0%**	International: **0.0%**
Unknown: **0.0%**	

Attrition rates for 2006-2007 full-time students
Percent of students discontinuing law school:

Men: 13%   Women: 13%
First-year students: 28%   Second-year students: 10%
Third-year students: 1%

LIBRARY RESOURCES
Total volumes: 117,104
Total seats available for library users: 285

INFORMATION TECHNOLOGY
Number of wired network connections available to students: 647 total (in the law library, excluding computer labs: 215; in classrooms: 350; in computer labs: 22; elsewhere in the law school: 60)
Law school doesn't have a wireless network.
Students are not required to own a computer.

EMPLOYMENT AND SALARIES
Proportion of 2006 graduates employed at graduation:
  N/A
Employed 9 months later, as of February 15, 2007: 73%
Salaries in the private sector (law firms, business, industry): $48,100–$90,000 (25th-75th percentile)
Median salary in the private sector: $58,000
Percentage in the private sector who reported salary information: 64%
Median salary in public service (government, judicial clerkships, academic posts, non-profits): $52,000

Percentage of 2006 graduates in:

Law firms: 40%   Government: 14%
Bus./industry: 24%   Judicial clerkship: 17%
Public interest: 3%   Unknown: 0%
Academia: 2%

2006 graduates employed in-state: 25%
2006 graduates employed in foreign countries: 0%
Number of states where graduates are employed: 17
Percentage of 2006 graduates working in: New England: 3%, Middle Atlantic: 10%, East North Central: 33%, West North Central: 14%, South Atlantic: 18%, East South Central: 3%, West South Central: 3%, Mountain: 3%, Pacific: 6%, Unknown: 6%

BAR PASSAGE RATES
Based on 2006 graduates taking Summer 2006 or Winter 2007 exams. Most of the school's first-time test takers took the bar in Michigan.

96%
School's bar passage rate for first-time test takers

89%
Statewide bar passage rate for first-time test takers

Barry University

- 6441 E. Colonial Drive, Orlando, FL, 32807
- http://www.barry.edu/law/
- Private
- Year founded: 1995
- 2007-2008 tuition: full-time: $29,300; part-time: $22,100
- Enrollment 2007-08 academic year: full-time: 536; part-time: 156
- U.S. News 2009 law specialty ranking: N/A

2.70-3.30 GPA, 25TH-75TH PERCENTILE

148-152 LSAT, 25TH-75TH PERCENTILE

55% ACCEPTANCE RATE

Tier 4 2009 U.S. NEWS LAW SCHOOL RANKING

ADMISSIONS
Admissions phone number: **(866) 532-2779**
Admissions email address: **lawinfo@mail.barry.edu**
Application website:
  http://www.barry.edu/law/pdf/application.pdf
Application deadline for Fall 2009 admission: **04/01**

Admissions statistics:
Number of applicants for Fall 2007: **1,896**
Number of acceptances: **1,048**
Number enrolled: **281**
Acceptance rate: **55%**
GPA, 25th-75th percentile, entering class Fall 2007: **2.70-3.30**
LSAT, 25th-75th percentile, entering class Fall 2007: **148-152**

Part-time program:
Number of applicants for Fall 2007: **211**
Number of acceptances: **119**
Number enrolled: **50**
Acceptance rate: **56%**
GPA, 25th-75th percentile, entering class Fall 2007: **2.30-3.40**
LSAT, 25th-75th percentile, entering class Fall 2007: **146-155**

FINANCIAL AID
Financial aid phone number: **(321) 206-5621**
Financial aid application deadline: **04/01**
Tuition 2007-2008 academic year: full-time: **$29,300**; part-time: **$22,100**
Room and board: **$12,600**; books: **$1,600**; miscellaneous expenses: **$6,300**
Total of room/board/books/miscellaneous expenses: **$20,500**
University does not offer graduate student housing for which law students are eligible.

Financial aid profile
Percent of students that received grants for the 2006-2007 academic year: full-time: **66%**; part-time **76%**
Median grant amount: full-time: **$5,000**; part-time: **$3,750**
The average law-school debt of those in the Class of 2007 who borrowed: **$99,832**. Proportion who borrowed: **91%**

ACADEMIC PROGRAMS
Calendar: **semester**
Joint degrees awarded: **J.D./M.A. Human Resource Development**
Typical first-year section size: Full-time: **82**; Part-time: **47**
Is there typically a "small section" of the first year class, other than Legal Writing, taught by full-time faculty?: Full-time: **no**; Part-time: **no**
Number of course titles, beyond the first year curriculum, offered last year: **138**
Percentages of upper division course sections, excluding seminars, with an enrollment of:

Under 25: **60%**	25 to 49: **27%**
50 to 74: **10%**	75 to 99: **2%**
100+: **1%**	

Areas of specialization: appellate advocacy, clinical training, dispute resolution, environmental law, healthcare law, intellectual property law, international law, tax law, trial advocacy

Fall 2007 faculty profile
Total teaching faculty: **62**. Full-time: **40%**; **60%** men, **40%** women, **12%** minorities. Part-time: **60%**; **68%** men, **32%** women, **8%** minorities
Student-to-faculty ratio: **20.7**

SPECIAL PROGRAMS (as provided by law school):
Barry University Dwayne O. Andreas School of Law offers clinical programs focusing on children and families. It also offers courses in intellectual property such as Trademarks, Patents, Copyrights, Sports Law, Internet Law, and Entertainment Law.

STUDENT BODY

Fall 2007 full-time enrollment: 536

Men: 53%	Women: 47%
African-American: 4.5%	American Indian: 0.2%
Asian-American: 4.3%	Mexican-American: 0.0%
Puerto Rican: 0.0%	Other Hisp-Amer: 8.6%
White: 65.7%	International: 0.0%
Unknown: 16.8%	

Fall 2007 part-time enrollment: 156

Men: 54%	Women: 46%
African-American: 6.4%	American Indian: 2.6%
Asian-American: 1.9%	Mexican-American: 0.0%
Puerto Rican: 0.0%	Other Hisp-Amer: 8.3%
White: 63.5%	International: 0.0%
Unknown: 17.3%	

Attrition rates for 2006-2007 full-time students
Percent of students discontinuing law school:

Men: 3%	Women: 0%
First-year students: 3%	Second-year students: 1%
Third-year students: 1%	

LIBRARY RESOURCES

Total volumes: 269,812
Total seats available for library users: 338

INFORMATION TECHNOLOGY

Number of wired network connections available to students: 0 total (in the law library, excluding computer labs: 0; in classrooms: 0; in computer labs: 0; elsewhere in the law school: 0)
Law school has a wireless network.
Students are not required to own a computer.

EMPLOYMENT AND SALARIES

Proportion of 2006 graduates employed at graduation: N/A
Employed 9 months later, as of February 15, 2007: 80%

Salaries in the private sector (law firms, business, industry): $45,000–$55,000 (25th-75th percentile)
Median salary in the private sector: $50,000
Percentage in the private sector who reported salary information: 62%
Median salary in public service (government, judicial clerkships, academic posts, non-profits): $40,000

Percentage of 2006 graduates in:

Law firms: 43%	Government: 24%
Bus./industry: 8%	Judicial clerkship: 1%
Public interest: 16%	Unknown: 6%
Academia: 2%	

2006 graduates employed in-state: 91%
2006 graduates employed in foreign countries: 0%
Number of states where graduates are employed: 8
Percentage of 2006 graduates working in: New England: 1%, Middle Atlantic: 1%, East North Central: N/A, West North Central: N/A, South Atlantic: 96%, East South Central: N/A, West South Central: 2%, Mountain: N/A, Pacific: N/A, Unknown: 0%

BAR PASSAGE RATES

Based on 2006 graduates taking Summer 2006 or Winter 2007 exams. Most of the school's first-time test takers took the bar in Florida.

71%
School's bar passage rate for first-time test takers

74%
Statewide bar passage rate for first-time test takers

Baylor University (Umphrey)

- 1114 S. University Parks Drive, 1 Bear Place #97288, Waco, TX, 76798-7288
- http://law.baylor.edu
- Private
- Year founded: 1857
- 2007-2008 tuition: full-time: $33,294; part-time: $33,294
- Enrollment 2007-08 academic year: full-time: 411
- U.S. News 2009 law specialty ranking: trial advocacy: 8

3.38-3.78 GPA, 25TH-75TH PERCENTILE

157-162 LSAT, 25TH-75TH PERCENTILE

30% ACCEPTANCE RATE

55 2009 U.S. NEWS LAW SCHOOL RANKING

ADMISSIONS

Admissions phone number: **(254) 710-1911**
Admissions email address: **Becky_Beck@baylor.edu**
Application website:
http://law.baylor.edu/ProspectiveStudents/PS_appinstructions.html
Application deadline for Fall 2009 admission: **03/01**

Admissions statistics:

Number of applicants for Fall 2007: **3,807**
Number of acceptances: **1,159**
Number enrolled: **171**
Acceptance rate: **30%**
GPA, 25th-75th percentile, entering class Fall 2007: **3.38-3.78**
LSAT, 25th-75th percentile, entering class Fall 2007: **157-162**

FINANCIAL AID

Financial aid phone number: **(254) 710-2611**
Financial aid application deadline: **N/A**
Tuition 2007-2008 academic year: full-time: **$33,294**; part-time: **$33,294**
Room and board: **$9,936**; books: **$1,839**; miscellaneous expenses: **$5,148**
Total of room/board/books/miscellaneous expenses: **$16,923**
University offers graduate student housing for which law students are eligible.

Financial aid profile

Percent of students that received grants for the 2006-2007 academic year: full-time: **91%**
Median grant amount: full-time: **$3,000**
The average law-school debt of those in the Class of 2007 who borrowed: **$83,338.** Proportion who borrowed: **87%**

ACADEMIC PROGRAMS

Calendar: **quarter**
Joint degrees awarded: **J.D./M.P.P.A.; J.D./M.B.A.; J.D./M.Tax**

Typical first-year section size: Full-time: **57**
Is there typically a "small section" of the first year class, other than Legal Writing, taught by full-time faculty?: Full-time: **yes**
Number of course titles, beyond the first year curriculum, offered last year: **85**
Percentages of upper division course sections, excluding seminars, with an enrollment of:

Under 25: **52%**	25 to 49: **32%**
50 to 74: **10%**	75 to 99: **5%**
100+: **1%**	

Areas of specialization: appellate advocacy, clinical training, dispute resolution, environmental law, healthcare law, intellectual property law, international law, tax law, trial advocacy

Fall 2007 faculty profile

Total teaching faculty: **50.** Full-time: **42%**; 81% men, 19% women, 5% minorities. Part-time: **58%**; 83% men, 17% women, 3% minorities
Student-to-faculty ratio: **16.6**

SPECIAL PROGRAMS (as provided by law school):

The Baylor curriculum is rigorous and unique. Baylor offers six areas of concentration (general civil litigation, business litigation, criminal practice, business transactions, estate planning, and administrative practice), three joint-degree programs (J.D./M.B.A., J.D./M.Tax, and J.D./M.P.P.A.), and a two-week summer program in Guadalajara, Mexico.

STUDENT BODY

Fall 2007 full-time enrollment: 411

Men: **60%**	Women: **40%**
African-American: **1.0%**	American Indian: **0.2%**
Asian-American: **5.4%**	Mexican-American: **3.2%**
Puerto Rican: **0.5%**	Other Hisp-Amer: **1.5%**
White: **88.3%**	International: **0.0%**
Unknown: **0.0%**	

Attrition rates for 2006-2007 full-time students

Percent of students discontinuing law school:

Men: **6%**   Women: **3%**
First-year students: **11%**   Second-year students: **N/A**
Third-year students: **1%**

LIBRARY RESOURCES
Total volumes: **232,766**
Total seats available for library users: **279**

INFORMATION TECHNOLOGY
Number of wired network connections available to students: **733** total (in the law library, excluding computer labs: **125**; in classrooms: **564**; in computer labs: **12**; elsewhere in the law school: **32**)
Law school has a wireless network.
Students are not required to own a computer.

EMPLOYMENT AND SALARIES
Proportion of 2006 graduates employed at graduation: **68%**
Employed 9 months later, as of February 15, 2007: **96%**
Salaries in the private sector (law firms, business, industry): **$60,000–$90,000** (25th-75th percentile)
Median salary in the private sector: **$75,000**
Percentage in the private sector who reported salary information: **80%**
Median salary in public service (government, judicial clerkships, academic posts, non-profits): **$49,000**

Percentage of 2006 graduates in:
Law firms: **61%**   Government: **16%**
Bus./industry: **14%**   Judicial clerkship: **7%**
Public interest: **1%**   Unknown: **0%**
Academia: **1%**

2006 graduates employed in-state: **86%**
2006 graduates employed in foreign countries: **0%**
Number of states where graduates are employed: **17**
Percentage of 2006 graduates working in: New England: **0%**, Middle Atlantic: **0%**, East North Central: **3%**, West North Central: **1%**, South Atlantic: **2%**, East South Central: **0%**, West South Central: **89%**, Mountain: **4%**, Pacific: **2%**, Unknown: **0%**

BAR PASSAGE RATES
Based on 2006 graduates taking Summer 2006 or Winter 2007 exams. Most of the school's first-time test takers took the bar in Texas.

99%
School's bar passage rate for first-time test takers

82%
Statewide bar passage rate for first-time test takers

Boston College

■ 885 Centre Street, Newton, MA, 02459-1154
■ http://www.bc.edu/lawschool
■ Private
■ Year founded: 1929
■ 2007-2008 tuition: full-time: $36,590; part-time: N/A
■ Enrollment 2007-08 academic year: full-time: 778; part-time: 5
■ U.S. News 2009 law specialty ranking: environmental law: 22, tax law: 25

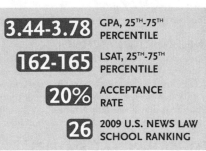

3.44-3.78	GPA, 25TH-75TH PERCENTILE
162-165	LSAT, 25TH-75TH PERCENTILE
20%	ACCEPTANCE RATE
26	2009 U.S. NEWS LAW SCHOOL RANKING

ADMISSIONS

Admissions phone number: **(617) 552-4351**
Admissions email address: **bclawadm@bc.edu**
Application website:
http://www.bc.edu/schools/law/admission
Application deadline for Fall 2009 admission: **03/01**

Admissions statistics:
Number of applicants for Fall 2007: **6,670**
Number of acceptances: **1,347**
Number enrolled: **269**
Acceptance rate: **20%**
GPA, 25th-75th percentile, entering class Fall 2007: **3.44-3.78**
LSAT, 25th-75th percentile, entering class Fall 2007: **162-165**

Part-time program:
Number of applicants for Fall 2007: **N/A**
Number of acceptances: **1**
Number enrolled: **1**
Acceptance rate: **N/A**
GPA, 25th-75th percentile, entering class Fall 2007: **N/A**
LSAT, 25th-75th percentile, entering class Fall 2007: **N/A**

FINANCIAL AID

Financial aid phone number: **(617) 552-4243**
Financial aid application deadline: **03/01**
Tuition 2007-2008 academic year: full-time: **$36,590**; part-time: **N/A**
Room and board: **$12,785**; books: **$1,000**; miscellaneous expenses: **$4,605**
Total of room/board/books/miscellaneous expenses: **$18,390**
University offers graduate student housing for which law students are eligible.

Financial aid profile
Percent of students that received grants for the 2006-2007 academic year: full-time: **57%**
Median grant amount: full-time: **$12,500**

The average law-school debt of those in the Class of 2007 who borrowed: **$80,497**. Proportion who borrowed: **90%**

ACADEMIC PROGRAMS

Calendar: **semester**
Joint degrees awarded: **J.D./M.B.A.; J.D./M.A. Education; J.D./M.S.W.; J.D./M.A.**
Typical first-year section size: Full-time: **84**
Is there typically a "small section" of the first year class, other than Legal Writing, taught by full-time faculty?: Full-time: **yes**
Number of course titles, beyond the first year curriculum, offered last year: **120**
Percentages of upper division course sections, excluding seminars, with an enrollment of:
Under 25: **65%**   25 to 49: **17%**
50 to 74: **10%**   75 to 99: **5%**
100+: **2%**
Areas of specialization: appellate advocacy, clinical training, dispute resolution, environmental law, healthcare law, intellectual property law, international law, tax law, trial advocacy

Fall 2007 faculty profile
Total teaching faculty: **136**. Full-time: **45%**; **49%** men, **51%** women, **15%** minorities. Part-time: **55%**; **75%** men, **25%** women, **11%** minorities
Student-to-faculty ratio: **12.6**

SPECIAL PROGRAMS *(as provided by law school)*:

Clinic/program subjects include: immigration, civil litigation, criminal justice, homelessness, juvenile rights, women and the law, attorney general, international criminal tribunal, London semester, semester in practice, judge and community courts, and judicial process. Also offered: dual-degree programs, cross-registration, and other studies abroad.

STUDENT BODY

Fall 2007 full-time enrollment: **778**
Men: **55%**   Women: **45%**
African-American: **4.5%**   American Indian: **0.4%**

Asian-American: **11.2%**
Puerto Rican: **0.8%**
White: **64.5%**
Unknown: **10.3%**

Mexican-American: **1.8%**
Other Hisp-Amer: **4.5%**
International: **2.1%**

Fall 2007 part-time enrollment: 5
Men: **60%**   Women: **40%**
African-American: **0.0%**   American Indian: **0.0%**
Asian-American: **0.0%**   Mexican-American: **0.0%**
Puerto Rican: **0.0%**   Other Hisp-Amer: **0.0%**
White: **100.0%**   International: **0.0%**
Unknown: **0.0%**

Attrition rates for 2006-2007 full-time students
Percent of students discontinuing law school:
Men: **2%**   Women: **3%**
First-year students: **7%**   Second-year students: **0%**
Third-year students: **N/A**

LIBRARY RESOURCES
Total volumes: **467,825**
Total seats available for library users: **653**

INFORMATION TECHNOLOGY
Number of wired network connections available to students: **1226** total (in the law library, excluding computer labs: **439**; in classrooms: **608**; in computer labs: **0**; elsewhere in the law school: **179**)
Law school has a wireless network.
Students are not required to own a computer.

EMPLOYMENT AND SALARIES
Proportion of 2006 graduates employed at graduation: **83%**
Employed 9 months later, as of February 15, 2007: **98%**
Salaries in the private sector (law firms, business, industry): **$125,000–$135,000** (25th-75th percentile)
Median salary in the private sector: **$135,000**

Percentage in the private sector who reported salary information: **79%**
Median salary in public service (government, judicial clerkships, academic posts, non-profits): **$47,018**

Percentage of 2006 graduates in:
Law firms: **65%**   Government: **9%**
Bus./industry: **6%**   Judicial clerkship: **14%**
Public interest: **5%**   Unknown: **0%**
Academia: **1%**

2006 graduates employed in-state: **51%**
2006 graduates employed in foreign countries: **1%**
Number of states where graduates are employed: **23**
Percentage of 2006 graduates working in: New England: **58%**, Middle Atlantic: **21%**, East North Central: **5%**, West North Central: **1%**, South Atlantic: **8%**, East South Central: **0%**, West South Central: **1%**, Mountain: **1%**, Pacific: **4%**, Unknown: **0%**

BAR PASSAGE RATES
Based on 2006 graduates taking Summer 2006 or Winter 2007 exams. Most of the school's first-time test takers took the bar in Massachusetts.

95%
School's bar passage rate for first-time test takers

86%
Statewide bar passage rate for first-time test takers

Boston University

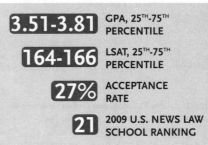

- 765 Commonwealth Avenue, Boston, MA, 02215
- http://www.bu.edu/law/
- Private
- Year founded: 1872
- 2007-2008 tuition: full-time: $36,806; part-time: N/A
- Enrollment 2007-08 academic year: full-time: 815; part-time: 19
- U.S. News 2009 law specialty ranking: healthcare law: 7, intellectual property law: 9, tax law: 8

3.51-3.81 GPA, 25TH-75TH PERCENTILE

164-166 LSAT, 25TH-75TH PERCENTILE

27% ACCEPTANCE RATE

21 2009 U.S. NEWS LAW SCHOOL RANKING

ADMISSIONS
Admissions phone number: **(617) 353-3100**
Admissions email address: **bulawadm@bu.edu**
Application website:
  http://www.bu.edu/law/prospective/apply
Application deadline for Fall 2009 admission: **03/01**

Admissions statistics:
Number of applicants for Fall 2007: **5,933**
Number of acceptances: **1,588**
Number enrolled: **278**
Acceptance rate: **27%**
GPA, 25th-75th percentile, entering class Fall 2007: **3.51-3.81**
LSAT, 25th-75th percentile, entering class Fall 2007: **164-166**

FINANCIAL AID
Financial aid phone number: **(617) 353-3160**
Financial aid application deadline: **03/01**
Tuition 2007-2008 academic year: full-time: **$36,806**; part-time: **N/A**
Room and board: **$11,305**; books: **$1,254**; miscellaneous expenses: **$4,500**
Total of room/board/books/miscellaneous expenses: **$17,059**
University offers graduate student housing for which law students are eligible.

Financial aid profile
Percent of students that received grants for the 2006-2007 academic year: full-time: **57%**
Median grant amount: full-time: **$15,000**
The average law-school debt of those in the Class of 2007 who borrowed: **$89,198**. Proportion who borrowed: **84%**

ACADEMIC PROGRAMS
Calendar: **semester**
Joint degrees awarded: **J.D./M.S.W.; J.D./M.B.A.; J.D./M.P.H.; J.D./M.S.; J.D./M.A.; J.D./LL.M.**
Typical first-year section size: Full-time: **89**

Is there typically a "small section" of the first year class, other than Legal Writing, taught by full-time faculty?: Full-time: **yes**
Number of course titles, beyond the first year curriculum, offered last year: **172**
Percentages of upper division course sections, excluding seminars, with an enrollment of:
  Under 25: **54%**   25 to 49: **24%**
  50 to 74: **11%**   75 to 99: **8%**
  100+: **3%**
Areas of specialization: appellate advocacy, clinical training, dispute resolution, environmental law, healthcare law, intellectual property law, international law, tax law, trial advocacy

Fall 2007 faculty profile
Total teaching faculty: **180**. Full-time: **32%**; **69%** men, **31%** women, **9%** minorities. Part-time: **68%**; **75%** men, **25%** women, **9%** minorities
Student-to-faculty ratio: **12.3**

SPECIAL PROGRAMS *(as provided by law school):*
The school offers three clinical programs (civil, criminal, and legislative) and three internship/externship programs. There are 12 academic-year programs that allow students to study abroad at leading universities in Oxford, Paris, Florence, Hong Kong, Buenos Aires, Tel Aviv, Leiden, Lyon, Hamburg, Beijing, Madrid, and Singapore.

STUDENT BODY
Fall 2007 full-time enrollment: 815
Men: **51%**	Women: **49%**
African-American: **3.6%**	American Indian: **0.4%**
Asian-American: **12.0%**	Mexican-American: **0.7%**
Puerto Rican: **0.4%**	Other Hisp-Amer: **2.1%**
White: **77.3%**	International: **3.6%**
Unknown: **0.0%**	

Fall 2007 part-time enrollment: 19
Men: **47%**	Women: **53%**
African-American: **0.0%**	American Indian: **0.0%**

Asian-American: 15.8% Mexican-American: 0.0%
Puerto Rican: 0.0% Other Hisp-Amer: 0.0%
White: 84.2% International: 0.0%
Unknown: 0.0%

Attrition rates for 2006-2007 full-time students
Percent of students discontinuing law school:
Men: 2% Women: 2%
First-year students: 4% Second-year students: 1%
Third-year students: N/A

LIBRARY RESOURCES
Total volumes: 646,119
Total seats available for library users: 634

INFORMATION TECHNOLOGY
Number of wired network connections available to students: 25 total (in the law library, excluding computer labs: 0; in classrooms: 0; in computer labs: 0; elsewhere in the law school: 25)
Law school has a wireless network.
Students are not required to own a computer.

EMPLOYMENT AND SALARIES
Proportion of 2006 graduates employed at graduation: 96%
Employed 9 months later, as of February 15, 2007: 99%
Salaries in the private sector (law firms, business, industry): $95,000–$135,000 (25th-75th percentile)
Median salary in the private sector: $135,000
Percentage in the private sector who reported salary information: 61%
Median salary in public service (government, judicial clerkships, academic posts, non-profits): $46,500

Percentage of 2006 graduates in:
Law firms: 61% Government: 6%
Bus./industry: 8% Judicial clerkship: 9%
Public interest: 3% Unknown: 12%
Academia: 1%

2006 graduates employed in-state: 37%
2006 graduates employed in foreign countries: 1%
Number of states where graduates are employed: 28
Percentage of 2006 graduates working in: New England: 43%, Middle Atlantic: 23%, East North Central: 3%, West North Central: 1%, South Atlantic: 7%, East South Central: 1%, West South Central: 2%, Mountain: 3%, Pacific: 12%, Unknown: 5%

BAR PASSAGE RATES
Based on 2006 graduates taking Summer 2006 or Winter 2007 exams. Most of the school's first-time test takers took the bar in Massachusetts.

95%
School's bar passage rate for first-time test takers

86%
Statewide bar passage rate for first-time test takers

Brigham Young University (Clark)

- 340 JRCB, Provo, UT, 84602-8000
- http://www.law.byu.edu
- Private
- **Year founded:** 1972
- **2007-2008 tuition:** full-time: $8,700; part-time: N/A
- **Enrollment 2007-08 academic year:** full-time: 457
- **U.S. News 2009 law specialty ranking:** N/A

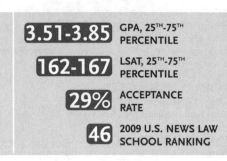

3.51-3.85 GPA, 25ᵀᴴ-75ᵀᴴ PERCENTILE

162-167 LSAT, 25ᵀᴴ-75ᵀᴴ PERCENTILE

29% ACCEPTANCE RATE

46 2009 U.S. NEWS LAW SCHOOL RANKING

ADMISSIONS
Admissions phone number: **(801) 422-4277**
Admissions email address: **kucharg@lawgate.byu.edu**
Application website:
http://www.law2.byu.edu/Admissions/application_form.htm
Application deadline for Fall 2009 admission: **03/01**

Admissions statistics:
Number of applicants for Fall 2007: **859**
Number of acceptances: **246**
Number enrolled: **146**
Acceptance rate: **29%**
GPA, 25th-75th percentile, entering class Fall 2007: **3.51-3.85**
LSAT, 25th-75th percentile, entering class Fall 2007: **162-167**

FINANCIAL AID
Financial aid phone number: **(801) 422-6386**
Financial aid application deadline:
Tuition 2007-2008 academic year: full-time: **$8,700**; part-time: **N/A**
Room and board: **$6,460**; books: **$1,760**; miscellaneous expenses: **$3,888**
Total of room/board/books/miscellaneous expenses: **$12,108**
University offers graduate student housing for which law students are eligible.

Financial aid profile
Percent of students that received grants for the 2006-2007 academic year: full-time: **43%**
Median grant amount: full-time: **$2,500**
The average law-school debt of those in the Class of 2007 who borrowed: **$44,128**. Proportion who borrowed: **86%**

ACADEMIC PROGRAMS
Calendar: **semester**
Joint degrees awarded: **J.D./M.B.A.; J.D./M.A.C.C.; J.D./M.A. Education; J.D./M.P.A.**

Typical first-year section size: Full-time: **104**
Is there typically a "small section" of the first year class, other than Legal Writing, taught by full-time faculty?: Full-time: **yes**
Number of course titles, beyond the first year curriculum, offered last year: **100**
Percentages of upper division course sections, excluding seminars, with an enrollment of:
Under 25: **44%**   25 to 49: **39%**
50 to 74: **11%**   75 to 99: **5%**
100+: **1%**
Areas of specialization: appellate advocacy, clinical training, dispute resolution, environmental law, healthcare law, intellectual property law, international law, tax law, trial advocacy

Fall 2007 faculty profile
Total teaching faculty: **54**. Full-time: **37%**; **90%** men, **10%** women, **15%** minorities. Part-time: **63%**; **65%** men, **35%** women, **3%** minorities
Student-to-faculty ratio: **18.9**

SPECIAL PROGRAMS *(as provided by law school):*
The Law and Religion Center works with scholars, government leaders, and nongovernmental organizations in promoting religious liberty. The World Family Policy Center provides opportunities to promote the natural family as the fundamental unit of society in national and international policy. Summer externships provide over 150 students per class with legal experience following their first year.

STUDENT BODY
Fall 2007 full-time enrollment: 457
Men: **66%**   Women: **34%**
African-American: **1.3%**   American Indian: **1.8%**
Asian-American: **7.2%**   Mexican-American: **0.9%**
Puerto Rican: **0.2%**   Other Hisp-Amer: **5.7%**
White: **80.3%**   International: **0.9%**
Unknown: **1.8%**

Attrition rates for 2006-2007 full-time students
Percent of students discontinuing law school:
Men: 1%   Women: 1%
First-year students: 1%   Second-year students: 2%
Third-year students: 1%

LIBRARY RESOURCES
Total volumes: 496,897
Total seats available for library users: 906

INFORMATION TECHNOLOGY
Number of wired network connections available to students: 533 total (in the law library, excluding computer labs: 505; in classrooms: 28; in computer labs: 0; elsewhere in the law school: 0)
Law school has a wireless network.
Students are required to own a computer.

EMPLOYMENT AND SALARIES
Proportion of 2006 graduates employed at graduation: 75%
Employed 9 months later, as of February 15, 2007: 91%
Salaries in the private sector (law firms, business, industry): $70,000–$110,000 (25th-75th percentile)
Median salary in the private sector: $92,500
Percentage in the private sector who reported salary information: 49%
Median salary in public service (government, judicial clerkships, academic posts, non-profits): $46,440

Percentage of 2006 graduates in:
Law firms: 57%   Government: 11%
Bus./industry: 17%   Judicial clerkship: 13%
Public interest: 1%   Unknown: 0%
Academia: 1%

2006 graduates employed in-state: 43%
2006 graduates employed in foreign countries: 1%
Number of states where graduates are employed: 26
Percentage of 2006 graduates working in: New England: 1%, Middle Atlantic: 3%, East North Central: 3%, West North Central: 1%, South Atlantic: 6%, East South Central: 2%, West South Central: 6%, Mountain: 60%, Pacific: 18%, Unknown: 0%

BAR PASSAGE RATES
Based on 2006 graduates taking Summer 2006 or Winter 2007 exams. Most of the school's first-time test takers took the bar in Utah.

| 96% |

School's bar passage rate for first-time test takers

| 87% |

Statewide bar passage rate for first-time test takers

Brooklyn Law School

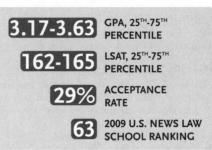

- 250 Joralemon Street, Brooklyn, NY, 11201
- http://www.brooklaw.edu
- Private
- **Year founded:** 1901
- **2007-2008 tuition:** full-time: $39,625; part-time: $29,807
- **Enrollment 2007-08 academic year:** full-time: 1,186; part-time: 310
- **U.S. News 2009 law specialty ranking:** clinical training: 28

3.17-3.63 GPA, 25TH-75TH PERCENTILE

162-165 LSAT, 25TH-75TH PERCENTILE

29% ACCEPTANCE RATE

63 2009 U.S. NEWS LAW SCHOOL RANKING

ADMISSIONS

Admissions phone number: **(718) 780-7906**
Admissions email address: **admitq@brooklaw.edu**
Application website: **http://www.brooklaw.edu/
  admissions/howto/materials.php**
Application deadline for Fall 2009 admission: **rolling**

Admissions statistics:
Number of applicants for Fall 2007: **4,037**
Number of acceptances: **1,188**
Number enrolled: **307**
Acceptance rate: **29%**
GPA, 25th-75th percentile, entering class Fall 2007: **3.17-
  3.63**
LSAT, 25th-75th percentile, entering class Fall 2007: **162-
  165**

FINANCIAL AID

Financial aid phone number: **(718) 780-7915**
Financial aid application deadline: **N/A**
Tuition 2007-2008 academic year: full-time: **$39,625**; part-
  time: **$29,807**
Room and board: **$15,725**; books: **$1,100**; miscellaneous
  expenses: **$3,741**
Total of room/board/books/miscellaneous expenses:
  $20,566
University does not offer graduate student housing for
  which law students are eligible.

Financial aid profile
Percent of students that received grants for the 2006-2007
  academic year: full-time: **71%**; part-time **28%**
Median grant amount: full-time: **$15,860**; part-time:
  $11,985
The average law-school debt of those in the Class of 2007
  who borrowed: **$92,447**. Proportion who borrowed: **79%**

ACADEMIC PROGRAMS

Calendar: **semester**
Joint degrees awarded: **J.D./M.A. Political Science;
  J.D./M.B.A.; J.D./M.S. Library & Information Science;**
J.D./M.S. City & Regional Planning; J.D./M.U.P.
Typical first-year section size: Full-time: **51**; Part-time: **41**
Is there typically a "small section" of the first year class,
  other than Legal Writing, taught by full-time faculty?:
  Full-time: **yes**; Part-time: **no**
Number of course titles, beyond the first year curriculum,
  offered last year: **169**
Percentages of upper division course sections, excluding
  seminars, with an enrollment of:
  Under 25: **59%**   25 to 49: **21%**
  50 to 74: **10%**   75 to 99: **4%**
  100+: **7%**
Areas of specialization: appellate advocacy, clinical training,
  dispute resolution, environmental law, healthcare law,
  intellectual property law, international law, tax law, trial
  advocacy

Fall 2007 faculty profile
Total teaching faculty: **205**. Full-time: **37%**; **51%** men, **49%**
  women, **9%** minorities. Part-time: **63%**; **70%** men, **30%**
  women, **7%** minorities
Student-to-faculty ratio: **19.9**

SPECIAL PROGRAMS *(as provided by law school):*
Clinics ranked 29th in the nation in criminal justice, individual
client and group/business representation, and dispute resolution. Fellowships: international business, public interest,
human rights, and bankruptcy. Centers: international business
law; health, science, and public policy; law, language, and cogni-
tion. Legal writing program ranks 14th in nation. Study abroad:
China, Italy, Germany.

STUDENT BODY
Fall 2007 full-time enrollment: **1,186**
Men: **53%**   Women: **47%**
African-American: **5.0%**   American Indian: **0.3%**
Asian-American: **15.8%**   Mexican-American: **1.0%**
Puerto Rican: **1.6%**   Other Hisp-Amer: **3.7%**
White: **70.5%**   International: **0.8%**
Unknown: **1.4%**

Fall 2007 part-time enrollment: 310

Men: 49%	Women: 51%
African-American: 11.0%	American Indian: 0.0%
Asian-American: 12.6%	Mexican-American: 0.0%
Puerto Rican: 1.0%	Other Hisp-Amer: 3.9%
White: 69.4%	International: 0.6%
Unknown: 1.6%	

Attrition rates for 2006-2007 full-time students
Percent of students discontinuing law school:

Men: 2%	Women: 1%
First-year students: 5%	Second-year students: 0%
Third-year students: N/A	

LIBRARY RESOURCES
Total volumes: 559,441
Total seats available for library users: 665

INFORMATION TECHNOLOGY
Number of wired network connections available to students: 1,984 total (in the law library, excluding computer labs: 216; in classrooms: 1,584; in computer labs: 110; elsewhere in the law school: 74)
Law school has a wireless network.
Students are not required to own a computer.

EMPLOYMENT AND SALARIES
Proportion of 2006 graduates employed at graduation: 67%
Employed 9 months later, as of February 15, 2007: 97%
Salaries in the private sector (law firms, business, industry): $65,000–$145,000 (25th-75th percentile)
Median salary in the private sector: $104,000
Percentage in the private sector who reported salary information: 58%

Median salary in public service (government, judicial clerkships, academic posts, non-profits): $50,000

Percentage of 2006 graduates in:

Law firms: 56%	Government: 15%
Bus./industry: 19%	Judicial clerkship: 5%
Public interest: 4%	Unknown: 1%
Academia: 0%	

2006 graduates employed in-state: 90%
2006 graduates employed in foreign countries: 1%
Number of states where graduates are employed: 14
Percentage of 2006 graduates working in: New England: 2%, Middle Atlantic: 92%, East North Central: 0%, West North Central: 0%, South Atlantic: 2%, East South Central: 0%, West South Central: 0%, Mountain: 0%, Pacific: 3%, Unknown: 0%

BAR PASSAGE RATES
Based on 2006 graduates taking Summer 2006 or Winter 2007 exams. Most of the school's first-time test takers took the bar in New York.

85%
School's bar passage rate for first-time test takers

77%
Statewide bar passage rate for first-time test takers

California Western School of Law

■ 225 Cedar Street, San Diego, CA, 92101-3090
■ http://www.cwsl.edu
■ Private
■ Year founded: 1924
■ 2007-2008 tuition: full-time: $34,300; part-time: $24,220
■ Enrollment 2007-08 academic year: full-time: 755; part-time: 92
■ U.S. News 2009 law specialty ranking: N/A

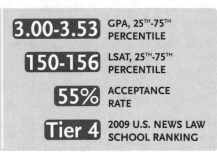

3.00-3.53 GPA, 25TH-75TH PERCENTILE

150-156 LSAT, 25TH-75TH PERCENTILE

55% ACCEPTANCE RATE

Tier 4 2009 U.S. NEWS LAW SCHOOL RANKING

ADMISSIONS

Admissions phone number: **(619) 525-1401**
Admissions email address: **admissions@cwsl.edu**
Application website:
**http://www.cwsl.edu/main/default.asp?nav=
admissions.asp&body=admissions/application.asp**
Application deadline for Fall 2009 admission: **04/01**

Admissions statistics:
Number of applicants for Fall 2007: **2,459**
Number of acceptances: **1,350**
Number enrolled: **363**
Acceptance rate: **55%**
GPA, 25th-75th percentile, entering class Fall 2007: **3.00-3.53**
LSAT, 25th-75th percentile, entering class Fall 2007: **150-156**

Part-time program:
Number of applicants for Fall 2007: **210**
Number of acceptances: **79**
Number enrolled: **28**
Acceptance rate: **38%**
GPA, 25th-75th percentile, entering class Fall 2007: **3.25-3.60**
LSAT, 25th-75th percentile, entering class Fall 2007: **149-154**

FINANCIAL AID

Financial aid phone number: **(619) 525-7060**
Financial aid application deadline: **04/01**
Tuition 2007-2008 academic year: full-time: **$34,300**; part-time: **$24,220**
Room and board: **$10,800**; books: **$1,088**; miscellaneous expenses: **$8,194**
Total of room/board/books/miscellaneous expenses: **$20,082**
University does not offer graduate student housing for which law students are eligible.

Financial aid profile
Percent of students that received grants for the 2006-2007 academic year: full-time: **34%**; part-time **41%**
Median grant amount: full-time: **$16,140**; part-time: **$8,550**
The average law-school debt of those in the Class of 2007 who borrowed: **$104,338**. Proportion who borrowed: **86%**

ACADEMIC PROGRAMS

Calendar: **semester**
Joint degrees awarded: **J.D./M.S.W.; J.D./Ph.D. History; J.D./M.B.A.; J.D./Ph.D. Political Science**
Typical first-year section size: Full-time: **80**
Is there typically a "small section" of the first year class, other than Legal Writing, taught by full-time faculty?: Full-time: **no**; Part-time: **no**
Number of course titles, beyond the first year curriculum, offered last year: **94**
Percentages of upper division course sections, excluding seminars, with an enrollment of:

Under 25: **61%**	25 to 49: **20%**
50 to 74: **10%**	75 to 99: **5%**
100+: **3%**	

Areas of specialization: appellate advocacy, clinical training, dispute resolution, environmental law, healthcare law, intellectual property law, international law, tax law, trial advocacy

Fall 2007 faculty profile
Total teaching faculty: **59**. Full-time: **63%**; 70% men, 30% women, 16% minorities. Part-time: **37%**; 68% men, 32% women, 5% minorities
Student-to-faculty ratio: **17.7**

SPECIAL PROGRAMS *(as provided by law school):*
Special programs include the Bail Project, California Innocence Project, Street Law and Community Law Project. Areas of concentration are health, international, intellectual property, family, and employment law. Students participate in study abroad programs, dual-degree programs with University of California–San Diego and San Diego State University, and a variety of clinical internships.

STUDENT BODY

Fall 2007 full-time enrollment: 755

Men: 48%	Women: 52%
African-American: 2.5%	American Indian: 0.9%
Asian-American: 14.8%	Mexican-American: 6.5%
Puerto Rican: 0.5%	Other Hisp-Amer: 3.0%
White: 57.5%	International: 0.9%
Unknown: 13.2%	

Fall 2007 part-time enrollment: 92

Men: 41%	Women: 59%
African-American: 5.4%	American Indian: 0.0%
Asian-American: 4.3%	Mexican-American: 13.0%
Puerto Rican: 0.0%	Other Hisp-Amer: 2.2%
White: 57.6%	International: 0.0%
Unknown: 17.4%	

Attrition rates for 2006-2007 full-time students
Percent of students discontinuing law school:

Men: 15%	Women: 13%
First-year students: 30%	Second-year students: 5%
Third-year students: 2%	

LIBRARY RESOURCES

Total volumes: 334,867
Total seats available for library users: 533

INFORMATION TECHNOLOGY

Number of wired network connections available to students: 566 total (in the law library, excluding computer labs: 355; in classrooms: 122; in computer labs: 9; elsewhere in the law school: 80)
Law school has a wireless network.
Students are not required to own a computer.

EMPLOYMENT AND SALARIES

Proportion of 2006 graduates employed at graduation: N/A

Employed 9 months later, as of February 15, 2007: 84%
Salaries in the private sector (law firms, business, industry): $60,000–$70,000 (25th-75th percentile)
Median salary in the private sector: $65,000
Percentage in the private sector who reported salary information: 58%
Median salary in public service (government, judicial clerkships, academic posts, non-profits): $54,900

Percentage of 2006 graduates in:

Law firms: 63%	Government: 10%
Bus./industry: 15%	Judicial clerkship: 5%
Public interest: 5%	Unknown: 0%
Academia: 2%	

2006 graduates employed in-state: 74%
2006 graduates employed in foreign countries: 1%
Number of states where graduates are employed: 21
Percentage of 2006 graduates working in: New England: 3%, Middle Atlantic: 4%, East North Central: 2%, West North Central: 1%, South Atlantic: 2%, East South Central: 0%, West South Central: 1%, Mountain: 10%, Pacific: 76%, Unknown: 0%

BAR PASSAGE RATES

Based on 2006 graduates taking Summer 2006 or Winter 2007 exams. Most of the school's first-time test takers took the bar in California.

68%
School's bar passage rate for first-time test takers

65%
Statewide bar passage rate for first-time test takers

Campbell University (Wiggins)

- PO Box 158, Buies Creek, NC, 27506
- http://www.law.campbell.edu
- Private
- **Year founded:** 1976
- **2007-2008 tuition:** full-time: $26,800; part-time: N/A
- **Enrollment 2007-08 academic year:** full-time: 339
- **U.S. News 2009 law specialty ranking:** N/A

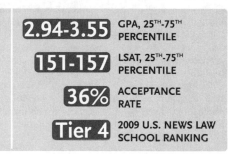

2.94-3.55 GPA, 25TH-75TH PERCENTILE

151-157 LSAT, 25TH-75TH PERCENTILE

36% ACCEPTANCE RATE

Tier 4 2009 U.S. NEWS LAW SCHOOL RANKING

ADMISSIONS

Admissions phone number: **(910) 893-1754**
Admissions email address: **admissions@law.campbell.edu**
Application website: **http://www.applyweb.com/apply /camplaw/index.html**
Application deadline for Fall 2009 admission: **05/05**

Admissions statistics:

Number of applicants for Fall 2007: **1,116**
Number of acceptances: **404**
Number enrolled: **129**
Acceptance rate: **36%**
GPA, 25th-75th percentile, entering class Fall 2007: **2.94-3.55**
LSAT, 25th-75th percentile, entering class Fall 2007: **151-157**

FINANCIAL AID

Financial aid phone number: **(910) 893-1310**
Financial aid application deadline: **N/A**
Tuition 2007-2008 academic year: full-time: **$26,800**; part-time: **N/A**
Room and board: **$8,922**; books: **$1,400**; miscellaneous expenses: **$2,500**
Total of room/board/books/miscellaneous expenses: **$12,822**
University offers graduate student housing for which law students are eligible.

Financial aid profile

Percent of students that received grants for the 2006-2007 academic year: full-time: **52%**
Median grant amount: full-time: **$6,600**
The average law-school debt of those in the Class of 2007 who borrowed: **$89,500**. Proportion who borrowed: **94%**

ACADEMIC PROGRAMS

Calendar: **semester**
Joint degrees awarded: **J.D./M.B.A.; J.D./M.T.I.M.**
Typical first-year section size: Full-time: **80**
Is there typically a "small section" of the first year class, other than Legal Writing, taught by full-time faculty?:
Full-time: **yes**
Number of course titles, beyond the first year curriculum, offered last year: **67**
Percentages of upper division course sections, excluding seminars, with an enrollment of:
Under 25: **51%**   25 to 49: **31%**
50 to 74: **4%**   75 to 99: **7%**
100+: **7%**
Areas of specialization: appellate advocacy, clinical training, dispute resolution, environmental law, healthcare law, intellectual property law, international law, tax law, trial advocacy

Fall 2007 faculty profile

Total teaching faculty: **40**. Full-time: **43%**; **82%** men, **18%** women, **12%** minorities. Part-time: **58%**; **87%** men, **13%** women, **4%** minorities
Student-to-faculty ratio: **16.5**

SPECIAL PROGRAMS (as provided by law school):

The Juvenile Justice Project exposes students to both the theoretical and the practical aspects of the mediation process in the context of restorative justice. The Korean cooperative summer program is a cooperative program with Handong International Law School, which allows Campbell students to attend summer school at Handong International Law School in South Korea.

STUDENT BODY

Fall 2007 full-time enrollment: 339
Men: **54%**   Women: **46%**
African-American: **2.9%**   American Indian: **0.6%**
Asian-American: **1.5%**   Mexican-American: **0.9%**
Puerto Rican: **0.0%**   Other Hisp-Amer: **1.5%**
White: **92.6%**   International: **0.0%**
Unknown: **0.0%**

Attrition rates for 2006-2007 full-time students

Percent of students discontinuing law school:
Men: **6%**   Women: **10%**
First-year students: **21%**   Second-year students: **N/A**
Third-year students: **N/A**

LIBRARY RESOURCES

Total volumes: **191,519**
Total seats available for library users: **429**

INFORMATION TECHNOLOGY

Number of wired network connections available to students: **150** total (in the law library, excluding computer labs: **150**; in classrooms: **0**; in computer labs: **0**; elsewhere in the law school: **0**)
Law school has a wireless network.
Students are not required to own a computer.

EMPLOYMENT AND SALARIES

Proportion of 2006 graduates employed at graduation: **63%**
Employed 9 months later, as of February 15, 2007: **94%**
Salaries in the private sector (law firms, business, industry): **$48,000–$75,000** (25th-75th percentile)
Median salary in the private sector: **$55,000**
Percentage in the private sector who reported salary information: **77%**
Median salary in public service (government, judicial clerkships, academic posts, non-profits): **N/A**

Percentage of 2006 graduates in:

Law firms: **69%**
Bus./industry: **9%**
Public interest: **5%**
Academia: **0%**

Government: **12%**
Judicial clerkship: **5%**
Unknown: **0%**

2006 graduates employed in-state: **86%**
2006 graduates employed in foreign countries: **0%**
Number of states where graduates are employed: **8**
Percentage of 2006 graduates working in: New England: **N/A**, Middle Atlantic: **N/A**, East North Central: **1%**, West North Central: **N/A**, South Atlantic: **98%**, East South Central: **N/A**, West South Central: **N/A**, Mountain: **N/A**, Pacific: **1%**, Unknown: **0%**

BAR PASSAGE RATES

Based on 2006 graduates taking Summer 2006 or Winter 2007 exams. Most of the school's first-time test takers took the bar in North Carolina.

97%
School's bar passage rate for first-time test takers

74%
Statewide bar passage rate for first-time test takers

Capital University

- 303 E. Broad Street, Columbus, OH, 43215-3200
- http://www.law.capital.edu
- Private
- Year founded: 1903
- 2007-2008 tuition: full-time: $975/credit hour; part-time: $975/credit hour
- Enrollment 2007-08 academic year: full-time: 459; part-time: 216
- U.S. News 2009 law specialty ranking: N/A

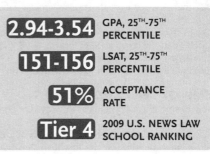

2.94-3.54 GPA, 25TH-75TH PERCENTILE

151-156 LSAT, 25TH-75TH PERCENTILE

51% ACCEPTANCE RATE

Tier 4 2009 U.S. NEWS LAW SCHOOL RANKING

ADMISSIONS

Admissions phone number: **(614) 236-6310**
Admissions email address: **admissions@law.capital.edu**
Application website:
https://secure.law.capital.edu/application/
Application deadline for Fall 2009 admission: **rolling**

Admissions statistics:
Number of applicants for Fall 2007: **1,056**
Number of acceptances: **541**
Number enrolled: **176**
Acceptance rate: **51%**
GPA, 25th-75th percentile, entering class Fall 2007: **2.94-3.54**
LSAT, 25th-75th percentile, entering class Fall 2007: **151-156**

Part-time program:
Number of applicants for Fall 2007: **242**
Number of acceptances: **101**
Number enrolled: **61**
Acceptance rate: **42%**
GPA, 25th-75th percentile, entering class Fall 2007: **2.75-3.50**
LSAT, 25th-75th percentile, entering class Fall 2007: **150-155**

FINANCIAL AID

Financial aid phone number: **(614) 236-6350**
Financial aid application deadline: **N/A**
Tuition 2007-2008 academic year: full-time: **$975/credit hour**; part-time: **$975/credit hour**
Room and board: **$11,558**; books: **$1,350**; miscellaneous expenses: **$567**
Total of room/board/books/miscellaneous expenses: **$13,475**
University does not offer graduate student housing for which law students are eligible.

Financial aid profile
Percent of students that received grants for the 2006-2007 academic year: full-time: **58%**; part-time **34%**

Median grant amount: full-time: **$11,000**; part-time: **$5,000**
The average law-school debt of those in the Class of 2007 who borrowed: **$74,598**. Proportion who borrowed: **90%**

ACADEMIC PROGRAMS

Calendar: **semester**
Joint degrees awarded: **J.D./LL.M. Business; J.D./LL.M. Tax; J.D./LL.M. Tax & Business; J.D./M.B.A.; J.D./M.T.S.; J.D./M.S.A.; J.D./M.S.N.**
Typical first-year section size: Full-time: **85**; Part-time: **70**
Is there typically a "small section" of the first year class, other than Legal Writing, taught by full-time faculty?: Full-time: **yes**; Part-time: **yes**
Number of course titles, beyond the first year curriculum, offered last year: **168**
Percentages of upper division course sections, excluding seminars, with an enrollment of:

Under 25: **65%**	25 to 49: **15%**
50 to 74: **15%**	75 to 99: **5%**
100+: **0%**	

Areas of specialization: appellate advocacy, clinical training, dispute resolution, environmental law, healthcare law, intellectual property law, international law, tax law, trial advocacy

Fall 2007 faculty profile
Total teaching faculty: **58**. Full-time: **45%**; **69%** men, **31%** women, **12%** minorities. Part-time: **55%**; **81%** men, **19%** women, **9%** minorities
Student-to-faculty ratio: **16.2**

SPECIAL PROGRAMS *(as provided by law school):*
Concentrations in governmental affairs, labor/employment, small-business entities, publicly held companies, dispute resolution, environmental law, family law. Joint degrees in Tax, Business, Nursing, Sports Administration, Theological Studies. National Center for Adoption Law and Policy; Tobacco Public Policy Center. Externships, legal and family advocacy clinics, legal research/writing program.

STUDENT BODY

Fall 2007 full-time enrollment: 459

Men: 55% Women: 45%
African-American: 7.0% American Indian: 0.9%
Asian-American: 1.5% Mexican-American: 0.0%
Puerto Rican: 0.0% Other Hisp-Amer: 1.3%
White: 77.8% International: 0.4%
Unknown: 11.1%

Fall 2007 part-time enrollment: 216

Men: 59% Women: 41%
African-American: 9.3% American Indian: 0.0%
Asian-American: 3.2% Mexican-American: 0.0%
Puerto Rican: 0.0% Other Hisp-Amer: 1.4%
White: 75.9% International: 0.0%
Unknown: 10.2%

Attrition rates for 2006-2007 full-time students

Percent of students discontinuing law school:
Men: 8% Women: 10%
First-year students: 23% Second-year students: 2%
Third-year students: 1%

LIBRARY RESOURCES

Total volumes: 258,223
Total seats available for library users: 460

INFORMATION TECHNOLOGY

Number of wired network connections available to students: 664 total (in the law library, excluding computer labs: 467; in classrooms: 186; in computer labs: 2; elsewhere in the law school: 9)
Law school has a wireless network.
Students are not required to own a computer.

EMPLOYMENT AND SALARIES

Proportion of 2006 graduates employed at graduation: N/A
Employed 9 months later, as of February 15, 2007: 82%

Salaries in the private sector (law firms, business, industry): $50,000–$85,000 (25th-75th percentile)
Median salary in the private sector: $65,000
Percentage in the private sector who reported salary information: 43%
Median salary in public service (government, judicial clerkships, academic posts, non-profits): $42,000

Percentage of 2006 graduates in:

Law firms: 47% Government: 21%
Bus./industry: 19% Judicial clerkship: 3%
Public interest: 6% Unknown: 0%
Academia: 4%

2006 graduates employed in-state: 88%
2006 graduates employed in foreign countries: 1%
Number of states where graduates are employed: 13
Percentage of 2006 graduates working in: New England: 0%, Middle Atlantic: 1%, East North Central: 90%, West North Central: 0%, South Atlantic: 4%, East South Central: 1%, West South Central: 0%, Mountain: 3%, Pacific: 0%, Unknown: 0%

BAR PASSAGE RATES

Based on 2006 graduates taking Summer 2006 or Winter 2007 exams. Most of the school's first-time test takers took the bar in Ohio.

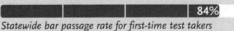

84%
School's bar passage rate for first-time test takers

84%
Statewide bar passage rate for first-time test takers

Case Western Reserve University

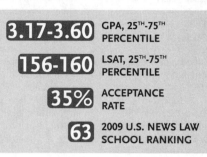

- 11075 E. Boulevard, Cleveland, OH, 44106-7148
- http://www.law.case.edu
- Private
- Year founded: 1892
- 2007-2008 tuition: full-time: $35,220; part-time: $1,446/credit hour
- Enrollment 2007-08 academic year: full-time: 678; part-time: 24
- U.S. News 2009 law specialty ranking: healthcare law: 4, international law: 16

3.17-3.60 GPA, 25TH-75TH PERCENTILE

156-160 LSAT, 25TH-75TH PERCENTILE

35% ACCEPTANCE RATE

63 2009 U.S. NEWS LAW SCHOOL RANKING

ADMISSIONS

Admissions phone number: **(800) 756-0036**
Admissions email address: **lawadmissions@case.edu**
Application website: **http://www.law.case.edu/admissions/**
Application deadline for Fall 2009 admission: **04/01**

Admissions statistics:
Number of applicants for Fall 2007: **2,298**
Number of acceptances: **800**
Number enrolled: **225**
Acceptance rate: **35%**
GPA, 25th-75th percentile, entering class Fall 2007: **3.17-3.60**
LSAT, 25th-75th percentile, entering class Fall 2007: **156-160**

Part-time program:
Number of applicants for Fall 2007: **32**
Number of acceptances: **32**
Number enrolled: **23**
Acceptance rate: **100%**
GPA, 25th-75th percentile, entering class Fall 2007: **2.99-3.43**
LSAT, 25th-75th percentile, entering class Fall 2007: **154-156**

FINANCIAL AID

Financial aid phone number: **(877) 889-4279**
Financial aid application deadline: **05/01**
Tuition 2007-2008 academic year: full-time: **$35,220**; part-time: **$1,446/credit hour**
Room and board: **$14,120**; books: **$1,275**; miscellaneous expenses: **$1,240**
Total of room/board/books/miscellaneous expenses: **$16,635**
University does not offer graduate student housing for which law students are eligible.

Financial aid profile
Percent of students that received grants for the 2006-2007

academic year: full-time: **46%**
Median grant amount: full-time: **$11,000**
The average law-school debt of those in the Class of 2007 who borrowed: **$83,730**. Proportion who borrowed: **87%**

ACADEMIC PROGRAMS

Calendar: **semester**
Joint degrees awarded: **J.D./M.B.A.; J.D./M.S.S.A. Social Work; J.D./M.P.H. Public Health; J.D./M.N.O. Nonprofit Management; J.D./M.A. Bioethics; J.D./M.D. Medicine; J.D./M.S. Biochemistry; J.D./M.A. Legal History; J.D./Certificate in Nonprofit Management; J.D./M.A. Political Science**
Typical first-year section size: Full-time: **80**
Is there typically a "small section" of the first year class, other than Legal Writing, taught by full-time faculty?: Full-time: **no**
Number of course titles, beyond the first year curriculum, offered last year: **154**
Percentages of upper division course sections, excluding seminars, with an enrollment of:
Under 25: **63%**　　25 to 49: **24%**
50 to 74: **6%**　　75 to 99: **5%**
100+: **1%**
Areas of specialization: appellate advocacy, clinical training, dispute resolution, environmental law, healthcare law, intellectual property law, international law, tax law, trial advocacy

Fall 2007 faculty profile
Total teaching faculty: **127**. Full-time: **43%**; **65%** men, **35%** women, **9%** minorities. Part-time: **57%**; **68%** men, **32%** women, **8%** minorities
Student-to-faculty ratio: **13.7**

SPECIAL PROGRAMS *(as provided by law school)*:
Capstone experiences: seven labs, four clinics, seven externships. Concentration options: law and technology; law and the arts; criminal law; business organizations; litigation; health law; international law; individual rights and social reform; and

public and regulatory institutions. The school funds extensive international summer internships and postgraduate fellowships for work abroad.

STUDENT BODY

Fall 2007 full-time enrollment: 678

Men: 58%	Women: 42%
African-American: 4.4%	American Indian: 0.1%
Asian-American: 8.7%	Mexican-American: 0.0%
Puerto Rican: 0.3%	Other Hisp-Amer: 0.7%
White: 72.7%	International: 3.4%
Unknown: 9.6%	

Fall 2007 part-time enrollment: 24

Men: 63%	Women: 38%
African-American: 0.0%	American Indian: 0.0%
Asian-American: 12.5%	Mexican-American: 0.0%
Puerto Rican: 0.0%	Other Hisp-Amer: 0.0%
White: 83.3%	International: 4.2%
Unknown: 0.0%	

Attrition rates for 2006-2007 full-time students

Percent of students discontinuing law school:

Men: 7%	Women: 5%
First-year students: 1%	Second-year students: 15%
Third-year students: 1%	

LIBRARY RESOURCES

Total volumes: 411,804
Total seats available for library users: 346

INFORMATION TECHNOLOGY

Number of wired network connections available to students: 100 total (in the law library, excluding computer labs: 68; in classrooms: 32; in computer labs: 0; elsewhere in the law school: 0)
Law school has a wireless network.
Students are not required to own a computer.

EMPLOYMENT AND SALARIES

Proportion of 2006 graduates employed at graduation: 71%
Employed 9 months later, as of February 15, 2007: 97%
Salaries in the private sector (law firms, business, industry): $70,000–$110,000 (25th-75th percentile)
Median salary in the private sector: $91,000
Percentage in the private sector who reported salary information: 54%
Median salary in public service (government, judicial clerkships, academic posts, non-profits): $45,000

Percentage of 2006 graduates in:

Law firms: 50%	Government: 12%
Bus./industry: 20%	Judicial clerkship: 6%
Public interest: 9%	Unknown: 1%
Academia: 2%	

2006 graduates employed in-state: 43%
2006 graduates employed in foreign countries: 2%
Number of states where graduates are employed: 27
Percentage of 2006 graduates working in: New England: 3%, Middle Atlantic: 16%, East North Central: 52%, West North Central: 0%, South Atlantic: 15%, East South Central: 0%, West South Central: 2%, Mountain: 4%, Pacific: 5%, Unknown: 0%

BAR PASSAGE RATES

Based on 2006 graduates taking Summer 2006 or Winter 2007 exams. Most of the school's first-time test takers took the bar in Ohio.

83%
School's bar passage rate for first-time test takers

84%
Statewide bar passage rate for first-time test takers

Catholic University of America

- 3600 John McCormack Road NE, Washington, DC, 20064
- http://www.law.edu
- Private
- Year founded: 1925
- 2007-2008 tuition: full-time: $34,505; part-time: $26,225
- Enrollment 2007-08 academic year: full-time: 607; part-time: 295
- U.S. News 2009 law specialty ranking: clinical training: 16

3.08-3.57 GPA, 25TH-75TH PERCENTILE

156-160 LSAT, 25TH-75TH PERCENTILE

34% ACCEPTANCE RATE

88 2009 U.S. NEWS LAW SCHOOL RANKING

ADMISSIONS

Admissions phone number: **(202) 319-5151**
Admissions email address: **admissions@law.edu**
Application website: **http://law.cua.edu/admissions/CSL**
Application deadline for Fall 2009 admission: **03/13**

Admissions statistics:
Number of applicants for Fall 2007: **2,262**
Number of acceptances: **775**
Number enrolled: **201**
Acceptance rate: **34%**
GPA, 25th-75th percentile, entering class Fall 2007: **3.08-3.57**
LSAT, 25th-75th percentile, entering class Fall 2007: **156-160**

Part-time program:
Number of applicants for Fall 2007: **628**
Number of acceptances: **239**
Number enrolled: **100**
Acceptance rate: **38%**
GPA, 25th-75th percentile, entering class Fall 2007: **3.02-3.47**
LSAT, 25th-75th percentile, entering class Fall 2007: **153-158**

FINANCIAL AID

Financial aid phone number: **(202) 319-5143**
Financial aid application deadline: **06/15**
Tuition 2007-2008 academic year: full-time: **$34,505**; part-time: **$26,225**
Room and board: **$14,600**; books: **$1,500**; miscellaneous expenses: **$7,724**
Total of room/board/books/miscellaneous expenses: **$23,824**
University does not offer graduate student housing for which law students are eligible.

Financial aid profile
Percent of students that received grants for the 2006-2007 academic year: full-time: **29%**; part-time **16%**

Median grant amount: full-time: **$10,000**; part-time: **$6,000**
The average law-school debt of those in the Class of 2007 who borrowed: **$112,589**. Proportion who borrowed: **88%**

ACADEMIC PROGRAMS

Calendar: **semester**
Joint degrees awarded: **J.D./M.S.W.; J.D./M.A. Politics; J.D./M.A. Psychology; J.D./M.S. Library & Information Science**
Typical first-year section size: Full-time: **48**; Part-time: **56**
Is there typically a "small section" of the first year class, other than Legal Writing, taught by full-time faculty?: Full-time: **yes**; Part-time: **yes**
Number of course titles, beyond the first year curriculum, offered last year: **139**
Percentages of upper division course sections, excluding seminars, with an enrollment of:

Under 25: **70%**	25 to 49: **18%**
50 to 74: **9%**	75 to 99: **3%**
100+: **0%**	

Areas of specialization: appellate advocacy, clinical training, dispute resolution, environmental law, healthcare law, intellectual property law, international law, tax law, trial advocacy

Fall 2007 faculty profile
Total teaching faculty: **120**. Full-time: **41%**; 51% men, 49% women, 12% minorities. Part-time: **59%**; 76% men, 24% women, 7% minorities
Student-to-faculty ratio: **13.6**

SPECIAL PROGRAMS *(as provided by law school)*:
Clinics: general practice; families and law; advocacy for the elderly; criminal prosecution; D.C. law students in court. Externships and Securities and Exchange Commission student observer program. Institutes include: communications, international, public policy. Interdisciplinary program in law and religion; Center for Law, Philosophy and Culture. Summer-abroad program in Krakow, Poland.

STUDENT BODY

Fall 2007 full-time enrollment: 607

Men: 48%	Women: 52%
African-American: 4.0%	American Indian: 0.8%
Asian-American: 6.9%	Mexican-American: 0.3%
Puerto Rican: 0.2%	Other Hisp-Amer: 4.8%
White: 65.6%	International: 0.0%
Unknown: 17.5%	

Fall 2007 part-time enrollment: 295

Men: 59%	Women: 41%
African-American: 6.8%	American Indian: 0.3%
Asian-American: 9.8%	Mexican-American: 0.0%
Puerto Rican: 1.4%	Other Hisp-Amer: 3.1%
White: 64.4%	International: 0.7%
Unknown: 13.6%	

Attrition rates for 2006-2007 full-time students
Percent of students discontinuing law school:

Men: 5%	Women: 3%
First-year students: 12%	Second-year students: 1%
Third-year students: 0%	

LIBRARY RESOURCES

Total volumes: 421,113
Total seats available for library users: 502

INFORMATION TECHNOLOGY

Number of wired network connections available to students: 368 total (in the law library, excluding computer labs: 220; in classrooms: 128; in computer labs: 0; elsewhere in the law school: 20)
Law school has a wireless network.
Students are not required to own a computer.

EMPLOYMENT AND SALARIES

Proportion of 2006 graduates employed at graduation: 70%

Employed 9 months later, as of February 15, 2007: 94%
Salaries in the private sector (law firms, business, industry): $60,000–$125,000 (25th-75th percentile)
Median salary in the private sector: $80,000
Percentage in the private sector who reported salary information: 66%
Median salary in public service (government, judicial clerkships, academic posts, non-profits): $53,000

Percentage of 2006 graduates in:

Law firms: 36%	Government: 26%
Bus./industry: 20%	Judicial clerkship: 14%
Public interest: 5%	Unknown: 0%
Academia: 0%	

2006 graduates employed in-state: 48%
2006 graduates employed in foreign countries: 1%
Number of states where graduates are employed: 25
Percentage of 2006 graduates working in: New England: 2%, Middle Atlantic: 7%, East North Central: 2%, West North Central: 0%, South Atlantic: 82%, East South Central: 0%, West South Central: 0%, Mountain: 1%, Pacific: 5%, Unknown: 0%

BAR PASSAGE RATES

Based on 2006 graduates taking Summer 2006 or Winter 2007 exams. Most of the school's first-time test takers took the bar in Maryland.

80%
School's bar passage rate for first-time test takers

77%
Statewide bar passage rate for first-time test takers

Chapman University

- 1 University Drive, Orange, CA, 92866
- http://www.chapman.edu/law
- Private
- **Year founded:** 1995
- **2007-2008 tuition:** full-time: $34,250; part-time: $29,468
- **Enrollment 2007-08 academic year:** full-time: 474; part-time: 71
- **U.S. News 2009 law specialty ranking:** N/A

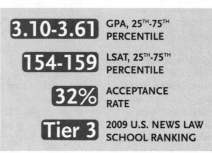

3.10-3.61 GPA, 25TH-75TH PERCENTILE

154-159 LSAT, 25TH-75TH PERCENTILE

32% ACCEPTANCE RATE

Tier 3 2009 U.S. NEWS LAW SCHOOL RANKING

ADMISSIONS

Admissions phone number: **(714) 628-2500**
Admissions email address: **lawadm@chapman.edu**
Application website:
http://web.chapman.edu/law_asp/RegForm.html
Application deadline for Fall 2009 admission: **04/15**

Admissions statistics:
Number of applicants for Fall 2007: **2,327**
Number of acceptances: **734**
Number enrolled: **136**
Acceptance rate: **32%**
GPA, 25th-75th percentile, entering class Fall 2007: **3.10-3.61**
LSAT, 25th-75th percentile, entering class Fall 2007: **154-159**

Part-time program:
Number of applicants for Fall 2007: **171**
Number of acceptances: **171**
Number enrolled: **53**
Acceptance rate: **100%**
GPA, 25th-75th percentile, entering class Fall 2007: **2.84-3.33**
LSAT, 25th-75th percentile, entering class Fall 2007: **149-154**

FINANCIAL AID

Financial aid phone number: **(714) 628-2510**
Financial aid application deadline: **04/01**
Tuition 2007-2008 academic year: full-time: **$34,250**; part-time: **$29,468**
Room and board: **$13,752**; books: **$1,500**; miscellaneous expenses: **$5,868**
Total of room/board/books/miscellaneous expenses: **$21,120**
University does not offer graduate student housing for which law students are eligible.

Financial aid profile
Percent of students that received grants for the 2006-2007 academic year: full-time: **44%**; part-time **1%**
Median grant amount: full-time: **$19,222**
The average law-school debt of those in the Class of 2007 who borrowed: **$94,397**. Proportion who borrowed: **71%**

ACADEMIC PROGRAMS

Calendar: **semester**
Joint degrees awarded: **J.D./M.B.A.**
Typical first-year section size: Full-time: **65**; Part-time: **65**
Is there typically a "small section" of the first year class, other than Legal Writing, taught by full-time faculty?: Full-time: **no**; Part-time: **no**
Number of course titles, beyond the first year curriculum, offered last year: **95**
Percentages of upper division course sections, excluding seminars, with an enrollment of:
Under 25: **58%**   25 to 49: **26%**
50 to 74: **16%**   75 to 99: **1%**
100+: **0%**
Areas of specialization: appellate advocacy, clinical training, dispute resolution, environmental law, intellectual property law, international law, tax law, trial advocacy

Fall 2007 faculty profile
Total teaching faculty: **98**. Full-time: **44%**; **56%** men, **44%** women, **12%** minorities. Part-time: **56%**; **84%** men, **16%** women, **0%** minorities
Student-to-faculty ratio: **12.6**

SPECIAL PROGRAMS *(as provided by law school):*
Chapman has five Certificate programs: Taxation; Environmental, Land Use and Real Estate; Advocacy and Dispute Resolution; Entertainment Law; and International Law. It has a joint J.D.-M.B.A. program. It offers clinical programs in elder law, taxation law, constitutional litigation, domestic violence, and a Ninth Circuit appellate law clinic. It cosponsors a summer law program in England.

STUDENT BODY

Fall 2007 full-time enrollment: 474

Men: 54%	Women: 46%
African-American: 1.1%	American Indian: 0.4%
Asian-American: 15.2%	Mexican-American: 4.2%
Puerto Rican: 0.0%	Other Hisp-Amer: 1.9%
White: 57.4%	International: 0.8%
Unknown: 19.0%	

Fall 2007 part-time enrollment: 71

Men: 58%	Women: 42%
African-American: 5.6%	American Indian: 0.0%
Asian-American: 15.5%	Mexican-American: 8.5%
Puerto Rican: 0.0%	Other Hisp-Amer: 1.4%
White: 50.7%	International: 1.4%
Unknown: 16.9%	

Attrition rates for 2006-2007 full-time students
Percent of students discontinuing law school:

Men: 6%	Women: 5%
First-year students: 9%	Second-year students: 6%
Third-year students: 1%	

LIBRARY RESOURCES

Total volumes: 292,974
Total seats available for library users: 294

INFORMATION TECHNOLOGY

Number of wired network connections available to students: 488 total (in the law library, excluding computer labs: 152; in classrooms: 236; in computer labs: 30; elsewhere in the law school: 70)
Law school has a wireless network.
Students are not required to own a computer.

EMPLOYMENT AND SALARIES

Proportion of 2006 graduates employed at graduation: 51%
Employed 9 months later, as of February 15, 2007: 95%

Salaries in the private sector (law firms, business, industry): $62,500–$75,000 (25th-75th percentile)
Median salary in the private sector: $70,000
Percentage in the private sector who reported salary information: 44%
Median salary in public service (government, judicial clerkships, academic posts, non-profits): $58,000

Percentage of 2006 graduates in:

Law firms: 55%	Government: 7%
Bus./industry: 21%	Judicial clerkship: 2%
Public interest: 2%	Unknown: 4%
Academia: 9%	

2006 graduates employed in-state: 91%
2006 graduates employed in foreign countries: 0%
Number of states where graduates are employed: 9
Percentage of 2006 graduates working in: New England: 0%, Middle Atlantic: 1%, East North Central: 1%, West North Central: 0%, South Atlantic: 1%, East South Central: 0%, West South Central: 0%, Mountain: 6%, Pacific: 92%, Unknown: 0%

BAR PASSAGE RATES

Based on 2006 graduates taking Summer 2006 or Winter 2007 exams. Most of the school's first-time test takers took the bar in California.

61%
School's bar passage rate for first-time test takers

65%
Statewide bar passage rate for first-time test takers

Charleston School of Law

- PO Box 535, Charleston, SC, 29402
- http://www.charlestonlaw.org
- Private
- **Year founded:** N/A
- **2007-2008 tuition:** full-time: $30,598; part-time: $23,188
- **Enrollment 2007-08 academic year:** full-time: 394; part-time: 197
- **U.S. News 2009 law specialty ranking:** N/A

2.96-3.49 GPA, 25TH-75TH PERCENTILE

153-157 LSAT, 25TH-75TH PERCENTILE

34% ACCEPTANCE RATE

Unranked 2009 U.S. NEWS LAW SCHOOL RANKING

ADMISSIONS

Admissions phone number: **(843) 329-1000**
Admissions email address: **info@charlestonlaw.org**
Application website: **N/A**
Application deadline for Fall 2009 admission: **03/01**

Admissions statistics:

Number of applicants for Fall 2007: **870**
Number of acceptances: **298**
Number enrolled: **134**
Acceptance rate: **34%**
GPA, 25th-75th percentile, entering class Fall 2007: **2.96-3.49**
LSAT, 25th-75th percentile, entering class Fall 2007: **153-157**

Part-time program:

Number of applicants for Fall 2007: **240**
Number of acceptances: **99**
Number enrolled: **71**
Acceptance rate: **41%**
GPA, 25th-75th percentile, entering class Fall 2007: **2.71-3.34**
LSAT, 25th-75th percentile, entering class Fall 2007: **147-152**

FINANCIAL AID

Financial aid phone number: **(843) 377-4901**
Financial aid application deadline: **04/01**
Tuition 2007-2008 academic year: full-time: **$30,598**; part-time: **$23,188**
Room and board: **$7,700**; books: **$1,020**; miscellaneous expenses: **$4,300**
Total of room/board/books/miscellaneous expenses: **$13,020**
University does not offer graduate student housing for which law students are eligible.

Financial aid profile

Percent of students that received grants for the 2006-2007 academic year: full-time: **40%**; part-time **10%**

Median grant amount: full-time: **$7,500**; part-time: **$5,000**
The average law-school debt of those in the Class of 2007 who borrowed: **$91,015**. Proportion who borrowed: **74%**

ACADEMIC PROGRAMS

Calendar: **semester**
Joint degrees awarded: **N/A**
Typical first-year section size: Full-time: **65**; Part-time: **65**
Is there typically a "small section" of the first year class, other than Legal Writing, taught by full-time faculty?: Full-time: **no**; Part-time: **no**
Number of course titles, beyond the first year curriculum, offered last year: **62**
Percentages of upper division course sections, excluding seminars, with an enrollment of:

Under 25: **48%**	25 to 49: **28%**
50 to 74: **15%**	75 to 99: **9%**
100+: **0%**	

Areas of specialization: appellate advocacy, dispute resolution, environmental law, healthcare law, intellectual property law, international law, tax law, trial advocacy

Fall 2007 faculty profile

Total teaching faculty: **44**. Full-time: **50%**; **73%** men, **27%** women, **9%** minorities. Part-time: **50%**; **73%** men, **27%** women, **41%** minorities
Student-to-faculty ratio: **19.8**

SPECIAL PROGRAMS (as provided by law school):

The Charleston School of Law offers an extensive externship program providing students with practical experience in more than 110 placement sites. The school is developing a Maritime Law Institute. All students are required to complete a minimum of 30 hours of pro bono work prior to graduation.

STUDENT BODY

Fall 2007 full-time enrollment: 394

Men: **57%**	Women: **43%**
African-American: **2.8%**	American Indian: **0.3%**
Asian-American: **1.3%**	Mexican-American: **0.0%**

Puerto Rican: **0.0%**
White: **87.6%**
Unknown: **8.1%**

Other Hisp-Amer: **0.0%**
International: **0.0%**

Fall 2007 part-time enrollment: 197
Men: **61%**
African-American: **6.6%**
Asian-American: **1.0%**
Puerto Rican: **0.0%**
White: **76.6%**
Unknown: **14.7%**

Women: **39%**
American Indian: **0.5%**
Mexican-American: **0.0%**
Other Hisp-Amer: **0.5%**
International: **0.0%**

Attrition rates for 2006-2007 full-time students
Percent of students discontinuing law school:
Men: **N/A**
First-year students: **N/A**
Third-year students: **N/A**

Women: **N/A**
Second-year students: **N/A**

LIBRARY RESOURCES
Total volumes: **25,096**
Total seats available for library users: **220**

INFORMATION TECHNOLOGY
Number of wired network connections available to students: **0** total (in the law library, excluding computer labs: **N/A**; in classrooms: **N/A**; in computer labs: **N/A**; elsewhere in the law school: **N/A**)
Law school has a wireless network.
Students are required to own a computer.

EMPLOYMENT AND SALARIES
Proportion of 2006 graduates employed at graduation: **N/A**
Employed 9 months later, as of February 15, 2007: **N/A**

Salaries in the private sector (law firms, business, industry): **N/A**
Median salary in the private sector: **N/A**
Percentage in the private sector who reported salary information: **N/A**
Median salary in public service (government, judicial clerkships, academic posts, non-profits): **N/A**

Percentage of 2006 graduates in:
Law firms: **N/A**
Bus./industry: **N/A**
Public interest: **N/A**
Academia: **N/A**

Government: **N/A**
Judicial clerkship: **N/A**
Unknown: **N/A**

2006 graduates employed in-state: **N/A**
2006 graduates employed in foreign countries: **N/A**
Number of states where graduates are employed: **N/A**
Percentage of 2006 graduates working in: New England: **N/A**, Middle Atlantic: **N/A**, East North Central: **N/A**, West North Central: **N/A**, South Atlantic: **N/A**, East South Central: **N/A**, West South Central: **N/A**, Mountain: **N/A**, Pacific: **N/A**, Unknown: **N/A**

BAR PASSAGE RATES
Based on 2006 graduates taking Summer 2006 or Winter 2007 exams. Most of the school's first-time test takers took the bar in N/A.

| N/A |
School's bar passage rate for first-time test takers

| N/A |
Statewide bar passage rate for first-time test takers

Cleveland State University (Marshall)

- 2121 Euclid Avenue, LB 138, Cleveland, OH, 44115-2214
- http://www.law.csuohio.edu
- Public
- **Year founded:** 1897
- **2007-2008 tuition:** In-state: full-time: $16,478; part-time: $12,675; Out-of-state: full-time: $22,608
- **Enrollment 2007-08 academic year:** full-time: 503; part-time: 203
- **U.S. News 2009 law specialty ranking:** N/A

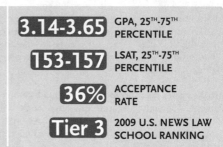

3.14-3.65 GPA, 25TH-75TH PERCENTILE

153-157 LSAT, 25TH-75TH PERCENTILE

36% ACCEPTANCE RATE

Tier 3 2009 U.S. NEWS LAW SCHOOL RANKING

ADMISSIONS

Admissions phone number: **(216) 687-2304**
Admissions email address: **admissions@law.csuohio.edu**
Application website:
  http://www.law.csuohio.edu/admissions/apply/
Application deadline for Fall 2009 admission: **05/01**

Admissions statistics:
Number of applicants for Fall 2007: **1,182**
Number of acceptances: **429**
Number enrolled: **151**
Acceptance rate: **36%**
GPA, 25th-75th percentile, entering class Fall 2007: **3.14-3.65**
LSAT, 25th-75th percentile, entering class Fall 2007: **153-157**

Part-time program:
Number of applicants for Fall 2007: **234**
Number of acceptances: **98**
Number enrolled: **64**
Acceptance rate: **42%**
GPA, 25th-75th percentile, entering class Fall 2007: **2.96-3.50**
LSAT, 25th-75th percentile, entering class Fall 2007: **148-154**

FINANCIAL AID

Financial aid phone number: **(216) 687-2304**
Financial aid application deadline: **05/01**
Tuition 2007-2008 academic year: In-state: full-time: **$16,478**; part-time: **$12,675**; Out-of-state: full-time: **$22,608**
Room and board: **$10,630**; books: **$1,300**; miscellaneous expenses: **$4,332**
Total of room/board/books/miscellaneous expenses: **$16,262**
University offers graduate student housing for which law students are eligible.

Financial aid profile
Percent of students that received grants for the 2006-2007

academic year: full-time: **35%**; part-time **15%**
Median grant amount: full-time: **$3,840**; part-time: **$1,920**
The average law-school debt of those in the Class of 2007 who borrowed: **$66,118**. Proportion who borrowed: **93%**

ACADEMIC PROGRAMS

Calendar: **semester**
Joint degrees awarded: **J.D./M.B.A.; J.D./M.P.A.; J.D./M.U.P.D.D.; J.D./M.A.E.S.; J.D./M.S.E.S.**
Typical first-year section size: Full-time: **59**; Part-time: **47**
Is there typically a "small section" of the first year class, other than Legal Writing, taught by full-time faculty?: Full-time: **no**; Part-time: **no**
Number of course titles, beyond the first year curriculum, offered last year: **73**
Percentages of upper division course sections, excluding seminars, with an enrollment of:
  Under 25: **65%**   25 to 49: **27%**
  50 to 74: **7%**   75 to 99: **1%**
  100+: **0%**
Areas of specialization: appellate advocacy, clinical training, dispute resolution, environmental law, healthcare law, intellectual property law, international law, tax law, trial advocacy

Fall 2007 faculty profile
Total teaching faculty: **79**. Full-time: **56%**; **59%** men, **41%** women, **9%** minorities. Part-time: **44%**; **74%** men, **26%** women, **9%** minorities
Student-to-faculty ratio: **13.0**

SPECIAL PROGRAMS *(as provided by law school):*

Clinics: employment law, environmental, fair housing, urban development. Externships include: judicial, public interest, U.S. attorney. Concentrations: business; civil litigation and dispute resolution; criminal law; employment and labor law. Joint-degree programs: M.B.A, M.P.A., M.U.P.D.D. (planning/design), M.A.E.S. and M.S.E.S. (environmental). Summer Law Institute in St. Petersburg, Russia.

STUDENT BODY

Fall 2007 full-time enrollment: 503

Men: 54%	Women: 46%
African-American: 5.8%	American Indian: 0.6%
Asian-American: 2.4%	Mexican-American: 0.0%
Puerto Rican: 0.0%	Other Hisp-Amer: 2.8%
White: 85.5%	International: 1.2%
Unknown: 1.8%	

Fall 2007 part-time enrollment: 203

Men: 51%	Women: 49%
African-American: 10.3%	American Indian: 0.0%
Asian-American: 5.4%	Mexican-American: 0.0%
Puerto Rican: 0.0%	Other Hisp-Amer: 3.0%
White: 78.3%	International: 0.0%
Unknown: 3.0%	

Attrition rates for 2006-2007 full-time students
Percent of students discontinuing law school:

Men: 7%	Women: 2%
First-year students: 13%	Second-year students: 2%
Third-year students: 0%	

LIBRARY RESOURCES

Total volumes: 531,290
Total seats available for library users: 481

INFORMATION TECHNOLOGY

Number of wired network connections available to students: 148 total (in the law library, excluding computer labs: 148; in classrooms: 0; in computer labs: 0; elsewhere in the law school: 0)
Law school has a wireless network.
Students are not required to own a computer.

EMPLOYMENT AND SALARIES

Proportion of 2006 graduates employed at graduation: 63%
Employed 9 months later, as of February 15, 2007: 93%

Salaries in the private sector (law firms, business, industry): $50,000–$90,000 (25th-75th percentile)
Median salary in the private sector: $60,000
Percentage in the private sector who reported salary information: 32%
Median salary in public service (government, judicial clerkships, academic posts, non-profits): $48,500

Percentage of 2006 graduates in:

Law firms: 47%	Government: 14%
Bus./industry: 29%	Judicial clerkship: 5%
Public interest: 5%	Unknown: 0%
Academia: 1%	

2006 graduates employed in-state: 85%
2006 graduates employed in foreign countries: 1%
Number of states where graduates are employed: 19
Percentage of 2006 graduates working in: New England: 1%, Middle Atlantic: 2%, East North Central: 86%, West North Central: 1%, South Atlantic: 5%, East South Central: 1%, West South Central: 1%, Mountain: 1%, Pacific: 1%, Unknown: 0%

BAR PASSAGE RATES

Based on 2006 graduates taking Summer 2006 or Winter 2007 exams. Most of the school's first-time test takers took the bar in Ohio.

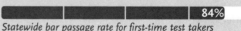

82%
School's bar passage rate for first-time test takers

84%
Statewide bar passage rate for first-time test takers

College of William and Mary

■ PO Box 8795, Williamsburg, VA, 23187-8795
■ http://www.wm.edu/law
■ Public
■ Year founded: 1779
■ 2007-2008 tuition: In-state: full-time: $18,336; part-time: N/A; Out-of-state: full-time: $28,536
■ Enrollment 2007-08 academic year: full-time: 617
■ U.S. News 2009 law specialty ranking: N/A

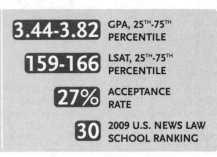

3.44-3.82 GPA, 25TH-75TH PERCENTILE

159-166 LSAT, 25TH-75TH PERCENTILE

27% ACCEPTANCE RATE

30 2009 U.S. NEWS LAW SCHOOL RANKING

ADMISSIONS
Admissions phone number: **(757) 221-3785**
Admissions email address: **lawadm@wm.edu**
Application website:
   http://www.wm.edu/law/prospective/admissions/jdprog ram_procedure.shtml
Application deadline for Fall 2009 admission: **03/01**

Admissions statistics:
Number of applicants for Fall 2007: **4,250**
Number of acceptances: **1,151**
Number enrolled: **217**
Acceptance rate: **27%**
GPA, 25th-75th percentile, entering class Fall 2007: **3.44-3.82**
LSAT, 25th-75th percentile, entering class Fall 2007: **159-166**

FINANCIAL AID
Financial aid phone number: **(757) 221-2420**
Financial aid application deadline: **02/15**
Tuition 2007-2008 academic year: In-state: full-time: **$18,336**; part-time: N/A; Out-of-state: full-time: **$28,536**
Room and board: **$8,134**; books: **$1,250**; miscellaneous expenses: **$1,350**
Total of room/board/books/miscellaneous expenses: **$10,734**
University offers graduate student housing for which law students are eligible.

Financial aid profile
Percent of students that received grants for the 2006-2007 academic year: full-time: **23%**
Median grant amount: full-time: **$5,000**
The average law-school debt of those in the Class of 2007 who borrowed: **$68,270**. Proportion who borrowed: **82%**

ACADEMIC PROGRAMS
Calendar: **semester**
Joint degrees awarded: **J.D./M.B.A.; J.D./M.P.P.; J.D./M.A.**

Typical first-year section size: Full-time: **72**
Is there typically a "small section" of the first year class, other than Legal Writing, taught by full-time faculty?: Full-time: **yes**
Number of course titles, beyond the first year curriculum, offered last year: **116**
Percentages of upper division course sections, excluding seminars, with an enrollment of:
   Under 25: **62%**   25 to 49: **28%**
   50 to 74: **6%**   75 to 99: **1%**
   100+: **3%**
Areas of specialization: appellate advocacy, clinical training, dispute resolution, environmental law, healthcare law, intellectual property law, international law, tax law, trial advocacy

Fall 2007 faculty profile
Total teaching faculty: **71**. Full-time: **54%**; **63%** men, **37%** women, **13%** minorities. Part-time: **46%**; **73%** men, **27%** women, **12%** minorities
Student-to-faculty ratio: **14.8**

SPECIAL PROGRAMS *(as provided by law school):*
Students select from numerous externship and clinical opportunities with placements in Norfolk, Richmond, and Williamsburg. Students participate in programs including: Institute of Bill of Rights Law; Center for Legal and Court Technology; human rights and national security law program. Summer abroad in Madrid. Joint degrees offered: J.D./M.B.A., J.D./M.P.P., and J.D./M.A. in American Culture.

STUDENT BODY
Fall 2007 full-time enrollment: **617**
Men: **51%**	Women: **49%**
African-American: **10.5%**	American Indian: **0.5%**
Asian-American: **4.4%**	Mexican-American: **0.0%**
Puerto Rican: **0.0%**	Other Hisp-Amer: **1.3%**
White: **68.6%**	International: **0.6%**
Unknown: **14.1%**	

Attrition rates for 2006-2007 full-time students
Percent of students discontinuing law school:
Men: 3%   Women: 2%
First-year students: 1%   Second-year students: 7%
Third-year students: N/A

LIBRARY RESOURCES
Total volumes: 390,317
Total seats available for library users: 568

INFORMATION TECHNOLOGY
Number of wired network connections available to students: 66 total (in the law library, excluding computer labs: 6; in classrooms: 10; in computer labs: 0; elsewhere in the law school: 50)
Law school has a wireless network.
Students are not required to own a computer.

EMPLOYMENT AND SALARIES
Proportion of 2006 graduates employed at graduation: 82%
Employed 9 months later, as of February 15, 2007: 96%
Salaries in the private sector (law firms, business, industry): $80,000–$135,000 (25th-75th percentile)
Median salary in the private sector: $115,000
Percentage in the private sector who reported salary information: 77%
Median salary in public service (government, judicial clerk-ships, academic posts, non-profits): $50,000

Percentage of 2006 graduates in:
Law firms: 53%   Government: 15%
Bus./industry: 11%   Judicial clerkship: 16%
Public interest: 5%   Unknown: 0%
Academia: 1%

2006 graduates employed in-state: 31%
2006 graduates employed in foreign countries: 1%
Number of states where graduates are employed: 29
Percentage of 2006 graduates working in: New England: 2%, Middle Atlantic: 13%, East North Central: 5%, West North Central: 0%, South Atlantic: 64%, East South Central: 2%, West South Central: 3%, Mountain: 3%, Pacific: 5%, Unknown: 2%

BAR PASSAGE RATES
Based on 2006 graduates taking Summer 2006 or Winter 2007 exams. Most of the school's first-time test takers took the bar in Virginia.

87%

School's bar passage rate for first-time test takers

74%

Statewide bar passage rate for first-time test takers

Columbia University

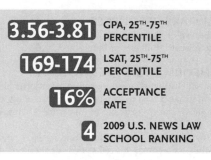

- 435 W. 116th Street, New York, NY, 10027
- http://www.law.columbia.edu
- Private
- Year founded: 1858
- 2007-2008 tuition: full-time: $43,470; part-time: N/A
- Enrollment 2007-08 academic year: full-time: 1,236
- U.S. News 2009 law specialty ranking: clinical training: 16, intellectual property law: 4, international law: 2, tax law: 19

3.56-3.81 GPA, 25TH-75TH PERCENTILE

169-174 LSAT, 25TH-75TH PERCENTILE

16% ACCEPTANCE RATE

4 2009 U.S. NEWS LAW SCHOOL RANKING

ADMISSIONS

Admissions phone number: (212) 854-2670
Admissions email address: **admissions@law.columbia.edu**
Application website:
   https://www-app.law.columbia.edu/admissions/index.jsp
Application deadline for Fall 2009 admission: **02/15**

Admissions statistics:

Number of applicants for Fall 2007: **7,292**
Number of acceptances: **1,159**
Number enrolled: **373**
Acceptance rate: **16%**
GPA, 25th-75th percentile, entering class Fall 2007: **3.56-3.81**
LSAT, 25th-75th percentile, entering class Fall 2007: **169-174**

FINANCIAL AID

Financial aid phone number: (212) 854-7730
Financial aid application deadline: 03/01
Tuition 2007-2008 academic year: full-time: **$43,470**; part-time: **N/A**
Room and board: **$15,035**; books: **$1,263**; miscellaneous expenses: **$3,300**
Total of room/board/books/miscellaneous expenses: **$19,598**
University offers graduate student housing for which law students are eligible.

Financial aid profile

Percent of students that received grants for the 2006-2007 academic year: full-time: **44%**
Median grant amount: full-time: **$10,000**
The average law-school debt of those in the Class of 2007 who borrowed: **$113,540**. Proportion who borrowed: **81%**

ACADEMIC PROGRAMS

Calendar: **semester**
Joint degrees awarded: **M.A. Economics; M.A. History; M.A. Philosophy; M.A. Politics; M.A. Psychology; M.A. Sociology; M.B.A.; M.F.A.; M.I.A.; M.P.A.; M.P.H.; M.S.** Journalism; M.U.P.; M.S.W.; Ph.D. Anthropology; Ph.D. History; Ph.D. Philosophy; Ph.D. Politics; Ph.D. Sociology; Ph.D. Economics; M.P.H.I.L.; Ph.D. Engineering; PH.D. Religion; M.A. Anthropology
Typical first-year section size: Full-time: **108**
Is there typically a "small section" of the first year class, other than Legal Writing, taught by full-time faculty?: Full-time: **yes**
Number of course titles, beyond the first year curriculum, offered last year: **228**
Percentages of upper division course sections, excluding seminars, with an enrollment of:

Under 25: **45%**		25 to 49: **22%**
50 to 74: **14%**		75 to 99: **9%**
100+: **10%**		

Areas of specialization: appellate advocacy, clinical training, dispute resolution, environmental law, healthcare law, intellectual property law, international law, tax law, trial advocacy

Fall 2007 faculty profile

Total teaching faculty: **298**. Full-time: **46%; 68%** men, **32%** women, **10%** minorities. Part-time: **54%; 73%** men, **27%** women, **9%** minorities
Student-to-faculty ratio: **9.5**

SPECIAL PROGRAMS *(as provided by law school):*

Columbia's clinics are dedicated to benefiting a broad range of societal interests, from environmental neglect to racial discrimination. Centers include Chinese Legal Studies and Corporate Governance. Externships include United Nations. Joint and foreign dual degrees. Study-abroad programs in 10 countries.

STUDENT BODY

Fall 2007 full-time enrollment: 1,236

Men: **56%**	Women: **44%**
African-American: **8.0%**	American Indian: **0.6%**
Asian-American: **14.1%**	Mexican-American: **2.4%**
Puerto Rican: **2.1%**	Other Hisp-Amer: **1.6%**
White: **60.2%**	International: **9.1%**
Unknown: **1.8%**	

Attrition rates for 2006-2007 full-time students
Percent of students discontinuing law school:
Men: 0%   Women: 1%
First-year students: 0%   Second-year students: 2%
Third-year students: N/A

LIBRARY RESOURCES
Total volumes: 1,126,199
Total seats available for library users: 369

INFORMATION TECHNOLOGY
Number of wired network connections available to students: 3,132 total (in the law library, excluding computer labs: 40; in classrooms: 2,478; in computer labs: 188; elsewhere in the law school: 426)
Law school has a wireless network.
Students are not required to own a computer.

EMPLOYMENT AND SALARIES
Proportion of 2006 graduates employed at graduation: 99%
Employed 9 months later, as of February 15, 2007: 99%
Salaries in the private sector (law firms, business, industry): $145,000–$145,000 (25th-75th percentile)
Median salary in the private sector: $145,000
Percentage in the private sector who reported salary information: 100%
Median salary in public service (government, judicial clerkships, academic posts, non-profits): $55,000

Percentage of 2006 graduates in:
Law firms: 80%   Government: 2%
Bus./industry: 3%   Judicial clerkship: 9%
Public interest: 6%   Unknown: 0%
Academia: 1%

2006 graduates employed in-state: 69%
2006 graduates employed in foreign countries: 4%
Number of states where graduates are employed: 18
Percentage of 2006 graduates working in: New England: 1%, Middle Atlantic: 73%, East North Central: 1%, West North Central: 0%, South Atlantic: 11%, East South Central: 0%, West South Central: 1%, Mountain: 0%, Pacific: 10%, Unknown: 0%

BAR PASSAGE RATES
Based on 2006 graduates taking Summer 2006 or Winter 2007 exams. Most of the school's first-time test takers took the bar in New York.

96%
School's bar passage rate for first-time test takers

77%
Statewide bar passage rate for first-time test takers

Cornell University

■ Myron Taylor Hall, Ithaca, NY, 14853-4901
■ http://www.lawschool.cornell.edu
■ Private
■ Year founded: 1887
■ 2007-2008 tuition: full-time: $42,683; part-time: N/A
■ Enrollment 2007-08 academic year: full-time: 583
■ U.S. News 2009 law specialty ranking: international law: 16

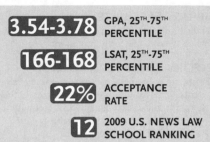

3.54-3.78 GPA, 25ᵀᴴ-75ᵀᴴ PERCENTILE

166-168 LSAT, 25ᵀᴴ-75ᵀᴴ PERCENTILE

22% ACCEPTANCE RATE

12 2009 U.S. NEWS LAW SCHOOL RANKING

ADMISSIONS
Admissions phone number: **(607) 255-5141**
Admissions email address:
  lawadmit@postoffice.law.cornell.edu
Application website:
  http://www.lawschool.cornell.edu/admissions
Application deadline for Fall 2009 admission: **02/01**

Admissions statistics:
Number of applicants for Fall 2007: **3,977**
Number of acceptances: **859**
Number enrolled: **199**
Acceptance rate: **22%**
GPA, 25th-75th percentile, entering class Fall 2007: **3.54-3.78**
LSAT, 25th-75th percentile, entering class Fall 2007: **166-168**

FINANCIAL AID
Financial aid phone number: **(607) 255-5141**
Financial aid application deadline: **03/14**
Tuition 2007-2008 academic year: full-time: **$42,683**; part-time: **N/A**
Room and board: **$10,300**; books: **$850**; miscellaneous expenses: **$6,200**
Total of room/board/books/miscellaneous expenses: **$17,350**
University offers graduate student housing for which law students are eligible.

Financial aid profile
Percent of students that received grants for the 2006-2007 academic year: full-time: **38%**
Median grant amount: full-time: **$13,000**
The average law-school debt of those in the Class of 2007 who borrowed: **$102,000**. Proportion who borrowed: **81%**

ACADEMIC PROGRAMS
Calendar: **semester**
Joint degrees awarded: **J.D./LL.M. International Legal Studies; J.D./Master en Droit French Law Degree; J.D./M. Global Business Law; J.D./M.LL.P. German Law Degree; J.D./M.B.A.; J.D./Ph.D.; J.D./M.P.A.; J.D./M.A.**
Typical first-year section size: Full-time: **93**
Is there typically a "small section" of the first year class, other than Legal Writing, taught by full-time faculty?: Full-time: **yes**
Number of course titles, beyond the first year curriculum, offered last year: **116**
Percentages of upper division course sections, excluding seminars, with an enrollment of:
  Under 25: **62%**   25 to 49: **22%**
  50 to 74: **6%**   75 to 99: **4%**
  100+: **6%**
Areas of specialization: appellate advocacy, clinical training, dispute resolution, environmental law, healthcare law, intellectual property law, international law, tax law, trial advocacy

Fall 2007 faculty profile
Total teaching faculty: **137**. Full-time: **61%**; **64%** men, **36%** women, **16%** minorities. Part-time: **39%**; **76%** men, **24%** women, **6%** minorities
Student-to-faculty ratio: **11.2**

SPECIAL PROGRAMS *(as provided by law school):*
Students benefit not only from the small class size and well-known collegial learning environment but also from a surprising array of externships, study-abroad programs, clinics, centers, and institutes. Cornell educates "lawyers in the best sense."

STUDENT BODY
Fall 2007 full-time enrollment: 583

Men: **50%**	Women: **50%**
African-American: **5.1%**	American Indian: **1.4%**
Asian-American: **9.8%**	Mexican-American: **1.4%**
Puerto Rican: **1.2%**	Other Hisp-Amer: **2.6%**
White: **73.8%**	International: **4.8%**
Unknown: **0.0%**	

Attrition rates for 2006-2007 full-time students
Percent of students discontinuing law school:
Men: 2%   Women: 1%
First-year students: 4%   Second-year students: 2%
Third-year students: N/A

LIBRARY RESOURCES
Total volumes: 735,476
Total seats available for library users: 434

INFORMATION TECHNOLOGY
Number of wired network connections available to students: 105 total (in the law library, excluding computer labs: 0; in classrooms: 34; in computer labs: 45; elsewhere in the law school: 26)
Law school has a wireless network.
Students are not required to own a computer.

EMPLOYMENT AND SALARIES
Proportion of 2006 graduates employed at graduation: 97%
Employed 9 months later, as of February 15, 2007: 99%
Salaries in the private sector (law firms, business, industry): $135,000–$145,000 (25th-75th percentile)
Median salary in the private sector: $145,000
Percentage in the private sector who reported salary information: 79%
Median salary in public service (government, judicial clerkships, academic posts, non-profits): $46,000

Percentage of 2006 graduates in:

Law firms: 82%	Government: 2%
Bus./industry: 4%	Judicial clerkship: 9%
Public interest: 2%	Unknown: 0%
Academia: 1%	

2006 graduates employed in-state: 58%
2006 graduates employed in foreign countries: 1%
Number of states where graduates are employed: 21
Percentage of 2006 graduates working in: New England: 7%, Middle Atlantic: 58%, East North Central: 5%, West North Central: 2%, South Atlantic: 8%, East South Central: 1%, West South Central: 2%, Mountain: 4%, Pacific: 12%, Unknown: 0%

BAR PASSAGE RATES
Based on 2006 graduates taking Summer 2006 or Winter 2007 exams. Most of the school's first-time test takers took the bar in New York.

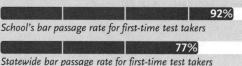

92%
School's bar passage rate for first-time test takers

77%
Statewide bar passage rate for first-time test takers

Creighton University

- 2500 California Plaza, Omaha, NE, 68178
- http://law.creighton.edu/
- Private
- Year founded: 1904
- 2007-2008 tuition: full-time: $25,850; part-time: $15,948
- Enrollment 2007-08 academic year: full-time: 451; part-time: 18
- U.S. News 2009 law specialty ranking: dispute resolution: 12

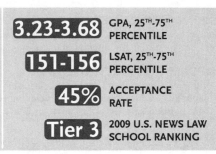

3.23-3.68 GPA, 25TH-75TH PERCENTILE

151-156 LSAT, 25TH-75TH PERCENTILE

45% ACCEPTANCE RATE

Tier 3 2009 U.S. NEWS LAW SCHOOL RANKING

ADMISSIONS

Admissions phone number: (800) 282-5835
Admissions email address: **lawadmit@creighton.edu**
Application website: **http://law.creighton.edu/pdf/ admissions/Application.pdf**
Application deadline for Fall 2009 admission: **03/01**

Admissions statistics:

Number of applicants for Fall 2007: **1,243**
Number of acceptances: **563**
Number enrolled: **159**
Acceptance rate: **45%**
GPA, 25th-75th percentile, entering class Fall 2007: **3.23-3.68**
LSAT, 25th-75th percentile, entering class Fall 2007: **151-156**

Part-time program:

Number of applicants for Fall 2007: **52**
Number of acceptances: **18**
Number enrolled: **11**
Acceptance rate: **35%**
GPA, 25th-75th percentile, entering class Fall 2007: **3.02-3.55**
LSAT, 25th-75th percentile, entering class Fall 2007: **147-150**

FINANCIAL AID

Financial aid phone number: **(402) 280-2352**
Financial aid application deadline: **07/01**
Tuition 2007-2008 academic year: full-time: **$25,850**; part-time: **$15,948**
Room and board: **$12,500**; books: **$1,350**; miscellaneous expenses: **$2,680**
Total of room/board/books/miscellaneous expenses: **$16,530**
University offers graduate student housing for which law students are eligible.

Financial aid profile

Percent of students that received grants for the 2006-2007 academic year: full-time: **38%**; part-time **11%**

Median grant amount: full-time: **$8,000**; part-time: **$4,750**
The average law-school debt of those in the Class of 2007 who borrowed: **$91,517**. Proportion who borrowed: **78%**

ACADEMIC PROGRAMS

Calendar: **semester**
Joint degrees awarded: **J.D./M.B.A.; J.D./M.S. Information Tech. Management; J.D./M.S. Negotiation/Dispute Resolution; J.D./M.A. International Relations**
Typical first-year section size: Full-time: **78**
Is there typically a "small section" of the first year class, other than Legal Writing, taught by full-time faculty?: Full-time: **no**
Number of course titles, beyond the first year curriculum, offered last year: **85**
Percentages of upper division course sections, excluding seminars, with an enrollment of:

Under 25: **70%** 25 to 49: **22%**
50 to 74: **7%** 75 to 99: **1%**
100+: **1%**

Areas of specialization: appellate advocacy, clinical training, dispute resolution, environmental law, healthcare law, intellectual property law, international law, tax law, trial advocacy

Fall 2007 faculty profile

Total teaching faculty: **N/A**. Full-time: **N/A**; **N/A** men, **N/A** women, **N/A** minorities. Part-time: **N/A**; **N/A** men, **N/A** women, **N/A** minorities
Student-to-faculty ratio: **18.1**

SPECIAL PROGRAMS (as provided by law school):

Clinics: Abrahams clinic for civil matters; community economic development clinic advising nonprofits. Internships for upper-class students with governmental, nonprofit, and public interest organizations. With other schools and Werner Institute: Combined-degree programs include M.B.A., M.S. in Information Technology, M.S. in Dispute Resolution, and M.S. in International Relations.

STUDENT BODY

Fall 2007 full-time enrollment: 451

Men: 60%   Women: 40%
African-American: 2.4%   American Indian: 0.2%
Asian-American: 4.0%   Mexican-American: 1.8%
Puerto Rican: 0.2%   Other Hisp-Amer: 0.9%
White: 89.6%   International: 0.4%
Unknown: 0.4%

Fall 2007 part-time enrollment: 18

Men: 33%   Women: 67%
African-American: 0.0%   American Indian: 0.0%
Asian-American: 0.0%   Mexican-American: 5.6%
Puerto Rican: 0.0%   Other Hisp-Amer: 5.6%
White: 88.9%   International: 0.0%
Unknown: 0.0%

Attrition rates for 2006-2007 full-time students
Percent of students discontinuing law school:
Men: 5%   Women: 2%
First-year students: 11%   Second-year students: N/A
Third-year students: N/A

LIBRARY RESOURCES

Total volumes: 370,427
Total seats available for library users: 363

INFORMATION TECHNOLOGY

Number of wired network connections available to students: 160 total (in the law library, excluding computer labs: 38; in classrooms: 114; in computer labs: 0; elsewhere in the law school: 8)
Law school has a wireless network.
Students are not required to own a computer.

EMPLOYMENT AND SALARIES

Proportion of 2006 graduates employed at graduation: 73%

Employed 9 months later, as of February 15, 2007: 97%
Salaries in the private sector (law firms, business, industry): $50,000–$78,000 (25th-75th percentile)
Median salary in the private sector: $70,000
Percentage in the private sector who reported salary information: 70%
Median salary in public service (government, judicial clerkships, academic posts, non-profits): $50,600

Percentage of 2006 graduates in:
Law firms: 47%   Government: 15%
Bus./industry: 23%   Judicial clerkship: 9%
Public interest: 5%   Unknown: 0%
Academia: 1%

2006 graduates employed in-state: 47%
2006 graduates employed in foreign countries: 1%
Number of states where graduates are employed: 23
Percentage of 2006 graduates working in: New England: N/A, Middle Atlantic: N/A, East North Central: 9%, West North Central: 68%, South Atlantic: 2%, East South Central: N/A, West South Central: N/A, Mountain: 16%, Pacific: 4%, Unknown: 0%

BAR PASSAGE RATES

Based on 2006 graduates taking Summer 2006 or Winter 2007 exams. Most of the school's first-time test takers took the bar in Nebraska.

75%
School's bar passage rate for first-time test takers

83%
Statewide bar passage rate for first-time test takers

CUNY–Queens College

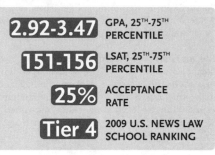

- 65-21 Main Street, Flushing, NY, 11367
- http://www.law.cuny.edu/
- Public
- Year founded: 1983
- **2007-2008 tuition:** In-state: full-time: $10,562; part-time: N/A; Out-of-state: full-time: $16,462
- **Enrollment 2007-08 academic year:** full-time: 412
- **U.S. News 2009 law specialty ranking:** clinical training: 4

2.92-3.47 GPA, 25TH-75TH PERCENTILE

151-156 LSAT, 25TH-75TH PERCENTILE

25% ACCEPTANCE RATE

Tier 4 2009 U.S. NEWS LAW SCHOOL RANKING

ADMISSIONS

Admissions phone number: **(718) 340-4210**
Admissions email address: **admissions@mail.law.cuny.edu**
Application website: **N/A**
Application deadline for Fall 2009 admission: **03/16**

Admissions statistics:

Number of applicants for Fall 2007: **2,322**
Number of acceptances: **572**
Number enrolled: **143**
Acceptance rate: **25%**
GPA, 25th-75th percentile, entering class Fall 2007: **2.92-3.47**
LSAT, 25th-75th percentile, entering class Fall 2007: **151-156**

FINANCIAL AID

Financial aid phone number: **(718) 340-4284**
Financial aid application deadline: **N/A**
Tuition 2007-2008 academic year: In-state: full-time: **$10,562**; part-time: **N/A**; Out-of-state: full-time: **$16,462**
Room and board: **$5,311**; books: **$938**; miscellaneous expenses: **$7,057**
Total of room/board/books/miscellaneous expenses: **$13,306**
University does not offer graduate student housing for which law students are eligible.

Financial aid profile

Percent of students that received grants for the 2006-2007 academic year: full-time: **42%**
Median grant amount: full-time: **$2,290**
The average law-school debt of those in the Class of 2007 who borrowed: **$57,262**. Proportion who borrowed: **77%**

ACADEMIC PROGRAMS

Calendar: **semester**
Joint degrees awarded: **N/A**
Typical first-year section size: Full-time: **80**
Is there typically a "small section" of the first year class, other than Legal Writing, taught by full-time faculty?: Full-time: **yes**
Number of course titles, beyond the first year curriculum, offered last year: **61**
Percentages of upper division course sections, excluding seminars, with an enrollment of:
Under 25: **51%**   25 to 49: **34%**
50 to 74: **10%**   75 to 99: **3%**
100+: **1%**
Areas of specialization: appellate advocacy, clinical training, dispute resolution, environmental law, healthcare law, intellectual property law, international law, trial advocacy

Fall 2007 faculty profile

Total teaching faculty: **78**. Full-time: **65%**; **49%** men, **51%** women, **39%** minorities. Part-time: **35%**; **30%** men, **70%** women, **41%** minorities
Student-to-faculty ratio: **13.0**

SPECIAL PROGRAMS (as provided by law school):

CUNY Law's nationally ranked clinical program offers 12 to 16 credits of supervised live-client representation to every third-year law student. In-house clinics and external placements include battered women's rights, criminal defense, immigrant and refugees' rights, international women's human rights, elder law, mediation, equality, and health law.

STUDENT BODY

Fall 2007 full-time enrollment: 412

Men: **35%**	Women: **65%**
African-American: **7.0%**	American Indian: **0.2%**
Asian-American: **15.5%**	Mexican-American: **0.0%**
Puerto Rican: **0.5%**	Other Hisp-Amer: **7.8%**
White: **55.3%**	International: **2.7%**
Unknown: **10.9%**	

Attrition rates for 2006-2007 full-time students

Percent of students discontinuing law school:
Men: **8%**   Women: **5%**

First-year students: **10%**   Second-year students: **8%**
Third-year students: **1%**

LIBRARY RESOURCES
Total volumes: **284,829**
Total seats available for library users: **239**

INFORMATION TECHNOLOGY
Number of wired network connections available to students: **62** total (in the law library, excluding computer labs: **0**; in classrooms: **20**; in computer labs: **6**; elsewhere in the law school: **36**)
Law school has a wireless network.
Students are not required to own a computer.

EMPLOYMENT AND SALARIES
Proportion of 2006 graduates employed at graduation: **37%**
Employed 9 months later, as of February 15, 2007: **88%**
Salaries in the private sector (law firms, business, industry): **$51,003–$80,000** (25th-75th percentile)
Median salary in the private sector: **$65,000**
Percentage in the private sector who reported salary information: **36%**
Median salary in public service (government, judicial clerkships, academic posts, non-profits): **$51,125**

Percentage of 2006 graduates in:

Law firms: **21%**	Government: **14%**
Bus./industry: **15%**	Judicial clerkship: **17%**
Public interest: **28%**	Unknown: **0%**
Academia: **5%**	

2006 graduates employed in-state: **74%**
2006 graduates employed in foreign countries: **4%**
Number of states where graduates are employed: **17**
Percentage of 2006 graduates working in: New England: **2%**, Middle Atlantic: **86%**, East North Central: **0%**, West North Central: **0%**, South Atlantic: **5%**, East South Central: **0%**, West South Central: **1%**, Mountain: **1%**, Pacific: **2%**, Unknown: **0%**

BAR PASSAGE RATES
Based on 2006 graduates taking Summer 2006 or Winter 2007 exams. Most of the school's first-time test takers took the bar in New York.

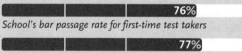

76%
School's bar passage rate for first-time test takers

77%
Statewide bar passage rate for first-time test takers

DePaul University

- 25 E. Jackson Boulevard, Chicago, IL, 60604
- http://www.law.depaul.edu
- Private
- Year founded: 1912
- 2007-2008 tuition: full-time: $33,110; part-time: $21,545
- Enrollment 2007-08 academic year: full-time: 745; part-time: 248
- U.S. News 2009 law specialty ranking: intellectual property law: 11

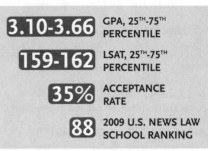

3.10-3.66 GPA, 25TH-75TH PERCENTILE

159-162 LSAT, 25TH-75TH PERCENTILE

35% ACCEPTANCE RATE

88 2009 U.S. NEWS LAW SCHOOL RANKING

ADMISSIONS
Admissions phone number: **(312) 362-6831**
Admissions email address: **lawinfo@depaul.edu**
Application website: **http://www.law.depaul.edu/apply**
Application deadline for Fall 2009 admission: **03/01**

Admissions statistics:
Number of applicants for Fall 2007: **4,029**
Number of acceptances: **1,419**
Number enrolled: **232**
Acceptance rate: **35%**
GPA, 25th-75th percentile, entering class Fall 2007: **3.10-3.66**
LSAT, 25th-75th percentile, entering class Fall 2007: **159-162**

Part-time program:
Number of applicants for Fall 2007: **665**
Number of acceptances: **316**
Number enrolled: **79**
Acceptance rate: **48%**
GPA, 25th-75th percentile, entering class Fall 2007: **3.01-3.51**
LSAT, 25th-75th percentile, entering class Fall 2007: **154-158**

FINANCIAL AID
Financial aid phone number: **(312) 362-8091**
Financial aid application deadline: **04/01**
Tuition 2007-2008 academic year: full-time: **$33,110**; part-time: **$21,545**
Room and board: **$21,604**; books: **$1,300**; miscellaneous expenses: **N/A**
Total of room/board/books/miscellaneous expenses: **$22,904**
University offers graduate student housing for which law students are eligible.

Financial aid profile
Percent of students that received grants for the 2006-2007 academic year: full-time: **60%**; part-time **26%**

Median grant amount: full-time: **$12,000**; part-time: **$4,000**
The average law-school debt of those in the Class of 2007 who borrowed: **$104,715**. Proportion who borrowed: **85%**

ACADEMIC PROGRAMS
Calendar: **semester**
Joint degrees awarded: **J.D./M.B.A.; J.D./M.S. Public Service Management; J.D./M.A. International Studies; J.D./M.A. Computer Science; J.D./M.S. Computer Science**
Typical first-year section size: Full-time: **84**; Part-time: **67**
Is there typically a "small section" of the first year class, other than Legal Writing, taught by full-time faculty?: Full-time: **no**; Part-time: **no**
Number of course titles, beyond the first year curriculum, offered last year: **145**
Percentages of upper division course sections, excluding seminars, with an enrollment of:
Under 25: **72%**   25 to 49: **16%**
50 to 74: **4%**   75 to 99: **8%**
100+: **0%**
Areas of specialization: appellate advocacy, clinical training, dispute resolution, environmental law, healthcare law, intellectual property law, international law, tax law, trial advocacy

Fall 2007 faculty profile
Total teaching faculty: **N/A**. Full-time: **N/A**; **N/A** men, **N/A** women, **N/A** minorities. Part-time: **N/A**; **N/A** men, **N/A** women, **N/A** minorities
Student-to-faculty ratio: **13.6**

SPECIAL PROGRAMS *(as provided by law school):*
DePaul is home to 13 academic research centers and institutes that focus on major legal issues of national and international scope. Additionally, DePaul offers six legal clinics, 10 Certificate programs, five joint-degree programs, and five study-abroad programs.

STUDENT BODY

Fall 2007 full-time enrollment: 745

Men: 50%	Women: 50%
African-American: 6.7%	American Indian: 0.5%
Asian-American: 4.8%	Mexican-American: 0.0%
Puerto Rican: 0.0%	Other Hisp-Amer: 10.1%
White: 73.3%	International: 1.1%
Unknown: 3.5%	

Fall 2007 part-time enrollment: 248

Men: 48%	Women: 52%
African-American: 6.9%	American Indian: 0.0%
Asian-American: 7.7%	Mexican-American: 0.0%
Puerto Rican: 0.0%	Other Hisp-Amer: 8.1%
White: 71.4%	International: 1.6%
Unknown: 4.4%	

Attrition rates for 2006-2007 full-time students
Percent of students discontinuing law school:

Men: 4%	Women: 3%
First-year students: 11%	Second-year students: 0%
Third-year students: N/A	

LIBRARY RESOURCES

Total volumes: 391,709
Total seats available for library users: 447

INFORMATION TECHNOLOGY

Number of wired network connections available to students: 55 total (in the law library, excluding computer labs: 35; in classrooms: 0; in computer labs: 10; elsewhere in the law school: 10)
Law school has a wireless network.
Students are not required to own a computer.

EMPLOYMENT AND SALARIES

Proportion of 2006 graduates employed at graduation: 83%

Employed 9 months later, as of February 15, 2007: 90%
Salaries in the private sector (law firms, business, industry): $50,000–$86,000 (25th-75th percentile)
Median salary in the private sector: $65,000
Percentage in the private sector who reported salary information: 78%
Median salary in public service (government, judicial clerkships, academic posts, non-profits): $47,650

Percentage of 2006 graduates in:

Law firms: 57%	Government: 12%
Bus./industry: 21%	Judicial clerkship: 3%
Public interest: 4%	Unknown: 1%
Academia: 2%	

2006 graduates employed in-state: 87%
2006 graduates employed in foreign countries: 1%
Number of states where graduates are employed: 21
Percentage of 2006 graduates working in: New England: 1%, Middle Atlantic: 1%, East North Central: 89%, West North Central: 1%, South Atlantic: 3%, East South Central: 0%, West South Central: 1%, Mountain: 0%, Pacific: 2%, Unknown: 2%

BAR PASSAGE RATES

Based on 2006 graduates taking Summer 2006 or Winter 2007 exams. Most of the school's first-time test takers took the bar in Illinois.

87%
School's bar passage rate for first-time test takers

87%
Statewide bar passage rate for first-time test takers

Drake University

- 2507 University Avenue, Des Moines, IA, 50311
- http://www.law.drake.edu/
- Private
- Year founded: 1881
- 2007-2008 tuition: full-time: $27,756; part-time: $950/credit hour
- Enrollment 2007-08 academic year: full-time: 414; part-time: 7
- U.S. News 2009 law specialty ranking: clinical training: 25

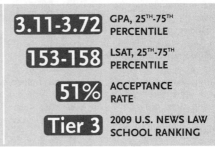

3.11-3.72 GPA, 25TH-75TH PERCENTILE

153-158 LSAT, 25TH-75TH PERCENTILE

51% ACCEPTANCE RATE

Tier 3 2009 U.S. NEWS LAW SCHOOL RANKING

ADMISSIONS
Admissions phone number: **(515) 271-2782**
Admissions email address: **lawadmit@drake.edu**
Application website:
http://www.law.drake.edu/admissions/
Application deadline for Fall 2009 admission: **04/01**

Admissions statistics:
Number of applicants for Fall 2007: **1,178**
Number of acceptances: **597**
Number enrolled: **146**
Acceptance rate: **51%**
GPA, 25th-75th percentile, entering class Fall 2007: **3.11-3.72**
LSAT, 25th-75th percentile, entering class Fall 2007: **153-158**

Part-time program:
Number of applicants for Fall 2007: **28**
Number of acceptances: **5**
Number enrolled: **2**
Acceptance rate: **18%**
GPA, 25th-75th percentile, entering class Fall 2007: **N/A**
LSAT, 25th-75th percentile, entering class Fall 2007: **N/A**

FINANCIAL AID
Financial aid phone number: **(515) 271-2782**
Financial aid application deadline: **03/01**
Tuition 2007-2008 academic year: full-time: **$27,756**; part-time: **$950/credit hour**
Room and board: **$7,125**; books: **$1,125**; miscellaneous expenses: **$3,900**
Total of room/board/books/miscellaneous expenses: **$12,150**
University does not offer graduate student housing for which law students are eligible.

Financial aid profile
Percent of students that received grants for the 2006-2007 academic year: full-time: **61%**

Median grant amount: full-time: **$11,000**
The average law-school debt of those in the Class of 2007 who borrowed: **$81,702**. Proportion who borrowed: **91%**

ACADEMIC PROGRAMS
Calendar: **semester**
Joint degrees awarded: **J.D./M.B.A.; J.D./M.P.A.; J.D./M.A. Political Science; J.D./M.A. Agricultural Economics; J.D./M.S.W.; J.D./Ph.D.; J.D./Pharm.D.**
Typical first-year section size: Full-time: **72**
Is there typically a "small section" of the first year class, other than Legal Writing, taught by full-time faculty?: Full-time: **no**; Part-time: **no**
Number of course titles, beyond the first year curriculum, offered last year: **112**
Percentages of upper division course sections, excluding seminars, with an enrollment of:
Under 25: **56%**   25 to 49: **31%**
50 to 74: **9%**   75 to 99: **4%**
100+: **0%**
Areas of specialization: appellate advocacy, clinical training, dispute resolution, environmental law, healthcare law, intellectual property law, international law, tax law, trial advocacy

Fall 2007 faculty profile
Total teaching faculty: **53**. Full-time: **53%**; **64%** men, **36%** women, **14%** minorities. Part-time: **47%**; **64%** men, **36%** women, **8%** minorities
Student-to-faculty ratio: **12.9**

SPECIAL PROGRAMS *(as provided by law school):*
Drake offers live-client clinics in civil practice, criminal defense, mediation, elder law, and children's rights. It has five centers: Constitutional Law, Children's Rights, Agricultural Law, Legislative Practice, and Intellectual Property Law. It offers a unique first-year trial practicum, a summer-in-France program, nearly 20 internships, and over 30 paid summer public interest internships.

STUDENT BODY

Fall 2007 full-time enrollment: 414

Men: 55%	Women: 45%
African-American: 6.0%	American Indian: 0.5%
Asian-American: 2.7%	Mexican-American: 0.7%
Puerto Rican: 0.5%	Other Hisp-Amer: 1.4%
White: 78.5%	International: 0.0%
Unknown: 9.7%	

Fall 2007 part-time enrollment: 7

Men: 0%	Women: 100%
African-American: 14.3%	American Indian: 0.0%
Asian-American: 0.0%	Mexican-American: 0.0%
Puerto Rican: 0.0%	Other Hisp-Amer: 0.0%
White: 85.7%	International: 0.0%
Unknown: 0.0%	

Attrition rates for 2006-2007 full-time students
Percent of students discontinuing law school:

Men: 3%	Women: 2%
First-year students: 7%	Second-year students: N/A
Third-year students: N/A	

LIBRARY RESOURCES

Total volumes: 330,382
Total seats available for library users: 705

INFORMATION TECHNOLOGY

Number of wired network connections available to students: 160 total (in the law library, excluding computer labs: 160; in classrooms: 0; in computer labs: 0; elsewhere in the law school: 0)
Law school has a wireless network.
Students are not required to own a computer.

EMPLOYMENT AND SALARIES

Proportion of 2006 graduates employed at graduation: N/A
Employed 9 months later, as of February 15, 2007: 95%

Salaries in the private sector (law firms, business, industry): $43,300–$66,875 (25th-75th percentile)
Median salary in the private sector: $54,250
Percentage in the private sector who reported salary information: 40%
Median salary in public service (government, judicial clerkships, academic posts, non-profits): $43,250

Percentage of 2006 graduates in:

Law firms: 59%	Government: 9%
Bus./industry: 17%	Judicial clerkship: 9%
Public interest: 5%	Unknown: 0%
Academia: 1%	

2006 graduates employed in-state: 68%
2006 graduates employed in foreign countries: 1%
Number of states where graduates are employed: 24
Percentage of 2006 graduates working in: New England: 1%, Middle Atlantic: 1%, East North Central: 7%, West North Central: 75%, South Atlantic: 5%, East South Central: 1%, West South Central: 4%, Mountain: 3%, Pacific: 1%, Unknown: 0%

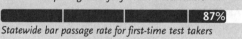

BAR PASSAGE RATES

Based on 2006 graduates taking Summer 2006 or Winter 2007 exams. Most of the school's first-time test takers took the bar in Iowa.

91%
School's bar passage rate for first-time test takers

87%
Statewide bar passage rate for first-time test takers

Duke University

■ Towerview and Science Drive, Box 90362, Durham, NC, 27708-0362
■ http://www.law.duke.edu
■ Private
■ Year founded: 1930
■ 2007-2008 tuition: full-time: $40,748; part-time: N/A
■ Enrollment 2007-08 academic year: full-time: 583; part-time: 37
■ U.S. News 2009 law specialty ranking: environmental law: 5, intellectual property law: 6, international law: 11, tax law: 18

3.61-3.82 GPA, 25TH-75TH PERCENTILE

167-170 LSAT, 25TH-75TH PERCENTILE

27% ACCEPTANCE RATE

12 2009 U.S. NEWS LAW SCHOOL RANKING

ADMISSIONS
Admissions phone number: **(919) 613-7020**
Admissions email address: **admissions@law.duke.edu**
Application website:
  http://admissions.law.duke.edu/admis/appform.html
Application deadline for Fall 2009 admission: **02/16**

Admissions statistics:
Number of applicants for Fall 2007: **5,803**
Number of acceptances: **1,546**
Number enrolled: **207**
Acceptance rate: **27%**
GPA, 25th-75th percentile, entering class Fall 2007: **3.61-3.82**
LSAT, 25th-75th percentile, entering class Fall 2007: **167-170**

FINANCIAL AID
Financial aid phone number: **(919) 613-7026**
Financial aid application deadline: **03/15**
Tuition 2007-2008 academic year: full-time: **$40,748**; part-time: **N/A**
Room and board: **$9,180**; books: **$1,140**; miscellaneous expenses: **$6,309**
Total of room/board/books/miscellaneous expenses: **$16,629**
University does not offer graduate student housing for which law students are eligible.

Financial aid profile
Percent of students that received grants for the 2006-2007 academic year: full-time: **79%**
Median grant amount: full-time: **$10,000**
The average law-school debt of those in the Class of 2007 who borrowed: **$108,596**. Proportion who borrowed: **86%**

ACADEMIC PROGRAMS
Calendar: **semester**
Joint degrees awarded: **J.D./M.A. Cultural Anthropology; J.D./M.A. East Asian Studies; J.D./M.S. Electrical &** Computer Eng.; **J.D./M.A. Environmental Sci./Policy; J.D./M.A. Economics; J.D./M.A. History; J.D./M.A. Humanities; J.D./LL.M. Int'l and Comparative Law; J.D/.M.B.A.; J.D./M.D.; J.D./M.S. Mechanical Engineering; J.D./M.E.M.; J.D./M.P.P.; J.D./M.T.S.; J.D./M.A. Philosophy; J.D./M.A. Political Science; J.D./M.A. Public Policy Studies; J.D./M.A. Psychology; J.D./M.S. Biomedical Engineering; J.D./M.A. Classical Studies; J.D./M.A. Romance Studies; J.D./M.A. Sociology; J.D./M.A. Religion; J.D./M.A. English; J.D./Ph.D History; J.D./Ph.D Political Science**
Typical first-year section size: Full-time: **69**
Is there typically a "small section" of the first year class, other than Legal Writing, taught by full-time faculty?: Full-time: **yes**
Number of course titles, beyond the first year curriculum, offered last year: **168**
Percentages of upper division course sections, excluding seminars, with an enrollment of:
  Under 25: **61%**   25 to 49: **25%**
  50 to 74: **7%**   75 to 99: **4%**
  100+: **4%**
Areas of specialization: appellate advocacy, clinical training, dispute resolution, environmental law, healthcare law, intellectual property law, international law, tax law, trial advocacy

Fall 2007 faculty profile
Total teaching faculty: **112**. Full-time: **43%**; **75%** men, **25%** women, **8%** minorities. Part-time: **57%**; **67%** men, **33%** women, **6%** minorities
Student-to-faculty ratio: **13.9**

SPECIAL PROGRAMS *(as provided by law school):*
Duke leads in interdisciplinary study with almost 25 percent of students in joint degrees. Interdisciplinary centers offer conferences, research, and teaching. A clinical education leader, Duke operates seven, soon eight, clinics; capstone projects integrate academics and hands-on practice. Opportunities abroad include externships, foreign exchanges, and summer institutes in Geneva and Hong Kong.

STUDENT BODY

Fall 2007 full-time enrollment: 583

Men: 55%	Women: 45%
African-American: 8.2%	American Indian: 0.2%
Asian-American: 5.8%	Mexican-American: 1.2%
Puerto Rican: 0.0%	Other Hisp-Amer: 2.1%
White: 64.3%	International: 4.6%
Unknown: 13.6%	

Fall 2007 part-time enrollment: 37

Men: 73%	Women: 27%
African-American: 8.1%	American Indian: 0.0%
Asian-American: 5.4%	Mexican-American: 0.0%
Puerto Rican: 0.0%	Other Hisp-Amer: 0.0%
White: 64.9%	International: 2.7%
Unknown: 18.9%	

Attrition rates for 2006-2007 full-time students

Percent of students discontinuing law school:

Men: 1%	Women: 0%
First-year students: 0%	Second-year students: 2%
Third-year students: N/A	

LIBRARY RESOURCES

Total volumes: 637,435

Total seats available for library users: 503

INFORMATION TECHNOLOGY

Number of wired network connections available to students: 818 total (in the law library, excluding computer labs: 138; in classrooms: 650; in computer labs: 0; elsewhere in the law school: 30)

Law school has a wireless network.

Students are not required to own a computer.

EMPLOYMENT AND SALARIES

Proportion of 2006 graduates employed at graduation: 92%

Employed 9 months later, as of February 15, 2007: 98%

Salaries in the private sector (law firms, business, industry): $115,000–$145,000 (25th-75th percentile)

Median salary in the private sector: $135,000

Percentage in the private sector who reported salary information: 91%

Median salary in public service (government, judicial clerkships, academic posts, non-profits): $50,000

Percentage of 2006 graduates in:

Law firms: 66%	Government: 6%
Bus./industry: 6%	Judicial clerkship: 19%
Public interest: 3%	Unknown: 0%
Academia: 0%	

2006 graduates employed in-state: 13%

2006 graduates employed in foreign countries: 2%

Number of states where graduates are employed: 32

Percentage of 2006 graduates working in: New England: 7%, Middle Atlantic: 25%, East North Central: 1%, West North Central: 2%, South Atlantic: 42%, East South Central: 2%, West South Central: 7%, Mountain: 4%, Pacific: 8%, Unknown: 0%

BAR PASSAGE RATES

Based on 2006 graduates taking Summer 2006 or Winter 2007 exams. Most of the school's first-time test takers took the bar in New York.

97%

School's bar passage rate for first-time test takers

77%

Statewide bar passage rate for first-time test takers

Duquesne University

■ 600 Forbes Avenue, Pittsburgh, PA, 15282
■ http://www.duq.edu/law
■ Private
■ Year founded: 1911
■ 2007-2008 tuition: full-time: $27,230; part-time: $21,078
■ Enrollment 2007-08 academic year: full-time: 470; part-time: 209
■ U.S. News 2009 law specialty ranking: N/A

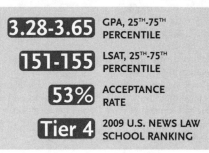

3.28-3.65 GPA, 25TH-75TH PERCENTILE

151-155 LSAT, 25TH-75TH PERCENTILE

53% ACCEPTANCE RATE

Tier 4 2009 U.S. NEWS LAW SCHOOL RANKING

ADMISSIONS
Admissions phone number: (412) 396-6296
Admissions email address: ricci@duq.edu
Application website: N/A
Application deadline for Fall 2009 admission: 04/01

Admissions statistics:
Number of applicants for Fall 2007: 911
Number of acceptances: 481
Number enrolled: 161
Acceptance rate: 53%
GPA, 25th-75th percentile, entering class Fall 2007: 3.28-3.65
LSAT, 25th-75th percentile, entering class Fall 2007: 151-155

Part-time program:
Number of applicants for Fall 2007: 184
Number of acceptances: 147
Number enrolled: 82
Acceptance rate: 80%
GPA, 25th-75th percentile, entering class Fall 2007: 3.24-3.61
LSAT, 25th-75th percentile, entering class Fall 2007: 149-154

FINANCIAL AID
Financial aid phone number: (412) 396-6607
Financial aid application deadline: 05/31
Tuition 2007-2008 academic year: full-time: $27,230; part-time: $21,078
Room and board: $8,054; books: $1,254; miscellaneous expenses: $1,750
Total of room/board/books/miscellaneous expenses: $11,058
University offers graduate student housing for which law students are eligible.

Financial aid profile
Percent of students that received grants for the 2006-2007 academic year: full-time: 37%; part-time 14%
Median grant amount: full-time: $8,564; part-time: $4,265

The average law-school debt of those in the Class of 2007 who borrowed: $75,760. Proportion who borrowed: 91%

ACADEMIC PROGRAMS
Calendar: **semester**
Joint degrees awarded: **J.D./M.B.A.; J.D./M.S.E.S.M.; J.D./M.Div.; J.D./M.S.T.**
Typical first-year section size: Full-time: **90**; Part-time: **85**
Is there typically a "small section" of the first year class, other than Legal Writing, taught by full-time faculty?: Full-time: **yes**; Part-time: **no**
Number of course titles, beyond the first year curriculum, offered last year: **82**
Percentages of upper division course sections, excluding seminars, with an enrollment of:
Under 25: **45%**   25 to 49: **25%**
50 to 74: **16%**   75 to 99: **12%**
100+: **1%**
Areas of specialization: appellate advocacy, clinical training, dispute resolution, environmental law, healthcare law, intellectual property law, international law, tax law, trial advocacy

Fall 2007 faculty profile
Total teaching faculty: **52**. Full-time: **52%**; **78%** men, **22%** women, **7%** minorities. Part-time: **48%**; **72%** men, **28%** women, **N/A** minorities
Student-to-faculty ratio: **18.2**

SPECIAL PROGRAMS *(as provided by law school)*:
Summer programs: Beijing, Rome, Dublin. Clinics: low-income taxation, securities, family justice, economic/community development, post-conviction DNA. Center: Prof. Jan Levine, a nationally known expert in legal writing and research, joined Duquesne from Temple Law School in 2007 as a tenured member of the faculty. With his guidance, a major legal research and writing center is under design.

STUDENT BODY
Fall 2007 full-time enrollment: 470
Men: 52%   Women: 48%

African-American: 4.7% American Indian: 0.2%
Asian-American: 1.5% Mexican-American: 0.0%
Puerto Rican: 0.0% Other Hisp-Amer: 1.3%
White: 91.1% International: 0.0%
Unknown: 1.3%

Fall 2007 part-time enrollment: 209
Men: 45% Women: 55%
African-American: 5.3% American Indian: 0.5%
Asian-American: 0.5% Mexican-American: 0.0%
Puerto Rican: 0.0% Other Hisp-Amer: 0.5%
White: 91.9% International: 0.0%
Unknown: 1.4%

Attrition rates for 2006-2007 full-time students
Percent of students discontinuing law school:
Men: 2% Women: 2%
First-year students: 4% Second-year students: 1%
Third-year students: N/A

LIBRARY RESOURCES
Total volumes: 302,165
Total seats available for library users: 411

INFORMATION TECHNOLOGY
Number of wired network connections available to students: 81 total (in the law library, excluding computer labs: 38; in classrooms: 0; in computer labs: 25; elsewhere in the law school: 18)
Law school has a wireless network.
Students are not required to own a computer.

EMPLOYMENT AND SALARIES
Proportion of 2006 graduates employed at graduation: N/A
Employed 9 months later, as of February 15, 2007: 86%

Salaries in the private sector (law firms, business, industry): $50,000–$80,000 (25th-75th percentile)
Median salary in the private sector: $60,000
Percentage in the private sector who reported salary information: 55%
Median salary in public service (government, judicial clerkships, academic posts, non-profits): $39,000

Percentage of 2006 graduates in:
Law firms: 55% Government: 8%
Bus./industry: 23% Judicial clerkship: 8%
Public interest: 4% Unknown: N/A
Academia: 2%

2006 graduates employed in-state: 86%
2006 graduates employed in foreign countries: 0%
Number of states where graduates are employed: 12
Percentage of 2006 graduates working in: New England: 2%, Middle Atlantic: 86%, East North Central: 2%, West North Central: N/A, South Atlantic: 8%, East South Central: N/A, West South Central: 1%, Mountain: 1%, Pacific: N/A, Unknown: 0%

BAR PASSAGE RATES
Based on 2006 graduates taking Summer 2006 or Winter 2007 exams. Most of the school's first-time test takers took the bar in Pennsylvania.

88%
School's bar passage rate for first-time test takers

83%
Statewide bar passage rate for first-time test takers

Emory University

- 1301 Clifton Road, Atlanta, GA, 30322-2770
- http://www.law.emory.edu
- Private
- Year founded: 1916
- 2007-2008 tuition: full-time: $38,176; part-time: N/A
- Enrollment 2007-08 academic year: full-time: 709
- U.S. News 2009 law specialty ranking: N/A

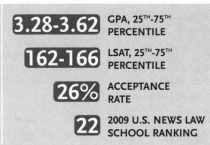

3.28-3.62 GPA, 25TH-75TH PERCENTILE

162-166 LSAT, 25TH-75TH PERCENTILE

26% ACCEPTANCE RATE

22 2009 U.S. NEWS LAW SCHOOL RANKING

ADMISSIONS
Admissions phone number: **(404) 727-6802**
Admissions email address: **lawinfo@law.emory.edu**
Application website:
http://www.law.emory.edu/admissions/application.html
Application deadline for Fall 2009 admission: **03/01**

Admissions statistics:
Number of applicants for Fall 2007: **3,913**
Number of acceptances: **1,025**
Number enrolled: **254**
Acceptance rate: **26%**
GPA, 25th-75th percentile, entering class Fall 2007: **3.28-3.62**
LSAT, 25th-75th percentile, entering class Fall 2007: **162-166**

FINANCIAL AID
Financial aid phone number: **(404) 727-6039**
Financial aid application deadline: **03/01**
Tuition 2007-2008 academic year: full-time: **$38,176**; part-time: **N/A**
Room and board: **$16,516**; books: **$2,250**; miscellaneous expenses: **$3,046**
Total of room/board/books/miscellaneous expenses: **$21,812**
University offers graduate student housing for which law students are eligible.

Financial aid profile
Percent of students that received grants for the 2006-2007 academic year: full-time: **35%**
Median grant amount: full-time: **$16,000**
The average law-school debt of those in the Class of 2007 who borrowed: **$94,326**. Proportion who borrowed: **79%**

ACADEMIC PROGRAMS
Calendar: **semester**
Joint degrees awarded: **J.D./M.B.A.; J.D./M.Div.; J.D./M.T.S.; J.D./M.P.H.; J.D./R.E.E.S.; J.D./Ph.D.; J.D./M.A.**

Typical first-year section size: Full-time: **70**
Is there typically a "small section" of the first year class, other than Legal Writing, taught by full-time faculty?: Full-time: **yes**
Number of course titles, beyond the first year curriculum, offered last year: **97**
Percentages of upper division course sections, excluding seminars, with an enrollment of:
Under 25: **64%**   25 to 49: **17%**
50 to 74: **12%**   75 to 99: **7%**
100+: **1%**
Areas of specialization: appellate advocacy, clinical training, dispute resolution, environmental law, healthcare law, intellectual property law, international law, tax law, trial advocacy

Fall 2007 faculty profile
Total teaching faculty: **99**. Full-time: **56%**; **53%** men, **47%** women, **15%** minorities. Part-time: **44%**; **73%** men, **27%** women, **32%** minorities
Student-to-faculty ratio: **10.8**

SPECIAL PROGRAMS *(as provided by law school):*
Interdisciplinary programs of study. Centers of Excellence in Law and Religion, International Law, Feminist Jurisprudence, Health Law. Trial techniques program and extensive field placement program. Clinics: Barton child law and policy; juvenile defender; indigent criminal defense; Turner environmental law; TI:GER program of technology and business law cosponsored by Emory and Georgia Tech.

STUDENT BODY
Fall 2007 full-time enrollment: **709**
Men: **53%**   Women: **47%**
African-American: **9.2%**   American Indian: **0.3%**
Asian-American: **9.9%**   Mexican-American: **0.0%**
Puerto Rican: **0.0%**   Other Hisp-Amer: **8.2%**
White: **67.1%**   International: **3.5%**
Unknown: **1.8%**

Attrition rates for 2006-2007 full-time students
Percent of students discontinuing law school:
Men: **2%**   Women: **3%**
First-year students: **2%**   Second-year students: **6%**
Third-year students: **N/A**

LIBRARY RESOURCES
Total volumes: **403,662**
Total seats available for library users: **498**

INFORMATION TECHNOLOGY
Number of wired network connections available to students: **123** total (in the law library, excluding computer labs: **37**; in classrooms: **86**; in computer labs: **0**; elsewhere in the law school: **0**)
Law school has a wireless network.
Students are not required to own a computer.

EMPLOYMENT AND SALARIES
Proportion of 2006 graduates employed at graduation: **96%**
Employed 9 months later, as of February 15, 2007: **98%**
Salaries in the private sector (law firms, business, industry): **$75,000–$125,000** (25th-75th percentile)
Median salary in the private sector: **$115,000**
Percentage in the private sector who reported salary information: **100%**
Median salary in public service (government, judicial clerkships, academic posts, non-profits): **$48,000**

Percentage of 2006 graduates in:
Law firms: **70%**   Government: **5%**
Bus./industry: **7%**   Judicial clerkship: **11%**
Public interest: **7%**   Unknown: **1%**
Academia: **0%**

2006 graduates employed in-state: **49%**
2006 graduates employed in foreign countries: **0%**
Number of states where graduates are employed: **19**
Percentage of 2006 graduates working in: New England: **2%**, Middle Atlantic: **23%**, East North Central: **2%**, West North Central: **1%**, South Atlantic: **61%**, East South Central: **4%**, West South Central: **3%**, Mountain: **0%**, Pacific: **4%**, Unknown: **0%**

BAR PASSAGE RATES
Based on 2006 graduates taking Summer 2006 or Winter 2007 exams. Most of the school's first-time test takers took the bar in Georgia.

95%
School's bar passage rate for first-time test takers

85%
Statewide bar passage rate for first-time test takers

Faulkner University (Jones)

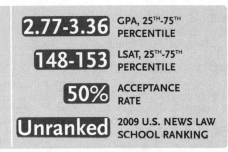

- 5345 Atlanta Highway, Montgomery, AL, 36109
- http://www.faulkner.edu/admissions/jonesLaw.asp
- Private
- Year founded: 1928
- 2007-2008 tuition: full-time: $22,000; part-time: $16,500
- Enrollment 2007-08 academic year: full-time: 228; part-time: 63
- U.S. News 2009 law specialty ranking: N/A

2.77-3.36 GPA, 25TH-75TH PERCENTILE

148-153 LSAT, 25TH-75TH PERCENTILE

50% ACCEPTANCE RATE

Unranked 2009 U.S. NEWS LAW SCHOOL RANKING

ADMISSIONS

Admissions phone number: **(334) 386-7210**
Admissions email address: **law@faulkner.edu**
Application website: **N/A**
Application deadline for Fall 2009 admission: **06/15**

Admissions statistics:
Number of applicants for Fall 2007: **453**
Number of acceptances: **225**
Number enrolled: **118**
Acceptance rate: **50%**
GPA, 25th-75th percentile, entering class Fall 2007: **2.77-3.36**
LSAT, 25th-75th percentile, entering class Fall 2007: **148-153**

Part-time program:
Number of applicants for Fall 2007: **89**
Number of acceptances: **26**
Number enrolled: **20**
Acceptance rate: **29%**
GPA, 25th-75th percentile, entering class Fall 2007: **2.52-3.26**
LSAT, 25th-75th percentile, entering class Fall 2007: **148-152**

FINANCIAL AID

Financial aid application deadline: **06/01**
Tuition 2007-2008 academic year: full-time: **$22,000**; part-time: **$16,500**
Room and board: **$12,000**; books: **$2,400**; miscellaneous expenses: **$4,500**
Total of room/board/books/miscellaneous expenses: **$18,900**
University does not offer graduate student housing for which law students are eligible.

Financial aid profile
Percent of students that received grants for the 2006-2007 academic year: full-time: **26%**; part-time **30%**

Median grant amount: full-time: **$7,500**; part-time: **$4,500**
The average law-school debt of those in the Class of 2007 who borrowed: **$62,400**. Proportion who borrowed: **86%**

ACADEMIC PROGRAMS

Calendar: **semester**
Joint degrees awarded: **N/A**
Typical first-year section size: Full-time: **75**; Part-time: **20**
Is there typically a "small section" of the first year class, other than Legal Writing, taught by full-time faculty?: Full-time: **no**; Part-time: **no**
Number of course titles, beyond the first year curriculum, offered last year: **48**
Percentages of upper division course sections, excluding seminars, with an enrollment of:

Under 25: **78%**	25 to 49: **22%**
50 to 74: **0%**	75 to 99: **0%**
100+: **0%**	

Areas of specialization: appellate advocacy, clinical training, dispute resolution, environmental law, healthcare law, intellectual property law, international law, tax law, trial advocacy

Fall 2007 faculty profile
Total teaching faculty: **28**. Full-time: **86%**; **71%** men, **29%** women, **17%** minorities. Part-time: **14%**; **75%** men, **25%** women, **0%** minorities
Student-to-faculty ratio: **10.0**

SPECIAL PROGRAMS *(as provided by law school)*:

Clinics: elder law clinic, family violence clinic, and mediation clinic. Programs: academic success program, advocacy programs, alternative dispute resolution program, externship program, and public interest program.

STUDENT BODY

Fall 2007 full-time enrollment: **228**

Men: **55%**	Women: **45%**
African-American: **5.7%**	American Indian: **1.3%**
Asian-American: **0.4%**	Mexican-American: **0.0%**

Puerto Rican: **0.0%**
White: **90.8%**
Unknown: **0.9%**

Other Hisp-Amer: **0.9%**
International: **0.0%**

Fall 2007 part-time enrollment: 63

Men: **57%**
African-American: **11.1%**
Asian-American: **4.8%**
Puerto Rican: **0.0%**
White: **82.5%**
Unknown: **0.0%**

Women: **43%**
American Indian: **0.0%**
Mexican-American: **0.0%**
Other Hisp-Amer: **1.6%**
International: **0.0%**

Attrition rates for 2006-2007 full-time students
Percent of students discontinuing law school:
Men: **N/A**
First-year students: **N/A**
Third-year students: **N/A**

Women: **N/A**
Second-year students: **N/A**

LIBRARY RESOURCES
Total volumes: **183,604**
Total seats available for library users: **213**

INFORMATION TECHNOLOGY
Number of wired network connections available to students: **205** total (in the law library, excluding computer labs: **151**; in classrooms: **54**; in computer labs: **0**; elsewhere in the law school: **0**)
Law school has a wireless network.
Students are not required to own a computer.

EMPLOYMENT AND SALARIES
Proportion of 2006 graduates employed at graduation: **N/A**
Employed 9 months later, as of February 15, 2007: **N/A**

Salaries in the private sector (law firms, business, industry): **N/A**
Median salary in the private sector: **N/A**
Percentage in the private sector who reported salary information: **N/A**
Median salary in public service (government, judicial clerkships, academic posts, non-profits): **N/A**

Percentage of 2006 graduates in:
Law firms: **54%**
Bus./industry: **6%**
Public interest: **2%**
Academia: **0%**

Government: **28%**
Judicial clerkship: **10%**
Unknown: **0%**

2006 graduates employed in-state: **94%**
2006 graduates employed in foreign countries: **0%**
Number of states where graduates are employed: **3**
Percentage of 2006 graduates working in: New England: **0%**, Middle Atlantic: **0%**, East North Central: **0%**, West North Central: **0%**, South Atlantic: **4%**, East South Central: **94%**, West South Central: **2%**, Mountain: **0%**, Pacific: **0%**, Unknown: **0%**

BAR PASSAGE RATES
Based on 2006 graduates taking Summer 2006 or Winter 2007 exams. Most of the school's first-time test takers took the bar in Alabama.

N/A
School's bar passage rate for first-time test takers

N/A
Statewide bar passage rate for first-time test takers

Florida A&M University

- 1 N. Orange Avenue, Orlando, FL, 32801
- http://www.famu.edu/acad/colleges/law
- Public
- **Year founded:** N/A
- **2007-2008 tuition:** In-state: full-time: $7,567; part-time: $6,344; Out-of-state: full-time: $26,828
- **Enrollment 2007-08 academic year:** full-time: 357; part-time: 213
- **U.S. News 2009 law specialty ranking:** N/A

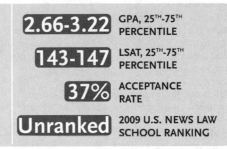

2.66-3.22 GPA, 25TH-75TH PERCENTILE

143-147 LSAT, 25TH-75TH PERCENTILE

37% ACCEPTANCE RATE

Unranked 2009 U.S. NEWS LAW SCHOOL RANKING

ADMISSIONS

Admissions phone number: **(407) 254-3263**
Admissions email address: **famu-law.admissions@famu.edu**
Application website: **N/A**
Application deadline for Fall 2009 admission: **rolling**

Admissions statistics:
Number of applicants for Fall 2007: **1,210**
Number of acceptances: **448**
Number enrolled: **145**
Acceptance rate: **37%**
GPA, 25th-75th percentile, entering class Fall 2007: **2.66-3.22**
LSAT, 25th-75th percentile, entering class Fall 2007: **143-147**

Part-time program:
Number of applicants for Fall 2007: **188**
Number of acceptances: **104**
Number enrolled: **57**
Acceptance rate: **55%**
GPA, 25th-75th percentile, entering class Fall 2007: **2.82-3.33**
LSAT, 25th-75th percentile, entering class Fall 2007: **143-151**

FINANCIAL AID

Financial aid phone number: **(850) 599-3730**
Financial aid application deadline: **N/A**
Tuition 2007-2008 academic year: In-state: full-time: **$7,567**; part-time: **$6,344**; Out-of-state: full-time: **$26,828**
Room and board: **$10,450**; books: **$1,000**; miscellaneous expenses: **$6,000**
Total of room/board/books/miscellaneous expenses: **$17,450**
University does not offer graduate student housing for which law students are eligible.

Financial aid profile
Percent of students that received grants for the 2006-2007 academic year: full-time: **N/A**
Median grant amount: full-time: **N/A**
The average law-school debt of those in the Class of 2007 who borrowed: **$18,500**. Proportion who borrowed: **84%**

ACADEMIC PROGRAMS

Calendar: **semester**
Joint degrees awarded: **N/A**
Typical first-year section size: Full-time: **60**; Part-time: **60**
Is there typically a "small section" of the first year class, other than Legal Writing, taught by full-time faculty?: Full-time: **no**; Part-time: **no**
Number of course titles, beyond the first year curriculum, offered last year: **52**
Percentages of upper division course sections, excluding seminars, with an enrollment of:
Under 25: **51%**   25 to 49: **22%**
50 to 74: **25%**   75 to 99: **2%**
100+: **0%**
Areas of specialization: clinical training, dispute resolution, environmental law, healthcare law, intellectual property law, international law, tax law, trial advocacy

Fall 2007 faculty profile
Total teaching faculty: **29**. Full-time: **69%**; **40%** men, **60%** women, **75%** minorities. Part-time: **31%**; **89%** men, **11%** women, **67%** minorities
Student-to-faculty ratio: **19.2**

SPECIAL PROGRAMS *(as provided by law school):*
N/A

STUDENT BODY
Fall 2007 full-time enrollment: **357**
Men: **43%**   Women: **57%**
African-American: **49.6%**   American Indian: **0.8%**
Asian-American: **3.9%**   Mexican-American: **0.6%**
Puerto Rican: **2.5%**   Other Hisp-Amer: **11.8%**
White: **29.7%**   International: **0.6%**
Unknown: **0.6%**

Fall 2007 part-time enrollment: 213

Men: 44%	Women: 56%
African-American: 41.3%	American Indian: 0.9%
Asian-American: 3.3%	Mexican-American: 0.0%
Puerto Rican: 1.9%	Other Hisp-Amer: 17.4%
White: 33.3%	International: 0.9%
Unknown: 0.9%	

Attrition rates for 2006-2007 full-time students
Percent of students discontinuing law school:

Men: 15%	Women: 13%
First-year students: 28%	Second-year students: 2%
Third-year students: 1%	

LIBRARY RESOURCES

Total volumes: 344,406
Total seats available for library users: 558

INFORMATION TECHNOLOGY

Number of wired network connections available to students: 18 total (in the law library, excluding computer labs: 0; in classrooms: 0; in computer labs: 18; elsewhere in the law school: 0)
Law school has a wireless network.
Students are not required to own a computer.

EMPLOYMENT AND SALARIES

Proportion of 2006 graduates employed at graduation: N/A
Employed 9 months later, as of February 15, 2007: N/A
Salaries in the private sector (law firms, business, industry): N/A

Median salary in the private sector: **N/A**
Percentage in the private sector who reported salary information: **N/A**
Median salary in public service (government, judicial clerkships, academic posts, non-profits): **N/A**

Percentage of 2006 graduates in:

Law firms: 32%	Government: 6%
Bus./industry: 13%	Judicial clerkship: 2%
Public interest: 30%	Unknown: 13%
Academia: 4%	

2006 graduates employed in-state: 96%
2006 graduates employed in foreign countries: 0%
Number of states where graduates are employed: 1
Percentage of 2006 graduates working in: New England: 0%, Middle Atlantic: 0%, East North Central: 0%, West North Central: 0%, South Atlantic: 96%, East South Central: 0%, West South Central: 0%, Mountain: 0%, Pacific: 0%, Unknown: 4%

BAR PASSAGE RATES

Based on 2006 graduates taking Summer 2006 or Winter 2007 exams. Most of the school's first-time test takers took the bar in Florida.

N/A
School's bar passage rate for first-time test takers

N/A
Statewide bar passage rate for first-time test takers

Florida Coastal School of Law

- 8787 Baypine Road, Jacksonville, FL, 32256
- http://www.fcsl.edu
- Private
- Year founded: 1996
- 2007-2008 tuition: full-time: $28,870; part-time: $23,360
- Enrollment 2007-08 academic year: full-time: 1,231; part-time: 164
- U.S. News 2009 law specialty ranking: N/A

2.81-3.47 GPA, 25TH-75TH PERCENTILE

149-154 LSAT, 25TH-75TH PERCENTILE

55% ACCEPTANCE RATE

Tier 4 2009 U.S. NEWS LAW SCHOOL RANKING

ADMISSIONS

Admissions phone number: **(904) 680-7710**
Admissions email address: **admissions@fcsl.edu**
Application website: **N/A**
Application deadline for Fall 2009 admission: **rolling**

Admissions statistics:
Number of applicants for Fall 2007: **4,970**
Number of acceptances: **2,730**
Number enrolled: **613**
Acceptance rate: **55%**
GPA, 25th-75th percentile, entering class Fall 2007: **2.81-3.47**
LSAT, 25th-75th percentile, entering class Fall 2007: **149-154**

Part-time program:
Number of applicants for Fall 2007: **69**
Number of acceptances: **20**
Number enrolled: **7**
Acceptance rate: **29%**
GPA, 25th-75th percentile, entering class Fall 2007: **2.77-3.49**
LSAT, 25th-75th percentile, entering class Fall 2007: **147-151**

FINANCIAL AID

Financial aid phone number: **(904) 680-7717**
Financial aid application deadline: **N/A**
Tuition 2007-2008 academic year: full-time: **$28,870**; part-time: **$23,360**
Room and board: **$8,820**; books: **$1,200**; miscellaneous expenses: **$8,100**
Total of room/board/books/miscellaneous expenses: **$18,120**
University does not offer graduate student housing for which law students are eligible.

Financial aid profile
Percent of students that received grants for the 2006-2007 academic year: full-time: **48%**; part-time **13%**

Median grant amount: full-time: **$5,000**; part-time: **$8,000**
The average law-school debt of those in the Class of 2007 who borrowed: **$91,861**. Proportion who borrowed: **90%**

ACADEMIC PROGRAMS

Calendar: **semester**
Joint degrees awarded: **N/A**
Typical first-year section size: Full-time: **75**; Part-time: **75**
Is there typically a "small section" of the first year class, other than Legal Writing, taught by full-time faculty?: Full-time: **no**; Part-time: **no**
Number of course titles, beyond the first year curriculum, offered last year: **203**
Percentages of upper division course sections, excluding seminars, with an enrollment of:
Under 25: **52%**	25 to 49: **27%**
50 to 74: **19%**	75 to 99: **2%**
100+: **0%**	
Areas of specialization: appellate advocacy, clinical training, dispute resolution, environmental law, healthcare law, intellectual property law, international law, tax law, trial advocacy

Fall 2007 faculty profile
Total teaching faculty: **126**. Full-time: **53%**; 37% men, 63% women, 19% minorities. Part-time: **47%**; 71% men, 29% women, 5% minorities
Student-to-faculty ratio: **19.7**

SPECIAL PROGRAMS *(as provided by law school):*

FCSL has four clinical programs, as well as externships for over 75 students per semester. In addition, it offers Certificates in Sports Law, International Law, Family Law, Environmental Law, and Legal Writing.

STUDENT BODY

Fall 2007 full-time enrollment: 1,231
Men: **52%**	Women: **48%**
African-American: **6.7%**	American Indian: **1.1%**
Asian-American: **6.0%**	Mexican-American: **0.5%**

Puerto Rican: 0.5% Other Hisp-Amer: 5.3%
White: 54.3% International: 0.0%
Unknown: 25.6%

Fall 2007 part-time enrollment: 164
Men: 54% Women: 46%
African-American: 6.7% American Indian: 6.1%
Asian-American: 4.9% Mexican-American: 0.0%
Puerto Rican: 0.0% Other Hisp-Amer: 3.7%
White: 56.7% International: 0.0%
Unknown: 22.0%

Attrition rates for 2006-2007 full-time students
Percent of students discontinuing law school:
Men: 7% Women: 5%
First-year students: 11% Second-year students: 4%
Third-year students: 1%

LIBRARY RESOURCES
Total volumes: 223,820
Total seats available for library users: 516

INFORMATION TECHNOLOGY
Number of wired network connections available to students: 3,780 total (in the law library, excluding computer labs: 500; in classrooms: 2,180; in computer labs: 60; elsewhere in the law school: 1,040)
Law school has a wireless network.
Students are not required to own a computer.

EMPLOYMENT AND SALARIES
Proportion of 2006 graduates employed at graduation: N/A
Employed 9 months later, as of February 15, 2007: 88%

Salaries in the private sector (law firms, business, industry): $39,000–$55,000 (25th-75th percentile)
Median salary in the private sector: $48,500
Percentage in the private sector who reported salary information: 36%
Median salary in public service (government, judicial clerkships, academic posts, non-profits): $40,000

Percentage of 2006 graduates in:
Law firms: 48% Government: 17%
Bus./industry: 15% Judicial clerkship: 5%
Public interest: 12% Unknown: 2%
Academia: 1%

2006 graduates employed in-state: 75%
2006 graduates employed in foreign countries: 0%
Number of states where graduates are employed: 26
Percentage of 2006 graduates working in: New England: 0%, Middle Atlantic: 1%, East North Central: 2%, West North Central: 1%, South Atlantic: 90%, East South Central: 3%, West South Central: 1%, Mountain: 0%, Pacific: 1%, Unknown: 0%

BAR PASSAGE RATES
Based on 2006 graduates taking Summer 2006 or Winter 2007 exams. Most of the school's first-time test takers took the bar in Florida.

74%
School's bar passage rate for first-time test takers

74%
Statewide bar passage rate for first-time test takers

Florida International University

■ University Park, GL 485, Miami, FL, 33199
■ http://www.fiu.edu/law
■ Public
■ Year founded: 2002
■ 2007-2008 tuition: In-state: full-time: $306/credit hour; part-time: $306/credit hour; Out-of-state: full-time: $766/credit hour
■ Enrollment 2007-08 academic year: full-time: 307; part-time: 143
■ U.S. News 2009 law specialty ranking: N/A

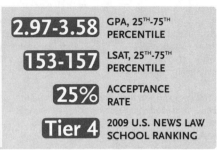

2.97-3.58 GPA, 25TH-75TH PERCENTILE

153-157 LSAT, 25TH-75TH PERCENTILE

25% ACCEPTANCE RATE

Tier 4 2009 U.S. NEWS LAW SCHOOL RANKING

ADMISSIONS

Admissions phone number: (305) 348-8006
Admissions email address: **lawadmit@fiu.edu**
Application website:
 http://law.fiu.edu/admissions/apply.htm
Application deadline for Fall 2009 admission: 05/01

Admissions statistics:

Number of applicants for Fall 2007: **1,709**
Number of acceptances: **420**
Number enrolled: **130**
Acceptance rate: **25%**
GPA, 25th-75th percentile, entering class Fall 2007: **2.97-3.58**
LSAT, 25th-75th percentile, entering class Fall 2007: **153-157**

Part-time program:

Number of applicants for Fall 2007: **426**
Number of acceptances: **163**
Number enrolled: **63**
Acceptance rate: **38%**
GPA, 25th-75th percentile, entering class Fall 2007: **2.91-3.54**
LSAT, 25th-75th percentile, entering class Fall 2007: **151-154**

FINANCIAL AID

Financial aid phone number: (305) 348-8006
Financial aid application deadline: N/A
Tuition 2007-2008 academic year: In-state: full-time: **$306/credit hour**; part-time: **$306/credit hour**; Out-of-state: full-time: **$766/credit hour**
Room and board: $10,258; books: $2,280; miscellaneous expenses: $2,128
Total of room/board/books/miscellaneous expenses: **$14,666**
University offers graduate student housing for which law students are eligible.

Financial aid profile

Percent of students that received grants for the 2006-2007 academic year: full-time: **30%**; part-time **14%**

Median grant amount: full-time: **$5,000**; part-time: **$5,000**
The average law-school debt of those in the Class of 2007 who borrowed: **$17,774**. Proportion who borrowed: **76%**

ACADEMIC PROGRAMS

Calendar: **semester**
Joint degrees awarded: **J.D./M.B.A.; J.D./M.S.W.; J.D./M.A. Latin Amer./Caribbean Studies; J.D./M.A. International Business; J.D./M.P.A.; J.D./M.S. Psychology; J.D./M.S. Criminal Justice; J.D./M.S. Environmental Studies**
Typical first-year section size: Full-time: **65**; Part-time: **64**
Is there typically a "small section" of the first year class, other than Legal Writing, taught by full-time faculty?: Full-time: **no**; Part-time: **no**
Number of course titles, beyond the first year curriculum, offered last year: **57**
Percentages of upper division course sections, excluding seminars, with an enrollment of:

Under 25: **80%**	25 to 49: **16%**
50 to 74: **4%**	75 to 99: **0%**
100+: **0%**	

Areas of specialization: appellate advocacy, clinical training, dispute resolution, environmental law, healthcare law, intellectual property law, international law, tax law, trial advocacy

Fall 2007 faculty profile

Total teaching faculty: **32**. Full-time: **75%**; 50% men, 50% women, 58% minorities. Part-time: **25%**; 75% men, 25% women, 50% minorities
Student-to-faculty ratio: **15.0**

SPECIAL PROGRAMS *(as provided by law school):*

The program emphasizes international and comparative law, which includes: a required first-year course in international law, a requirement that all courses include an international component, and a rich array of upper-level international electives. The school offers four clinics: immigration, community development, juvenile justice, and criminal law.

STUDENT BODY

Fall 2007 full-time enrollment: 307

Men: 57%	Women: 43%
African-American: 5.9%	American Indian: 1.0%
Asian-American: 2.0%	Mexican-American: 0.0%
Puerto Rican: 0.0%	Other Hisp-Amer: 41.4%
White: 44.6%	International: 2.0%
Unknown: 3.3%	

Fall 2007 part-time enrollment: 143

Men: 52%	Women: 48%
African-American: 11.9%	American Indian: 0.0%
Asian-American: 1.4%	Mexican-American: 0.0%
Puerto Rican: 0.0%	Other Hisp-Amer: 42.0%
White: 38.5%	International: 0.0%
Unknown: 6.3%	

Attrition rates for 2006-2007 full-time students
Percent of students discontinuing law school:

Men: 8%	Women: 9%
First-year students: 18%	Second-year students: N/A
Third-year students: 1%	

LIBRARY RESOURCES

Total volumes: 203,936
Total seats available for library users: 322

INFORMATION TECHNOLOGY

Number of wired network connections available to students: 51 total (in the law library, excluding computer labs: 9; in classrooms: 16; in computer labs: 10; elsewhere in the law school: 16)
Law school has a wireless network.
Students are not required to own a computer.

EMPLOYMENT AND SALARIES

Proportion of 2006 graduates employed at graduation: 21%

Employed 9 months later, as of February 15, 2007: 84%
Salaries in the private sector (law firms, business, industry): $55,000–$92,000 (25th-75th percentile)
Median salary in the private sector: $60,000
Percentage in the private sector who reported salary information: 17%
Median salary in public service (government, judicial clerkships, academic posts, non-profits): $40,000

Percentage of 2006 graduates in:

Law firms: 34%	Government: 17%
Bus./industry: 9%	Judicial clerkship: 3%
Public interest: 4%	Unknown: 33%
Academia: 0%	

2006 graduates employed in-state: 87%
2006 graduates employed in foreign countries: 1%
Number of states where graduates are employed: 2
Percentage of 2006 graduates working in: New England: N/A, Middle Atlantic: N/A, East North Central: N/A, West North Central: N/A, South Atlantic: 88%, East South Central: N/A, West South Central: N/A, Mountain: N/A, Pacific: N/A, Unknown: 11%

BAR PASSAGE RATES

Based on 2006 graduates taking Summer 2006 or Winter 2007 exams. Most of the school's first-time test takers took the bar in Florida.

83%
School's bar passage rate for first-time test takers

74%
Statewide bar passage rate for first-time test takers

Florida State University

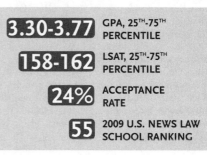

- 425 W. Jefferson Street, Tallahassee, FL, 32306-1601
- http://www.law.fsu.edu
- Public
- Year founded: 1966
- 2007-2008 tuition: In-state: full-time: $10,770; part-time: N/A; Out-of-state: full-time: $30,782
- Enrollment 2007-08 academic year: full-time: 764
- U.S. News 2009 law specialty ranking: environmental law: 10

3.30-3.77 GPA, 25TH-75TH PERCENTILE

158-162 LSAT, 25TH-75TH PERCENTILE

24% ACCEPTANCE RATE

55 2009 U.S. NEWS LAW SCHOOL RANKING

ADMISSIONS

Admissions phone number: **(850) 644-3787**
Admissions email address: **admissions@law.fsu.edu**
Application website:
https://www.law.fsu.edu/prospective_students/index.html
Application deadline for Fall 2009 admission: 03/15

Admissions statistics:
Number of applicants for Fall 2007: **3,296**
Number of acceptances: **785**
Number enrolled: **194**
Acceptance rate: **24%**
GPA, 25th-75th percentile, entering class Fall 2007: **3.30-3.77**
LSAT, 25th-75th percentile, entering class Fall 2007: **158-162**

FINANCIAL AID

Financial aid phone number: **(850) 644-5716**
Financial aid application deadline: **01/01**
Tuition 2007-2008 academic year: In-state: full-time: **$10,770**; part-time: **N/A**; Out-of-state: full-time: **$30,782**
Room and board: **$11,000**; books: **$1,200**; miscellaneous expenses: **$5,500**
Total of room/board/books/miscellaneous expenses: **$17,700**
University offers graduate student housing for which law students are eligible.

Financial aid profile
Percent of students that received grants for the 2006-2007 academic year: full-time: **33%**
Median grant amount: full-time: **$2,000**
The average law-school debt of those in the Class of 2007 who borrowed: **$56,270**. Proportion who borrowed: **84%**

ACADEMIC PROGRAMS

Calendar: **semester**
Joint degrees awarded: **J.D./M.B.A.; J.D./M.S. International Affairs; J.D./M.P.A.; J.D./M.S. Economics; J.D./M.URP.;**
J.D./M.S.W.; J.D./M.S. Library & Information Science
Typical first-year section size: Full-time: **66**
Is there typically a "small section" of the first year class, other than Legal Writing, taught by full-time faculty?: Full-time: **no**
Number of course titles, beyond the first year curriculum, offered last year: **124**
Percentages of upper division course sections, excluding seminars, with an enrollment of:
Under 25: **54%**   25 to 49: **21%**
50 to 74: **18%**   75 to 99: **4%**
100+: **2%**
Areas of specialization: appellate advocacy, clinical training, dispute resolution, environmental law, healthcare law, intellectual property law, international law, tax law, trial advocacy

Fall 2007 faculty profile
Total teaching faculty: **88**. Full-time: **56%**; **63%** men, **37%** women, **10%** minorities. Part-time: **44%**; **69%** men, **31%** women, **10%** minorities
Student-to-faculty ratio: **13.7**

SPECIAL PROGRAMS *(as provided by law school):*
The Law School offers seven joint-degree programs; a law, business, and economics program; an LL.M. program for foreign lawyers, and Certificates in Environmental Law, Natural Resources and Land Use Law, and International Law. It has an extensive clinical externship program with domestic and international placements, an in-house legal clinic, and summer-abroad study at Oxford University in England.

STUDENT BODY
Fall 2007 full-time enrollment: **764**
Men: **60%**   Women: **40%**
African-American: **5.4%**   American Indian: **0.5%**
Asian-American: **3.7%**   Mexican-American: **0.1%**
Puerto Rican: **1.3%**   Other Hisp-Amer: **5.9%**
White: **81.2%**   International: **2.0%**
Unknown: **0.0%**

Attrition rates for 2006-2007 full-time students
Percent of students discontinuing law school:
Men: 2%   Women: 1%
First-year students: 5%   Second-year students: 0%
Third-year students: 0%

LIBRARY RESOURCES
Total volumes: 516,850
Total seats available for library users: 413

INFORMATION TECHNOLOGY
Number of wired network connections available to students: 1 total (in the law library, excluding computer labs: 1; in classrooms: 0; in computer labs: 0; elsewhere in the law school: 0)
Law school has a wireless network.
Students are required to own a computer.

EMPLOYMENT AND SALARIES
Proportion of 2006 graduates employed at graduation: 82%
Employed 9 months later, as of February 15, 2007: 95%
Salaries in the private sector (law firms, business, industry): $56,000–$80,000 (25th-75th percentile)
Median salary in the private sector: $68,000
Percentage in the private sector who reported salary information: 51%
Median salary in public service (government, judicial clerkships, academic posts, non-profits): $40,000

Percentage of 2006 graduates in:
Law firms: 44%   Government: 31%
Bus./industry: 7%   Judicial clerkship: 7%
Public interest: 9%   Unknown: 0%
Academia: 1%

2006 graduates employed in-state: 85%
2006 graduates employed in foreign countries: 0%
Number of states where graduates are employed: 16
Percentage of 2006 graduates working in: New England: 0%, Middle Atlantic: 1%, East North Central: 0%, West North Central: 0%, South Atlantic: 92%, East South Central: 0%, West South Central: 1%, Mountain: 1%, Pacific: 1%, Unknown: 2%

BAR PASSAGE RATES
Based on 2006 graduates taking Summer 2006 or Winter 2007 exams. Most of the school's first-time test takers took the bar in Florida.

88%
School's bar passage rate for first-time test takers

74%
Statewide bar passage rate for first-time test takers

Fordham University

- 140 W. 62nd Street, New York, NY, 10023-7485
- http://law.fordham.edu
- Private
- **Year founded:** 1905
- **2007-2008 tuition:** full-time: $39,450; part-time: $29,650
- **Enrollment 2007-08 academic year:** full-time: 1,191; part-time: 318
- **U.S. News 2009 law specialty ranking:** clinical training: 10, dispute resolution: 10, intellectual property law: 22, international law: 13

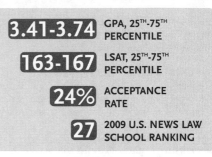

3.41-3.74 GPA, 25TH-75TH PERCENTILE

163-167 LSAT, 25TH-75TH PERCENTILE

24% ACCEPTANCE RATE

27 2009 U.S. NEWS LAW SCHOOL RANKING

ADMISSIONS

Admissions phone number: **(212) 636-6810**
Admissions email address: **lawadmissions@law.fordham.edu**
Application website: **http://law.fordham.edu/admissions**
Application deadline for Fall 2009 admission: **03/01**

Admissions statistics:
Number of applicants for Fall 2007: **5,884**
Number of acceptances: **1,384**
Number enrolled: **337**
Acceptance rate: **24%**
GPA, 25th-75th percentile, entering class Fall 2007: **3.41-3.74**
LSAT, 25th-75th percentile, entering class Fall 2007: **163-167**

Part-time program:
Number of applicants for Fall 2007: **1,328**
Number of acceptances: **241**
Number enrolled: **161**
Acceptance rate: **18%**
GPA, 25th-75th percentile, entering class Fall 2007: **3.20-3.66**
LSAT, 25th-75th percentile, entering class Fall 2007: **160-163**

FINANCIAL AID

Financial aid phone number: **(212) 636-6815**
Financial aid application deadline: **04/01**
Tuition 2007-2008 academic year: full-time: **$39,450**; part-time: **$29,650**
Room and board: **N/A**; books: **N/A**; miscellaneous expenses: **N/A**
Total of room/board/books/miscellaneous expenses: **$22,000**
University offers graduate student housing for which law students are eligible.

Financial aid profile
Percent of students that received grants for the 2006-2007 academic year: full-time: **34%**; part-time **19%**
Median grant amount: full-time: **$9,600**; part-time: **$5,300**
The average law-school debt of those in the Class of 2007 who borrowed: **$100,554.** Proportion who borrowed: **82%**

ACADEMIC PROGRAMS

Calendar: **semester**
Joint degrees awarded: **J.D./M.B.A.; J.D./M.S.W.; J.D./M.A.**
Typical first-year section size: Full-time: **80**; Part-time: **80**
Is there typically a "small section" of the first year class, other than Legal Writing, taught by full-time faculty?: Full-time: **yes**; Part-time: **yes**
Number of course titles, beyond the first year curriculum, offered last year: **237**
Percentages of upper division course sections, excluding seminars, with an enrollment of:

Under 25: **43%**	25 to 49: **30%**
50 to 74: **14%**	75 to 99: **7%**
100+: **6%**	

Areas of specialization: appellate advocacy, clinical training, dispute resolution, environmental law, healthcare law, intellectual property law, international law, tax law, trial advocacy

Fall 2007 faculty profile
Total teaching faculty: **285.** Full-time: **24%**; **63%** men, **37%** women, **15%** minorities. Part-time: **76%**; **64%** men, **36%** women, **11%** minorities
Student-to-faculty ratio: **14.6**

SPECIAL PROGRAMS *(as provided by law school):*
Centers include: International Law and Justice; Competition Law Institute; Forum on Law, Culture and Society; Corporate Law; Law and Ethics. Clinics include: community development, criminal defense, family advocacy, federal litigation, housing, immigration, mediation, securities arbitration, tax and consumer litigation, urban policy. Summer study abroad is offered in Ireland and South Korea.

STUDENT BODY

Fall 2007 full-time enrollment: 1,191

Men: 53%
African-American: 5.5%
Asian-American: 7.5%
Puerto Rican: 0.8%
White: 56.5%
Unknown: 17.7%

Women: 47%
American Indian: 0.5%
Mexican-American: 0.3%
Other Hisp-Amer: 8.9%
International: 2.4%

Fall 2007 part-time enrollment: 318

Men: 55%
African-American: 6.0%
Asian-American: 10.1%
Puerto Rican: 1.3%
White: 51.9%
Unknown: 22.6%

Women: 45%
American Indian: 0.6%
Mexican-American: 0.9%
Other Hisp-Amer: 5.7%
International: 0.9%

Attrition rates for 2006-2007 full-time students
Percent of students discontinuing law school:

Men: 2%
First-year students: 1%
Third-year students: 0%

Women: 2%
Second-year students: 4%

LIBRARY RESOURCES

Total volumes: 638,561
Total seats available for library users: 442

INFORMATION TECHNOLOGY

Number of wired network connections available to students: 601 total (in the law library, excluding computer labs: 282; in classrooms: 287; in computer labs: 0; elsewhere in the law school: 32)
Law school has a wireless network.
Students are not required to own a computer.

EMPLOYMENT AND SALARIES

Proportion of 2006 graduates employed at graduation: 82%

Employed 9 months later, as of February 15, 2007: 95%
Salaries in the private sector (law firms, business, industry): $125,000–$145,000 (25th-75th percentile)
Median salary in the private sector: $145,000
Percentage in the private sector who reported salary information: 92%
Median salary in public service (government, judicial clerkships, academic posts, non-profits): $47,733

Percentage of 2006 graduates in:

Law firms: 69%
Bus./industry: 8%
Public interest: 7%
Academia: 1%

Government: 8%
Judicial clerkship: 4%
Unknown: 3%

2006 graduates employed in-state: 78%
2006 graduates employed in foreign countries: 1%
Number of states where graduates are employed: 15
Percentage of 2006 graduates working in: New England: 3%, Middle Atlantic: 80%, East North Central: 0%, West North Central: 0%, South Atlantic: 3%, East South Central: 0%, West South Central: 0%, Mountain: 0%, Pacific: 3%, Unknown: 9%

BAR PASSAGE RATES
Based on 2006 graduates taking Summer 2006 or Winter 2007 exams. Most of the school's first-time test takers took the bar in New York.

89%
School's bar passage rate for first-time test takers

77%
Statewide bar passage rate for first-time test takers

Franklin Pierce Law Center

- 2 White Street, Concord, NH, 03301
- http://www.piercelaw.edu
- Private
- Year founded: 1973
- 2007-2008 tuition: full-time: $30,780; part-time: N/A
- Enrollment 2007-08 academic year: full-time: 400
- U.S. News 2009 law specialty ranking: intellectual property law: 5

3.00-3.50 GPA, 25TH-75TH PERCENTILE

150-155 LSAT, 25TH-75TH PERCENTILE

50% ACCEPTANCE RATE

Tier 3 2009 U.S. NEWS LAW SCHOOL RANKING

ADMISSIONS

Admissions phone number: **(603) 228-9217**
Admissions email address: **admissions@piercelaw.edu**
Application website: **http://www.piercelaw.edu/apply/**
Application deadline for Fall 2009 admission: **06/30**

Admissions statistics:
Number of applicants for Fall 2007: **1,123**
Number of acceptances: **559**
Number enrolled: **138**
Acceptance rate: **50%**
GPA, 25th-75th percentile, entering class Fall 2007: **3.00-3.50**
LSAT, 25th-75th percentile, entering class Fall 2007: **150-155**

FINANCIAL AID

Financial aid phone number: **(603) 228-1541**
Financial aid application deadline: **N/A**
Tuition 2007-2008 academic year: full-time: **$30,780**; part-time: **N/A**
Room and board: **$9,450**; books: **$1,250**; miscellaneous expenses: **$4,850**
Total of room/board/books/miscellaneous expenses: **$15,550**
University offers graduate student housing for which law students are eligible.

Financial aid profile
Percent of students that received grants for the 2006-2007 academic year: full-time: **65%**
Median grant amount: full-time: **$3,500**
The average law-school debt of those in the Class of 2007 who borrowed: **$97,592**. Proportion who borrowed: **89%**

ACADEMIC PROGRAMS

Calendar: **semester**
Joint degrees awarded: **J.D./M.I.P. Commerce**
Typical first-year section size: Full-time: **71**
Is there typically a "small section" of the first year class,

other than Legal Writing, taught by full-time faculty?: Full-time: **yes**
Number of course titles, beyond the first year curriculum, offered last year: **93**
Percentages of upper division course sections, excluding seminars, with an enrollment of:
Under 25: **71%**   25 to 49: **16%**
50 to 74: **11%**   75 to 99: **2%**
100+: **0%**
Areas of specialization: appellate advocacy, clinical training, dispute resolution, environmental law, healthcare law, intellectual property law, international law, tax law, trial advocacy

Fall 2007 faculty profile
Total teaching faculty: **104**. Full-time: **45%**; **64%** men, **36%** women, **13%** minorities. Part-time: **55%**; **67%** men, **33%** women, **N/A** minorities
Student-to-faculty ratio: **14.4**

SPECIAL PROGRAMS *(as provided by law school):*
Students enroll in clinics focused on intellectual property, commercial, and criminal law or spend a semester in an externship in the United States or abroad. Summer programs in IP and E-law are available in China, Ireland, and New Hampshire, and a course in international criminal law and justice is offered in Washington, D.C. An honors program offers an alternative to the New Hampshire bar exam.

STUDENT BODY

Fall 2007 full-time enrollment: **400**
Men: **66%**   Women: **35%**
African-American: **3.5%**   American Indian: **0.5%**
Asian-American: **8.0%**   Mexican-American: **1.5%**
Puerto Rican: **0.5%**   Other Hisp-Amer: **2.0%**
White: **65.5%**   International: **7.0%**
Unknown: **11.5%**

Attrition rates for 2006-2007 full-time students
Percent of students discontinuing law school:
Men: 5%   Women: 6%
First-year students: 14%   Second-year students: 1%
Third-year students: N/A

LIBRARY RESOURCES
Total volumes: 300,037
Total seats available for library users: 327

INFORMATION TECHNOLOGY
Number of wired network connections available to students: 338 total (in the law library, excluding computer labs: 108; in classrooms: 158; in computer labs: 31; elsewhere in the law school: 41)
Law school has a wireless network.
Students are not required to own a computer.

EMPLOYMENT AND SALARIES
Proportion of 2006 graduates employed at graduation: 66%
Employed 9 months later, as of February 15, 2007: 96%
Salaries in the private sector (law firms, business, industry): $60,000–$125,000 (25th-75th percentile)
Median salary in the private sector: $95,000
Percentage in the private sector who reported salary information: 73%
Median salary in public service (government, judicial clerkships, academic posts, non-profits): $48,500

Percentage of 2006 graduates in:
Law firms: 58%   Government: 12%
Bus./industry: 14%   Judicial clerkship: 9%
Public interest: 4%   Unknown: 1%
Academia: 1%

2006 graduates employed in-state: 21%
2006 graduates employed in foreign countries: 2%
Number of states where graduates are employed: 24
Percentage of 2006 graduates working in: New England: 41%, Middle Atlantic: 15%, East North Central: 6%, West North Central: 4%, South Atlantic: 23%, East South Central: 1%, West South Central: 1%, Mountain: 2%, Pacific: 5%, Unknown: 0%

BAR PASSAGE RATES
Based on 2006 graduates taking Summer 2006 or Winter 2007 exams. Most of the school's first-time test takers took the bar in Massachusetts.

96%
School's bar passage rate for first-time test takers

86%
Statewide bar passage rate for first-time test takers

George Mason University

■ 3301 Fairfax Drive, Arlington, VA, 22201-4426
■ http://www.law.gmu.edu
■ Public
■ **Year founded:** 1980
■ **2007-2008 tuition:** In-state: full-time: $16,716; part-time: $597/credit hour; Out-of-state: full-time: $28,532
■ **Enrollment 2007-08 academic year:** full-time: 503; part-time: 285
■ **U.S. News 2009 law specialty ranking:** N/A

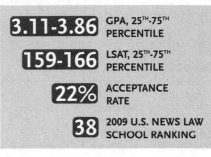

3.11-3.86 GPA, 25TH-75TH PERCENTILE

159-166 LSAT, 25TH-75TH PERCENTILE

22% ACCEPTANCE RATE

38 2009 U.S. NEWS LAW SCHOOL RANKING

ADMISSIONS
Admissions phone number: **(703) 993-8010**
Admissions email address: **aprice1@gmu.edu**
Application website:
http://www.law.gmu.edu/admission/onlineapp.html
Application deadline for Fall 2009 admission: **04/01**

Admissions statistics:
Number of applicants for Fall 2007: **4,527**
Number of acceptances: **1,011**
Number enrolled: **176**
Acceptance rate: **22%**
GPA, 25th-75th percentile, entering class Fall 2007: **3.11-3.86**
LSAT, 25th-75th percentile, entering class Fall 2007: **159-166**

Part-time program:
Number of applicants for Fall 2007: **1,551**
Number of acceptances: **221**
Number enrolled: **91**
Acceptance rate: **14%**
GPA, 25th-75th percentile, entering class Fall 2007: **2.92-3.63**
LSAT, 25th-75th percentile, entering class Fall 2007: **158-165**

FINANCIAL AID
Financial aid phone number: **(703) 993-2353**
Financial aid application deadline: **03/01**
Tuition 2007-2008 academic year: In-state: full-time: **$16,716**; part-time: **$597/credit hour**; Out-of-state: full-time: **$28,532**
Room and board: **$15,000**; books: **$990**; miscellaneous expenses: **$5,144**
Total of room/board/books/miscellaneous expenses: **$21,134**
University does not offer graduate student housing for which law students are eligible.

Financial aid profile
Percent of students that received grants for the 2006-2007 academic year: full-time: **13%**; part-time **2%**
Median grant amount: full-time: **$5,000**; part-time: **$4,250**
The average law-school debt of those in the Class of 2007 who borrowed: **$62,589**. Proportion who borrowed: **80%**

ACADEMIC PROGRAMS
Calendar: **semester**
Joint degrees awarded: **J.D./M.A. Economics; J.D./Ph.D. Economics; J.D./M.P.P.**
Typical first-year section size: Full-time: **90**; Part-time: **80**
Is there typically a "small section" of the first year class, other than Legal Writing, taught by full-time faculty?: Full-time: **no**; Part-time: **no**
Number of course titles, beyond the first year curriculum, offered last year: **168**
Percentages of upper division course sections, excluding seminars, with an enrollment of:

Under 25: **77%**	25 to 49: **15%**
50 to 74: **6%**	75 to 99: **1%**
100+: **0%**	

Areas of specialization: appellate advocacy, clinical training, dispute resolution, environmental law, healthcare law, intellectual property law, international law, tax law, trial advocacy

Fall 2007 faculty profile
Total teaching faculty: **165**. Full-time: **18%**; **87%** men, **13%** women, **10%** minorities. Part-time: **82%**; **75%** men, **25%** women, **6%** minorities
Student-to-faculty ratio: **16.7**

SPECIAL PROGRAMS *(as provided by law school):*
Mason's curriculum integrates economic and quantitative methods and requires extensive research and writing. Field programs include the clinic for legal assistance to service members and regulatory, patent, immigration, and Virginia practice programs. Mason's centers and programs include the intellectual property

program, Law and Economics Center, and National Center for Technology and Law.

STUDENT BODY

Fall 2007 full-time enrollment: 503

Men: 59%	Women: 41%
African-American: 3.0%	American Indian: 0.2%
Asian-American: 7.4%	Mexican-American: 0.0%
Puerto Rican: 0.0%	Other Hisp-Amer: 4.2%
White: 82.3%	International: 2.6%
Unknown: 0.4%	

Fall 2007 part-time enrollment: 285

Men: 62%	Women: 38%
African-American: 4.9%	American Indian: 0.7%
Asian-American: 9.1%	Mexican-American: 0.0%
Puerto Rican: 0.0%	Other Hisp-Amer: 6.7%
White: 76.8%	International: 0.4%
Unknown: 1.4%	

Attrition rates for 2006-2007 full-time students
Percent of students discontinuing law school:

Men: 4%	Women: 4%
First-year students: 11%	Second-year students: 1%
Third-year students: N/A	

LIBRARY RESOURCES

Total volumes: 458,270
Total seats available for library users: 363

INFORMATION TECHNOLOGY

Number of wired network connections available to students: **888** total (in the law library, excluding computer labs: **216**; in classrooms: **637**; in computer labs: **0**; elsewhere in the law school: **35**)
Law school has a wireless network.
Students are not required to own a computer.

EMPLOYMENT AND SALARIES

Proportion of 2006 graduates employed at graduation: **93%**

Employed 9 months later, as of February 15, 2007: **98%**
Salaries in the private sector (law firms, business, industry): **$75,000–$135,000** (25th-75th percentile)
Median salary in the private sector: **$128,750**
Percentage in the private sector who reported salary information: **65%**
Median salary in public service (government, judicial clerkships, academic posts, non-profits): **$53,000**

Percentage of 2006 graduates in:

Law firms: 41%	Government: 25%
Bus./industry: 14%	Judicial clerkship: 12%
Public interest: 5%	Unknown: 0%
Academia: 3%	

2006 graduates employed in-state: **38%**
2006 graduates employed in foreign countries: **3%**
Number of states where graduates are employed: **19**
Percentage of 2006 graduates working in: New England: **2%**, Middle Atlantic: **3%**, East North Central: **2%**, West North Central: **0%**, South Atlantic: **86%**, East South Central: **0%**, West South Central: **2%**, Mountain: **1%**, Pacific: **3%**, Unknown: **0%**

BAR PASSAGE RATES

Based on 2006 graduates taking Summer 2006 or Winter 2007 exams. Most of the school's first-time test takers took the bar in Virginia.

84%
School's bar passage rate for first-time test takers

74%
Statewide bar passage rate for first-time test takers

George Washington University

- 2000 H Street NW, Washington, DC, 20052
- http://www.law.gwu.edu
- Private
- Year founded: 1865
- 2007-2008 tuition: full-time: $38,198; part-time: $26,860
- Enrollment 2007-08 academic year: full-time: 1,412; part-time: 250
- U.S. News 2009 law specialty ranking: environmental law: 16, intellectual property law: 3, international law: 8

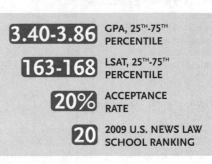

3.40-3.86 GPA, 25TH-75TH PERCENTILE

163-168 LSAT, 25TH-75TH PERCENTILE

20% ACCEPTANCE RATE

20 2009 U.S. NEWS LAW SCHOOL RANKING

ADMISSIONS
Admissions phone number: (202) 739-0648
Admissions email address: jdadmit@law.gwu.edu
Application website:
http://www.law.gwu.edu/admissions/JD+Admissions/appform.htm
Application deadline for Fall 2009 admission: 03/01

Admissions statistics:
Number of applicants for Fall 2007: 10,311
Number of acceptances: 2,039
Number enrolled: 383
Acceptance rate: 20%
GPA, 25th-75th percentile, entering class Fall 2007: 3.40-3.86
LSAT, 25th-75th percentile, entering class Fall 2007: 163-168

Part-time program:
Number of applicants for Fall 2007: 1,179
Number of acceptances: 229
Number enrolled: 121
Acceptance rate: 19%
GPA, 25th-75th percentile, entering class Fall 2007: 3.22-3.77
LSAT, 25th-75th percentile, entering class Fall 2007: 160-165

FINANCIAL AID
Financial aid phone number: (202) 994-7230
Financial aid application deadline: 01/01
Tuition 2007-2008 academic year: full-time: $38,198; part-time: $26,860
Room and board: $12,900; books: $1,100; miscellaneous expenses: $6,500
Total of room/board/books/miscellaneous expenses: $20,500
University offers graduate student housing for which law students are eligible.

Financial aid profile
Percent of students that received grants for the 2006-2007 academic year: full-time: 47%; part-time 19%
Median grant amount: full-time: $11,000; part-time: $8,000
The average law-school debt of those in the Class of 2007 who borrowed: $104,468. Proportion who borrowed: 89%

ACADEMIC PROGRAMS
Calendar: semester
Joint degrees awarded: J.D./M.A.; J.D./M.B.A.; J.D./M.P.H.; J.D./M.P.A.; J.D./M.P.P.; LL.M./M.A.; LL.M./M.P.H.
Typical first-year section size: Full-time: 108; Part-time: 117
Is there typically a "small section" of the first year class, other than Legal Writing, taught by full-time faculty?: Full-time: yes; Part-time: no
Number of course titles, beyond the first year curriculum, offered last year: 200
Percentages of upper division course sections, excluding seminars, with an enrollment of:

Under 25: 61%	25 to 49: 23%
50 to 74: 7%	75 to 99: 5%
100+: 4%	

Areas of specialization: appellate advocacy, clinical training, dispute resolution, environmental law, healthcare law, intellectual property law, international law, tax law, trial advocacy

Fall 2007 faculty profile
Total teaching faculty: 387. Full-time: 26%; 65% men, 35% women, 11% minorities. Part-time: 74%; 68% men, 32% women, 10% minorities
Student-to-faculty ratio: 14.9

SPECIAL PROGRAMS (as provided by law school):
Ten legal clinics, an externship program, and other experiential learning projects let students provide critically needed legal

services while gaining skills. Summer study in Oxford, England, and in Augsburg and Munich in Germany; exchange program with select Canadian and Mexican law schools. Joint degrees include J.D./M.B.A., J.D./M.P.H., and J.D./M.A. in International Affairs.

STUDENT BODY

Fall 2007 full-time enrollment: 1,412

Men: 56%	Women: 44%
African-American: 7.9%	American Indian: 0.8%
Asian-American: 9.1%	Mexican-American: 0.0%
Puerto Rican: 0.0%	Other Hisp-Amer: 7.9%
White: 62.9%	International: 0.5%
Unknown: 10.9%	

Fall 2007 part-time enrollment: 250

Men: 64%	Women: 36%
African-American: 5.2%	American Indian: 0.8%
Asian-American: 14.4%	Mexican-American: 0.0%
Puerto Rican: 0.0%	Other Hisp-Amer: 2.8%
White: 62.4%	International: 0.0%
Unknown: 14.4%	

Attrition rates for 2006-2007 full-time students

Percent of students discontinuing law school:

Men: 5%	Women: 1%
First-year students: 8%	Second-year students: 2%
Third-year students: 0%	

LIBRARY RESOURCES

Total volumes: 611,190
Total seats available for library users: 643

INFORMATION TECHNOLOGY

Number of wired network connections available to students: 54 total (in the law library, excluding computer labs: 54; in classrooms: 0; in computer labs: 0; elsewhere in the law school: 0)
Law school has a wireless network.
Students are required to own a computer.

EMPLOYMENT AND SALARIES

Proportion of 2006 graduates employed at graduation: 95%
Employed 9 months later, as of February 15, 2007: 97%
Salaries in the private sector (law firms, business, industry): $115,000–$135,000 (25th-75th percentile)
Median salary in the private sector: $135,000
Percentage in the private sector who reported salary information: 73%
Median salary in public service (government, judicial clerkships, academic posts, non-profits): $52,000

Percentage of 2006 graduates in:

Law firms: 63%	Government: 11%
Bus./industry: 9%	Judicial clerkship: 11%
Public interest: 4%	Unknown: 3%
Academia: 0%	

2006 graduates employed in-state: 45%
2006 graduates employed in foreign countries: 0%
Number of states where graduates are employed: 31
Percentage of 2006 graduates working in: New England: 3%, Middle Atlantic: 16%, East North Central: 2%, West North Central: 1%, South Atlantic: 64%, East South Central: 0%, West South Central: 1%, Mountain: 1%, Pacific: 7%, Unknown: 5%

BAR PASSAGE RATES

Based on 2006 graduates taking Summer 2006 or Winter 2007 exams. Most of the school's first-time test takers took the bar in New York.

94%
School's bar passage rate for first-time test takers

77%
Statewide bar passage rate for first-time test takers

Georgetown University

■ 600 New Jersey Avenue NW, Washington, DC, 20001-2075
■ http://www.law.georgetown.edu
■ Private
■ Year founded: 1870
■ 2007-2008 tuition: full-time: $39,390; part-time: $34,680
■ Enrollment 2007-08 academic year: full-time: 1,605; part-time: 385
■ U.S. News 2009 law specialty ranking: clinical training: 1, dispute resolution: 11, environmental law: 4, healthcare law: 8, intellectual property law: 19, international law: 4, tax law: 3, trial advocacy: 5

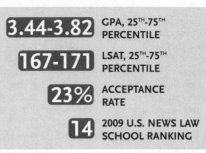

3.44-3.82 GPA, 25TH-75TH PERCENTILE

167-171 LSAT, 25TH-75TH PERCENTILE

23% ACCEPTANCE RATE

14 2009 U.S. NEWS LAW SCHOOL RANKING

ADMISSIONS

Admissions phone number: **(202) 662-9015**
Admissions email address: **admis@law.georgetown.edu**
Application website:
   http://www.law.georgetown.edu/admissions
Application deadline for Fall 2009 admission: **02/01**

Admissions statistics:

Number of applicants for Fall 2007: **10,032**
Number of acceptances: **2,326**
Number enrolled: **450**
Acceptance rate: **23%**
GPA, 25th-75th percentile, entering class Fall 2007: **3.44-3.82**
LSAT, 25th-75th percentile, entering class Fall 2007: **167-171**

Part-time program:

Number of applicants for Fall 2007: **864**
Number of acceptances: **185**
Number enrolled: **132**
Acceptance rate: **21%**
GPA, 25th-75th percentile, entering class Fall 2007: **3.33-3.75**
LSAT, 25th-75th percentile, entering class Fall 2007: **160-167**

FINANCIAL AID

Financial aid phone number: **(202) 662-9210**
Financial aid application deadline: **03/01**
Tuition 2007-2008 academic year: full-time: **$39,390**; part-time: **$34,680**
Room and board: **$14,600**; books: **$970**; miscellaneous expenses: **$4,640**
Total of room/board/books/miscellaneous expenses: **$20,210**
University does not offer graduate student housing for which law students are eligible.

Financial aid profile

Percent of students that received grants for the 2006-2007 academic year: full-time: **32%**; part-time **2%**
Median grant amount: full-time: **$14,550**; part-time: **$8,425**
The average law-school debt of those in the Class of 2007 who borrowed: **$108,074.** Proportion who borrowed: **81%**

ACADEMIC PROGRAMS

Calendar: **semester**
Joint degrees awarded: **J.D./M.S.F.S.; J.D./M.B.A.; J.D./M.P.H.; J.D./M.P.P.; J.D./M.A. Government; J.D./M.A. Philosophy; J.D./M.A. Arab Studies; J.D./M.A. Russian & E. European Studies; J.D./M.A. Latin American Studies; J.D./M.A. Security Studies; J.D./M.A. German & European Studies**
Typical first-year section size: Full-time: **112**; Part-time: **125**
Is there typically a "small section" of the first year class, other than Legal Writing, taught by full-time faculty?: Full-time: **yes**; Part-time: **yes**
Number of course titles, beyond the first year curriculum, offered last year: **354**
Percentages of upper division course sections, excluding seminars, with an enrollment of:
   Under 25: **49%**   25 to 49: **30%**
   50 to 74: **9%**   75 to 99: **6%**
   100+: **5%**
Areas of specialization: appellate advocacy, clinical training, dispute resolution, environmental law, healthcare law, intellectual property law, international law, tax law, trial advocacy

Fall 2007 faculty profile

Total teaching faculty: **368.** Full-time: **39%**; **69%** men, **31%** women, **5%** minorities. Part-time: **61%**; **78%** men, **22%** women, **6%** minorities
Student-to-faculty ratio: **13.2**

SPECIAL PROGRAMS *(as provided by law school):*

With more than 100 full-time faculty who have a broad range of scholarly interests and legal backgrounds, Georgetown is able to offer a comprehensive legal curriculum with more than 350 courses, seminars, and other programs including the largest in-house clinical program of any law school in the nation, the public interest law scholars program, and the global law scholars program.

STUDENT BODY

Fall 2007 full-time enrollment: 1,605

Men: 57%	Women: 43%
African-American: 9.3%	American Indian: 0.1%
Asian-American: 9.4%	Mexican-American: 0.7%
Puerto Rican: 0.2%	Other Hisp-Amer: 3.8%
White: 63.4%	International: 2.5%
Unknown: 10.6%	

Fall 2007 part-time enrollment: 385

Men: 57%	Women: 43%
African-American: 9.1%	American Indian: 1.0%
Asian-American: 10.4%	Mexican-American: 1.3%
Puerto Rican: 0.8%	Other Hisp-Amer: 2.6%
White: 65.7%	International: 3.9%
Unknown: 5.2%	

Attrition rates for 2006-2007 full-time students

Percent of students discontinuing law school:

Men: 1%	Women: 1%
First-year students: 1%	Second-year students: 1%
Third-year students: 0%	

LIBRARY RESOURCES

Total volumes: 1,152,501
Total seats available for library users: 1,121

INFORMATION TECHNOLOGY

Number of wired network connections available to students: 1178 total (in the law library, excluding computer labs: 288; in classrooms: 550; in computer labs: 20; elsewhere in the law school: 320)

Law school has a wireless network.
Students are not required to own a computer.

EMPLOYMENT AND SALARIES

Proportion of 2006 graduates employed at graduation: 95%

Employed 9 months later, as of February 15, 2007: 98%

Salaries in the private sector (law firms, business, industry): $135,000–$145,000 (25th-75th percentile)

Median salary in the private sector: $135,000

Percentage in the private sector who reported salary information: 64%

Median salary in public service (government, judicial clerkships, academic posts, non-profits): $50,000

Percentage of 2006 graduates in:

Law firms: 71%	Government: 8%
Bus./industry: 4%	Judicial clerkship: 10%
Public interest: 4%	Unknown: 2%
Academia: 1%	

2006 graduates employed in-state: 32%
2006 graduates employed in foreign countries: 2%
Number of states where graduates are employed: 48
Percentage of 2006 graduates working in: New England: 3%, Middle Atlantic: 28%, East North Central: 3%, West North Central: 2%, South Atlantic: 44%, East South Central: 1%, West South Central: 2%, Mountain: 2%, Pacific: 10%, Unknown: 2%

BAR PASSAGE RATES

Based on 2006 graduates taking Summer 2006 or Winter 2007 exams. Most of the school's first-time test takers took the bar in New York.

91%

School's bar passage rate for first-time test takers

77%

Statewide bar passage rate for first-time test takers

Georgia State University

- PO Box 4049, Atlanta, GA, 30302-4049
- http://law.gsu.edu
- Public
- Year founded: 1982
- 2007-2008 tuition: In-state: full-time: $9,530; part-time: $8,846; Out-of-state: full-time: $27,916
- Enrollment 2007-08 academic year: full-time: 473; part-time: 192
- U.S. News 2009 law specialty ranking: healthcare law: 10

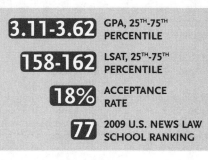

3.11-3.62 GPA, 25TH-75TH PERCENTILE

158-162 LSAT, 25TH-75TH PERCENTILE

18% ACCEPTANCE RATE

77 2009 U.S. NEWS LAW SCHOOL RANKING

ADMISSIONS
Admissions phone number: **(404) 651-2048**
Admissions email address: **admissions@gsulaw.gsu.edu**
Application website:
https://www.applyweb.com/aw?gsulaw
Application deadline for Fall 2009 admission: **03/15**

Admissions statistics:
Number of applicants for Fall 2007: **2,281**
Number of acceptances: **403**
Number enrolled: **163**
Acceptance rate: **18%**
GPA, 25th-75th percentile, entering class Fall 2007: **3.11-3.62**
LSAT, 25th-75th percentile, entering class Fall 2007: **158-162**

Part-time program:
Number of applicants for Fall 2007: **194**
Number of acceptances: **149**
Number enrolled: **57**
Acceptance rate: **77%**
GPA, 25th-75th percentile, entering class Fall 2007: **2.92-3.48**
LSAT, 25th-75th percentile, entering class Fall 2007: **156-160**

FINANCIAL AID
Financial aid phone number: **(404) 651-2227**
Financial aid application deadline: **04/01**
Tuition 2007-2008 academic year: In-state: full-time: **$9,530**; part-time: **$8,846**; Out-of-state: full-time: **$27,916**
Room and board: **$9,000**; books: **$1,500**; miscellaneous expenses: **$4,474**
Total of room/board/books/miscellaneous expenses: **$14,974**
University offers graduate student housing for which law students are eligible.

Financial aid profile
Percent of students that received grants for the 2006-2007 academic year: full-time: **15%**; part-time **22%**
Median grant amount: full-time: **$9,350**; part-time: **$2,000**
The average law-school debt of those in the Class of 2007 who borrowed: **$52,245**. Proportion who borrowed: **71%**

ACADEMIC PROGRAMS
Calendar: **semester**
Joint degrees awarded: **J.D./M.S.H.A.; J.D./M.B.A.; J.D./M.P.A.; J.D./M.A. Philosophy; J.D./M.C.R.P.**
Typical first-year section size: Full-time: **70**; Part-time: **70**
Is there typically a "small section" of the first year class, other than Legal Writing, taught by full-time faculty?: Full-time: **no**; Part-time: **no**
Number of course titles, beyond the first year curriculum, offered last year: **114**
Percentages of upper division course sections, excluding seminars, with an enrollment of:
Under 25: **59%**   25 to 49: **26%**
50 to 74: **12%**   75 to 99: **3%**
100+: **N/A**
Areas of specialization: appellate advocacy, clinical training, dispute resolution, environmental law, healthcare law, intellectual property law, international law, tax law, trial advocacy

Fall 2007 faculty profile
Total teaching faculty: **96**. Full-time: **47%**; **56%** men, **44%** women, **11%** minorities. Part-time: **53%**; **71%** men, **29%** women, **18%** minorities
Student-to-faculty ratio: **12.8**

SPECIAL PROGRAMS *(as provided by law school):*
The College of Law offers several special programs including: an externship program; five joint-degree programs; the Consortium on Negotiation and Conflict Resolution, three international programs; two accredited foreign law programs; trial advocacy program; litigation workshop; national mock trial

competitions; appellate advocacy program; moot court; and a legislation clinic and practicum.

STUDENT BODY

Fall 2007 full-time enrollment: 473

Men: 52%	Women: 48%
African-American: 10.8%	American Indian: 0.6%
Asian-American: 7.0%	Mexican-American: 0.0%
Puerto Rican: 0.0%	Other Hisp-Amer: 1.9%
White: 65.5%	International: 0.0%
Unknown: 14.2%	

Fall 2007 part-time enrollment: 192

Men: 53%	Women: 47%
African-American: 14.1%	American Indian: 0.0%
Asian-American: 2.6%	Mexican-American: 0.0%
Puerto Rican: 0.0%	Other Hisp-Amer: 2.6%
White: 67.7%	International: 0.0%
Unknown: 13.0%	

Attrition rates for 2006-2007 full-time students
Percent of students discontinuing law school:

Men: 5%	Women: 3%
First-year students: 12%	Second-year students: 0%
Third-year students: N/A	

LIBRARY RESOURCES

Total volumes: 349,854
Total seats available for library users: 354

INFORMATION TECHNOLOGY

Number of wired network connections available to students: **882** total (in the law library, excluding computer labs: **191**; in classrooms: **665**; in computer labs: **6**; elsewhere in the law school: **20**)
Law school has a wireless network.
Students are not required to own a computer.

EMPLOYMENT AND SALARIES

Proportion of 2006 graduates employed at graduation: N/A

Employed 9 months later, as of February 15, 2007: **98%**
Salaries in the private sector (law firms, business, industry): **$55,500–$115,000** (25th-75th percentile)
Median salary in the private sector: **$70,000**
Percentage in the private sector who reported salary information: **77%**
Median salary in public service (government, judicial clerkships, academic posts, non-profits): **$48,070**

Percentage of 2006 graduates in:

Law firms: 62%	Government: 14%
Bus./industry: 12%	Judicial clerkship: 4%
Public interest: 6%	Unknown: 0%
Academia: 2%	

2006 graduates employed in-state: **88%**
2006 graduates employed in foreign countries: **0%**
Number of states where graduates are employed: **14**
Percentage of 2006 graduates working in: New England: **1%**, Middle Atlantic: **1%**, East North Central: **1%**, West North Central: **1%**, South Atlantic: **92%**, East South Central: **4%**, West South Central: **1%**, Mountain: **0%**, Pacific: **1%**, Unknown: **0%**

BAR PASSAGE RATES

Based on 2006 graduates taking Summer 2006 or Winter 2007 exams. Most of the school's first-time test takers took the bar in Georgia.

93%
School's bar passage rate for first-time test takers

85%
Statewide bar passage rate for first-time test takers

Golden Gate University

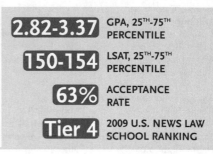

- 536 Mission Street, San Francisco, CA, 94105
- http://www.ggu.edu/law/
- Private
- Year founded: 1901
- 2007-2008 tuition: full-time: $32,940; part-time: $23,130
- Enrollment 2007-08 academic year: full-time: 538; part-time: 150
- U.S. News 2009 law specialty ranking: environmental law: 22

2.82-3.37 GPA, 25TH-75TH PERCENTILE

150-154 LSAT, 25TH-75TH PERCENTILE

63% ACCEPTANCE RATE

Tier 4 2009 U.S. NEWS LAW SCHOOL RANKING

ADMISSIONS
Admissions phone number: (415) 442-6630
Admissions email address: **lawadmit@ggu.edu**
Application website: **http://www.lsac.org**
Application deadline for Fall 2009 admission: 04/01

Admissions statistics:
Number of applicants for Fall 2007: 2,474
Number of acceptances: 1,556
Number enrolled: 225
Acceptance rate: 63%
GPA, 25th-75th percentile, entering class Fall 2007: 2.82-3.37
LSAT, 25th-75th percentile, entering class Fall 2007: 150-154

Part-time program:
Number of applicants for Fall 2007: 273
Number of acceptances: 139
Number enrolled: 46
Acceptance rate: 51%
GPA, 25th-75th percentile, entering class Fall 2007: 2.74-3.20
LSAT, 25th-75th percentile, entering class Fall 2007: 149-153

FINANCIAL AID
Financial aid phone number: (415) 442-6635
Financial aid application deadline: N/A
Tuition 2007-2008 academic year: full-time: $32,940; part-time: $23,130
Room and board: $13,500; books: $1,200; miscellaneous expenses: $6,615
Total of room/board/books/miscellaneous expenses: $21,315
University does not offer graduate student housing for which law students are eligible.

Financial aid profile
Percent of students that received grants for the 2006-2007 academic year: full-time: 43%; part-time 21%

Median grant amount: full-time: $7,500; part-time: $7,500
The average law-school debt of those in the Class of 2007 who borrowed: $112,477. Proportion who borrowed: 96%

ACADEMIC PROGRAMS
Calendar: **semester**
Joint degrees awarded: **J.D./M.B.A.; J.D./Ph.D.**
Typical first-year section size: Full-time: **89**; Part-time: **46**
Is there typically a "small section" of the first year class, other than Legal Writing, taught by full-time faculty?: Full-time: **yes**; Part-time: **no**
Number of course titles, beyond the first year curriculum, offered last year: **122**
Percentages of upper division course sections, excluding seminars, with an enrollment of:

Under 25: **73%**	25 to 49: **18%**
50 to 74: **8%**	75 to 99: **1%**
100+: **0%**	

Areas of specialization: appellate advocacy, clinical training, dispute resolution, environmental law, intellectual property law, international law, tax law, trial advocacy

Fall 2007 faculty profile
Total teaching faculty: **96**. Full-time: **30%**; **59%** men, **41%** women, **17%** minorities. Part-time: **70%**; **60%** men, **40%** women, **16%** minorities
Student-to-faculty ratio: **18.9**

SPECIAL PROGRAMS *(as provided by law school):*
GGU Law students study a practice-oriented curriculum that enables them to understand legal theory and provide meaningful legal assistance both during and after law school. Through simulation exercises, clinics, externships, trial practice teams, specialization programs, and the competitive honors lawyering program, GGU students start thinking and working like lawyers from the day they arrive.

STUDENT BODY
Fall 2007 full-time enrollment: 538
Men: 44% — Women: 56%
African-American: 1.9% — American Indian: 0.7%

Asian-American: 16.9%   Mexican-American: 1.7%
Puerto Rican: 0.0%   Other Hisp-Amer: 2.8%
White: 61.5%   International: 1.1%
Unknown: 13.4%

Fall 2007 part-time enrollment: 150
Men: 47%   Women: 53%
African-American: 6.0% American Indian: 0.7%
Asian-American: 22.0%   Mexican-American: 5.3%
Puerto Rican: 0.7%   Other Hisp-Amer: 6.0%
White: 52.0%   International: 0.0%
Unknown: 7.3%

Attrition rates for 2006-2007 full-time students
Percent of students discontinuing law school:
Men: 10%   Women: 13%
First-year students: 28% Second-year students: 3%
Third-year students: 2%

LIBRARY RESOURCES
Total volumes: 376,991
Total seats available for library users: 308

INFORMATION TECHNOLOGY
Number of wired network connections available to students: 520 total (in the law library, excluding computer
   labs: 93; in classrooms: 427; in computer labs: 0; elsewhere in the law school: 0)
Law school has a wireless network.
Students are not required to own a computer.

EMPLOYMENT AND SALARIES
Proportion of 2006 graduates employed at graduation:
   N/A
Employed 9 months later, as of February 15, 2007: 78%

Salaries in the private sector (law firms, business, industry): $52,000–$75,000 (25th-75th percentile)
Median salary in the private sector: $65,000
Percentage in the private sector who reported salary
   information: 71%
Median salary in public service (government, judicial clerkships, academic posts, non-profits): $59,700

Percentage of 2006 graduates in:
Law firms: 53%   Government: 12%
Bus./industry: 25%   Judicial clerkship: 2%
Public interest: 3%   Unknown: 1%
Academia: 5%

2006 graduates employed in-state: 92%
2006 graduates employed in foreign countries: 0%
Number of states where graduates are employed: 9
Percentage of 2006 graduates working in: New England:
   0%, Middle Atlantic: 2%, East North Central: 1%, West
   North Central: 0%, South Atlantic: 3%, East South
   Central: 0%, West South Central: 0%, Mountain: 2%,
   Pacific: 92%, Unknown: 0%

BAR PASSAGE RATES
Based on 2006 graduates taking Summer 2006 or
Winter 2007 exams. Most of the school's first-time test
takers took the bar in California.

60%
School's bar passage rate for first-time test takers

65%
Statewide bar passage rate for first-time test takers

Gonzaga University

■ PO Box 3528, Spokane, WA, 99220-3528
■ http://www.law.gonzaga.edu
■ Private
■ **Year founded:** 1912
■ **2007-2008 tuition:** full-time: $29,397; part-time: $17,667
■ **Enrollment 2007-08 academic year:** full-time: 549; part-time: 16
■ **U.S. News 2009 law specialty ranking:** N/A

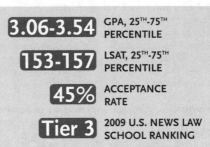

3.06-3.54 GPA, 25TH-75TH PERCENTILE

153-157 LSAT, 25TH-75TH PERCENTILE

45% ACCEPTANCE RATE

Tier 3 2009 U.S. NEWS LAW SCHOOL RANKING

ADMISSIONS
Admissions phone number: **(800) 793-1710**
Admissions email address:
  admissions@lawschool.gonzaga.edu
Application website: **http://www.law.gonzaga.edu/
  admissions/ApplicationInformation**
Application deadline for Fall 2009 admission: **04/15**

Admissions statistics:
Number of applicants for Fall 2007: **1,631**
Number of acceptances: **741**
Number enrolled: **207**
Acceptance rate: **45%**
GPA, 25th-75th percentile, entering class Fall 2007: **3.06-3.54**
LSAT, 25th-75th percentile, entering class Fall 2007: **153-157**

FINANCIAL AID
Financial aid phone number: **(800) 448-2138**
Financial aid application deadline: **02/01**
Tuition 2007-2008 academic year: full-time: **$29,397**; part-time: **$17,667**
Room and board: **$8,775**; books: **$1,000**; miscellaneous expenses: **$4,600**
Total of room/board/books/miscellaneous expenses: **$14,375**
University does not offer graduate student housing for which law students are eligible.

Financial aid profile
Percent of students that received grants for the 2006-2007 academic year: full-time: **67%**
Median grant amount: full-time: **$10,000**
The average law-school debt of those in the Class of 2007 who borrowed: **$87,458**. Proportion who borrowed: **94%**

ACADEMIC PROGRAMS
Calendar: **semester**
Joint degrees awarded: **J.D./M.B.A.; J.D./M.A.C.C.; J.D./M.S.W.**

Typical first-year section size: Full-time: **75**
Is there typically a "small section" of the first year class, other than Legal Writing, taught by full-time faculty?: Full-time: **no**
Number of course titles, beyond the first year curriculum, offered last year: **90**
Percentages of upper division course sections, excluding seminars, with an enrollment of:
  Under 25: **49%**   25 to 49: **20%**
  50 to 74: **24%**   75 to 99: **7%**
  100+: **0%**
Areas of specialization: appellate advocacy, clinical training, dispute resolution, environmental law, healthcare law, intellectual property law, international law, tax law, trial advocacy

Fall 2007 faculty profile
Total teaching faculty: **64**. Full-time: **48%**; 58% men, 42% women, 6% minorities. Part-time: **52%**; 70% men, 30% women, 3% minorities
Student-to-faculty ratio: **14.8**

SPECIAL PROGRAMS *(as provided by law school):*
Gonzaga students receive two years of extensive training in legal research and writing. Special programs include the clinical law program, which gives students the opportunity to practice law under the close supervision of attorneys; a four-week summer law program in Florence, Italy; and three joint-degree programs. Gonzaga boasts a distinguished record in interscholastic advocacy competitions.

STUDENT BODY
Fall 2007 full-time enrollment: **549**
Men: **58%**   Women: **42%**
African-American: **0.5%**   American Indian: **1.1%**
Asian-American: **4.2%**   Mexican-American: **0.2%**
Puerto Rican: **0.0%**   Other Hisp-Amer: **2.0%**
White: **86.3%**   International: **0.2%**
Unknown: **5.5%**

Fall 2007 part-time enrollment: 16

Men: 38%	Women: 63%
African-American: 6.3%	American Indian: 12.5%
Asian-American: 0.0%	Mexican-American: 0.0%
Puerto Rican: 0.0%	Other Hisp-Amer: 12.5%
White: 68.8%	International: 0.0%
Unknown: 0.0%	

Attrition rates for 2006-2007 full-time students
Percent of students discontinuing law school:

Men: 6%	Women: 3%
First-year students: 12%	Second-year students: 1%
Third-year students: N/A	

LIBRARY RESOURCES

Total volumes: 297,941
Total seats available for library users: 507

INFORMATION TECHNOLOGY

Number of wired network connections available to students: 140 total (in the law library, excluding computer labs: 87; in classrooms: 18; in computer labs: 10; elsewhere in the law school: 25)
Law school has a wireless network.
Students are not required to own a computer.

EMPLOYMENT AND SALARIES

Proportion of 2006 graduates employed at graduation: N/A
Employed 9 months later, as of February 15, 2007: 93%
Salaries in the private sector (law firms, business, industry): $45,000–$68,500 (25th-75th percentile)
Median salary in the private sector: $55,000

Percentage in the private sector who reported salary information: 61%
Median salary in public service (government, judicial clerkships, academic posts, non-profits): $49,000

Percentage of 2006 graduates in:

Law firms: 48%	Government: 20%
Bus./industry: 13%	Judicial clerkship: 12%
Public interest: 6%	Unknown: 0%
Academia: 1%	

2006 graduates employed in-state: 48%
2006 graduates employed in foreign countries: 0%
Number of states where graduates are employed: 18
Percentage of 2006 graduates working in: New England: 0%, Middle Atlantic: 0%, East North Central: 1%, West North Central: 1%, South Atlantic: 4%, East South Central: 2%, West South Central: 3%, Mountain: 31%, Pacific: 58%, Unknown: 0%

BAR PASSAGE RATES

Based on 2006 graduates taking Summer 2006 or Winter 2007 exams. Most of the school's first-time test takers took the bar in Washington.

84%
School's bar passage rate for first-time test takers

82%
Statewide bar passage rate for first-time test takers

Hamline University

- 1536 Hewitt Avenue, St. Paul, MN, 55104-1284
- http://www.hamline.edu/law
- Private
- Year founded: 1973
- 2007-2008 tuition: full-time: $28,682; part-time: $20,682
- Enrollment 2007-08 academic year: full-time: 489; part-time: 211
- U.S. News 2009 law specialty ranking: dispute resolution: 4

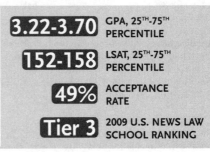

3.22-3.70 GPA, 25TH-75TH PERCENTILE

152-158 LSAT, 25TH-75TH PERCENTILE

49% ACCEPTANCE RATE

Tier 3 2009 U.S. NEWS LAW SCHOOL RANKING

ADMISSIONS
Admissions phone number: (651) 523-2461
Admissions email address: **lawadm@hamline.edu**
Application website:
   http://www.hamline.edu/law/apply.htm
Application deadline for Fall 2009 admission: 04/01

Admissions statistics:
Number of applicants for Fall 2007: 1,182
Number of acceptances: 574
Number enrolled: 152
Acceptance rate: 49%
GPA, 25th-75th percentile, entering class Fall 2007: 3.22-3.70
LSAT, 25th-75th percentile, entering class Fall 2007: 152-158

Part-time program:
Number of applicants for Fall 2007: 221
Number of acceptances: 135
Number enrolled: 73
Acceptance rate: 61%
GPA, 25th-75th percentile, entering class Fall 2007: 3.13-3.56
LSAT, 25th-75th percentile, entering class Fall 2007: 148-154

FINANCIAL AID
Financial aid phone number: (651) 523-3000
Financial aid application deadline: 04/01
Tuition 2007-2008 academic year: full-time: **$28,682**; part-time: **$20,682**
Room and board: **$14,353**; books: **$1,200**; miscellaneous expenses: **N/A**
Total of room/board/books/miscellaneous expenses: **$15,553**
University offers graduate student housing for which law students are eligible.

Financial aid profile
Percent of students that received grants for the 2006-2007 academic year: full-time: **50%**; part-time **18%**
Median grant amount: full-time: **$20,000**; part-time: **$9,090**
The average law-school debt of those in the Class of 2007 who borrowed: **$86,882**. Proportion who borrowed: **91%**

ACADEMIC PROGRAMS
Calendar: **semester**
Joint degrees awarded: **J.D./M.A.P.A.; J.D./M.A.O.L.; J.D./M.L.I.S.; J.D./M.A.M.; J.D./M.A.N.M.; J.D./M.F.A**
Typical first-year section size: Full-time: **60**; Part-time: **48**
Is there typically a "small section" of the first year class, other than Legal Writing, taught by full-time faculty?: Full-time: **no**; Part-time: **no**
Number of course titles, beyond the first year curriculum, offered last year: **141**
Percentages of upper division course sections, excluding seminars, with an enrollment of:

Under 25: **56%**	25 to 49: **31%**
50 to 74: **12%**	75 to 99: **0%**
100+: **0%**	

Areas of specialization: appellate advocacy, clinical training, dispute resolution, environmental law, healthcare law, intellectual property law, international law, tax law, trial advocacy

Fall 2007 faculty profile
Total teaching faculty: **75**. Full-time: **47%**; **57%** men, **43%** women, **14%** minorities. Part-time: **53%**; **60%** men, **40%** women, **0%** minorities
Student-to-faculty ratio: **14.6**

SPECIAL PROGRAMS *(as provided by law school):*
Hamline offers 11 clinics, six study-abroad programs, and externships in eight fields. Hamline is home to the nationally recognized Dispute Resolution Institute and the Health Law

Institute, offering courses, research opportunities, and other programs for students and the community. Joint degree/dual-degree options are available in business, management, library science, and a new J.D./M.F.A.

STUDENT BODY

Fall 2007 full-time enrollment: 489

Men: 46%	Women: 54%
African-American: 2.0%	American Indian: 0.4%
Asian-American: 5.3%	Mexican-American: 0.0%
Puerto Rican: 0.0%	Other Hisp-Amer: 3.1%
White: 80.2%	International: 1.4%
Unknown: 7.6%	

Fall 2007 part-time enrollment: 211

Men: 53%	Women: 47%
African-American: 4.3%	American Indian: 1.4%
Asian-American: 4.7%	Mexican-American: 0.0%
Puerto Rican: 0.0%	Other Hisp-Amer: 7.1%
White: 75.4%	International: 0.5%
Unknown: 6.6%	

Attrition rates for 2006-2007 full-time students
Percent of students discontinuing law school:

Men: 2%	Women: 2%
First-year students: 4%	Second-year students: 2%
Third-year students: N/A	

LIBRARY RESOURCES

Total volumes: 277,221
Total seats available for library users: 335

INFORMATION TECHNOLOGY

Number of wired network connections available to students: 506 total (in the law library, excluding computer labs: 42; in classrooms: 457; in computer labs: 0; elsewhere in the law school: 7)
Law school has a wireless network.
Students are required to own a computer.

EMPLOYMENT AND SALARIES

Proportion of 2006 graduates employed at graduation: N/A
Employed 9 months later, as of February 15, 2007: 92%
Salaries in the private sector (law firms, business, industry): **$46,000–$90,000** (25th-75th percentile)
Median salary in the private sector: **$54,000**
Percentage in the private sector who reported salary information: 61%
Median salary in public service (government, judicial clerkships, academic posts, non-profits): **$42,000**

Percentage of 2006 graduates in:

Law firms: 36%	Government: 15%
Bus./industry: 24%	Judicial clerkship: 13%
Public interest: 5%	Unknown: 4%
Academia: 3%	

2006 graduates employed in-state: 73%
2006 graduates employed in foreign countries: 1%
Number of states where graduates are employed: 33
Percentage of 2006 graduates working in: New England: 1%, Middle Atlantic: 3%, East North Central: 9%, West North Central: 76%, South Atlantic: 1%, East South Central: 0%, West South Central: 1%, Mountain: 2%, Pacific: 3%, Unknown: 4%

BAR PASSAGE RATES

Based on 2006 graduates taking Summer 2006 or Winter 2007 exams. Most of the school's first-time test takers took the bar in Minnesota.

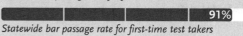

86%
School's bar passage rate for first-time test takers

91%
Statewide bar passage rate for first-time test takers

Harvard University

- 1563 Massachusetts Avenue, Cambridge, MA, 02138
- http://www.law.harvard.edu
- Private
- Year founded: 1817
- 2007-2008 tuition: full-time: $39,325; part-time: N/A
- Enrollment 2007-08 academic year: full-time: 1,734
- U.S. News 2009 law specialty ranking: clinical training: 19, dispute resolution: 2, intellectual property law: 17, international law: 3, tax law: 6, trial advocacy: 12

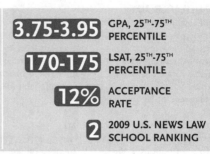

3.75-3.95 GPA, 25TH-75TH PERCENTILE

170-175 LSAT, 25TH-75TH PERCENTILE

12% ACCEPTANCE RATE

2 2009 U.S. NEWS LAW SCHOOL RANKING

ADMISSIONS
Admissions phone number: **(617) 495-3109**
Admissions email address: **jdadmiss@law.harvard.edu**
Application website:
  http://www.law.harvard.edu/Admissions/JD/apply.php
Application deadline for Fall 2009 admission: **02/01**

Admissions statistics:
Number of applicants for Fall 2007: **6,928**
Number of acceptances: **817**
Number enrolled: **555**
Acceptance rate: **12%**
GPA, 25th-75th percentile, entering class Fall 2007: **3.75-3.95**
LSAT, 25th-75th percentile, entering class Fall 2007: **170-175**

FINANCIAL AID
Financial aid phone number: **(617) 495-4606**
Financial aid application deadline: **03/01**
Tuition 2007-2008 academic year: full-time: **$39,325**; part-time: **N/A**
Room and board: **$17,497**; books: **$1,075**; miscellaneous expenses: **$4,503**
Total of room/board/books/miscellaneous expenses: **$23,075**
University offers graduate student housing for which law students are eligible.

Financial aid profile
Percent of students that received grants for the 2006-2007 academic year: full-time: **41%**
Median grant amount: full-time: **$16,705**
The average law-school debt of those in the Class of 2007 who borrowed: **$105,494**. Proportion who borrowed: **85%**

ACADEMIC PROGRAMS
Calendar: **semester**
Joint degrees awarded: **J.D./M.B.A.; J.D./M.P.P.; J.D./M.A.L.D.; J.D./M.P.A.; J.D./M.Div.; J.D./Ed.M.; J.D./Ph.D.; J.D./M.P.H.; J.D./M.U.P.; J.D./LL.M.**

Typical first-year section size: Full-time: **80**
Is there typically a "small section" of the first year class, other than Legal Writing, taught by full-time faculty?: Full-time: **no**
Number of course titles, beyond the first year curriculum, offered last year: **N/A**
Percentages of upper division course sections, excluding seminars, with an enrollment of:
  Under 25: **46%**   25 to 49: **23%**
  50 to 74: **16%**   75 to 99: **9%**
  100+: **5%**
Areas of specialization: appellate advocacy, clinical training, dispute resolution, environmental law, healthcare law, intellectual property law, international law, tax law, trial advocacy

Fall 2007 faculty profile
Total teaching faculty: **85**. Full-time: **100%**; **80%** men, **20%** women, **12%** minorities. Part-time: **N/A**; **N/A** men, **N/A** women, **N/A** minorities
Student-to-faculty ratio: **10.3**

SPECIAL PROGRAMS *(as provided by law school):*
Harvard Law School is the world's premier center for legal education and research. At the center of the HLS experience is learning from and working with teachers who shape the landscape of the law. Each year, HLS offers more than 150 seminars and classes with fewer than 25 students, an extensive clinical program, study abroad, and joint-degree programs. It is home to more than 15 research centers.

STUDENT BODY
Fall 2007 full-time enrollment: 1,734
Men: **53%**   Women: **47%**
African-American: **11.5%**   American Indian: **0.8%**
Asian-American: **10.8%**   Mexican-American: **1.5%**
Puerto Rican: **0.9%**   Other Hisp-Amer: **4.6%**
White: **52.1%**   International: **4.2%**
Unknown: **13.7%**

Attrition rates for 2006-2007 full-time students
Percent of students discontinuing law school:
Men: 0%   Women: 1%
First-year students: 0%   Second-year students: 1%
Third-year students: 0%

LIBRARY RESOURCES
Total volumes: 2,258,142
Total seats available for library users: 802

INFORMATION TECHNOLOGY
Number of wired network connections available to students: 2,750 total (in the law library, excluding computer labs: 1,000; in classrooms: 800; in computer labs: 100; elsewhere in the law school: 850)
Law school has a wireless network.
Students are not required to own a computer.

EMPLOYMENT AND SALARIES
Proportion of 2006 graduates employed at graduation: 96%
Employed 9 months later, as of February 15, 2007: 98%
Salaries in the private sector (law firms, business, industry): $135,000–$145,000 (25th-75th percentile)
Median salary in the private sector: $135,000
Percentage in the private sector who reported salary information: 99%
Median salary in public service (government, judicial clerkships, academic posts, non-profits): $51,000

Percentage of 2006 graduates in:
Law firms: 66%   Government: 2%
Bus./industry: 4%   Judicial clerkship: 23%
Public interest: 5%   Unknown: 0%
Academia: 0%

2006 graduates employed in-state: 11%
2006 graduates employed in foreign countries: 2%
Number of states where graduates are employed: 39
Percentage of 2006 graduates working in: New England: 13%, Middle Atlantic: 31%, East North Central: 7%, West North Central: 1%, South Atlantic: 20%, East South Central: 1%, West South Central: 5%, Mountain: 3%, Pacific: 17%, Unknown: 0%

BAR PASSAGE RATES
Based on 2006 graduates taking Summer 2006 or Winter 2007 exams. Most of the school's first-time test takers took the bar in New York.

97%
School's bar passage rate for first-time test takers

77%
Statewide bar passage rate for first-time test takers

Hofstra University

■ 121 Hofstra University, Hempstead, NY, 11549
■ http://law.hofstra.edu
■ Private
■ Year founded: 1970
■ 2007-2008 tuition: full-time: $37,600; part-time: $1,320/credit hour
■ Enrollment 2007-08 academic year: full-time: 870; part-time: 272
■ U.S. News 2009 law specialty ranking: N/A

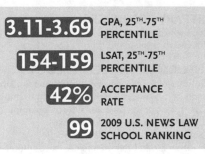

3.11-3.69 GPA, 25TH-75TH PERCENTILE

154-159 LSAT, 25TH-75TH PERCENTILE

42% ACCEPTANCE RATE

99 2009 U.S. NEWS LAW SCHOOL RANKING

ADMISSIONS

Admissions phone number: **(516) 463-5916**
Admissions email address: **lawadmissions@hofstra.edu**
Application website:
  https://law.hofstra.edu/pdf/apply_jd_application.pdf
Application deadline for Fall 2009 admission: **04/15**

Admissions statistics:

Number of applicants for Fall 2007: **4,214**
Number of acceptances: **1,768**
Number enrolled: **276**
Acceptance rate: **42%**
GPA, 25th-75th percentile, entering class Fall 2007: **3.11-3.69**
LSAT, 25th-75th percentile, entering class Fall 2007: **154-159**

Part-time program:

Number of applicants for Fall 2007: **623**
Number of acceptances: **183**
Number enrolled: **89**
Acceptance rate: **29%**
GPA, 25th-75th percentile, entering class Fall 2007: **2.98-3.54**
LSAT, 25th-75th percentile, entering class Fall 2007: **152-156**

FINANCIAL AID

Financial aid phone number: **(516) 463-5929**
Financial aid application deadline: **04/01**
Tuition 2007-2008 academic year: full-time: **$37,600**; part-time: **$1,320/credit hour**
Room and board: **$11,116**; books: **$1,400**; miscellaneous expenses: **$3,160**
Total of room/board/books/miscellaneous expenses: **$15,676**
University offers graduate student housing for which law students are eligible.

Financial aid profile

Percent of students that received grants for the 2006-2007 academic year: full-time: **50%**; part-time **17%**
Median grant amount: full-time: **$13,540**; part-time: **$10,000**
The average law-school debt of those in the Class of 2007 who borrowed: **$100,915**. Proportion who borrowed: **79%**

ACADEMIC PROGRAMS

Calendar: **semester**
Joint degrees awarded: **J.D./M.B.A.**
Typical first-year section size: Full-time: **104**; Part-time: **91**
Is there typically a "small section" of the first year class, other than Legal Writing, taught by full-time faculty?: Full-time: **yes**; Part-time: **yes**
Number of course titles, beyond the first year curriculum, offered last year: **147**
Percentages of upper division course sections, excluding seminars, with an enrollment of:
  Under 25: **61%**   25 to 49: **17%**
  50 to 74: **10%**   75 to 99: **4%**
  100+: **7%**
Areas of specialization: appellate advocacy, clinical training, dispute resolution, environmental law, healthcare law, intellectual property law, international law, tax law, trial advocacy

Fall 2007 faculty profile

Total teaching faculty: **205**. Full-time: **54%**; **63%** men, **37%** women, **16%** minorities. Part-time: **46%**; **74%** men, **26%** women, **18%** minorities
Student-to-faculty ratio: **15.5**

SPECIAL PROGRAMS (as provided by law school):

Fellowships in child and family advocacy, sexual orientation rights, and health law. Clinics in criminal justice, immigrant defense, child advocacy, economic development, housing rights, political asylum, securities arbitration, and mediation. Summer programs in Italy and Australia; winter program in Netherlands Antilles. Summer Litigation Institute; advanced programs in international and family law.

STUDENT BODY

Fall 2007 full-time enrollment: 870
Men: 53%	Women: 47%
African-American: 7.9%	American Indian: 0.2%
Asian-American: 6.2%	Mexican-American: 0.7%
Puerto Rican: 1.7%	Other Hisp-Amer: 6.1%
White: 63.4%	International: 1.0%
Unknown: 12.6%	

Fall 2007 part-time enrollment: 272
Men: 53%	Women: 47%
African-American: 11.4%	American Indian: 0.0%
Asian-American: 9.6%	Mexican-American: 0.0%
Puerto Rican: 1.8%	Other Hisp-Amer: 3.7%
White: 58.1%	International: 0.0%
Unknown: 15.4%	

Attrition rates for 2006-2007 full-time students
Percent of students discontinuing law school:
Men: 2%	Women: 2%
First-year students: 6%	Second-year students: N/A
Third-year students: N/A	

LIBRARY RESOURCES
Total volumes: 566,232
Total seats available for library users: 463

INFORMATION TECHNOLOGY
Number of wired network connections available to students: 166 total (in the law library, excluding computer labs: 120; in classrooms: 36; in computer labs: 0; elsewhere in the law school: 10)
Law school has a wireless network.
Students are not required to own a computer.

EMPLOYMENT AND SALARIES
Proportion of 2006 graduates employed at graduation: N/A
Employed 9 months later, as of February 15, 2007: 93%
Salaries in the private sector (law firms, business, industry): $70,000–$160,000 (25th-75th percentile)
Median salary in the private sector: $86,000
Percentage in the private sector who reported salary information: 26%
Median salary in public service (government, judicial clerkships, academic posts, non-profits): $49,000

Percentage of 2006 graduates in:
Law firms: 56%	Government: 11%
Bus./industry: 22%	Judicial clerkship: 5%
Public interest: 3%	Unknown: 2%
Academia: 2%	

2006 graduates employed in-state: 71%
2006 graduates employed in foreign countries: 0%
Number of states where graduates are employed: 15
Percentage of 2006 graduates working in: New England: 1%, Middle Atlantic: 75%, East North Central: 1%, West North Central: 0%, South Atlantic: 6%, East South Central: 0%, West South Central: 0%, Mountain: 1%, Pacific: 2%, Unknown: 15%

BAR PASSAGE RATES
Based on 2006 graduates taking Summer 2006 or Winter 2007 exams. Most of the school's first-time test takers took the bar in New York.

74%
School's bar passage rate for first-time test takers

77%
Statewide bar passage rate for first-time test takers

Howard University

■ 2900 Van Ness Street NW, Washington, DC, 20008
■ http://www.law.howard.edu
■ Private
■ Year founded: 1869
■ 2007-2008 tuition: full-time: $20,445; part-time: N/A
■ Enrollment 2007-08 academic year: full-time: 428
■ U.S. News 2009 law specialty ranking: N/A

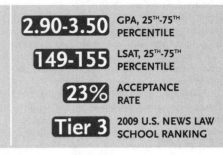

2.90-3.50 GPA, 25ᵀᴴ-75ᵀᴴ PERCENTILE

149-155 LSAT, 25ᵀᴴ-75ᵀᴴ PERCENTILE

23% ACCEPTANCE RATE

Tier 3 2009 U.S. NEWS LAW SCHOOL RANKING

ADMISSIONS
Admissions phone number: (202) 806-8009
Admissions email address: **admissions@law.howard.edu**
Application website:
  http://www4.lsac.org/school/howard.htm
Application deadline for Fall 2009 admission: **07/31**

Admissions statistics:
Number of applicants for Fall 2007: **2,373**
Number of acceptances: **538**
Number enrolled: **150**
Acceptance rate: **23%**
GPA, 25th-75th percentile, entering class Fall 2007: **2.90-3.50**
LSAT, 25th-75th percentile, entering class Fall 2007: **149-155**

FINANCIAL AID
Financial aid phone number: (202) 806-8005
Financial aid application deadline: 08/28
Tuition 2007-2008 academic year: full-time: **$20,445**; part-time: N/A
Room and board: **$14,722**; books: **$1,486**; miscellaneous expenses: **$4,176**
Total of room/board/books/miscellaneous expenses: **$20,384**
University offers graduate student housing for which law students are eligible.

Financial aid profile
Percent of students that received grants for the 2006-2007 academic year: full-time: **56%**
Median grant amount: full-time: **$10,000**
The average law-school debt of those in the Class of 2007 who borrowed: **$24,705**. Proportion who borrowed: **98%**

ACADEMIC PROGRAMS
Calendar: **semester**
Joint degrees awarded: **J.D./M.B.A.**
Typical first-year section size: Full-time: **50**
Is there typically a "small section" of the first year class, other than Legal Writing, taught by full-time faculty?:
  Full-time: **no**
Number of course titles, beyond the first year curriculum, offered last year: **108**
Percentages of upper division course sections, excluding seminars, with an enrollment of:
  Under 25: **39%**   25 to 49: **36%**
  50 to 74: **21%**   75 to 99: **3%**
  100+: **0%**
Areas of specialization: appellate advocacy, clinical training, dispute resolution, environmental law, healthcare law, intellectual property law, international law, tax law, trial advocacy

Fall 2007 faculty profile
Total teaching faculty: **63**. Full-time: **32%**; **60%** men, **40%** women, **70%** minorities. Part-time: **68%**; **65%** men, **35%** women, **72%** minorities
Student-to-faculty ratio: **18.7**

SPECIAL PROGRAMS *(as provided by law school):*
The Clinical Law Center offers students the opportunity to gain professional skills training and practical lawyering experiences in criminal justice, fair housing, alternative dispute resolution, civil rights, and D.C. law students in court clinics. There are many externships that permit students to work pro bono for credit, a South African summer-abroad program, and a J.D./M.B.A. degree program.

STUDENT BODY
Fall 2007 full-time enrollment: **428**
Men: **41%**   Women: **59%**
African-American: **76.4%**   American Indian: **1.6%**
Asian-American: **4.4%**   Mexican-American: **0.0%**
Puerto Rican: **0.2%**   Other Hisp-Amer: **2.1%**
White: **4.9%**   International: **7.9%**
Unknown: **2.3%**

Attrition rates for 2006-2007 full-time students
Percent of students discontinuing law school:
Men: **4%**   Women: **1%**

First-year students: **4%**   Second-year students: **1%**
Third-year students: **1%**

LIBRARY RESOURCES
Total volumes: **643,115**
Total seats available for library users: **374**

INFORMATION TECHNOLOGY
Number of wired network connections available to students: **607** total (in the law library, excluding computer labs: **319**; in classrooms: **145**; in computer labs: **78**; elsewhere in the law school: **65**)
Law school has a wireless network.
Students are not required to own a computer.

EMPLOYMENT AND SALARIES
Proportion of 2006 graduates employed at graduation: **88%**
Employed 9 months later, as of February 15, 2007: **94%**
Salaries in the private sector (law firms, business, industry): **$100,000–$145,000** (25th-75th percentile)
Median salary in the private sector: **$135,000**
Percentage in the private sector who reported salary information: **54%**
Median salary in public service (government, judicial clerkships, academic posts, non-profits): **$49,185**

Percentage of 2006 graduates in:
Law firms: **48%**   Government: **14%**
Bus./industry: **16%**   Judicial clerkship: **13%**
Public interest: **7%**   Unknown: **0%**
Academia: **2%**

2006 graduates employed in-state: **32%**
2006 graduates employed in foreign countries: **3%**
Number of states where graduates are employed: **22**
Percentage of 2006 graduates working in: New England: **5%**, Middle Atlantic: **25%**, East North Central: **5%**, West North Central: **2%**, South Atlantic: **48%**, East South Central: **4%**, West South Central: **3%**, Mountain: **3%**, Pacific: **4%**, Unknown: **0%**

BAR PASSAGE RATES
Based on 2006 graduates taking Summer 2006 or Winter 2007 exams. Most of the school's first-time test takers took the bar in New York.

62%
School's bar passage rate for first-time test takers

77%
Statewide bar passage rate for first-time test takers

Ill. Institute of Tech. (Chicago-Kent)

- 565 W. Adams Street, Chicago, IL, 60661-3691
- http://www.kentlaw.edu/
- Private
- Year founded: 1888
- 2007-2008 tuition: full-time: $33,879; part-time: $24,775
- Enrollment 2007-08 academic year: full-time: 751; part-time: 224
- U.S. News 2009 law specialty ranking: intellectual property law: 10, trial advocacy: 15

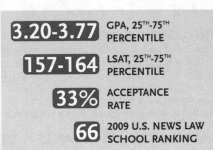

3.20-3.77 GPA, 25TH-75TH PERCENTILE

157-164 LSAT, 25TH-75TH PERCENTILE

33% ACCEPTANCE RATE

66 2009 U.S. NEWS LAW SCHOOL RANKING

ADMISSIONS
Admissions phone number: (312) 906-5020
Admissions email address: **admit@kentlaw.edu**
Application website: **https://www.kentlaw.edu/ admissions/jd_application.html**
Application deadline for Fall 2009 admission: 03/01

Admissions statistics:
Number of applicants for Fall 2007: **2,825**
Number of acceptances: **942**
Number enrolled: **217**
Acceptance rate: **33%**
GPA, 25th-75th percentile, entering class Fall 2007: **3.20-3.77**
LSAT, 25th-75th percentile, entering class Fall 2007: **157-164**

Part-time program:
Number of applicants for Fall 2007: **709**
Number of acceptances: **270**
Number enrolled: **102**
Acceptance rate: **38%**
GPA, 25th-75th percentile, entering class Fall 2007: **3.06-3.47**
LSAT, 25th-75th percentile, entering class Fall 2007: **156-159**

FINANCIAL AID
Financial aid phone number: (312) 906-5180
Financial aid application deadline: 04/15
Tuition 2007-2008 academic year: full-time: **$33,879**; part-time: **$24,775**
Room and board: **$14,247**; books: **$1,000**; miscellaneous expenses: **$3,780**
Total of room/board/books/miscellaneous expenses: **$19,027**
University offers graduate student housing for which law students are eligible.

Financial aid profile
Percent of students that received grants for the 2006-2007 academic year: full-time: **56%**; part-time **49%**
Median grant amount: full-time: **$15,000**; part-time: **$4,000**
The average law-school debt of those in the Class of 2007 who borrowed: **$98,981**. Proportion who borrowed: **89%**

ACADEMIC PROGRAMS
Calendar: **semester**
Joint degrees awarded: **J.D./M.B.A.; J.D./LL.M. Taxation; J.D./M.S. Financial Markets; J.D./LL.M. Financial Services Law; J.D./M.S. Environmental Management; J.D./M.P.A.; J.D./M.P.H.; JD/LL.M. Family Law**
Typical first-year section size: Full-time: **50**; Part-time: **52**
Is there typically a "small section" of the first year class, other than Legal Writing, taught by full-time faculty?: Full-time: **no**; Part-time: **no**
Number of course titles, beyond the first year curriculum, offered last year: **135**
Percentages of upper division course sections, excluding seminars, with an enrollment of:
Under 25: **73%**   25 to 49: **16%**
50 to 74: **6%**   75 to 99: **3%**
100+: **2%**
Areas of specialization: appellate advocacy, clinical training, dispute resolution, environmental law, healthcare law, intellectual property law, international law, tax law, trial advocacy

Fall 2007 faculty profile
Total teaching faculty: **207**. Full-time: **35%**; **65%** men, **35%** women, **10%** minorities. Part-time: **65%**; **73%** men, **27%** women, **7%** minorities
Student-to-faculty ratio: **11.5**

SPECIAL PROGRAMS *(as provided by law school):*

Clinical: criminal, employment, family, health/disability, intellectual property, immigration, low-income taxpayer, mediation/alternative dispute resolution, advice desk, legal and judicial externships. Certificates: IP, Criminal Litigation, Labor/Employment, International/Comparative, Environmental, Public Interest, Litigation/ADR. Institute for Science, Law and Technology. Study abroad: London.

STUDENT BODY

Fall 2007 full-time enrollment: 751

Men: 49%	Women: 51%
African-American: 5.7%	American Indian: 0.3%
Asian-American: 6.9%	Mexican-American: 2.5%
Puerto Rican: 0.3%	Other Hisp-Amer: 2.7%
White: 73.6%	International: 1.5%
Unknown: 6.5%	

Fall 2007 part-time enrollment: 224

Men: 62%	Women: 38%
African-American: 5.8%	American Indian: 0.0%
Asian-American: 12.1%	Mexican-American: 2.2%
Puerto Rican: 0.4%	Other Hisp-Amer: 1.8%
White: 67.9%	International: 3.6%
Unknown: 6.3%	

Attrition rates for 2006-2007 full-time students

Percent of students discontinuing law school:

Men: 2%	Women: 1%
First-year students: 4%	Second-year students: 1%
Third-year students: 0%	

LIBRARY RESOURCES

Total volumes: 550,789
Total seats available for library users: 463

INFORMATION TECHNOLOGY

Number of wired network connections available to students: 1,770 total (in the law library, excluding computer labs: 175; in classrooms: 1,048; in computer labs: 32; elsewhere in the law school: 515)

Law school has a wireless network.
Students are required to own a computer.

EMPLOYMENT AND SALARIES

Proportion of 2006 graduates employed at graduation: 72%
Employed 9 months later, as of February 15, 2007: 91%
Salaries in the private sector (law firms, business, industry): $55,000–$135,000 (25th-75th percentile)
Median salary in the private sector: $75,000
Percentage in the private sector who reported salary information: 65%
Median salary in public service (government, judicial clerkships, academic posts, non-profits): $50,500

Percentage of 2006 graduates in:

Law firms: 56%	Government: 14%
Bus./industry: 18%	Judicial clerkship: 5%
Public interest: 3%	Unknown: 3%
Academia: 1%	

2006 graduates employed in-state: 88%
2006 graduates employed in foreign countries: 0%
Number of states where graduates are employed: 17
Percentage of 2006 graduates working in: New England: 0%, Middle Atlantic: 1%, East North Central: 90%, West North Central: 1%, South Atlantic: 4%, East South Central: 0%, West South Central: 1%, Mountain: 1%, Pacific: 1%, Unknown: 0%

BAR PASSAGE RATES

Based on 2006 graduates taking Summer 2006 or Winter 2007 exams. Most of the school's first-time test takers took the bar in Illinois.

90%
School's bar passage rate for first-time test takers

87%
Statewide bar passage rate for first-time test takers

Indiana University—Bloomington

■ 211 S. Indiana Avenue, Bloomington, IN, 47405-1001
■ http://www.law.indiana.edu
■ Public
■ Year founded: 1842
■ 2007-2008 tuition: In-state: full-time: $17,912; part-time: N/A; Out-of-state: full-time: $34,486
■ Enrollment 2007-08 academic year: full-time: 619; part-time: 1
■ U.S. News 2009 law specialty ranking: N/A

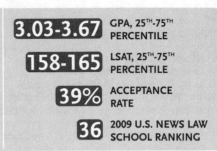

3.03-3.67 GPA, 25TH-75TH PERCENTILE

158-165 LSAT, 25TH-75TH PERCENTILE

39% ACCEPTANCE RATE

36 2009 U.S. NEWS LAW SCHOOL RANKING

ADMISSIONS

Admissions phone number: **(812) 855-4765**
Admissions email address: **lawadmis@indiana.edu**
Application website: **http://www.law.indiana.edu/ prospective/application.shtml**
Application deadline for Fall 2009 admission: **rolling**

Admissions statistics:

Number of applicants for Fall 2007: **2,517**
Number of acceptances: **978**
Number enrolled: **214**
Acceptance rate: **39%**
GPA, 25th-75th percentile, entering class Fall 2007: **3.03-3.67**
LSAT, 25th-75th percentile, entering class Fall 2007: **158-165**

FINANCIAL AID

Financial aid phone number: **(812) 855-7746**
Financial aid application deadline: **03/01**
Tuition 2007-2008 academic year: In-state: full-time: **$17,912**; part-time: N/A; Out-of-state: full-time: **$34,486**
Room and board: **$8,732**; books: **$1,558**; miscellaneous expenses: **$4,498**
Total of room/board/books/miscellaneous expenses: **$14,788**
University offers graduate student housing for which law students are eligible.

Financial aid profile

Percent of students that received grants for the 2006-2007 academic year: full-time: **74%**
Median grant amount: full-time: **$7,484**
The average law-school debt of those in the Class of 2007 who borrowed: **$82,400**. Proportion who borrowed: **92%**

ACADEMIC PROGRAMS

Calendar: **semester**
Joint degrees awarded: **J.D./M.P.A. Environmental Affairs; J.D./M.P.A. Accounting; J.D./M.A.Telecommunications; J.D./M.B.A.; J.D./M.L.S.; Ph.D. Law & Social Science**

Typical first-year section size: Full-time: **73**
Is there typically a "small section" of the first year class, other than Legal Writing, taught by full-time faculty?: Full-time: **no**
Number of course titles, beyond the first year curriculum, offered last year: **137**
Percentages of upper division course sections, excluding seminars, with an enrollment of:

Under 25: **65%**	25 to 49: **23%**
50 to 74: **8%**	75 to 99: **2%**
100+: **1%**	

Areas of specialization: appellate advocacy, clinical training, dispute resolution, environmental law, healthcare law, intellectual property law, international law, tax law, trial advocacy

Fall 2007 faculty profile

Total teaching faculty: **66**. Full-time: **70%**; **63%** men, **37%** women, **9%** minorities. Part-time: **30%**; **70%** men, **30%** women, **0%** minorities
Student-to-faculty ratio: **11.4**

SPECIAL PROGRAMS (as provided by law school):

Joint degrees in business, public affairs, environmental science, journalism, telecommunications, and library science. Special joint degrees arranged. Clinics in family law, mediation, business law, environmental law, criminal law, elder law, disability law, and others. Semesters abroad: Poland, Germany (two), France, Spain, England, Hong Kong, China (two), and New Zealand. Summer start available.

STUDENT BODY

Fall 2007 full-time enrollment: 619

Men: **61%**	Women: **39%**
African-American: **8.1%**	American Indian: **0.3%**
Asian-American: **4.7%**	Mexican-American: **5.2%**
Puerto Rican: **0.0%**	Other Hisp-Amer: **0.0%**
White: **78.4%**	International: **0.0%**
Unknown: **3.4%**	

Fall 2007 part-time enrollment: 1

Men: 100%	Women: 0%
African-American: 0.0%	American Indian: 0.0%
Asian-American: 0.0%	Mexican-American: 0.0%
Puerto Rican: 0.0%	Other Hisp-Amer: 0.0%
White: 100.0%	International: 0.0%
Unknown: 0.0%	

Attrition rates for 2006-2007 full-time students
Percent of students discontinuing law school:

Men: 3%	Women: 4%
First-year students: 11%	Second-year students: N/A
Third-year students: N/A	

LIBRARY RESOURCES
Total volumes: 745,343
Total seats available for library users: 684

INFORMATION TECHNOLOGY
Number of wired network connections available to students: 192 total (in the law library, excluding computer labs: 177; in classrooms: 15; in computer labs: 0; elsewhere in the law school: 0)
Law school has a wireless network.
Students are required to own a computer.

EMPLOYMENT AND SALARIES
Proportion of 2006 graduates employed at graduation: 88%
Employed 9 months later, as of February 15, 2007: 98%
Salaries in the private sector (law firms, business, industry): $60,000–$110,000 (25th-75th percentile)
Median salary in the private sector: $85,000

Percentage in the private sector who reported salary information: 36%
Median salary in public service (government, judicial clerkships, academic posts, non-profits): $50,000

Percentage of 2006 graduates in:

Law firms: 53%	Government: 11%
Bus./industry: 19%	Judicial clerkship: 9%
Public interest: 5%	Unknown: 0%
Academia: 3%	

2006 graduates employed in-state: 37%
2006 graduates employed in foreign countries: 0%
Number of states where graduates are employed: 32
Percentage of 2006 graduates working in: New England: 1%, Middle Atlantic: 3%, East North Central: 58%, West North Central: 5%, South Atlantic: 12%, East South Central: 3%, West South Central: 6%, Mountain: 3%, Pacific: 10%, Unknown: 0%

BAR PASSAGE RATES
Based on 2006 graduates taking Summer 2006 or Winter 2007 exams. Most of the school's first-time test takers took the bar in Indiana.

86%
School's bar passage rate for first-time test takers

83%
Statewide bar passage rate for first-time test takers

Indiana University–Indianapolis

- 530 W. New York Street, Indianapolis, IN, 46202-3225
- http://www.indylaw.indiana.edu
- Public
- Year founded: 1894
- 2007-2008 tuition: In-state: full-time: $14,638; part-time: $10,926; Out-of-state: full-time: $31,993
- Enrollment 2007-08 academic year: full-time: 647; part-time: 305
- U.S. News 2009 law specialty ranking: healthcare law: 11

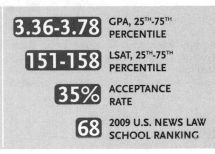

3.36-3.78 GPA, 25TH-75TH PERCENTILE

151-158 LSAT, 25TH-75TH PERCENTILE

35% ACCEPTANCE RATE

68 2009 U.S. NEWS LAW SCHOOL RANKING

ADMISSIONS
Admissions phone number: **(317) 274-2459**
Admissions email address: **pkkinney@iupui.edu**
Application website:
 http://www.indylaw.indiana.edu/admissions/app.htm
Application deadline for Fall 2009 admission: **03/01**

Admissions statistics:
Number of applicants for Fall 2007: **1,350**
Number of acceptances: **472**
Number enrolled: **199**
Acceptance rate: **35%**
GPA, 25th-75th percentile, entering class Fall 2007: **3.36-3.78**
LSAT, 25th-75th percentile, entering class Fall 2007: **151-158**

Part-time program:
Number of applicants for Fall 2007: **225**
Number of acceptances: **153**
Number enrolled: **101**
Acceptance rate: **68%**
GPA, 25th-75th percentile, entering class Fall 2007: **3.15-3.54**
LSAT, 25th-75th percentile, entering class Fall 2007: **149-155**

FINANCIAL AID
Financial aid phone number: **(317) 278-2862**
Financial aid application deadline: **03/01**
Tuition 2007-2008 academic year: In-state: full-time: **$14,638**; part-time: **$10,926**; Out-of-state: full-time: **$31,993**
Room and board: **$11,296**; books: **$1,700**; miscellaneous expenses: **$8,928**
Total of room/board/books/miscellaneous expenses: **$21,924**
University offers graduate student housing for which law students are eligible.

Financial aid profile
Percent of students that received grants for the 2006-2007 academic year: full-time: **47%**; part-time **12%**
Median grant amount: full-time: **$5,010**; part-time: **$2,000**
The average law-school debt of those in the Class of 2007 who borrowed: **$64,571**. Proportion who borrowed: **65%**

ACADEMIC PROGRAMS
Calendar: **semester**
Joint degrees awarded: **J.D./M.B.A.; J.D./M.P.A.; J.D./M.H.A.; J.D./M.P.H.; J.D./M.L.S.; J.D./M.Phil**
Typical first-year section size: Full-time: **97**; Part-time: **88**
Is there typically a "small section" of the first year class, other than Legal Writing, taught by full-time faculty?: Full-time: **no**; Part-time: **no**
Number of course titles, beyond the first year curriculum, offered last year: **126**
Percentages of upper division course sections, excluding seminars, with an enrollment of:

Under 25: **41%**	25 to 49: **38%**
50 to 74: **10%**	75 to 99: **8%**
100+: **2%**	

Areas of specialization: appellate advocacy, clinical training, dispute resolution, environmental law, healthcare law, intellectual property law, international law, tax law, trial advocacy

Fall 2007 faculty profile
Total teaching faculty: **141**. Full-time: **35%**; **57%** men, **43%** women, **10%** minorities. Part-time: **65%**; **71%** men, **29%** women, **4%** minorities
Student-to-faculty ratio: **17.0**

SPECIAL PROGRAMS (as provided by law school):
IU School of Law–Indianapolis offers three in-house clinics (civil, disability, and criminal), each giving students real-world experience under faculty supervision. The school has the nationally recognized Hall Center for Law and Health, the

Center for Intellectual Property Law and Innovation, the Center for International and Comparative Law, and the program in international human-rights law.

STUDENT BODY

Fall 2007 full-time enrollment: 647

Men: 52%   Women: 48%
African-American: 4.6%   American Indian: 0.3%
Asian-American: 2.6%   Mexican-American: 0.9%
Puerto Rican: 0.2%   Other Hisp-Amer: 1.9%
White: 84.4%   International: 5.1%
Unknown: 0.0%

Fall 2007 part-time enrollment: 305

Men: 52%   Women: 48%
African-American: 8.9%   American Indian: 0.7%
Asian-American: 4.6%   Mexican-American: 1.0%
Puerto Rican: 0.3%   Other Hisp-Amer: 2.6%
White: 79.0%   International: 3.0%
Unknown: 0.0%

Attrition rates for 2006-2007 full-time students

Percent of students discontinuing law school:
Men: 2%   Women: 3%
First-year students: 2%   Second-year students: 4%
Third-year students: 2%

LIBRARY RESOURCES

Total volumes: 599,038
Total seats available for library users: 506

INFORMATION TECHNOLOGY

Number of wired network connections available to students: 1,140 total (in the law library, excluding computer labs: 325; in classrooms: 686; in computer labs: 0; elsewhere in the law school: 129)
Law school has a wireless network.
Students are not required to own a computer.

EMPLOYMENT AND SALARIES

Proportion of 2006 graduates employed at graduation: 82%
Employed 9 months later, as of February 15, 2007: 96%
Salaries in the private sector (law firms, business, industry): $45,000–$90,000 (25th-75th percentile)
Median salary in the private sector: $60,000
Percentage in the private sector who reported salary information: 23%
Median salary in public service (government, judicial clerkships, academic posts, non-profits): $43,250

Percentage of 2006 graduates in:

Law firms: 50%   Government: 22%
Bus./industry: 22%   Judicial clerkship: 2%
Public interest: 2%   Unknown: 0%
Academia: 2%

2006 graduates employed in-state: 83%
2006 graduates employed in foreign countries: 1%
Number of states where graduates are employed: 17
Percentage of 2006 graduates working in: New England: 0%, Middle Atlantic: 0%, East North Central: 88%, West North Central: 1%, South Atlantic: 5%, East South Central: 1%, West South Central: 0%, Mountain: 2%, Pacific: 2%, Unknown: 0%

BAR PASSAGE RATES

Based on 2006 graduates taking Summer 2006 or Winter 2007 exams. Most of the school's first-time test takers took the bar in Indiana.

85%
School's bar passage rate for first-time test takers

83%
Statewide bar passage rate for first-time test takers

John Marshall Law School

■ 315 S. Plymouth Court, Chicago, IL, 60604
■ http://www.jmls.edu
■ Private
■ Year founded: 1899
■ 2007-2008 tuition: full-time: $31,460; part-time: $22,500
■ Enrollment 2007-08 academic year: full-time: 1,067; part-time: 317
■ U.S. News 2009 law specialty ranking: intellectual property law: 15

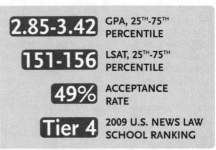

2.85-3.42 GPA, 25TH-75TH PERCENTILE

151-156 LSAT, 25TH-75TH PERCENTILE

49% ACCEPTANCE RATE

Tier 4 2009 U.S. NEWS LAW SCHOOL RANKING

ADMISSIONS

Admissions phone number: **(800) 537-4280**
Admissions email address: **admission@jmls.edu**
Application website:
   http://www.jmls.edu/supportdata/webviewbookapp.pdf
Application deadline for Fall 2009 admission: **03/01**

Admissions statistics:
Number of applicants for Fall 2007: **2,830**
Number of acceptances: **1,394**
Number enrolled: **366**
Acceptance rate: **49%**
GPA, 25th-75th percentile, entering class Fall 2007: **2.85-3.42**
LSAT, 25th-75th percentile, entering class Fall 2007: **151-156**

Part-time program:
Number of applicants for Fall 2007: **602**
Number of acceptances: **215**
Number enrolled: **110**
Acceptance rate: **36%**
GPA, 25th-75th percentile, entering class Fall 2007: **2.88-3.43**
LSAT, 25th-75th percentile, entering class Fall 2007: **152-156**

FINANCIAL AID

Financial aid phone number: **(800) 537-4280**
Financial aid application deadline: **06/14**
Tuition 2007-2008 academic year: full-time: **$31,460**; part-time: **$22,500**
Room and board: **$22,970**; books: **$2,060**; miscellaneous expenses: **$6,562**
Total of room/board/books/miscellaneous expenses: **$31,592**
University does not offer graduate student housing for which law students are eligible.

Financial aid profile
Percent of students that received grants for the 2006-2007 academic year: full-time: **38%**; part-time **35%**

Median grant amount: full-time: **$6,000**; part-time: **$3,800**
The average law-school debt of those in the Class of 2007 who borrowed: **$108,022.** Proportion who borrowed: **91%**

ACADEMIC PROGRAMS

Calendar: **semester**
Joint degrees awarded: **J.D./M.B.A.; J.D./M.P.A.; J.D./M.A.; J.D./LL.M. Employee Benefits Law; J.D./LL.M. Intellectual Property Law; J.D./LL.M. Information Technology Law; J.D./LL.M. International Business/Trade ; J.D./LL.M. Real Estate Law; J.D./LL.M. Tax Law**
Typical first-year section size: Full-time: **70**; Part-time: **60**
Is there typically a "small section" of the first year class, other than Legal Writing, taught by full-time faculty?: Full-time: **no**; Part-time: **no**
Number of course titles, beyond the first year curriculum, offered last year: **230**
Percentages of upper division course sections, excluding seminars, with an enrollment of:
   Under 25: **64%**   25 to 49: **22%**
   50 to 74: **7%**   75 to 99: **6%**
   100+: **0%**
Areas of specialization: appellate advocacy, clinical training, dispute resolution, environmental law, healthcare law, intellectual property law, international law, tax law, trial advocacy

Fall 2007 faculty profile
Total teaching faculty: **190.** Full-time: **28%**; **77%** men, **23%** women, **11%** minorities. Part-time: **72%**; **72%** men, **28%** women, **7%** minorities
Student-to-faculty ratio: **17.9**

SPECIAL PROGRAMS *(as provided by law school):*
The John Marshall Law School provides its students the opportunity to gain an understanding of the basic competencies expected of attorneys. In addition to the many courses that help meet this commitment, the Law School has established a clinical legal education program with two divisions: the fair housing legal clinic and the general externship program.

STUDENT BODY

Fall 2007 full-time enrollment: 1,067

Men: 58%   Women: 42%
African-American: 4.0%   American Indian: 1.2%
Asian-American: 6.9%   Mexican-American: 2.3%
Puerto Rican: 0.2%   Other Hisp-Amer: 2.6%
White: 74.9%   International: 1.3%
Unknown: 6.5%

Fall 2007 part-time enrollment: 317

Men: 56%   Women: 44%
African-American: 9.5%   American Indian: 0.9%
Asian-American: 5.7%   Mexican-American: 2.5%
Puerto Rican: 0.6%   Other Hisp-Amer: 3.5%
White: 69.4%   International: 1.9%
Unknown: 6.0%

Attrition rates for 2006-2007 full-time students
Percent of students discontinuing law school:
Men: 3%   Women: 2%
First-year students: 7%   Second-year students: 1%
Third-year students: N/A

LIBRARY RESOURCES

Total volumes: 400,155
Total seats available for library users: 681

INFORMATION TECHNOLOGY

Number of wired network connections available to students: 0 total (in the law library, excluding computer labs: 0; in classrooms: 0; in computer labs: 0; elsewhere in the law school: 0)
Law school has a wireless network.
Students are not required to own a computer.

EMPLOYMENT AND SALARIES

Proportion of 2006 graduates employed at graduation: N/A

Employed 9 months later, as of February 15, 2007: 88%
Salaries in the private sector (law firms, business, industry): $51,250–$90,000 (25th-75th percentile)
Median salary in the private sector: $70,000
Percentage in the private sector who reported salary information: 78%
Median salary in public service (government, judicial clerkships, academic posts, non-profits): $48,796

Percentage of 2006 graduates in:
Law firms: 54%   Government: 18%
Bus./industry: 24%   Judicial clerkship: 2%
Public interest: 1%   Unknown: 0%
Academia: 1%

2006 graduates employed in-state: 87%
2006 graduates employed in foreign countries: 1%
Number of states where graduates are employed: 19
Percentage of 2006 graduates working in: New England: 0%, Middle Atlantic: 2%, East North Central: 90%, West North Central: 1%, South Atlantic: 3%, East South Central: 0%, West South Central: 1%, Mountain: 0%, Pacific: 3%, Unknown: 0%

BAR PASSAGE RATES

Based on 2006 graduates taking Summer 2006 or Winter 2007 exams. Most of the school's first-time test takers took the bar in Illinois.

87%
School's bar passage rate for first-time test takers

87%
Statewide bar passage rate for first-time test takers

Lewis and Clark Coll. (Northwestern)

- 10015 S.W. Terwilliger Boulevard, Portland, OR, 97219
- http://law.lclark.edu
- Private
- Year founded: 1884
- 2007-2008 tuition: full-time: $28,984; part-time: $21,738
- Enrollment 2007-08 academic year: full-time: 537; part-time: 188
- U.S. News 2009 law specialty ranking: environmental law: 1, intellectual property law: 22

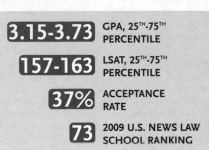

3.15-3.73 GPA, 25TH-75TH PERCENTILE

157-163 LSAT, 25TH-75TH PERCENTILE

37% ACCEPTANCE RATE

73 2009 U.S. NEWS LAW SCHOOL RANKING

ADMISSIONS
Admissions phone number: **(503) 768-6613**
Admissions email address: **lawadmss@lclark.edu**
Application website:
   http://law.lclark.edu/dept/lawadmss/requirements.html
Application deadline for Fall 2009 admission: **03/01**

Admissions statistics:
Number of applicants for Fall 2007: **2,328**
Number of acceptances: **862**
Number enrolled: **177**
Acceptance rate: **37%**
GPA, 25th-75th percentile, entering class Fall 2007: **3.15-3.73**
LSAT, 25th-75th percentile, entering class Fall 2007: **157-163**

Part-time program:
Number of applicants for Fall 2007: **194**
Number of acceptances: **75**
Number enrolled: **43**
Acceptance rate: **39%**
GPA, 25th-75th percentile, entering class Fall 2007: **2.82-3.62**
LSAT, 25th-75th percentile, entering class Fall 2007: **152-162**

FINANCIAL AID
Financial aid phone number: **(503) 768-7090**
Financial aid application deadline: **03/01**
Tuition 2007-2008 academic year: full-time: **$28,984**; part-time: **$21,738**
Room and board: **$10,395**; books: **$1,000**; miscellaneous expenses: **$4,950**
Total of room/board/books/miscellaneous expenses: **$16,345**
University does not offer graduate student housing for which law students are eligible.

Financial aid profile
Percent of students that received grants for the 2006-2007 academic year: full-time: **47%**; part-time **23%**
Median grant amount: full-time: **$9,000**; part-time: **$7,000**
The average law-school debt of those in the Class of 2007 who borrowed: **$94,341**. Proportion who borrowed: **92%**

ACADEMIC PROGRAMS
Calendar: **semester**
Joint degrees awarded: **N/A**
Typical first-year section size: Full-time: **74**; Part-time: **78**
Is there typically a "small section" of the first year class, other than Legal Writing, taught by full-time faculty?: Full-time: **yes**; Part-time: **yes**
Number of course titles, beyond the first year curriculum, offered last year: **122**
Percentages of upper division course sections, excluding seminars, with an enrollment of:
   Under 25: **54%**   25 to 49: **29%**
   50 to 74: **12%**   75 to 99: **4%**
   100+: **1%**
Areas of specialization: appellate advocacy, clinical training, dispute resolution, environmental law, healthcare law, intellectual property law, international law, tax law, trial advocacy

Fall 2007 faculty profile
Total teaching faculty: **118**. Full-time: **48%**; **56%** men, **44%** women, **9%** minorities. Part-time: **52%**; **62%** men, **38%** women, **2%** minorities
Student-to-faculty ratio: **10.6**

SPECIAL PROGRAMS *(as provided by law school):*
Certificates in Environmental, Criminal, Intellectual Property, Business, Tax, Public Interest, and Animal Law. Seven clinics; externships around the world; internships in several practice areas. Summer: environmental law, Indian law, summer-abroad

partnerships. Law centers: International Environmental Law, National Crime Victims Law Institute, National Animal Law, National Environmental Defense.

STUDENT BODY

Fall 2007 full-time enrollment: 537

Men: 54%	Women: 46%
African-American: 1.7%	American Indian: 1.3%
Asian-American: 7.8%	Mexican-American: 1.5%
Puerto Rican: 0.2%	Other Hisp-Amer: 3.9%
White: 73.7%	International: 1.3%
Unknown: 8.6%	

Fall 2007 part-time enrollment: 188

Men: 48%	Women: 52%
African-American: 3.7%	American Indian: 3.7%
Asian-American: 11.2%	Mexican-American: 3.7%
Puerto Rican: 0.0%	Other Hisp-Amer: 3.7%
White: 63.3%	International: 2.7%
Unknown: 8.0%	

Attrition rates for 2006-2007 full-time students
Percent of students discontinuing law school:

Men: 3%	Women: 5%
First-year students: 7%	Second-year students: 3%
Third-year students: 1%	

LIBRARY RESOURCES

Total volumes: 522,172
Total seats available for library users: 385

INFORMATION TECHNOLOGY

Number of wired network connections available to students: 959 total (in the law library, excluding computer labs: 269; in classrooms: 292; in computer labs: 31; elsewhere in the law school: 367)
Law school has a wireless network.
Students are not required to own a computer.

EMPLOYMENT AND SALARIES

Proportion of 2006 graduates employed at graduation: N/A
Employed 9 months later, as of February 15, 2007: 92%
Salaries in the private sector (law firms, business, industry): $57,000–$95,000 (25th-75th percentile)
Median salary in the private sector: $90,000
Percentage in the private sector who reported salary information: 64%
Median salary in public service (government, judicial clerkships, academic posts, non-profits): $42,533

Percentage of 2006 graduates in:

Law firms: 47%	Government: 16%
Bus./industry: 17%	Judicial clerkship: 7%
Public interest: 12%	Unknown: 0%
Academia: 1%	

2006 graduates employed in-state: 67%
2006 graduates employed in foreign countries: 0%
Number of states where graduates are employed: 20
Percentage of 2006 graduates working in: New England: N/A, Middle Atlantic: 4%, East North Central: 1%, West North Central: N/A, South Atlantic: 4%, East South Central: N/A, West South Central: 2%, Mountain: 6%, Pacific: 83%, Unknown: 0%

BAR PASSAGE RATES

Based on 2006 graduates taking Summer 2006 or Winter 2007 exams. Most of the school's first-time test takers took the bar in Oregon.

86%
School's bar passage rate for first-time test takers

82%
Statewide bar passage rate for first-time test takers

Louisiana State Univ.–Baton Rouge

■ 400 Paul M. Hebert Law Center, Baton Rouge, LA, 70803
■ http://www.law.lsu.edu
■ Public
■ Year founded: 1906
■ 2007-2008 tuition: In-state: full-time: $12,190; part-time: N/A; Out-of-state: full-time: $21,286
■ Enrollment 2007-08 academic year: full-time: 570; part-time: 13
■ U.S. News 2009 law specialty ranking: N/A

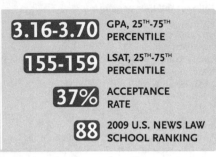

3.16-3.70 GPA, 25TH-75TH PERCENTILE

155-159 LSAT, 25TH-75TH PERCENTILE

37% ACCEPTANCE RATE

88 2009 U.S. NEWS LAW SCHOOL RANKING

ADMISSIONS

Admissions phone number: **(225) 578-8646**
Admissions email address: **admissions@law.lsu.edu**
Application website:
https://apploo8.lsu.edu/admissions/lawappl.nsf/admissionapplication?OpenForm
Application deadline for Fall 2009 admission: **07/01**

Admissions statistics:

Number of applicants for Fall 2007: **1,298**
Number of acceptances: **486**
Number enrolled: **201**
Acceptance rate: **37%**
GPA, 25th-75th percentile, entering class Fall 2007: **3.16-3.70**
LSAT, 25th-75th percentile, entering class Fall 2007: **155-159**

FINANCIAL AID

Financial aid phone number: **(225) 578-3103**
Financial aid application deadline: **N/A**
Tuition 2007-2008 academic year: In-state: full-time: **$12,190**; part-time: **N/A**; Out-of-state: full-time: **$21,286**
Room and board: **$11,354**; books: **$2,000**; miscellaneous expenses: **$3,162**
Total of room/board/books/miscellaneous expenses: **$16,516**
University does not offer graduate student housing for which law students are eligible.

Financial aid profile

Percent of students that received grants for the 2006-2007 academic year: full-time: **51%**
Median grant amount: full-time: **$2,981**
The average law-school debt of those in the Class of 2007 who borrowed: **$59,218**. Proportion who borrowed: **80%**

ACADEMIC PROGRAMS

Calendar: **semester**
Joint degrees awarded: **N/A**

Typical first-year section size: Full-time: **67**
Is there typically a "small section" of the first year class, other than Legal Writing, taught by full-time faculty?: Full-time: **yes**; Part-time: **no**
Number of course titles, beyond the first year curriculum, offered last year: **79**
Percentages of upper division course sections, excluding seminars, with an enrollment of:
Under 25: **59%**   25 to 49: **28%**
50 to 74: **7%**   75 to 99: **5%**
100+: **2%**
Areas of specialization: appellate advocacy, clinical training, dispute resolution, environmental law, healthcare law, intellectual property law, international law, tax law, trial advocacy

Fall 2007 faculty profile

Total teaching faculty: **78**. Full-time: **40%**; **77%** men, **23%** women, **10%** minorities. Part-time: **60%**; **94%** men, **6%** women, **9%** minorities
Student-to-faculty ratio: **16.2**

SPECIAL PROGRAMS (as provided by law school):

LSU law students have the opportunity to participate in summer programs in Lyon, France, or Buenos Aires, Argentina. Some students choose to participate in the LSU–Southern University Law Center co-op program. Externships are offered in some law courses, giving students the opportunity to work with government agencies, local prosecutors and public defenders, and state and federal revenue offices.

STUDENT BODY

Fall 2007 full-time enrollment: 570
Men: **52%**   Women: **48%**
African-American: **4.4%**   American Indian: **1.1%**
Asian-American: **0.5%**   Mexican-American: **0.0%**
Puerto Rican: **0.0%**   Other Hisp-Amer: **3.7%**
White: **79.5%**   International: **0.0%**
Unknown: **10.9%**

Fall 2007 part-time enrollment: 13

Men: 46%	Women: 54%
African-American: 15.4%	American Indian: 0.0%
Asian-American: 0.0%	Mexican-American: 0.0%
Puerto Rican: 0.0%	Other Hisp-Amer: 7.7%
White: 69.2%	International: 0.0%
Unknown: 7.7%	

Attrition rates for 2006-2007 full-time students
Percent of students discontinuing law school:

Men: 1%	Women: 3%
First-year students: 5%	Second-year students: N/A
Third-year students: N/A	

LIBRARY RESOURCES

Total volumes: 853,778
Total seats available for library users: 473

INFORMATION TECHNOLOGY

Number of wired network connections available to students: 107 total (in the law library, excluding computer labs: 85; in classrooms: 14; in computer labs: 8; elsewhere in the law school: 0)
Law school has a wireless network.
Students are not required to own a computer.

EMPLOYMENT AND SALARIES

Proportion of 2006 graduates employed at graduation: 74%
Employed 9 months later, as of February 15, 2007: 94%
Salaries in the private sector (law firms, business, industry): N/A

Median salary in the private sector: $65,000
Percentage in the private sector who reported salary information: 78%
Median salary in public service (government, judicial clerkships, academic posts, non-profits): $39,000

Percentage of 2006 graduates in:

Law firms: 60%	Government: 14%
Bus./industry: 7%	Judicial clerkship: 14%
Public interest: 2%	Unknown: 2%
Academia: 1%	

2006 graduates employed in-state: 80%
2006 graduates employed in foreign countries: 0%
Number of states where graduates are employed: 14
Percentage of 2006 graduates working in: New England: N/A, Middle Atlantic: 1%, East North Central: 0%, West North Central: 0%, South Atlantic: 8%, East South Central: 1%, West South Central: 86%, Mountain: 0%, Pacific: 2%, Unknown: 1%

BAR PASSAGE RATES

Based on 2006 graduates taking Summer 2006 or Winter 2007 exams. Most of the school's first-time test takers took the bar in Louisiana.

89%
School's bar passage rate for first-time test takers

75%
Statewide bar passage rate for first-time test takers

Loyola Marymount University

- 919 Albany Street, Los Angeles, CA, 90015-1211
- http://www.lls.edu
- Private
- **Year founded:** 1920
- **2007-2008 tuition:** full-time: $36,058; part-time: $24,188
- **Enrollment 2007-08 academic year:** full-time: 1,003; part-time: 291
- **U.S. News 2009 law specialty ranking:** tax law: 13, trial advocacy: 6

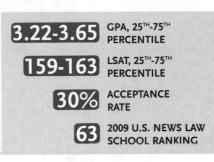

3.22-3.65 GPA, 25TH-75TH PERCENTILE

159-163 LSAT, 25TH-75TH PERCENTILE

30% ACCEPTANCE RATE

63 2009 U.S. NEWS LAW SCHOOL RANKING

ADMISSIONS

Admissions phone number: **(213) 736-1074**
Admissions email address: **Admissions@lls.edu**
Application website: **http://www.lls.edu/admissions**
Application deadline for Fall 2009 admission: **02/02**

Admissions statistics:
Number of applicants for Fall 2007: **4,372**
Number of acceptances: **1,298**
Number enrolled: **344**
Acceptance rate: **30%**
GPA, 25th-75th percentile, entering class Fall 2007: **3.22-3.65**
LSAT, 25th-75th percentile, entering class Fall 2007: **159-163**

Part-time program:
Number of applicants for Fall 2007: **2,221**
Number of acceptances: **135**
Number enrolled: **74**
Acceptance rate: **6%**
GPA, 25th-75th percentile, entering class Fall 2007: **3.02-3.42**
LSAT, 25th-75th percentile, entering class Fall 2007: **157-160**

FINANCIAL AID

Financial aid phone number: **(213) 736-1140**
Financial aid application deadline: **03/13**
Tuition 2007-2008 academic year: full-time: **$36,058**; part-time: **$24,188**
Room and board: **$13,500**; books: **$1,000**; miscellaneous expenses: **$5,720**
Total of room/board/books/miscellaneous expenses: **$20,220**
University does not offer graduate student housing for which law students are eligible.

Financial aid profile
Percent of students that received grants for the 2006-2007 academic year: full-time: **25%**; part-time **13%**

Median grant amount: full-time: **$26,900**; part-time: **$15,300**
The average law-school debt of those in the Class of 2007 who borrowed: **$101,800**. Proportion who borrowed: **81%**

ACADEMIC PROGRAMS

Calendar: **semester**
Joint degrees awarded: **J.D./M.B.A.**
Typical first-year section size: Full-time: **87**; Part-time: **70**
Is there typically a "small section" of the first year class, other than Legal Writing, taught by full-time faculty?: Full-time: **no**; Part-time: **no**
Number of course titles, beyond the first year curriculum, offered last year: **141**
Percentages of upper division course sections, excluding seminars, with an enrollment of:
Under 25: **59%**   25 to 49: **23%**
50 to 74: **7%**   75 to 99: **6%**
100+: **5%**
Areas of specialization: appellate advocacy, clinical training, dispute resolution, environmental law, healthcare law, intellectual property law, international law, tax law, trial advocacy

Fall 2007 faculty profile
Total teaching faculty: **176**. Full-time: **40%**; 57% men, 43% women, 20% minorities. Part-time: **60%**; 74% men, 26% women, 18% minorities
Student-to-faculty ratio: **15.8**

SPECIAL PROGRAMS *(as provided by law school):*
Academic support programs. Externships with federal, state, and local governments; public interest and entertainment firms; and district attorney. Clinics: juvenile justice, disability rights, conflict resolution, State Board of Equalization, nonprofit tax and transactions. Study abroad: Italy, Costa Rica, and London. Ethical Advocacy Center, alumni mentor program, and public interest program.

STUDENT BODY

Fall 2007 full-time enrollment: 1,003

Men: 50%	Women: 50%
African-American: 3.7%	American Indian: 0.1%
Asian-American: 25.2%	Mexican-American: 7.0%
Puerto Rican: 0.5%	Other Hisp-Amer: 3.9%
White: 48.2%	International: 1.1%
Unknown: 10.4%	

Fall 2007 part-time enrollment: 291

Men: 53%	Women: 47%
African-American: 3.8%	American Indian: 1.4%
Asian-American: 19.6%	Mexican-American: 4.5%
Puerto Rican: 0.7%	Other Hisp-Amer: 3.4%
White: 53.6%	International: 2.1%
Unknown: 11.0%	

Attrition rates for 2006-2007 full-time students
Percent of students discontinuing law school:

Men: 3%	Women: 5%
First-year students: 13%	Second-year students: N/A
Third-year students: 0%	

LIBRARY RESOURCES

Total volumes: 592,499
Total seats available for library users: 550

INFORMATION TECHNOLOGY

Number of wired network connections available to students: 640 total (in the law library, excluding computer labs: 520; in classrooms: 0; in computer labs: 0; elsewhere in the law school: 120)
Law school has a wireless network.
Students are not required to own a computer.

EMPLOYMENT AND SALARIES

Proportion of 2006 graduates employed at graduation: 67%

Employed 9 months later, as of February 15, 2007: **97%**
Salaries in the private sector (law firms, business, industry): **$67,650–$125,000** (25th-75th percentile)
Median salary in the private sector: **$80,000**
Percentage in the private sector who reported salary information: **59%**
Median salary in public service (government, judicial clerkships, academic posts, non-profits): **$58,000**

Percentage of 2006 graduates in:

Law firms: 59%	Government: 8%
Bus./industry: 21%	Judicial clerkship: 3%
Public interest: 8%	Unknown: 1%
Academia: 2%	

2006 graduates employed in-state: 92%
2006 graduates employed in foreign countries: 2%
Number of states where graduates are employed: 12
Percentage of 2006 graduates working in: New England: N/A, Middle Atlantic: 1%, East North Central: 1%, West North Central: N/A, South Atlantic: 0%, East South Central: N/A, West South Central: 0%, Mountain: 1%, Pacific: 95%, Unknown: 0%

BAR PASSAGE RATES

Based on 2006 graduates taking Summer 2006 or Winter 2007 exams. Most of the school's first-time test takers took the bar in California.

75%
School's bar passage rate for first-time test takers

65%
Statewide bar passage rate for first-time test takers

Loyola University Chicago

■ 25 E. Pearson Street, Chicago, IL, 60611
■ http://www.luc.edu/schools/law
■ Private
■ Year founded: 1908
■ 2007-2008 tuition: full-time: $33,300; part-time: $25,050
■ Enrollment 2007-08 academic year: full-time: 621; part-time: 244
■ U.S. News 2009 law specialty ranking: healthcare law: 6

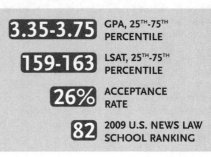

3.35-3.75 GPA, 25TH-75TH PERCENTILE

159-163 LSAT, 25TH-75TH PERCENTILE

26% ACCEPTANCE RATE

82 2009 U.S. NEWS LAW SCHOOL RANKING

ADMISSIONS
Admissions phone number: **(312) 915-7170**
Admissions email address: **law-admissions@luc.edu**
Application website:
  http://www.luc.edu/schools/law/admissions/index.html
Application deadline for Fall 2009 admission: **04/01**

Admissions statistics:
Number of applicants for Fall 2007: **3,581**
Number of acceptances: **924**
Number enrolled: **177**
Acceptance rate: **26%**
GPA, 25th-75th percentile, entering class Fall 2007: **3.35-3.75**
LSAT, 25th-75th percentile, entering class Fall 2007: **159-163**

Part-time program:
Number of applicants for Fall 2007: **540**
Number of acceptances: **228**
Number enrolled: **99**
Acceptance rate: **42%**
GPA, 25th-75th percentile, entering class Fall 2007: **2.95-3.42**
LSAT, 25th-75th percentile, entering class Fall 2007: **151-158**

FINANCIAL AID
Financial aid phone number: **(312) 915-7170**
Financial aid application deadline: **03/01**
Tuition 2007-2008 academic year: full-time: **$33,300**; part-time: **$25,050**
Room and board: **$13,200**; books: **$1,200**; miscellaneous expenses: **$5,300**
Total of room/board/books/miscellaneous expenses: **$19,700**
University offers graduate student housing for which law students are eligible.

Financial aid profile
Percent of students that received grants for the 2006-2007 academic year: full-time: **72%**; part-time **29%**

Median grant amount: full-time: **$10,000**; part-time: **$5,000**
The average law-school debt of those in the Class of 2007 who borrowed: **$90,518**. Proportion who borrowed: **84%**

ACADEMIC PROGRAMS
Calendar: **semester**
Joint degrees awarded: **J.D./M.S.W.; J.D./M.B.A.; J.D./M.S.H.R.; J.D./M.A.**
Typical first-year section size: Full-time: **62**; Part-time: **71**
Is there typically a "small section" of the first year class, other than Legal Writing, taught by full-time faculty?: Full-time: **no**; Part-time: **no**
Number of course titles, beyond the first year curriculum, offered last year: **155**
Percentages of upper division course sections, excluding seminars, with an enrollment of:
  Under 25: **70%**   25 to 49: **19%**
  50 to 74: **10%**   75 to 99: **2%**
  100+: **1%**
Areas of specialization: appellate advocacy, clinical training, dispute resolution, environmental law, healthcare law, intellectual property law, international law, tax law, trial advocacy

Fall 2007 faculty profile
Total teaching faculty: **154**. Full-time: **31%**; **60%** men, **40%** women, **15%** minorities. Part-time: **69%**; **52%** men, **48%** women, **5%** minorities
Student-to-faculty ratio: **14.5**

SPECIAL PROGRAMS *(as provided by law school):*
Loyola's clinics include the Community Law Center and the child law, tax, business law, and elder law clinics. Centers of excellence include the Beazeley Health Law Institute, Civitas ChildLaw Center, Advocacy Center, and the Institute for Consumer Antitrust Studies. Annual overseas programs include Rome; Strasbourg, France; Oxford; London; and Santiago, Chile.

STUDENT BODY

Fall 2007 full-time enrollment: 621

Men: 47%	Women: 53%
African-American: 6.1%	American Indian: 0.6%
Asian-American: 6.1%	Mexican-American: 2.7%
Puerto Rican: 0.2%	Other Hisp-Amer: 1.8%
White: 74.4%	International: 1.1%
Unknown: 6.9%	

Fall 2007 part-time enrollment: 244

Men: 50%	Women: 50%
African-American: 4.1%	American Indian: 0.8%
Asian-American: 9.0%	Mexican-American: 3.3%
Puerto Rican: 0.0%	Other Hisp-Amer: 1.2%
White: 73.4%	International: 0.8%
Unknown: 7.4%	

Attrition rates for 2006-2007 full-time students
Percent of students discontinuing law school:

Men: 2%	Women: 4%
First-year students: 2%	Second-year students: 8%
Third-year students: 0%	

LIBRARY RESOURCES

Total volumes: 401,282
Total seats available for library users: 456

INFORMATION TECHNOLOGY

Number of wired network connections available to students: 328 total (in the law library, excluding computer labs: 180; in classrooms: 148; in computer labs: 0; elsewhere in the law school: 0)
Law school has a wireless network.
Students are not required to own a computer.

EMPLOYMENT AND SALARIES

Proportion of 2006 graduates employed at graduation: 54%

Employed 9 months later, as of February 15, 2007: 89%
Salaries in the private sector (law firms, business, industry): $70,000–$135,000 (25th-75th percentile)
Median salary in the private sector: $100,000
Percentage in the private sector who reported salary information: 47%
Median salary in public service (government, judicial clerkships, academic posts, non-profits): $45,000

Percentage of 2006 graduates in:

Law firms: 54%	Government: 16%
Bus./industry: 23%	Judicial clerkship: 6%
Public interest: 1%	Unknown: 0%
Academia: 0%	

2006 graduates employed in-state: 87%
2006 graduates employed in foreign countries: 0%
Number of states where graduates are employed: 16
Percentage of 2006 graduates working in: New England: N/A, Middle Atlantic: 1%, East North Central: 91%, West North Central: 0%, South Atlantic: 3%, East South Central: N/A, West South Central: 1%, Mountain: 1%, Pacific: 2%, Unknown: 0%

BAR PASSAGE RATES

Based on 2006 graduates taking Summer 2006 or Winter 2007 exams. Most of the school's first-time test takers took the bar in Illinois.

90%
School's bar passage rate for first-time test takers

87%
Statewide bar passage rate for first-time test takers

Loyola University New Orleans

■ 7214 St. Charles Avenue, PO Box 901, New Orleans, LA, 70118
■ http://law.loyno.edu/
■ Private
■ Year founded: 1931
■ 2007-2008 tuition: full-time: $30,456; part-time: $20,596
■ Enrollment 2007-08 academic year: full-time: 700; part-time: 158
■ U.S. News 2009 law specialty ranking: clinical training: 25

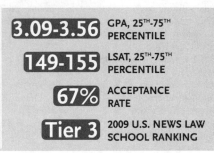

3.09-3.56 GPA, 25TH-75TH PERCENTILE

149-155 LSAT, 25TH-75TH PERCENTILE

67% ACCEPTANCE RATE

Tier 3 2009 U.S. NEWS LAW SCHOOL RANKING

ADMISSIONS

Admissions phone number: **(504) 861-5575**
Admissions email address: **ladmit@loyno.edu**
Application website:
  http://law.loyno.edu/admissions/application.php
Application deadline for Fall 2009 admission: **rolling**

Admissions statistics:
Number of applicants for Fall 2007: **1,191**
Number of acceptances: **800**
Number enrolled: **260**
Acceptance rate: **67%**
GPA, 25th-75th percentile, entering class Fall 2007: **3.09-3.56**
LSAT, 25th-75th percentile, entering class Fall 2007: **149-155**

Part-time program:
Number of applicants for Fall 2007: **142**
Number of acceptances: **93**
Number enrolled: **60**
Acceptance rate: **65%**
GPA, 25th-75th percentile, entering class Fall 2007: **3.24-3.50**
LSAT, 25th-75th percentile, entering class Fall 2007: **146-154**

FINANCIAL AID

Financial aid phone number: **(504) 865-3231**
Financial aid application deadline: **N/A**
Tuition 2007-2008 academic year: full-time: **$30,456**; part-time: **$20,596**
Room and board: **$12,600**; books: **$1,500**; miscellaneous expenses: **$5,150**
Total of room/board/books/miscellaneous expenses: **$19,250**
University offers graduate student housing for which law students are eligible.

Financial aid profile
Percent of students that received grants for the 2006-2007
academic year: full-time: **45%**; part-time **18%**
Median grant amount: full-time: **$14,000**; part-time: **$3,000**
The average law-school debt of those in the Class of 2007 who borrowed: **$84,155**. Proportion who borrowed: **87%**

ACADEMIC PROGRAMS

Calendar: **semester**
Joint degrees awarded: **J.D./M.B.A.; J.D./M.A. Mass Communication; J.D./MA Religious Studies; J.D./M.U.P.; J.D./M.P.A.**
Typical first-year section size: Full-time: **82**; Part-time: **55**
Is there typically a "small section" of the first year class, other than Legal Writing, taught by full-time faculty?: Full-time: **no**; Part-time: **no**
Number of course titles, beyond the first year curriculum, offered last year: **85**
Percentages of upper division course sections, excluding seminars, with an enrollment of:
  Under 25: **33%**   25 to 49: **39%**
  50 to 74: **23%**   75 to 99: **3%**
  100+: **2%**
Areas of specialization: appellate advocacy, clinical training, dispute resolution, environmental law, intellectual property law, international law, tax law, trial advocacy

Fall 2007 faculty profile
Total teaching faculty: **60**. Full-time: **62%**; **68%** men, **32%** women, **27%** minorities. Part-time: **38%**; **78%** men, **22%** women, **0%** minorities
Student-to-faculty ratio: **17.5**

SPECIAL PROGRAMS *(as provided by law school):*
Loyola has programs in civil and common law; summer programs in Vienna, Moscow, Budapest, Mexico, Brazil, Costa Rica; Certificate in International Legal Studies; joint degrees J.D./M.B.A. and J.D./M.A. in several disciplines; law clinic students represent clients in civil, criminal, and other cases; loan forgiveness for public service employment; externships with federal and state courts/agencies.

STUDENT BODY

Fall 2007 full-time enrollment: 700

Men: 47%	Women: 53%
African-American: 11.4%	American Indian: 1.0%
Asian-American: 5.1%	Mexican-American: 0.7%
Puerto Rican: 0.9%	Other Hisp-Amer: 6.1%
White: 68.1%	International: 0.6%
Unknown: 6.0%	

Fall 2007 part-time enrollment: 158

Men: 53%	Women: 47%
African-American: 11.4%	American Indian: 1.3%
Asian-American: 2.5%	Mexican-American: 1.3%
Puerto Rican: 0.6%	Other Hisp-Amer: 5.7%
White: 69.6%	International: 0.0%
Unknown: 7.6%	

Attrition rates for 2006-2007 full-time students

Percent of students discontinuing law school:

Men: 5%	Women: 2%
First-year students: 9%	Second-year students: 1%
Third-year students: N/A	

LIBRARY RESOURCES

Total volumes: 371,675

Total seats available for library users: 366

INFORMATION TECHNOLOGY

Number of wired network connections available to students: 40 total (in the law library, excluding computer labs: 28; in classrooms: 0; in computer labs: 0; elsewhere in the law school: 12)

Law school has a wireless network.

Students are not required to own a computer.

EMPLOYMENT AND SALARIES

Proportion of 2006 graduates employed at graduation: 63%

Employed 9 months later, as of February 15, 2007: **95%**

Salaries in the private sector (law firms, business, industry): **N/A**

Median salary in the private sector: **N/A**

Percentage in the private sector who reported salary information: **N/A**

Median salary in public service (government, judicial clerkships, academic posts, non-profits): **N/A**

Percentage of 2006 graduates in:

Law firms: **62%**	Government: **9%**
Bus./industry: **12%**	Judicial clerkship: **11%**
Public interest: **6%**	Unknown: **0%**
Academia: **0%**	

2006 graduates employed in-state: **63%**

2006 graduates employed in foreign countries: **0%**

Number of states where graduates are employed: **23**

Percentage of 2006 graduates working in: New England: **2%**, Middle Atlantic: **2%**, East North Central: **2%**, West North Central: **1%**, South Atlantic: **15%**, East South Central: **6%**, West South Central: **68%**, Mountain: **2%**, Pacific: **2%**, Unknown: **0%**

BAR PASSAGE RATES

Based on 2006 graduates taking Summer 2006 or Winter 2007 exams. Most of the school's first-time test takers took the bar in Louisiana.

80%

School's bar passage rate for first-time test takers

75%

Statewide bar passage rate for first-time test takers

Marquette University

■ Sensenbrenner Hall, PO Box 1881, Milwaukee, WI, 53201-1881
■ http://law.marquette.edu
■ Private
■ **Year founded:** 1892
■ **2007-2008 tuition:** full-time: $29,410; part-time: $17,625
■ **Enrollment 2007-08 academic year:** full-time: 530; part-time: 188
■ **U.S. News 2009 law specialty ranking:** dispute resolution: 6

3.20-3.65 GPA, 25TH-75TH PERCENTILE

155-159 LSAT, 25TH-75TH PERCENTILE

46% ACCEPTANCE RATE

95 2009 U.S. NEWS LAW SCHOOL RANKING

ADMISSIONS
Admissions phone number: **(414) 288-6767**
Admissions email address: **law.admission@marquette.edu**
Application website: **N/A**
Application deadline for Fall 2009 admission: **07/01**

Admissions statistics:
Number of applicants for Fall 2007: **1,581**
Number of acceptances: **721**
Number enrolled: **182**
Acceptance rate: **46%**
GPA, 25th-75th percentile, entering class Fall 2007: **3.20-3.65**
LSAT, 25th-75th percentile, entering class Fall 2007: **155-159**

Part-time program:
Number of applicants for Fall 2007: **187**
Number of acceptances: **51**
Number enrolled: **42**
Acceptance rate: **27%**
GPA, 25th-75th percentile, entering class Fall 2007: **2.86-3.55**
LSAT, 25th-75th percentile, entering class Fall 2007: **152-159**

FINANCIAL AID
Financial aid phone number: **(414) 288-7390**
Financial aid application deadline: **07/01**
Tuition 2007-2008 academic year: full-time: **$29,410**; part-time: **$17,625**
Room and board: **$10,130**; books: **$1,162**; miscellaneous expenses: **$5,314**
Total of room/board/books/miscellaneous expenses: **$16,606**
University does not offer graduate student housing for which law students are eligible.

Financial aid profile
Percent of students that received grants for the 2006-2007 academic year: full-time: **44%**; part-time **37%**

Median grant amount: full-time: **$6,500**; part-time: **$4,500**
The average law-school debt of those in the Class of 2007 who borrowed: **$81,722**. Proportion who borrowed: **87%**

ACADEMIC PROGRAMS
Calendar: **semester**
Joint degrees awarded: **J.D./M.B.A.; J.D./M.A. Political Science; J.D./M.A. International Affairs; J.D./M.A. History of Philosophy; J.D./M.A. Philosophy; J.D./Certificate in Dispute Resolution; J.D./M.B.A. Sports Business**
Typical first-year section size: Full-time: **89**; Part-time: **45**
Is there typically a "small section" of the first year class, other than Legal Writing, taught by full-time faculty?: Full-time: **yes**; Part-time: **yes**
Number of course titles, beyond the first year curriculum, offered last year: **127**
Percentages of upper division course sections, excluding seminars, with an enrollment of:
Under 25: **55%**   25 to 49: **31%**
50 to 74: **11%**   75 to 99: **3%**
100+: **0%**
Areas of specialization: appellate advocacy, clinical training, dispute resolution, environmental law, healthcare law, intellectual property law, international law, tax law, trial advocacy

Fall 2007 faculty profile
Total teaching faculty: **101**. Full-time: **31%**; **45%** men, **55%** women, **13%** minorities. Part-time: **69%**; **64%** men, **36%** women, **6%** minorities
Student-to-faculty ratio: **17.5**

SPECIAL PROGRAMS *(as provided by law school):*
Marquette students have the opportunity to develop legal skills in one of the school's clinical programs. Students participate in internships with a variety of governmental and legal services agencies, as well as in internships with trial and appellate judges. Students may focus their studies in specific doctrinal areas including dispute resolution, intellectual property, and sports law.

STUDENT BODY

Fall 2007 full-time enrollment: 530

Men: 58%   Women: 42%
African-American: 3.4%   American Indian: 0.6%
Asian-American: 3.0%   Mexican-American: 0.8%
Puerto Rican: 0.8%   Other Hisp-Amer: 3.0%
White: 87.7%   International: 0.6%
Unknown: 0.2%

Fall 2007 part-time enrollment: 188

Men: 51%   Women: 49%
African-American: 3.2%   American Indian: 2.1%
Asian-American: 3.7%   Mexican-American: 0.5%
Puerto Rican: 0.5%   Other Hisp-Amer: 1.6%
White: 87.8%   International: 0.5%
Unknown: 0.0%

Attrition rates for 2006-2007 full-time students
Percent of students discontinuing law school:
Men: 2%   Women: 3%
First-year students: 5%   Second-year students: 1%
Third-year students: N/A

LIBRARY RESOURCES

Total volumes: 350,710
Total seats available for library users: 396

INFORMATION TECHNOLOGY

Number of wired network connections available to students: 124 total (in the law library, excluding computer labs: 20; in classrooms: 96; in computer labs: 2; elsewhere in the law school: 6)
Law school has a wireless network.
Students are not required to own a computer.

EMPLOYMENT AND SALARIES

Proportion of 2006 graduates employed at graduation: 63%

Employed 9 months later, as of February 15, 2007: 96%
Salaries in the private sector (law firms, business, industry): $45,000–$84,000 (25th-75th percentile)
Median salary in the private sector: $54,000
Percentage in the private sector who reported salary information: 83%
Median salary in public service (government, judicial clerkships, academic posts, non-profits): $47,000

Percentage of 2006 graduates in:
Law firms: 65%   Government: 9%
Bus./industry: 14%   Judicial clerkship: 5%
Public interest: 5%   Unknown: 0%
Academia: 2%

2006 graduates employed in-state: 73%
2006 graduates employed in foreign countries: 0%
Number of states where graduates are employed: 18
Percentage of 2006 graduates working in: New England: 0%, Middle Atlantic: 1%, East North Central: 84%, West North Central: 5%, South Atlantic: 3%, East South Central: 1%, West South Central: 0%, Mountain: 5%, Pacific: 1%, Unknown: 0%

BAR PASSAGE RATES

Based on 2006 graduates taking Summer 2006 or Winter 2007 exams. Most of the school's first-time test takers took the bar in Wisconsin.

100%
School's bar passage rate for first-time test takers

89%
Statewide bar passage rate for first-time test takers

Mercer University

- 1021 Georgia Avenue, Macon, GA, 31207-0001
- http://www.law.mercer.edu
- Private
- Year founded: 1873
- 2007-2008 tuition: full-time: $32,292; part-time: N/A
- Enrollment 2007-08 academic year: full-time: 448
- U.S. News 2009 law specialty ranking: N/A

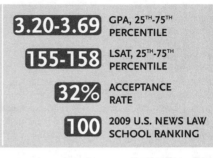

3.20-3.69 GPA, 25TH-75TH PERCENTILE

155-158 LSAT, 25TH-75TH PERCENTILE

32% ACCEPTANCE RATE

100 2009 U.S. NEWS LAW SCHOOL RANKING

ADMISSIONS
Admissions phone number: **(478) 301-2605**
Admissions email address: **martin_sv@mercer.edu**
Application website:
   http://www.law.mercer.edu/admissions/apply.cfm
Application deadline for Fall 2009 admission: **03/15**

Admissions statistics:
Number of applicants for Fall 2007: **1,317**
Number of acceptances: **419**
Number enrolled: **148**
Acceptance rate: **32%**
GPA, 25th-75th percentile, entering class Fall 2007: **3.20-3.69**
LSAT, 25th-75th percentile, entering class Fall 2007: **155-158**

FINANCIAL AID
Financial aid phone number: **(478) 301-2064**
Financial aid application deadline: **04/01**
Tuition 2007-2008 academic year: full-time: **$32,292**; part-time: **N/A**
Room and board: **$7,200**; books: **$1,000**; miscellaneous expenses: **$6,000**
Total of room/board/books/miscellaneous expenses: **$14,200**
University offers graduate student housing for which law students are eligible.

Financial aid profile
Percent of students that received grants for the 2006-2007 academic year: full-time: **28%**
Median grant amount: full-time: **$20,000**
The average law-school debt of those in the Class of 2007 who borrowed: **$76,293**. Proportion who borrowed: **81%**

ACADEMIC PROGRAMS
Calendar: **semester**
Joint degrees awarded: **J.D./M.B.A.**
Typical first-year section size: Full-time: **72**
Is there typically a "small section" of the first year class, other than Legal Writing, taught by full-time faculty?:

Full-time: **yes**
Number of course titles, beyond the first year curriculum, offered last year: **105**
Percentages of upper division course sections, excluding seminars, with an enrollment of:
Under 25: **73%**   25 to 49: **19%**
50 to 74: **6%**   75 to 99: **2%**
100+: **1%**
Areas of specialization: appellate advocacy, clinical training, dispute resolution, environmental law, healthcare law, intellectual property law, international law, tax law, trial advocacy

Fall 2007 faculty profile
Total teaching faculty: **61**. Full-time: **46%**; **64%** men, **36%** women, **11%** minorities. Part-time: **54%**; **79%** men, **21%** women, **3%** minorities
Student-to-faculty ratio: **13.3**

SPECIAL PROGRAMS *(as provided by law school):*
Mercer, home of the Legal Writing Institute, is the only school that offers a Legal Writing Certificate. The school also hosts the Mercer Center for Legal Ethics and Professionalism, and in fall 2006, the university instituted a new law and public service program to promote volunteerism and attention to public interest law.

STUDENT BODY
Fall 2007 full-time enrollment: **448**
Men: **57%**   Women: **43%**
African-American: **10.7%**   American Indian: **0.4%**
Asian-American: **2.9%**   Mexican-American: **0.2%**
Puerto Rican: **0.7%**   Other Hisp-Amer: **1.6%**
White: **72.8%**   International: **0.0%**
Unknown: **10.7%**

Attrition rates for 2006-2007 full-time students
Percent of students discontinuing law school:
Men: **3%**   Women: **5%**
First-year students: **9%**   Second-year students: **N/A**
Third-year students: **2%**

LIBRARY RESOURCES

Total volumes: 342,718
Total seats available for library users: 378

INFORMATION TECHNOLOGY

Number of wired network connections available to students: 726 total (in the law library, excluding computer labs: 92; in classrooms: 604; in computer labs: 22; elsewhere in the law school: 8)
Law school has a wireless network.
Students are required to own a computer.

EMPLOYMENT AND SALARIES

Proportion of 2006 graduates employed at graduation: 62%
Employed 9 months later, as of February 15, 2007: 94%
Salaries in the private sector (law firms, business, industry): $52,000–$85,000 (25th-75th percentile)
Median salary in the private sector: $60,000
Percentage in the private sector who reported salary information: 70%
Median salary in public service (government, judicial clerkships, academic posts, non-profits): $39,669

Percentage of 2006 graduates in:

Law firms: 70%	Government: 14%
Bus./industry: 4%	Judicial clerkship: 5%
Public interest: 4%	Unknown: 0%
Academia: 4%	

2006 graduates employed in-state: 68%
2006 graduates employed in foreign countries: 1%
Number of states where graduates are employed: 9
Percentage of 2006 graduates working in: New England: 0%, Middle Atlantic: 0%, East North Central: 1%, West North Central: 1%, South Atlantic: 87%, East South Central: 3%, West South Central: 0%, Mountain: 2%, Pacific: 0%, Unknown: 5%

BAR PASSAGE RATES

Based on 2006 graduates taking Summer 2006 or Winter 2007 exams. Most of the school's first-time test takers took the bar in Georgia.

88%
School's bar passage rate for first-time test takers

85%
Statewide bar passage rate for first-time test takers

Michigan State University

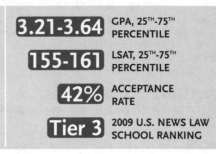

- ■ 368 Law College Building, East Lansing, MI, 48824-1300
- ■ http://www.law.msu.edu
- ■ Private
- ■ Year founded: 1891
- ■ 2007-2008 tuition: full-time: $30,124; part-time: $22,907
- ■ Enrollment 2007-08 academic year: full-time: 696; part-time: 310
- ■ U.S. News 2009 law specialty ranking: N/A

3.21-3.64 GPA, 25TH-75TH PERCENTILE

155-161 LSAT, 25TH-75TH PERCENTILE

42% ACCEPTANCE RATE

Tier 3 2009 U.S. NEWS LAW SCHOOL RANKING

ADMISSIONS
Admissions phone number: (517) 432-0222
Admissions email address: law@msu.edu
Application website:
   http://www.law.msu.edu/admissions/app.html
Application deadline for Fall 2009 admission: 03/01

Admissions statistics:
Number of applicants for Fall 2007: 1,622
Number of acceptances: 678
Number enrolled: 192
Acceptance rate: 42%
GPA, 25th-75th percentile, entering class Fall 2007: 3.21-3.64
LSAT, 25th-75th percentile, entering class Fall 2007: 155-161

Part-time program:
Number of applicants for Fall 2007: 315
Number of acceptances: 251
Number enrolled: 201
Acceptance rate: 80%
GPA, 25th-75th percentile, entering class Fall 2007: 2.91-3.39
LSAT, 25th-75th percentile, entering class Fall 2007: 148-153

FINANCIAL AID
Financial aid phone number: (517) 432-6810
Financial aid application deadline: 04/01
Tuition 2007-2008 academic year: full-time: $30,124; part-time: $22,907
Room and board: $9,962; books: $1,292; miscellaneous expenses: $1,640
Total of room/board/books/miscellaneous expenses: $12,894
University offers graduate student housing for which law students are eligible.

Financial aid profile
Percent of students that received grants for the 2006-2007 academic year: full-time: 37%; part-time 10%

Median grant amount: full-time: $20,968; part-time: $20,244
The average law-school debt of those in the Class of 2007 who borrowed: $71,762. Proportion who borrowed: 86%

ACADEMIC PROGRAMS
Calendar: **semester**
Joint degrees awarded: **J.D./M.B.A. (Eli Broad C.O.B.); J.D./M.A. English; J.D./M.A. Interdisciplinary Studies; J.D/M.A. Labor Relations/Human Resources; J.D./M.A. Forestry; J.D./M.S. Fisheries and Wildlife; J.D./M.S. Park, Rec., Tourism Resources; J.D./Ph.D. Park, Rec., Tourism Resources; J.D./M.URP.; J.D./M.B.A. (Seidman School of Business); J.D./M.S. Forestry/Urban Studies; J.D./LL.B. (University of Ottawa); J.D./M.P.A.; J.D./M.S.T. (Grand Valley State Univ.)**
Typical first-year section size: Full-time: **63**; Part-time: **80**
Is there typically a "small section" of the first year class, other than Legal Writing, taught by full-time faculty?: Full-time: **no**; Part-time: **no**
Number of course titles, beyond the first year curriculum, offered last year: **153**
Percentages of upper division course sections, excluding seminars, with an enrollment of:

Under 25: **54%**	25 to 49: **30%**
50 to 74: **8%**	75 to 99: **6%**
100+: **3%**	

Areas of specialization: appellate advocacy, clinical training, dispute resolution, environmental law, healthcare law, intellectual property law, international law, tax law, trial advocacy

Fall 2007 faculty profile
Total teaching faculty: **79**. Full-time: **48%**; **58%** men, **42%** women, **8%** minorities. Part-time: **52%**; **73%** men, **27%** women, **15%** minorities
Student-to-faculty ratio: **19.4**

SPECIAL PROGRAMS *(as provided by law school):*
MSU Law offers 10 concentrations including a nationally ranked intellectual property program. Students sharpen skills

and build credentials through five legal clinics, three certificates, and many externships. Dual-degree programs, including the J.D./LL.B. with the University of Ottawa, provide interdisciplinary study. The Fieger trial practice program trains students in a high-tech court setting.

STUDENT BODY

Fall 2007 full-time enrollment: 696

Men: 56%	Women: 44%
African-American: 3.6%	American Indian: 1.4%
Asian-American: 3.6%	Mexican-American: 0.3%
Puerto Rican: 0.0%	Other Hisp-Amer: 2.4%
White: 77.3%	International: 7.8%
Unknown: 3.6%	

Fall 2007 part-time enrollment: 310

Men: 61%	Women: 39%
African-American: 6.1%	American Indian: 1.0%
Asian-American: 5.5%	Mexican-American: 0.6%
Puerto Rican: 0.0%	Other Hisp-Amer: 2.9%
White: 77.1%	International: 1.6%
Unknown: 5.2%	

Attrition rates for 2006-2007 full-time students
Percent of students discontinuing law school:

Men: 4%	Women: 4%
First-year students: 7%	Second-year students: 6%
Third-year students: N/A	

LIBRARY RESOURCES
Total volumes: 284,804
Total seats available for library users: 455

INFORMATION TECHNOLOGY
Number of wired network connections available to students: 1,239 total (in the law library, excluding computer labs: 339; in classrooms: 800; in computer labs: 50; elsewhere in the law school: 50)
Law school has a wireless network.
Students are required to own a computer.

EMPLOYMENT AND SALARIES
Proportion of 2006 graduates employed at graduation: N/A
Employed 9 months later, as of February 15, 2007: 91%
Salaries in the private sector (law firms, business, industry): $48,000–$87,000 (25th-75th percentile)
Median salary in the private sector: $60,000
Percentage in the private sector who reported salary information: 65%
Median salary in public service (government, judicial clerkships, academic posts, non-profits): $42,000

Percentage of 2006 graduates in:

Law firms: 47%	Government: 14%
Bus./industry: 18%	Judicial clerkship: 5%
Public interest: 5%	Unknown: 9%
Academia: 2%	

2006 graduates employed in-state: 54%
2006 graduates employed in foreign countries: 3%
Number of states where graduates are employed: 31
Percentage of 2006 graduates working in: New England: 1%, Middle Atlantic: 5%, East North Central: 66%, West North Central: 1%, South Atlantic: 11%, East South Central: 0%, West South Central: 1%, Mountain: 7%, Pacific: 2%, Unknown: 3%

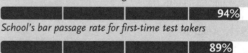

Mississippi College

- 151 E. Griffith Street, Jackson, MS, 39201
- http://www.law.mc.edu
- Private
- Year founded: 1975
- 2007-2008 tuition: full-time: $23,720; part-time: N/A
- Enrollment 2007-08 academic year: full-time: 528; part-time: 9
- U.S. News 2009 law specialty ranking: N/A

2.88-3.50 GPA, 25TH-75TH PERCENTILE

148-153 LSAT, 25TH-75TH PERCENTILE

52% ACCEPTANCE RATE

Tier 4 2009 U.S. NEWS LAW SCHOOL RANKING

ADMISSIONS
Admissions phone number: **(601) 925-7151**
Admissions email address: **hweaver@mc.edu**
Application website:
   http://www.law.mc.edu/admissions/apply_options.htm
Application deadline for Fall 2009 admission: **06/01**

Admissions statistics:
Number of applicants for Fall 2007: **1,153**
Number of acceptances: **603**
Number enrolled: **197**
Acceptance rate: **52%**
GPA, 25th-75th percentile, entering class Fall 2007: **2.88-3.50**
LSAT, 25th-75th percentile, entering class Fall 2007: **148-153**

FINANCIAL AID
Financial aid phone number: **(601) 925-7110**
Financial aid application deadline: **06/01**
Tuition 2007-2008 academic year: full-time: **$23,720**; part-time: **N/A**
Room and board: **$9,000**; books: **$900**; miscellaneous expenses: **$7,300**
Total of room/board/books/miscellaneous expenses: **$17,200**
University does not offer graduate student housing for which law students are eligible.

Financial aid profile
Percent of students that received grants for the 2006-2007 academic year: full-time: **28%**
Median grant amount: full-time: **$7,333**
The average law-school debt of those in the Class of 2007 who borrowed: **$77,716**. Proportion who borrowed: **84%**

ACADEMIC PROGRAMS
Calendar: **semester**
Joint degrees awarded: **J.D./M.B.A.**
Typical first-year section size: Full-time: **98**
Is there typically a "small section" of the first year class,
other than Legal Writing, taught by full-time faculty?:
  Full-time: **yes**
Number of course titles, beyond the first year curriculum, offered last year: **66**
Percentages of upper division course sections, excluding seminars, with an enrollment of:
  Under 25: **54%**   25 to 49: **24%**
  50 to 74: **18%**   75 to 99: **4%**
  100+: **0%**
Areas of specialization: appellate advocacy, clinical training, dispute resolution, environmental law, healthcare law, intellectual property law, international law, tax law, trial advocacy

Fall 2007 faculty profile
Total teaching faculty: **87**. Full-time: **21%**; **61%** men, **39%** women, **17%** minorities. Part-time: **79%**; **71%** men, **29%** women, **10%** minorities
Student-to-faculty ratio: **18.9**

SPECIAL PROGRAMS *(as provided by law school):*
The child advocacy program permits students to represent a child, interview parties, and make a court appearance. The Legal Aid Office gives students an opportunity to assist the under-served, acquire expertise in basic consumer issues, and gain experience in client interviewing. The externship program provides practical work experience with judges and government agencies.

STUDENT BODY
Fall 2007 full-time enrollment: 528
Men: **59%**	Women: **41%**
African-American: **7.0%**	American Indian: **0.2%**
Asian-American: **0.9%**	Mexican-American: **0.2%**
Puerto Rican: **0.9%**	Other Hisp-Amer: **0.0%**
White: **85.4%**	International: **0.0%**
Unknown: **5.3%**	

Fall 2007 part-time enrollment: 9
Men: **44%**	Women: **56%**
African-American: **11.1%**	American Indian: **0.0%**

Asian-American: 0.0% Mexican-American: 0.0%
Puerto Rican: 0.0% Other Hisp-Amer: 0.0%
White: 88.9% International: 0.0%
Unknown: 0.0%

Attrition rates for 2006-2007 full-time students
Percent of students discontinuing law school:
Men: 6% Women: 3%
First-year students: 12% Second-year students: 1%
Third-year students: N/A

LIBRARY RESOURCES
Total volumes: 346,941
Total seats available for library users: 394

INFORMATION TECHNOLOGY
Number of wired network connections available to students: 72 total (in the law library, excluding computer labs: 72; in classrooms: 0; in computer labs: 0; elsewhere in the law school: 0)
Law school has a wireless network.
Students are not required to own a computer.

EMPLOYMENT AND SALARIES
Proportion of 2006 graduates employed at graduation: 45%
Employed 9 months later, as of February 15, 2007: 87%
Salaries in the private sector (law firms, business, industry): $60,000–$85,000 (25th-75th percentile)
Median salary in the private sector: $65,000
Percentage in the private sector who reported salary information: 42%
Median salary in public service (government, judicial clerkships, academic posts, non-profits): $50,000

Percentage of 2006 graduates in:
Law firms: 61% Government: 11%
Bus./industry: 13% Judicial clerkship: 8%
Public interest: 5% Unknown: 0%
Academia: 2%

2006 graduates employed in-state: 75%
2006 graduates employed in foreign countries: 0%
Number of states where graduates are employed: 15
Percentage of 2006 graduates working in: New England: 0%, Middle Atlantic: 0%, East North Central: 0%, West North Central: 2%, South Atlantic: 8%, East South Central: 81%, West South Central: 6%, Mountain: 1%, Pacific: 2%, Unknown: 0%

BAR PASSAGE RATES
Based on 2006 graduates taking Summer 2006 or Winter 2007 exams. Most of the school's first-time test takers took the bar in Mississippi.

	83%

School's bar passage rate for first-time test takers

	88%

Statewide bar passage rate for first-time test takers

New England School of Law

- 154 Stuart Street, Boston, MA, 02116
- http://www.nesl.edu
- Private
- Year founded: 1908
- 2007-2008 tuition: full-time: $28,020; part-time: $21,030
- Enrollment 2007-08 academic year: full-time: 715; part-time: 386
- U.S. News 2009 law specialty ranking: N/A

3.02-3.52 GPA, 25ᵀᴴ-75ᵀᴴ PERCENTILE

150-153 LSAT, 25ᵀᴴ-75ᵀᴴ PERCENTILE

58% ACCEPTANCE RATE

Tier 4 2009 U.S. NEWS LAW SCHOOL RANKING

ADMISSIONS

Admissions phone number: **(617) 422-7210**
Admissions email address: **admit@admin.nesl.edu**
Application website: **N/A**
Application deadline for Fall 2009 admission: **03/15**

Admissions statistics:

Number of applicants for Fall 2007: **2,568**
Number of acceptances: **1,482**
Number enrolled: **255**
Acceptance rate: **58%**
GPA, 25th-75th percentile, entering class Fall 2007: **3.02-3.52**
LSAT, 25th-75th percentile, entering class Fall 2007: **150-153**

Part-time program:

Number of applicants for Fall 2007: **659**
Number of acceptances: **347**
Number enrolled: **124**
Acceptance rate: **53%**
GPA, 25th-75th percentile, entering class Fall 2007: **2.91-3.36**
LSAT, 25th-75th percentile, entering class Fall 2007: **149-151**

FINANCIAL AID

Financial aid phone number: **(617) 422-7298**
Financial aid application deadline: **04/01**
Tuition 2007-2008 academic year: full-time: **$28,020**; part-time: **$21,030**
Room and board: **$10,905**; books: **$1,200**; miscellaneous expenses: **$4,500**
Total of room/board/books/miscellaneous expenses: **$16,605**
University does not offer graduate student housing for which law students are eligible.

Financial aid profile

Percent of students that received grants for the 2006-2007 academic year: full-time: **46%**; part-time **26%**

Median grant amount: full-time: **$3,000**; part-time: **$4,000**
The average law-school debt of those in the Class of 2007 who borrowed: **$86,346**. Proportion who borrowed: **88%**

ACADEMIC PROGRAMS

Calendar: **semester**
Joint degrees awarded: **N/A**
Typical first-year section size: Full-time: **135**; Part-time: **125**
Is there typically a "small section" of the first year class, other than Legal Writing, taught by full-time faculty?: Full-time: **no**; Part-time: **no**
Number of course titles, beyond the first year curriculum, offered last year: **191**
Percentages of upper division course sections, excluding seminars, with an enrollment of:

Under 25: **53%**   25 to 49: **26%**
50 to 74: **9%**   75 to 99: **8%**
100+: **4%**

Areas of specialization: appellate advocacy, clinical training, dispute resolution, environmental law, intellectual property law, international law, tax law, trial advocacy

Fall 2007 faculty profile

Total teaching faculty: **109**. Full-time: **34%**; **62%** men, **38%** women, **14%** minorities. Part-time: **66%**; **63%** men, **38%** women, **6%** minorities
Student-to-faculty ratio: **23.2**

SPECIAL PROGRAMS (as provided by law school):

Clinics in 16 subject areas and in-house clinical law office; academic centers on International Law, Law and Social Responsibility, and Business Law, sponsoring conferences and research projects; three required semesters of legal research and writing; judicial clerkship opportunities; summer programs in Ireland, London/Edinburgh, Malta, Prague; semester programs in the Netherlands, Denmark, Paris.

STUDENT BODY

Fall 2007 full-time enrollment: 715
Men: **42%**   Women: **58%**
African-American: **1.8%**   American Indian: **0.7%**

Asian-American: **6.2%**
Puerto Rican: **0.6%**
White: **74.1%**
Unknown: **12.3%**

Mexican-American: **0.6%**
Other Hisp-Amer: **2.0%**
International: **1.8%**

Fall 2007 part-time enrollment: 386
Men: **52%**
African-American: **0.8%**
Asian-American: **2.8%**
Puerto Rican: **0.8%**
White: **81.3%**
Unknown: **13.0%**

Women: **48%**
American Indian: **0.3%**
Mexican-American: **0.8%**
Other Hisp-Amer: **0.0%**
International: **0.3%**

Attrition rates for 2006-2007 full-time students
Percent of students discontinuing law school:
Men: **5%**
First-year students: **16%**
Third-year students: **0%**

Women: **8%**
Second-year students: **2%**

LIBRARY RESOURCES
Total volumes: **357,068**
Total seats available for library users: **430**

INFORMATION TECHNOLOGY
Number of wired network connections available to students: **426** total (in the law library, excluding computer labs: **100**; in classrooms: **250**; in computer labs: **41**; elsewhere in the law school: **35**)
Law school has a wireless network.
Students are not required to own a computer.

EMPLOYMENT AND SALARIES
Proportion of 2006 graduates employed at graduation: **31%**
Employed 9 months later, as of February 15, 2007: **76%**
Salaries in the private sector (law firms, business, industry): **$40,000–$70,000** (25th-75th percentile)

Median salary in the private sector: **$50,000**
Percentage in the private sector who reported salary information: **64%**
Median salary in public service (government, judicial clerkships, academic posts, non-profits): **$47,000**

Percentage of 2006 graduates in:
Law firms: **45%**
Bus./industry: **20%**
Public interest: **5%**
Academia: **2%**

Government: **17%**
Judicial clerkship: **11%**
Unknown: **2%**

2006 graduates employed in-state: **63%**
2006 graduates employed in foreign countries: **0%**
Number of states where graduates are employed: **23**
Percentage of 2006 graduates working in: New England: **67%**, Middle Atlantic: **14%**, East North Central: **1%**, West North Central: **1%**, South Atlantic: **9%**, East South Central: **0%**, West South Central: **1%**, Mountain: **1%**, Pacific: **5%**, Unknown: **0%**

BAR PASSAGE RATES
Based on 2006 graduates taking Summer 2006 or Winter 2007 exams. Most of the school's first-time test takers took the bar in Massachusetts.

80%
School's bar passage rate for first-time test takers

86%
Statewide bar passage rate for first-time test takers

New York Law School

- 57 Worth Street, New York, NY, 10013-2960
- http://www.nyls.edu
- Private
- Year founded: 1891
- 2007-2008 tuition: full-time: $41,950; part-time: $32,250
- Enrollment 2007-08 academic year: full-time: 1,165; part-time: 407
- U.S. News 2009 law specialty ranking: N/A

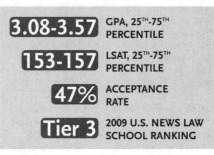

3.08-3.57 GPA, 25TH-75TH PERCENTILE

153-157 LSAT, 25TH-75TH PERCENTILE

47% ACCEPTANCE RATE

Tier 3 2009 U.S. NEWS LAW SCHOOL RANKING

ADMISSIONS

Admissions phone number: **(212) 431-2888**
Admissions email address: **admissions@nyls.edu**
Application website: **N/A**
Application deadline for Fall 2009 admission: **04/01**

Admissions statistics:

Number of applicants for Fall 2007: **4,587**
Number of acceptances: **2,159**
Number enrolled: **425**
Acceptance rate: **47%**
GPA, 25th-75th percentile, entering class Fall 2007: **3.08-3.57**
LSAT, 25th-75th percentile, entering class Fall 2007: **153-157**

Part-time program:

Number of applicants for Fall 2007: **861**
Number of acceptances: **288**
Number enrolled: **125**
Acceptance rate: **33%**
GPA, 25th-75th percentile, entering class Fall 2007: **2.90-3.45**
LSAT, 25th-75th percentile, entering class Fall 2007: **150-155**

FINANCIAL AID

Financial aid phone number: **(212) 431-2828**
Financial aid application deadline: **04/01**
Tuition 2007-2008 academic year: full-time: **$41,950**; part-time: **$32,250**
Room and board: **$15,750**; books: **$1,000**; miscellaneous expenses: **$4,035**
Total of room/board/books/miscellaneous expenses: **$20,785**
University offers graduate student housing for which law students are eligible.

Financial aid profile

Percent of students that received grants for the 2006-2007 academic year: full-time: **32%**; part-time **17%**
Median grant amount: full-time: **$8,750**; part-time: **$7,500**

The average law-school debt of those in the Class of 2007 who borrowed: **$105,793**. Proportion who borrowed: **90%**

ACADEMIC PROGRAMS

Calendar: **semester**
Joint degrees awarded: **J.D./M.B.A.**
Typical first-year section size: Full-time: **106**; Part-time: **106**
Is there typically a "small section" of the first year class, other than Legal Writing, taught by full-time faculty?: Full-time: **yes**; Part-time: **yes**
Number of course titles, beyond the first year curriculum, offered last year: **219**
Percentages of upper division course sections, excluding seminars, with an enrollment of:

Under 25: **55%**	25 to 49: **23%**
50 to 74: **5%**	75 to 99: **7%**
100+: **11%**	

Areas of specialization: appellate advocacy, clinical training, dispute resolution, environmental law, healthcare law, intellectual property law, international law, tax law, trial advocacy

Fall 2007 faculty profile

Total teaching faculty: **158**. Full-time: **41%**; **66%** men, **34%** women, **11%** minorities. Part-time: **59%**; **65%** men, **35%** women, **10%** minorities
Student-to-faculty ratio: **22.9**

SPECIAL PROGRAMS (as provided by law school):

A liaison program linking students to administrators and students; a faculty advising system; an alumni mentor program; John Marshall Harlan Scholars. The Lawyering Skills Center and seven academic centers: International Law; Business Law and Policy; New York City Law; Professional Values and Practice; Justice Action; Real Estate; Information Law and Policy.

STUDENT BODY

Fall 2007 full-time enrollment: 1,165

Men: **46%**	Women: **54%**
African-American: **5.0%**	American Indian: **0.3%**

Asian-American: 8.7% Mexican-American: 1.1%
Puerto Rican: 0.9% Other Hisp-Amer: 5.8%
White: 56.2% International: 0.0%
Unknown: 22.0%

Fall 2007 part-time enrollment: 407
Men: 54% Women: 46%
African-American: 8.4% American Indian: 0.0%
Asian-American: 10.3% Mexican-American: 0.7%
Puerto Rican: 2.2% Other Hisp-Amer: 4.4%
White: 56.0% International: 0.0%
Unknown: 17.9%

Attrition rates for 2006-2007 full-time students
Percent of students discontinuing law school:
Men: 6% Women: 5%
First-year students: 14% Second-year students: 2%
Third-year students: N/A

LIBRARY RESOURCES
Total volumes: 522,118
Total seats available for library users: 525

INFORMATION TECHNOLOGY
Number of wired network connections available to students: 0 total (in the law library, excluding computer labs: 0; in classrooms: 0; in computer labs: 0; elsewhere in the law school: 0)
Law school has a wireless network.
Students are not required to own a computer.

EMPLOYMENT AND SALARIES
Proportion of 2006 graduates employed at graduation: N/A
Employed 9 months later, as of February 15, 2007: 90%
Salaries in the private sector (law firms, business, industry): $65,000–$145,000 (25th-75th percentile)

Median salary in the private sector: $92,500
Percentage in the private sector who reported salary information: 25%
Median salary in public service (government, judicial clerkships, academic posts, non-profits): $45,000

Percentage of 2006 graduates in:
Law firms: 52% Government: 11%
Bus./industry: 18% Judicial clerkship: 5%
Public interest: 4% Unknown: 8%
Academia: 2%

2006 graduates employed in-state: 77%
2006 graduates employed in foreign countries: 1%
Number of states where graduates are employed: 15
Percentage of 2006 graduates working in: New England: 2%, Middle Atlantic: 90%, East North Central: 0%, West North Central: 0%, South Atlantic: 4%, East South Central: 0%, West South Central: 1%, Mountain: 0%, Pacific: 2%, Unknown: 0%

BAR PASSAGE RATES
Based on 2006 graduates taking Summer 2006 or Winter 2007 exams. Most of the school's first-time test takers took the bar in New York.

81%
School's bar passage rate for first-time test takers

77%
Statewide bar passage rate for first-time test takers

New York University

- 40 Washington Square S, New York, NY, 10012
- http://www.law.nyu.edu
- Private
- Year founded: 1835
- 2007-2008 tuition: full-time: $40,890; part-time: N/A
- Enrollment 2007-08 academic year: full-time: 1,424
- U.S. News 2009 law specialty ranking: clinical training: 3, environmental law: 15, intellectual property law: 11, international law: 1, tax law: 1, trial advocacy: 9

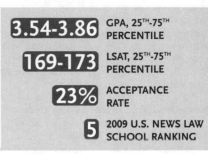

3.54-3.86 GPA, 25TH-75TH PERCENTILE

169-173 LSAT, 25TH-75TH PERCENTILE

23% ACCEPTANCE RATE

5 2009 U.S. NEWS LAW SCHOOL RANKING

ADMISSIONS

Admissions phone number: **(212) 998-6060**
Admissions email address: **law.moreinfo@nyu.edu**
Application website: **http://www.law.nyu.edu/depts/admissions/applications/online/jd.html**
Application deadline for Fall 2009 admission: **02/01**

Admissions statistics:
Number of applicants for Fall 2007: **7,095**
Number of acceptances: **1,628**
Number enrolled: **448**
Acceptance rate: **23%**
GPA, 25th-75th percentile, entering class Fall 2007: **3.54-3.86**
LSAT, 25th-75th percentile, entering class Fall 2007: **169-173**

FINANCIAL AID

Financial aid phone number: **(212) 998-6050**
Financial aid application deadline: **04/15**
Tuition 2007-2008 academic year: full-time: **$40,890**; part-time: **N/A**
Room and board: **$19,731**; books: **$1,050**; miscellaneous expenses: **$2,789**
Total of room/board/books/miscellaneous expenses: **$23,570**
University does not offer graduate student housing for which law students are eligible.

Financial aid profile
Percent of students that received grants for the 2006-2007 academic year: full-time: **33%**
Median grant amount: full-time: **$15,000**
The average law-school debt of those in the Class of 2007 who borrowed: **$117,636**. Proportion who borrowed: **81%**

ACADEMIC PROGRAMS

Calendar: **semester**
Joint degrees awarded: **J.D./M.A.; J.D./M.B.A.; J.D./M.P.A.; J.D./M.U.P.; J.D./M.S.W.; J.D./Ph.D.; J.D./M.P.A.K.S.; J.D./M.P.A. (Princeton); J.D./LL.B. (Osgoode)**

Typical first-year section size: Full-time: **112**
Is there typically a "small section" of the first year class, other than Legal Writing, taught by full-time faculty?: Full-time: **yes**
Number of course titles, beyond the first year curriculum, offered last year: **276**
Percentages of upper division course sections, excluding seminars, with an enrollment of:
Under 25: **44%**　　　25 to 49: **21%**
50 to 74: **13%**　　　75 to 99: **13%**
100+: **10%**
Areas of specialization: appellate advocacy, clinical training, dispute resolution, environmental law, healthcare law, intellectual property law, international law, tax law, trial advocacy

Fall 2007 faculty profile
Total teaching faculty: **268**. Full-time: **59%**; **72%** men, **28%** women, **8%** minorities. Part-time: **41%**; **76%** men, **24%** women, **4%** minorities
Student-to-faculty ratio: **10.4**

SPECIAL PROGRAMS *(as provided by law school):*

NYU School of Law's curriculum is distinguished by its strength in traditional areas of legal study, interdisciplinary study, and clinical education. The school has long been committed to educating lawyers who will use their degrees to serve the public. Students enjoy the intellectual and pedagogical diversity of NYU by mixing traditional courses with colloquia, research, clinics, and more.

STUDENT BODY

Fall 2007 full-time enrollment: **1,424**
Men: **53%**　　　　　　　　Women: **47%**
African-American: **7.1%**　　American Indian: **0.0%**
Asian-American: **10.7%**　　Mexican-American: **1.1%**
Puerto Rican: **0.5%**　　　　Other Hisp-Amer: **3.3%**
White: **50.6%**　　　　　　International: **3.6%**
Unknown: **23.2%**

Attrition rates for 2006-2007 full-time students
Percent of students discontinuing law school:
Men: 1%   Women: 1%
First-year students: 0%   Second-year students: 1%
Third-year students: 0%

LIBRARY RESOURCES
Total volumes: 1,097,926
Total seats available for library users: 850

INFORMATION TECHNOLOGY
Number of wired network connections available to students: 750 total (in the law library, excluding computer labs: 35; in classrooms: 700; in computer labs: 0; elsewhere in the law school: 15)
Law school has a wireless network.
Students are required to own a computer.

EMPLOYMENT AND SALARIES
Proportion of 2006 graduates employed at graduation: 96%
Employed 9 months later, as of February 15, 2007: 99%
Salaries in the private sector (law firms, business, industry): $135,000–$145,000 (25th-75th percentile)
Median salary in the private sector: $145,000
Percentage in the private sector who reported salary information: 95%
Median salary in public service (government, judicial clerkships, academic posts, non-profits): $54,272

Percentage of 2006 graduates in:
Law firms: 69%   Government: 3%
Bus./industry: 2%   Judicial clerkship: 12%
Public interest: 13%   Unknown: 1%
Academia: 0%

2006 graduates employed in-state: 66%
2006 graduates employed in foreign countries: 2%
Number of states where graduates are employed: 29
Percentage of 2006 graduates working in: New England: 4%, Middle Atlantic: 68%, East North Central: 3%, West North Central: 0%, South Atlantic: 8%, East South Central: 1%, West South Central: 2%, Mountain: 1%, Pacific: 12%, Unknown: 0%

BAR PASSAGE RATES
Based on 2006 graduates taking Summer 2006 or Winter 2007 exams. Most of the school's first-time test takers took the bar in New York.

95%
School's bar passage rate for first-time test takers

77%
Statewide bar passage rate for first-time test takers

North Carolina Central University

- 640 Nelson Street, Durham, NC, 27707
- http://web.nccu.edu/law
- Public
- Year founded: 1939
- 2007-2008 tuition: In-state: full-time: $5,709; part-time: $5,709; Out-of-state: full-time: $17,569
- Enrollment 2007-08 academic year: full-time: 478; part-time: 126
- U.S. News 2009 law specialty ranking: N/A

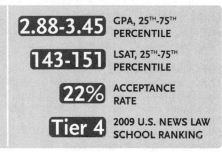

2.88-3.45 GPA, 25TH-75TH PERCENTILE

143-151 LSAT, 25TH-75TH PERCENTILE

22% ACCEPTANCE RATE

Tier 4 2009 U.S. NEWS LAW SCHOOL RANKING

ADMISSIONS
Admissions phone number: **(919) 530-5243**
Admissions email address: **recruiter@nccu.edu**
Application website: **N/A**
Application deadline for Fall 2009 admission: **03/31**

Admissions statistics:
Number of applicants for Fall 2007: **1,830**
Number of acceptances: **404**
Number enrolled: **190**
Acceptance rate: **22%**
GPA, 25th-75th percentile, entering class Fall 2007: **2.88-3.45**
LSAT, 25th-75th percentile, entering class Fall 2007: **143-151**

Part-time program:
Number of applicants for Fall 2007: **719**
Number of acceptances: **100**
Number enrolled: **43**
Acceptance rate: **14%**
GPA, 25th-75th percentile, entering class Fall 2007: **3.21-3.65**
LSAT, 25th-75th percentile, entering class Fall 2007: **148-157**

FINANCIAL AID
Financial aid phone number: **(919) 530-7173**
Financial aid application deadline: **07/01**
Tuition 2007-2008 academic year: In-state: full-time: **$5,709**; part-time: **$5,709**; Out-of-state: full-time: **$17,569**
Room and board: **$17,180**; books: **$2,000**; miscellaneous expenses: **$556**
Total of room/board/books/miscellaneous expenses: **$19,736**
University offers graduate student housing for which law students are eligible.

Financial aid profile
Percent of students that received grants for the 2006-2007 academic year: full-time: **27%**

Median grant amount: full-time: **$3,464**
The average law-school debt of those in the Class of 2007 who borrowed: **$19,886.** Proportion who borrowed: **96%**

ACADEMIC PROGRAMS
Calendar: **semester**
Joint degrees awarded: **J.D./M.B.A.; J.D./M.L.S.**
Typical first-year section size: Full-time: **63**; Part-time: **43**
Is there typically a "small section" of the first year class, other than Legal Writing, taught by full-time faculty?: Full-time: **no**; Part-time: **no**
Number of course titles, beyond the first year curriculum, offered last year: **72**
Percentages of upper division course sections, excluding seminars, with an enrollment of:
Under 25: **66%**   25 to 49: **19%**
50 to 74: **12%**   75 to 99: **1%**
100+: **2%**
Areas of specialization: appellate advocacy, clinical training, dispute resolution, environmental law, healthcare law, intellectual property law, international law, tax law, trial advocacy

Fall 2007 faculty profile
Total teaching faculty: **45.** Full-time: **53%**; **29%** men, **71%** women, **67%** minorities. Part-time: **47%**; **48%** men, **52%** women, **48%** minorities
Student-to-faculty ratio: **17.6**

SPECIAL PROGRAMS *(as provided by law school):*
NCCU School of Law offers top-notch clinics and externships, joint master's degree programs with the Business School and the Library School, and Certificates to J.D. graduates who complete related coursework in the school's Biotechnology and Pharmaceutical Law Institute and Dispute Resolution Institute.

STUDENT BODY
Fall 2007 full-time enrollment: **478**
Men: **39%**   Women: **61%**
African-American: **48.1%**   American Indian: **0.8%**
Asian-American: **2.9%**   Mexican-American: **0.2%**

Puerto Rican: 0.2%   Other Hisp-Amer: 2.9%
White: 38.3%   International: 1.9%
Unknown: 4.6%

Fall 2007 part-time enrollment: 126
Men: 48%   Women: 52%
African-American: 17.5%   American Indian: 1.6%
Asian-American: 5.6%   Mexican-American: 0.0%
Puerto Rican: 3.2%   Other Hisp-Amer: 0.8%
White: 65.9%   International: 1.6%
Unknown: 4.0%

Attrition rates for 2006-2007 full-time students
Percent of students discontinuing law school:
Men: 7%   Women: 4%
First-year students: 12%   Second-year students: 1%
Third-year students: N/A

LIBRARY RESOURCES
Total volumes: 365,452
Total seats available for library users: 296

INFORMATION TECHNOLOGY
Number of wired network connections available to students: 78 total (in the law library, excluding computer labs: 12; in classrooms: 4; in computer labs: 30; elsewhere in the law school: 32)
Law school has a wireless network.
Students are not required to own a computer.

EMPLOYMENT AND SALARIES
Proportion of 2006 graduates employed at graduation: N/A
Employed 9 months later, as of February 15, 2007: 81%
Salaries in the private sector (law firms, business, industry): N/A

Median salary in the private sector: N/A
Percentage in the private sector who reported salary information: N/A
Median salary in public service (government, judicial clerkships, academic posts, non-profits): N/A

Percentage of 2006 graduates in:
Law firms: 61%   Government: 16%
Bus./industry: 8%   Judicial clerkship: 5%
Public interest: 7%   Unknown: 0%
Academia: 3%

2006 graduates employed in-state: 86%
2006 graduates employed in foreign countries: 0%
Number of states where graduates are employed: 9
Percentage of 2006 graduates working in: New England: N/A, Middle Atlantic: 3%, East North Central: 2%, West North Central: N/A, South Atlantic: 92%, East South Central: 1%, West South Central: 2%, Mountain: N/A, Pacific: N/A, Unknown: 0%

BAR PASSAGE RATES
Based on 2006 graduates taking Summer 2006 or Winter 2007 exams. Most of the school's first-time test takers took the bar in North Carolina.

82%
School's bar passage rate for first-time test takers

74%
Statewide bar passage rate for first-time test takers

Northeastern University

■ 400 Huntington Avenue, Boston, MA, 02115
■ http://www.slaw.neu.edu
■ Private
■ Year founded: 1898
■ 2007-2008 tuition: full-time: $36,564; part-time: N/A
■ Enrollment 2007-08 academic year: full-time: 624
■ U.S. News 2009 law specialty ranking: clinical training: 28

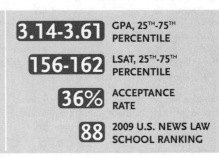

3.14-3.61 GPA, 25TH-75TH PERCENTILE

156-162 LSAT, 25TH-75TH PERCENTILE

36% ACCEPTANCE RATE

88 2009 U.S. NEWS LAW SCHOOL RANKING

ADMISSIONS
Admissions phone number: **(617) 373-2395**
Admissions email address: **lawadmissions@nunet.neu.edu**
Application website:
  http://www.slaw.neu.edu/admiss/appadmis.htm
Application deadline for Fall 2009 admission: **07/01**

Admissions statistics:
Number of applicants for Fall 2007: **3,034**
Number of acceptances: **1,098**
Number enrolled: **198**
Acceptance rate: **36%**
GPA, 25th-75th percentile, entering class Fall 2007: **3.14-3.61**
LSAT, 25th-75th percentile, entering class Fall 2007: **156-162**

FINANCIAL AID
Financial aid phone number: **(617) 373-4620**
Financial aid application deadline: **08/29**
Tuition 2007-2008 academic year: full-time: **$36,564**; part-time: **N/A**
Room and board: **$15,300**; books: **$1,200**; miscellaneous expenses: **$1,825**
Total of room/board/books/miscellaneous expenses: **$18,325**
University offers graduate student housing for which law students are eligible.

Financial aid profile
Percent of students that received grants for the 2006-2007 academic year: full-time: **84%**
Median grant amount: full-time: **$8,500**
The average law-school debt of those in the Class of 2007 who borrowed: **$93,775**. Proportion who borrowed: **93%**

ACADEMIC PROGRAMS
Calendar: **quarter**
Joint degrees awarded: **J.D./M.P.H.; J.D./M.B.A.; J.D./M.S./M.B.A.; J.D./L.P.S./Ph.D**

Typical first-year section size: Full-time: **67**
Is there typically a "small section" of the first year class, other than Legal Writing, taught by full-time faculty?: Full-time: **yes**
Number of course titles, beyond the first year curriculum, offered last year: **84**
Percentages of upper division course sections, excluding seminars, with an enrollment of:
  Under 25: **44%**   25 to 49: **32%**
  50 to 74: **19%**   75 to 99: **4%**
  100+: **0%**
Areas of specialization: appellate advocacy, clinical training, dispute resolution, environmental law, healthcare law, intellectual property law, international law, tax law, trial advocacy

Fall 2007 faculty profile
Total teaching faculty: **63**. Full-time: **37%**; **57%** men, **43%** women, **26%** minorities. Part-time: **63%**; **50%** men, **50%** women, **13%** minorities
Student-to-faculty ratio: **16.9**

SPECIAL PROGRAMS *(as provided by law school):*
The school's program is unique in its integration of classroom rigor and real-world experience. Each first-year student undertakes a team social justice project through the Legal Skills in Social Context course. Students graduate with a full year of legal experience through the co-op program with four 11-week, full-time jobs, offered in 54 countries; 45 percent also complete at least one clinic.

STUDENT BODY
Fall 2007 full-time enrollment: **624**

Men: **41%**	Women: **59%**
African-American: **6.4%**	American Indian: **1.0%**
Asian-American: **9.9%**	Mexican-American: **0.0%**
Puerto Rican: **0.0%**	Other Hisp-Amer: **9.5%**
White: **56.4%**	International: **0.0%**
Unknown: **16.8%**	

Attrition rates for 2006-2007 full-time students
Percent of students discontinuing law school:
Men: 1%   Women: 2%
First-year students: 3%   Second-year students: 3%
Third-year students: N/A

LIBRARY RESOURCES
Total volumes: 331,684
Total seats available for library users: 424

INFORMATION TECHNOLOGY
Number of wired network connections available to students: 65 total (in the law library, excluding computer labs: 35; in classrooms: 10; in computer labs: 0; elsewhere in the law school: 20)
Law school has a wireless network.
Students are not required to own a computer.

EMPLOYMENT AND SALARIES
Proportion of 2006 graduates employed at graduation: N/A
Employed 9 months later, as of February 15, 2007: **94%**
Salaries in the private sector (law firms, business, industry): **$52,250–$135,000** (25th-75th percentile)
Median salary in the private sector: **$87,500**
Percentage in the private sector who reported salary information: **57%**
Median salary in public service (government, judicial clerkships, academic posts, non-profits): **$45,000**

Percentage of 2006 graduates in:

Law firms: **40%**	Government: **10%**
Bus./industry: **18%**	Judicial clerkship: **14%**
Public interest: **16%**	Unknown: **1%**
Academia: **1%**	

2006 graduates employed in-state: **62%**
2006 graduates employed in foreign countries: **2%**
Number of states where graduates are employed: **23**
Percentage of 2006 graduates working in: New England: **65%**, Middle Atlantic: **13%**, East North Central: **1%**, West North Central: **1%**, South Atlantic: **10%**, East South Central: **1%**, West South Central: **1%**, Mountain: **1%**, Pacific: **6%**, Unknown: **0%**

BAR PASSAGE RATES
Based on 2006 graduates taking Summer 2006 or Winter 2007 exams. Most of the school's first-time test takers took the bar in Massachusetts.

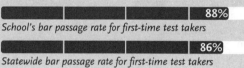

88%
School's bar passage rate for first-time test takers

86%
Statewide bar passage rate for first-time test takers

Northern Illinois University

■ Swen Parson Hall, Room 276, De Kalb, IL, 60115
■ http://law.niu.edu
■ Public
■ Year founded: 1975
■ 2007-2008 tuition: In-state: full-time: $13,036; part-time: $543/credit hour; Out-of-state: full-time: $23,620
■ Enrollment 2007-08 academic year: full-time: 310; part-time: 16
■ U.S. News 2009 law specialty ranking: N/A

3.09-3.66 GPA, 25TH-75TH PERCENTILE

150-157 LSAT, 25TH-75TH PERCENTILE

37% ACCEPTANCE RATE

Tier 4 2009 U.S. NEWS LAW SCHOOL RANKING

ADMISSIONS
Admissions phone number: **(815) 753-9485**
Admissions email address: **lawadm@niu.edu**
Application website: **http://law.niu.edu**
Application deadline for Fall 2009 admission: **05/15**

Admissions statistics:
Number of applicants for Fall 2007: **1,290**
Number of acceptances: **480**
Number enrolled: **111**
Acceptance rate: **37%**
GPA, 25th-75th percentile, entering class Fall 2007: **3.09-3.66**
LSAT, 25th-75th percentile, entering class Fall 2007: **150-157**

Part-time program:
Number of applicants for Fall 2007: **17**
Number of acceptances: **5**
Number enrolled: **4**
Acceptance rate: **29%**
GPA, 25th-75th percentile, entering class Fall 2007: **N/A**
LSAT, 25th-75th percentile, entering class Fall 2007: **N/A**

FINANCIAL AID
Financial aid phone number: **(815) 753-9485**
Financial aid application deadline: **03/01**
Tuition 2007-2008 academic year: In-state: full-time: **$13,036**; part-time: **$543/credit hour**; Out-of-state: full-time: **$23,620**
Room and board: **$8,568**; books: **$1,500**; miscellaneous expenses: **$2,536**
Total of room/board/books/miscellaneous expenses: **$12,604**
University offers graduate student housing for which law students are eligible.

Financial aid profile
Percent of students that received grants for the 2006-2007 academic year: full-time: **22%**
Median grant amount: full-time: **$8,910**

The average law-school debt of those in the Class of 2007 who borrowed: **$48,472**. Proportion who borrowed: **85%**

ACADEMIC PROGRAMS
Calendar: **semester**
Joint degrees awarded: **J.D./M.B.A.; J.D./M.P.A.**
Typical first-year section size: Full-time: **52**
Is there typically a "small section" of the first year class, other than Legal Writing, taught by full-time faculty?: Full-time: **no**
Number of course titles, beyond the first year curriculum, offered last year: **55**
Percentages of upper division course sections, excluding seminars, with an enrollment of:
Under 25: **49%**   25 to 49: **20%**
50 to 74: **24%**   75 to 99: **6%**
100+: **0%**
Areas of specialization: appellate advocacy, clinical training, dispute resolution, environmental law, healthcare law, intellectual property law, international law, tax law, trial advocacy

Fall 2007 faculty profile
Total teaching faculty: **27**. Full-time: **56%**; **67%** men, **33%** women, **33%** minorities. Part-time: **44%**; **92%** men, **8%** women, **17%** minorities
Student-to-faculty ratio: **18.6**

SPECIAL PROGRAMS *(as provided by law school)*:
Students who have been exposed to the fundamentals of legal practice in the simulation courses have the opportunity in the clinical experiences to refine their practice skills and begin the transition from classroom to practice. The College of Law offers one international program—located in Agen, France—as well as a selection of upper-level courses during the summer.

STUDENT BODY
Fall 2007 full-time enrollment: **310**
Men: **51%**   Women: **49%**
African-American: **8.1%**   American Indian: **0.0%**
Asian-American: **6.8%**   Mexican-American: **4.2%**

Puerto Rican: 0.3% Other Hisp-Amer: 2.3%
White: 75.2% International: 0.0%
Unknown: 3.2%

Fall 2007 part-time enrollment: 16
Men: 31% Women: 69%
African-American: 12.5% American Indian: 0.0%
Asian-American: 0.0% Mexican-American: 0.0%
Puerto Rican: 0.0% Other Hisp-Amer: 0.0%
White: 87.5% International: 0.0%
Unknown: 0.0%

Attrition rates for 2006-2007 full-time students
Percent of students discontinuing law school:
Men: 5% Women: 3%
First-year students: 9% Second-year students: 2%
Third-year students: 1%

LIBRARY RESOURCES
Total volumes: 252,709
Total seats available for library users: 215

INFORMATION TECHNOLOGY
Number of wired network connections available to students: 16 total (in the law library, excluding computer labs: 14; in classrooms: 2; in computer labs: 0; elsewhere in the law school: 0)
Law school has a wireless network.
Students are not required to own a computer.

EMPLOYMENT AND SALARIES
Proportion of 2006 graduates employed at graduation: 55%
Employed 9 months later, as of February 15, 2007: 90%
Salaries in the private sector (law firms, business, industry): $42,000–$60,000 (25th-75th percentile)
Median salary in the private sector: $55,023

Percentage in the private sector who reported salary information: 69%
Median salary in public service (government, judicial clerkships, academic posts, non-profits): $43,427

Percentage of 2006 graduates in:
Law firms: 51% Government: 25%
Bus./industry: 14% Judicial clerkship: 1%
Public interest: 9% Unknown: 0%
Academia: 0%

2006 graduates employed in-state: 88%
2006 graduates employed in foreign countries: 0%
Number of states where graduates are employed: 9
Percentage of 2006 graduates working in: New England: 0%, Middle Atlantic: 0%, East North Central: 91%, West North Central: 1%, South Atlantic: 3%, East South Central: 0%, West South Central: 2%, Mountain: 0%, Pacific: 2%, Unknown: 0%

BAR PASSAGE RATES
Based on 2006 graduates taking Summer 2006 or Winter 2007 exams. Most of the school's first-time test takers took the bar in Illinois.

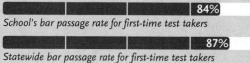

84%
School's bar passage rate for first-time test takers

87%
Statewide bar passage rate for first-time test takers

Northern Kentucky University (Chase)

- Nunn Hall, Highland Heights, KY, 41099-6031
- http://www.nku.edu/~chase
- Public
- Year founded: 1893
- 2007-2008 tuition: In-state: full-time: $12,168; part-time: $9,126; Out-of-state: full-time: $26,544
- Enrollment 2007-08 academic year: full-time: 304; part-time: 239
- U.S. News 2009 law specialty ranking: N/A

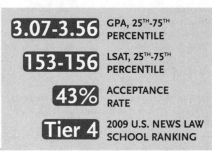

3.07-3.56 GPA, 25TH-75TH PERCENTILE

153-156 LSAT, 25TH-75TH PERCENTILE

43% ACCEPTANCE RATE

Tier 4 2009 U.S. NEWS LAW SCHOOL RANKING

ADMISSIONS
Admissions phone number: **(859) 572-5841**
Admissions email address: **folger@nku.edu**
Application website: **N/A**
Application deadline for Fall 2009 admission: **rolling**

Admissions statistics:
Number of applicants for Fall 2007: **796**
Number of acceptances: **345**
Number enrolled: **122**
Acceptance rate: **43%**
GPA, 25th-75th percentile, entering class Fall 2007: **3.07-3.56**
LSAT, 25th-75th percentile, entering class Fall 2007: **153-156**

Part-time program:
Number of applicants for Fall 2007: **176**
Number of acceptances: **113**
Number enrolled: **82**
Acceptance rate: **64%**
GPA, 25th-75th percentile, entering class Fall 2007: **2.76-3.45**
LSAT, 25th-75th percentile, entering class Fall 2007: **149-154**

FINANCIAL AID
Financial aid phone number: **(859) 572-6437**
Financial aid application deadline: **06/30**
Tuition 2007-2008 academic year: In-state: full-time: **$12,168**; part-time: **$9,126**; Out-of-state: full-time: **$26,544**
Room and board: **$9,278**; books: **$1,000**; miscellaneous expenses: **$0**
Total of room/board/books/miscellaneous expenses: **$10,278**
University offers graduate student housing for which law students are eligible.

Financial aid profile
Percent of students that received grants for the 2006-2007 academic year: full-time: **38%**; part-time **13%**
Median grant amount: full-time: **$11,112**; part-time: **$4,167**
The average law-school debt of those in the Class of 2007 who borrowed: **$61,857**. Proportion who borrowed: **63%**

ACADEMIC PROGRAMS
Calendar: **semester**
Joint degrees awarded: **J.D./M.B.A.**
Typical first-year section size: Full-time: **94**; Part-time: **58**
Is there typically a "small section" of the first year class, other than Legal Writing, taught by full-time faculty?: Full-time: **yes**; Part-time: **yes**
Number of course titles, beyond the first year curriculum, offered last year: **60**
Percentages of upper division course sections, excluding seminars, with an enrollment of:

Under 25: **43%**	25 to 49: **31%**
50 to 74: **21%**	75 to 99: **4%**
100+: **1%**	

Areas of specialization: appellate advocacy, clinical training, dispute resolution, environmental law, healthcare law, intellectual property law, international law, tax law, trial advocacy

Fall 2007 faculty profile
Total teaching faculty: **33**. Full-time: **70%**; **74%** men, **26%** women, **13%** minorities. Part-time: **30%**; **70%** men, **30%** women, **0%** minorities
Student-to-faculty ratio: **17.1**

SPECIAL PROGRAMS *(as provided by law school):*
Exceptional practical training is offered through clinical and pro bono programs, including: the Chase clinical externships and internships, federal trial practice seminar, constitutional litigation clinic, local government clinic, Kentucky Innocence Project, IRS chief counsel externship, tax clinic, public interest fellowship program, and volunteer income tax assistance program.

STUDENT BODY

Fall 2007 full-time enrollment: 304

Men: 56% Women: 44%
African-American: 4.3% American Indian: 0.7%
Asian-American: 2.3% Mexican-American: 0.0%
Puerto Rican: 0.0% Other Hisp-Amer: 1.6%
White: 87.5% International: 0.0%
Unknown: 3.6%

Fall 2007 part-time enrollment: 239

Men: 56% Women: 44%
African-American: 5.4% American Indian: 0.4%
Asian-American: 1.7% Mexican-American: 0.0%
Puerto Rican: 0.0% Other Hisp-Amer: 2.5%
White: 88.3% International: 0.0%
Unknown: 1.7%

Attrition rates for 2006-2007 full-time students

Percent of students discontinuing law school:
Men: 1% Women: 3%
First-year students: 4% Second-year students: 3%
Third-year students: N/A

LIBRARY RESOURCES

Total volumes: 333,975
Total seats available for library users: 222

INFORMATION TECHNOLOGY

Number of wired network connections available to students: 23 total (in the law library, excluding computer labs: 19; in classrooms: 0; in computer labs: 0; elsewhere in the law school: 4)
Law school has a wireless network.
Students are not required to own a computer.

EMPLOYMENT AND SALARIES

Proportion of 2006 graduates employed at graduation: 55%
Employed 9 months later, as of February 15, 2007: 89%

Salaries in the private sector (law firms, business, industry): $40,000–$63,000 (25th-75th percentile)
Median salary in the private sector: $52,000
Percentage in the private sector who reported salary information: 72%
Median salary in public service (government, judicial clerkships, academic posts, non-profits): $39,250

Percentage of 2006 graduates in:

Law firms: 53% Government: 10%
Bus./industry: 21% Judicial clerkship: 4%
Public interest: 9% Unknown: 0%
Academia: 3%

2006 graduates employed in-state: 46%
2006 graduates employed in foreign countries: 0%
Number of states where graduates are employed: 7
Percentage of 2006 graduates working in: New England: 0%, Middle Atlantic: 1%, East North Central: 50%, West North Central: 0%, South Atlantic: 1%, East South Central: 47%, West South Central: 0%, Mountain: 1%, Pacific: 0%, Unknown: 1%

BAR PASSAGE RATES

Based on 2006 graduates taking Summer 2006 or Winter 2007 exams. Most of the school's first-time test takers took the bar in Kentucky.

81%
School's bar passage rate for first-time test takers

83%
Statewide bar passage rate for first-time test takers

Northwestern University

- 357 E. Chicago Avenue, Chicago, IL, 60611
- http://www.law.northwestern.edu
- Private
- **Year founded:** 1859
- **2007-2008 tuition:** full-time: $42,942; part-time: N/A
- **Enrollment 2007-08 academic year:** full-time: 771
- **U.S. News 2009 law specialty ranking:** clinical training: 11, dispute resolution: 12, tax law: 4, trial advocacy: 3

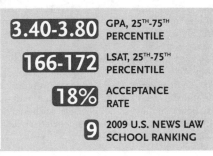

3.40-3.80 GPA, 25ᵀᴴ-75ᵀᴴ PERCENTILE

166-172 LSAT, 25ᵀᴴ-75ᵀᴴ PERCENTILE

18% ACCEPTANCE RATE

9 2009 U.S. NEWS LAW SCHOOL RANKING

ADMISSIONS

Admissions phone number: **(312) 503-8465**
Admissions email address:
  admissions@law.northwestern.edu
Application website:
  http://www.law.northwestern.edu/admissions/applying/
Application deadline for Fall 2009 admission: **02/15**

Admissions statistics:

Number of applicants for Fall 2007: **4,821**
Number of acceptances: **850**
Number enrolled: **238**
Acceptance rate: **18%**
GPA, 25th-75th percentile, entering class Fall 2007: **3.40-3.80**
LSAT, 25th-75th percentile, entering class Fall 2007: **166-172**

FINANCIAL AID

Financial aid phone number: **(312) 503-8465**
Financial aid application deadline: **02/15**
Tuition 2007-2008 academic year: full-time: **$42,942**; part-time: **N/A**
Room and board: **$12,376**; books: **$1,418**; miscellaneous expenses: **$7,680**
Total of room/board/books/miscellaneous expenses: **$21,474**
University offers graduate student housing for which law students are eligible.

Financial aid profile

Percent of students that received grants for the 2006-2007 academic year: full-time: **32%**
Median grant amount: full-time: **$20,000**
The average law-school debt of those in the Class of 2007 who borrowed: **$126,398**. Proportion who borrowed: **74%**

ACADEMIC PROGRAMS

Calendar: **semester**
Joint degrees awarded: **J.D./M.B.A.; J.D./Ph.D.; M.S.**
Law/M.S. Journalism; J.D./LL.M. Tax; LL.M.–Certificate in Management
Typical first-year section size: Full-time: **62**
Is there typically a "small section" of the first year class, other than Legal Writing, taught by full-time faculty?: Full-time: **no**
Number of course titles, beyond the first year curriculum, offered last year: **200**
Percentages of upper division course sections, excluding seminars, with an enrollment of:

Under 25: **53%**	25 to 49: **32%**
50 to 74: **13%**	75 to 99: **2%**
100+: **0%**	

Areas of specialization: appellate advocacy, clinical training, dispute resolution, environmental law, healthcare law, intellectual property law, international law, tax law, trial advocacy

Fall 2007 faculty profile

Total teaching faculty: **118**. Full-time: **49%**; **66%** men, **34%** women, **16%** minorities. Part-time: **51%**; **85%** men, **15%** women, **23%** minorities
Student-to-faculty ratio: **10.4**

SPECIAL PROGRAMS (as provided by law school):

In addition to traditional core courses, the first-year curriculum emphasizes communication and teamwork. Thereafter, students can focus on theory and research in the senior research and academic training programs, work on cases in the Bluhm Legal Clinic, explore different legal systems through international team projects, or cross-train in business in classes at the Kellogg School of Management.

STUDENT BODY

Fall 2007 full-time enrollment: 771

Men: **54%**	Women: **46%**
African-American: **8.2%**	American Indian: **0.9%**
Asian-American: **18.3%**	Mexican-American: **1.7%**
Puerto Rican: **0.9%**	Other Hisp-Amer: **6.1%**
White: **59.9%**	International: **4.0%**
Unknown: **0.0%**	

Attrition rates for 2006-2007 full-time students
Percent of students discontinuing law school:
Men: 2%   Women: 1%
First-year students: 2%   Second-year students: 3%
Third-year students: 1%

LIBRARY RESOURCES
Total volumes: 761,454
Total seats available for library users: 615

INFORMATION TECHNOLOGY
Number of wired network connections available to students: 255 total (in the law library, excluding computer labs: 72; in classrooms: 94; in computer labs: 2; elsewhere in the law school: 87)
Law school has a wireless network.
Students are required to own a computer.

EMPLOYMENT AND SALARIES
Proportion of 2006 graduates employed at graduation: 96%
Employed 9 months later, as of February 15, 2007: 99%
Salaries in the private sector (law firms, business, industry): $135,000–$135,000 (25th-75th percentile)
Median salary in the private sector: $135,000
Percentage in the private sector who reported salary information: 91%
Median salary in public service (government, judicial clerkships, academic posts, non-profits): $55,000

Percentage of 2006 graduates in:
Law firms: 74%   Government: 3%
Bus./industry: 8%   Judicial clerkship: 11%
Public interest: 2%   Unknown: 1%
Academia: 1%

2006 graduates employed in-state: 50%
2006 graduates employed in foreign countries: 2%
Number of states where graduates are employed: 23
Percentage of 2006 graduates working in: New England: 2%, Middle Atlantic: 15%, East North Central: 55%, West North Central: 1%, South Atlantic: 8%, East South Central: 0%, West South Central: 2%, Mountain: 2%, Pacific: 12%, Unknown: 1%

BAR PASSAGE RATES
Based on 2006 graduates taking Summer 2006 or Winter 2007 exams. Most of the school's first-time test takers took the bar in Illinois.

95%
School's bar passage rate for first-time test takers

87%
Statewide bar passage rate for first-time test takers

Nova Southeastern University (Broad)

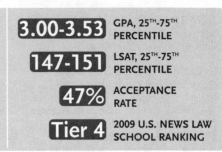

- 3305 College Avenue, Fort Lauderdale, FL, 33314-7721
- http://www.nsulaw.nova.edu/
- Private
- Year founded: 1974
- 2007-2008 tuition: full-time: $29,180; part-time: $22,010
- Enrollment 2007-08 academic year: full-time: 770; part-time: 176
- U.S. News 2009 law specialty ranking: N/A

3.00-3.53 GPA, 25TH-75TH PERCENTILE

147-151 LSAT, 25TH-75TH PERCENTILE

47% ACCEPTANCE RATE

Tier 4 2009 U.S. NEWS LAW SCHOOL RANKING

ADMISSIONS

Admissions phone number: **(954) 262-6117**
Admissions email address: **admission@nsu.law.nova.edu**
Application website:
  http://www.nsulaw.nova.edu/admissions/index.cfm
Application deadline for Fall 2009 admission: **03/01**

Admissions statistics:
Number of applicants for Fall 2007: **2,504**
Number of acceptances: **1,177**
Number enrolled: **320**
Acceptance rate: **47%**
GPA, 25th-75th percentile, entering class Fall 2007: **3.00-3.53**
LSAT, 25th-75th percentile, entering class Fall 2007: **147-151**

Part-time program:
Number of applicants for Fall 2007: **351**
Number of acceptances: **107**
Number enrolled: **64**
Acceptance rate: **30%**
GPA, 25th-75th percentile, entering class Fall 2007: **2.76-3.32**
LSAT, 25th-75th percentile, entering class Fall 2007: **146-151**

FINANCIAL AID

Financial aid phone number: **(954) 262-7412**
Financial aid application deadline: **04/01**
Tuition 2007-2008 academic year: full-time: **$29,180**; part-time: **$22,010**
Room and board: **$13,950**; books: **$2,325**; miscellaneous expenses: **$4,698**
Total of room/board/books/miscellaneous expenses: **$20,973**
University does not offer graduate student housing for which law students are eligible.

Financial aid profile
Percent of students that received grants for the 2006-2007 academic year: full-time: **10%**; part-time **16%**

Median grant amount: full-time: **$15,000**; part-time: **$8,320**
The average law-school debt of those in the Class of 2007 who borrowed: **$93,948**. Proportion who borrowed: **86%**

ACADEMIC PROGRAMS

Calendar: **semester**
Joint degrees awarded: **J.D./M.B.A.; J.D./M.S. Computers; J.D./M.S. Psychology; J.D./M.S. Dispute Resolution; J.D./M.URP.**
Typical first-year section size: Full-time: **51**; Part-time: **49**
Is there typically a "small section" of the first year class, other than Legal Writing, taught by full-time faculty?: Full-time: **no**; Part-time: **no**
Number of course titles, beyond the first year curriculum, offered last year: **115**
Percentages of upper division course sections, excluding seminars, with an enrollment of:

Under 25: **67%**	25 to 49: **18%**
50 to 74: **11%**	75 to 99: **4%**
100+: **0%**	

Areas of specialization: appellate advocacy, clinical training, dispute resolution, environmental law, healthcare law, intellectual property law, international law, tax law, trial advocacy

Fall 2007 faculty profile
Total teaching faculty: **112**. Full-time: **50%**; **46%** men, **54%** women, **21%** minorities. Part-time: **50%**; **71%** men, **29%** women, **14%** minorities
Student-to-faculty ratio: **14.1**

SPECIAL PROGRAMS *(as provided by law school):*
Every student has an opportunity to participate in an in-house clinic or an externship. Opportunities include alternative dispute resolution, business, children, criminal, international, and personal injury. Students fluent in Spanish can participate in a dual-degree opportunity offered with the University of Barcelona. Other semester-abroad opportunities are available in Prague and Venice.

STUDENT BODY

Fall 2007 full-time enrollment: 770

Men: 49%	Women: 51%
African-American: 4.4%	American Indian: 0.1%
Asian-American: 3.9%	Mexican-American: 0.1%
Puerto Rican: 0.8%	Other Hisp-Amer: 12.9%
White: 67.9%	International: 2.6%
Unknown: 7.3%	

Fall 2007 part-time enrollment: 176

Men: 45%	Women: 55%
African-American: 8.0%	American Indian: 0.6%
Asian-American: 1.1%	Mexican-American: 0.6%
Puerto Rican: 2.3%	Other Hisp-Amer: 27.8%
White: 53.4%	International: 1.7%
Unknown: 4.5%	

Attrition rates for 2006-2007 full-time students
Percent of students discontinuing law school:

Men: 4%	Women: 5%
First-year students: 11%	Second-year students: 1%
Third-year students: 0%	

LIBRARY RESOURCES

Total volumes: 365,269
Total seats available for library users: 514

INFORMATION TECHNOLOGY

Number of wired network connections available to students: 3 total (in the law library, excluding computer labs: 0; in classrooms: 0; in computer labs: 0; elsewhere in the law school: 3)
Law school has a wireless network.
Students are required to own a computer.

EMPLOYMENT AND SALARIES

Proportion of 2006 graduates employed at graduation:
N/A

Employed 9 months later, as of February 15, 2007: 85%
Salaries in the private sector (law firms, business, industry): $50,000–$75,000 (25th-75th percentile)
Median salary in the private sector: $55,000
Percentage in the private sector who reported salary information: 62%
Median salary in public service (government, judicial clerkships, academic posts, non-profits): $40,000

Percentage of 2006 graduates in:

Law firms: 58%	Government: 16%
Bus./industry: 15%	Judicial clerkship: 3%
Public interest: 7%	Unknown: 0%
Academia: 1%	

2006 graduates employed in-state: 86%
2006 graduates employed in foreign countries: 1%
Number of states where graduates are employed: 17
Percentage of 2006 graduates working in: New England: 1%, Middle Atlantic: 3%, East North Central: 0%, West North Central: 1%, South Atlantic: 89%, East South Central: 0%, West South Central: 1%, Mountain: 0%, Pacific: 1%, Unknown: 0%

BAR PASSAGE RATES

Based on 2006 graduates taking Summer 2006 or Winter 2007 exams. Most of the school's first-time test takers took the bar in Florida.

69%
School's bar passage rate for first-time test takers

74%
Statewide bar passage rate for first-time test takers

Ohio Northern University (Pettit)

- 525 S. Main Street, Ada, OH, 45810-1599
- http://www.law.onu.edu
- Private
- Year founded: 1885
- 2007-2008 tuition: full-time: $26,350; part-time: N/A
- Enrollment 2007-08 academic year: full-time: 311
- U.S. News 2009 law specialty ranking: N/A

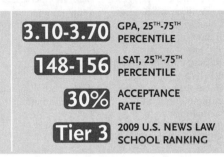

3.10-3.70 GPA, 25TH-75TH PERCENTILE

148-156 LSAT, 25TH-75TH PERCENTILE

30% ACCEPTANCE RATE

Tier 3 2009 U.S. NEWS LAW SCHOOL RANKING

ADMISSIONS

Admissions phone number: **(877) 452-9668**
Admissions email address: **law-admissions@onu.edu**
Application website: **N/A**
Application deadline for Fall 2009 admission: **08/01**

Admissions statistics:
Number of applicants for Fall 2007: **1,271**
Number of acceptances: **377**
Number enrolled: **116**
Acceptance rate: **30%**
GPA, 25th-75th percentile, entering class Fall 2007: **3.10-3.70**
LSAT, 25th-75th percentile, entering class Fall 2007: **148-156**

FINANCIAL AID

Financial aid phone number: **(419) 772-2272**
Financial aid application deadline: **06/01**
Tuition 2007-2008 academic year: full-time: **$26,350**; part-time: **N/A**
Room and board: **$8,865**; books: **$1,200**; miscellaneous expenses: **$2,250**
Total of room/board/books/miscellaneous expenses: **$12,315**
University offers graduate student housing for which law students are eligible.

Financial aid profile
Percent of students that received grants for the 2006-2007 academic year: full-time: **50%**
Median grant amount: full-time: **$15,000**
The average law-school debt of those in the Class of 2007 who borrowed: **$85,570**. Proportion who borrowed: **90%**

ACADEMIC PROGRAMS

Calendar: **semester**
Joint degrees awarded: **N/A**
Typical first-year section size: Full-time: **60**
Is there typically a "small section" of the first year class, other than Legal Writing, taught by full-time faculty?:
Full-time: **no**
Number of course titles, beyond the first year curriculum, offered last year: **77**
Percentages of upper division course sections, excluding seminars, with an enrollment of:
Under 25: **70%**   25 to 49: **19%**
50 to 74: **11%**   75 to 99: **0%**
100+: **0%**
Areas of specialization: appellate advocacy, clinical training, dispute resolution, environmental law, intellectual property law, international law, tax law, trial advocacy

Fall 2007 faculty profile
Total teaching faculty: **30**. Full-time: **70%**; **62%** men, **38%** women, **14%** minorities. Part-time: **30%**; **78%** men, **22%** women, **11%** minorities
Student-to-faculty ratio: **12.2**

SPECIAL PROGRAMS *(as provided by law school)*:
The ONU legal clinic offers a number of programs that provide students with practical and educational experience. A detailed listing of clinical offerings is on the school's website.

STUDENT BODY
Fall 2007 full-time enrollment: 311
Men: **53%**   Women: **47%**
African-American: **6.1%**   American Indian: **0.3%**
Asian-American: **3.2%**   Mexican-American: **0.0%**
Puerto Rican: **0.0%**   Other Hisp-Amer: **1.3%**
White: **89.1%**   International: **0.0%**
Unknown: **0.0%**

Attrition rates for 2006-2007 full-time students
Percent of students discontinuing law school:
Men: **8%**   Women: **8%**
First-year students: **20%**   Second-year students: **N/A**
Third-year students: **1%**

LIBRARY RESOURCES
Total volumes: **410,224**
Total seats available for library users: **337**

INFORMATION TECHNOLOGY

Number of wired network connections available to students: 230 total (in the law library, excluding computer labs: 176; in classrooms: 39; in computer labs: 0; elsewhere in the law school: 15)

Law school has a wireless network.

Students are not required to own a computer.

EMPLOYMENT AND SALARIES

Proportion of 2006 graduates employed at graduation: N/A

Employed 9 months later, as of February 15, 2007: 96%

Salaries in the private sector (law firms, business, industry): $42,000–$73,500 (25th-75th percentile)

Median salary in the private sector: $60,000

Percentage in the private sector who reported salary information: 30%

Median salary in public service (government, judicial clerkships, academic posts, non-profits): $45,000

Percentage of 2006 graduates in:

Law firms: 60%	Government: 17%
Bus./industry: 15%	Judicial clerkship: 3%
Public interest: 3%	Unknown: N/A
Academia: 2%	

2006 graduates employed in-state: 35%

2006 graduates employed in foreign countries: 0%

Number of states where graduates are employed: 20

Percentage of 2006 graduates working in: New England: 0%, Middle Atlantic: 9%, East North Central: 44%, West North Central: 4%, South Atlantic: 24%, East South Central: 7%, West South Central: 4%, Mountain: 5%, Pacific: 3%, Unknown: 0%

BAR PASSAGE RATES

Based on 2006 graduates taking Summer 2006 or Winter 2007 exams. Most of the school's first-time test takers took the bar in Ohio.

81%
School's bar passage rate for first-time test takers

84%
Statewide bar passage rate for first-time test takers

Ohio State University (Moritz)

- 55 W. 12th Avenue, Columbus, OH, 43210
- http://www.moritzlaw.osu.edu
- Public
- **Year founded:** 1891
- **2007-2008 tuition:** In-state: full-time: $19,246; part-time: N/A; Out-of-state: full-time: $33,946
- **Enrollment 2007-08 academic year:** full-time: 669
- **U.S. News 2009 law specialty ranking:** dispute resolution: 5

3.34-3.81 GPA, 25TH-75TH PERCENTILE

158-164 LSAT, 25TH-75TH PERCENTILE

29% ACCEPTANCE RATE

32 2009 U.S. NEWS LAW SCHOOL RANKING

ADMISSIONS
Admissions phone number: **(614) 292-8810**
Admissions email address: **lawadmit@osu.edu**
Application website: **N/A**
Application deadline for Fall 2009 admission: **03/15**

Admissions statistics:
Number of applicants for Fall 2007: **2,320**
Number of acceptances: **684**
Number enrolled: **202**
Acceptance rate: **29%**
GPA, 25th-75th percentile, entering class Fall 2007: **3.34-3.81**
LSAT, 25th-75th percentile, entering class Fall 2007: **158-164**

FINANCIAL AID
Financial aid phone number: **(614) 292-8807**
Financial aid application deadline: **03/01**
Tuition 2007-2008 academic year: In-state: full-time: **$19,246**; part-time: **N/A**; Out-of-state: full-time: **$33,946**
Room and board: **$7,490**; books: **$3,500**; miscellaneous expenses: **$6,880**
Total of room/board/books/miscellaneous expenses: **$17,870**
University offers graduate student housing for which law students are eligible.

Financial aid profile
Percent of students that received grants for the 2006-2007 academic year: full-time: **84%**
Median grant amount: full-time: **$4,302**
The average law-school debt of those in the Class of 2007 who borrowed: **$53,525.** Proportion who borrowed: **96%**

ACADEMIC PROGRAMS
Calendar: **semester**
Joint degrees awarded: **J.D./M.B.A.; J.D./M.A. Public Policy & Management; J.D./M.H.A.; J.D./M.A. City and Regional Planning; J.D./M.A. Education, Policy & Leadership**

Typical first-year section size: Full-time: **74**
Is there typically a "small section" of the first year class, other than Legal Writing, taught by full-time faculty?: Full-time: **yes**
Number of course titles, beyond the first year curriculum, offered last year: **109**
Percentages of upper division course sections, excluding seminars, with an enrollment of:
Under 25: **58%**   25 to 49: **27%**
50 to 74: **12%**   75 to 99: **2%**
100+: **2%**
Areas of specialization: appellate advocacy, clinical training, dispute resolution, environmental law, healthcare law, intellectual property law, international law, tax law, trial advocacy

Fall 2007 faculty profile
Total teaching faculty: **63.** Full-time: **71%**; **62%** men, **38%** women, **22%** minorities. Part-time: **29%**; **78%** men, **22%** women, **17%** minorities
Student-to-faculty ratio: **12.6**

SPECIAL PROGRAMS *(as provided by law school):*
Moritz offers clinics in civil, criminal, juvenile, mediation, and legislation; Certificates in Alternative Dispute Resolution, Children's Justice, and International Business/Trade; study abroad in Oxford, England; joint degrees including J.D./M.B.A., J.D./M.P.A., and J.D./M.H.A. Internship credit offered in judicial extern and Washington, D.C., summer programs (government and nonprofits).

STUDENT BODY
Fall 2007 full-time enrollment: **669**
Men: **57%**   Women: **43%**
African-American: **9.0%**   American Indian: **0.9%**
Asian-American: **9.3%**   Mexican-American: **0.9%**
Puerto Rican: **0.3%**   Other Hisp-Amer: **2.8%**
White: **74.7%**   International: **1.8%**
Unknown: **0.3%**

Attrition rates for 2006-2007 full-time students
Percent of students discontinuing law school:
Men: 2%   Women: 3%
First-year students: N/A   Second-year students: 4%
Third-year students: 4%

LIBRARY RESOURCES
Total volumes: 815,688
Total seats available for library users: 689

INFORMATION TECHNOLOGY
Number of wired network connections available to students: 0 total (in the law library, excluding computer labs: 0; in classrooms: 0; in computer labs: 0; elsewhere in the law school: 0)
Law school has a wireless network.
Students are not required to own a computer.

EMPLOYMENT AND SALARIES
Proportion of 2006 graduates employed at graduation: 86%
Employed 9 months later, as of February 15, 2007: 95%
Salaries in the private sector (law firms, business, industry): $63,000–$105,000 (25th-75th percentile)
Median salary in the private sector: $95,000
Percentage in the private sector who reported salary information: 66%
Median salary in public service (government, judicial clerkships, academic posts, non-profits): $45,000

Percentage of 2006 graduates in:
Law firms: 48%   Government: 15%
Bus./industry: 18%   Judicial clerkship: 7%
Public interest: 6%   Unknown: 2%
Academia: 4%

2006 graduates employed in-state: 59%
2006 graduates employed in foreign countries: 1%
Number of states where graduates are employed: 27
Percentage of 2006 graduates working in: New England: 1%, Middle Atlantic: 6%, East North Central: 66%, West North Central: 0%, South Atlantic: 13%, East South Central: 1%, West South Central: 3%, Mountain: 4%, Pacific: 3%, Unknown: 2%

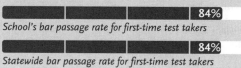

BAR PASSAGE RATES
Based on 2006 graduates taking Summer 2006 or Winter 2007 exams. Most of the school's first-time test takers took the bar in Ohio.

84%
School's bar passage rate for first-time test takers

84%
Statewide bar passage rate for first-time test takers

Oklahoma City University

- 2501 N. Blackwelder, Oklahoma City, OK, 73106-1493
- http://www.okcu.edu/law
- Private
- **Year founded:** 1907
- **2007-2008 tuition:** full-time: $930/credit hour; part-time: $930/credit hour
- **Enrollment 2007-08 academic year:** full-time: 501; part-time: 97
- **U.S. News 2009 law specialty ranking:** N/A

2.87-3.40	GPA, 25TH-75TH PERCENTILE
147-152	LSAT, 25TH-75TH PERCENTILE
57%	ACCEPTANCE RATE
Tier 4	2009 U.S. NEWS LAW SCHOOL RANKING

ADMISSIONS

Admissions phone number: **(866) 529-6281**
Admissions email address: **lawquestions@okcu.edu**
Application website: **http://www.okcu.edu/law/applynow**
Application deadline for Fall 2009 admission: **08/01**

Admissions statistics:
Number of applicants for Fall 2007: **1,107**
Number of acceptances: **633**
Number enrolled: **186**
Acceptance rate: **57%**
GPA, 25th-75th percentile, entering class Fall 2007: **2.87-3.40**
LSAT, 25th-75th percentile, entering class Fall 2007: **147-152**

Part-time program:
Number of applicants for Fall 2007: **130**
Number of acceptances: **59**
Number enrolled: **31**
Acceptance rate: **45%**
GPA, 25th-75th percentile, entering class Fall 2007: **2.80-3.49**
LSAT, 25th-75th percentile, entering class Fall 2007: **147-152**

FINANCIAL AID

Financial aid phone number: **(800) 633-7242**
Financial aid application deadline: **03/02**
Tuition 2007-2008 academic year: full-time: **$930/credit hour**; part-time: **$930/credit hour**
Room and board: **$8,400**; books: **$1,800**; miscellaneous expenses: **$6,400**
Total of room/board/books/miscellaneous expenses: **$16,600**
University does not offer graduate student housing for which law students are eligible.

Financial aid profile
Percent of students that received grants for the 2006-2007 academic year: full-time: **30%**; part-time **26%**

Median grant amount: full-time: **$14,000**; part-time: **$6,000**
The average law-school debt of those in the Class of 2007 who borrowed: **$96,522**. Proportion who borrowed: **90%**

ACADEMIC PROGRAMS

Calendar: **semester**
Joint degrees awarded: **J.D./M.B.A.**
Typical first-year section size: Full-time: **58**; Part-time: **59**
Is there typically a "small section" of the first year class, other than Legal Writing, taught by full-time faculty?: Full-time: **no**; Part-time: **no**
Number of course titles, beyond the first year curriculum, offered last year: **85**
Percentages of upper division course sections, excluding seminars, with an enrollment of:

Under 25: **63%**	25 to 49: **15%**
50 to 74: **15%**	75 to 99: **7%**
100+: **0%**	

Areas of specialization: appellate advocacy, clinical training, dispute resolution, environmental law, healthcare law, intellectual property law, international law, tax law, trial advocacy

Fall 2007 faculty profile
Total teaching faculty: **69**. Full-time: **39%**; **74%** men, **26%** women, **15%** minorities. Part-time: **61%**; **64%** men, **36%** women, **7%** minorities
Student-to-faculty ratio: **18.2**

SPECIAL PROGRAMS (as provided by law school):
Five international programs. Externships: judicial, governmental, Native American, and litigation. Licensed student internships. Certificates in Business Law, Alternative Dispute Resolution, and Public Law. Centers: Native American, Alternative Dispute Resolution, and State Constitutional Law. Public interest fellowships. Joint J.D./M.B.A.

STUDENT BODY
Fall 2007 full-time enrollment: **501**

Men: **60%**	Women: **40%**

African-American: 2.0%   American Indian: 4.2%
Asian-American: 3.2%   Mexican-American: 4.8%
Puerto Rican: 0.0%   Other Hisp-Amer: 0.0%
White: 82.8%   International: 0.0%
Unknown: 3.0%

Fall 2007 part-time enrollment: 97
Men: 56%   Women: 44%
African-American: 7.2%   American Indian: 12.4%
Asian-American: 1.0%   Mexican-American: 5.2%
Puerto Rican: 0.0%   Other Hisp-Amer: 0.0%
White: 72.2%   International: 0.0%
Unknown: 2.1%

Attrition rates for 2006-2007 full-time students
Percent of students discontinuing law school:
Men: 9%   Women: 5%
First-year students: 16%   Second-year students: 6%
Third-year students: N/A

LIBRARY RESOURCES
Total volumes: 321,561
Total seats available for library users: 345

INFORMATION TECHNOLOGY
Number of wired network connections available to students: 147 total (in the law library, excluding computer labs: 104; in classrooms: 26; in computer labs: 4; elsewhere in the law school: 13)
Law school has a wireless network.
Students are not required to own a computer.

EMPLOYMENT AND SALARIES
Proportion of 2006 graduates employed at graduation: N/A
Employed 9 months later, as of February 15, 2007: 84%

Salaries in the private sector (law firms, business, industry): $40,000–$70,000 (25th-75th percentile)
Median salary in the private sector: $50,000
Percentage in the private sector who reported salary information: 79%
Median salary in public service (government, judicial clerkships, academic posts, non-profits): $45,000

Percentage of 2006 graduates in:
Law firms: 60%   Government: 14%
Bus./industry: 19%   Judicial clerkship: 0%
Public interest: 4%   Unknown: 0%
Academia: 3%

2006 graduates employed in-state: 65%
2006 graduates employed in foreign countries: 0%
Number of states where graduates are employed: 24
Percentage of 2006 graduates working in: New England: 0%, Middle Atlantic: 2%, East North Central: 1%, West North Central: 7%, South Atlantic: 3%, East South Central: 1%, West South Central: 77%, Mountain: 3%, Pacific: 1%, Unknown: 5%

BAR PASSAGE RATES
Based on 2006 graduates taking Summer 2006 or Winter 2007 exams. Most of the school's first-time test takers took the bar in Oklahoma.

90%
School's bar passage rate for first-time test takers

92%
Statewide bar passage rate for first-time test takers

Pace University

- 78 N. Broadway, White Plains, NY, 10603
- http://www.law.pace.edu
- Private
- **Year founded:** 1976
- **2007-2008 tuition:** full-time: $37,430; part-time: $28,090
- **Enrollment 2007-08 academic year:** full-time: 533; part-time: 232
- **U.S. News 2009 law specialty ranking:** environmental law: 3

3.13-3.59 GPA, 25TH-75TH PERCENTILE

153-157 LSAT, 25TH-75TH PERCENTILE

37% ACCEPTANCE RATE

Tier 3 2009 U.S. NEWS LAW SCHOOL RANKING

ADMISSIONS

Admissions phone number: **(914) 422-4210**
Admissions email address: **admissions@law.pace.edu**
Application website: **http://appserv.pace.edu/execute/ page.cfm?doc_id=23688**
Application deadline for Fall 2009 admission: **03/01**

Admissions statistics:
Number of applicants for Fall 2007: **2,655**
Number of acceptances: **980**
Number enrolled: **188**
Acceptance rate: **37%**
GPA, 25th-75th percentile, entering class Fall 2007: **3.13-3.59**
LSAT, 25th-75th percentile, entering class Fall 2007: **153-157**

Part-time program:
Number of applicants for Fall 2007: **499**
Number of acceptances: **158**
Number enrolled: **75**
Acceptance rate: **32%**
GPA, 25th-75th percentile, entering class Fall 2007: **2.95-3.51**
LSAT, 25th-75th percentile, entering class Fall 2007: **151-155**

FINANCIAL AID

Financial aid phone number: **(914) 422-4050**
Financial aid application deadline: **02/15**
Tuition 2007-2008 academic year: full-time: **$37,430**; part-time: **$28,090**
Room and board: **$16,780**; books: **$1,120**; miscellaneous expenses: **$5,170**
Total of room/board/books/miscellaneous expenses: **$23,070**
University offers graduate student housing for which law students are eligible.

Financial aid profile
Percent of students that received grants for the 2006-2007 academic year: full-time: **51%**; part-time **34%**

Median grant amount: full-time: **$12,000**; part-time: **$6,000**
The average law-school debt of those in the Class of 2007 who borrowed: **$78,000**. Proportion who borrowed: **88%**

ACADEMIC PROGRAMS

Calendar: **semester**
Joint degrees awarded: **J.D./M.B.A.; J.D./M.P.A.; J.D./M.E.M.; J.D./M.S.**
Typical first-year section size: Full-time: **54**; Part-time: **61**
Is there typically a "small section" of the first year class, other than Legal Writing, taught by full-time faculty?: Full-time: **yes**; Part-time: **yes**
Number of course titles, beyond the first year curriculum, offered last year: **144**
Percentages of upper division course sections, excluding seminars, with an enrollment of:

Under 25: **79%**	25 to 49: **13%**
50 to 74: **3%**	75 to 99: **4%**
100+: **1%**	

Areas of specialization: appellate advocacy, clinical training, dispute resolution, environmental law, healthcare law, intellectual property law, international law, tax law, trial advocacy

Fall 2007 faculty profile
Total teaching faculty: **103**. Full-time: **38%**; **62%** men, **38%** women, **13%** minorities. Part-time: **62%**; **48%** men, **52%** women, **3%** minorities
Student-to-faculty ratio: **14.2**

SPECIAL PROGRAMS *(as provided by law school)*:
Pace offers a wide variety of special programs through the Pace Women's Justice Center, the Land Use Law Center, the federal judicial extern honors program, and its many direct representation clinics and externships. There are also opportunities for a semester in London as well as summer work for foreign law firms and at war crimes tribunals.

STUDENT BODY

Fall 2007 full-time enrollment: 533

Men: 37%   Women: 63%
African-American: 2.6%   American Indian: 0.0%
Asian-American: 10.5%   Mexican-American: 0.0%
Puerto Rican: 0.6%   Other Hisp-Amer: 1.7%
White: 72.4%   International: 1.3%
Unknown: 10.9%

Fall 2007 part-time enrollment: 232

Men: 51%   Women: 49%
African-American: 3.0%   American Indian: 0.0%
Asian-American: 5.2%   Mexican-American: 0.4%
Puerto Rican: 0.9%   Other Hisp-Amer: 4.7%
White: 70.7%   International: 0.0%
Unknown: 15.1%

Attrition rates for 2006-2007 full-time students

Percent of students discontinuing law school:
Men: 9%   Women: 6%
First-year students: 16%   Second-year students: 3%
Third-year students: 1%

LIBRARY RESOURCES

Total volumes: 389,357
Total seats available for library users: 551

INFORMATION TECHNOLOGY

Number of wired network connections available to students: 229 total (in the law library, excluding computer labs: 78; in classrooms: 115; in computer labs: 0; elsewhere in the law school: 36)
Law school has a wireless network.
Students are not required to own a computer.

EMPLOYMENT AND SALARIES

Proportion of 2006 graduates employed at graduation:
N/A

Employed 9 months later, as of February 15, 2007: 88%
Salaries in the private sector (law firms, business, industry): $54,000–$95,000 (25th-75th percentile)
Median salary in the private sector: $65,000
Percentage in the private sector who reported salary information: 39%
Median salary in public service (government, judicial clerkships, academic posts, non-profits): $54,548

Percentage of 2006 graduates in:

Law firms: 51%   Government: 15%
Bus./industry: 27%   Judicial clerkship: 3%
Public interest: 2%   Unknown: 1%
Academia: 1%

2006 graduates employed in-state: 61%
2006 graduates employed in foreign countries: 0%
Number of states where graduates are employed: 17
Percentage of 2006 graduates working in: New England: 5%, Middle Atlantic: 65%, East North Central: 1%, West North Central: 0%, South Atlantic: 6%, East South Central: 1%, West South Central: 0%, Mountain: 0%, Pacific: 3%, Unknown: 19%

BAR PASSAGE RATES

Based on 2006 graduates taking Summer 2006 or Winter 2007 exams. Most of the school's first-time test takers took the bar in New York.

81%
School's bar passage rate for first-time test takers

77%
Statewide bar passage rate for first-time test takers

Penn. State University (Dickinson)

■ 100 Beam Building, University Park, PA, 16802
■ http://www.dsl.psu.edu
■ Public
■ Year founded: 1834
■ 2007-2008 tuition: In-state: full-time: $29,674; part-time: $27,248; Out-of-state: full-time: $29,674
■ Enrollment 2007-08 academic year: full-time: 573; part-time: 82
■ U.S. News 2009 law specialty ranking: dispute resolution: 12

3.02-3.69 GPA, 25TH-75TH PERCENTILE

156-159 LSAT, 25TH-75TH PERCENTILE

33% ACCEPTANCE RATE

77 2009 U.S. NEWS LAW SCHOOL RANKING

ADMISSIONS

Admissions phone number: **(800) 840-1122**
Admissions email address: **dsladmit@psu.edu**
Application website:
  http://www.dsl.psu.edu/admissions/applyjd.cfm
Application deadline for Fall 2009 admission: **03/01**

Admissions statistics:
Number of applicants for Fall 2007: **2,459**
Number of acceptances: **819**
Number enrolled: **151**
Acceptance rate: **33%**
GPA, 25th-75th percentile, entering class Fall 2007: **3.02-3.69**
LSAT, 25th-75th percentile, entering class Fall 2007: **156-159**

Part-time program:
Number of applicants for Fall 2007: **583**
Number of acceptances: **251**
Number enrolled: **79**
Acceptance rate: **43%**
GPA, 25th-75th percentile, entering class Fall 2007: **3.38-3.67**
LSAT, 25th-75th percentile, entering class Fall 2007: **147-154**

FINANCIAL AID

Financial aid phone number: **(800) 840-1122**
Financial aid application deadline: **03/01**
Tuition 2007-2008 academic year: In-state: full-time: **$29,674**; part-time: **$27,248**; Out-of-state: full-time: **$29,674**
Room and board: **$9,378**; books: **$1,200**; miscellaneous expenses: **$7,456**
Total of room/board/books/miscellaneous expenses: **$18,034**
University offers graduate student housing for which law students are eligible.

Financial aid profile
Percent of students that received grants for the 2006-2007 academic year: full-time: **39%**; part-time **4%**
Median grant amount: full-time: **$4,800**; part-time: **$1,900**
The average law-school debt of those in the Class of 2007 who borrowed: **$89,529**. Proportion who borrowed: **85%**

ACADEMIC PROGRAMS

Calendar: **semester**
Joint degrees awarded: **J.D./M.P.A.; J.D./M.B.A. (University Park); J.D./M.E.P.C.; J.D./M.ENG.P.C.; J.D./M.S.I.S.; J.D./M.S. Forest Resources; J.D./M.Agr.; J.D./Ph.D. Forest Resources; J.D./M.B.A. (Harrisburg); J.D./M.A. Educational Theory & Policy; J.D./Ph.D. Educational Theory & Policy; J.D./M.Ed. College Student Affairs; J.D./M.Ed. Educational Leadership; J.D./M.S. Educational Leadership; J.D./D.Ed. Educational Leadership; J.D./Ph.D. Educational Leadership; J.D./Ph.D. Higher Education; J.D./D.Ed. Higher Education; J.D./M.Ed. Higher Education; J.D./M.S. Human Resources**
Typical first-year section size: Full-time: **56**; Part-time: **56**
Is there typically a "small section" of the first year class, other than Legal Writing, taught by full-time faculty?: Full-time: **no**; Part-time: **no**
Number of course titles, beyond the first year curriculum, offered last year: **126**
Percentages of upper division course sections, excluding seminars, with an enrollment of:
  Under 25: **77%**   25 to 49: **16%**
  50 to 74: **5%**   75 to 99: **3%**
  100+: **0%**
Areas of specialization: appellate advocacy, clinical training, dispute resolution, environmental law, healthcare law, intellectual property law, international law, tax law, trial advocacy

Fall 2007 faculty profile
Total teaching faculty: 53. Full-time: 79%; 50% men, 50% women, 7% minorities. Part-time: 21%; 55% men, 45% women, 9% minorities
Student-to-faculty ratio: 11.5

SPECIAL PROGRAMS *(as provided by law school):*
Students research through Institute of Arbitration Law and Practice; Miller Center for Public Interest Advocacy; Institute for Sports Law, Policy, and Research; Vinogradoff Institute (Russian law); and Agricultural Law Resource and Reference Center; represent clients in clinics (refugee, child advocacy, disability, elder law and consumer protection, and family law); and serve in key externships.

STUDENT BODY
Fall 2007 full-time enrollment: 573

Men: 57%	Women: 43%
African-American: 8.0%	American Indian: 0.2%
Asian-American: 7.5%	Mexican-American: 0.0%
Puerto Rican: 0.0%	Other Hisp-Amer: 6.3%
White: 67.5%	International: 3.0%
Unknown: 7.5%	

Fall 2007 part-time enrollment: 82

Men: 50%	Women: 50%
African-American: 14.6%	American Indian: 0.0%
Asian-American: 3.7%	Mexican-American: 11.0%
Puerto Rican: 0.0%	Other Hisp-Amer: 0.0%
White: 45.1%	International: 1.2%
Unknown: 24.4%	

Attrition rates for 2006-2007 full-time students
Percent of students discontinuing law school:

Men: 5%	Women: 4%
First-year students: 11%	Second-year students: N/A
Third-year students: 1%	

LIBRARY RESOURCES
Total volumes: 530,783
Total seats available for library users: 267

INFORMATION TECHNOLOGY
Number of wired network connections available to students: 24 total (in the law library, excluding computer labs: 0; in classrooms: 18; in computer labs: 0; elsewhere in the law school: 6)

Law school has a wireless network.
Students are not required to own a computer.

EMPLOYMENT AND SALARIES
Proportion of 2006 graduates employed at graduation: N/A
Employed 9 months later, as of February 15, 2007: 92%
Salaries in the private sector (law firms, business, industry): $50,000–$100,000 (25th-75th percentile)
Median salary in the private sector: $63,000
Percentage in the private sector who reported salary information: 64%
Median salary in public service (government, judicial clerkships, academic posts, non-profits): $41,000

Percentage of 2006 graduates in:

Law firms: 50%	Government: 12%
Bus./industry: 14%	Judicial clerkship: 14%
Public interest: 3%	Unknown: 5%
Academia: 2%	

2006 graduates employed in-state: 57%
2006 graduates employed in foreign countries: 0%
Number of states where graduates are employed: 22
Percentage of 2006 graduates working in: New England: 0%, Middle Atlantic: 66%, East North Central: 2%, West North Central: 2%, South Atlantic: 16%, East South Central: 1%, West South Central: 1%, Mountain: 1%, Pacific: 4%, Unknown: 7%

BAR PASSAGE RATES
Based on 2006 graduates taking Summer 2006 or Winter 2007 exams. Most of the school's first-time test takers took the bar in Pennsylvania.

87%
School's bar passage rate for first-time test takers

83%
Statewide bar passage rate for first-time test takers

Pepperdine University

- 24255 Pacific Coast Highway, Malibu, CA, 90263
- http://law.pepperdine.edu
- Private
- **Year founded:** 1969
- **2007-2008 tuition:** full-time: $35,520; part-time: N/A
- **Enrollment 2007-08 academic year:** full-time: 633
- **U.S. News 2009 law specialty ranking:** dispute resolution: 1

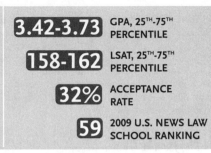

3.42-3.73 GPA, 25TH-75TH PERCENTILE

158-162 LSAT, 25TH-75TH PERCENTILE

32% ACCEPTANCE RATE

59 2009 U.S. NEWS LAW SCHOOL RANKING

ADMISSIONS

Admissions phone number: **(310) 506-4631**
Admissions email address: **soladmis@pepperdine.edu**
Application website:
   http://law.pepperdine.edu/admissions/applications
Application deadline for Fall 2009 admission: **02/01**

Admissions statistics:
Number of applicants for Fall 2007: **2,655**
Number of acceptances: **862**
Number enrolled: **226**
Acceptance rate: **32%**
GPA, 25th-75th percentile, entering class Fall 2007: **3.42-3.73**
LSAT, 25th-75th percentile, entering class Fall 2007: **158-162**

FINANCIAL AID

Financial aid phone number: **(310) 506-4633**
Financial aid application deadline: **02/01**
Tuition 2007-2008 academic year: full-time: **$35,520**; part-time: **N/A**
Room and board: **$15,110**; books: **$800**; miscellaneous expenses: **$4,700**
Total of room/board/books/miscellaneous expenses: **$20,610**
University offers graduate student housing for which law students are eligible.

Financial aid profile
Percent of students that received grants for the 2006-2007 academic year: full-time: **76%**
Median grant amount: full-time: **$6,000**
The average law-school debt of those in the Class of 2007 who borrowed: **$111,173**. Proportion who borrowed: **88%**

ACADEMIC PROGRAMS

Calendar: **semester**
Joint degrees awarded: **J.D./M.B.A.; J.D./M.D.R.; J.D./M.P.P.; J.D./M.Div.**

Typical first-year section size: Full-time: **75**
Is there typically a "small section" of the first year class, other than Legal Writing, taught by full-time faculty?: Full-time: **no**
Number of course titles, beyond the first year curriculum, offered last year: **108**
Percentages of upper division course sections, excluding seminars, with an enrollment of:
   Under 25: **65%**   25 to 49: **24%**
   50 to 74: **5%**   75 to 99: **2%**
   100+: **4%**
Areas of specialization: appellate advocacy, clinical training, dispute resolution, environmental law, healthcare law, intellectual property law, international law, tax law, trial advocacy

Fall 2007 faculty profile
Total teaching faculty: **154**. Full-time: **39%**; **78%** men, **22%** women, **18%** minorities. Part-time: **61%**; **76%** men, **24%** women, **9%** minorities
Student-to-faculty ratio: **16.9**

SPECIAL PROGRAMS *(as provided by law school):*
The school operates a summer/fall London program; a legal aid clinic at the Union Rescue Mission in Los Angeles; the Nootbaar Institute on Law, Religion, and Ethics exploring how religion influences the law; a special education clinic; the Palmer Center for Entrepreneurship and the Law; and the Straus Institute for Dispute Resolution. Exchange programs with the Universities of Augsburg and Copenhagen.

STUDENT BODY
Fall 2007 full-time enrollment: **633**
Men: **50%**   Women: **50%**
African-American: **3.5%**   American Indian: **0.8%**
Asian-American: **8.5%**   Mexican-American: **2.4%**
Puerto Rican: **0.2%**   Other Hisp-Amer: **1.6%**
White: **61.0%**   International: **0.0%**
Unknown: **22.1%**

Attrition rates for 2006-2007 full-time students
Percent of students discontinuing law school:
Men: 1%   Women: 2%
First-year students: 4%   Second-year students: N/A
Third-year students: N/A

LIBRARY RESOURCES
Total volumes: 386,418
Total seats available for library users: 470

INFORMATION TECHNOLOGY
Number of wired network connections available to students: 83 total (in the law library, excluding computer
labs: 70; in classrooms: 13; in computer labs: 0; elsewhere in the law school: 0)
Law school has a wireless network.
Students are not required to own a computer.

EMPLOYMENT AND SALARIES
Proportion of 2006 graduates employed at graduation:
N/A
Employed 9 months later, as of February 15, 2007: 95%
Salaries in the private sector (law firms, business, indus-
try): $65,000–$135,000 (25th-75th percentile)
Median salary in the private sector: $90,000
Percentage in the private sector who reported salary
information: 33%
Median salary in public service (government, judicial clerk-
ships, academic posts, non-profits): $57,600

Percentage of 2006 graduates in:
Law firms: 57%   Government: 15%
Bus./industry: 18%   Judicial clerkship: 5%
Public interest: 2%   Unknown: 1%
Academia: 2%

2006 graduates employed in-state: 77%
2006 graduates employed in foreign countries: 2%
Number of states where graduates are employed: 23
Percentage of 2006 graduates working in: New England:
2%, Middle Atlantic: 1%, East North Central: 1%, West
North Central: 1%, South Atlantic: 4%, East South
Central: 1%, West South Central: 4%, Mountain: 4%,
Pacific: 78%, Unknown: 2%

BAR PASSAGE RATES
Based on 2006 graduates taking Summer 2006 or
Winter 2007 exams. Most of the school's first-time test
takers took the bar in California.

83%
School's bar passage rate for first-time test takers

65%
Statewide bar passage rate for first-time test takers

Phoenix School of Law

■ 4041 N. Central Avenue, Suite 100, Phoenix, AZ, 85012
■ http://www.phoenixlaw.edu
■ Private
■ Year founded: 2005
■ 2007-2008 tuition: full-time: $28,640; part-time: $21,800
■ Enrollment 2007-08 academic year: full-time: 103; part-time: 91
■ U.S. News 2009 law specialty ranking: N/A

2.93-3.48 GPA, 25TH-75TH PERCENTILE

148-157 LSAT, 25TH-75TH PERCENTILE

62% ACCEPTANCE RATE

Unranked 2009 U.S. NEWS LAW SCHOOL RANKING

ADMISSIONS

Admissions phone number: **(602) 682-6800**
Admissions email address: **admissions@phoenixlaw.edu**
Application website:
   http://www.phoenixlaw.edu/Application.pdf
Application deadline for Fall 2009 admission: **rolling**

Admissions statistics:
Number of applicants for Fall 2007: **311**
Number of acceptances: **192**
Number enrolled: **56**
Acceptance rate: **62%**
GPA, 25th-75th percentile, entering class Fall 2007: **2.93-3.48**
LSAT, 25th-75th percentile, entering class Fall 2007: **148-157**

Part-time program:
Number of applicants for Fall 2007: **156**
Number of acceptances: **69**
Number enrolled: **35**
Acceptance rate: **44%**
GPA, 25th-75th percentile, entering class Fall 2007: **3.02-3.59**
LSAT, 25th-75th percentile, entering class Fall 2007: **149-154**

FINANCIAL AID

Financial aid phone number: **(602) 682-6800**
Financial aid application deadline: **N/A**
Tuition 2007-2008 academic year: full-time: **$28,640**; part-time: **$21,800**
Room and board: **N/A**; books: **N/A**; miscellaneous expenses: **N/A**
Total of room/board/books/miscellaneous expenses: **N/A**
University does not offer graduate student housing for which law students are eligible.

Financial aid profile
Percent of students that received grants for the 2006-2007 academic year: full-time: **37%**; part-time: **56%**

Median grant amount: full-time: **$8,995**; part-time: **$5,000**
The average law-school debt of those in the Class of 2007 who borrowed: **N/A**. Proportion who borrowed: **N/A**

ACADEMIC PROGRAMS

Calendar: **semester**
Joint degrees awarded: **N/A**
Typical first-year section size: Full-time: **27**; Part-time: **16**
Is there typically a "small section" of the first year class, other than Legal Writing, taught by full-time faculty?: Full-time: **no**; Part-time: **no**
Number of course titles, beyond the first year curriculum, offered last year: **3**
Percentages of upper division course sections, excluding seminars, with an enrollment of:

Under 25: **76%**	25 to 49: **24%**
50 to 74: **0%**	75 to 99: **0%**
100+: **0%**	

Areas of specialization: appellate advocacy, clinical training, dispute resolution, environmental law, trial advocacy

Fall 2007 faculty profile
Total teaching faculty: **21**. Full-time: **71%**; **47%** men, **53%** women, **40%** minorities. Part-time: **29%**; **83%** men, **17%** women, **0%** minorities
Student-to-faculty ratio: **16.8**

SPECIAL PROGRAMS *(as provided by law school):*
Mediation clinic, general practice skills course, externships (including judicial externships).

STUDENT BODY
Fall 2007 full-time enrollment: **103**

Men: **50%**	Women: **50%**
African-American: **3.9%**	American Indian: **0.0%**
Asian-American: **3.9%**	Mexican-American: **1.0%**
Puerto Rican: **0.0%**	Other Hisp-Amer: **9.7%**
White: **60.2%**	International: **0.0%**
Unknown: **21.4%**	

Fall 2007 part-time enrollment: 91

Men: 47%	Women: 53%
African-American: 2.2%	American Indian: 4.4%
Asian-American: 0.0%	Mexican-American: 5.5%
Puerto Rican: 0.0%	Other Hisp-Amer: 7.7%
White: 64.8%	International: 0.0%
Unknown: 15.4%	

Attrition rates for 2006-2007 full-time students

Percent of students discontinuing law school:

Men: **N/A**	Women: **N/A**
First-year students: **N/A**	Second-year students: **N/A**
Third-year students: **N/A**	

LIBRARY RESOURCES

Total volumes: 123,597
Total seats available for library users: 173

INFORMATION TECHNOLOGY

Number of wired network connections available to students: 0 total (in the law library, excluding computer labs: 0; in classrooms: 0; in computer labs: 0; elsewhere in the law school: 0)

Law school has a wireless network.

Students are required to own a computer.

EMPLOYMENT AND SALARIES

Proportion of 2006 graduates employed at graduation: **N/A**

Employed 9 months later, as of February 15, 2007: **N/A**

Salaries in the private sector (law firms, business, industry): **N/A**

Median salary in the private sector: **N/A**

Percentage in the private sector who reported salary information: **N/A**

Median salary in public service (government, judicial clerkships, academic posts, non-profits): **N/A**

Percentage of 2006 graduates in:

Law firms: **N/A**	Government: **N/A**
Bus./industry: **N/A**	Judicial clerkship: **N/A**
Public interest: **N/A**	Unknown: **N/A**
Academia: **N/A**	

2006 graduates employed in-state: **N/A**

2006 graduates employed in foreign countries: **N/A**

Number of states where graduates are employed: **N/A**

Percentage of 2006 graduates working in: New England: **N/A**, Middle Atlantic: **N/A**, East North Central: **N/A**, West North Central: **N/A**, South Atlantic: **N/A**, East South Central: **N/A**, West South Central: **N/A**, Mountain: **N/A**, Pacific: **N/A**, Unknown: **N/A**

BAR PASSAGE RATES

Based on 2006 graduates taking Summer 2006 or Winter 2007 exams. Most of the school's first-time test takers took the bar in N/A.

N/A
School's bar passage rate for first-time test takers

N/A
Statewide bar passage rate for first-time test takers

Quinnipiac University

- 275 Mount Carmel Avenue, Hamden, CT, 06518
- http://law.quinnipiac.edu
- Private
- Year founded: 1977
- 2007-2008 tuition: full-time: $36,240; part-time: $25,440
- Enrollment 2007-08 academic year: full-time: 235; part-time: 153
- U.S. News 2009 law specialty ranking: N/A

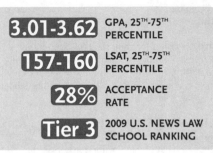

3.01-3.62 GPA, 25TH-75TH PERCENTILE

157-160 LSAT, 25TH-75TH PERCENTILE

28% ACCEPTANCE RATE

Tier 3 2009 U.S. NEWS LAW SCHOOL RANKING

ADMISSIONS

Admissions phone number: **(203) 582-3400**
Admissions email address: **ladm@quinnipiac.edu**
Application website: **http://law.quinnipiac.edu/x53.xml**
Application deadline for Fall 2009 admission: **rolling**

Admissions statistics:
Number of applicants for Fall 2007: **2,331**
Number of acceptances: **644**
Number enrolled: **66**
Acceptance rate: **28%**
GPA, 25th-75th percentile, entering class Fall 2007: **3.01-3.62**
LSAT, 25th-75th percentile, entering class Fall 2007: **157-160**

Part-time program:
Number of applicants for Fall 2007: **654**
Number of acceptances: **189**
Number enrolled: **62**
Acceptance rate: **29%**
GPA, 25th-75th percentile, entering class Fall 2007: **3.00-3.53**
LSAT, 25th-75th percentile, entering class Fall 2007: **152-156**

FINANCIAL AID

Financial aid phone number: **(203) 582-3405**
Financial aid application deadline: **N/A**
Tuition 2007-2008 academic year: full-time: **$36,240**; part-time: **$25,440**
Room and board: **$8,919**; books: **$1,200**; miscellaneous expenses: **$7,597**
Total of room/board/books/miscellaneous expenses: **$17,716**
University does not offer graduate student housing for which law students are eligible.

Financial aid profile
Percent of students that received grants for the 2006-2007 academic year: full-time: **89%**; part-time **54%**

Median grant amount: full-time: **$12,000**; part-time: **$6,000**
The average law-school debt of those in the Class of 2007 who borrowed: **$77,288**. Proportion who borrowed: **83%**

ACADEMIC PROGRAMS

Calendar: **semester**
Joint degrees awarded: **J.D./M.B.A.; J.D./M.H.A.**
Typical first-year section size: Full-time: **30**; Part-time: **64**
Is there typically a "small section" of the first year class, other than Legal Writing, taught by full-time faculty?: Full-time: **no**; Part-time: **no**
Number of course titles, beyond the first year curriculum, offered last year: **104**
Percentages of upper division course sections, excluding seminars, with an enrollment of:

Under 25: **81%**	25 to 49: **15%**
50 to 74: **3%**	75 to 99: **1%**
100+: **0%**	

Areas of specialization: appellate advocacy, clinical training, dispute resolution, environmental law, healthcare law, intellectual property law, international law, tax law, trial advocacy

Fall 2007 faculty profile
Total teaching faculty: **73**. Full-time: **41%**; 63% men, 37% women, 13% minorities. Part-time: **59%**; 63% men, 37% women, 2% minorities
Student-to-faculty ratio: **10.4**

SPECIAL PROGRAMS *(as provided by law school):*
Six concentrations: civil advocacy and dispute resolution; criminal law and advocacy; family and juvenile law; health law; intellectual property; and tax. J.D./M.B.A. Center for Health Law and Policy; Center on Dispute Resolution. Summer study in Ireland; 15 clinics and externships.

STUDENT BODY
Fall 2007 full-time enrollment: 235

Men: **51%**	Women: **49%**
African-American: **1.7%**	American Indian: **1.3%**

Asian-American: **8.9%**   Mexican-American: **0.0%**
Puerto Rican: **0.0%**   Other Hisp-Amer: **3.8%**
White: **79.1%**   International: **0.0%**
Unknown: **5.1%**

Fall 2007 part-time enrollment: 153
Men: **45%**   Women: **55%**
African-American: **5.2%**   American Indian: **0.0%**
Asian-American: **5.2%**   Mexican-American: **0.0%**
Puerto Rican: **0.0%**   Other Hisp-Amer: **3.3%**
White: **83.0%**   International: **0.0%**
Unknown: **3.3%**

Attrition rates for 2006-2007 full-time students
Percent of students discontinuing law school:
Men: **3%**   Women: **1%**
First-year students: **6%**   Second-year students: **3%**
Third-year students: **N/A**

LIBRARY RESOURCES
Total volumes: **420,553**
Total seats available for library users: **350**

INFORMATION TECHNOLOGY
Number of wired network connections available to students: **327** total (in the law library, excluding computer labs: **237**; in classrooms: **22**; in computer labs: **0**; elsewhere in the law school: **68**)
Law school has a wireless network.
Students are not required to own a computer.

EMPLOYMENT AND SALARIES
Proportion of 2006 graduates employed at graduation: **N/A**
Employed 9 months later, as of February 15, 2007: **94%**

Salaries in the private sector (law firms, business, industry): **$47,500–$78,000** (25th-75th percentile)
Median salary in the private sector: **$60,000**
Percentage in the private sector who reported salary information: **70%**
Median salary in public service (government, judicial clerkships, academic posts, non-profits): **$42,500**

Percentage of 2006 graduates in:
Law firms: **49%**   Government: **14%**
Bus./industry: **20%**   Judicial clerkship: **5%**
Public interest: **5%**   Unknown: **3%**
Academia: **3%**

2006 graduates employed in-state: **67%**
2006 graduates employed in foreign countries: **0%**
Number of states where graduates are employed: **14**
Percentage of 2006 graduates working in: New England: **69%**, Middle Atlantic: **19%**, East North Central: **1%**, West North Central: **2%**, South Atlantic: **2%**, East South Central: **1%**, West South Central: **0%**, Mountain: **0%**, Pacific: **1%**, Unknown: **6%**

BAR PASSAGE RATES
Based on 2006 graduates taking Summer 2006 or Winter 2007 exams. Most of the school's first-time test takers took the bar in Connecticut.

83%
School's bar passage rate for first-time test takers

83%
Statewide bar passage rate for first-time test takers

Regent University

■ 1000 Regent University Drive, Virginia Beach, VA, 23464-9880
■ http://www.regent.edu/law/admissions
■ Private
■ Year founded: 1986
■ 2007-2008 tuition: full-time: $26,862; part-time: $19,982
■ Enrollment 2007-08 academic year: full-time: 437; part-time: 22
■ U.S. News 2009 law specialty ranking: N/A

2.95-3.66 GPA, 25TH-75TH PERCENTILE

150-156 LSAT, 25TH-75TH PERCENTILE

53% ACCEPTANCE RATE

Tier 4 2009 U.S. NEWS LAW SCHOOL RANKING

ADMISSIONS
Admissions phone number: **(757) 226-4584**
Admissions email address: **lawschool@regent.edu**
Application website:
http://www.regent.edu/acad/schlaw/admissions/apply.cfm
Application deadline for Fall 2009 admission: **06/01**

Admissions statistics:
Number of applicants for Fall 2007: **562**
Number of acceptances: **297**
Number enrolled: **149**
Acceptance rate: **53%**
GPA, 25th-75th percentile, entering class Fall 2007: **2.95-3.66**
LSAT, 25th-75th percentile, entering class Fall 2007: **150-156**

Part-time program:
Number of applicants for Fall 2007: **13**
Number of acceptances: **4**
Number enrolled: **4**
Acceptance rate: **31%**
GPA, 25th-75th percentile, entering class Fall 2007: **3.09-3.26**
LSAT, 25th-75th percentile, entering class Fall 2007: **149-150**

FINANCIAL AID
Financial aid phone number: **(757) 226-4559**
Financial aid application deadline: **06/01**
Tuition 2007-2008 academic year: full-time: **$26,862**; part-time: **$19,982**
Room and board: **$6,752**; books: **$1,509**; miscellaneous expenses: **$8,231**
Total of room/board/books/miscellaneous expenses: **$16,492**
University offers graduate student housing for which law students are eligible.

Financial aid profile
Percent of students that received grants for the 2006-2007 academic year: full-time: **78%**; part-time **100%**
Median grant amount: full-time: **$6,000**; part-time: **$1,000**
The average law-school debt of those in the Class of 2007 who borrowed: **$90,193**. Proportion who borrowed: **83%**

ACADEMIC PROGRAMS
Calendar: **semester**
Joint degrees awarded: **J.D./M.A. Communications; J.D./M.A. Management; J.D./M.A. Journalism; J.D./M.A. Counseling; J.D./M.B.A.; J.D./M.Div.; J.D./M.A. Government; J.D./M.A. Public Policy**
Typical first-year section size: Full-time: **80**; Part-time: **80**
Is there typically a "small section" of the first year class, other than Legal Writing, taught by full-time faculty?: Full-time: **yes**; Part-time: **yes**
Number of course titles, beyond the first year curriculum, offered last year: **82**
Percentages of upper division course sections, excluding seminars, with an enrollment of:
Under 25: **69%**   25 to 49: **17%**
50 to 74: **9%**   75 to 99: **5%**
100+: **0%**
Areas of specialization: appellate advocacy, clinical training, dispute resolution, environmental law, healthcare law, intellectual property law, international law, tax law, trial advocacy

Fall 2007 faculty profile
Total teaching faculty: **52**. Full-time: **44%**; **74%** men, **26%** women, **17%** minorities. Part-time: **56%**; **86%** men, **14%** women, **0%** minorities
Student-to-faculty ratio: **20.0**

SPECIAL PROGRAMS *(as provided by law school):*
Special programs include a summer program in Strasbourg, France, focusing on international law and human rights; student-client contact through litigation and family mediation

clinics; public interest opportunities involving the defense of religious liberties; the American Center for Law and Justice spring semester program in Washington, D.C.; and exchange programs with law schools in Korea and Spain.

STUDENT BODY

Fall 2007 full-time enrollment: 437

Men: 51%	Women: 49%
African-American: 5.7%	American Indian: 2.5%
Asian-American: 3.9%	Mexican-American: 0.0%
Puerto Rican: 0.0%	Other Hisp-Amer: 1.6%
White: 83.5%	International: 1.4%
Unknown: 1.4%	

Fall 2007 part-time enrollment: 22

Men: 45%	Women: 55%
African-American: 9.1%	American Indian: 0.0%
Asian-American: 0.0%	Mexican-American: 0.0%
Puerto Rican: 0.0%	Other Hisp-Amer: 0.0%
White: 90.9%	International: 0.0%
Unknown: 0.0%	

Attrition rates for 2006-2007 full-time students
Percent of students discontinuing law school:

Men: 7%	Women: 4%
First-year students: 7%	Second-year students: 9%
Third-year students: 1%	

LIBRARY RESOURCES

Total volumes: 395,655
Total seats available for library users: 325

INFORMATION TECHNOLOGY

Number of wired network connections available to students: 241 total (in the law library, excluding computer labs: 214; in classrooms: 10; in computer labs: 4; elsewhere in the law school: 13)
Law school has a wireless network.
Students are not required to own a computer.

EMPLOYMENT AND SALARIES

Proportion of 2006 graduates employed at graduation: 41%
Employed 9 months later, as of February 15, 2007: 83%
Salaries in the private sector (law firms, business, industry): $40,000–$65,000 (25th-75th percentile)
Median salary in the private sector: $50,000
Percentage in the private sector who reported salary information: 58%
Median salary in public service (government, judicial clerkships, academic posts, non-profits): $44,000

Percentage of 2006 graduates in:

Law firms: 44%	Government: 23%
Bus./industry: 14%	Judicial clerkship: 6%
Public interest: 6%	Unknown: 0%
Academia: 6%	

2006 graduates employed in-state: 38%
2006 graduates employed in foreign countries: 0%
Number of states where graduates are employed: 32
Percentage of 2006 graduates working in: New England: 2%, Middle Atlantic: 0%, East North Central: 7%, West North Central: 2%, South Atlantic: 64%, East South Central: 9%, West South Central: 4%, Mountain: 9%, Pacific: 4%, Unknown: 0%

BAR PASSAGE RATES

Based on 2006 graduates taking Summer 2006 or Winter 2007 exams. Most of the school's first-time test takers took the bar in Virginia.

74%
School's bar passage rate for first-time test takers

74%
Statewide bar passage rate for first-time test takers

Roger Williams University

- 10 Metacom Avenue, Bristol, RI, 02809-5171
- http://law.rwu.edu
- Private
- Year founded: 1992
- 2007-2008 tuition: full-time: $1,050/credit hour; part-time: N/A
- Enrollment 2007-08 academic year: full-time: 556; part-time: 30
- U.S. News 2009 law specialty ranking: N/A

2.90-3.50 GPA, 25TH-75TH PERCENTILE

151-155 LSAT, 25TH-75TH PERCENTILE

57% ACCEPTANCE RATE

Tier 4 2009 U.S. NEWS LAW SCHOOL RANKING

ADMISSIONS

Admissions phone number: **(401) 254-4555**
Admissions email address: **Admissions@rwu.edu**
Application website: **http://law.rwu.edu/apply**
Application deadline for Fall 2009 admission: **03/15**

Admissions statistics:

Number of applicants for Fall 2007: **1,391**
Number of acceptances: **793**
Number enrolled: **192**
Acceptance rate: **57%**
GPA, 25th-75th percentile, entering class Fall 2007: **2.90-3.50**
LSAT, 25th-75th percentile, entering class Fall 2007: **151-155**

FINANCIAL AID

Financial aid phone number: **(401) 254-4641**
Financial aid application deadline: **03/15**
Tuition 2007-2008 academic year: full-time: **$1,050/credit hour**; part-time: **N/A**
Room and board: **N/A**; books: **N/A**; miscellaneous expenses: **N/A**
Total of room/board/books/miscellaneous expenses: **$20,144**
University offers graduate student housing for which law students are eligible.

Financial aid profile

Percent of students that received grants for the 2006-2007 academic year: full-time: **43%**; part-time **50%**
Median grant amount: full-time: **$11,000**; part-time: **$8,500**
The average law-school debt of those in the Class of 2007 who borrowed: **$99,573**. Proportion who borrowed: **90%**

ACADEMIC PROGRAMS

Calendar: **semester**
Joint degrees awarded: **J.D./M.M.A.; J.D./M.L.R.H.R.; J.D./M.S.C.J.**
Typical first-year section size: Full-time: **70**
Is there typically a "small section" of the first year class, other than Legal Writing, taught by full-time faculty?:
Full-time: **no**; Part-time: **no**
Number of course titles, beyond the first year curriculum, offered last year: **105**
Percentages of upper division course sections, excluding seminars, with an enrollment of:

Under 25: **50%**	25 to 49: **23%**
50 to 74: **20%**	75 to 99: **5%**
100+: **2%**	

Areas of specialization: appellate advocacy, clinical training, dispute resolution, environmental law, healthcare law, intellectual property law, international law, tax law, trial advocacy

Fall 2007 faculty profile

Total teaching faculty: **45**. Full-time: **58%**; **62%** men, **38%** women, **15%** minorities. Part-time: **42%**; **84%** men, **16%** women, **0%** minorities
Student-to-faculty ratio: **18.3**

SPECIAL PROGRAMS (as provided by law school):

RWU School of Law offers a rich environment of opportunities, including the Marine Affairs Institute and the Feinstein Institute; an honors program; clinics that include criminal defense and mediation; and study abroad in London and in Lisbon, Portugal. Joint-degree programs include J.D./Master of Marine Affairs and J.D./Master of Science in Criminal Justice.

STUDENT BODY

Fall 2007 full-time enrollment: 556

Men: **52%**	Women: **48%**
African-American: **3.1%**	American Indian: **0.7%**
Asian-American: **4.0%**	Mexican-American: **0.7%**
Puerto Rican: **0.7%**	Other Hisp-Amer: **2.9%**
White: **72.5%**	International: **0.5%**
Unknown: **14.9%**	

Fall 2007 part-time enrollment: 30

Men: **63%**	Women: **37%**
African-American: **3.3%**	American Indian: **0.0%**
Asian-American: **3.3%**	Mexican-American: **0.0%**

Puerto Rican: **0.0%** Other Hisp-Amer: **3.3%**
White: **66.7%** International: **0.0%**
Unknown: **23.3%**

Attrition rates for 2006-2007 full-time students
Percent of students discontinuing law school:
Men: **3%** Women: **4%**
First-year students: **9%** Second-year students: **1%**
Third-year students: **N/A**

LIBRARY RESOURCES
Total volumes: **299,744**
Total seats available for library users: **403**

INFORMATION TECHNOLOGY
Number of wired network connections available to students: **196** total (in the law library, excluding computer labs: **120**; in classrooms: **0**; in computer labs: **44**; elsewhere in the law school: **32**)
Law school has a wireless network.
Students are not required to own a computer.

EMPLOYMENT AND SALARIES
Proportion of 2006 graduates employed at graduation: **N/A**
Employed 9 months later, as of February 15, 2007: **84%**
Salaries in the private sector (law firms, business, industry): **$45,000–$70,000** (25th-75th percentile)
Median salary in the private sector: **$55,000**
Percentage in the private sector who reported salary information: **35%**
Median salary in public service (government, judicial clerkships, academic posts, non-profits): **$46,000**

Percentage of 2006 graduates in:
Law firms: **48%** Government: **8%**
Bus./industry: **18%** Judicial clerkship: **12%**
Public interest: **9%** Unknown: **2%**
Academia: **3%**

2006 graduates employed in-state: **37%**
2006 graduates employed in foreign countries: **0%**
Number of states where graduates are employed: **21**
Percentage of 2006 graduates working in: New England: **69%**, Middle Atlantic: **17%**, East North Central: **1%**, West North Central: **1%**, South Atlantic: **5%**, East South Central: **1%**, West South Central: **0%**, Mountain: **2%**, Pacific: **3%**, Unknown: **2%**

BAR PASSAGE RATES
Based on 2006 graduates taking Summer 2006 or Winter 2007 exams. Most of the school's first-time test takers took the bar in Massachusetts.

85%
School's bar passage rate for first-time test takers

86%
Statewide bar passage rate for first-time test takers

Rutgers State University—Camden

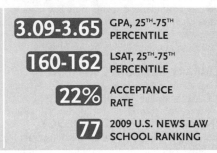

- 217 N. Fifth Street, Camden, NJ, 08102-1203
- http://www-camlaw.rutgers.edu
- Public
- Year founded: 1926
- 2007-2008 tuition: In-state: full-time: $21,488; part-time: $17,144; Out-of-state: full time: $30,492
- Enrollment 2007-08 academic year: full-time: 561; part-time: 229
- U.S. News 2009 law specialty ranking: N/A

3.09-3.65 GPA, 25TH-75TH PERCENTILE

160-162 LSAT, 25TH-75TH PERCENTILE

22% ACCEPTANCE RATE

77 2009 U.S. NEWS LAW SCHOOL RANKING

ADMISSIONS

Admissions phone number: **(800) 466-7561**
Admissions email address: **admissions@camlaw.rutgers.edu**
Application website:
http://www-camlaw.rutgers.edu/admissions/
Application deadline for Fall 2009 admission: **03/01**

Admissions statistics:
Number of applicants for Fall 2007: **2,173**
Number of acceptances: **488**
Number enrolled: **113**
Acceptance rate: **22%**
GPA, 25th-75th percentile, entering class Fall 2007: **3.09-3.65**
LSAT, 25th-75th percentile, entering class Fall 2007: **160-162**

Part-time program:
Number of applicants for Fall 2007: **2,173**
Number of acceptances: **169**
Number enrolled: **122**
Acceptance rate: **8%**
GPA, 25th-75th percentile, entering class Fall 2007: **3.02-3.64**
LSAT, 25th-75th percentile, entering class Fall 2007: **154-160**

FINANCIAL AID

Financial aid phone number: **(856) 225-6039**
Financial aid application deadline: **03/15**
Tuition 2007-2008 academic year: In-state: full-time: **$21,488**; part-time: **$17,144**; Out-of-state: full-time: **$30,492**
Room and board: **$10,683**; books: **$1,285**; miscellaneous expenses: **$1,795**
Total of room/board/books/miscellaneous expenses: **$13,763**
University offers graduate student housing for which law students are eligible.

Financial aid profile
Percent of students that received grants for the 2006-2007 academic year: full-time: **39%**; part-time **10%**
Median grant amount: full-time: **$4,500**; part-time: **$1,350**
The average law-school debt of those in the Class of 2007 who borrowed: **$71,113**. Proportion who borrowed: **89%**

ACADEMIC PROGRAMS

Calendar: **semester**
Joint degrees awarded: **J.D./M.B.A.; J.D./M.P.A.P.; J.D./M.S.W.; J.D./D.O.; J.D./M.D.; J.D./M.C.R.P.; J.D./M.P.A.**
Typical first-year section size: Full-time: **52**; Part-time: **54**
Is there typically a "small section" of the first year class, other than Legal Writing, taught by full-time faculty?: Full-time: **no**; Part-time: **no**
Number of course titles, beyond the first year curriculum, offered last year: **109**
Percentages of upper division course sections, excluding seminars, with an enrollment of:

Under 25: **60%**	25 to 49: **30%**
50 to 74: **6%**	75 to 99: **3%**
100+: **1%**	

Areas of specialization: appellate advocacy, clinical training, dispute resolution, environmental law, healthcare law, intellectual property law, international law, tax law, trial advocacy

Fall 2007 faculty profile
Total teaching faculty: **80**. Full-time: **50%**; **65%** men, **35%** women, **5%** minorities. Part-time: **50%**; **73%** men, **28%** women, **3%** minorities
Student-to-faculty ratio: **14.1**

SPECIAL PROGRAMS *(as provided by law school):*
Rutgers-Camden has special programs including business concentrations, outstanding externships, pro bono activities, and joint-degree programs. The legal writing program provides excellent communications skills. The Law School's clinical program enables students to learn lawyering skills in a variety of

areas. The school has one of the highest percentages of students obtaining judicial clerkships.

STUDENT BODY

Fall 2007 full-time enrollment: 561

Men: 58%	Women: 42%
African-American: 6.8%	American Indian: 0.2%
Asian-American: 8.6%	Mexican-American: 1.6%
Puerto Rican: 0.9%	Other Hisp-Amer: 6.1%
White: 75.6%	International: 0.4%
Unknown: 0.0%	

Fall 2007 part-time enrollment: 229

Men: 61%	Women: 39%
African-American: 3.1%	American Indian: 0.4%
Asian-American: 3.9%	Mexican-American: 0.0%
Puerto Rican: 0.0%	Other Hisp-Amer: 1.3%
White: 90.8%	International: 0.4%
Unknown: 0.0%	

Attrition rates for 2006-2007 full-time students
Percent of students discontinuing law school:

Men: 0%	Women: 0%
First-year students: 0%	Second-year students: N/A
Third-year students: 0%	

LIBRARY RESOURCES

Total volumes: 449,612
Total seats available for library users: 403

INFORMATION TECHNOLOGY

Number of wired network connections available to students: 170 total (in the law library, excluding computer labs: 60; in classrooms: 10; in computer labs: 50; elsewhere in the law school: 50)
Law school has a wireless network.
Students are required to own a computer.

EMPLOYMENT AND SALARIES

Proportion of 2006 graduates employed at graduation: 72%
Employed 9 months later, as of February 15, 2007: 92%
Salaries in the private sector (law firms, business, industry): $60,001–$115,000 (25th-75th percentile)
Median salary in the private sector: $100,000
Percentage in the private sector who reported salary information: 54%
Median salary in public service (government, judicial clerkships, academic posts, non-profits): $38,040

Percentage of 2006 graduates in:

Law firms: 41%	Government: 6%
Bus./industry: 8%	Judicial clerkship: 40%
Public interest: 2%	Unknown: 3%
Academia: 0%	

2006 graduates employed in-state: 61%
2006 graduates employed in foreign countries: 1%
Number of states where graduates are employed: 17
Percentage of 2006 graduates working in: New England: 1%, Middle Atlantic: 82%, East North Central: 1%, West North Central: 1%, South Atlantic: 6%, East South Central: 0%, West South Central: 1%, Mountain: 1%, Pacific: 4%, Unknown: 3%

BAR PASSAGE RATES

Based on 2006 graduates taking Summer 2006 or Winter 2007 exams. Most of the school's first-time test takers took the bar in New Jersey.

79%
School's bar passage rate for first-time test takers

79%
Statewide bar passage rate for first-time test takers

Rutgers State University—Newark

- 123 Washington Street, Newark, NJ, 07102
- http://law.newark.rutgers.edu
- Public
- **Year founded:** 1908
- **2007-2008 tuition:** In-state: full-time: $21,302; part-time: $13,803; Out-of-state: full-time: $30,307
- **Enrollment 2007-08 academic year:** full-time: 558; part-time: 260
- **U.S. News 2009 law specialty ranking:** clinical training: 28

3.08-3.55 GPA, 25TH-75TH PERCENTILE

155-161 LSAT, 25TH-75TH PERCENTILE

30% ACCEPTANCE RATE

77 2009 U.S. NEWS LAW SCHOOL RANKING

ADMISSIONS
Admissions phone number: **(973) 353-5554**
Admissions email address: **awalton@andromeda.rutgers.edu**
Application website:
http://law.newark.rutgers.edu/admissions.html
Application deadline for Fall 2009 admission: **03/15**

Admissions statistics:
Number of applicants for Fall 2007: **2,893**
Number of acceptances: **863**
Number enrolled: **195**
Acceptance rate: **30%**
GPA, 25th-75th percentile, entering class Fall 2007: **3.08-3.55**
LSAT, 25th-75th percentile, entering class Fall 2007: **155-161**

Part-time program:
Number of applicants for Fall 2007: **631**
Number of acceptances: **118**
Number enrolled: **67**
Acceptance rate: **19%**
GPA, 25th-75th percentile, entering class Fall 2007: **3.06-3.59**
LSAT, 25th-75th percentile, entering class Fall 2007: **153-158**

FINANCIAL AID
Financial aid phone number: **(973) 353-1702**
Financial aid application deadline: **03/01**
Tuition 2007-2008 academic year: In-state: full-time: **$21,302**; part-time: **$13,803**; Out-of-state: full-time: **$30,307**
Room and board: **$10,683**; books: **$1,285**; miscellaneous expenses: **$1,980**
Total of room/board/books/miscellaneous expenses: **$13,948**
University offers graduate student housing for which law students are eligible.

Financial aid profile
Percent of students that received grants for the 2006-2007 academic year: full-time: **46%**; part-time **15%**
Median grant amount: full-time: **$4,000**; part-time: **$4,000**
The average law-school debt of those in the Class of 2007 who borrowed: **$64,775.** Proportion who borrowed: **81%**

ACADEMIC PROGRAMS
Calendar: **semester**
Joint degrees awarded: **J.D./M.A.; J.D./M.C.R.P.; J.D./M.D.; J.D./Ph.D.; J.D./M.B.A.; J.D./M.S.W.**
Typical first-year section size: Full-time: **60**; Part-time: **70**
Is there typically a "small section" of the first year class, other than Legal Writing, taught by full-time faculty?: Full-time: **yes**; Part-time: **yes**
Number of course titles, beyond the first year curriculum, offered last year: **101**
Percentages of upper division course sections, excluding seminars, with an enrollment of:
Under 25: **47%**   25 to 49: **33%**
50 to 74: **12%**   75 to 99: **4%**
100+: **3%**
Areas of specialization: appellate advocacy, clinical training, dispute resolution, environmental law, healthcare law, intellectual property law, international law, tax law, trial advocacy

Fall 2007 faculty profile
Total teaching faculty: **63**. Full-time: **44%**; **64%** men, **36%** women, **21%** minorities. Part-time: **56%**; **74%** men, **26%** women, **6%** minorities
Student-to-faculty ratio: **14.8**

SPECIAL PROGRAMS *(as provided by law school)*:
Minority student program is a post-admissions program for students who, regardless of race or ethnicity, demonstrate educational, cultural, or socioeconomic disadvantage. The clinical

program, begun in 1970, offers faculty-supervised experience representing real clients. Eric Neisser public interest fellowships; summer placement; loan repayment program; externships including judicial, labor law.

STUDENT BODY

Fall 2007 full-time enrollment: 558

Men: 56%	Women: 44%
African-American: 13.4%	American Indian: 0.2%
Asian-American: 11.6%	Mexican-American: 2.2%
Puerto Rican: 2.7%	Other Hisp-Amer: 7.3%
White: 61.8%	International: 0.7%
Unknown: 0.0%	

Fall 2007 part-time enrollment: 260

Men: 58%	Women: 42%
African-American: 13.1%	American Indian: 0.4%
Asian-American: 12.7%	Mexican-American: 0.8%
Puerto Rican: 4.6%	Other Hisp-Amer: 5.4%
White: 60.0%	International: 3.1%
Unknown: 0.0%	

Attrition rates for 2006-2007 full-time students

Percent of students discontinuing law school:

Men: 3%	Women: 3%
First-year students: 6%	Second-year students: 3%
Third-year students: 1%	

LIBRARY RESOURCES

Total volumes: 533,200
Total seats available for library users: 522

INFORMATION TECHNOLOGY

Number of wired network connections available to students: 570 total (in the law library, excluding computer labs: 160; in classrooms: 350; in computer labs: 0; elsewhere in the law school: 60)
Law school has a wireless network.
Students are not required to own a computer.

EMPLOYMENT AND SALARIES

Proportion of 2006 graduates employed at graduation: 82%
Employed 9 months later, as of February 15, 2007: 95%
Salaries in the private sector (law firms, business, industry): $90,000–$145,000 (25th-75th percentile)
Median salary in the private sector: $115,000
Percentage in the private sector who reported salary information: 77%
Median salary in public service (government, judicial clerkships, academic posts, non-profits): $39,000

Percentage of 2006 graduates in:

Law firms: 45%	Government: 7%
Bus./industry: 14%	Judicial clerkship: 28%
Public interest: 3%	Unknown: 0%
Academia: 2%	

2006 graduates employed in-state: 63%
2006 graduates employed in foreign countries: 1%
Number of states where graduates are employed: 10
Percentage of 2006 graduates working in: New England: 1%, Middle Atlantic: 93%, East North Central: 1%, West North Central: 0%, South Atlantic: 4%, East South Central: 0%, West South Central: 0%, Mountain: 0%, Pacific: 1%, Unknown: 0%

BAR PASSAGE RATES

Based on 2006 graduates taking Summer 2006 or Winter 2007 exams. Most of the school's first-time test takers took the bar in New Jersey.

80%
School's bar passage rate for first-time test takers

79%
Statewide bar passage rate for first-time test takers

Samford University (Cumberland)

- 800 Lakeshore Drive, Birmingham, AL, 35229
- http://cumberland.samford.edu
- Private
- Year founded: 1847
- 2007-2008 tuition: full-time: $27,892; part-time: $16,740
- Enrollment 2007-08 academic year: full-time: 495
- U.S. News 2009 law specialty ranking: N/A

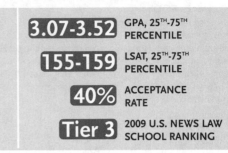

3.07-3.52 GPA, 25TH-75TH PERCENTILE

155-159 LSAT, 25TH-75TH PERCENTILE

40% ACCEPTANCE RATE

Tier 3 2009 U.S. NEWS LAW SCHOOL RANKING

ADMISSIONS

Admissions phone number: **(205) 726-2702**
Admissions email address: **law.admissions@samford.edu**
Application website:
http://cumberland.samford.edu/application
Application deadline for Fall 2009 admission: **05/01**

Admissions statistics:

Number of applicants for Fall 2007: **1,240**
Number of acceptances: **499**
Number enrolled: **159**
Acceptance rate: **40%**
GPA, 25th-75th percentile, entering class Fall 2007: **3.07-3.52**
LSAT, 25th-75th percentile, entering class Fall 2007: **155-159**

FINANCIAL AID

Financial aid phone number: **(205) 726-2905**
Financial aid application deadline: **03/01**
Tuition 2007-2008 academic year: full-time: **$27,892**; part-time: **$16,740**
Room and board: **$13,300**; books: **$1,550**; miscellaneous expenses: **$4,850**
Total of room/board/books/miscellaneous expenses: **$19,700**
University does not offer graduate student housing for which law students are eligible.

Financial aid profile

Percent of students that received grants for the 2006-2007 academic year: full-time: **36%**
Median grant amount: full-time: **$18,000**
The average law-school debt of those in the Class of 2007 who borrowed: **$94,263**. Proportion who borrowed: **85%**

ACADEMIC PROGRAMS

Calendar: **semester**
Joint degrees awarded: **J.D./M.P.H.; J.D./M.B.A.;**
J.D./M.Acc.; J.D./M.Div; J.D./M.S. Environmental Management; J.D./M.P.A.; J.D./M.T.S.
Typical first-year section size: Full-time: **56**
Is there typically a "small section" of the first year class, other than Legal Writing, taught by full-time faculty?: Full-time: **no**
Number of course titles, beyond the first year curriculum, offered last year: **96**
Percentages of upper division course sections, excluding seminars, with an enrollment of:

Under 25: **47%**	25 to 49: **36%**
50 to 74: **18%**	75 to 99: **0%**
100+: **0%**	

Areas of specialization: appellate advocacy, clinical training, dispute resolution, environmental law, healthcare law, intellectual property law, international law, tax law, trial advocacy

Fall 2007 faculty profile

Total teaching faculty: **49**. Full-time: **49%**; **75%** men, **25%** women, **13%** minorities. Part-time: **51%**; **72%** men, **28%** women, **4%** minorities
Student-to-faculty ratio: **17.6**

SPECIAL PROGRAMS (as provided by law school):

Semester-long and summer externships; judicial externships; trial advocacy and advanced trial advocacy program; the Center for Biotechnology, Law and Ethics; Cumberland Community Mediation Center; summer study-abroad program in Sidney-Sussex College in Cambridge, England.

STUDENT BODY

Fall 2007 full-time enrollment: 495

Men: **54%**	Women: **46%**
African-American: **7.3%**	American Indian: **0.8%**
Asian-American: **1.2%**	Mexican-American: **0.0%**
Puerto Rican: **0.0%**	Other Hisp-Amer: **1.4%**
White: **79.0%**	International: **0.0%**
Unknown: **10.3%**	

Attrition rates for 2006-2007 full-time students
Percent of students discontinuing law school:
Men: 3%   Women: 2%
First-year students: 7%   Second-year students: 1%
Third-year students: 1%

LIBRARY RESOURCES

Total volumes: 301,840
Total seats available for library users: 474

INFORMATION TECHNOLOGY

Number of wired network connections available to students: 200 total (in the law library, excluding computer labs: 200; in classrooms: 0; in computer labs: 0; elsewhere in the law school: 0)
Law school has a wireless network.
Students are not required to own a computer.

EMPLOYMENT AND SALARIES

Proportion of 2006 graduates employed at graduation: 66%
Employed 9 months later, as of February 15, 2007: 90%
Salaries in the private sector (law firms, business, industry): $50,000–$82,500 (25th-75th percentile)
Median salary in the private sector: $62,500
Percentage in the private sector who reported salary information: 49%
Median salary in public service (government, judicial clerkships, academic posts, non-profits): $40,000

Percentage of 2006 graduates in:
Law firms: 67%   Government: 14%
Bus./industry: 9%   Judicial clerkship: 7%
Public interest: 3%   Unknown: 0%
Academia: 0%

2006 graduates employed in-state: 55%
2006 graduates employed in foreign countries: 0%
Number of states where graduates are employed: 13
Percentage of 2006 graduates working in: New England: 0%, Middle Atlantic: 1%, East North Central: 0%, West North Central: 0%, South Atlantic: 32%, East South Central: 65%, West South Central: 1%, Mountain: 0%, Pacific: 1%, Unknown: 0%

BAR PASSAGE RATES

Based on 2006 graduates taking Summer 2006 or Winter 2007 exams. Most of the school's first-time test takers took the bar in Alabama.

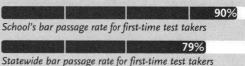

90%
School's bar passage rate for first-time test takers

79%
Statewide bar passage rate for first-time test takers

Santa Clara University

- 500 El Camino Real, Santa Clara, CA, 95053-0421
- http://www.scu.edu/law
- Private
- **Year founded:** 1851
- **2007-2008 tuition:** full-time: $1,175/credit hour; part-time: $1,175/credit hour
- **Enrollment 2007-08 academic year:** full-time: 728; part-time: 217
- **U.S. News 2009 law specialty ranking:** intellectual property law: 8

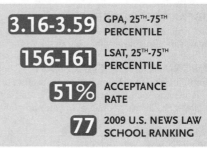

3.16-3.59 GPA, 25TH-75TH PERCENTILE

156-161 LSAT, 25TH-75TH PERCENTILE

51% ACCEPTANCE RATE

77 2009 U.S. NEWS LAW SCHOOL RANKING

ADMISSIONS
Admissions phone number: **(408) 554-4800**
Admissions email address: **lawadmissions@scu.edu**
Application website:
  http://www.scu.edu/law/admissions/how_to_apply.html
Application deadline for Fall 2009 admission: **02/01**

Admissions statistics:
Number of applicants for Fall 2007: **3,399**
Number of acceptances: **1,742**
Number enrolled: **241**
Acceptance rate: **51%**
GPA, 25th-75th percentile, entering class Fall 2007: **3.16-3.59**
LSAT, 25th-75th percentile, entering class Fall 2007: **156-161**

Part-time program:
Number of applicants for Fall 2007: **318**
Number of acceptances: **146**
Number enrolled: **85**
Acceptance rate: **46%**
GPA, 25th-75th percentile, entering class Fall 2007: **3.28-3.48**
LSAT, 25th-75th percentile, entering class Fall 2007: **153-158**

FINANCIAL AID
Financial aid phone number: **(408) 554-4447**
Financial aid application deadline: **03/01**
Tuition 2007-2008 academic year: full-time: **$1,175/credit hour**; part-time: **$1,175/credit hour**
Room and board: **$12,528**; books: **$674**; miscellaneous expenses: **$6,376**
Total of room/board/books/miscellaneous expenses: **$19,578**
University offers graduate student housing for which law students are eligible.

Financial aid profile
Percent of students that received grants for the 2006-2007 academic year: full-time: **40%**; part-time **25%**

Median grant amount: full-time: **$10,000**; part-time: **$8,000**
The average law-school debt of those in the Class of 2007 who borrowed: **$98,307**. Proportion who borrowed: **76%**

ACADEMIC PROGRAMS
Calendar: **semester**
Joint degrees awarded: **J.D./M.B.A.**
Typical first-year section size: Full-time: **78**; Part-time: **52**
Is there typically a "small section" of the first year class, other than Legal Writing, taught by full-time faculty?: Full-time: **yes**; Part-time: **no**
Number of course titles, beyond the first year curriculum, offered last year: **186**
Percentages of upper division course sections, excluding seminars, with an enrollment of:

Under 25: **69%**	25 to 49: **19%**
50 to 74: **9%**	75 to 99: **4%**
100+: **0%**	

Areas of specialization: appellate advocacy, clinical training, dispute resolution, environmental law, healthcare law, intellectual property law, international law, tax law, trial advocacy

Fall 2007 faculty profile
Total teaching faculty: **76**. Full-time: **59%**; **51%** men, **49%** women, **27%** minorities. Part-time: **41%**; **58%** men, **42%** women, **13%** minorities
Student-to-faculty ratio: **15.9**

SPECIAL PROGRAMS *(as provided by law school):*
The Center for Social Justice and Public Service, the Northern California Innocence Project, and the Alexander Community Law Center offer innovative courses and clinics under the supervision of experienced attorneys. The high-tech law curriculum is one of the richest in the nation. The Center for Global Law and Policy offers 13 summer study-abroad programs, most of which include field placement.

STUDENT BODY

Fall 2007 full-time enrollment: 728

Men: 52%	Women: 48%
African-American: 4.0%	American Indian: 0.1%
Asian-American: 26.1%	Mexican-American: 0.0%
Puerto Rican: 0.0%	Other Hisp-Amer: 8.7%
White: 60.4%	International: 0.5%
Unknown: 0.1%	

Fall 2007 part-time enrollment: 217

Men: 62%	Women: 38%
African-American: 6.0%	American Indian: 0.9%
Asian-American: 31.8%	Mexican-American: 0.0%
Puerto Rican: 0.0%	Other Hisp-Amer: 9.2%
White: 52.1%	International: 0.0%
Unknown: 0.0%	

Attrition rates for 2006-2007 full-time students
Percent of students discontinuing law school:

Men: 4%	Women: 6%
First-year students: 15%	Second-year students: 1%
Third-year students: N/A	

LIBRARY RESOURCES

Total volumes: 369,154
Total seats available for library users: 448

INFORMATION TECHNOLOGY

Number of wired network connections available to students: 707 total (in the law library, excluding computer labs: 257; in classrooms: 427; in computer labs: 0; elsewhere in the law school: 23)
Law school has a wireless network.
Students are not required to own a computer.

EMPLOYMENT AND SALARIES

Proportion of 2006 graduates employed at graduation: 72%

Employed 9 months later, as of February 15, 2007: 93%
Salaries in the private sector (law firms, business, industry): $70,000–$135,000 (25th-75th percentile)
Median salary in the private sector: $110,000
Percentage in the private sector who reported salary information: 78%
Median salary in public service (government, judicial clerkships, academic posts, non-profits): $52,000

Percentage of 2006 graduates in:

Law firms: 52%	Government: 9%
Bus./industry: 27%	Judicial clerkship: 1%
Public interest: 3%	Unknown: 7%
Academia: 1%	

2006 graduates employed in-state: 92%
2006 graduates employed in foreign countries: 1%
Number of states where graduates are employed: 12
Percentage of 2006 graduates working in: New England: 0%, Middle Atlantic: 0%, East North Central: 0%, West North Central: 0%, South Atlantic: 2%, East South Central: 0%, West South Central: 0%, Mountain: 2%, Pacific: 95%, Unknown: 0%

BAR PASSAGE RATES

Based on 2006 graduates taking Summer 2006 or Winter 2007 exams. Most of the school's first-time test takers took the bar in California.

77%
School's bar passage rate for first-time test takers

65%
Statewide bar passage rate for first-time test takers

Seattle University

- 901 12th Avenue, Seattle, WA, 98122-1090
- http://www.law.seattleu.edu
- Private
- **Year founded:** 1972
- **2007-2008 tuition:** full-time: $29,938; part-time: $19,958
- **Enrollment 2007-08 academic year:** full-time: 845; part-time: 226
- **U.S. News 2009 law specialty ranking:** N/A

3.17-3.62 GPA, 25TH-75TH PERCENTILE

155-161 LSAT, 25TH-75TH PERCENTILE

28% ACCEPTANCE RATE

82 2009 U.S. NEWS LAW SCHOOL RANKING

ADMISSIONS

Admissions phone number: (206) 398-4200
Admissions email address: **lawadmin@seattleu.edu**
Application website:
http://www.law.seattleu.edu/admission/admissionapp.asp
Application deadline for Fall 2009 admission: **03/01**

Admissions statistics:
Number of applicants for Fall 2007: **2,919**
Number of acceptances: **822**
Number enrolled: **252**
Acceptance rate: **28%**
GPA, 25th-75th percentile, entering class Fall 2007: **3.17-3.62**
LSAT, 25th-75th percentile, entering class Fall 2007: **155-161**

Part-time program:
Number of applicants for Fall 2007: **265**
Number of acceptances: **98**
Number enrolled: **70**
Acceptance rate: **37%**
GPA, 25th-75th percentile, entering class Fall 2007: **3.04-3.46**
LSAT, 25th-75th percentile, entering class Fall 2007: **154-161**

FINANCIAL AID

Financial aid phone number: (206) 398-4250
Financial aid application deadline: **N/A**
Tuition 2007-2008 academic year: full-time: **$29,938**; part-time: **$19,958**
Room and board: **$10,575**; books: **$1,258**; miscellaneous expenses: **$4,486**
Total of room/board/books/miscellaneous expenses: **$16,319**
University offers graduate student housing for which law students are eligible.

Financial aid profile
Percent of students that received grants for the 2006-2007

academic year: full-time: **56%**; part-time **29%**
Median grant amount: full-time: **$7,000**; part-time: **$7,000**
The average law-school debt of those in the Class of 2007 who borrowed: **$86,253**. Proportion who borrowed: **91%**

ACADEMIC PROGRAMS

Calendar: **semester**
Joint degrees awarded: **J.D./M.B.A.; J.D./M.I.B.; J.D./M.S.F.; J.D./M.Acc.; J.D./M.P.A.; J.D./M.S.A.L.**
Typical first-year section size: Full-time: **86**; Part-time: **63**
Is there typically a "small section" of the first year class, other than Legal Writing, taught by full-time faculty?: Full-time: **no**; Part-time: **no**
Number of course titles, beyond the first year curriculum, offered last year: **161**
Percentages of upper division course sections, excluding seminars, with an enrollment of:
Under 25: **55%**   25 to 49: **26%**
50 to 74: **12%**   75 to 99: **4%**
100+: **3%**
Areas of specialization: appellate advocacy, clinical training, dispute resolution, environmental law, healthcare law, intellectual property law, international law, tax law, trial advocacy

Fall 2007 faculty profile
Total teaching faculty: **105**. Full-time: **57%**; 57% men, 43% women, 25% minorities. Part-time: **43%**; 73% men, 27% women, 13% minorities
Student-to-faculty ratio: **14.4**

SPECIAL PROGRAMS *(as provided by law school):*

Clinics: administrative; arts legal; bankruptcy; community development; family law; immigration; human rights; predatory lending; trusts and estates; youth advocacy. Centers/institutes: Academic Resource; Access to Justice; Corporations, Law and Society; Global Justice; Indian Estate Planning and Probate. Summer study in Brazil and South Africa; international public interest internships.

STUDENT BODY

Fall 2007 full-time enrollment: 845

Men: 47%	Women: 53%
African-American: 3.3%	American Indian: 1.1%
Asian-American: 15.6%	Mexican-American: 3.2%
Puerto Rican: 0.6%	Other Hisp-Amer: 2.7%
White: 68.2%	International: 1.4%
Unknown: 3.9%	

Fall 2007 part-time enrollment: 226

Men: 51%	Women: 49%
African-American: 3.1%	American Indian: 2.7%
Asian-American: 12.8%	Mexican-American: 0.9%
Puerto Rican: 0.0%	Other Hisp-Amer: 1.3%
White: 72.6%	International: 0.4%
Unknown: 6.2%	

Attrition rates for 2006-2007 full-time students
Percent of students discontinuing law school:

Men: 4%	Women: 1%
First-year students: 6%	Second-year students: 3%
Third-year students: N/A	

LIBRARY RESOURCES

Total volumes: 377,397
Total seats available for library users: 429

INFORMATION TECHNOLOGY

Number of wired network connections available to students: **2,116** total (in the law library, excluding computer labs: **367**; in classrooms: **665**; in computer labs: **0**; elsewhere in the law school: **1,084**)
Law school has a wireless network.
Students are required to own a computer.

EMPLOYMENT AND SALARIES

Proportion of 2006 graduates employed at graduation: 67%

Employed 9 months later, as of February 15, 2007: **99%**
Salaries in the private sector (law firms, business, industry): **$45,000–$90,000** (25th-75th percentile)
Median salary in the private sector: **$67,500**
Percentage in the private sector who reported salary information: **13%**
Median salary in public service (government, judicial clerkships, academic posts, non-profits): **$45,000**

Percentage of 2006 graduates in:

Law firms: 43%	Government: 15%
Bus./industry: 30%	Judicial clerkship: 3%
Public interest: 7%	Unknown: 0%
Academia: 2%	

2006 graduates employed in-state: **85%**
2006 graduates employed in foreign countries: **2%**
Number of states where graduates are employed: **17**
Percentage of 2006 graduates working in: New England: **1%**, Middle Atlantic: **2%**, East North Central: **1%**, West North Central: **0%**, South Atlantic: **2%**, East South Central: **0%**, West South Central: **0%**, Mountain: **3%**, Pacific: **90%**, Unknown: **0%**

BAR PASSAGE RATES

Based on 2006 graduates taking Summer 2006 or Winter 2007 exams. Most of the school's first-time test takers took the bar in Washington.

82%	
School's bar passage rate for first-time test takers	
82%	
Statewide bar passage rate for first-time test takers	

Seton Hall University

- 1 Newark Center, Newark, NJ, 07102-5210
- http://law.shu.edu
- Private
- Year founded: 1951
- 2007-2008 tuition: full-time: $38,040; part-time: $28,725
- Enrollment 2007-08 academic year: full-time: 722; part-time: 342
- U.S. News 2009 law specialty ranking: healthcare law: 4

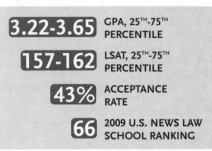

3.22-3.65 GPA, 25TH-75TH PERCENTILE

157-162 LSAT, 25TH-75TH PERCENTILE

43% ACCEPTANCE RATE

66 2009 U.S. NEWS LAW SCHOOL RANKING

ADMISSIONS
Admissions phone number: **(888) 415-7271**
Admissions email address: **admitme@shu.edu**
Application website:
   http://www4.lsac.org/school/setonHall.htm
Application deadline for Fall 2009 admission: **04/01**

Admissions statistics:
Number of applicants for Fall 2007: **2,638**
Number of acceptances: **1,125**
Number enrolled: **214**
Acceptance rate: **43%**
GPA, 25th-75th percentile, entering class Fall 2007: **3.22-3.65**
LSAT, 25th-75th percentile, entering class Fall 2007: **157-162**

Part-time program:
Number of applicants for Fall 2007: **571**
Number of acceptances: **392**
Number enrolled: **151**
Acceptance rate: **69%**
GPA, 25th-75th percentile, entering class Fall 2007: **3.02-3.57**
LSAT, 25th-75th percentile, entering class Fall 2007: **151-155**

FINANCIAL AID
Financial aid phone number: **(973) 642-8850**
Financial aid application deadline: **04/01**
Tuition 2007-2008 academic year: full-time: **$38,040**; part-time: **$28,725**
Room and board: **$12,150**; books: **$1,000**; miscellaneous expenses: **$4,140**
Total of room/board/books/miscellaneous expenses: **$17,290**
University offers graduate student housing for which law students are eligible.

Financial aid profile
Percent of students that received grants for the 2006-2007 academic year: full-time: **42%**; part-time **9%**

Median grant amount: full-time: **$17,500**; part-time: **$3,500**
The average law-school debt of those in the Class of 2007 who borrowed: **$91,500**. Proportion who borrowed: **88%**

ACADEMIC PROGRAMS
Calendar: **semester**
Joint degrees awarded: **J.D./M.B.A.; J.D./M.D.; M.S.J./M.D.; J.D./M.A.D.I.R.**
Typical first-year section size: Full-time: **70**; Part-time: **110**
Is there typically a "small section" of the first year class, other than Legal Writing, taught by full-time faculty?: Full-time: **no**; Part-time: **no**
Number of course titles, beyond the first year curriculum, offered last year: **137**
Percentages of upper division course sections, excluding seminars, with an enrollment of:

Under 25: **51%**	25 to 49: **29%**	
50 to 74: **14%**	75 to 99: **6%**	
100+: **0%**		

Areas of specialization: appellate advocacy, clinical training, dispute resolution, environmental law, healthcare law, intellectual property law, international law, tax law, trial advocacy

Fall 2007 faculty profile
Total teaching faculty: **265**. Full-time: **36%**; **66%** men, **34%** women, **17%** minorities. Part-time: **64%**; **69%** men, **31%** women, **8%** minorities
Student-to-faculty ratio: **15.4**

SPECIAL PROGRAMS *(as provided by law school):*
The Center for Social Justice represents disadvantaged clients in diverse legal matters. A J.D. concentration and LL.M. in Health Law are available through the health law and policy program. Students may pursue a J.D. concentration in intellectual property through the Institute of Law, Science and Technology. For-credit internships in state, federal, and international courts and agencies.

STUDENT BODY

Fall 2007 full-time enrollment: 722
Men: 58%   Women: 42%
African-American: 1.8%   American Indian: 0.1%
Asian-American: 6.0%   Mexican-American: 0.0%
Puerto Rican: 0.0%   Other Hisp-Amer: 2.5%
White: 88.0%   International: 1.7%
Unknown: 0.0%

Fall 2007 part-time enrollment: 342
Men: 54%   Women: 46%
African-American: 4.7%   American Indian: 0.3%
Asian-American: 8.2%   Mexican-American: 0.0%
Puerto Rican: 0.0%   Other Hisp-Amer: 8.8%
White: 75.1%   International: 2.9%
Unknown: 0.0%

Attrition rates for 2006-2007 full-time students
Percent of students discontinuing law school:
Men: 5%   Women: 4%
First-year students: 12%   Second-year students: 1%
Third-year students: 1%

LIBRARY RESOURCES

Total volumes: 454,534
Total seats available for library users: 564

INFORMATION TECHNOLOGY

Number of wired network connections available to students: 126 total (in the law library, excluding computer labs: 72; in classrooms: 18; in computer labs: 18; elsewhere in the law school: 18)
Law school has a wireless network.
Students are required to own a computer.

EMPLOYMENT AND SALARIES

Proportion of 2006 graduates employed at graduation: 90%

Employed 9 months later, as of February 15, 2007: 98%
Salaries in the private sector (law firms, business, industry): $55,000–$105,000 (25th-75th percentile)
Median salary in the private sector: $70,000
Percentage in the private sector who reported salary information: 55%
Median salary in public service (government, judicial clerkships, academic posts, non-profits): $38,038

Percentage of 2006 graduates in:
Law firms: 39%   Government: 7%
Bus./industry: 16%   Judicial clerkship: 33%
Public interest: 1%   Unknown: 2%
Academia: 1%

2006 graduates employed in-state: 70%
2006 graduates employed in foreign countries: 0%
Number of states where graduates are employed: 15
Percentage of 2006 graduates working in: New England: 1%, Middle Atlantic: 85%, East North Central: 0%, West North Central: N/A, South Atlantic: 4%, East South Central: N/A, West South Central: 1%, Mountain: 1%, Pacific: 0%, Unknown: 8%

BAR PASSAGE RATES

Based on 2006 graduates taking Summer 2006 or Winter 2007 exams. Most of the school's first-time test takers took the bar in New Jersey.

85%
School's bar passage rate for first-time test takers

79%
Statewide bar passage rate for first-time test takers

South Texas College of Law

- 1303 San Jacinto Street, Houston, TX, 77002-7000
- http://www.stcl.edu
- Private
- **Year founded:** 1923
- **2007-2008 tuition:** full-time: $23,610; part-time: $15,940
- **Enrollment 2007-08 academic year:** full-time: 936; part-time: 316
- **U.S. News 2009 law specialty ranking:** trial advocacy: 6

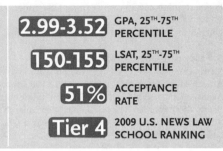

2.99-3.52 GPA, 25TH-75TH PERCENTILE

150-155 LSAT, 25TH-75TH PERCENTILE

51% ACCEPTANCE RATE

Tier 4 2009 U.S. NEWS LAW SCHOOL RANKING

ADMISSIONS
Admissions phone number: **(713) 646-1810**
Admissions email address: **admissions@stcl.edu**
Application website: **http://www.stcl.edu**
Application deadline for Fall 2009 admission: **02/15**

Admissions statistics:
Number of applicants for Fall 2007: **1,991**
Number of acceptances: **1,006**
Number enrolled: **352**
Acceptance rate: **51%**
GPA, 25th-75th percentile, entering class Fall 2007: **2.99-3.52**
LSAT, 25th-75th percentile, entering class Fall 2007: **150-155**

Part-time program:
Number of applicants for Fall 2007: **339**
Number of acceptances: **163**
Number enrolled: **102**
Acceptance rate: **48%**
GPA, 25th-75th percentile, entering class Fall 2007: **2.70-3.40**
LSAT, 25th-75th percentile, entering class Fall 2007: **149-154**

FINANCIAL AID
Financial aid phone number: **(713) 646-1820**
Financial aid application deadline: **05/01**
Tuition 2007-2008 academic year: full-time: **$23,610**; part-time: **$15,940**
Room and board: **$9,000**; books: **$1,700**; miscellaneous expenses: **$6,000**
Total of room/board/books/miscellaneous expenses: **$16,700**
University does not offer graduate student housing for which law students are eligible.

Financial aid profile
Percent of students that received grants for the 2006-2007 academic year: full-time: **34%**; part-time **19%**

Median grant amount: full-time: **$2,040**; part-time: **$1,503**
The average law-school debt of those in the Class of 2007 who borrowed: **$72,381**. Proportion who borrowed: **88%**

ACADEMIC PROGRAMS
Calendar: **semester**
Joint degrees awarded: **J.D./M.B.A.**
Typical first-year section size: Full-time: **95**; Part-time: **60**
Is there typically a "small section" of the first year class, other than Legal Writing, taught by full-time faculty?: Full-time: **no**; Part-time: **no**
Number of course titles, beyond the first year curriculum, offered last year: **120**
Percentages of upper division course sections, excluding seminars, with an enrollment of:
Under 25: **60%**   25 to 49: **18%**
50 to 74: **10%**   75 to 99: **11%**
100+: **0%**
Areas of specialization: appellate advocacy, clinical training, dispute resolution, environmental law, healthcare law, intellectual property law, international law, tax law, trial advocacy

Fall 2007 faculty profile
Total teaching faculty: **119**. Full-time: **46%**; **64%** men, **36%** women, **11%** minorities. Part-time: **54%**; **72%** men, **28%** women, **11%** minorities
Student-to-faculty ratio: **20.4**

SPECIAL PROGRAMS *(as provided by law school)*:
Development of strong legal skills is important at South Texas, as evidenced by its nationally recognized advocacy program and its other three centers of excellence. South Texas offers numerous off-site clinics, placing students in the real world of lawyering. For students interested in the increased globalization of law, South Texas offers a wide variety of foreign programs throughout the year.

STUDENT BODY
Fall 2007 full-time enrollment: 936
Men: **54%**   Women: **46%**

African-American: **1.8%**
Asian-American: **11.0%**
Puerto Rican: **0.3%**
White: **77.8%**
Unknown: **0.0%**

American Indian: **0.6%**
Mexican-American: **4.2%**
Other Hisp-Amer: **4.0%**
International: **0.3%**

Fall 2007 part-time enrollment: **316**
Men: **57%**
African-American: **9.5%**
Asian-American: **12.0%**
Puerto Rican: **0.0%**
White: **67.7%**
Unknown: **0.0%**

Women: **43%**
American Indian: **1.9%**
Mexican-American: **4.4%**
Other Hisp-Amer: **4.1%**
International: **0.3%**

Attrition rates for 2006-2007 full-time students
Percent of students discontinuing law school:
Men: **3%**
First-year students: **6%**
Third-year students: **N/A**

Women: **4%**
Second-year students: **1%**

LIBRARY RESOURCES
Total volumes: **523,272**
Total seats available for library users: **877**

INFORMATION TECHNOLOGY
Number of wired network connections available to students: **1,150** total (in the law library, excluding computer labs: **1,100**; in classrooms: **0**; in computer labs: **0**; elsewhere in the law school: **50**)
Law school has a wireless network.
Students are not required to own a computer.

EMPLOYMENT AND SALARIES
Proportion of 2006 graduates employed at graduation: **N/A**
Employed 9 months later, as of February 15, 2007: **78%**

Salaries in the private sector (law firms, business, industry): **$70,000–$135,000** (25th-75th percentile)
Median salary in the private sector: **$79,000**
Percentage in the private sector who reported salary information: **44%**
Median salary in public service (government, judicial clerkships, academic posts, non-profits): **$46,125**

Percentage of 2006 graduates in:
Law firms: **63%**
Bus./industry: **16%**
Public interest: **2%**
Academia: **1%**

Government: **11%**
Judicial clerkship: **3%**
Unknown: **4%**

2006 graduates employed in-state: **95%**
2006 graduates employed in foreign countries: **1%**
Number of states where graduates are employed: **7**
Percentage of 2006 graduates working in: New England: **N/A**, Middle Atlantic: **N/A**, East North Central: **1%**, West North Central: **N/A**, South Atlantic: **1%**, East South Central: **N/A**, West South Central: **95%**, Mountain: **1%**, Pacific: **N/A**, Unknown: **1%**

BAR PASSAGE RATES
Based on 2006 graduates taking Summer 2006 or Winter 2007 exams. Most of the school's first-time test takers took the bar in Texas.

82%
School's bar passage rate for first-time test takers

82%
Statewide bar passage rate for first-time test takers

Southern Illinois Univ.—Carbondale

■ Lesar Law Building, Carbondale, IL, 62901
■ http://www.law.siu.edu
■ Public
■ Year founded: 1973
■ 2007-2008 tuition: In-state: full-time: $12,265; part-time: N/A; Out-of-state: full-time: $29,185
■ Enrollment 2007-08 academic year: full-time: 352; part-time: 2
■ U.S. News 2009 law specialty ranking: N/A

2.90-3.60 GPA, 25TH-75TH PERCENTILE

151-156 LSAT, 25TH-75TH PERCENTILE

52% ACCEPTANCE RATE

Tier 4 2009 U.S. NEWS LAW SCHOOL RANKING

ADMISSIONS
Admissions phone number: **(800) 739-9187**
Admissions email address: **lawadmit@siu.edu**
Application website: **http://www.law.siu.edu**
Application deadline for Fall 2009 admission: **03/01**

Admissions statistics:
Number of applicants for Fall 2007: **660**
Number of acceptances: **343**
Number enrolled: **135**
Acceptance rate: **52%**
GPA, 25th-75th percentile, entering class Fall 2007: **2.90-3.60**
LSAT, 25th-75th percentile, entering class Fall 2007: **151-156**

FINANCIAL AID
Financial aid phone number: **(618) 453-4334**
Financial aid application deadline: **04/01**
Tuition 2007-2008 academic year: In-state: full-time: **$12,265**; part-time: **N/A**; Out-of-state: full-time: **$29,185**
Room and board: **$8,800**; books: **$1,150**; miscellaneous expenses: **$2,435**
Total of room/board/books/miscellaneous expenses: **$12,385**
University offers graduate student housing for which law students are eligible.

Financial aid profile
Percent of students that received grants for the 2006-2007 academic year: full-time: **53%**
Median grant amount: full-time: **$6,000**
The average law-school debt of those in the Class of 2007 who borrowed: **$52,167**. Proportion who borrowed: **91%**

ACADEMIC PROGRAMS
Calendar: **semester**
Joint degrees awarded: **J.D./M.B.A.; J.D./M.Acc; J.D./M.P.A.; J.D./M.D.; J.D./Ph.D; J.D./M.S.W.; J.D./M.S.Ed.; J.D./ECE**
Typical first-year section size: Full-time: **60**

Is there typically a "small section" of the first year class, other than Legal Writing, taught by full-time faculty?: Full-time: **no**
Number of course titles, beyond the first year curriculum, offered last year: **82**
Percentages of upper division course sections, excluding seminars, with an enrollment of:
Under 25: **69%**　　25 to 49: **20%**
50 to 74: **8%**　　75 to 99: **3%**
100+: **0%**
Areas of specialization: appellate advocacy, clinical training, dispute resolution, environmental law, healthcare law, intellectual property law, international law, tax law, trial advocacy

Fall 2007 faculty profile
Total teaching faculty: **39**. Full-time: **74%**; **59%** men, **41%** women, **7%** minorities. Part-time: **26%**; **70%** men, **30%** women, **0%** minorities
Student-to-faculty ratio: **11.7**

SPECIAL PROGRAMS (as provided by law school):
Two in-house clinics: civil practice/elder law and domestic violence. Externships in public interest offices (legal services, prosecutors, public defenders, judges, local and state agencies). Other programs: Center for Health Law and Policy and the Self Help Legal Center.

STUDENT BODY
Fall 2007 full-time enrollment: 352
Men: **63%**　　　　　　Women: **38%**
African-American: **4.0%**　　American Indian: **0.0%**
Asian-American: **3.1%**　　Mexican-American: **0.6%**
Puerto Rican: **0.6%**　　Other Hisp-Amer: **0.9%**
White: **80.4%**　　　　International: **0.0%**
Unknown: **10.5%**

Fall 2007 part-time enrollment: 2
Men: **100%**　　　　　Women: **0%**
African-American: **0.0%**　　American Indian: **0.0%**

Asian-American: **0.0%** Mexican-American: **0.0%**
Puerto Rican: **0.0%** Other Hisp-Amer: **0.0%**
White: **100.0%** International: **0.0%**
Unknown: **0.0%**

Attrition rates for 2006-2007 full-time students
Percent of students discontinuing law school:
Men: **6%** Women: **7%**
First-year students: **16%** Second-year students: **2%**
Third-year students: **1%**

LIBRARY RESOURCES
Total volumes: **408,628**
Total seats available for library users: **349**

INFORMATION TECHNOLOGY
Number of wired network connections available to students: **14** total (in the law library, excluding computer labs: **3**; in classrooms: **0**; in computer labs: **0**; elsewhere in the law school: **11**)
Law school has a wireless network.
Students are not required to own a computer.

EMPLOYMENT AND SALARIES
Proportion of 2006 graduates employed at graduation: **N/A**
Employed 9 months later, as of February 15, 2007: **85%**
Salaries in the private sector (law firms, business, industry): **$38,000–$61,000** (25th-75th percentile)
Median salary in the private sector: **$46,250**
Percentage in the private sector who reported salary information: **100%**
Median salary in public service (government, judicial clerkships, academic posts, non-profits): **$36,500**

Percentage of 2006 graduates in:
Law firms: **61%** Government: **20%**
Bus./industry: **9%** Judicial clerkship: **1%**
Public interest: **9%** Unknown: **0%**
Academia: **0**

2006 graduates employed in-state: **77%**
2006 graduates employed in foreign countries: **0%**
Number of states where graduates are employed: **10**
Percentage of 2006 graduates working in: New England: **N/A**, Middle Atlantic: **N/A**, East North Central: **82%**, West North Central: **6%**, South Atlantic: **5%**, East South Central: **6%**, West South Central: **N/A**, Mountain: **N/A**, Pacific: **1%**, Unknown: **0%**

BAR PASSAGE RATES
Based on 2006 graduates taking Summer 2006 or Winter 2007 exams. Most of the school's first-time test takers took the bar in Illinois.

86%
School's bar passage rate for first-time test takers

87%
Statewide bar passage rate for first-time test takers

Southern Methodist University

- PO Box 750116, Dallas, TX, 75275-0116
- http://www.law.smu.edu
- Private
- Year founded: 1911
- 2007-2008 tuition: full-time: $34,576; part-time: $25,932
- Enrollment 2007-08 academic year: full-time: 562; part-time: 425
- U.S. News 2009 law specialty ranking: tax law: 22

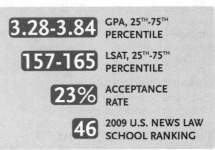

3.28-3.84 GPA, 25TH-75TH PERCENTILE

157-165 LSAT, 25TH-75TH PERCENTILE

23% ACCEPTANCE RATE

46 2009 U.S. NEWS LAW SCHOOL RANKING

ADMISSIONS

Admissions phone number: **(214) 768-2550**
Admissions email address: **lawadmit@mail.smu.edu**
Application website: **N/A**
Application deadline for Fall 2009 admission: **02/15**

Admissions statistics:

Number of applicants for Fall 2007: **2,113**
Number of acceptances: **483**
Number enrolled: **177**
Acceptance rate: **23%**
GPA, 25th-75th percentile, entering class Fall 2007: **3.28-3.84**
LSAT, 25th-75th percentile, entering class Fall 2007: **157-165**

Part-time program:

Number of applicants for Fall 2007: **552**
Number of acceptances: **152**
Number enrolled: **105**
Acceptance rate: **28%**
GPA, 25th-75th percentile, entering class Fall 2007: **3.09-3.69**
LSAT, 25th-75th percentile, entering class Fall 2007: **152-160**

FINANCIAL AID

Financial aid phone number: **(214) 768-4119**
Financial aid application deadline: **04/01**
Tuition 2007-2008 academic year: full-time: **$34,576**; part-time: **$25,932**
Room and board: **$14,400**; books: **$1,900**; miscellaneous expenses: **$2,700**
Total of room/board/books/miscellaneous expenses: **$19,000**
University offers graduate student housing for which law students are eligible.

Financial aid profile

Percent of students that received grants for the 2006-2007 academic year: full-time: **92%**; part-time **8%**

Median grant amount: full-time: **$8,500**; part-time: **$3,000**
The average law-school debt of those in the Class of 2007 who borrowed: **$75,831**. Proportion who borrowed: **78%**

ACADEMIC PROGRAMS

Calendar: **semester**
Joint degrees awarded: **J.D./M.B.A.**
Typical first-year section size: Full-time: **97**; Part-time: **94**
Is there typically a "small section" of the first year class, other than Legal Writing, taught by full-time faculty?: Full-time: **no**; Part-time: **no**
Number of course titles, beyond the first year curriculum, offered last year: **117**
Percentages of upper division course sections, excluding seminars, with an enrollment of:

Under 25: **52%**	25 to 49: **26%**
50 to 74: **9%**	75 to 99: **12%**
100+: **1%**	

Areas of specialization: appellate advocacy, clinical training, dispute resolution, environmental law, healthcare law, intellectual property law, international law, tax law, trial advocacy

Fall 2007 faculty profile

Total teaching faculty: **97**. Full-time: **49%**; **67%** men, **33%** women, **21%** minorities. Part-time: **51%**; **78%** men, **22%** women, **N/A** minorities
Student-to-faculty ratio: **14.7**

SPECIAL PROGRAMS *(as provided by law school):*

Criminal, consumer, civil, child advocacy, taxpayers clinics. Criminal clinic is joint with the Dallas County district attorney to provide legal service to indigent individuals. Students choose faculty-approved externship in state and federal courts; local, state, and federal agencies; and various legal departments. There is a seven-week summer session and the summer program in Oxford, England.

STUDENT BODY

Fall 2007 full-time enrollment: **562**

Men: **52%**	Women: **48%**

African-American: 3.6% American Indian: 0.2%
Asian-American: 10.9% Mexican-American: 0.5%
Puerto Rican: 0.2% Other Hisp-Amer: 7.8%
White: 76.3% International: 0.4%
Unknown: 0.2%

Fall 2007 part-time enrollment: 425
Men: 58% Women: 42%
African-American: 4.5% American Indian: 0.9%
Asian-American: 8.7% Mexican-American: 0.7%
Puerto Rican: 0.0% Other Hisp-Amer: 7.3%
White: 72.9% International: 0.2%
Unknown: 4.7%

Attrition rates for 2006-2007 full-time students
Percent of students discontinuing law school:
Men: 0% Women: N/A
First-year students: N/A Second-year students: N/A
Third-year students: 0%

LIBRARY RESOURCES
Total volumes: 622,702
Total seats available for library users: 731

INFORMATION TECHNOLOGY
Number of wired network connections available to students: 0 total (in the law library, excluding computer labs: 0; in classrooms: 0; in computer labs: 0; elsewhere in the law school: 0)
Law school has a wireless network.
Students are not required to own a computer.

EMPLOYMENT AND SALARIES
Proportion of 2006 graduates employed at graduation: 70%
Employed 9 months later, as of February 15, 2007: 95%

Salaries in the private sector (law firms, business, industry): $65,000–$135,000 (25th-75th percentile)
Median salary in the private sector: $85,000
Percentage in the private sector who reported salary information: 85%
Median salary in public service (government, judicial clerkships, academic posts, non-profits): $47,500

Percentage of 2006 graduates in:
Law firms: 69% Government: 7%
Bus./industry: 16% Judicial clerkship: 5%
Public interest: 1% Unknown: 0%
Academia: 2%

2006 graduates employed in-state: 89%
2006 graduates employed in foreign countries: 1%
Number of states where graduates are employed: 24
Percentage of 2006 graduates working in: New England: 1%, Middle Atlantic: 1%, East North Central: 1%, West North Central: 1%, South Atlantic: 2%, East South Central: 0%, West South Central: 91%, Mountain: 2%, Pacific: 1%, Unknown: 0%

BAR PASSAGE RATES
Based on 2006 graduates taking Summer 2006 or Winter 2007 exams. Most of the school's first-time test takers took the bar in Texas.

90%
School's bar passage rate for first-time test takers

82%
Statewide bar passage rate for first-time test takers

Southern University

- PO Box 9294, Baton Rouge, LA, 70813
- http://www.sulc.edu/index.html
- Public
- Year founded: 1947
- 2007-2008 tuition: In-state: full-time: $6,611; part-time: $5,494; Out-of-state: full-time: $11,211
- Enrollment 2007-08 academic year: full-time: 377; part-time: 111
- U.S. News 2009 law specialty ranking: N/A

2.52-3.26 GPA, 25TH-75TH PERCENTILE

143-149 LSAT, 25TH-75TH PERCENTILE

37% ACCEPTANCE RATE

Tier 4 2009 U.S. NEWS LAW SCHOOL RANKING

ADMISSIONS

Admissions phone number: **(225) 771-5340**
Admissions email address: **Admission@sulc.edu**
Application website: **http://www.sulc.edu**
Application deadline for Fall 2009 admission: **02/28**

Admissions statistics:
Number of applicants for Fall 2007: **731**
Number of acceptances: **271**
Number enrolled: **131**
Acceptance rate: **37%**
GPA, 25th-75th percentile, entering class Fall 2007: **2.52-3.26**
LSAT, 25th-75th percentile, entering class Fall 2007: **143-149**

Part-time program:
Number of applicants for Fall 2007: **143**
Number of acceptances: **73**
Number enrolled: **54**
Acceptance rate: **51%**
GPA, 25th-75th percentile, entering class Fall 2007: **2.66-2.88**
LSAT, 25th-75th percentile, entering class Fall 2007: **142-148**

FINANCIAL AID

Financial aid phone number: **(225) 771-2141**
Financial aid application deadline: **04/15**
Tuition 2007-2008 academic year: In-state: full-time: **$6,611**; part-time: **$5,494**; Out-of-state: full-time: **$11,211**
Room and board: **$9,059**; books: **$2,081**; miscellaneous expenses: **$1,693**
Total of room/board/books/miscellaneous expenses: **$12,833**
University offers graduate student housing for which law students are eligible.

Financial aid profile
Percent of students that received grants for the 2006-2007 academic year: full-time: **42%**

Median grant amount: full-time: **$1,567**
The average law-school debt of those in the Class of 2007 who borrowed: **$16,793**. Proportion who borrowed: **100%**

ACADEMIC PROGRAMS

Calendar: **semester**
Joint degrees awarded: **J.D./M.P.A.**
Typical first-year section size: Full-time: **45**; Part-time: **51**
Is there typically a "small section" of the first year class, other than Legal Writing, taught by full-time faculty?: Full-time: **no**; Part-time: **no**
Number of course titles, beyond the first year curriculum, offered last year: **37**
Percentages of upper division course sections, excluding seminars, with an enrollment of:
Under 25: **44%**   25 to 49: **36%**
50 to 74: **19%**   75 to 99: **0%**
100+: **0%**
Areas of specialization: appellate advocacy, clinical training, dispute resolution, environmental law, healthcare law, intellectual property law, international law, tax law, trial advocacy

Fall 2007 faculty profile
Total teaching faculty: **59**. Full-time: **63%**; **57%** men, **43%** women, **62%** minorities. Part-time: **37%**; **68%** men, **32%** women, **86%** minorities
Student-to-faculty ratio: **13.0**

SPECIAL PROGRAMS *(as provided by law school):*
The juris doctor degree is offered through a full-time and a part-time day/evening program requiring completion of 96 hours of academic credit. A J.D./Master of Public Administration joint degree is available and requires 123 hours of academic credit. There is also a clinical education program, a Certificate in Public Law, and a summer studies-abroad program in London.

STUDENT BODY

Fall 2007 full-time enrollment: **377**
Men: **50%**   Women: **50%**
African-American: **57.6%**   American Indian: **0.0%**

Asian-American: 0.5% Mexican-American: 0.0%
Puerto Rican: 0.0% Other Hisp-Amer: 1.1%
White: 40.8% International: 0.0%
Unknown: 0.0%

Fall 2007 part-time enrollment: 111
Men: 41% Women: 59%
African-American: 42.3% American Indian: 0.0%
Asian-American: 0.0% Mexican-American: 0.0%
Puerto Rican: 0.0% Other Hisp-Amer: 4.5%
White: 53.2% International: 0.0%
Unknown: 0.0%

Attrition rates for 2006-2007 full-time students
Percent of students discontinuing law school:
Men: 6% Women: 4%
First-year students: 12% Second-year students: 1%
Third-year students: 1%

LIBRARY RESOURCES
Total volumes: 480,937
Total seats available for library users: 284

INFORMATION TECHNOLOGY
Number of wired network connections available to students: 76 total (in the law library, excluding computer labs: 25; in classrooms: 0; in computer labs: 21; elsewhere in the law school: 30)
Law school has a wireless network.
Students are not required to own a computer.

EMPLOYMENT AND SALARIES
Proportion of 2006 graduates employed at graduation: 79%
Employed 9 months later, as of February 15, 2007: 84%

Salaries in the private sector (law firms, business, industry): $70,000–$135,000 (25th-75th percentile)
Median salary in the private sector: $92,500
Percentage in the private sector who reported salary information: 59%
Median salary in public service (government, judicial clerkships, academic posts, non-profits): $42,000

Percentage of 2006 graduates in:
Law firms: 45% Government: 26%
Bus./industry: 9% Judicial clerkship: 12%
Public interest: 3% Unknown: 2%
Academia: 3%

2006 graduates employed in-state: 73%
2006 graduates employed in foreign countries: 0%
Number of states where graduates are employed: 13
Percentage of 2006 graduates working in: New England: 0%, Middle Atlantic: 2%, East North Central: 7%, West North Central: 2%, South Atlantic: 7%, East South Central: 2%, West South Central: 80%, Mountain: 0%, Pacific: 2%, Unknown: 0%

BAR PASSAGE RATES
Based on 2006 graduates taking Summer 2006 or Winter 2007 exams. Most of the school's first-time test takers took the bar in Louisiana.

63%
School's bar passage rate for first-time test takers

75%
Statewide bar passage rate for first-time test takers

Southwestern Law School

■ 3050 Wilshire Boulevard, Los Angeles, CA, 90010-1106
■ http://www.swlaw.edu
■ Private
■ Year founded: 1911
■ 2007-2008 tuition: full-time: $33,410; part-time: $20,126
■ Enrollment 2007-08 academic year: full-time: 698; part-time: 274
■ U.S. News 2009 law specialty ranking: N/A

3.06-3.58 GPA, 25TH-75TH PERCENTILE

153-157 LSAT, 25TH-75TH PERCENTILE

33% ACCEPTANCE RATE

Tier 4 2009 U.S. NEWS LAW SCHOOL RANKING

ADMISSIONS
Admissions phone number: **(213) 738-6717**
Admissions email address: **admissions@swlaw.edu**
Application website: **http://www.swlaw.edu/studentservices/jdadmin/applicants**
Application deadline for Fall 2009 admission: **04/01**

Admissions statistics:
Number of applicants for Fall 2007: **2,890**
Number of acceptances: **968**
Number enrolled: **252**
Acceptance rate: **33%**
GPA, 25th-75th percentile, entering class Fall 2007: **3.06-3.58**
LSAT, 25th-75th percentile, entering class Fall 2007: **153-157**

Part-time program:
Number of applicants for Fall 2007: **465**
Number of acceptances: **174**
Number enrolled: **100**
Acceptance rate: **37%**
GPA, 25th-75th percentile, entering class Fall 2007: **2.90-3.40**
LSAT, 25th-75th percentile, entering class Fall 2007: **151-154**

FINANCIAL AID
Financial aid phone number: **(213) 738-6719**
Financial aid application deadline: **06/01**
Tuition 2007-2008 academic year: full-time: **$33,410**; part-time: **$20,126**
Room and board: **$14,220**; books: **$1,250**; miscellaneous expenses: **$5,580**
Total of room/board/books/miscellaneous expenses: **$21,050**
University does not offer graduate student housing for which law students are eligible.

Financial aid profile
Percent of students that received grants for the 2006-2007

academic year: full-time: **29%**; part-time **22%**
Median grant amount: full-time: **$10,000**; part-time: **$7,500**
The average law-school debt of those in the Class of 2007 who borrowed: **$105,029**. Proportion who borrowed: **87%**

ACADEMIC PROGRAMS
Calendar: **semester**
Joint degrees awarded: **N/A**
Typical first-year section size: Full-time: **73**; Part-time: **87**
Is there typically a "small section" of the first year class, other than Legal Writing, taught by full-time faculty?: Full-time: **no**; Part-time: **no**
Number of course titles, beyond the first year curriculum, offered last year: **136**
Percentages of upper division course sections, excluding seminars, with an enrollment of:

Under 25: **52%**	25 to 49: **21%**
50 to 74: **13%**	75 to 99: **13%**
100+: **0%**	

Areas of specialization: appellate advocacy, clinical training, dispute resolution, environmental law, healthcare law, intellectual property law, international law, tax law, trial advocacy

Fall 2007 faculty profile
Total teaching faculty: **95**. Full-time: **47%**; **64%** men, **36%** women, **22%** minorities. Part-time: **53%**; **74%** men, **26%** women, **14%** minorities
Student-to-faculty ratio: **16.3**

SPECIAL PROGRAMS *(as provided by law school):*
Entertainment and Media Law Institute offering 40-plus entertainment/sports law courses, 50 entertainment externships, and a law firm practicum. SCALE two-year alternative J.D. program. Foreign summer programs in Vancouver; Buenos Aires; London; and Guanajuato, Mexico. Clinics for children's rights, and immigration and international human rights.

STUDENT BODY

Fall 2007 full-time enrollment: 698

Men: 47%	Women: 53%
African-American: 4.6%	American Indian: 1.0%
Asian-American: 15.5%	Mexican-American: 7.2%
Puerto Rican: 0.1%	Other Hisp-Amer: 5.3%
White: 50.7%	International: 0.7%
Unknown: 14.9%	

Fall 2007 part-time enrollment: 274

Men: 54%	Women: 46%
African-American: 6.6%	American Indian: 0.0%
Asian-American: 18.2%	Mexican-American: 8.4%
Puerto Rican: 0.4%	Other Hisp-Amer: 3.3%
White: 44.5%	International: 0.7%
Unknown: 17.9%	

Attrition rates for 2006-2007 full-time students

Percent of students discontinuing law school:

Men: 7%	Women: 5%
First-year students: 8%	Second-year students: 11%
Third-year students: 0%	

LIBRARY RESOURCES

Total volumes: 483,433
Total seats available for library users: 610

INFORMATION TECHNOLOGY

Number of wired network connections available to students: 442 total (in the law library, excluding computer labs: 442; in classrooms: 0; in computer labs: 0; elsewhere in the law school: 0)
Law school has a wireless network.
Students are not required to own a computer.

EMPLOYMENT AND SALARIES

Proportion of 2006 graduates employed at graduation: 76%

Employed 9 months later, as of February 15, 2007: 85%
Salaries in the private sector (law firms, business, industry): $65,000–$87,500 (25th-75th percentile)
Median salary in the private sector: $75,000
Percentage in the private sector who reported salary information: 44%
Median salary in public service (government, judicial clerkships, academic posts, non-profits): $60,000

Percentage of 2006 graduates in:

Law firms: 57%	Government: 13%
Bus./industry: 14%	Judicial clerkship: 4%
Public interest: 1%	Unknown: 9%
Academia: 2%	

2006 graduates employed in-state: 93%
2006 graduates employed in foreign countries: 1%
Number of states where graduates are employed: 11
Percentage of 2006 graduates working in: New England: 0%, Middle Atlantic: 0%, East North Central: 1%, West North Central: 1%, South Atlantic: 1%, East South Central: 1%, West South Central: 1%, Mountain: 2%, Pacific: 93%, Unknown: 1%

BAR PASSAGE RATES

Based on 2006 graduates taking Summer 2006 or Winter 2007 exams. Most of the school's first-time test takers took the bar in California.

64%
School's bar passage rate for first-time test takers

65%
Statewide bar passage rate for first-time test takers

St. John's University

- 8000 Utopia Parkway, Jamaica, NY, 11439
- http://www.law.stjohns.edu/
- Private
- **Year founded:** 1925
- **2007-2008 tuition:** full-time: $38,400; part-time: $28,800
- **Enrollment 2007-08 academic year:** full-time: 748; part-time: 166
- **U.S. News 2009 law specialty ranking:** N/A

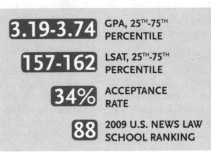

3.19-3.74 GPA, 25TH-75TH PERCENTILE

157-162 LSAT, 25TH-75TH PERCENTILE

34% ACCEPTANCE RATE

88 2009 U.S. NEWS LAW SCHOOL RANKING

ADMISSIONS

Admissions phone number: **(718) 990-6474**
Admissions email address: **lawinfo@stjohns.edu**
Application website: **http://www.law.stjohns.edu/**
Application deadline for Fall 2009 admission: **04/01**

Admissions statistics:

Number of applicants for Fall 2007: **3,094**
Number of acceptances: **1,058**
Number enrolled: **232**
Acceptance rate: **34%**
GPA, 25th-75th percentile, entering class Fall 2007: **3.19-3.74**
LSAT, 25th-75th percentile, entering class Fall 2007: **157-162**

Part-time program:

Number of applicants for Fall 2007: **742**
Number of acceptances: **239**
Number enrolled: **88**
Acceptance rate: **32%**
GPA, 25th-75th percentile, entering class Fall 2007: **3.23-3.57**
LSAT, 25th-75th percentile, entering class Fall 2007: **150-157**

FINANCIAL AID

Financial aid phone number: **(718) 990-1485**
Financial aid application deadline: **03/01**
Tuition 2007-2008 academic year: full-time: **$38,400**; part-time: **$28,800**
Room and board: **$13,670**; books: **$1,400**; miscellaneous expenses: **$4,140**
Total of room/board/books/miscellaneous expenses: **$19,210**
University offers graduate student housing for which law students are eligible.

Financial aid profile

Percent of students that received grants for the 2006-2007 academic year: full-time: **42%**; part-time **15%**

Median grant amount: full-time: **$20,000**; part-time: **$10,000**
The average law-school debt of those in the Class of 2007 who borrowed: **$93,619**. Proportion who borrowed: **80%**

ACADEMIC PROGRAMS

Calendar: **semester**
Joint degrees awarded: **J.D./M.A.; J.D./M.B.A.; J.D./LL.M.**
Typical first-year section size: Full-time: **85**; Part-time: **61**
Is there typically a "small section" of the first year class, other than Legal Writing, taught by full-time faculty?: Full-time: **yes**; Part-time: **no**
Number of course titles, beyond the first year curriculum, offered last year: **116**
Percentages of upper division course sections, excluding seminars, with an enrollment of:
Under 25: **58%**   25 to 49: **23%**
50 to 74: **8%**   75 to 99: **10%**
100+: **1%**
Areas of specialization: appellate advocacy, clinical training, dispute resolution, environmental law, healthcare law, intellectual property law, international law, tax law, trial advocacy

Fall 2007 faculty profile

Total teaching faculty: **131**. Full-time: **42%**; **58%** men, **42%** women, **18%** minorities. Part-time: **58%**; **72%** men, **28%** women, **5%** minorities
Student-to-faculty ratio: **16.4**

SPECIAL PROGRAMS *(as provided by law school):*

A summer program in Rome began in 2007. The Law School sponsors seven clinics in the areas of elder law; securities arbitration; child advocacy; domestic violence litigation; refugee and immigrant rights; immigrant tenant advocacy; and prosecution. Externship offerings include placements in governmental agencies, public defenders' offices, and judicial chambers.

STUDENT BODY

Fall 2007 full-time enrollment: **748**
Men: **53%**   Women: **47%**

African-American: 4.9%   American Indian: 0.1%
Asian-American: 8.6%   Mexican-American: 0.3%
Puerto Rican: 0.9%   Other Hisp-Amer: 5.1%
White: 65.1%   International: 1.1%
Unknown: 13.9%

Fall 2007 part-time enrollment: 166
Men: 48%   Women: 52%
African-American: 8.4%   American Indian: 0.0%
Asian-American: 14.5%   Mexican-American: 0.0%
Puerto Rican: 1.8%   Other Hisp-Amer: 10.2%
White: 47.6%   International: 1.2%
Unknown: 16.3%

Attrition rates for 2006-2007 full-time students
Percent of students discontinuing law school:
Men: 4%   Women: 2%
First-year students: 3% Second-year students: 6%
Third-year students: 0%

LIBRARY RESOURCES
Total volumes: 376,546
Total seats available for library users: 507

INFORMATION TECHNOLOGY
Number of wired network connections available to students: 0 total (in the law library, excluding computer labs: N/A; in classrooms: N/A; in computer labs: N/A; elsewhere in the law school: N/A)
Law school has a wireless network.
Students are not required to own a computer.

EMPLOYMENT AND SALARIES
Proportion of 2006 graduates employed at graduation: 66%

Employed 9 months later, as of February 15, 2007: 89%
Salaries in the private sector (law firms, business, industry): $60,000–$145,000 (25th-75th percentile)
Median salary in the private sector: $80,000
Percentage in the private sector who reported salary information: 72%
Median salary in public service (government, judicial clerkships, academic posts, non-profits): $49,000

Percentage of 2006 graduates in:
Law firms: 58%   Government: 20%
Bus./industry: 14%   Judicial clerkship: 4%
Public interest: 3%   Unknown: 1%
Academia: 1%

2006 graduates employed in-state: 89%
2006 graduates employed in foreign countries: 0%
Number of states where graduates are employed: 12
Percentage of 2006 graduates working in: New England: 2%, Middle Atlantic: 93%, East North Central: 0%, West North Central: N/A, South Atlantic: 2%, East South Central: N/A, West South Central: N/A, Mountain: 1%, Pacific: 1%, Unknown: 1%

BAR PASSAGE RATES
Based on 2006 graduates taking Summer 2006 or Winter 2007 exams. Most of the school's first-time test takers took the bar in New York.

89%
School's bar passage rate for first-time test takers

77%
Statewide bar passage rate for first-time test takers

St. Louis University

- 3700 Lindell Boulevard, St. Louis, MO, 63108
- http://law.slu.edu
- Private
- Year founded: 1843
- 2007-2008 tuition: full-time: $31,750; part-time: $23,135
- Enrollment 2007-08 academic year: full-time: 750; part-time: 218
- U.S. News 2009 law specialty ranking: healthcare law: 1

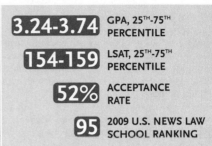

3.24-3.74 GPA, 25TH-75TH PERCENTILE

154-159 LSAT, 25TH-75TH PERCENTILE

52% ACCEPTANCE RATE

95 2009 U.S. NEWS LAW SCHOOL RANKING

ADMISSIONS

Admissions phone number: **(314) 977-2800**
Admissions email address: **admissions@law.slu.edu**
Application website:
  http://law.slu.edu/admissions/index.html
Application deadline for Fall 2009 admission: **rolling**

Admissions statistics:
Number of applicants for Fall 2007: **1,774**
Number of acceptances: **928**
Number enrolled: **240**
Acceptance rate: **52%**
GPA, 25th-75th percentile, entering class Fall 2007: **3.24-3.74**
LSAT, 25th-75th percentile, entering class Fall 2007: **154-159**

Part-time program:
Number of applicants for Fall 2007: **375**
Number of acceptances: **154**
Number enrolled: **92**
Acceptance rate: **41%**
GPA, 25th-75th percentile, entering class Fall 2007: **3.16-3.60**
LSAT, 25th-75th percentile, entering class Fall 2007: **151-155**

FINANCIAL AID

Financial aid phone number: **(314) 977-3369**
Financial aid application deadline: **03/01**
Tuition 2007-2008 academic year: full-time: **$31,750**; part-time: **$23,135**
Room and board: **$11,988**; books: **$1,300**; miscellaneous expenses: **$5,589**
Total of room/board/books/miscellaneous expenses: **$18,877**
University does not offer graduate student housing for which law students are eligible.

Financial aid profile
Percent of students that received grants for the 2006-2007 academic year: full-time: **44%**; part-time **27%**

Median grant amount: full-time: **$13,000**; part-time: **$4,000**
The average law-school debt of those in the Class of 2007 who borrowed: **$89,682**. Proportion who borrowed: **90%**

ACADEMIC PROGRAMS

Calendar: **semester**
Joint degrees awarded: **J.D./M.H.A.; J.D./M.B.A.; J.D./M.A.Urban Affairs; J.D./M.P.A.; J.D./M.P.H.; J.D./Ph.D.**
Typical first-year section size: Full-time: **85**; Part-time: **90**
Is there typically a "small section" of the first year class, other than Legal Writing, taught by full-time faculty?: Full-time: **yes**; Part-time: **no**
Number of course titles, beyond the first year curriculum, offered last year: **105**
Percentages of upper division course sections, excluding seminars, with an enrollment of:

Under 25: **60%**   25 to 49: **25%**
50 to 74: **6%**   75 to 99: **4%**
100+: **6%**

Areas of specialization: appellate advocacy, clinical training, dispute resolution, environmental law, healthcare law, intellectual property law, international law, tax law, trial advocacy

Fall 2007 faculty profile
Total teaching faculty: **84**. Full-time: **49%**; **63%** men, **37%** women, **7%** minorities. Part-time: **51%**; **67%** men, **33%** women, **5%** minorities
Student-to-faculty ratio: **17.6**

SPECIAL PROGRAMS *(as provided by law school)*:
The Saint Louis University School of Law provides a broad array of opportunities for students to practice law through clinical programs; it has three centers of excellence: Health Law, Employment Law, and International and Comparative Law; it offers summer programs in St. Louis and two programs abroad: Madrid and Berlin; and it offers six joint-degree programs.

STUDENT BODY

Fall 2007 full-time enrollment: 750

Men: 50%	Women: 50%
African-American: 5.7%	American Indian: 0.5%
Asian-American: 5.1%	Mexican-American: 0.9%
Puerto Rican: 0.0%	Other Hisp-Amer: 1.7%
White: 79.5%	International: 0.5%
Unknown: 6.0%	

Fall 2007 part-time enrollment: 218

Men: 58%	Women: 42%
African-American: 6.4%	American Indian: 0.9%
Asian-American: 2.8%	Mexican-American: 0.0%
Puerto Rican: 0.0%	Other Hisp-Amer: 0.9%
White: 76.6%	International: 1.4%
Unknown: 11.0%	

Attrition rates for 2006-2007 full-time students
Percent of students discontinuing law school:

Men: 5%	Women: 3%
First-year students: 9%	Second-year students: 1%
Third-year students: N/A	

LIBRARY RESOURCES

Total volumes: 654,307
Total seats available for library users: 410

INFORMATION TECHNOLOGY

Number of wired network connections available to students: 610 total (in the law library, excluding computer labs: 178; in classrooms: 373; in computer labs: 5; elsewhere in the law school: 54)
Law school has a wireless network.
Students are not required to own a computer.

EMPLOYMENT AND SALARIES

Proportion of 2006 graduates employed at graduation: 71%

Employed 9 months later, as of February 15, 2007: 93%
Salaries in the private sector (law firms, business, industry): $52,000–$90,000 (25th-75th percentile)
Median salary in the private sector: $65,000
Percentage in the private sector who reported salary information: 77%
Median salary in public service (government, judicial clerkships, academic posts, non-profits): $42,000

Percentage of 2006 graduates in:

Law firms: 62%	Government: 12%
Bus./industry: 16%	Judicial clerkship: 3%
Public interest: 6%	Unknown: 0%
Academia: 1%	

2006 graduates employed in-state: 67%
2006 graduates employed in foreign countries: 1%
Number of states where graduates are employed: 21
Percentage of 2006 graduates working in: New England: 1%, Middle Atlantic: 17%, East North Central: 71%, West North Central: 5%, South Atlantic: 1%, East South Central: 1%, West South Central: 1%, Mountain: 1%, Pacific: 1%, Unknown: 0%

BAR PASSAGE RATES

Based on 2006 graduates taking Summer 2006 or Winter 2007 exams. Most of the school's first-time test takers took the bar in Missouri.

86%
School's bar passage rate for first-time test takers

86%
Statewide bar passage rate for first-time test takers

St. Mary's University

- ■ 1 Camino Santa Maria, San Antonio, TX, 78228-8602
- ■ http://law.stmarytx.edu
- ■ Private
- ■ Year founded: 1927
- ■ 2007-2008 tuition: full-time: $23,440; part-time: $16,040
- ■ Enrollment 2007-08 academic year: full-time: 699; part-time: 63
- ■ U.S. News 2009 law specialty ranking: N/A

2.80-3.41 GPA, 25TH-75TH PERCENTILE

149-156 LSAT, 25TH-75TH PERCENTILE

51% ACCEPTANCE RATE

Tier 4 2009 U.S. NEWS LAW SCHOOL RANKING

ADMISSIONS

Admissions phone number: **(210) 436-3523**
Admissions email address: **lawadmissions@stmarytx.edu**
Application website: **N/A**
Application deadline for Fall 2009 admission: **03/01**

Admissions statistics:
Number of applicants for Fall 2007: **1,655**
Number of acceptances: **846**
Number enrolled: **264**
Acceptance rate: **51%**
GPA, 25th-75th percentile, entering class Fall 2007: **2.80-3.41**
LSAT, 25th-75th percentile, entering class Fall 2007: **149-156**

Part-time program:
Number of applicants for Fall 2007: **237**
Number of acceptances: **88**
Number enrolled: **64**
Acceptance rate: **37%**
GPA, 25th-75th percentile, entering class Fall 2007: **2.52-3.30**
LSAT, 25th-75th percentile, entering class Fall 2007: **148-154**

FINANCIAL AID

Financial aid phone number: **(210) 431-6743**
Financial aid application deadline: **08/28**
Tuition 2007-2008 academic year: full-time: **$23,440**; part-time: **$16,040**
Room and board: **$7,730**; books: **$1,300**; miscellaneous expenses: **$5,482**
Total of room/board/books/miscellaneous expenses: **$14,512**
University offers graduate student housing for which law students are eligible.

Financial aid profile
Percent of students that received grants for the 2006-2007 academic year: full-time: **44%**

Median grant amount: full-time: **$1,432**
The average law-school debt of those in the Class of 2007 who borrowed: **$84,124**. Proportion who borrowed: **86%**

ACADEMIC PROGRAMS

Calendar: **semester**
Joint degrees awarded: **J.D./M.B.A.; J.D./M.A International Relations; J.D./M.P.A.; J.D./M.A. Theology; J.D./M.A. Communication Studies; J.D./M.Acc.; J.D./M.A. Economics; J.D./M.A. Engineering; J.D./M.A. English Literature; J.D./M.S. Computer Information Systems**
Typical first-year section size: Full-time: **87**; Part-time: **66**
Is there typically a "small section" of the first year class, other than Legal Writing, taught by full-time faculty?: Full-time: **no**; Part-time: **no**
Number of course titles, beyond the first year curriculum, offered last year: **112**
Percentages of upper division course sections, excluding seminars, with an enrollment of:

Under 25: **51%**	25 to 49: **21%**
50 to 74: **18%**	75 to 99: **11%**
100+: **0%**	

Areas of specialization: appellate advocacy, clinical training, dispute resolution, environmental law, healthcare law, intellectual property law, international law, tax law, trial advocacy

Fall 2007 faculty profile
Total teaching faculty: **69**. Full-time: **42%**; **72%** men, **28%** women, **17%** minorities. Part-time: **58%**; **60%** men, **40%** women, **13%** minorities
Student-to-faculty ratio: **22.1**

SPECIAL PROGRAMS *(as provided by law school):*
Please see the School of Law's website.

STUDENT BODY
Fall 2007 full-time enrollment: **699**

Men: **54%**	Women: **46%**
African-American: **3.3%**	American Indian: **1.1%**

Asian-American: 5.3% Mexican-American: 12.0%
Puerto Rican: 0.6% Other Hisp-Amer: 11.3%
White: 66.2% International: 0.1%
Unknown: 0.0%

Fall 2007 part-time enrollment: 63
Men: 65% Women: 35%
African-American: 6.3% American Indian: 1.6%
Asian-American: 4.8% Mexican-American: 12.7%
Puerto Rican: 0.0% Other Hisp-Amer: 15.9%
White: 58.7% International: 0.0%
Unknown: 0.0%

Attrition rates for 2006-2007 full-time students
Percent of students discontinuing law school:
Men: 8% Women: 9%
First-year students: 16% Second-year students: 9%
Third-year students: N/A

LIBRARY RESOURCES
Total volumes: 415,495
Total seats available for library users: 390

INFORMATION TECHNOLOGY
Number of wired network connections available to students: 619 total (in the law library, excluding computer labs: 173; in classrooms: 400; in computer labs: 30; elsewhere in the law school: 16)
Law school has a wireless network.
Students are not required to own a computer.

EMPLOYMENT AND SALARIES
Proportion of 2006 graduates employed at graduation: N/A
Employed 9 months later, as of February 15, 2007: 82%

Salaries in the private sector (law firms, business, industry): $45,000–$75,000 (25th-75th percentile)
Median salary in the private sector: $67,500
Percentage in the private sector who reported salary information: 22%
Median salary in public service (government, judicial clerkships, academic posts, non-profits): $41,334

Percentage of 2006 graduates in:
Law firms: 56% Government: 11%
Bus./industry: 15% Judicial clerkship: 4%
Public interest: 1% Unknown: 12%
Academia: 1%

2006 graduates employed in-state: 93%
2006 graduates employed in foreign countries: N/A
Number of states where graduates are employed: 8
Percentage of 2006 graduates working in: New England: N/A, Middle Atlantic: 1%, East North Central: N/A, West North Central: 1%, South Atlantic: 2%, East South Central: N/A, West South Central: 91%, Mountain: 1%, Pacific: N/A, Unknown: 4%

BAR PASSAGE RATES
Based on 2006 graduates taking Summer 2006 or Winter 2007 exams. Most of the school's first-time test takers took the bar in Texas.

| 83% |
School's bar passage rate for first-time test takers

| 82% |
Statewide bar passage rate for first-time test takers

St. Thomas University

- 16401 N.W. 37th Avenue, Miami Gardens, FL, 33054
- http://www.stu.edu
- Private
- Year founded: 1984
- 2007-2008 tuition: full-time: $27,840; part-time: N/A
- Enrollment 2007-08 academic year: full-time: 625
- U.S. News 2009 law specialty ranking: N/A

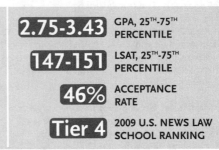

2.75-3.43 GPA, 25TH-75TH PERCENTILE

147-151 LSAT, 25TH-75TH PERCENTILE

46% ACCEPTANCE RATE

Tier 4 2009 U.S. NEWS LAW SCHOOL RANKING

ADMISSIONS

Admissions phone number: **(305) 623-2311**
Admissions email address: **admitme@stu.edu**
Application website: **N/A**
Application deadline for Fall 2009 admission: **05/01**

Admissions statistics:
Number of applicants for Fall 2007: **2,712**
Number of acceptances: **1,235**
Number enrolled: **228**
Acceptance rate: **46%**
GPA, 25th-75th percentile, entering class Fall 2007: **2.75-3.43**
LSAT, 25th-75th percentile, entering class Fall 2007: **147-151**

FINANCIAL AID

Financial aid phone number: **(305) 628-6725**
Financial aid application deadline: **05/01**
Tuition 2007-2008 academic year: full-time: **$27,840**; part-time: **N/A**
Room and board: **$13,000**; books: **$1,250**; miscellaneous expenses: **$5,595**
Total of room/board/books/miscellaneous expenses: **$19,845**
University offers graduate student housing for which law students are eligible.

Financial aid profile
Percent of students that received grants for the 2006-2007 academic year: full-time: **29%**
Median grant amount: full-time: **$11,000**
The average law-school debt of those in the Class of 2007 who borrowed: **$93,000**. Proportion who borrowed: **83%**

ACADEMIC PROGRAMS

Calendar: **semester**
Joint degrees awarded: **J.D./M.B.A. Accounting; J.D./M.B.A. International Business; J.D./M.B.A. Sports Administration; J.D./M.S. Marriage and Family Counseling; J.D./M.B.A. Business Administration**

Typical first-year section size: Full-time: **60**
Is there typically a "small section" of the first year class, other than Legal Writing, taught by full-time faculty?: Full-time: **no**
Number of course titles, beyond the first year curriculum, offered last year: **97**
Percentages of upper division course sections, excluding seminars, with an enrollment of:
Under 25: **71%**   25 to 49: **18%**
50 to 74: **7%**   75 to 99: **4%**
100+: **0%**
Areas of specialization: appellate advocacy, clinical training, dispute resolution, environmental law, healthcare law, intellectual property law, international law, tax law, trial advocacy

Fall 2007 faculty profile
Total teaching faculty: **61**. Full-time: **48%**; **45%** men, **55%** women, **14%** minorities. Part-time: **52%**; **75%** men, **25%** women, **25%** minorities
Student-to-faculty ratio: **18.0**

SPECIAL PROGRAMS *(as provided by law school):*

Appellate litigation, bankruptcy, civil, family court, tax clinics; Human Rights Institute; J.D./M.B.A. Accounting, International Business; J.D./M.S. Marriage-Family Counseling, Sports Administration; and J.D./B.S. Environmental Justice. Summer: Royal College Univ. Escorial Maria Cristina, Spain. Individual and small-group academic support and assistance to graduates with bar exam preparation.

STUDENT BODY

Fall 2007 full-time enrollment: **625**
Men: **53%**   Women: **47%**
African-American: **8.5%**   American Indian: **0.0%**
Asian-American: **3.8%**   Mexican-American: **0.5%**
Puerto Rican: **1.6%**   Other Hisp-Amer: **29.3%**
White: **50.1%**   International: **2.4%**
Unknown: **3.8%**

Attrition rates for 2006-2007 full-time students
Percent of students discontinuing law school:
Men: 11%   Women: 7%
First-year students: 23%   Second-year students: 4%
Third-year students: 1%

LIBRARY RESOURCES
Total volumes: 330,143
Total seats available for library users: 472

INFORMATION TECHNOLOGY
Number of wired network connections available to students: 60 total (in the law library, excluding computer labs: 20; in classrooms: 30; in computer labs: 5; elsewhere in the law school: 5)
Law school has a wireless network.
Students are not required to own a computer.

EMPLOYMENT AND SALARIES
Proportion of 2006 graduates employed at graduation: N/A
Employed 9 months later, as of February 15, 2007: 83%
Salaries in the private sector (law firms, business, industry): $40,000–$70,000 (25th-75th percentile)
Median salary in the private sector: $60,000
Percentage in the private sector who reported salary information: 90%
Median salary in public service (government, judicial clerkships, academic posts, non-profits): $39,000

Percentage of 2006 graduates in:
Law firms: 53%   Government: 13%
Bus./industry: 21%   Judicial clerkship: 2%
Public interest: 8%   Unknown: 2%
Academia: 1%

2006 graduates employed in-state: 87%
2006 graduates employed in foreign countries: 0%
Number of states where graduates are employed: 16
Percentage of 2006 graduates working in: New England: 1%, Middle Atlantic: 2%, East North Central: 3%, West North Central: 0%, South Atlantic: 90%, East South Central: 0%, West South Central: 2%, Mountain: 2%, Pacific: 2%, Unknown: 0%

BAR PASSAGE RATES
Based on 2006 graduates taking Summer 2006 or Winter 2007 exams. Most of the school's first-time test takers took the bar in Florida.

65%

School's bar passage rate for first-time test takers

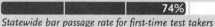

74%

Statewide bar passage rate for first-time test takers

Stanford University

- ■ Crown Quadrangle, 559 Nathan Abbott Way, Stanford, CA, 94305-8610
- ■ http://www.law.stanford.edu/
- ■ Private
- ■ Year founded: 1893
- ■ 2007-2008 tuition: full-time: $39,916; part-time: N/A
- ■ Enrollment 2007-08 academic year: full-time: 538
- ■ U.S. News 2009 law specialty ranking: clinical training: 13, environmental law: 7, intellectual property law: 2, international law: 16, tax law: 13

3.74-3.95 GPA, 25TH-75TH PERCENTILE

167-172 LSAT, 25TH-75TH PERCENTILE

9% ACCEPTANCE RATE

2 2009 U.S. NEWS LAW SCHOOL RANKING

ADMISSIONS

Admissions phone number: **(650) 723-4985**
Admissions email address: **admissions@law.stanford.edu**
Application website:
  http://www.law.stanford.edu/prospective/
Application deadline for Fall 2009 admission: **02/02**

Admissions statistics:
Number of applicants for Fall 2007: **4,052**
Number of acceptances: **366**
Number enrolled: **170**
Acceptance rate: **9%**
GPA, 25th-75th percentile, entering class Fall 2007: **3.74-3.95**
LSAT, 25th-75th percentile, entering class Fall 2007: **167-172**

FINANCIAL AID

Financial aid phone number: **(650) 723-9247**
Financial aid application deadline: **03/15**
Tuition 2007-2008 academic year: full-time: **$39,916**; part-time: **N/A**
Room and board: **$16,218**; books: **$1,640**; miscellaneous expenses: **$2,842**
Total of room/board/books/miscellaneous expenses: **$20,700**
University offers graduate student housing for which law students are eligible.

Financial aid profile
Percent of students that received grants for the 2006-2007 academic year: full-time: **41%**
Median grant amount: full-time: **$16,613**
The average law-school debt of those in the Class of 2007 who borrowed: **$101,379**. Proportion who borrowed: **82%**

ACADEMIC PROGRAMS

Calendar: **semester**
Joint degrees awarded: **J.D./M.B.A.; J.D./Ph.D.; J.D./M.D.; J.D./M.P.A.; J.D./M.A.; J.D./M.S.**

Typical first-year section size: Full-time: **60**
Is there typically a "small section" of the first year class, other than Legal Writing, taught by full-time faculty?: Full-time: **yes**
Number of course titles, beyond the first year curriculum, offered last year: **168**
Percentages of upper division course sections, excluding seminars, with an enrollment of:

Under 25: **75%**	25 to 49: **15%**
50 to 74: **6%**	75 to 99: **2%**
100+: **1%**	

Areas of specialization: appellate advocacy, clinical training, dispute resolution, environmental law, healthcare law, intellectual property law, international law, tax law, trial advocacy

Fall 2007 faculty profile
Total teaching faculty: **0**. Full-time: **N/A**; **N/A** men, **N/A** women, **N/A** minorities. Part-time: **N/A**; **N/A** men, **N/A** women, **N/A** minorities
Student-to-faculty ratio: **8.3**

SPECIAL PROGRAMS *(as provided by law school):*
A leader in interdisciplinary education, SLS offers 27 joint degrees and virtually limitless opportunities to customize. With 10 clinics, SLS enables students to take on the roles and responsibilities of practicing lawyers. Students can engage in research and policy-oriented study through SLS's programs and centers.

STUDENT BODY
Fall 2007 full-time enrollment: 538

Men: **54%**	Women: **46%**
African-American: **8.6%**	American Indian: **1.7%**
Asian-American: **13.4%**	Mexican-American: **8.4%**
Puerto Rican: **0.9%**	Other Hisp-Amer: **0.4%**
White: **56.1%**	International: **1.5%**
Unknown: **9.1%**	

Attrition rates for 2006-2007 full-time students
Percent of students discontinuing law school:
Men: 0%   Women: N/A
First-year students: N/A   Second-year students: 1%
Third-year students: N/A

LIBRARY RESOURCES
Total volumes: 480,130
Total seats available for library users: 528

INFORMATION TECHNOLOGY
Number of wired network connections available to students: 94 total (in the law library, excluding computer labs: 7; in classrooms: 87; in computer labs: 0; elsewhere in the law school: 0)
Law school has a wireless network.
Students are required to own a computer.

EMPLOYMENT AND SALARIES
Proportion of 2006 graduates employed at graduation: 98%
Employed 9 months later, as of February 15, 2007: 99%
Salaries in the private sector (law firms, business, industry): $135,000–$145,000 (25th-75th percentile)
Median salary in the private sector: $135,000
Percentage in the private sector who reported salary information: 97%
Median salary in public service (government, judicial clerkships, academic posts, non-profits): $54,272

Percentage of 2006 graduates in:
Law firms: 66%   Government: 2%
Bus./industry: 2%   Judicial clerkship: 27%
Public interest: 2%   Unknown: 0%
Academia: 1%

2006 graduates employed in-state: 46%
2006 graduates employed in foreign countries: 2%
Number of states where graduates are employed: 25
Percentage of 2006 graduates working in: New England: 2%, Middle Atlantic: 21%, East North Central: 2%, West North Central: 1%, South Atlantic: 15%, East South Central: 1%, West South Central: 3%, Mountain: 4%, Pacific: 48%, Unknown: 0%

BAR PASSAGE RATES
Based on 2006 graduates taking Summer 2006 or Winter 2007 exams. Most of the school's first-time test takers took the bar in California.

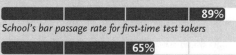

89%
School's bar passage rate for first-time test takers

65%
Statewide bar passage rate for first-time test takers

Stetson University

- 1401 61st Street S, Gulfport, FL, 33707
- http://www.law.stetson.edu
- Private
- **Year founded:** 1900
- **2007-2008 tuition:** full-time: $29,240; part-time: $20,260
- **Enrollment 2007-08 academic year:** full-time: 765; part-time: 229
- **U.S. News 2009 law specialty ranking:** trial advocacy: 1

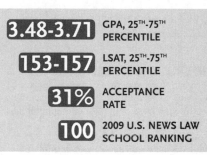

3.48-3.71 GPA, 25TH-75TH PERCENTILE

153-157 LSAT, 25TH-75TH PERCENTILE

31% ACCEPTANCE RATE

100 2009 U.S. NEWS LAW SCHOOL RANKING

ADMISSIONS

Admissions phone number: **(727) 562-7802**
Admissions email address: **lawadmit@law.stetson.edu**
Application website:
   http://www.law.stetson.edu/admissions/
Application deadline for Fall 2009 admission: **03/15**

Admissions statistics:

Number of applicants for Fall 2007: **2,560**
Number of acceptances: **796**
Number enrolled: **257**
Acceptance rate: **31%**
GPA, 25th-75th percentile, entering class Fall 2007: **3.48-3.71**
LSAT, 25th-75th percentile, entering class Fall 2007: **153-157**

Part-time program:

Number of applicants for Fall 2007: **506**
Number of acceptances: **172**
Number enrolled: **69**
Acceptance rate: **34%**
GPA, 25th-75th percentile, entering class Fall 2007: **3.32-3.64**
LSAT, 25th-75th percentile, entering class Fall 2007: **150-155**

FINANCIAL AID

Financial aid phone number: **(727) 562-7813**
Financial aid application deadline: **N/A**
Tuition 2007-2008 academic year: full-time: **$29,240**; part-time: **$20,260**
Room and board: **$8,212**; books: **$1,200**; miscellaneous expenses: **$4,847**
Total of room/board/books/miscellaneous expenses: **$14,259**
University does not offer graduate student housing for which law students are eligible.

Financial aid profile

Percent of students that received grants for the 2006-2007 academic year: full-time: **21%**; part-time **7%**

Median grant amount: full-time: **$17,479**; part-time: **$9,431**
The average law-school debt of those in the Class of 2007 who borrowed: **$105,900**. Proportion who borrowed: **86%**

ACADEMIC PROGRAMS

Calendar: **semester**
Joint degrees awarded: **J.D./M.B.A.**
Typical first-year section size: Full-time: **67**; Part-time: **80**
Is there typically a "small section" of the first year class, other than Legal Writing, taught by full-time faculty?: Full-time: **no**; Part-time: **no**
Number of course titles, beyond the first year curriculum, offered last year: **118**
Percentages of upper division course sections, excluding seminars, with an enrollment of:

Under 25: **57%**	25 to 49: **32%**
50 to 74: **9%**	75 to 99: **2%**
100+: **0%**	

Areas of specialization: appellate advocacy, clinical training, dispute resolution, environmental law, healthcare law, intellectual property law, international law, tax law, trial advocacy

Fall 2007 faculty profile

Total teaching faculty: **80**. Full-time: **55%**; **57%** men, **43%** women, **18%** minorities. Part-time: **45%**; **81%** men, **19%** women, **6%** minorities
Student-to-faculty ratio: **17.9**

SPECIAL PROGRAMS (as provided by law school):

Advocacy, elder law, higher education law, and international law centers. National Clearinghouse for Science, Technology and Law. Two institutes. Internships and clinics. Part-time and J.D./M.B.A., J.D./M.P.H., and J.D./M.D. programs. Honors program. Summer abroad in Spain, Argentina, Germany, Netherlands, and China. Winter intercession in Cayman Islands. Summer internship in Washington, D.C.

STUDENT BODY

Fall 2007 full-time enrollment: 765

Men: 47%	Women: 53%
African-American: 5.4%	American Indian: 0.4%
Asian-American: 2.7%	Mexican-American: 0.3%
Puerto Rican: 1.7%	Other Hisp-Amer: 8.5%
White: 75.7%	International: 1.0%
Unknown: 4.3%	

Fall 2007 part-time enrollment: 229

Men: 45%	Women: 55%
African-American: 10.5%	American Indian: 1.3%
Asian-American: 2.6%	Mexican-American: 0.4%
Puerto Rican: 1.7%	Other Hisp-Amer: 4.4%
White: 76.0%	International: 0.0%
Unknown: 3.1%	

Attrition rates for 2006-2007 full-time students
Percent of students discontinuing law school:

Men: 0%	Women: 0%
First-year students: 1%	Second-year students: N/A
Third-year students: N/A	

LIBRARY RESOURCES

Total volumes: 419,501
Total seats available for library users: 628

INFORMATION TECHNOLOGY

Number of wired network connections available to students: 1,367 total (in the law library, excluding computer labs: 348; in classrooms: 835; in computer labs: 54; elsewhere in the law school: 130)
Law school has a wireless network.
Students are required to own a computer.

EMPLOYMENT AND SALARIES

Proportion of 2006 graduates employed at graduation: N/A

Employed 9 months later, as of February 15, 2007: 98%
Salaries in the private sector (law firms, business, industry): $65,000–$90,000 (25th-75th percentile)
Median salary in the private sector: $75,000
Percentage in the private sector who reported salary information: 65%
Median salary in public service (government, judicial clerkships, academic posts, non-profits): $41,000

Percentage of 2006 graduates in:

Law firms: 52%	Government: 21%
Bus./industry: 13%	Judicial clerkship: 5%
Public interest: 7%	Unknown: 0%
Academia: 2%	

2006 graduates employed in-state: 89%
2006 graduates employed in foreign countries: 0%
Number of states where graduates are employed: 15
Percentage of 2006 graduates working in: New England: 0%, Middle Atlantic: 1%, East North Central: 1%, West North Central: 0%, South Atlantic: 96%, East South Central: 1%, West South Central: 0%, Mountain: 0%, Pacific: 1%, Unknown: 0%

BAR PASSAGE RATES

Based on 2006 graduates taking Summer 2006 or Winter 2007 exams. Most of the school's first-time test takers took the bar in Florida.

82%
School's bar passage rate for first-time test takers

74%
Statewide bar passage rate for first-time test takers

Suffolk University

■ 120 Tremont Street, Boston, MA, 02108
■ http://www.law.suffolk.edu/
■ Private
■ Year founded: 1906
■ 2007-2008 tuition: full-time: $36,068; part-time: $27,051
■ Enrollment 2007-08 academic year: full-time: 1,021; part-time: 604
■ U.S. News 2009 law specialty ranking: clinical training: 20

3.03-3.49 GPA, 25TH-75TH PERCENTILE

154-158 LSAT, 25TH-75TH PERCENTILE

50% ACCEPTANCE RATE

Tier 3 2009 U.S. NEWS LAW SCHOOL RANKING

ADMISSIONS
Admissions phone number: **(617) 573-8144**
Admissions email address: **lawadm@admin.suffolk.edu**
Application website: **http://www.law.suffolk.edu/admiss/**
Application deadline for Fall 2009 admission: **03/01**

Admissions statistics:
Number of applicants for Fall 2007: **2,402**
Number of acceptances: **1,196**
Number enrolled: **337**
Acceptance rate: **50%**
GPA, 25th-75th percentile, entering class Fall 2007: **3.03-3.49**
LSAT, 25th-75th percentile, entering class Fall 2007: **154-158**

Part-time program:
Number of applicants for Fall 2007: **653**
Number of acceptances: **339**
Number enrolled: **199**
Acceptance rate: **52%**
GPA, 25th-75th percentile, entering class Fall 2007: **2.99-3.50**
LSAT, 25th-75th percentile, entering class Fall 2007: **151-156**

FINANCIAL AID
Financial aid phone number: **(617) 573-8147**
Financial aid application deadline: **03/01**
Tuition 2007-2008 academic year: full-time: **$36,068**; part-time: **$27,051**
Room and board: **$11,503**; books: **$900**; miscellaneous expenses: **$1,711**
Total of room/board/books/miscellaneous expenses: **$14,114**
University does not offer graduate student housing for which law students are eligible.

Financial aid profile
Percent of students that received grants for the 2006-2007 academic year: full-time: **49%**; part-time **21%**
Median grant amount: full-time: **$6,500**; part-time: **$4,170**

The average law-school debt of those in the Class of 2007 who borrowed: **$94,360**. Proportion who borrowed: **88%**

ACADEMIC PROGRAMS
Calendar: **semester**
Joint degrees awarded: **J.D./M.B.A.; J.D./M.P.A.; J.D./M.S.F.; J.D./M.S.I.E.; J.D./M.S.C.J.**
Typical first-year section size: Full-time: **85**; Part-time: **100**
Is there typically a "small section" of the first year class, other than Legal Writing, taught by full-time faculty?: Full-time: **yes**; Part-time: **yes**
Number of course titles, beyond the first year curriculum, offered last year: **280**
Percentages of upper division course sections, excluding seminars, with an enrollment of:

Under 25: **60%**		25 to 49: **23%**
50 to 74: **9%**		75 to 99: **3%**
100+: **5%**		

Areas of specialization: appellate advocacy, clinical training, dispute resolution, environmental law, healthcare law, intellectual property law, international law, tax law, trial advocacy

Fall 2007 faculty profile
Total teaching faculty: **N/A**. Full-time: **N/A**; **N/A** men, **N/A** women, **N/A** minorities. Part-time: **N/A**; **N/A** men, **N/A** women, **N/A** minorities
Student-to-faculty ratio: **16.5**

SPECIAL PROGRAMS (as provided by law school):
Law students may take courses in intellectual property, civil litigation, health and biomedical law, international law, and business and financial services. They may enroll in a broad array of clinical and internship programs, including international internships at law firms worldwide. The Rappaport Center for Law and Public Service offers opportunities in public policy and public service work.

STUDENT BODY
Fall 2007 full-time enrollment: 1,021
Men: **49%**   Women: **51%**

African-American: 2.7%   American Indian: 0.7%
Asian-American: 7.3%   Mexican-American: 0.0%
Puerto Rican: 0.0%   Other Hisp-Amer: 3.9%
White: 74.0%   International: 2.0%
Unknown: 9.3%

Fall 2007 part-time enrollment: 604
Men: 53%   Women: 47%
African-American: 3.0%   American Indian: 0.3%
Asian-American: 5.8%   Mexican-American: 0.0%
Puerto Rican: 0.0%   Other Hisp-Amer: 3.8%
White: 77.6%   International: 2.2%
Unknown: 7.3%

Attrition rates for 2006-2007 full-time students
Percent of students discontinuing law school:
Men: 1%   Women: 2%
First-year students: 4%   Second-year students: 0%
Third-year students: N/A

LIBRARY RESOURCES
Total volumes: 374,469
Total seats available for library users: 880

INFORMATION TECHNOLOGY
Number of wired network connections available to students: 3,650 total (in the law library, excluding computer labs: 2,000; in classrooms: 1,400; in computer labs: 100; elsewhere in the law school: 150)
Law school has a wireless network.
Students are not required to own a computer.

EMPLOYMENT AND SALARIES
Proportion of 2006 graduates employed at graduation: 57%

Employed 9 months later, as of February 15, 2007: 91%
Salaries in the private sector (law firms, business, industry): $52,000–$125,000 (25th-75th percentile)
Median salary in the private sector: $70,000
Percentage in the private sector who reported salary information: 69%
Median salary in public service (government, judicial clerkships, academic posts, non-profits): $45,000

Percentage of 2006 graduates in:
Law firms: 46%   Government: 13%
Bus./industry: 23%   Judicial clerkship: 10%
Public interest: 2%   Unknown: 4%
Academia: 2%

2006 graduates employed in-state: 85%
2006 graduates employed in foreign countries: 0%
Number of states where graduates are employed: 25
Percentage of 2006 graduates working in: New England: 91%, Middle Atlantic: 3%, East North Central: 1%, West North Central: 0%, South Atlantic: 2%, East South Central: 0%, West South Central: 0%, Mountain: 1%, Pacific: 1%, Unknown: 0%

BAR PASSAGE RATES
Based on 2006 graduates taking Summer 2006 or Winter 2007 exams. Most of the school's first-time test takers took the bar in Massachusetts.

| 82% |
School's bar passage rate for first-time test takers

| 86% |
Statewide bar passage rate for first-time test takers

Syracuse University

- Suite 340, Syracuse, NY, 13244-1030
- http://www.law.syr.edu
- Private
- Year founded: 1895
- 2007-2008 tuition: full-time: $41,694; part-time: $1,800/credit hour
- Enrollment 2007-08 academic year: full-time: 659; part-time: 7
- U.S. News 2009 law specialty ranking: trial advocacy: 12

3.09-3.59 GPA, 25TH-75TH PERCENTILE

152-156 LSAT, 25TH-75TH PERCENTILE

50% ACCEPTANCE RATE

100 2009 U.S. NEWS LAW SCHOOL RANKING

ADMISSIONS

Admissions phone number: (315) 443-1962
Admissions email address: **admissions@law.syr.edu**
Application website: **N/A**
Application deadline for Fall 2009 admission: **04/01**

Admissions statistics:
Number of applicants for Fall 2007: **2,022**
Number of acceptances: **1,003**
Number enrolled: **221**
Acceptance rate: **50%**
GPA, 25th-75th percentile, entering class Fall 2007: **3.09-3.59**
LSAT, 25th-75th percentile, entering class Fall 2007: **152-156**

Part-time program:
Number of applicants for Fall 2007: **46**
Number of acceptances: **10**
Number enrolled: **2**
Acceptance rate: **22%**
GPA, 25th-75th percentile, entering class Fall 2007: **N/A**
LSAT, 25th-75th percentile, entering class Fall 2007: **N/A**

FINANCIAL AID

Financial aid phone number: (315) 443-1963
Financial aid application deadline: **02/15**
Tuition 2007-2008 academic year: full-time: **$41,694**; part-time: **$1,800/credit hour**
Room and board: **$11,270**; books: **$1,250**; miscellaneous expenses: **$4,296**
Total of room/board/books/miscellaneous expenses: **$16,816**
University offers graduate student housing for which law students are eligible.

Financial aid profile
Percent of students that received grants for the 2006-2007 academic year: full-time: **72%**
Median grant amount: full-time: **$7,600**

The average law-school debt of those in the Class of 2007 who borrowed: **$99,886**. Proportion who borrowed: **91%**

ACADEMIC PROGRAMS

Calendar: **semester**
Joint degrees awarded: **J.D./M.B.A.; J.D./M.A. Economics; J.D./M.A. International Relations; J.D./M.P.A.; J.D./M.S. Information Management; J.D./M.A. TV, Radio and Film; J.D./M.A. History; J.D./M.A. Political Science; J.D/M.A. Journalism; J.D./M.S. Cultural Foundations of Edu.; J.D./M.S. Bioengineering; J.D./M.S. Media Management; J.D./M.S. Electrical Engineering; J.D./M.A. Advertising; J.D./M.S. Computer Science; J.D./M.S. Education, Disability Studies; J.D./M.S.W.**
Typical first-year section size: Full-time: **62**
Is there typically a "small section" of the first year class, other than Legal Writing, taught by full-time faculty?: Full-time: **yes**
Number of course titles, beyond the first year curriculum, offered last year: **144**
Percentages of upper division course sections, excluding seminars, with an enrollment of:

Under 25: **77%**	25 to 49: **14%**	
50 to 74: **7%**	75 to 99: **2%**	
100+: **0%**		

Areas of specialization: appellate advocacy, clinical training, dispute resolution, environmental law, healthcare law, intellectual property law, international law, tax law, trial advocacy

Fall 2007 faculty profile
Total teaching faculty: **82**. Full-time: **56%**; **63%** men, **37%** women, **20%** minorities. Part-time: **44%**; **83%** men, **17%** women, **19%** minorities
Student-to-faculty ratio: **12.7**

SPECIAL PROGRAMS *(as provided by law school):*
Syracuse University College of Law offers innovative interdisciplinary programs with seven centers and two institutes; a distinguished clinical program with six in-house clinics and an

externship program with more than 40 placements; a highly competitive advocacy skills training program with award-winning student teams; and 10 joint-degree programs.

STUDENT BODY

Fall 2007 full-time enrollment: 659

Men: 55%	Women: 45%
African-American: 4.4%	American Indian: 1.1%
Asian-American: 10.3%	Mexican-American: 0.5%
Puerto Rican: 0.3%	Other Hisp-Amer: 2.4%
White: 55.2%	International: 2.9%
Unknown: 22.9%	

Fall 2007 part-time enrollment: 7

Men: 29%	Women: 71%
African-American: 0.0%	American Indian: 0.0%
Asian-American: 0.0%	Mexican-American: 0.0%
Puerto Rican: 0.0%	Other Hisp-Amer: 0.0%
White: 100.0%	International: 0.0%
Unknown: 0.0%	

Attrition rates for 2006-2007 full-time students

Percent of students discontinuing law school:

Men: 9%	Women: 3%
First-year students: 15%	Second-year students: 2%
Third-year students: N/A	

LIBRARY RESOURCES

Total volumes: 473,076
Total seats available for library users: 388

INFORMATION TECHNOLOGY

Number of wired network connections available to students: 19 total (in the law library, excluding computer labs: 14; in classrooms: 0; in computer labs: 0; elsewhere in the law school: 5)
Law school has a wireless network.
Students are required to own a computer.

EMPLOYMENT AND SALARIES

Proportion of 2006 graduates employed at graduation: 63%
Employed 9 months later, as of February 15, 2007: 93%
Salaries in the private sector (law firms, business, industry): $45,000–$85,000 (25th-75th percentile)
Median salary in the private sector: $65,000
Percentage in the private sector who reported salary information: 76%
Median salary in public service (government, judicial clerkships, academic posts, non-profits): $42,000

Percentage of 2006 graduates in:

Law firms: 46%	Government: 16%
Bus./industry: 16%	Judicial clerkship: 15%
Public interest: 4%	Unknown: 0%
Academia: 3%	

2006 graduates employed in-state: 37%
2006 graduates employed in foreign countries: 1%
Number of states where graduates are employed: 31
Percentage of 2006 graduates working in: New England: 5%, Middle Atlantic: 54%, East North Central: 4%, West North Central: 1%, South Atlantic: 24%, East South Central: 1%, West South Central: 2%, Mountain: 2%, Pacific: 6%, Unknown: 0%

BAR PASSAGE RATES

Based on 2006 graduates taking Summer 2006 or Winter 2007 exams. Most of the school's first-time test takers took the bar in New York.

80%
School's bar passage rate for first-time test takers

77%
Statewide bar passage rate for first-time test takers

Temple University (Beasley)

■ 1719 N. Broad Street, Philadelphia, PA, 19122
■ http://www.law.temple.edu
■ Public
■ Year founded: 1895
■ 2007-2008 tuition: In-state: full-time: $15,800; part-time: $12,756; Out-of-state: full-time: $27,078
■ Enrollment 2007-08 academic year: full-time: 754; part-time: 214
■ U.S. News 2009 law specialty ranking: international law: 16, tax law: 25, trial advocacy: 2

3.27-3.65 GPA, 25TH-75TH PERCENTILE

160-164 LSAT, 25TH-75TH PERCENTILE

41% ACCEPTANCE RATE

59 2009 U.S. NEWS LAW SCHOOL RANKING

ADMISSIONS
Admissions phone number: (800) 560-1428
Admissions email address: **lawadmis@temple.edu**
Application website:
  http://www.law.temple.edu/admissions
Application deadline for Fall 2009 admission: **03/01**

Admissions statistics:
Number of applicants for Fall 2007: **4,434**
Number of acceptances: **1,820**
Number enrolled: **252**
Acceptance rate: **41%**
GPA, 25th-75th percentile, entering class Fall 2007: **3.27-3.65**
LSAT, 25th-75th percentile, entering class Fall 2007: **160-164**

Part-time program:
Number of applicants for Fall 2007: **350**
Number of acceptances: **116**
Number enrolled: **62**
Acceptance rate: **33%**
GPA, 25th-75th percentile, entering class Fall 2007: **2.98-3.58**
LSAT, 25th-75th percentile, entering class Fall 2007: **157-161**

FINANCIAL AID
Financial aid phone number: (800) 560-1428
Financial aid application deadline: **03/01**
Tuition 2007-2008 academic year: In-state: full-time: **$15,800**; part-time: **$12,756**; Out-of-state: full-time: **$27,078**
Room and board: **$11,162**; books: **$1,500**; miscellaneous expenses: **$6,546**
Total of room/board/books/miscellaneous expenses: **$19,208**
University offers graduate student housing for which law students are eligible.

Financial aid profile
Percent of students that received grants for the 2006-2007 academic year: full-time: **44%**; part-time **20%**
Median grant amount: full-time: **$6,000**; part-time: **$3,000**
The average law-school debt of those in the Class of 2007 who borrowed: **$72,529**. Proportion who borrowed: **82%**

ACADEMIC PROGRAMS
Calendar: **semester**
Joint degrees awarded: **J.D./M.B.A.**
Typical first-year section size: Full-time: **60**; Part-time: **60**
Is there typically a "small section" of the first year class, other than Legal Writing, taught by full-time faculty?: Full-time: **no**; Part-time: **no**
Number of course titles, beyond the first year curriculum, offered last year: **185**
Percentages of upper division course sections, excluding seminars, with an enrollment of:
  Under 25: **68%**   25 to 49: **22%**
  50 to 74: **5%**   75 to 99: **4%**
  100+: **0%**
Areas of specialization: appellate advocacy, clinical training, dispute resolution, environmental law, healthcare law, intellectual property law, international law, tax law, trial advocacy

Fall 2007 faculty profile
Total teaching faculty: **343**. Full-time: **34%**; **60%** men, **40%** women, **27%** minorities. Part-time: **66%**; **70%** men, **30%** women, **12%** minorities
Student-to-faculty ratio: **12.8**

SPECIAL PROGRAMS *(as provided by law school):*
Temple's curriculum integrates critical thinking and practical legal skills. Temple boasts a prize-winning trial advocacy program, an extensive clinical program, business and transactional skills courses, unique opportunities to study international law at home and abroad, traditional intellectual property law and the law of emerging technologies, and a long-standing tradition of public service.

STUDENT BODY

Fall 2007 full-time enrollment: 754

Men: 50%
African-American: 7.8%
Asian-American: 10.1%
Puerto Rican: 0.8%
White: 74.1%
Unknown: 2.4%

Women: 50%
American Indian: 0.9%
Mexican-American: 0.5%
Other Hisp-Amer: 1.9%
International: 1.5%

Fall 2007 part-time enrollment: 214

Men: 63%
African-American: 6.5%
Asian-American: 8.9%
Puerto Rican: 0.5%
White: 79.9%
Unknown: 0.5%

Women: 37%
American Indian: 0.5%
Mexican-American: 0.0%
Other Hisp-Amer: 1.9%
International: 1.4%

Attrition rates for 2006-2007 full-time students
Percent of students discontinuing law school:
Men: 3%
First-year students: 7%
Third-year students: N/A

Women: 2%
Second-year students: 1%

LIBRARY RESOURCES

Total volumes: 598,212
Total seats available for library users: 700

INFORMATION TECHNOLOGY

Number of wired network connections available to students: 425 total (in the law library, excluding computer labs: 160; in classrooms: 143; in computer labs: 56; elsewhere in the law school: 66)
Law school has a wireless network.
Students are not required to own a computer.

EMPLOYMENT AND SALARIES

Proportion of 2006 graduates employed at graduation: 67%
Employed 9 months later, as of February 15, 2007: 94%

Salaries in the private sector (law firms, business, industry): $57,000–$120,000 (25th-75th percentile)
Median salary in the private sector: $80,000
Percentage in the private sector who reported salary information: 68%
Median salary in public service (government, judicial clerkships, academic posts, non-profits): $47,000

Percentage of 2006 graduates in:
Law firms: 49%
Bus./industry: 19%
Public interest: 6%
Academia: 2%

Government: 11%
Judicial clerkship: 12%
Unknown: 1%

2006 graduates employed in-state: 73%
2006 graduates employed in foreign countries: 1%
Number of states where graduates are employed: 18
Percentage of 2006 graduates working in: New England: 1%, Middle Atlantic: 86%, East North Central: 0%, West North Central: 0%, South Atlantic: 8%, East South Central: 0%, West South Central: 1%, Mountain: 1%, Pacific: 1%, Unknown: 1%

BAR PASSAGE RATES

Based on 2006 graduates taking Summer 2006 or Winter 2007 exams. Most of the school's first-time test takers took the bar in Pennsylvania.

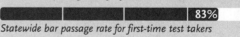

90%
School's bar passage rate for first-time test takers

83%
Statewide bar passage rate for first-time test takers

Texas Southern University (Marshall)

- 3100 Cleburne Street, Houston, TX, 77004
- http://www.tsu.edu/academics/law/index.asp
- Public
- Year founded: 1947
- 2007-2008 tuition: In-state: full-time: $11,528; part-time: N/A; Out-of-state: full-time: $15,278
- Enrollment 2007-08 academic year: full-time: 583
- U.S. News 2009 law specialty ranking: N/A

2.83-3.29 GPA, 25TH-75TH PERCENTILE

146-151 LSAT, 25TH-75TH PERCENTILE

36% ACCEPTANCE RATE

Tier 4 2009 U.S. NEWS LAW SCHOOL RANKING

ADMISSIONS
Admissions phone number: **(713) 313-7114**
Admissions email address: **lawadmit@tsulaw.edu**
Application website: **N/A**
Application deadline for Fall 2009 admission: **04/01**

Admissions statistics:
Number of applicants for Fall 2007: **2,100**
Number of acceptances: **754**
Number enrolled: **187**
Acceptance rate: **36%**
GPA, 25th-75th percentile, entering class Fall 2007: **2.83-3.29**
LSAT, 25th-75th percentile, entering class Fall 2007: **146-151**

FINANCIAL AID
Financial aid phone number: **(713) 313-7243**
Financial aid application deadline: **04/01**
Tuition 2007-2008 academic year: In-state: full-time: **$11,528**; part-time: **N/A**; Out-of-state: full-time: **$15,278**
Room and board: **$7,000**; books: **$1,900**; miscellaneous expenses: **$3,600**
Total of room/board/books/miscellaneous expenses: **$12,500**
University does not offer graduate student housing for which law students are eligible.

Financial aid profile
Percent of students that received grants for the 2006-2007 academic year: full-time: **43%**
Median grant amount: full-time: **$3,000**
The average law-school debt of those in the Class of 2007 who borrowed: **$20,000**. Proportion who borrowed: **98%**

ACADEMIC PROGRAMS
Calendar: **semester**
Joint degrees awarded: **M.P.A.; M.B.A.**
Typical first-year section size: Full-time: **65**
Is there typically a "small section" of the first year class, other than Legal Writing, taught by full-time faculty?:
Full-time: **no**
Number of course titles, beyond the first year curriculum, offered last year: **123**
Percentages of upper division course sections, excluding seminars, with an enrollment of:
Under 25: **57%**   25 to 49: **22%**
50 to 74: **18%**   75 to 99: **3%**
100+: **0%**
Areas of specialization: appellate advocacy, clinical training, dispute resolution, environmental law, healthcare law, intellectual property law, international law, tax law, trial advocacy

Fall 2007 faculty profile
Total teaching faculty: **61**. Full-time: **64%**; **49%** men, **51%** women, **69%** minorities. Part-time: **36%**; **86%** men, **14%** women, **86%** minorities
Student-to-faculty ratio: **14.5**

SPECIAL PROGRAMS (as provided by law school):
The law school is proud of its wide array of special programs offered to the student body. The school offers a successful and thriving legal clinical program, the Institute for International and Immigration Law, the Earl Carl Institute for Legal and Social Policy, and the Center for Government Law, and provides several internship and externship programs.

STUDENT BODY
Fall 2007 full-time enrollment: 583
Men: **50%**   Women: **50%**
African-American: **47.2%**   American Indian: **0.5%**
Asian-American: **7.9%**   Mexican-American: **21.3%**
Puerto Rican: **0.0%**   Other Hisp-Amer: **1.9%**
White: **20.9%**   International: **0.0%**
Unknown: **0.3%**

Attrition rates for 2006-2007 full-time students
Percent of students discontinuing law school:
Men: **9%**   Women: **9%**
First-year students: **22%**   Second-year students: **2%**
Third-year students: **N/A**

LIBRARY RESOURCES
Total volumes: **682,372**
Total seats available for library users: **372**

INFORMATION TECHNOLOGY
Number of wired network connections available to students: **945** total (in the law library, excluding computer labs: **300**; in classrooms: **560**; in computer labs: **65**; elsewhere in the law school: **20**)
Law school has a wireless network.
Students are not required to own a computer.

EMPLOYMENT AND SALARIES
Proportion of 2006 graduates employed at graduation: **N/A**
Employed 9 months later, as of February 15, 2007: **88%**
Salaries in the private sector (law firms, business, industry): **$65,000–$105,000** (25th-75th percentile)
Median salary in the private sector: **$85,000**
Percentage in the private sector who reported salary information: **0%**
Median salary in public service (government, judicial clerkships, academic posts, non-profits): **$41,018**

Percentage of 2006 graduates in:
Law firms: **71%**	Government: **10%**
Bus./industry: **13%**	Judicial clerkship: **1%**
Public interest: **1%**	Unknown: **2%**
Academia: **2%**	

2006 graduates employed in-state: **74%**
2006 graduates employed in foreign countries: **1%**
Number of states where graduates are employed: **23**
Percentage of 2006 graduates working in: New England: **0%**, Middle Atlantic: **3%**, East North Central: **4%**, West North Central: **1%**, South Atlantic: **6%**, East South Central: **2%**, West South Central: **76%**, Mountain: **4%**, Pacific: **3%**, Unknown: **0%**

BAR PASSAGE RATES
Based on 2006 graduates taking Summer 2006 or Winter 2007 exams. Most of the school's first-time test takers took the bar in Texas.

56%
School's bar passage rate for first-time test takers

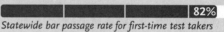

82%
Statewide bar passage rate for first-time test takers

Texas Tech University

- 1802 Hartford Avenue, Lubbock, TX, 79409-0004
- http://www.law.ttu.edu
- Public
- **Year founded:** 1967
- **2007-2008 tuition:** In-state: full-time: $13,654; part-time: N/A; Out-of-state: full-time: $20,759
- **Enrollment 2007-08 academic year:** full-time: 692
- **U.S. News 2009 law specialty ranking:** N/A

3.34-3.75 GPA, 25TH-75TH PERCENTILE

151-157 LSAT, 25TH-75TH PERCENTILE

43% ACCEPTANCE RATE

Tier 3 2009 U.S. NEWS LAW SCHOOL RANKING

ADMISSIONS
Admissions phone number: **(806) 742-3791**
Admissions email address: **donna.williams@ttu.edu**
Application website: **N/A**
Application deadline for Fall 2009 admission: **02/01**

Admissions statistics:
Number of applicants for Fall 2007: **1,747**
Number of acceptances: **758**
Number enrolled: **238**
Acceptance rate: **43%**
GPA, 25th-75th percentile, entering class Fall 2007: **3.34-3.75**
LSAT, 25th-75th percentile, entering class Fall 2007: **151-157**

FINANCIAL AID
Financial aid phone number: **(806) 742-3990**
Financial aid application deadline: **02/01**
Tuition 2007-2008 academic year: In-state: full-time: **$13,654**; part-time: N/A; Out-of-state: full-time: **$20,759**
Room and board: **$7,680**; books: **$1,000**; miscellaneous expenses: **$4,310**
Total of room/board/books/miscellaneous expenses: **$12,990**
University offers graduate student housing for which law students are eligible.

Financial aid profile
Percent of students that received grants for the 2006-2007 academic year: full-time: **75%**
Median grant amount: full-time: **$3,400**
The average law-school debt of those in the Class of 2007 who borrowed: **$50,716**. Proportion who borrowed: **90%**

ACADEMIC PROGRAMS
Calendar: **semester**
Joint degrees awarded: **J.D./M.B.A.; J.D./M.P.A.; J.D./M.S. Taxation; J.D./M.S. Agr. & Applied Economics; J.D./M.S. Environmental Toxicology; J.D./M.S. Personal Financial Planning; J.D./M.S. Biotechnology; J.D./M.S. C.S./H./S.S./E.**

Typical first-year section size: Full-time: **56**
Is there typically a "small section" of the first year class, other than Legal Writing, taught by full-time faculty?: Full-time: **no**
Number of course titles, beyond the first year curriculum, offered last year: **90**
Percentages of upper division course sections, excluding seminars, with an enrollment of:
Under 25: **48%**   25 to 49: **27%**
50 to 74: **12%**   75 to 99: **9%**
100+: **4%**
Areas of specialization: appellate advocacy, clinical training, dispute resolution, environmental law, healthcare law, intellectual property law, international law, tax law, trial advocacy

Fall 2007 faculty profile
Total teaching faculty: **53**. Full-time: **72%**; **66%** men, **34%** women, **21%** minorities. Part-time: **28%**; **73%** men, **27%** women, **20%** minorities
Student-to-faculty ratio: **15.4**

SPECIAL PROGRAMS (as provided by law school):
Clinical programs: to represent clients in real cases through clinical courses. Summer Law Institute: Guanajuato, Mexico. Semester abroad: University of Lyon in France; Universidad Pablo de Olavide in Seville, Spain; La Trobe University in Australia. Center for Military Law and Policy; Center for Biodefense Law and Public Policy; Center for Water Law and Policy.

STUDENT BODY
Fall 2007 full-time enrollment: 692
Men: **57%**   Women: **43%**
African-American: **3.8%**   American Indian: **0.7%**
Asian-American: **3.6%**   Mexican-American: **12.6%**
Puerto Rican: **0.3%**   Other Hisp-Amer: **0.0%**
White: **78.9%**   International: **0.0%**
Unknown: **0.1%**

Attrition rates for 2006-2007 full-time students
Percent of students discontinuing law school:
Men: 1%   Women: 1%
First-year students: 3%   Second-year students: 0%
Third-year students: N/A

LIBRARY RESOURCES
Total volumes: 314,124
Total seats available for library users: 580

INFORMATION TECHNOLOGY
Number of wired network connections available to students: 891 total (in the law library, excluding computer labs: 474; in classrooms: 386; in computer labs: 5; elsewhere in the law school: 26)
Law school has a wireless network.
Students are required to own a computer.

EMPLOYMENT AND SALARIES
Proportion of 2006 graduates employed at graduation: 41%
Employed 9 months later, as of February 15, 2007: 92%
Salaries in the private sector (law firms, business, industry): $36,000–$101,000 (25th-75th percentile)
Median salary in the private sector: $77,000
Percentage in the private sector who reported salary information: 40%
Median salary in public service (government, judicial clerkships, academic posts, non-profits): $41,000

Percentage of 2006 graduates in:
Law firms: 86%   Government: 8%
Bus./industry: 1%   Judicial clerkship: 2%
Public interest: 3%   Unknown: 0%
Academia: 0%

2006 graduates employed in-state: 96%
2006 graduates employed in foreign countries: 0%
Number of states where graduates are employed: 5
Percentage of 2006 graduates working in: New England: N/A, Middle Atlantic: 1%, East North Central: N/A, West North Central: N/A, South Atlantic: 1%, East South Central: N/A, West South Central: 96%, Mountain: 3%, Pacific: 1%, Unknown: N/A

BAR PASSAGE RATES
Based on 2006 graduates taking Summer 2006 or Winter 2007 exams. Most of the school's first-time test takers took the bar in Texas.

87%
School's bar passage rate for first-time test takers

82%
Statewide bar passage rate for first-time test takers

Texas Wesleyan University

■ 1515 Commerce Street, Fort Worth, TX, 76102
■ http://www.law.txwes.edu/
■ Private
■ Year founded: 1992
■ 2007-2008 tuition: full-time: $23,250; part-time: $16,800
■ Enrollment 2007-08 academic year: full-time: 443; part-time: 314
■ U.S. News 2009 law specialty ranking: N/A

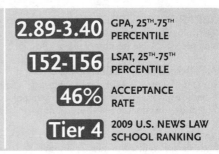

2.89-3.40 GPA, 25ᵀᴴ-75ᵀᴴ PERCENTILE

152-156 LSAT, 25ᵀᴴ-75ᵀᴴ PERCENTILE

46% ACCEPTANCE RATE

Tier 4 2009 U.S. NEWS LAW SCHOOL RANKING

ADMISSIONS

Admissions phone number: **(817) 212-4040**
Admissions email address: **lawadmissions@law.txwes.edu**
Application website:
   http://www.law.txwes.edu/application.htm
Application deadline for Fall 2009 admission: **05/15**

Admissions statistics:
Number of applicants for Fall 2007: **1,522**
Number of acceptances: **697**
Number enrolled: **169**
Acceptance rate: **46%**
GPA, 25th-75th percentile, entering class Fall 2007: **2.89-3.40**
LSAT, 25th-75th percentile, entering class Fall 2007: **152-156**

Part-time program:
Number of applicants for Fall 2007: **412**
Number of acceptances: **247**
Number enrolled: **118**
Acceptance rate: **60%**
GPA, 25th-75th percentile, entering class Fall 2007: **2.76-3.35**
LSAT, 25th-75th percentile, entering class Fall 2007: **149-154**

FINANCIAL AID

Financial aid phone number: **(817) 212-4090**
Financial aid application deadline: **03/15**
Tuition 2007-2008 academic year: full-time: **$23,250**; part-time: **$16,800**
Room and board: **$10,521**; books: **$1,740**; miscellaneous expenses: **$2,034**
Total of room/board/books/miscellaneous expenses: **$14,295**
University offers graduate student housing for which law students are eligible.

Financial aid profile
Percent of students that received grants for the 2006-2007 academic year: full-time: **37%**; part-time **26%**
Median grant amount: full-time: **$7,500**; part-time: **$5,000**
The average law-school debt of those in the Class of 2007 who borrowed: **$57,231**. Proportion who borrowed: **66%**

ACADEMIC PROGRAMS

Calendar: **semester**
Joint degrees awarded: **N/A**
Typical first-year section size: Full-time: **79**; Part-time: **70**
Is there typically a "small section" of the first year class, other than Legal Writing, taught by full-time faculty?: Full-time: **no**; Part-time: **no**
Number of course titles, beyond the first year curriculum, offered last year: **87**
Percentages of upper division course sections, excluding seminars, with an enrollment of:
   Under 25: **66%**   25 to 49: **19%**
   50 to 74: **8%**   75 to 99: **6%**
   100+: **1%**
Areas of specialization: appellate advocacy, clinical training, dispute resolution, environmental law, healthcare law, intellectual property law, tax law, trial advocacy

Fall 2007 faculty profile
Total teaching faculty: **60**. Full-time: **42%**; **64%** men, **36%** women, **20%** minorities. Part-time: **58%**; **63%** men, **37%** women, **9%** minorities
Student-to-faculty ratio: **20.8**

SPECIAL PROGRAMS *(as provided by law school):*
Texas Wesleyan Law School provides many opportunities for learning skills. In clinics, students represent clients in Social Security and family law cases. In the externship program, students work with practicing attorneys in many different areas of law. In the practicums, students learn practical skills such as drafting and negotiations.

STUDENT BODY

Fall 2007 full-time enrollment: 443

Men: 52%	Women: 48%
African-American: 3.4%	American Indian: 1.6%
Asian-American: 6.1%	Mexican-American: 0.0%
Puerto Rican: 0.0%	Other Hisp-Amer: 6.3%
White: 77.2%	International: 0.0%
Unknown: 5.4%	

Fall 2007 part-time enrollment: 314

Men: 53%	Women: 47%
African-American: 6.7%	American Indian: 2.2%
Asian-American: 6.4%	Mexican-American: 0.0%
Puerto Rican: 0.0%	Other Hisp-Amer: 12.4%
White: 69.4%	International: 0.0%
Unknown: 2.9%	

Attrition rates for 2006-2007 full-time students
Percent of students discontinuing law school:

Men: 6%	Women: 3%
First-year students: 12%	Second-year students: 0%
Third-year students: N/A	

LIBRARY RESOURCES

Total volumes: 255,467
Total seats available for library users: 383

INFORMATION TECHNOLOGY

Number of wired network connections available to students: 0 total (in the law library, excluding computer labs: 0; in classrooms: 0; in computer labs: 0; elsewhere in the law school: 0)
Law school has a wireless network.
Students are not required to own a computer.

EMPLOYMENT AND SALARIES

Proportion of 2006 graduates employed at graduation: 54%

Employed 9 months later, as of February 15, 2007: 83%
Salaries in the private sector (law firms, business, industry): $48,000–$80,000 (25th-75th percentile)
Median salary in the private sector: $62,000
Percentage in the private sector who reported salary information: 36%
Median salary in public service (government, judicial clerkships, academic posts, non-profits): $50,000

Percentage of 2006 graduates in:

Law firms: 42%	Government: 12%
Bus./industry: 26%	Judicial clerkship: 2%
Public interest: 4%	Unknown: 13%
Academia: 1%	

2006 graduates employed in-state: 95%
2006 graduates employed in foreign countries: 0%
Number of states where graduates are employed: 8
Percentage of 2006 graduates working in: New England: 0%, Middle Atlantic: 1%, East North Central: 1%, West North Central: 0%, South Atlantic: 1%, East South Central: 1%, West South Central: 94%, Mountain: 1%, Pacific: 1%, Unknown: 0%

BAR PASSAGE RATES

Based on 2006 graduates taking Summer 2006 or Winter 2007 exams. Most of the school's first-time test takers took the bar in Texas.

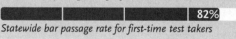

86%
School's bar passage rate for first-time test takers

82%
Statewide bar passage rate for first-time test takers

Thomas Jefferson School of Law

■ 2121 San Diego Avenue, San Diego, CA, 92110
■ http://www.tjsl.edu
■ Private
■ Year founded: 1969
■ 2007-2008 tuition: full-time: $31,770; part-time: $20,010
■ Enrollment 2007-08 academic year: full-time: 581; part-time: 196
■ U.S. News 2009 law specialty ranking: N/A

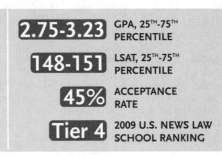

2.75-3.23 GPA, 25ᵀᴴ-75ᵀᴴ PERCENTILE

148-151 LSAT, 25ᵀᴴ-75ᵀᴴ PERCENTILE

45% ACCEPTANCE RATE

Tier 4 2009 U.S. NEWS LAW SCHOOL RANKING

ADMISSIONS
Admissions phone number: **(619) 297-9700**
Admissions email address: **info@tjsl.edu**
Application website: **N/A**
Application deadline for Fall 2009 admission: **06/01**

Admissions statistics:
Number of applicants for Fall 2007: **2,657**
Number of acceptances: **1,205**
Number enrolled: **252**
Acceptance rate: **45%**
GPA, 25th-75th percentile, entering class Fall 2007: **2.75-3.23**
LSAT, 25th-75th percentile, entering class Fall 2007: **148-151**

Part-time program:
Number of applicants for Fall 2007: **325**
Number of acceptances: **124**
Number enrolled: **52**
Acceptance rate: **38%**
GPA, 25th-75th percentile, entering class Fall 2007: **2.61-3.22**
LSAT, 25th-75th percentile, entering class Fall 2007: **146-148**

FINANCIAL AID
Financial aid phone number: **(619) 297-9700**
Financial aid application deadline: **04/30**
Tuition 2007-2008 academic year: full-time: **$31,770**; part-time: **$20,010**
Room and board: **N/A**; books: **N/A**; miscellaneous expenses: **N/A**
Total of room/board/books/miscellaneous expenses: **$24,566**
University does not offer graduate student housing for which law students are eligible.

Financial aid profile
Percent of students that received grants for the 2006-2007 academic year: full-time: **45%**; part-time **43%**

Median grant amount: full-time: **$12,000**; part-time: **$6,000**
The average law-school debt of those in the Class of 2007 who borrowed: **$92,397**. Proportion who borrowed: **96%**

ACADEMIC PROGRAMS
Calendar: **semester**
Joint degrees awarded: **N/A**
Typical first-year section size: Full-time: **98**; Part-time: **48**
Is there typically a "small section" of the first year class, other than Legal Writing, taught by full-time faculty?: Full-time: **no**; Part-time: **no**
Number of course titles, beyond the first year curriculum, offered last year: **107**
Percentages of upper division course sections, excluding seminars, with an enrollment of:
Under 25: **63%**   25 to 49: **20%**
50 to 74: **13%**   75 to 99: **2%**
100+: **2%**
Areas of specialization: appellate advocacy, clinical training, dispute resolution, environmental law, healthcare law, intellectual property law, international law, tax law, trial advocacy

Fall 2007 faculty profile
Total teaching faculty: **80**. Full-time: **50%**; **53%** men, **48%** women, **20%** minorities. Part-time: **50%**; **73%** men, **28%** women, **5%** minorities
Student-to-faculty ratio: **14.9**

SPECIAL PROGRAMS *(as provided by law school):*
To provide an institutional framework for the study of technological change and globalization, the law school has established three academic centers: the Centers for Law Technology and Communications, Global Legal Studies, and Law and Social Justice. Each center combines the scholarship of the faculty with special programs that attract leading legal experts from throughout the world.

STUDENT BODY

Fall 2007 full-time enrollment: 581

Men: 52%	Women: 48%
African-American: 7.7%	American Indian: 0.9%
Asian-American: 10.2%	Mexican-American: 7.7%
Puerto Rican: 1.2%	Other Hisp-Amer: 5.0%
White: 65.2%	International: 0.0%
Unknown: 2.1%	

Fall 2007 part-time enrollment: 196

Men: 53%	Women: 47%
African-American: 6.1%	American Indian: 1.0%
Asian-American: 7.7%	Mexican-American: 6.6%
Puerto Rican: 1.5%	Other Hisp-Amer: 3.6%
White: 71.4%	International: 0.0%
Unknown: 2.0%	

Attrition rates for 2006-2007 full-time students
Percent of students discontinuing law school:

Men: 12%	Women: 11%
First-year students: 11%	Second-year students: 25%
Third-year students: 4%	

LIBRARY RESOURCES

Total volumes: 255,510
Total seats available for library users: 266

INFORMATION TECHNOLOGY

Number of wired network connections available to students: 46 total (in the law library, excluding computer labs: 46; in classrooms: 0; in computer labs: 0; elsewhere in the law school: 0)
Law school has a wireless network.
Students are required to own a computer.

EMPLOYMENT AND SALARIES

Proportion of 2006 graduates employed at graduation: N/A

Employed 9 months later, as of February 15, 2007: 80%
Salaries in the private sector (law firms, business, industry): $40,000–$65,000 (25th-75th percentile)
Median salary in the private sector: $54,000
Percentage in the private sector who reported salary information: 36%
Median salary in public service (government, judicial clerkships, academic posts, non-profits): $49,500

Percentage of 2006 graduates in:

Law firms: 50%	Government: 11%
Bus./industry: 24%	Judicial clerkship: 2%
Public interest: 6%	Unknown: 4%
Academia: 3%	

2006 graduates employed in-state: 65%
2006 graduates employed in foreign countries: 2%
Number of states where graduates are employed: 24
Percentage of 2006 graduates working in: New England: 1%, Middle Atlantic: 3%, East North Central: 4%, West North Central: 2%, South Atlantic: 5%, East South Central: 0%, West South Central: 4%, Mountain: 10%, Pacific: 67%, Unknown: 2%

BAR PASSAGE RATES

Based on 2006 graduates taking Summer 2006 or Winter 2007 exams. Most of the school's first-time test takers took the bar in California.

55%
School's bar passage rate for first-time test takers

65%
Statewide bar passage rate for first-time test takers

Thomas M. Cooley Law School

■ 300 S. Capitol Avenue, PO Box 13038, Lansing, MI, 48901
■ http://www.cooley.edu
■ Private
■ Year founded: 1972
■ 2007-2008 tuition: full-time: $25,436; part-time: $21,808
■ Enrollment 2007-08 academic year: full-time: 535; part-time: 3,129
■ U.S. News 2009 law specialty ranking: N/A

2.75-3.35 GPA, 25ᵀᴴ-75ᵀᴴ PERCENTILE

145-154 LSAT, 25ᵀᴴ-75ᵀᴴ PERCENTILE

74% ACCEPTANCE RATE

Tier 4 2009 U.S. NEWS LAW SCHOOL RANKING

ADMISSIONS

Admissions phone number: (517) 371-5140
Admissions email address: **admissions@cooley.edu**
Application website: **http://www.cooley.edu/admissions**
Application deadline for Fall 2009 admission: **09/01**

Admissions statistics:
Number of applicants for Fall 2007: 4,202
Number of acceptances: 3,103
Number enrolled: 307
Acceptance rate: 74%
GPA, 25th-75th percentile, entering class Fall 2007: 2.75-3.35
LSAT, 25th-75th percentile, entering class Fall 2007: 145-154

Part-time program:
Number of applicants for Fall 2007: 776
Number of acceptances: 596
Number enrolled: 1,273
Acceptance rate: 77%
GPA, 25th-75th percentile, entering class Fall 2007: 2.61-3.28
LSAT, 25th-75th percentile, entering class Fall 2007: 144-149

FINANCIAL AID

Financial aid phone number: (517) 371-5140
Financial aid application deadline: 09/01
Tuition 2007-2008 academic year: full-time: **$25,436**; part-time: **$21,808**
Room and board: **$6,860**; books: **$800**; miscellaneous expenses: **$3,500**
Total of room/board/books/miscellaneous expenses: **$11,160**
University offers graduate student housing for which law students are eligible.

Financial aid profile
Percent of students that received grants for the 2006-2007 academic year: full-time: **86%**; part-time **49%**

Median grant amount: full-time: **$7,872**; part-time: **$5,190**
The average law-school debt of those in the Class of 2007 who borrowed: **$85,450**. Proportion who borrowed: **90%**

ACADEMIC PROGRAMS

Calendar: **semester**
Joint degrees awarded: **J.D./M.P.A.; J.D./LL.M. Taxation; J.D./LL.M. Intellectual Property; J.D./M.B.A.**
Typical first-year section size: Full-time: **57**; Part-time: **57**
Is there typically a "small section" of the first year class, other than Legal Writing, taught by full-time faculty?: Full-time: **no**; Part-time: **no**
Number of course titles, beyond the first year curriculum, offered last year: **247**
Percentages of upper division course sections, excluding seminars, with an enrollment of:

Under 25: **64%**		25 to 49: **14%**	
50 to 74: **9%**		75 to 99: **8%**	
100+: **5%**			

Areas of specialization: appellate advocacy, clinical training, dispute resolution, environmental law, healthcare law, intellectual property law, international law, tax law, trial advocacy

Fall 2007 faculty profile
Total teaching faculty: 231. Full-time: **39%**; **63%** men, **37%** women, **12%** minorities. Part-time: **61%**; **68%** men, **32%** women, **7%** minorities
Student-to-faculty ratio: **24.3**

SPECIAL PROGRAMS *(as provided by law school):*

Cooley offers day, evening, and weekend schedules year-round at three campuses. Students may select from seven areas of concentration. Joint J.D./LL.M., J.D./M.P.A., and J.D./M.B.A. degrees available. Clinics include estate planning, public defender, domestic violence, and civil justice as well as the Sixty Plus Elderlaw Clinic and national externships. Several study-abroad opportunities.

STUDENT BODY

Fall 2007 full-time enrollment: 535

Men: 61%	Women: 39%
African-American: 6.7%	American Indian: 0.4%
Asian-American: 4.3%	Mexican-American: 2.4%
Puerto Rican: 0.4%	Other Hisp-Amer: 2.6%
White: 72.0%	International: 5.6%
Unknown: 5.6%	

Fall 2007 part-time enrollment: 3,129

Men: 52%	Women: 48%
African-American: 10.7%	American Indian: 0.3%
Asian-American: 5.4%	Mexican-American: 1.8%
Puerto Rican: 0.4%	Other Hisp-Amer: 2.7%
White: 69.4%	International: 4.1%
Unknown: 5.3%	

Attrition rates for 2006-2007 full-time students
Percent of students discontinuing law school:

Men: 10%	Women: 13%
First-year students: 14%	Second-year students: 9%
Third-year students: 5%	

LIBRARY RESOURCES

Total volumes: 577,975
Total seats available for library users: 946

INFORMATION TECHNOLOGY

Number of wired network connections available to students: 48 total (in the law library, excluding computer labs: 48; in classrooms: 0; in computer labs: 0; elsewhere in the law school: 0)
Law school has a wireless network.
Students are not required to own a computer.

EMPLOYMENT AND SALARIES

Proportion of 2006 graduates employed at graduation: N/A

Employed 9 months later, as of February 15, 2007: 73%
Salaries in the private sector (law firms, business, industry): $40,000–$67,000 (25th-75th percentile)
Median salary in the private sector: $51,000
Percentage in the private sector who reported salary information: 67%
Median salary in public service (government, judicial clerkships, academic posts, non-profits): $43,000

Percentage of 2006 graduates in:

Law firms: 48%	Government: 17%
Bus./industry: 20%	Judicial clerkship: 7%
Public interest: 5%	Unknown: 1%
Academia: 2%	

2006 graduates employed in-state: 34%
2006 graduates employed in foreign countries: 1%
Number of states where graduates are employed: 37
Percentage of 2006 graduates working in: New England: 1%, Middle Atlantic: 10%, East North Central: 44%, West North Central: 3%, South Atlantic: 19%, East South Central: 2%, West South Central: 3%, Mountain: 7%, Pacific: 4%, Unknown: 7%

BAR PASSAGE RATES

Based on 2006 graduates taking Summer 2006 or Winter 2007 exams. Most of the school's first-time test takers took the bar in Michigan.

80%
School's bar passage rate for first-time test takers

89%
Statewide bar passage rate for first-time test takers

Touro College (Fuchsberg)

■ 225 Eastview Drive, Central Islip, NY, 11722
■ http://www.tourolaw.edu
■ Private
■ Year founded: 1980
■ 2007-2008 tuition: full-time: $33,920; part-time: $25,520
■ Enrollment 2007-08 academic year: full-time: 513; part-time: 234
■ U.S. News 2009 law specialty ranking: N/A

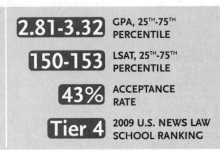

2.81-3.32 GPA, 25TH-75TH PERCENTILE

150-153 LSAT, 25TH-75TH PERCENTILE

43% ACCEPTANCE RATE

Tier 4 2009 U.S. NEWS LAW SCHOOL RANKING

ADMISSIONS
Admissions phone number: **(631) 761-7010**
Admissions email address: **admissions@tourolaw.edu**
Application website:
   http://www.tourolaw.edu/admissions/app.asp
Application deadline for Fall 2009 admission: **08/01**

Admissions statistics:
Number of applicants for Fall 2007: **1,736**
Number of acceptances: **753**
Number enrolled: **204**
Acceptance rate: **43%**
GPA, 25th-75th percentile, entering class Fall 2007: **2.81-3.32**
LSAT, 25th-75th percentile, entering class Fall 2007: **150-153**

Part-time program:
Number of applicants for Fall 2007: **468**
Number of acceptances: **162**
Number enrolled: **80**
Acceptance rate: **35%**
GPA, 25th-75th percentile, entering class Fall 2007: **2.71-3.26**
LSAT, 25th-75th percentile, entering class Fall 2007: **149-151**

FINANCIAL AID
Financial aid phone number: **(631) 761-7020**
Financial aid application deadline: **04/15**
Tuition 2007-2008 academic year: full-time: **$33,920**; part-time: **$25,520**
Room and board: **$17,151**; books: **$1,874**; miscellaneous expenses: **$3,981**
Total of room/board/books/miscellaneous expenses: **$23,006**
University does not offer graduate student housing for which law students are eligible.

Financial aid profile
Percent of students that received grants for the 2006-2007 academic year: full-time: **64%**; part-time **54%**
Median grant amount: full-time: **$3,628**; part-time: **$2,250**
The average law-school debt of those in the Class of 2007 who borrowed: **$88,249**. Proportion who borrowed: **83%**

ACADEMIC PROGRAMS
Calendar: **semester**
Joint degrees awarded: **J.D./M.P.A.; J.D./M.B.A. (C.W. Post); J.D./M.S.W.; J.D./M.B.A. (Dowling)**
Typical first-year section size: Full-time: **69**; Part-time: **58**
Is there typically a "small section" of the first year class, other than Legal Writing, taught by full-time faculty?:
   Full-time: **no**; Part-time: **no**
Number of course titles, beyond the first year curriculum, offered last year: **72**
Percentages of upper division course sections, excluding seminars, with an enrollment of:
   Under 25: **63%**   25 to 49: **16%**
   50 to 74: **17%**   75 to 99: **2%**
   100+: **2%**
Areas of specialization: appellate advocacy, clinical training, dispute resolution, environmental law, healthcare law, intellectual property law, international law, tax law, trial advocacy

Fall 2007 faculty profile
Total teaching faculty: **59**. Full-time: **61%**; **53%** men, **47%** women, **11%** minorities. Part-time: **39%**; **83%** men, **17%** women, **9%** minorities
Student-to-faculty ratio: **15.7**

SPECIAL PROGRAMS (as provided by law school):
N/A

STUDENT BODY

Fall 2007 full-time enrollment: 513

Men: 55%   Women: 45%
African-American: 7.4%   American Indian: 0.2%
Asian-American: 7.2%   Mexican-American: 0.4%
Puerto Rican: 0.0%   Other Hisp-Amer: 3.1%
White: 75.8%   International: 2.1%
Unknown: 3.7%

Fall 2007 part-time enrollment: 234

Men: 48%   Women: 52%
African-American: 13.7%   American Indian: 1.7%
Asian-American: 6.8%   Mexican-American: 0.0%
Puerto Rican: 1.3%   Other Hisp-Amer: 4.3%
White: 65.4%   International: 0.0%
Unknown: 6.8%

Attrition rates for 2006-2007 full-time students
Percent of students discontinuing law school:
Men: 8%   Women: 9%
First-year students: 21%   Second-year students: 3%
Third-year students: N/A

LIBRARY RESOURCES

Total volumes: 441,273
Total seats available for library users: 476

INFORMATION TECHNOLOGY

Number of wired network connections available to students: 60 total (in the law library, excluding computer labs: 0; in classrooms: 0; in computer labs: 40; elsewhere in the law school: 20)
Law school has a wireless network.
Students are not required to own a computer.

EMPLOYMENT AND SALARIES

Proportion of 2006 graduates employed at graduation: N/A

Employed 9 months later, as of February 15, 2007: 74%
Salaries in the private sector (law firms, business, industry): $48,000–$75,500 (25th-75th percentile)
Median salary in the private sector: $62,500
Percentage in the private sector who reported salary information: 47%
Median salary in public service (government, judicial clerkships, academic posts, non-profits): $50,000

Percentage of 2006 graduates in:
Law firms: 60%   Government: 16%
Bus./industry: 15%   Judicial clerkship: 3%
Public interest: 5%   Unknown: 0%
Academia: 1%

2006 graduates employed in-state: 84%
2006 graduates employed in foreign countries: 0%
Number of states where graduates are employed: 10
Percentage of 2006 graduates working in: New England: 0%, Middle Atlantic: 94%, East North Central: 1%, West North Central: 0%, South Atlantic: 3%, East South Central: 0%, West South Central: 0%, Mountain: 1%, Pacific: 1%, Unknown: 0%

BAR PASSAGE RATES

Based on 2006 graduates taking Summer 2006 or Winter 2007 exams. Most of the school's first-time test takers took the bar in New York.

78%
School's bar passage rate for first-time test takers

77%
Statewide bar passage rate for first-time test takers

Tulane University

- 6329 Freret Street, John Giffen Weinmann Hall, New Orleans, LA, 70118-6231
- http://www.law.tulane.edu
- Private
- Year founded: 1847
- 2007-2008 tuition: full-time: $36,670; part-time: N/A
- Enrollment 2007-08 academic year: full-time: 752
- U.S. News 2009 law specialty ranking: clinical training: 24, environmental law: 12

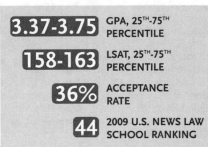

3.37-3.75 GPA, 25TH-75TH PERCENTILE

158-163 LSAT, 25TH-75TH PERCENTILE

36% ACCEPTANCE RATE

44 2009 U.S. NEWS LAW SCHOOL RANKING

ADMISSIONS

Admissions phone number: **(504) 865-5930**
Admissions email address: **admissions@law.tulane.edu**
Application website:
  https://www4.lsac.org/school/Tulane.htm
Application deadline for Fall 2009 admission: **02/15**

Admissions statistics:
Number of applicants for Fall 2007: **2,303**
Number of acceptances: **821**
Number enrolled: **245**
Acceptance rate: **36%**
GPA, 25th-75th percentile, entering class Fall 2007: **3.37-3.75**
LSAT, 25th-75th percentile, entering class Fall 2007: **158-163**

FINANCIAL AID

Financial aid phone number: **(504) 865-5931**
Financial aid application deadline: **02/15**
Tuition 2007-2008 academic year: full-time: **$36,670**; part-time: **N/A**
Room and board: **$11,690**; books: **$1,500**; miscellaneous expenses: **$5,530**
Total of room/board/books/miscellaneous expenses: **$18,720**
University offers graduate student housing for which law students are eligible.

Financial aid profile
Percent of students that received grants for the 2006-2007 academic year: full-time: **66%**
Median grant amount: full-time: **$10,000**
The average law-school debt of those in the Class of 2007 who borrowed: **$102,095**. Proportion who borrowed: **80%**

ACADEMIC PROGRAMS

Calendar: **semester**
Joint degrees awarded: **J.D./M.B.A.; J.D./M.P.H.; J.D./M.A.** Political Science/International Affairs; J.D./M.A. Classical Studies; J.D./M.S. International Development; J.D./B.S.; J.D./B.A.; J.D./M.H.A.; J.D./M.S.W.; J.D./M.A. Latin American Studies; J.D./M.Acc.; J.D./Ph.D.
Typical first-year section size: Full-time: **74**
Is there typically a "small section" of the first year class, other than Legal Writing, taught by full-time faculty?: Full-time: **no**
Number of course titles, beyond the first year curriculum, offered last year: **160**
Percentages of upper division course sections, excluding seminars, with an enrollment of:
  Under 25: **46%**   25 to 49: **35%**
  50 to 74: **11%**   75 to 99: **4%**
  100+: **3%**
Areas of specialization: appellate advocacy, clinical training, dispute resolution, environmental law, healthcare law, intellectual property law, international law, tax law, trial advocacy

Fall 2007 faculty profile
Total teaching faculty: **79**. Full-time: **52%**; **71%** men, **29%** women, **10%** minorities. Part-time: **48%**; **84%** men, **16%** women, **3%** minorities
Student-to-faculty ratio: **15.4**

SPECIAL PROGRAMS *(as provided by law school)*:

Clinics include: criminal, civil, environmental, juvenile, legislative, mediation. Institute on Water Resources Law and Policy. Summer abroad in five countries; semester abroad in nine. Externships: federal and state judges, National Labor Relations Board, public interest. Certificates: Environmental Law, Admiralty Law, Sports Law, European Legal Studies, Civil Law. Mandatory pro bono program.

STUDENT BODY

Fall 2007 full-time enrollment: **752**
Men: **60%**   Women: **40%**
African-American: **6.9%**   American Indian: **1.2%**
Asian-American: **3.5%**   Mexican-American: **0.7%**

Puerto Rican: 0.9%   Other Hisp-Amer: 2.8%
White: 75.4%   International: 2.1%
Unknown: 6.5%

Attrition rates for 2006-2007 full-time students
Percent of students discontinuing law school:
Men: 6%   Women: 3%
First-year students: 7% Second-year students: 1%
Third-year students: 6%

LIBRARY RESOURCES
Total volumes: 643,967
Total seats available for library users: 557

INFORMATION TECHNOLOGY
Number of wired network connections available to students: 308 total (in the law library, excluding computer labs: 293; in classrooms: 0; in computer labs: 15; elsewhere in the law school: 0)
Law school has a wireless network.
Students are not required to own a computer.

EMPLOYMENT AND SALARIES
Proportion of 2006 graduates employed at graduation: 78%
Employed 9 months later, as of February 15, 2007: 96%
Salaries in the private sector (law firms, business, industry): $85,000–$145,000 (25th-75th percentile)
Median salary in the private sector: $115,000
Percentage in the private sector who reported salary information: 42%

Median salary in public service (government, judicial clerkships, academic posts, non-profits): $49,000

Percentage of 2006 graduates in:
Law firms: 55%   Government: 13%
Bus./industry: 12%   Judicial clerkship: 9%
Public interest: 7%   Unknown: 3%
Academia: 1%

2006 graduates employed in-state: 23%
2006 graduates employed in foreign countries: 1%
Number of states where graduates are employed: 33
Percentage of 2006 graduates working in: New England: 3%, Middle Atlantic: 9%, East North Central: 4%, West North Central: 2%, South Atlantic: 23%, East South Central: 5%, West South Central: 32%, Mountain: 4%, Pacific: 11%, Unknown: 6%

BAR PASSAGE RATES
Based on 2006 graduates taking Summer 2006 or Winter 2007 exams. Most of the school's first-time test takers took the bar in Louisiana.

83%
School's bar passage rate for first-time test takers

75%
Statewide bar passage rate for first-time test takers

University at Buffalo–SUNY

- John Lord O'Brian Hall, Buffalo, NY, 14260
- http://www.law.buffalo.edu
- Public
- Year founded: 1887
- 2007-2008 tuition: In-state: full-time: $14,633; part-time: N/A; Out-of-state: full-time: $21,433
- Enrollment 2007-08 academic year: full-time: 746; part-time: 5
- U.S. News 2009 law specialty ranking: N/A

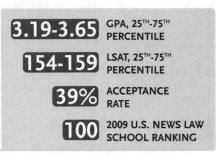

3.19-3.65 GPA, 25TH-75TH PERCENTILE

154-159 LSAT, 25TH-75TH PERCENTILE

39% ACCEPTANCE RATE

100 2009 U.S. NEWS LAW SCHOOL RANKING

ADMISSIONS

Admissions phone number: **(716) 645-2907**
Admissions email address: **law-admissions@buffalo.edu**
Application website:
http://www.law.buffalo.edu/admissions
Application deadline for Fall 2009 admission: **03/15**

Admissions statistics:

Number of applicants for Fall 2007: **1,516**
Number of acceptances: **584**
Number enrolled: **246**
Acceptance rate: **39%**
GPA, 25th-75th percentile, entering class Fall 2007: **3.19-3.65**
LSAT, 25th-75th percentile, entering class Fall 2007: **154-159**

FINANCIAL AID

Financial aid phone number: **(716) 645-7324**
Financial aid application deadline: **03/01**
Tuition 2007-2008 academic year: In-state: full-time: **$14,633**; part-time: **N/A**; Out-of-state: full-time: **$21,433**
Room and board: **$9,581**; books: **$1,534**; miscellaneous expenses: **$3,329**
Total of room/board/books/miscellaneous expenses: **$14,444**
University offers graduate student housing for which law students are eligible.

Financial aid profile

Percent of students that received grants for the 2006-2007 academic year: full-time: **72%**
Median grant amount: full-time: **$5,340**
The average law-school debt of those in the Class of 2007 who borrowed: **$54,294**. Proportion who borrowed: **88%**

ACADEMIC PROGRAMS

Calendar: **semester**
Joint degrees awarded: **N/A**
Typical first-year section size: Full-time: **83**

Is there typically a "small section" of the first year class, other than Legal Writing, taught by full-time faculty?:
Full-time: **no**
Number of course titles, beyond the first year curriculum, offered last year: **208**
Percentages of upper division course sections, excluding seminars, with an enrollment of:
Under 25: **69%** 25 to 49: **22%**
50 to 74: **7%** 75 to 99: **2%**
100+: **0%**
Areas of specialization: appellate advocacy, clinical training, dispute resolution, environmental law, healthcare law, intellectual property law, international law, tax law, trial advocacy

Fall 2007 faculty profile

Total teaching faculty: **153**. Full-time: **22%**; **71%** men, **29%** women, **15%** minorities. Part-time: **78%**; **66%** men, **34%** women, **9%** minorities
Student-to-faculty ratio: **15.6**

SPECIAL PROGRAMS *(as provided by law school)*:

Ten concentrations (including civil litigation, finance transactions, and intellectual property); seven nationally renowned clinics (including affordable housing, community economic development, and family violence); numerous joint degrees (J.D./M.B.A., J.D./Pharm.D., J.D./M.P.H); a New York City–based semester on international finance (includes projects with banking, investment, and law firms).

STUDENT BODY

Fall 2007 full-time enrollment: 746

Men: **51%** Women: **49%**
African-American: **4.8%** American Indian: **0.4%**
Asian-American: **6.8%** Mexican-American: **0.1%**
Puerto Rican: **1.1%** Other Hisp-Amer: **2.9%**
White: **72.5%** International: **0.0%**
Unknown: **11.3%**

Fall 2007 part-time enrollment: 5
Men: 20%   Women: 80%
African-American: 0.0%   American Indian: 0.0%
Asian-American: 0.0%   Mexican-American: 0.0%
Puerto Rican: 0.0%   Other Hisp-Amer: 0.0%
White: 100.0%   International: 0.0%
Unknown: 0.0%

Attrition rates for 2006-2007 full-time students
Percent of students discontinuing law school:
Men: 5%   Women: 4%
First-year students: 1%   Second-year students: 11%
Third-year students: 0%

LIBRARY RESOURCES
Total volumes: 578,882
Total seats available for library users: 510

INFORMATION TECHNOLOGY
Number of wired network connections available to students: 70 total (in the law library, excluding computer
   labs: 45; in classrooms: 0; in computer labs: 0; elsewhere in the law school: 25)
Law school has a wireless network.
Students are not required to own a computer.

EMPLOYMENT AND SALARIES
Proportion of 2006 graduates employed at graduation:
   74%
Employed 9 months later, as of February 15, 2007: 93%
Salaries in the private sector (law firms, business, indus-
   try): $50,000–$83,000 (25th-75th percentile)
Median salary in the private sector: $75,000

Percentage in the private sector who reported salary
   information: 60%
Median salary in public service (government, judicial clerkships, academic posts, non-profits): $49,432

Percentage of 2006 graduates in:
Law firms: 54%   Government: 14%
Bus./industry: 11%   Judicial clerkship: 6%
Public interest: 11%   Unknown: 2%
Academia: 2%

2006 graduates employed in-state: 73%
2006 graduates employed in foreign countries: 2%
Number of states where graduates are employed: 19
Percentage of 2006 graduates working in: New England:
   2%, Middle Atlantic: 78%, East North Central: 2%, West
   North Central: 0%, South Atlantic: 7%, East South
   Central: 1%, West South Central: 1%, Mountain: 2%,
   Pacific: 4%, Unknown: 1%

BAR PASSAGE RATES
Based on 2006 graduates taking Summer 2006 or
Winter 2007 exams. Most of the school's first-time test
takers took the bar in New York.

81%
School's bar passage rate for first-time test takers

77%
Statewide bar passage rate for first-time test takers

University of Akron

- C. Blake McDowell Law Center, Akron, OH, 44325-2901
- http://www.uakron.edu/law
- Public
- Year founded: 1921
- 2007-2008 tuition: In-state: full-time: $16,497; part-time: $10,506; Out-of-state: full-time: $26,089
- Enrollment 2007-08 academic year: full-time: 308; part-time: 221
- U.S. News 2009 law specialty ranking: trial advocacy: 15

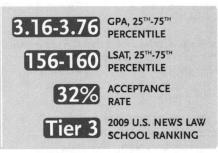

3.16-3.76 GPA, 25TH-75TH PERCENTILE

156-160 LSAT, 25TH-75TH PERCENTILE

32% ACCEPTANCE RATE

Tier 3 2009 U.S. NEWS LAW SCHOOL RANKING

ADMISSIONS

Admissions phone number: **(800) 425-7668**
Admissions email address: **lawadmissions@uakron.edu**
Application website:
http://www.uakron.edu/law/lawadmissions/application. php
Application deadline for Fall 2009 admission: **03/01**

Admissions statistics:

Number of applicants for Fall 2007: **1,581**
Number of acceptances: **507**
Number enrolled: **108**
Acceptance rate: **32%**
GPA, 25th-75th percentile, entering class Fall 2007: **3.16-3.76**
LSAT, 25th-75th percentile, entering class Fall 2007: **156-160**

Part-time program:

Number of applicants for Fall 2007: **338**
Number of acceptances: **225**
Number enrolled: **67**
Acceptance rate: **67%**
GPA, 25th-75th percentile, entering class Fall 2007: **3.10-3.61**
LSAT, 25th-75th percentile, entering class Fall 2007: **150-155**

FINANCIAL AID

Financial aid phone number: **(800) 621-3847**
Financial aid application deadline: **03/01**
Tuition 2007-2008 academic year: In-state: full-time: **$16,497**; part-time: **$10,506**; Out-of-state: full-time: **$26,089**
Room and board: **$13,320**; books: **$1,082**; miscellaneous expenses: **N/A**
Total of room/board/books/miscellaneous expenses: **$14,402**
University offers graduate student housing for which law students are eligible.

Financial aid profile

Percent of students that received grants for the 2006-2007 academic year: full-time: **55%**; part-time **17%**
Median grant amount: full-time: **$12,738**; part-time: **$4,500**
The average law-school debt of those in the Class of 2007 who borrowed: **$57,669**. Proportion who borrowed: **92%**

ACADEMIC PROGRAMS

Calendar: **semester**
Joint degrees awarded: **J.D./M.B.A.; J.D./M.Tax; J.D./M.P.A.; J.D./M.B.A. Human Resources; J.D./M.A.P.**
Typical first-year section size: Full-time: **58**; Part-time: **64**
Is there typically a "small section" of the first year class, other than Legal Writing, taught by full-time faculty?: Full-time: **yes**; Part-time: **yes**
Number of course titles, beyond the first year curriculum, offered last year: **97**
Percentages of upper division course sections, excluding seminars, with an enrollment of:

Under 25: **69%**		25 to 49: **23%**	
50 to 74: **6%**		75 to 99: **1%**	
100+: **1%**			

Areas of specialization: appellate advocacy, clinical training, dispute resolution, environmental law, healthcare law, intellectual property law, international law, tax law, trial advocacy

Fall 2007 faculty profile

Total teaching faculty: **74**. Full-time: **38%**; **68%** men, **32%** women, **11%** minorities. Part-time: **62%**; **63%** men, **37%** women, **2%** minorities
Student-to-faculty ratio: **13.3**

SPECIAL PROGRAMS *(as provided by law school)*:

Clinical programs: appellate review; jail inmate assistance; new business legal clinic; civil litigation; trial litigation. Certificates: Intellectual Property and Technology; Litigation. Joint degrees: J.D./M.B.A.; J.D./M.S., Management in H.R.; J.D./M.P.A.; J.D./M.Tax.; J.D./M.A.P. Centers: Intellectual Property and Technology Law; Constitutional Law; Institute for Professional Responsibility.

STUDENT BODY

Fall 2007 full-time enrollment: 308
Men: 56%   Women: 44%
African-American: 8.1%   American Indian: 0.3%
Asian-American: 3.9%   Mexican-American: 0.0%
Puerto Rican: 0.0%   Other Hisp-Amer: 1.9%
White: 71.1%   International: 1.3%
Unknown: 13.3%

Fall 2007 part-time enrollment: 221
Men: 57%   Women: 43%
African-American: 3.6%   American Indian: 0.0%
Asian-American: 4.5%   Mexican-American: 0.0%
Puerto Rican: 0.0%   Other Hisp-Amer: 2.3%
White: 81.9%   International: 0.0%
Unknown: 7.7%

Attrition rates for 2006-2007 full-time students
Percent of students discontinuing law school:
Men: 9%   Women: 9%
First-year students: 21%   Second-year students: 3%
Third-year students: 2%

LIBRARY RESOURCES

Total volumes: 293,934
Total seats available for library users: 295

INFORMATION TECHNOLOGY

Number of wired network connections available to stu-
    dents: 16 total (in the law library, excluding computer
    labs: 0; in classrooms: 0; in computer labs: 16; else-
    where in the law school: 0)
Law school has a wireless network.
Students are not required to own a computer.

EMPLOYMENT AND SALARIES

Proportion of 2006 graduates employed at graduation:
    75%
Employed 9 months later, as of February 15, 2007: 92%

Salaries in the private sector (law firms, business, indus-
    try): **$46,253–$87,912** (25th-75th percentile)
Median salary in the private sector: **$65,824**
Percentage in the private sector who reported salary
    information: 48%
Median salary in public service (government, judicial clerk-
    ships, academic posts, non-profits): **$58,280**

Percentage of 2006 graduates in:
Law firms: 41%   Government: 16%
Bus./industry: 30%   Judicial clerkship: 7%
Public interest: 4%   Unknown: N/A
Academia: 2%

2006 graduates employed in-state: 85%
2006 graduates employed in foreign countries: 0%
Number of states where graduates are employed: 10
Percentage of 2006 graduates working in: New England:
    N/A, Middle Atlantic: 5%, East North Central: 85%, West
    North Central: N/A, South Atlantic: 9%, East South
    Central: N/A, West South Central: 1%, Mountain: 1%,
    Pacific: N/A, Unknown: 0%

BAR PASSAGE RATES

Based on 2006 graduates taking Summer 2006 or
Winter 2007 exams. Most of the school's first-time test
takers took the bar in Ohio.

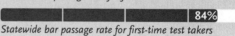

| | 85% |

School's bar passage rate for first-time test takers

| | 84% |

Statewide bar passage rate for first-time test takers

University of Alabama

- Box 870382, Tuscaloosa, AL, 35487
- http://www.law.ua.edu
- Public
- Year founded: 1872
- **2007-2008 tuition:** In-state: full-time: $11,190; part-time: N/A; Out-of-state: full-time: $22,170
- **Enrollment 2007-08 academic year:** full-time: 492; part-time: 23
- **U.S. News 2009 law specialty ranking:** N/A

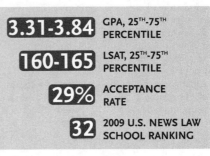

3.31-3.84 GPA, 25TH-75TH PERCENTILE

160-165 LSAT, 25TH-75TH PERCENTILE

29% ACCEPTANCE RATE

32 2009 U.S. NEWS LAW SCHOOL RANKING

ADMISSIONS
Admissions phone number: **(205) 348-5440**
Admissions email address: **admissions@law.ua.edu**
Application website:
http://www.law.ua.edu/admissions/info.php?re=onlineapp
Application deadline for Fall 2009 admission: **03/01**

Admissions statistics:
Number of applicants for Fall 2007: **1,197**
Number of acceptances: **350**
Number enrolled: **159**
Acceptance rate: **29%**
GPA, 25th-75th percentile, entering class Fall 2007: **3.31-3.84**
LSAT, 25th-75th percentile, entering class Fall 2007: **160-165**

Part-time program:
Number of applicants for Fall 2007: **N/A**
Number of acceptances: **N/A**
Number enrolled: **23**
Acceptance rate: **N/A**
GPA, 25th-75th percentile, entering class Fall 2007: **2.97-3.54**
LSAT, 25th-75th percentile, entering class Fall 2007: **150-156**

FINANCIAL AID
Financial aid phone number: **(205) 348-6756**
Financial aid application deadline: **N/A**
Tuition 2007-2008 academic year: In-state: full-time: **$11,190**; part-time: N/A; Out-of-state: full-time: **$22,170**
Room and board: **$8,950**; books: **$1,300**; miscellaneous expenses: **$4,704**
Total of room/board/books/miscellaneous expenses: **$14,954**
University offers graduate student housing for which law students are eligible.

Financial aid profile
Percent of students that received grants for the 2006-2007 academic year: full-time: **45%**
Median grant amount: full-time: **$6,603**
The average law-school debt of those in the Class of 2007 who borrowed: **$37,611**. Proportion who borrowed: **69%**

ACADEMIC PROGRAMS
Calendar: **semester**
Joint degrees awarded: **J.D./M.B.A.; J.D./MPA**
Typical first-year section size: Full-time: **57**
Is there typically a "small section" of the first year class, other than Legal Writing, taught by full-time faculty?: Full-time: **no**; Part-time: **no**
Number of course titles, beyond the first year curriculum, offered last year: **105**
Percentages of upper division course sections, excluding seminars, with an enrollment of:

Under 25: **68%**	25 to 49: **23%**	
50 to 74: **6%**	75 to 99: **2%**	
100+: **1%**		

Areas of specialization: appellate advocacy, clinical training, dispute resolution, environmental law, healthcare law, intellectual property law, international law, tax law, trial advocacy

Fall 2007 faculty profile
Total teaching faculty: **105**. Full-time: **52%**; **62%** men, **38%** women, **13%** minorities. Part-time: **48%**; **92%** men, **8%** women, **4%** minorities
Student-to-faculty ratio: **9.8**

SPECIAL PROGRAMS *(as provided by law school):*
Clinics: civil, elder, domestic violence, community development, capital representation, criminal defense. Summer externships; academic year judicial externships; summer abroad in Canberra, Australia; summer abroad in Fribourg, Switzerland; Public Interest Institute; courses in other parts of the University; J.D./M.B.A.; dual enrollment in other departments; Certificate in Public Interest.

STUDENT BODY

Fall 2007 full-time enrollment: 492

Men: 62%	Women: 38%
African-American: 6.5%	American Indian: 0.6%
Asian-American: 2.8%	Mexican-American: 0.0%
Puerto Rican: 0.0%	Other Hisp-Amer: 2.0%
White: 88.0%	International: 0.0%
Unknown: 0.0%	

Fall 2007 part-time enrollment: 23

Men: 39%	Women: 61%
African-American: 43.5%	American Indian: 0.0%
Asian-American: 0.0%	Mexican-American: 0.0%
Puerto Rican: 0.0%	Other Hisp-Amer: 0.0%
White: 56.5%	International: 0.0%
Unknown: 0.0%	

Attrition rates for 2006-2007 full-time students
Percent of students discontinuing law school:

Men: 3%	Women: 1%
First-year students: 4%	Second-year students: 2%
Third-year students: N/A	

LIBRARY RESOURCES

Total volumes: 602,463
Total seats available for library users: 545

INFORMATION TECHNOLOGY

Number of wired network connections available to students: 81 total (in the law library, excluding computer labs: 6; in classrooms: 7; in computer labs: 45; elsewhere in the law school: 23)
Law school has a wireless network.
Students are not required to own a computer.

EMPLOYMENT AND SALARIES

Proportion of 2006 graduates employed at graduation: 84%

Employed 9 months later, as of February 15, 2007: 97%
Salaries in the private sector (law firms, business, industry): $45,000–$95,000 (25th-75th percentile)
Median salary in the private sector: $85,000
Percentage in the private sector who reported salary information: 42%
Median salary in public service (government, judicial clerkships, academic posts, non-profits): $54,000

Percentage of 2006 graduates in:

Law firms: 69%	Government: 9%
Bus./industry: 7%	Judicial clerkship: 8%
Public interest: 4%	Unknown: 2%
Academia: 1%	

2006 graduates employed in-state: 70%
2006 graduates employed in foreign countries: 0%
Number of states where graduates are employed: 16
Percentage of 2006 graduates working in: New England: 0%, Middle Atlantic: 0%, East North Central: 2%, West North Central: 0%, South Atlantic: 17%, East South Central: 73%, West South Central: 6%, Mountain: 2%, Pacific: N/A, Unknown: 0%

BAR PASSAGE RATES

Based on 2006 graduates taking Summer 2006 or Winter 2007 exams. Most of the school's first-time test takers took the bar in Alabama.

97%
School's bar passage rate for first-time test takers

79%
Statewide bar passage rate for first-time test takers

University of Arizona (Rogers)

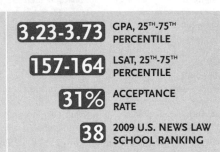

- PO Box 210176, Tucson, AZ, 85721-0176
- http://www.law.arizona.edu
- Public
- Year founded: 1915
- 2007-2008 tuition: In-state: full-time: $17,768; part-time: N/A; Out-of-state: full-time: $28,574
- Enrollment 2007-08 academic year: full-time: 453
- U.S. News 2009 law specialty ranking: N/A

3.23-3.73 GPA, 25TH-75TH PERCENTILE

157-164 LSAT, 25TH-75TH PERCENTILE

31% ACCEPTANCE RATE

38 2009 U.S. NEWS LAW SCHOOL RANKING

ADMISSIONS

Admissions phone number: **(520) 621-3477**
Admissions email address: **admissions@law.arizona.edu**
Application website: **http://www.law.arizona.edu/ admissions/PDF/application.pdf**
Application deadline for Fall 2009 admission: **02/15**

Admissions statistics:

Number of applicants for Fall 2007: **2,278**
Number of acceptances: **704**
Number enrolled: **158**
Acceptance rate: **31%**
GPA, 25th-75th percentile, entering class Fall 2007: **3.23-3.73**
LSAT, 25th-75th percentile, entering class Fall 2007: **157-164**

FINANCIAL AID

Financial aid phone number: **(520) 626-8101**
Financial aid application deadline: **03/01**
Tuition 2007-2008 academic year: In-state: full-time: **$17,768**; part-time: N/A; Out-of-state: full-time: **$28,574**
Room and board: **$11,840**; books: **$816**; miscellaneous expenses: **$5,050**
Total of room/board/books/miscellaneous expenses: **$17,706**
University offers graduate student housing for which law students are eligible.

Financial aid profile

Percent of students that received grants for the 2006-2007 academic year: full-time: **79%**
Median grant amount: full-time: **$7,000**
The average law-school debt of those in the Class of 2007 who borrowed: **$61,912**. Proportion who borrowed: **89%**

ACADEMIC PROGRAMS

Calendar: **semester**
Joint degrees awarded: **J.D./Ph.D. Economics; J.D./Ph.D. Philosophy; J.D./Ph.D. Psychology; J.D./M.B.A.; J.D./M.P.A.; J.D./M.A. American Indian Studies;** J.D./M.A. Economics; J.D./M.A. Latin American Studies; J.D./M.A. Women's Studies; J.D./M.M.F. Finance
Typical first-year section size: Full-time: **79**
Is there typically a "small section" of the first year class, other than Legal Writing, taught by full-time faculty?: Full-time: **yes**
Number of course titles, beyond the first year curriculum, offered last year: **131**
Percentages of upper division course sections, excluding seminars, with an enrollment of:

Under 25: **76%**	25 to 49: **19%**
50 to 74: **2%**	75 to 99: **2%**
100+: **1%**	

Areas of specialization: appellate advocacy, clinical training, dispute resolution, environmental law, healthcare law, intellectual property law, international law, tax law, trial advocacy

Fall 2007 faculty profile

Total teaching faculty: **143**. Full-time: **45%**; **69%** men, **31%** women, **20%** minorities. Part-time: **55%**; **68%** men, **32%** women, **6%** minorities
Student-to-faculty ratio: **11.7**

SPECIAL PROGRAMS (as provided by law school):

Programs: environmental law, science, and policy; indigenous peoples law and policy; intellectual property and business law; criminal justice and security; trial advocacy. Clinics: child advocacy, domestic violence, immigration, indigenous peoples, Ninth Circuit pro bono, and bankruptcy. Rehnquist Center on Constitutional Structures of Government. Ten dual-degree programs. National internships.

STUDENT BODY

Fall 2007 full-time enrollment: 453

Men: **49%**	Women: **51%**
African-American: **2.6%**	American Indian: **5.7%**
Asian-American: **8.4%**	Mexican-American: **0.7%**
Puerto Rican: **0.0%**	Other Hisp-Amer: **9.9%**
White: **70.4%**	International: **0.7%**
Unknown: **1.5%**	

Attrition rates for 2006-2007 full-time students
Percent of students discontinuing law school:
Men: 3%   Women: 2%
First-year students: N/A Second-year students: 7%
Third-year students: 1%

LIBRARY RESOURCES
Total volumes: 392,588
Total seats available for library users: 368

INFORMATION TECHNOLOGY
Number of wired network connections available to students: 0 total (in the law library, excluding computer
   labs: 0; in classrooms: 0; in computer labs: 0; elsewhere
   in the law school: 0)
Law school has a wireless network.
Students are not required to own a computer.

EMPLOYMENT AND SALARIES
Proportion of 2006 graduates employed at graduation:
   79%
Employed 9 months later, as of February 15, 2007: 95%
Salaries in the private sector (law firms, business, indus-
   try): $65,000–$110,000 (25th-75th percentile)
Median salary in the private sector: $90,000
Percentage in the private sector who reported salary
   information: 67%
Median salary in public service (government, judicial clerk-
   ships, academic posts, non-profits): $49,900

Percentage of 2006 graduates in:
Law firms: 41%   Government: 16%
Bus./industry: 13%   Judicial clerkship: 23%
Public interest: 3%   Unknown: 1%
Academia: 4%

2006 graduates employed in-state: 62%
2006 graduates employed in foreign countries: 3%
Number of states where graduates are employed: 18
Percentage of 2006 graduates working in: New England:
   0%, Middle Atlantic: 4%, East North Central: 1%, West
   North Central: 3%, South Atlantic: 4%, East South
   Central: 1%, West South Central: 2%, Mountain: 73%,
   Pacific: 10%, Unknown: 2%

BAR PASSAGE RATES
Based on 2006 graduates taking Summer 2006 or
Winter 2007 exams. Most of the school's first-time test
takers took the bar in Arizona.

87%
School's bar passage rate for first-time test takers

75%
Statewide bar passage rate for first-time test takers

University of Arkansas–Fayetteville

■ Robert A. Leflar Law Center, Fayetteville, AR, 72701
■ http://law.uark.edu/
■ Public
■ Year founded: 1928
■ 2007-2008 tuition: In-state: full-time: $338/credit hour; part-time: N/A; Out-of-state: full-time: $677/credit hour
■ Enrollment 2007-08 academic year: full-time: 407
■ U.S. News 2009 law specialty ranking: N/A

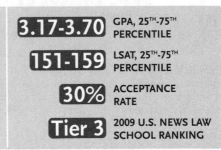

3.17-3.70 GPA, 25TH-75TH PERCENTILE

151-159 LSAT, 25TH-75TH PERCENTILE

30% ACCEPTANCE RATE

Tier 3 2009 U.S. NEWS LAW SCHOOL RANKING

ADMISSIONS
Admissions phone number: **(479) 575-3102**
Admissions email address: **jkmiller@uark.edu**
Application website: **N/A**
Application deadline for Fall 2009 admission: **07/01**

Admissions statistics:
Number of applicants for Fall 2007: **1,231**
Number of acceptances: **373**
Number enrolled: **145**
Acceptance rate: **30%**
GPA, 25th-75th percentile, entering class Fall 2007: **3.17-3.70**
LSAT, 25th-75th percentile, entering class Fall 2007: **151-159**

FINANCIAL AID
Financial aid phone number: **(479) 575-3806**
Financial aid application deadline: **N/A**
Tuition 2007-2008 academic year: In-state: full-time: **$338/credit hour**; part-time: **N/A**; Out-of-state: full-time: **$677/credit hour**
Room and board: **$7,968**; books: **$1,000**; miscellaneous expenses: **$5,346**
Total of room/board/books/miscellaneous expenses: **$14,314**
University does not offer graduate student housing for which law students are eligible.

Financial aid profile
Percent of students that received grants for the 2006-2007 academic year: full-time: **39%**
Median grant amount: full-time: **$6,000**
The average law-school debt of those in the Class of 2007 who borrowed: **$50,031**. Proportion who borrowed: **81%**

ACADEMIC PROGRAMS
Calendar: **semester**
Joint degrees awarded: **J.D./M.B.A.; J.D./M.P.A.; LL.M./M.S.C.; J.D./M.A.**

Typical first-year section size: Full-time: **75**
Is there typically a "small section" of the first year class, other than Legal Writing, taught by full-time faculty?: Full-time: **no**
Number of course titles, beyond the first year curriculum, offered last year: **93**
Percentages of upper division course sections, excluding seminars, with an enrollment of:

Under 25: **79%**   25 to 49: **11%**
50 to 74: **7%**   75 to 99: **3%**
100+: **1%**

Areas of specialization: appellate advocacy, clinical training, dispute resolution, environmental law, healthcare law, intellectual property law, international law, tax law, trial advocacy

Fall 2007 faculty profile
Total teaching faculty: **57**. Full-time: **46%**; **58%** men, **42%** women, **15%** minorities. Part-time: **54%**; **84%** men, **16%** women, **N/A** minorities
Student-to-faculty ratio: **13.8**

SPECIAL PROGRAMS (as provided by law school):
Nine clinics are available, representing a broad range of practice experiences. Students must earn at least three credits in certified skills courses from a variety of offerings designed specifically for this purpose. Summer curriculum is extensive, with foreign programs in England, Russia, and Belize. Judicial, legislative, and corporate externships are available.

STUDENT BODY
Fall 2007 full-time enrollment: 407
Men: **61%**   Women: **39%**
African-American: **16.2%**   American Indian: **2.5%**
Asian-American: **3.2%**   Mexican-American: **0.5%**
Puerto Rican: **0.5%**   Other Hisp-Amer: **1.2%**
White: **75.4%**   International: **0.0%**
Unknown: **0.5%**

Attrition rates for 2006-2007 full-time students
Percent of students discontinuing law school:

Men: **1%**   Women: **3%**

First-year students: **5%**   Second-year students: **1%**

Third-year students: **N/A**

LIBRARY RESOURCES

Total volumes: **331,745**
Total seats available for library users: **379**

INFORMATION TECHNOLOGY

Number of wired network connections available to students: **26** total (in the law library, excluding computer labs: **18**; in classrooms: **0**; in computer labs: **0**; elsewhere in the law school: **8**)
Law school has a wireless network.
Students are not required to own a computer.

EMPLOYMENT AND SALARIES

Proportion of 2006 graduates employed at graduation: **N/A**
Employed 9 months later, as of February 15, 2007: **89%**
Salaries in the private sector (law firms, business, industry): **$44,500–$62,000** (25th-75th percentile)
Median salary in the private sector: **$50,000**
Percentage in the private sector who reported salary information: **100%**
Median salary in public service (government, judicial clerkships, academic posts, non-profits): **$42,000**

Percentage of 2006 graduates in:

Law firms: **60%**   Government: **12%**

Bus./industry: **14%**   Judicial clerkship: **5%**

Public interest: **8%**   Unknown: **0%**

Academia: **1%**

2006 graduates employed in-state: **72%**
2006 graduates employed in foreign countries: **0%**
Number of states where graduates are employed: **15**
Percentage of 2006 graduates working in: New England: **N/A**, Middle Atlantic: **2%**, East North Central: **N/A**, West North Central: **6%**, South Atlantic: **7%**, East South Central: **3%**, West South Central: **79%**, Mountain: **2%**, Pacific: **1%**, Unknown: **0%**

BAR PASSAGE RATES

Based on 2006 graduates taking Summer 2006 or Winter 2007 exams. Most of the school's first-time test takers took the bar in Arkansas.

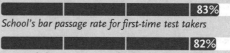

83%

School's bar passage rate for first-time test takers

82%

Statewide bar passage rate for first-time test takers

University of Ark.–Little Rock (Bowen)

- 1201 McMath Avenue, Little Rock, AR, 72202-5142
- http://www.law.ualr.edu/
- Public
- **Year founded:** 1969
- **2007-2008 tuition:** In-state: full-time: $10,201; part-time: $7,135; Out-of-state: full-time: $20,524
- **Enrollment 2007-08 academic year:** full-time: 292; part-time: 150
- **U.S. News 2009 law specialty ranking:** N/A

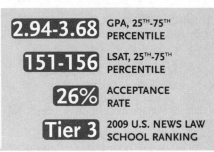

2.94-3.68 GPA, 25TH-75TH PERCENTILE

151-156 LSAT, 25TH-75TH PERCENTILE

26% ACCEPTANCE RATE

Tier 3 2009 U.S. NEWS LAW SCHOOL RANKING

ADMISSIONS
Admissions phone number: **(501) 324-9439**
Admissions email address: **lawadm@ualr.edu**
Application website:
http://www.law.ualr.edu/admissions.html
Application deadline for Fall 2009 admission: **04/15**

Admissions statistics:
Number of applicants for Fall 2007: **1,320**
Number of acceptances: **345**
Number enrolled: **95**
Acceptance rate: **26%**
GPA, 25th-75th percentile, entering class Fall 2007: **2.94-3.68**
LSAT, 25th-75th percentile, entering class Fall 2007: **151-156**

Part-time program:
Number of applicants for Fall 2007: **187**
Number of acceptances: **74**
Number enrolled: **59**
Acceptance rate: **40%**
GPA, 25th-75th percentile, entering class Fall 2007: **2.76-3.48**
LSAT, 25th-75th percentile, entering class Fall 2007: **147-155**

FINANCIAL AID
Financial aid phone number: **(501) 569-3035**
Financial aid application deadline: **03/01**
Tuition 2007-2008 academic year: In-state: full-time: **$10,201**; part-time: **$7,135**; Out-of-state: full-time: **$20,524**
Room and board: **$7,454**; books: **$1,250**; miscellaneous expenses: **$3,508**
Total of room/board/books/miscellaneous expenses: **$12,212**
University does not offer graduate student housing for which law students are eligible.

Financial aid profile
Percent of students that received grants for the 2006-2007 academic year: full-time: **34%**; part-time **14%**
Median grant amount: full-time: **$3,500**; part-time: **$3,500**
The average law-school debt of those in the Class of 2007 who borrowed: **$49,730**. Proportion who borrowed: **83%**

ACADEMIC PROGRAMS
Calendar: **semester**
Joint degrees awarded: **J.D./M.B.A.; J.D./M.P.A.; J.D./M.P.H.; J.D./M.D.; J.D./M.P.S.**
Typical first-year section size: Full-time: **87**; Part-time: **44**
Is there typically a "small section" of the first year class, other than Legal Writing, taught by full-time faculty?: Full-time: **no**; Part-time: **no**
Number of course titles, beyond the first year curriculum, offered last year: **79**
Percentages of upper division course sections, excluding seminars, with an enrollment of:

Under 25: **72%**	25 to 49: **23%**
50 to 74: **3%**	75 to 99: **2%**
100+: **N/A**	

Areas of specialization: appellate advocacy, clinical training, dispute resolution, environmental law, healthcare law, intellectual property law, international law, tax law, trial advocacy

Fall 2007 faculty profile
Total teaching faculty: **92**. Full-time: **24%**; **50%** men, **50%** women, **27%** minorities. Part-time: **76%**; **67%** men, **33%** women, **7%** minorities
Student-to-faculty ratio: **14.3**

SPECIAL PROGRAMS *(as provided by law school):*
Five joint degrees: J.D./M.B.A., J.D./M.P.A., J.D./M.P.H., J.D./M.P.S., and J.D./M.D. Three clinics: litigation, tax, and mediation.

STUDENT BODY

Fall 2007 full-time enrollment: 292

Men: 52%	Women: 48%
African-American: 10.3%	American Indian: 1.7%
Asian-American: 1.0%	Mexican-American: 2.1%
Puerto Rican: 0.0%	Other Hisp-Amer: 1.4%
White: 79.1%	International: 2.1%
Unknown: 2.4%	

Fall 2007 part-time enrollment: 150

Men: 52%	Women: 48%
African-American: 18.0%	American Indian: 0.7%
Asian-American: 4.0%	Mexican-American: 0.0%
Puerto Rican: 0.0%	Other Hisp-Amer: 3.3%
White: 72.7%	International: 1.3%
Unknown: 0.0%	

Attrition rates for 2006-2007 full-time students
Percent of students discontinuing law school:

Men: 6%	Women: 6%
First-year students: 11%	Second-year students: 7%
Third-year students: N/A	

LIBRARY RESOURCES

Total volumes: 303,839
Total seats available for library users: 357

INFORMATION TECHNOLOGY

Number of wired network connections available to students: 1 total (in the law library, excluding computer labs: 0; in classrooms: 0; in computer labs: 1; elsewhere in the law school: 0)
Law school has a wireless network.
Students are not required to own a computer.

EMPLOYMENT AND SALARIES

Proportion of 2006 graduates employed at graduation: N/A

Employed 9 months later, as of February 15, 2007: **88%**
Salaries in the private sector (law firms, business, industry): **$45,000–$58,000** (25th-75th percentile)
Median salary in the private sector: **$52,200**
Percentage in the private sector who reported salary information: 25%
Median salary in public service (government, judicial clerkships, academic posts, non-profits): **$42,000**

Percentage of 2006 graduates in:

Law firms: 57%	Government: 15%
Bus./industry: 12%	Judicial clerkship: 8%
Public interest: 2%	Unknown: 4%
Academia: 2%	

2006 graduates employed in-state: 83%
2006 graduates employed in foreign countries: 0%
Number of states where graduates are employed: 11
Percentage of 2006 graduates working in: New England: 0%, Middle Atlantic: 1%, East North Central: 1%, West North Central: 0%, South Atlantic: 2%, East South Central: 6%, West South Central: 89%, Mountain: 1%, Pacific: 1%, Unknown: 0%

BAR PASSAGE RATES

Based on 2006 graduates taking Summer 2006 or Winter 2007 exams. Most of the school's first-time test takers took the bar in Arkansas.

86%
School's bar passage rate for first-time test takers

82%
Statewide bar passage rate for first-time test takers

University of Baltimore

■ 1420 N. Charles Street, Baltimore, MD, 21201-5779
■ http://law.ubalt.edu
■ Public
■ Year founded: 1925
■ 2007-2008 tuition: In-state: full-time: $20,597; part-time: $873/credit hour; Out-of-state: full-time: $32,754
■ Enrollment 2007-08 academic year: full-time: 657; part-time: 425
■ U.S. News 2009 law specialty ranking: N/A

3.00-3.57 GPA, 25TH-75TH PERCENTILE

153-157 LSAT, 25TH-75TH PERCENTILE

41% ACCEPTANCE RATE

Tier 3 2009 U.S. NEWS LAW SCHOOL RANKING

ADMISSIONS
Admissions phone number: **(410) 837-4459**
Admissions email address: **lwadmiss@ubalt.edu**
Application website: **http://law.ubalt.edu/admissions**
Application deadline for Fall 2009 admission: **rolling**

Admissions statistics:
Number of applicants for Fall 2007: **1,835**
Number of acceptances: **750**
Number enrolled: **211**
Acceptance rate: **41%**
GPA, 25th-75th percentile, entering class Fall 2007: **3.00-3.57**
LSAT, 25th-75th percentile, entering class Fall 2007: **153-157**

Part-time program:
Number of applicants for Fall 2007: **680**
Number of acceptances: **352**
Number enrolled: **170**
Acceptance rate: **52%**
GPA, 25th-75th percentile, entering class Fall 2007: **2.82-3.42**
LSAT, 25th-75th percentile, entering class Fall 2007: **149-154**

FINANCIAL AID
Financial aid phone number: **(410) 837-4763**
Financial aid application deadline: **N/A**
Tuition 2007-2008 academic year: In-state: full-time: **$20,597**; part-time: **$873/credit hour**; Out-of-state: full-time: **$32,754**
Room and board: **$12,124**; books: **$1,376**; miscellaneous expenses: **$3,698**
Total of room/board/books/miscellaneous expenses: **$17,198**
University does not offer graduate student housing for which law students are eligible.

Financial aid profile
Percent of students that received grants for the 2006-2007 academic year: full-time: **11%**; part-time **4%**

Median grant amount: full-time: **$3,000**; part-time: **$3,000**
The average law-school debt of those in the Class of 2007 who borrowed: **$33,928**. Proportion who borrowed: **92%**

ACADEMIC PROGRAMS
Calendar: **semester**
Joint degrees awarded: **J.D./M.S. Criminal Science; J.D./M.B.A.; J.D./M.P.A.; J.D./Ph.D; J.D./M.S. Negotiation**
Typical first-year section size: Full-time: **73**; Part-time: **95**
Is there typically a "small section" of the first year class, other than Legal Writing, taught by full-time faculty?: Full-time: **no**; Part-time: **no**
Number of course titles, beyond the first year curriculum, offered last year: **124**
Percentages of upper division course sections, excluding seminars, with an enrollment of:
Under 25: **69%**   25 to 49: **16%**
50 to 74: **11%**   75 to 99: **3%**
100+: **1%**
Areas of specialization: appellate advocacy, clinical training, dispute resolution, environmental law, healthcare law, intellectual property law, international law, tax law, trial advocacy

Fall 2007 faculty profile
Total teaching faculty: **134**. Full-time: **31%**; **60%** men, **40%** women, **21%** minorities. Part-time: **69%**; **70%** men, **30%** women, **13%** minorities
Student-to-faculty ratio: **18.9**

SPECIAL PROGRAMS *(as provided by law school):*
At the University of Baltimore School of Law, students learn doctrine, perspective, and skills through traditional study and through clinical and lawyering courses. Their education is enriched by work on journals, membership in student organizations and government, and by centers focused on local, national, and global issues.

STUDENT BODY

Fall 2007 full-time enrollment: 657

Men: 50%
African-American: 5.0%
Asian-American: 5.8%
Puerto Rican: 0.0%
White: 68.3%
Unknown: 19.0%

Women: 50%
American Indian: 0.2%
Mexican-American: 0.0%
Other Hisp-Amer: 1.4%
International: 0.3%

Fall 2007 part-time enrollment: 425

Men: 44%
African-American: 13.2%
Asian-American: 5.2%
Puerto Rican: 0.0%
White: 64.5%
Unknown: 14.4%

Women: 56%
American Indian: 0.5%
Mexican-American: 0.0%
Other Hisp-Amer: 1.6%
International: 0.7%

Attrition rates for 2006-2007 full-time students
Percent of students discontinuing law school:
Men: 6%
First-year students: 14%
Third-year students: N/A

Women: 5%
Second-year students: 2%

LIBRARY RESOURCES

Total volumes: 365,150
Total seats available for library users: 317

INFORMATION TECHNOLOGY

Number of wired network connections available to students: 30 total (in the law library, excluding computer labs: 1; in classrooms: 0; in computer labs: 28; elsewhere in the law school: 1)
Law school has a wireless network.
Students are not required to own a computer.

EMPLOYMENT AND SALARIES

Proportion of 2006 graduates employed at graduation: 94%

Employed 9 months later, as of February 15, 2007: 95%
Salaries in the private sector (law firms, business, industry): $50,625–$95,000 (25th-75th percentile)
Median salary in the private sector: $65,000
Percentage in the private sector who reported salary information: 41%
Median salary in public service (government, judicial clerkships, academic posts, non-profits): $42,223

Percentage of 2006 graduates in:

Law firms: 36%
Bus./industry: 18%
Public interest: 5%
Academia: 3%

Government: 14%
Judicial clerkship: 23%
Unknown: 1%

2006 graduates employed in-state: 71%
2006 graduates employed in foreign countries: 0%
Number of states where graduates are employed: 19
Percentage of 2006 graduates working in: New England: 0%, Middle Atlantic: 2%, East North Central: 1%, West North Central: 0%, South Atlantic: 87%, East South Central: 0%, West South Central: 0%, Mountain: 1%, Pacific: 1%, Unknown: 7%

BAR PASSAGE RATES

Based on 2006 graduates taking Summer 2006 or Winter 2007 exams. Most of the school's first-time test takers took the bar in Maryland.

75%
School's bar passage rate for first-time test takers

77%
Statewide bar passage rate for first-time test takers

University of California (Hastings)

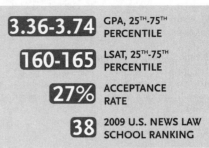

- 200 McAllister Street, San Francisco, CA, 94102
- http://www.uchastings.edu
- Public
- Year founded: 1878
- 2007-2008 tuition: In-state: full-time: $24,120; part-time: N/A; Out-of-state: full-time: $35,345
- Enrollment 2007-08 academic year: full-time: 1,215
- U.S. News 2009 law specialty ranking: clinical training: 25, tax law: 25

3.36-3.74 GPA, 25TH-75TH PERCENTILE

160-165 LSAT, 25TH-75TH PERCENTILE

27% ACCEPTANCE RATE

38 2009 U.S. NEWS LAW SCHOOL RANKING

ADMISSIONS
Admissions phone number: **(415) 565-4623**
Admissions email address: **admiss@uchastings.edu**
Application website:
 http://www.uchastings.edu/admwelcome_01
Application deadline for Fall 2009 admission: **03/01**

Admissions statistics:
Number of applicants for Fall 2007: **5,142**
Number of acceptances: **1,364**
Number enrolled: **401**
Acceptance rate: **27%**
GPA, 25th-75th percentile, entering class Fall 2007: **3.36-3.74**
LSAT, 25th-75th percentile, entering class Fall 2007: **160-165**

FINANCIAL AID
Financial aid phone number: **(415) 565-4624**
Financial aid application deadline: **03/01**
Tuition 2007-2008 academic year: In-state: full-time: **$24,120**; part-time: N/A; Out-of-state: full-time: **$35,345**
Room and board: **$14,040**; books: **$1,150**; miscellaneous expenses: **$4,103**
Total of room/board/books/miscellaneous expenses: **$19,293**
University does not offer graduate student housing for which law students are eligible.

Financial aid profile
Percent of students that received grants for the 2006-2007 academic year: full-time: **75%**
Median grant amount: full-time: **$5,500**
The average law-school debt of those in the Class of 2007 who borrowed: **$83,000**. Proportion who borrowed: **88%**

ACADEMIC PROGRAMS
Calendar: **semester**
Joint degrees awarded: **J.D./M.S.; J.D./M.C.P.**
Typical first-year section size: Full-time: **83**

Is there typically a "small section" of the first year class, other than Legal Writing, taught by full-time faculty?:
 Full-time: **no**
Number of course titles, beyond the first year curriculum, offered last year: **153**
Percentages of upper division course sections, excluding seminars, with an enrollment of:
 Under 25: **62%**   25 to 49: **15%**
 50 to 74: **12%**   75 to 99: **10%**
 100+: **1%**
Areas of specialization: appellate advocacy, clinical training, dispute resolution, environmental law, healthcare law, intellectual property law, international law, tax law, trial advocacy

Fall 2007 faculty profile
Total teaching faculty: **128**. Full-time: **50%**; **63%** men, **38%** women, **20%** minorities. Part-time: **50%**; **64%** men, **36%** women, **19%** minorities
Student-to-faculty ratio: **16.2**

SPECIAL PROGRAMS *(as provided by law school)*:
Hastings's strengths include civil, criminal, and transactional clinical programs and cutting-edge research and advocacy centers. The school has study-abroad programs in Argentina, Australia, China, Denmark, England, Germany, Hungary, Italy, and the Netherlands. It offers joint degrees and concentrations in Civil Litigation, Family Law, International Law, Tax, Criminal Law, and Public Interest Law.

STUDENT BODY
Fall 2007 full-time enrollment: **1,215**
Men: **47%**   Women: **53%**
African-American: **3.2%**   American Indian: **0.5%**
Asian-American: **23.7%**   Mexican-American: **3.1%**
Puerto Rican: **0.3%**   Other Hisp-Amer: **3.0%**
White: **45.2%**   International: **1.5%**
Unknown: **19.4%**

Attrition rates for 2006-2007 full-time students
Percent of students discontinuing law school:
Men: **4%**   Women: **3%**
First-year students: **4%**   Second-year students: **6%**
Third-year students: **0%**

LIBRARY RESOURCES
Total volumes: **707,264**
Total seats available for library users: **792**

INFORMATION TECHNOLOGY
Number of wired network connections available to students: **533** total (in the law library, excluding computer labs: **264**; in classrooms: **174**; in computer labs: **11**; elsewhere in the law school: **84**)
Law school has a wireless network.
Students are not required to own a computer.

EMPLOYMENT AND SALARIES
Proportion of 2006 graduates employed at graduation: **68%**
Employed 9 months later, as of February 15, 2007: **93%**
Salaries in the private sector (law firms, business, industry): **$76,500–$135,000** (25th-75th percentile)
Median salary in the private sector: **$120,000**
Percentage in the private sector who reported salary information: **75%**
Median salary in public service (government, judicial clerkships, academic posts, non-profits): **$52,000**

Percentage of 2006 graduates in:

Law firms: **68%**	Government: **8%**
Bus./industry: **8%**	Judicial clerkship: **3%**
Public interest: **10%**	Unknown: **1%**
Academia: **2%**	

2006 graduates employed in-state: **88%**
2006 graduates employed in foreign countries: **2%**
Number of states where graduates are employed: **16**
Percentage of 2006 graduates working in: New England: **1%**, Middle Atlantic: **4%**, East North Central: **0%**, West North Central: **0%**, South Atlantic: **1%**, East South Central: **0%**, West South Central: **1%**, Mountain: **2%**, Pacific: **90%**, Unknown: **0%**

BAR PASSAGE RATES
Based on 2006 graduates taking Summer 2006 or Winter 2007 exams. Most of the school's first-time test takers took the bar in California.

82%
School's bar passage rate for first-time test takers

65%
Statewide bar passage rate for first-time test takers

University of California–Berkeley

■ Boalt Hall, Berkeley, CA, 94720-7200
■ http://www.law.berkeley.edu
■ Public
■ Year founded: 1894
■ 2007-2008 tuition: In-state: full-time: $26,896; part-time: N/A; Out-of-state: full-time: $39,141
■ Enrollment 2007-08 academic year: full-time: 864
■ U.S. News 2009 law specialty ranking: clinical training: 15, environmental law: 11, intellectual property law: 1, international law: 9

3.64-3.90 GPA, 25TH-75TH PERCENTILE

163-170 LSAT, 25TH-75TH PERCENTILE

12% ACCEPTANCE RATE

6 2009 U.S. NEWS LAW SCHOOL RANKING

ADMISSIONS

Admissions phone number: **(510) 642-2274**
Admissions email address: **admissions@law.berkeley.edu**
Application website:
　http://www.law.berkeley.edu/prospectives/admissions/
Application deadline for Fall 2009 admission: **02/01**

Admissions statistics:

Number of applicants for Fall 2007: **6,980**
Number of acceptances: **839**
Number enrolled: **269**
Acceptance rate: **12%**
GPA, 25th-75th percentile, entering class Fall 2007: **3.64-3.90**
LSAT, 25th-75th percentile, entering class Fall 2007: **163-170**

FINANCIAL AID

Financial aid phone number: **(510) 642-1563**
Financial aid application deadline: **03/01**
Tuition 2007-2008 academic year: In-state: full-time: **$26,896**; part-time: N/A; Out-of-state: full-time: **$39,141**
Room and board: **$15,104**; books: **$1,495**; miscellaneous expenses: **$4,908**
Total of room/board/books/miscellaneous expenses: **$21,507**
University offers graduate student housing for which law students are eligible.

Financial aid profile

Percent of students that received grants for the 2006-2007 academic year: full-time: **69%**
Median grant amount: full-time: **$8,300**
The average law-school debt of those in the Class of 2007 who borrowed: **$74,802.** Proportion who borrowed: **70%**

ACADEMIC PROGRAMS

Calendar: **semester**
Joint degrees awarded: **J.D./Ph.D. Jurisprudence & Social Policy; J.D./M.A. Public Policy; J.D./M.A. International & Area Studies; J.D./M.A. Social Welfare; J.D./M.A. Economics; J.D./Ph.D. English; J.D./M.A. Journalism; J.D./Ph.D. Computer Science; J.D./M.A. Psychology; J.D./M.A. Political Science; J.D./M.A. City and Regional Planning; J.D./M.A. Business Administration**
Typical first-year section size: Full-time: **90**
Is there typically a "small section" of the first year class, other than Legal Writing, taught by full-time faculty?: Full-time: **yes**
Number of course titles, beyond the first year curriculum, offered last year: **209**
Percentages of upper division course sections, excluding seminars, with an enrollment of:
　Under 25: **68%**　　25 to 49: **16%**
　50 to 74: **8%**　　75 to 99: **4%**
　100+: **4%**
Areas of specialization: appellate advocacy, clinical training, dispute resolution, environmental law, healthcare law, intellectual property law, international law, tax law, trial advocacy

Fall 2007 faculty profile

Total teaching faculty: **128.** Full-time: **45%; 63%** men, **37%** women, **12%** minorities. Part-time: **55%; 72%** men, **28%** women, **6%** minorities
Student-to-faculty ratio: **12.3**

SPECIAL PROGRAMS (as provided by law school):

Boalt offers a wide array of special programs for J.D. students, including guaranteed funding for summer public interest fellowships, an array of employment opportunities at cutting-edge research centers, and a clinical education program. Boalt's financial aid programs, including the loan repayment assistance program, are quite possibly the best in the nation.

STUDENT BODY

Fall 2007 full-time enrollment: 864
Men: **45%**　　　　　　　　Women: **55%**
African-American: **4.3%**　　American Indian: **1.4%**
Asian-American: **17.4%**　　Mexican-American: **4.1%**

Puerto Rican: **0.0%**   Other Hisp-Amer: **4.9%**
White: **49.0%**   International: **0.0%**
Unknown: **19.1%**

Attrition rates for 2006-2007 full-time students
Percent of students discontinuing law school:
Men: **1%**   Women: **1%**
First-year students: **1%**   Second-year students: **2%**
Third-year students: **0%**

LIBRARY RESOURCES
Total volumes: **871,280**
Total seats available for library users: **325**

INFORMATION TECHNOLOGY
Number of wired network connections available to students: **164** total (in the law library, excluding computer labs: **96**; in classrooms: **0**; in computer labs: **3**; elsewhere in the law school: **65**)
Law school has a wireless network.
Students are not required to own a computer.

EMPLOYMENT AND SALARIES
Proportion of 2006 graduates employed at graduation: **99%**
Employed 9 months later, as of February 15, 2007: **99%**
Salaries in the private sector (law firms, business, industry): **$135,000–$135,000** (25th-75th percentile)
Median salary in the private sector: **$135,000**
Percentage in the private sector who reported salary information: **92%**
Median salary in public service (government, judicial clerkships, academic posts, non-profits): **$50,000**

Percentage of 2006 graduates in:
Law firms: **67%**   Government: **5%**
Bus./industry: **3%**   Judicial clerkship: **14%**
Public interest: **11%**   Unknown: **0%**
Academia: **0%**

2006 graduates employed in-state: **67%**
2006 graduates employed in foreign countries: **2%**
Number of states where graduates are employed: **21**
Percentage of 2006 graduates working in: New England: **1%**, Middle Atlantic: **11%**, East North Central: **1%**, West North Central: **0%**, South Atlantic: **9%**, East South Central: **0%**, West South Central: **2%**, Mountain: **3%**, Pacific: **71%**, Unknown: **0%**

BAR PASSAGE RATES
Based on 2006 graduates taking Summer 2006 or Winter 2007 exams. Most of the school's first-time test takers took the bar in California.

85%
School's bar passage rate for first-time test takers

65%
Statewide bar passage rate for first-time test takers

University of California–Davis

- 400 Mrak Hall Drive, Davis, CA, 95616-5201
- http://www.law.ucdavis.edu
- Public
- Year founded: 1965
- 2007-2008 tuition: In-state: full-time: $25,489; part-time: N/A; Out-of-state: full-time: $37,734
- Enrollment 2007-08 academic year: full-time: 577
- U.S. News 2009 law specialty ranking: environmental law: 17

3.38-3.75 GPA, 25TH-75TH PERCENTILE

159-165 LSAT, 25TH-75TH PERCENTILE

29% ACCEPTANCE RATE

44 2009 U.S. NEWS LAW SCHOOL RANKING

ADMISSIONS

Admissions phone number: **(530) 752-6477**
Admissions email address: **admissions@law.ucdavis.edu**
Application website: **http://www.law.ucdavis.edu/ admissions/applicationForms.shtml**
Application deadline for Fall 2009 admission: **02/01**

Admissions statistics:
Number of applicants for Fall 2007: **3,315**
Number of acceptances: **955**
Number enrolled: **201**
Acceptance rate: **29%**
GPA, 25th-75th percentile, entering class Fall 2007: **3.38-3.75**
LSAT, 25th-75th percentile, entering class Fall 2007: **159-165**

FINANCIAL AID

Financial aid phone number: **(530) 752-6573**
Financial aid application deadline: **03/02**
Tuition 2007-2008 academic year: In-state: full-time: **$25,489**; part-time: **N/A**; Out-of-state: full-time: **$37,734**
Room and board: **$11,279**; books: **$987**; miscellaneous expenses: **$3,637**
Total of room/board/books/miscellaneous expenses: **$15,903**
University offers graduate student housing for which law students are eligible.

Financial aid profile
Percent of students that received grants for the 2006-2007 academic year: full-time: **69%**
Median grant amount: full-time: **$8,300**
The average law-school debt of those in the Class of 2007 who borrowed: **$62,077**. Proportion who borrowed: **91%**

ACADEMIC PROGRAMS

Calendar: **semester**
Joint degrees awarded: **J.D./M.B.A.; J.D./M.S.; J.D./M.A.; J.D./M.C.P.**

Typical first-year section size: Full-time: **65**
Is there typically a "small section" of the first year class, other than Legal Writing, taught by full-time faculty?: Full-time: **yes**
Number of course titles, beyond the first year curriculum, offered last year: **84**
Percentages of upper division course sections, excluding seminars, with an enrollment of:

Under 25: **50%**	25 to 49: **22%**
50 to 74: **13%**	75 to 99: **4%**
100+: **11%**	

Areas of specialization: appellate advocacy, clinical training, dispute resolution, environmental law, healthcare law, intellectual property law, international law, tax law, trial advocacy

Fall 2007 faculty profile
Total teaching faculty: **77**. Full-time: **53%**; **51%** men, **49%** women, **37%** minorities. Part-time: **47%**; **69%** men, **31%** women, **19%** minorities
Student-to-faculty ratio: **12.4**

SPECIAL PROGRAMS *(as provided by law school)*:

Nationally renowned faculty; talented, diverse students; small classes (one first-year course of 30-35 students; the largest usually 70). Clinics: immigration, civil rights, prison, family law. Externships: employment, tax, criminal, government, judicial. Litigation and nonlitigation skills courses; Public Service Law Certificate, externship, program; Environmental Law Certificate, externship.

STUDENT BODY

Fall 2007 full-time enrollment: 577

Men: **45%**	Women: **55%**
African-American: **2.3%**	American Indian: **0.5%**
Asian-American: **24.3%**	Mexican-American: **5.9%**
Puerto Rican: **0.0%**	Other Hisp-Amer: **2.6%**
White: **46.6%**	International: **1.4%**
Unknown: **16.5%**	

Attrition rates for 2006-2007 full-time students
Percent of students discontinuing law school:
Men: **3%**   Women: **2%**
First-year students: **7%**   Second-year students: **N/A**
Third-year students: **N/A**

LIBRARY RESOURCES
Total volumes: **446,959**
Total seats available for library users: **311**

INFORMATION TECHNOLOGY
Number of wired network connections available to students: **0** total (in the law library, excluding computer labs: **0**; in classrooms: **0**; in computer labs: **0**; elsewhere in the law school: **0**)
Law school has a wireless network.
Students are not required to own a computer.

EMPLOYMENT AND SALARIES
Proportion of 2006 graduates employed at graduation: **79%**
Employed 9 months later, as of February 15, 2007: **87%**
Salaries in the private sector (law firms, business, industry): **$78,500–$135,000** (25th-75th percentile)
Median salary in the private sector: **$103,500**
Percentage in the private sector who reported salary information: **77%**
Median salary in public service (government, judicial clerkships, academic posts, non-profits): **$50,000**

Percentage of 2006 graduates in:
Law firms: **63%**   Government: **6%**
Bus./industry: **14%**   Judicial clerkship: **3%**
Public interest: **11%**   Unknown: **2%**
Academia: **1%**

2006 graduates employed in-state: **90%**
2006 graduates employed in foreign countries: **0%**
Number of states where graduates are employed: **11**
Percentage of 2006 graduates working in: New England: **0%**, Middle Atlantic: **3%**, East North Central: **0%**, West North Central: **0%**, South Atlantic: **1%**, East South Central: **1%**, West South Central: **1%**, Mountain: **1%**, Pacific: **92%**, Unknown: **1%**

BAR PASSAGE RATES
Based on 2006 graduates taking Summer 2006 or Winter 2007 exams. Most of the school's first-time test takers took the bar in California.

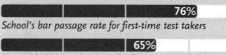

School's bar passage rate for first-time test takers
76%

Statewide bar passage rate for first-time test takers
65%

University of California—Los Angeles

- 71 Dodd Hall, PO Box 951445, Los Angeles, CA, 90095-1445
- http://www.law.ucla.edu
- Public
- **Year founded:** 1949
- **2007-2008 tuition:** In-state: full-time: $26,855; part-time: N/A; Out-of-state: full-time: $37,648
- **Enrollment 2007-08 academic year:** full-time: 1,025
- **U.S. News 2009 law specialty ranking:** clinical training: 20, environmental law: 20, intellectual property law: 16, international law: 11, tax law: 5

3.54-3.85 GPA, 25TH-75TH PERCENTILE

163-169 LSAT, 25TH-75TH PERCENTILE

18% ACCEPTANCE RATE

16 2009 U.S. NEWS LAW SCHOOL RANKING

ADMISSIONS

Admissions phone number: **(310) 825-2080**
Admissions email address: **admissions@law.ucla.edu**
Application website:
http://www1.law.ucla.edu/~admissions/
Application deadline for Fall 2009 admission: **02/01**

Admissions statistics:
Number of applicants for Fall 2007: **6,499**
Number of acceptances: **1,140**
Number enrolled: **313**
Acceptance rate: **18%**
GPA, 25th-75th percentile, entering class Fall 2007: **3.54-3.85**
LSAT, 25th-75th percentile, entering class Fall 2007: **163-169**

FINANCIAL AID

Financial aid phone number: **(310) 825-2459**
Financial aid application deadline: **03/02**
Tuition 2007-2008 academic year: In-state: full-time: **$26,855**; part-time: **N/A**; Out-of-state: full-time: **$37,648**
Room and board: **$13,002**; books: **$1,836**; miscellaneous expenses: **$4,887**
Total of room/board/books/miscellaneous expenses: **$19,725**
University offers graduate student housing for which law students are eligible.

Financial aid profile
Percent of students that received grants for the 2006-2007 academic year: full-time: **61%**
Median grant amount: full-time: **$8,760**
The average law-school debt of those in the Class of 2007 who borrowed: **$91,435**. Proportion who borrowed: **84%**

ACADEMIC PROGRAMS

Calendar: **semester**
Joint degrees awarded: **J.D./M.B.A.; J.D./M.A. Urban Planning; J.D./M.A. American Indian Studies;**
J.D./M.S.W.; J.D./M.P.P.; J.D./M.A. African American Studies; J.D./M.P.H.
Typical first-year section size: Full-time: **80**
Is there typically a "small section" of the first year class, other than Legal Writing, taught by full-time faculty?: Full-time: **yes**
Number of course titles, beyond the first year curriculum, offered last year: **161**
Percentages of upper division course sections, excluding seminars, with an enrollment of:

Under 25: **43%**	25 to 49: **28%**
50 to 74: **14%**	75 to 99: **9%**
100+: **6%**	

Areas of specialization: appellate advocacy, clinical training, dispute resolution, environmental law, healthcare law, intellectual property law, international law, tax law, trial advocacy

Fall 2007 faculty profile
Total teaching faculty: **84**. Full-time: **75%**; **73%** men, **27%** women, **14%** minorities. Part-time: **25%**; **76%** men, **24%** women, **5%** minorities
Student-to-faculty ratio: **12.9**

SPECIAL PROGRAMS *(as provided by law school):*

UCLA Law students can participate in supervised educational experiences in the school's renowned clinical program. They can choose academic specializations in business law, critical race studies, entertainment law, and public interest law. Students can also participate in a variety of academic centers in areas of real estate, environmental law, Indian law, and sexual orientation law.

STUDENT BODY

Fall 2007 full-time enrollment: **1,025**

Men: **51%**	Women: **49%**
African-American: **3.6%**	American Indian: **1.3%**
Asian-American: **19.4%**	Mexican-American: **6.0%**
Puerto Rican: **0.3%**	Other Hisp-Amer: **2.7%**
White: **42.2%**	International: **0.9%**
Unknown: **23.6%**	

Attrition rates for 2006-2007 full-time students
Percent of students discontinuing law school:
Men: **N/A**   Women: **N/A**
First-year students: **N/A**   Second-year students: **N/A**
Third-year students: **N/A**

LIBRARY RESOURCES
Total volumes: **641,468**
Total seats available for library users: **774**

INFORMATION TECHNOLOGY
Number of wired network connections available to students: **1,610** total (in the law library, excluding computer labs: **400**; in classrooms: **1,200**; in computer labs: **10**; elsewhere in the law school: **0**)
Law school has a wireless network.
Students are not required to own a computer.

EMPLOYMENT AND SALARIES
Proportion of 2006 graduates employed at graduation: **95%**
Employed 9 months later, as of February 15, 2007: **98%**
Salaries in the private sector (law firms, business, industry): **$100,000–$135,000** (25th-75th percentile)
Median salary in the private sector: **$135,000**
Percentage in the private sector who reported salary information: **86%**
Median salary in public service (government, judicial clerkships, academic posts, non-profits): **$56,896**

Percentage of 2006 graduates in:
Law firms: **64%**   Government: **8%**
Bus./industry: **9%**   Judicial clerkship: **11%**
Public interest: **6%**   Unknown: **1%**
Academia: **1%**

2006 graduates employed in-state: **78%**
2006 graduates employed in foreign countries: **1%**
Number of states where graduates are employed: **22**
Percentage of 2006 graduates working in: New England: **0%**, Middle Atlantic: **3%**, East North Central: **2%**, West North Central: **0%**, South Atlantic: **5%**, East South Central: **0%**, West South Central: **3%**, Mountain: **3%**, Pacific: **83%**, Unknown: **1%**

BAR PASSAGE RATES
Based on 2006 graduates taking Summer 2006 or Winter 2007 exams. Most of the school's first-time test takers took the bar in California.

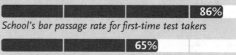

86%
School's bar passage rate for first-time test takers

65%
Statewide bar passage rate for first-time test takers

University of Chicago

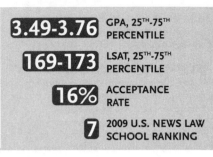

- 1111 E. 60th Street, Chicago, IL, 60637
- http://www.law.uchicago.edu
- Private
- Year founded: 1902
- 2007-2008 tuition: full-time: $39,198; part-time: N/A
- Enrollment 2007-08 academic year: full-time: 607
- U.S. News 2009 law specialty ranking: clinical training: 20, tax law: 17

3.49-3.76 GPA, 25TH-75TH PERCENTILE

169-173 LSAT, 25TH-75TH PERCENTILE

16% ACCEPTANCE RATE

7 2009 U.S. NEWS LAW SCHOOL RANKING

ADMISSIONS

Admissions phone number: **(773) 702-9484**
Admissions email address: **admissions@law.uchicago.edu**
Application website: **https://grad-application.uchicago.edu/intro/law/intro1.cfm**
Application deadline for Fall 2009 admission: **02/01**

Admissions statistics:
Number of applicants for Fall 2007: **4,798**
Number of acceptances: **777**
Number enrolled: **190**
Acceptance rate: **16%**
GPA, 25th-75th percentile, entering class Fall 2007: **3.49-3.76**
LSAT, 25th-75th percentile, entering class Fall 2007: **169-173**

FINANCIAL AID

Financial aid phone number: **(773) 702-9484**
Financial aid application deadline: **03/01**
Tuition 2007-2008 academic year: full-time: **$39,198**; part-time: **N/A**
Room and board: **$13,466**; books: **$1,654**; miscellaneous expenses: **$7,186**
Total of room/board/books/miscellaneous expenses: **$22,306**
University offers graduate student housing for which law students are eligible.

Financial aid profile
Percent of students that received grants for the 2006-2007 academic year: full-time: **55%**
Median grant amount: full-time: **$10,800**
The average law-school debt of those in the Class of 2007 who borrowed: **$121,782**. Proportion who borrowed: **82%**

ACADEMIC PROGRAMS

Calendar: **quarter**
Joint degrees awarded: **J.D./M.B.A.; J.D./M.P.P.; J.D./A.M. INR; J.D./Ph.D.**

Typical first-year section size: Full-time: **96**
Is there typically a "small section" of the first year class, other than Legal Writing, taught by full-time faculty?: Full-time: **no**
Number of course titles, beyond the first year curriculum, offered last year: **159**
Percentages of upper division course sections, excluding seminars, with an enrollment of:

Under 25: **26%**   25 to 49: **41%**
50 to 74: **16%**   75 to 99: **13%**
100+: **3%**

Areas of specialization: appellate advocacy, clinical training, dispute resolution, environmental law, healthcare law, intellectual property law, international law, tax law, trial advocacy

Fall 2007 faculty profile
Total teaching faculty: **102**. Full-time: **48%**; **76%** men, **24%** women, **10%** minorities. Part-time: **52%**; **81%** men, **19%** women, **8%** minorities
Student-to-faculty ratio: **10.3**

SPECIAL PROGRAMS (as provided by law school):
The Chicago Policy Initiatives encourage faculty members and students to think hard about important social problems and to propose solutions. Centers on Civil Justice, Comparative Constitutionalism, Studies in Criminal Justice, and the John M. Olin program in law and economics. The Mandel Legal Aid Clinic continues to serve the people of Chicago to this day.

STUDENT BODY
Fall 2007 full-time enrollment: 607
Men: **55%**   Women: **45%**
African-American: **6.6%**   American Indian: **0.3%**
Asian-American: **11.4%**   Mexican-American: **2.6%**
Puerto Rican: **1.0%**   Other Hisp-Amer: **4.0%**
White: **55.8%**   International: **2.0%**
Unknown: **16.3%**

Attrition rates for 2006-2007 full-time students

Percent of students discontinuing law school:

Men: **0%**   Women: **0%**

First-year students: **1%**   Second-year students: **N/A**

Third-year students: **N/A**

LIBRARY RESOURCES

Total volumes: **632,325**

Total seats available for library users: **447**

INFORMATION TECHNOLOGY

Number of wired network connections available to students: **1,115** total (in the law library, excluding computer labs: **307**; in classrooms: **800**; in computer labs: **0**; elsewhere in the law school: **8**)

Law school has a wireless network.

Students are required to own a computer.

EMPLOYMENT AND SALARIES

Proportion of 2006 graduates employed at graduation: **96%**

Employed 9 months later, as of February 15, 2007: **99%**

Salaries in the private sector (law firms, business, industry): **$120,000–$135,000** (25th-75th percentile)

Median salary in the private sector: **$135,000**

Percentage in the private sector who reported salary information: **98%**

Median salary in public service (government, judicial clerkships, academic posts, non-profits): **$53,000**

Percentage of 2006 graduates in:

Law firms: **76%**   Government: **6%**

Bus./industry: **3%**   Judicial clerkship: **14%**

Public interest: **1%**   Unknown: **1%**

Academia: **1%**

2006 graduates employed in-state: **34%**

2006 graduates employed in foreign countries: **1%**

Number of states where graduates are employed: **22**

Percentage of 2006 graduates working in: New England: **2%**, Middle Atlantic: **22%**, East North Central: **37%**, West North Central: **1%**, South Atlantic: **16%**, East South Central: **0%**, West South Central: **3%**, Mountain: **3%**, Pacific: **14%**, Unknown: **1%**

BAR PASSAGE RATES

Based on 2006 graduates taking Summer 2006 or Winter 2007 exams. Most of the school's first-time test takers took the bar in Illinois.

98%

School's bar passage rate for first-time test takers

87%

Statewide bar passage rate for first-time test takers

University of Cincinnati

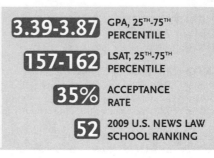

- PO Box 210040, Cincinnati, OH, 45221-0040
- http://www.law.uc.edu
- Public
- Year founded: 1833
- 2007-2008 tuition: In-state: full-time: $18,982; part-time: N/A; Out-of-state: full-time: $33,102
- Enrollment 2007-08 academic year: full-time: 356
- U.S. News 2009 law specialty ranking: N/A

3.39-3.87 GPA, 25TH-75TH PERCENTILE

157-162 LSAT, 25TH-75TH PERCENTILE

35% ACCEPTANCE RATE

52 2009 U.S. NEWS LAW SCHOOL RANKING

ADMISSIONS

Admissions phone number: **(513) 556-6805**
Admissions email address: **admissions@law.uc.edu**
Application website: **http://www.law.uc.edu/admissions**
Application deadline for Fall 2009 admission: **03/01**

Admissions statistics:

Number of applicants for Fall 2007: **1,293**
Number of acceptances: **454**
Number enrolled: **120**
Acceptance rate: **35%**
GPA, 25th-75th percentile, entering class Fall 2007: **3.39-3.87**
LSAT, 25th-75th percentile, entering class Fall 2007: **157-162**

FINANCIAL AID

Financial aid phone number: **(513) 556-6805**
Financial aid application deadline: **03/01**
Tuition 2007-2008 academic year: In-state: full-time: **$18,982**; part-time: N/A; Out-of-state: full-time: **$33,102**
Room and board: **$9,765**; books: **$1,227**; miscellaneous expenses: **$4,386**
Total of room/board/books/miscellaneous expenses: **$15,378**
University offers graduate student housing for which law students are eligible.

Financial aid profile

Percent of students that received grants for the 2006-2007 academic year: full-time: **71%**
Median grant amount: full-time: **$6,500**
The average law-school debt of those in the Class of 2007 who borrowed: **$53,982**. Proportion who borrowed: **89%**

ACADEMIC PROGRAMS

Calendar: **semester**
Joint degrees awarded: **J.D./M.B.A.; J.D./M.C.P.; J.D./M.A. Women's Studies; J.D./M.S. Political Science; J.D./Ph.D Political Science; J.D./M.S. Economics; J.D./M.S.W.**

Typical first-year section size: Full-time: **54**
Is there typically a "small section" of the first year class, other than Legal Writing, taught by full-time faculty?: Full-time: **yes**
Number of course titles, beyond the first year curriculum, offered last year: **112**
Percentages of upper division course sections, excluding seminars, with an enrollment of:
Under 25: **64%**   25 to 49: **19%**
50 to 74: **15%**   75 to 99: **1%**
100+: **0%**
Areas of specialization: appellate advocacy, clinical training, dispute resolution, environmental law, healthcare law, intellectual property law, international law, tax law, trial advocacy

Fall 2007 faculty profile

Total teaching faculty: **89**. Full-time: **39%**; **51%** men, **49%** women, **20%** minorities. Part-time: **61%**; **81%** men, **19%** women, **4%** minorities
Student-to-faculty ratio: **9.6**

SPECIAL PROGRAMS *(as provided by law school):*

Institutes/centers include: Center for Corporate Law, Center for Practice in Negotiation and Problem Solving, Glenn M. Weaver Institute of Law and Psychiatry, Lois and Richard Rosenthal/Ohio Institute for Justice. Clinics: Sixth Circuit appellate practice clinic, domestic relations/domestic violence. Joint-degree programs: M.B.A., M.C.P., M.S.W, Women's Studies and Political Science.

STUDENT BODY

Fall 2007 full-time enrollment: 356

Men: **54%**   Women: **46%**
African-American: **7.0%**   American Indian: **0.3%**
Asian-American: **6.5%**   Mexican-American: **0.3%**
Puerto Rican: **0.3%**   Other Hisp-Amer: **3.1%**
White: **82.6%**   International: **0.0%**
Unknown: **0.0%**

Attrition rates for 2006-2007 full-time students
Percent of students discontinuing law school:
Men: **3%**   Women: **2%**
First-year students: **8%**   Second-year students: **N/A**
Third-year students: **N/A**

LIBRARY RESOURCES
Total volumes: **428,753**
Total seats available for library users: **333**

INFORMATION TECHNOLOGY
Number of wired network connections available to students: **6** total (in the law library, excluding computer labs: **6**; in classrooms: **0**; in computer labs: **0**; elsewhere in the law school: **0**)
Law school has a wireless network.
Students are not required to own a computer.

EMPLOYMENT AND SALARIES
Proportion of 2006 graduates employed at graduation: **73%**
Employed 9 months later, as of February 15, 2007: **96%**
Salaries in the private sector (law firms, business, industry): **$65,000–$100,000** (25th-75th percentile)
Median salary in the private sector: **$90,000**
Percentage in the private sector who reported salary information: **62%**
Median salary in public service (government, judicial clerkships, academic posts, non-profits): **$43,000**

Percentage of 2006 graduates in:
Law firms: **56%**   Government: **9%**
Bus./industry: **16%**   Judicial clerkship: **8%**
Public interest: **5%**   Unknown: **2%**
Academia: **4%**

2006 graduates employed in-state: **76%**
2006 graduates employed in foreign countries: **0%**
Number of states where graduates are employed: **17**
Percentage of 2006 graduates working in: New England: **0%**, Middle Atlantic: **1%**, East North Central: **81%**, West North Central: **1%**, South Atlantic: **7%**, East South Central: **3%**, West South Central: **1%**, Mountain: **3%**, Pacific: **4%**, Unknown: **1%**

BAR PASSAGE RATES
Based on 2006 graduates taking Summer 2006 or Winter 2007 exams. Most of the school's first-time test takers took the bar in Ohio.

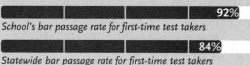

92%
School's bar passage rate for first-time test takers

84%
Statewide bar passage rate for first-time test takers

University of Colorado—Boulder

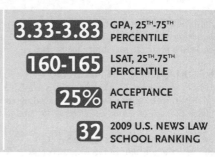

- Box 401, Boulder, CO, 80309-0401
- http://www.colorado.edu/law/
- Public
- Year founded: 1892
- 2007-2008 tuition: In-state: full-time: $18,594; part-time: N/A; Out-of-state: full-time: $31,278
- Enrollment 2007-08 academic year: full-time: 530
- U.S. News 2009 law specialty ranking: environmental law: 6

3.33-3.83 GPA, 25TH-75TH PERCENTILE

160-165 LSAT, 25TH-75TH PERCENTILE

25% ACCEPTANCE RATE

32 2009 U.S. NEWS LAW SCHOOL RANKING

ADMISSIONS

Admissions phone number: **(303) 492-7203**
Admissions email address: **lawadmin@colorado.edu**
Application website: **http://www.colorado.edu/law/ admissions/request.htm**
Application deadline for Fall 2009 admission: **03/15**

Admissions statistics:
Number of applicants for Fall 2007: **2,579**
Number of acceptances: **651**
Number enrolled: **175**
Acceptance rate: **25%**
GPA, 25th-75th percentile, entering class Fall 2007: **3.33-3.83**
LSAT, 25th-75th percentile, entering class Fall 2007: **160-165**

FINANCIAL AID

Financial aid phone number: **(303) 492-8223**
Financial aid application deadline: **04/01**
Tuition 2007-2008 academic year: In-state: full-time: **$18,594**; part-time: **N/A**; Out-of-state: full-time: **$31,278**
Room and board: **$7,465**; books: **$1,567**; miscellaneous expenses: **$3,888**
Total of room/board/books/miscellaneous expenses: **$12,920**
University offers graduate student housing for which law students are eligible.

Financial aid profile
Percent of students that received grants for the 2006-2007 academic year: full-time: **36%**
Median grant amount: full-time: **$2,500**
The average law-school debt of those in the Class of 2007 who borrowed: **$62,485**. Proportion who borrowed: **89%**

ACADEMIC PROGRAMS

Calendar: **semester**
Joint degrees awarded: **J.D./M.B.A.; J.D./M.P.A.; J.D./M.A. International Affairs; J.D./M.S. EnvS.; J.D./M.D.; J.D./M.URP.; J.D./Ph.D. EnvS.; J.D./M.S.T.**

Typical first-year section size: Full-time: **87**
Is there typically a "small section" of the first year class, other than Legal Writing, taught by full-time faculty?: Full-time: **yes**
Number of course titles, beyond the first year curriculum, offered last year: **101**
Percentages of upper division course sections, excluding seminars, with an enrollment of:
Under 25: **66%**   25 to 49: **19%**
50 to 74: **14%**   75 to 99: **1%**
100+: **0%**
Areas of specialization: appellate advocacy, clinical training, dispute resolution, environmental law, healthcare law, intellectual property law, international law, tax law, trial advocacy

Fall 2007 faculty profile
Total teaching faculty: **55**. Full-time: **69%**; **55%** men, **45%** women, **18%** minorities. Part-time: **31%**; **71%** men, **29%** women, **6%** minorities
Student-to-faculty ratio: **12.2**

SPECIAL PROGRAMS *(as provided by law school):*
Colorado Law students work with legal, legislative, and business professionals through 18 clinics, centers, and programs covering appellate advocacy, constitutional, energy and environment, entrepreneurial, Indian, international, juvenile and family, natural resources, telecommunications, tax, legal aid, and wrongful convictions issues. Dual-degree programs include: J.D./M.B.A, J.D./M.P.A.

STUDENT BODY
Fall 2007 full-time enrollment: 530
Men: **52%**   Women: **48%**
African-American: **3.8%**   American Indian: **2.3%**
Asian-American: **8.3%**   Mexican-American: **2.6%**
Puerto Rican: **0.2%**   Other Hisp-Amer: **5.1%**
White: **77.2%**   International: **0.6%**
Unknown: **0.0%**

Attrition rates for 2006-2007 full-time students
Percent of students discontinuing law school:
Men: **0%**   Women: **0%**
First-year students: **1%**   Second-year students: **1%**
Third-year students: **N/A**

LIBRARY RESOURCES
Total volumes: **676,949**
Total seats available for library users: **444**

INFORMATION TECHNOLOGY
Number of wired network connections available to students: **24** total (in the law library, excluding computer labs: **0**; in classrooms: **16**; in computer labs: **0**; elsewhere in the law school: **8**)
Law school has a wireless network.
Students are not required to own a computer.

EMPLOYMENT AND SALARIES
Proportion of 2006 graduates employed at graduation: **89%**
Employed 9 months later, as of February 15, 2007: **97%**
Salaries in the private sector (law firms, business, industry): **$52,000–$105,000** (25th-75th percentile)
Median salary in the private sector: **$80,000**
Percentage in the private sector who reported salary information: **57%**
Median salary in public service (government, judicial clerkships, academic posts, non-profits): **$45,000**

Percentage of 2006 graduates in:
Law firms: **43%**   Government: **18%**
Bus./industry: **9%**   Judicial clerkship: **19%**
Public interest: **3%**   Unknown: **8%**
Academia: **1%**

2006 graduates employed in-state: **79%**
2006 graduates employed in foreign countries: **1%**
Number of states where graduates are employed: **16**
Percentage of 2006 graduates working in: New England: **0%**, Middle Atlantic: **2%**, East North Central: **2%**, West North Central: **0%**, South Atlantic: **4%**, East South Central: **0%**, West South Central: **1%**, Mountain: **84%**, Pacific: **6%**, Unknown: **1%**

BAR PASSAGE RATES
Based on 2006 graduates taking Summer 2006 or Winter 2007 exams. Most of the school's first-time test takers took the bar in Colorado.

91%
School's bar passage rate for first-time test takers

76%
Statewide bar passage rate for first-time test takers

University of Connecticut

■ 55 Elizabeth Street, Hartford, CT, 06105-2296
■ http://www.law.uconn.edu
■ Public
■ Year founded: 1921
■ 2007-2008 tuition: In-state: full-time: $17,520; part-time: $12,220;
  Out-of-state: full-time: $36,960
■ Enrollment 2007-08 academic year: full-time: 484; part-time: 179
■ U.S. News 2009 law specialty ranking: N/A

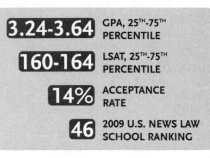

3.24-3.64 GPA, 25TH-75TH PERCENTILE

160-164 LSAT, 25TH-75TH PERCENTILE

14% ACCEPTANCE RATE

46 2009 U.S. NEWS LAW SCHOOL RANKING

ADMISSIONS

Admissions phone number: **(860) 570-5100**
Admissions email address: **admit@law.uconn.edu**
Application website: **http://www.law.uconn.edu/
admissions/admsfin/forms.html**
Application deadline for Fall 2009 admission: **03/01**

Admissions statistics:

Number of applicants for Fall 2007: **2,001**
Number of acceptances: **282**
Number enrolled: **141**
Acceptance rate: **14%**
GPA, 25th-75th percentile, entering class Fall 2007: **3.24-3.64**
LSAT, 25th-75th percentile, entering class Fall 2007: **160-164**

Part-time program:

Number of applicants for Fall 2007: **823**
Number of acceptances: **144**
Number enrolled: **75**
Acceptance rate: **17%**
GPA, 25th-75th percentile, entering class Fall 2007: **3.23-3.65**
LSAT, 25th-75th percentile, entering class Fall 2007: **155-159**

FINANCIAL AID

Financial aid phone number: **(860) 570-5147**
Financial aid application deadline: **03/01**
Tuition 2007-2008 academic year: In-state: full-time:
  $17,520; part-time: **$12,220**; Out-of-state: full-time:
  $36,960
Room and board: **$10,930**; books: **$1,100**; miscellaneous
  expenses: **$5,170**
Total of room/board/books/miscellaneous expenses:
  $17,200
University does not offer graduate student housing for
  which law students are eligible.

Financial aid profile

Percent of students that received grants for the 2006-2007
  academic year: full-time: **73%**; part-time **15%**
Median grant amount: full-time: **$9,000**; part-time:
  $2,800
The average law-school debt of those in the Class of 2007
  who borrowed: **$72,421**. Proportion who borrowed: **86%**

ACADEMIC PROGRAMS

Calendar: **semester**
Joint degrees awarded: **J.D./M.S.W.; J.D./M.B.A.;
  J.D./M.L.S.; J.D./M.P.A.; J.D./M.P.H.; J.D./LL.M.
  Insurance Law**
Typical first-year section size: Full-time: **71**; Part-time: **72**
Is there typically a "small section" of the first year class,
  other than Legal Writing, taught by full-time faculty?:
  Full-time: **yes**; Part-time: **yes**
Number of course titles, beyond the first year curriculum,
  offered last year: **151**
Percentages of upper division course sections, excluding
  seminars, with an enrollment of:
  Under 25: **71%**   25 to 49: **21%**
  50 to 74: **8%**   75 to 99: **0%**
  100+: **0%**
Areas of specialization: appellate advocacy, clinical training,
  dispute resolution, environmental law, healthcare law,
  intellectual property law, international law, tax law, trial
  advocacy

Fall 2007 faculty profile

Total teaching faculty: **91**. Full-time: **48%**; **64%** men, **36%**
  women, **14%** minorities. Part-time: **52%**; **85%** men, **15%**
  women, **6%** minorities
Student-to-faculty ratio: **11.0**

SPECIAL PROGRAMS (as provided by law school):

In-house clinics represent low-income taxpayers, political asylum seekers, entrepreneurs, and criminal defendants. Others
focus on mediation, children's advocacy, urban revitalization,

environmental law, women's rights, GLBTQ rights, and criminal prosecution. Certificates offered in Tax; Intellectual Property; Law and Public Policy; Human Rights. Foreign study and dual-degree programs available.

STUDENT BODY

Fall 2007 full-time enrollment: 484

Men: 51%	Women: 49%
African-American: 5.6%	American Indian: 0.6%
Asian-American: 4.3%	Mexican-American: 0.2%
Puerto Rican: 2.7%	Other Hisp-Amer: 3.5%
White: 70.2%	International: 0.4%
Unknown: 12.4%	

Fall 2007 part-time enrollment: 179

Men: 55%	Women: 45%
African-American: 5.0%	American Indian: 0.0%
Asian-American: 10.1%	Mexican-American: 0.0%
Puerto Rican: 2.8%	Other Hisp-Amer: 3.9%
White: 66.5%	International: 0.6%
Unknown: 11.2%	

Attrition rates for 2006-2007 full-time students

Percent of students discontinuing law school:

Men: 2%	Women: 1%
First-year students: 4%	Second-year students: 1%
Third-year students: N/A	

LIBRARY RESOURCES

Total volumes: 545,754
Total seats available for library users: 822

INFORMATION TECHNOLOGY

Number of wired network connections available to students: 779 total (in the law library, excluding computer labs: 388; in classrooms: 371; in computer labs: 0; elsewhere in the law school: 20)
Law school has a wireless network.
Students are not required to own a computer.

EMPLOYMENT AND SALARIES

Proportion of 2006 graduates employed at graduation: 74%
Employed 9 months later, as of February 15, 2007: 96%
Salaries in the private sector (law firms, business, industry): $73,000–$125,000 (25th-75th percentile)
Median salary in the private sector: $74,000
Percentage in the private sector who reported salary information: 58%
Median salary in public service (government, judicial clerkships, academic posts, non-profits): $47,500

Percentage of 2006 graduates in:

Law firms: 50%	Government: 12%
Bus./industry: 16%	Judicial clerkship: 13%
Public interest: 6%	Unknown: 0%
Academia: 3%	

2006 graduates employed in-state: 55%
2006 graduates employed in foreign countries: 0%
Number of states where graduates are employed: 21
Percentage of 2006 graduates working in: New England: 72%, Middle Atlantic: 15%, East North Central: 1%, West North Central: 1%, South Atlantic: 9%, East South Central: 1%, West South Central: 0%, Mountain: 2%, Pacific: 1%, Unknown: 1%

BAR PASSAGE RATES

Based on 2006 graduates taking Summer 2006 or Winter 2007 exams. Most of the school's first-time test takers took the bar in Connecticut.

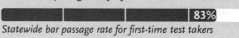

87%
School's bar passage rate for first-time test takers

83%
Statewide bar passage rate for first-time test takers

University of Dayton

■ 300 College Park, Dayton, OH, 45469-2772
■ http://law.udayton.edu
■ Private
■ Year founded: 1974
■ 2007-2008 tuition: full-time: $910/credit hour; part-time: N/A
■ Enrollment 2007-08 academic year: full-time: 424
■ U.S. News 2009 law specialty ranking: N/A

2.96-3.50 GPA, 25TH-75TH PERCENTILE

149-154 LSAT, 25TH-75TH PERCENTILE

51% ACCEPTANCE RATE

Tier 4 2009 U.S. NEWS LAW SCHOOL RANKING

ADMISSIONS

Admissions phone number: **(937) 229-3555**
Admissions email address: **lawinfo@notes.udayton.edu**
Application website: **http://131.238.103.185/onlineapp/**
Application deadline for Fall 2009 admission: **rolling**

Admissions statistics:
Number of applicants for Fall 2007: **1,881**
Number of acceptances: **953**
Number enrolled: **177**
Acceptance rate: **51%**
GPA, 25th-75th percentile, entering class Fall 2007: **2.96-3.50**
LSAT, 25th-75th percentile, entering class Fall 2007: **149-154**

FINANCIAL AID

Financial aid phone number: **(937) 229-3555**
Financial aid application deadline: **N/A**
Tuition 2007-2008 academic year: full-time: **$910/credit hour**; part-time: **N/A**
Room and board: **$10,500**; books: **$1,200**; miscellaneous expenses: **$0**
Total of room/board/books/miscellaneous expenses: **$11,700**
University offers graduate student housing for which law students are eligible.

Financial aid profile
Percent of students that received grants for the 2006-2007 academic year: full-time: **62%**
Median grant amount: full-time: **$11,000**
The average law-school debt of those in the Class of 2007 who borrowed: **$83,575**. Proportion who borrowed: **88%**

ACADEMIC PROGRAMS

Calendar: **semester**
Joint degrees awarded: **J.D./M.B.A.; J.D./M.S. Education**
Typical first-year section size: Full-time: **80**

Is there typically a "small section" of the first year class, other than Legal Writing, taught by full-time faculty?: Full-time: **yes**
Number of course titles, beyond the first year curriculum, offered last year: **74**
Percentages of upper division course sections, excluding seminars, with an enrollment of:

Under 25: **69%**		25 to 49: **16%**	
50 to 74: **9%**		75 to 99: **5%**	
100+: **1%**			

Areas of specialization: appellate advocacy, clinical training, dispute resolution, environmental law, healthcare law, intellectual property law, international law, tax law, trial advocacy

Fall 2007 faculty profile
Total teaching faculty: **46**. Full-time: **54%**; **56%** men, **44%** women, **12%** minorities. Part-time: **46%**; **57%** men, **43%** women, **10%** minorities
Student-to-faculty ratio: **14.5**

SPECIAL PROGRAMS (as provided by law school):
Clinic, summer study, externships.

STUDENT BODY
Fall 2007 full-time enrollment: 424

Men: **57%**	Women: **43%**
African-American: **6.1%**	American Indian: **0.7%**
Asian-American: **4.5%**	Mexican-American: **1.7%**
Puerto Rican: **0.7%**	Other Hisp-Amer: **1.9%**
White: **84.4%**	International: **0.0%**
Unknown: **0.0%**	

Attrition rates for 2006-2007 full-time students
Percent of students discontinuing law school:

Men: **1%**	Women: **2%**
First-year students: **3%**	Second-year students: **1%**
Third-year students: **1%**	

LIBRARY RESOURCES

Total volumes: 318,825
Total seats available for library users: 489

INFORMATION TECHNOLOGY

Number of wired network connections available to students: 43 total (in the law library, excluding computer labs: 6; in classrooms: 0; in computer labs: 30; elsewhere in the law school: 7)
Law school has a wireless network.
Students are not required to own a computer.

EMPLOYMENT AND SALARIES

Proportion of 2006 graduates employed at graduation: N/A
Employed 9 months later, as of February 15, 2007: 88%
Salaries in the private sector (law firms, business, industry): $45,000–$60,000 (25th-75th percentile)
Median salary in the private sector: $55,892
Percentage in the private sector who reported salary information: 91%
Median salary in public service (government, judicial clerkships, academic posts, non-profits): $40,000

Percentage of 2006 graduates in:

Law firms: 61%
Bus./industry: 15%
Public interest: 11%
Academia: 3%

Government: 2%
Judicial clerkship: 6%
Unknown: 2%

2006 graduates employed in-state: 52%
2006 graduates employed in foreign countries: 0%
Number of states where graduates are employed: 19
Percentage of 2006 graduates working in: New England: 1%, Middle Atlantic: 8%, East North Central: 67%, West North Central: 1%, South Atlantic: 14%, East South Central: 4%, West South Central: 1%, Mountain: 2%, Pacific: 1%, Unknown: 0%

BAR PASSAGE RATES

Based on 2006 graduates taking Summer 2006 or Winter 2007 exams. Most of the school's first-time test takers took the bar in Ohio.

78%
School's bar passage rate for first-time test takers

84%
Statewide bar passage rate for first-time test takers

University of Denver (Sturm)

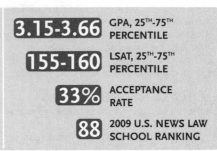

- 2255 E. Evans Avenue, Denver, CO, 80208
- http://www.law.du.edu
- Private
- Year founded: 1864
- 2007-2008 tuition: full-time: $32,752; part-time: $24,136
- Enrollment 2007-08 academic year: full-time: 855; part-time: 279
- U.S. News 2009 law specialty ranking: environmental law: 13, tax law: 19

3.15-3.66 GPA, 25TH-75TH PERCENTILE

155-160 LSAT, 25TH-75TH PERCENTILE

33% ACCEPTANCE RATE

88 2009 U.S. NEWS LAW SCHOOL RANKING

ADMISSIONS

Admissions phone number: (303) 871-6135
Admissions email address: admissions@law.du.edu
Application website: http://www.law.du.edu/ad/
Application deadline for Fall 2009 admission: rolling

Admissions statistics:
Number of applicants for Fall 2007: 2,960
Number of acceptances: 988
Number enrolled: 284
Acceptance rate: 33%
GPA, 25th-75th percentile, entering class Fall 2007: 3.15-3.66
LSAT, 25th-75th percentile, entering class Fall 2007: 155-160

Part-time program:
Number of applicants for Fall 2007: 381
Number of acceptances: 150
Number enrolled: 96
Acceptance rate: 39%
GPA, 25th-75th percentile, entering class Fall 2007: 3.09-3.56
LSAT, 25th-75th percentile, entering class Fall 2007: 151-157

FINANCIAL AID

Financial aid phone number: (303) 871-6136
Financial aid application deadline: N/A
Tuition 2007-2008 academic year: full-time: $32,752; part-time: $24,136
Room and board: $9,585; books: $1,698; miscellaneous expenses: $4,550
Total of room/board/books/miscellaneous expenses: $15,833
University offers graduate student housing for which law students are eligible.

Financial aid profile
Percent of students that received grants for the 2006-2007 academic year: full-time: 41%; part-time 19%

Median grant amount: full-time: $10,000; part-time: $5,750
The average law-school debt of those in the Class of 2007 who borrowed: $91,062. Proportion who borrowed: 85%

ACADEMIC PROGRAMS

Calendar: semester
Joint degrees awarded: J.D./M.B.A.; J.D./M.A. International Studies; J.D./M.S.W.; J.D./M.A. Philosophy; J.D./M.A. Economics; J.D./MIM; J.D./MSLA; J.D./Psy.; J.D./L.L.M. Tax; J.D./MMP; J.D./M.A. Mass Communications; J.D./M.S. Computer Science; J.D./RECM
Typical first-year section size: Full-time: 90; Part-time: 90
Is there typically a "small section" of the first year class, other than Legal Writing, taught by full-time faculty?: Full-time: yes; Part-time: no
Number of course titles, beyond the first year curriculum, offered last year: 161
Percentages of upper division course sections, excluding seminars, with an enrollment of:

Under 25: 71%	25 to 49: 20%
50 to 74: 6%	75 to 99: 3%
100+: 0%	

Areas of specialization: appellate advocacy, clinical training, dispute resolution, environmental law, healthcare law, intellectual property law, international law, tax law, trial advocacy

Fall 2007 faculty profile
Total teaching faculty: 97. Full-time: 51%; 59% men, 41% women, 24% minorities. Part-time: 49%; 85% men, 15% women, 4% minorities
Student-to-faculty ratio: 18.7

SPECIAL PROGRAMS (as provided by law school):
The University of Denver College of Law has an internship program. To better prepare students for the internationalization of legal practice, the College of Law offers law courses in Spanish that train students to operate in a global economy. The law

school offers a variety of opportunities for practical legal experience through its clinical and affiliated programs.

STUDENT BODY

Fall 2007 full-time enrollment: 855

Men: 57%	Women: 43%
African-American: 2.1%	American Indian: 2.2%
Asian-American: 4.8%	Mexican-American: 0.0%
Puerto Rican: 0.0%	Other Hisp-Amer: 5.3%
White: 75.7%	International: 0.2%
Unknown: 9.7%	

Fall 2007 part-time enrollment: 279

Men: 49%	Women: 51%
African-American: 6.5%	American Indian: 3.9%
Asian-American: 3.6%	Mexican-American: 0.0%
Puerto Rican: 0.0%	Other Hisp-Amer: 9.3%
White: 72.4%	International: 0.0%
Unknown: 4.3%	

Attrition rates for 2006-2007 full-time students

Percent of students discontinuing law school:

Men: 4%	Women: 5%
First-year students: 3%	Second-year students: 7%
Third-year students: 3%	

LIBRARY RESOURCES

Total volumes: 400,814
Total seats available for library users: 333

INFORMATION TECHNOLOGY

Number of wired network connections available to students: 1,575 total (in the law library, excluding computer labs: 167; in classrooms: 878; in computer labs: 40; elsewhere in the law school: 490)
Law school has a wireless network.
Students are required to own a computer.

EMPLOYMENT AND SALARIES

Proportion of 2006 graduates employed at graduation: 67%
Employed 9 months later, as of February 15, 2007: 96%
Salaries in the private sector (law firms, business, industry): $52,000–$95,000 (25th-75th percentile)
Median salary in the private sector: $65,000
Percentage in the private sector who reported salary information: 56%
Median salary in public service (government, judicial clerkships, academic posts, non-profits): $46,000

Percentage of 2006 graduates in:

Law firms: 46%	Government: 17%
Bus./industry: 12%	Judicial clerkship: 9%
Public interest: 4%	Unknown: 11%
Academia: 1%	

2006 graduates employed in-state: 80%
2006 graduates employed in foreign countries: 0%
Number of states where graduates are employed: 31
Percentage of 2006 graduates working in: New England: 1%, Middle Atlantic: 2%, East North Central: 1%, West North Central: 1%, South Atlantic: 5%, East South Central: 1%, West South Central: 2%, Mountain: 83%, Pacific: 2%, Unknown: 2%

BAR PASSAGE RATES

Based on 2006 graduates taking Summer 2006 or Winter 2007 exams. Most of the school's first-time test takers took the bar in Colorado.

66%
School's bar passage rate for first-time test takers

76%
Statewide bar passage rate for first-time test takers

University of Detroit Mercy

- 651 E. Jefferson Avenue, Detroit, MI, 48226
- http://www.law.udmercy.edu
- Private
- **Year founded:** 1912
- **2007-2008 tuition:** full-time: $28,500; part-time: $950/credit hour
- **Enrollment 2007-08 academic year:** full-time: 591; part-time: 160
- **U.S. News 2009 law specialty ranking:** N/A

2.95-3.36 GPA, 25TH-75TH PERCENTILE

146-154 LSAT, 25TH-75TH PERCENTILE

47% ACCEPTANCE RATE

Tier 4 2009 U.S. NEWS LAW SCHOOL RANKING

ADMISSIONS

Admissions phone number: **(313) 596-0264**
Admissions email address: **udmlawao@udmercy.edu**
Application website:
   https://www4.lsac.org/LSACD_on_the_Web/login/open.aspx
Application deadline for Fall 2009 admission: **04/15**

Admissions statistics:
Number of applicants for Fall 2007: **1,714**
Number of acceptances: **799**
Number enrolled: **216**
Acceptance rate: **47%**
GPA, 25th-75th percentile, entering class Fall 2007: **2.95-3.36**
LSAT, 25th-75th percentile, entering class Fall 2007: **146-154**

Part-time program:
Number of applicants for Fall 2007: **234**
Number of acceptances: **118**
Number enrolled: **65**
Acceptance rate: **50%**
GPA, 25th-75th percentile, entering class Fall 2007: **2.62-3.36**
LSAT, 25th-75th percentile, entering class Fall 2007: **144-150**

FINANCIAL AID

Financial aid phone number: **(313) 596-0214**
Financial aid application deadline: **04/01**
Tuition 2007-2008 academic year: full-time: **$28,500**; part-time: **$950/credit hour**
Room and board: **$11,166**; books: **$1,800**; miscellaneous expenses: **$5,590**
Total of room/board/books/miscellaneous expenses: **$18,556**
University offers graduate student housing for which law students are eligible.

Financial aid profile
Percent of students that received grants for the 2006-2007 academic year: full-time: **15%**; part-time **16%**
Median grant amount: full-time: **$6,270**; part-time: **$5,532**
The average law-school debt of those in the Class of 2007 who borrowed: **$86,431**. Proportion who borrowed: **61%**

ACADEMIC PROGRAMS

Calendar: **semester**
Joint degrees awarded: **J.D./M.B.A.; J.D./LL.B.**
Typical first-year section size: Full-time: **61**; Part-time: **42**
Is there typically a "small section" of the first year class, other than Legal Writing, taught by full-time faculty?: Full-time: **no**; Part-time: **no**
Number of course titles, beyond the first year curriculum, offered last year: **98**
Percentages of upper division course sections, excluding seminars, with an enrollment of:

Under 25: **52%**	25 to 49: **39%**
50 to 74: **9%**	75 to 99: **0%**
100+: **0%**	

Areas of specialization: appellate advocacy, clinical training, dispute resolution, environmental law, healthcare law, intellectual property law, international law, tax law, trial advocacy

Fall 2007 faculty profile
Total teaching faculty: **56**. Full-time: **46%**; **62%** men, **38%** women, **8%** minorities. Part-time: **54%**; **83%** men, **17%** women, **7%** minorities
Student-to-faculty ratio: **16.8**

SPECIAL PROGRAMS *(as provided by law school)*:
Veterans clinic; environmental law clinic; mediation training and clinic; immigration law clinic; mobile law office; appellate advocacy clinic; urban law clinic; National Institute for Trial Advocacy; American Inns of Court; public service fellowships; teaching law in high school.

STUDENT BODY

Fall 2007 full-time enrollment: 591

Men: 57%	Women: 43%
African-American: 5.6%	American Indian: 0.2%
Asian-American: 3.6%	Mexican-American: 0.0%
Puerto Rican: 0.0%	Other Hisp-Amer: 1.2%
White: 69.0%	International: 19.3%
Unknown: 1.2%	

Fall 2007 part-time enrollment: 160

Men: 45%	Women: 55%
African-American: 23.8%	American Indian: 0.0%
Asian-American: 1.9%	Mexican-American: 0.0%
Puerto Rican: 0.0%	Other Hisp-Amer: 1.9%
White: 68.1%	International: 1.9%
Unknown: 2.5%	

Attrition rates for 2006-2007 full-time students

Percent of students discontinuing law school:

Men: 5%	Women: 6%
First-year students: 14%	Second-year students: 3%
Third-year students: N/A	

LIBRARY RESOURCES

Total volumes: 373,844
Total seats available for library users: 316

INFORMATION TECHNOLOGY

Number of wired network connections available to students: 0 total (in the law library, excluding computer labs: 0; in classrooms: 0; in computer labs: 0; elsewhere in the law school: 0)
Law school has a wireless network.
Students are not required to own a computer.

EMPLOYMENT AND SALARIES

Proportion of 2006 graduates employed at graduation: N/A
Employed 9 months later, as of February 15, 2007: 86%

Salaries in the private sector (law firms, business, industry): $55,000–$100,000 (25th-75th percentile)
Median salary in the private sector: $62,500
Percentage in the private sector who reported salary information: 17%
Median salary in public service (government, judicial clerkships, academic posts, non-profits): $45,000

Percentage of 2006 graduates in:

Law firms: 59%	Government: 7%
Bus./industry: 24%	Judicial clerkship: 4%
Public interest: 3%	Unknown: 2%
Academia: 1%	

2006 graduates employed in-state: 73%
2006 graduates employed in foreign countries: 18%
Number of states where graduates are employed: 11
Percentage of 2006 graduates working in: New England: 1%, Middle Atlantic: 1%, East North Central: 75%, West North Central: 0%, South Atlantic: 3%, East South Central: 0%, West South Central: 1%, Mountain: 1%, Pacific: 0%, Unknown: 0%

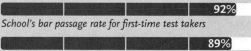

BAR PASSAGE RATES

Based on 2006 graduates taking Summer 2006 or Winter 2007 exams. Most of the school's first-time test takers took the bar in Michigan.

92%
School's bar passage rate for first-time test takers

89%
Statewide bar passage rate for first-time test takers

University of Florida (Levin)

■ PO Box 117620, Gainesville, FL, 32611-7620
■ http://www.law.ufl.edu
■ Public
■ Year founded: 1909
■ 2007-2008 tuition: In-state: full-time: $10,809; part-time: N/A; Out-of-state: full-time: $30,174
■ Enrollment 2007-08 academic year: full-time: 1,290
■ U.S. News 2009 law specialty ranking: environmental law: 13, tax law: 2

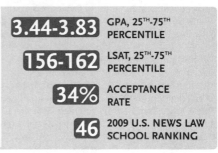

3.44-3.83 GPA, 25TH-75TH PERCENTILE

156-162 LSAT, 25TH-75TH PERCENTILE

34% ACCEPTANCE RATE

46 2009 U.S. NEWS LAW SCHOOL RANKING

ADMISSIONS

Admissions phone number: **(352) 273-0890**
Admissions email address: **patrick@law.ufl.edu**
Application website: **http://www.law.ufl.edu/admissions**
Application deadline for Fall 2009 admission: **01/15**

Admissions statistics:

Number of applicants for Fall 2007: **2,781**
Number of acceptances: **955**
Number enrolled: **378**
Acceptance rate: **34%**
GPA, 25th-75th percentile, entering class Fall 2007: **3.44-3.83**
LSAT, 25th-75th percentile, entering class Fall 2007: **156-162**

FINANCIAL AID

Financial aid phone number: **(352) 273-0628**
Financial aid application deadline: **04/01**
Tuition 2007-2008 academic year: In-state: full-time: **$10,809**; part-time: N/A; Out-of-state: full-time: **$30,174**
Room and board: **N/A**; books: **N/A**; miscellaneous expenses: **N/A**
Total of room/board/books/miscellaneous expenses: **$13,545**
University offers graduate student housing for which law students are eligible.

Financial aid profile

Percent of students that received grants for the 2006-2007 academic year: full-time: **17%**
Median grant amount: full-time: **$2,100**
The average law-school debt of those in the Class of 2007 who borrowed: **$53,949**. Proportion who borrowed: **82%**

ACADEMIC PROGRAMS

Calendar: **semester**
Joint degrees awarded: **J.D./M.S. Accounting; J.D./M.B.A.; J.D./M.S. or Ph.D. Political Science; J.D./M.D.; J.D./M.S. or Ph.D. Sociology; J.D./M.A. or Ph.D. Mass Communication; J.D./M.A. or Ph.D. History; J.D./Ph.D.**
Education Leadership; J.D./M.S. Urban Planning; J.D./Ph.D. Psychology; J.D./M.A. Real Estate; J.D./M.A. Finance; J.D./M.S. Sports Management; J.D./M.S. Forest Conservation; J.D./M.A. Women's Studies; J.D./M.A. or Ph.D. Anthropology; J.D./M.S. Environmental Engineering; J.D./M.A. Latin American Studies; J.D./M.A. or Ph.D. Medical Science; J.D./M.A. Public Administration; J.D./D.V.M.; J.D./M.S. Family, Youth & Comm. Services; J.D./M.S. Electrical & Computer Engineer; J.D./M.S. Public Health; J.D./M.A. International Relations

Typical first-year section size: Full-time: **100**
Is there typically a "small section" of the first year class, other than Legal Writing, taught by full-time faculty?: Full-time: **no**
Number of course titles, beyond the first year curriculum, offered last year: **145**
Percentages of upper division course sections, excluding seminars, with an enrollment of:

Under 25: **37%**	25 to 49: **25%**
50 to 74: **25%**	75 to 99: **4%**
100+: **8%**	

Areas of specialization: appellate advocacy, clinical training, dispute resolution, environmental law, healthcare law, intellectual property law, international law, tax law, trial advocacy

Fall 2007 faculty profile

Total teaching faculty: **98**. Full-time: **61%**; **55%** men, **45%** women, **15%** minorities. Part-time: **39%**; **82%** men, **18%** women, **8%** minorities
Student-to-faculty ratio: **15.7**

SPECIAL PROGRAMS (as provided by law school):

The college offers both civil and criminal clinics as well as numerous simulation courses. It also offers Certificates in Children and Family Law, International Law, Estates and Trusts Practice, Intellectual Property Law, and Environmental and Land Use Law. The college also has a number of academic-year exchange and summer-abroad programs.

STUDENT BODY

Fall 2007 full-time enrollment: 1,290

Men: 53%	Women: 47%
African-American: 6.0%	American Indian: 0.4%
Asian-American: 4.7%	Mexican-American: 0.0%
Puerto Rican: 0.0%	Other Hisp-Amer: 9.5%
White: 75.5%	International: 1.3%
Unknown: 2.6%	

Attrition rates for 2006-2007 full-time students
Percent of students discontinuing law school:

Men: 1%	Women: 0%
First-year students: 3%	Second-year students: 0%
Third-year students: N/A	

LIBRARY RESOURCES

Total volumes: 635,308
Total seats available for library users: 765

INFORMATION TECHNOLOGY

Number of wired network connections available to students: 0 total (in the law library, excluding computer labs: 0; in classrooms: 0; in computer labs: 0; elsewhere in the law school: 0)
Law school has a wireless network.
Students are required to own a computer.

EMPLOYMENT AND SALARIES

Proportion of 2006 graduates employed at graduation: 78%
Employed 9 months later, as of February 15, 2007: 97%
Salaries in the private sector (law firms, business, industry): $60,000–$100,000 (25th-75th percentile)

Median salary in the private sector: $80,000
Percentage in the private sector who reported salary information: 65%
Median salary in public service (government, judicial clerkships, academic posts, non-profits): $39,000

Percentage of 2006 graduates in:

Law firms: 56%	Government: 16%
Bus./industry: 13%	Judicial clerkship: 4%
Public interest: 9%	Unknown: 1%
Academia: 1%	

2006 graduates employed in-state: 83%
2006 graduates employed in foreign countries: 0%
Number of states where graduates are employed: 18
Percentage of 2006 graduates working in: New England: 0%, Middle Atlantic: 2%, East North Central: 1%, West North Central: 0%, South Atlantic: 90%, East South Central: 1%, West South Central: 1%, Mountain: 1%, Pacific: 2%, Unknown: 3%

BAR PASSAGE RATES

Based on 2006 graduates taking Summer 2006 or Winter 2007 exams. Most of the school's first-time test takers took the bar in Florida.

78%
School's bar passage rate for first-time test takers

74%
Statewide bar passage rate for first-time test takers

University of Georgia

- Herty Drive, Athens, GA, 30602
- http://www.lawsch.uga.edu
- Public
- **Year founded:** 1859
- **2007-2008 tuition:** In-state: full-time: $12,058; part-time: N/A; Out-of-state: full-time: $29,054
- **Enrollment 2007-08 academic year:** full-time: 642
- **U.S. News 2009 law specialty ranking:** N/A

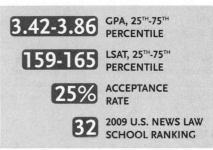

3.42-3.86 GPA, 25TH-75TH PERCENTILE

159-165 LSAT, 25TH-75TH PERCENTILE

25% ACCEPTANCE RATE

32 2009 U.S. NEWS LAW SCHOOL RANKING

ADMISSIONS

Admissions phone number: **(706) 542-7060**
Admissions email address: **ugajd@uga.edu**
Application website:
   http://www.law.uga.edu/admissions/jd/apply/lawapp.pdf
Application deadline for Fall 2009 admission: **02/01**

Admissions statistics:
Number of applicants for Fall 2007: **2,309**
Number of acceptances: **574**
Number enrolled: **222**
Acceptance rate: **25%**
GPA, 25th-75th percentile, entering class Fall 2007: **3.42-3.86**
LSAT, 25th-75th percentile, entering class Fall 2007: **159-165**

FINANCIAL AID

Financial aid phone number: **(706) 542-6147**
Financial aid application deadline: **03/01**
Tuition 2007-2008 academic year: In-state: full-time: **$12,058**; part-time: **N/A**; Out-of-state: full-time: **$29,054**
Room and board: **$5,600**; books: **$1,200**; miscellaneous expenses: **$5,900**
Total of room/board/books/miscellaneous expenses: **$12,700**
University offers graduate student housing for which law students are eligible.

Financial aid profile
Percent of students that received grants for the 2006-2007 academic year: full-time: **49%**
Median grant amount: full-time: **$2,000**
The average law-school debt of those in the Class of 2007 who borrowed: **$57,545**. Proportion who borrowed: **75%**

ACADEMIC PROGRAMS

Calendar: **semester**
Joint degrees awarded: **J.D./M.B.A.; J.D./M.A. Historical Preservation; J.D./M.P.A.; J.D./M.A. Sports Management; J.D./M.S.W.**

Typical first-year section size: Full-time: **77**
Is there typically a "small section" of the first year class, other than Legal Writing, taught by full-time faculty?: Full-time: **no**
Number of course titles, beyond the first year curriculum, offered last year: **127**
Percentages of upper division course sections, excluding seminars, with an enrollment of:

Under 25: **57%**	25 to 49: **27%**
50 to 74: **9%**	75 to 99: **6%**
100+: **1%**	

Areas of specialization: appellate advocacy, clinical training, dispute resolution, environmental law, healthcare law, intellectual property law, international law, tax law, trial advocacy

Fall 2007 faculty profile
Total teaching faculty: **N/A**. Full-time: **N/A**; **N/A** men, **N/A** women, **N/A** minorities. Part-time: **N/A**; **N/A** men, **N/A** women, **N/A** minorities
Student-to-faculty ratio: **14.8**

SPECIAL PROGRAMS (as provided by law school):
Georgia Law operates eight clinics, with a ninth in operation on a pilot basis in 2007-08. Georgia is part of a spring term overseas (a joint program with Ohio State at Oxford University, England). A summer program in China began in 2006, and a program in Brussels, Belgium, was recently approved by the American Bar Association. Overseas internships also provide international experience.

STUDENT BODY
Fall 2007 full-time enrollment: 642

Men: **54%**	Women: **46%**
African-American: **13.7%**	American Indian: **0.0%**
Asian-American: **4.2%**	Mexican-American: **0.0%**
Puerto Rican: **0.0%**	Other Hisp-Amer: **1.7%**
White: **64.5%**	International: **0.6%**
Unknown: **15.3%**	

Attrition rates for 2006-2007 full-time students
Percent of students discontinuing law school:
Men: 1%   Women: N/A
First-year students: 1%   Second-year students: N/A
Third-year students: N/A

LIBRARY RESOURCES
Total volumes: 529,036
Total seats available for library users: 433

INFORMATION TECHNOLOGY
Number of wired network connections available to students: 0 total (in the law library, excluding computer labs: 0; in classrooms: 0; in computer labs: 0; elsewhere in the law school: 0)
Law school has a wireless network.
Students are not required to own a computer.

EMPLOYMENT AND SALARIES
Proportion of 2006 graduates employed at graduation: 88%
Employed 9 months later, as of February 15, 2007: 98%
Salaries in the private sector (law firms, business, industry): $70,000–$115,000 (25th-75th percentile)
Median salary in the private sector: $100,000
Percentage in the private sector who reported salary information: 56%
Median salary in public service (government, judicial clerkships, academic posts, non-profits): $50,500

Percentage of 2006 graduates in:
Law firms: 58%   Government: 6%
Bus./industry: 6%   Judicial clerkship: 19%
Public interest: 9%   Unknown: 0%
Academia: 1%

2006 graduates employed in-state: 79%
2006 graduates employed in foreign countries: N/A
Number of states where graduates are employed: 24
Percentage of 2006 graduates working in: New England: 1%, Middle Atlantic: 3%, East North Central: 2%, West North Central: 0%, South Atlantic: 88%, East South Central: 3%, West South Central: 0%, Mountain: 2%, Pacific: 2%, Unknown: 0%

BAR PASSAGE RATES
Based on 2006 graduates taking Summer 2006 or Winter 2007 exams. Most of the school's first-time test takers took the bar in Georgia.

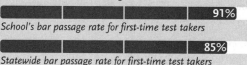

91%
School's bar passage rate for first-time test takers

85%
Statewide bar passage rate for first-time test takers

University of Hawaii (Richardson)

- 2515 Dole Street, Honolulu, HI, 96822
- http://www.hawaii.edu/law
- Public
- Year founded: 1973
- 2007-2008 tuition: In-state: full-time: $13,656; part-time: N/A; Out-of-state: full-time: $24,480
- Enrollment 2007-08 academic year: full-time: 257; part-time: 15
- U.S. News 2009 law specialty ranking: environmental law: 22

3.09-3.62 GPA, 25TH-75TH PERCENTILE

155-160 LSAT, 25TH-75TH PERCENTILE

19% ACCEPTANCE RATE

82 2009 U.S. NEWS LAW SCHOOL RANKING

ADMISSIONS

Admissions phone number: **(808) 956-3000**
Admissions email address: **lawadm@hawaii.edu**
Application website:
   http://www.hawaii.edu/law/admissions/forms
Application deadline for Fall 2009 admission: **03/01**

Admissions statistics:

Number of applicants for Fall 2007: **1,049**
Number of acceptances: **196**
Number enrolled: **76**
Acceptance rate: **19%**
GPA, 25th-75th percentile, entering class Fall 2007: **3.09-3.62**
LSAT, 25th-75th percentile, entering class Fall 2007: **155-160**

Part-time program:

Number of applicants for Fall 2007: **N/A**
Number of acceptances: **13**
Number enrolled: **11**
Acceptance rate: **N/A**
GPA, 25th-75th percentile, entering class Fall 2007: **2.99-3.43**
LSAT, 25th-75th percentile, entering class Fall 2007: **148-152**

FINANCIAL AID

Financial aid phone number: **(808) 956-7251**
Financial aid application deadline: **03/01**
Tuition 2007-2008 academic year: In-state: full-time: **$13,656**; part-time: **N/A**; Out-of-state: full-time: **$24,480**
Room and board: **$12,125**; books: **$1,179**; miscellaneous expenses: **$1,693**
Total of room/board/books/miscellaneous expenses: **$14,997**
University offers graduate student housing for which law students are eligible.

Financial aid profile

Percent of students that received grants for the 2006-2007 academic year: full-time: **40%**
Median grant amount: full-time: **$6,444**
The average law-school debt of those in the Class of 2007 who borrowed: **$51,702**. Proportion who borrowed: **66%**

ACADEMIC PROGRAMS

Calendar: **semester**
Joint degrees awarded: **J.D./M.B.A.; J.D./M.A.**
Typical first-year section size: Full-time: **93**
Is there typically a "small section" of the first year class, other than Legal Writing, taught by full-time faculty?: Full-time: **no**
Number of course titles, beyond the first year curriculum, offered last year: **83**
Percentages of upper division course sections, excluding seminars, with an enrollment of:

Under 25: **74%**	25 to 49: **15%**
50 to 74: **7%**	75 to 99: **4%**
100+: **0%**	

Areas of specialization: appellate advocacy, clinical training, dispute resolution, environmental law, healthcare law, intellectual property law, international law, tax law, trial advocacy

Fall 2007 faculty profile

Total teaching faculty: **69**. Full-time: **36%**; **56%** men, **44%** women, **28%** minorities. Part-time: **64%**; **77%** men, **23%** women, **48%** minorities
Student-to-faculty ratio: **8.5**

SPECIAL PROGRAMS (as provided by law school):

Richardson offers certificate programs in Environmental Law and Pacific Asian Legal Studies. The Center for Excellence in Native Hawaiian Law and the elder law program also provide unique opportunities for students to engage in exciting legal issues.

STUDENT BODY

Fall 2007 full-time enrollment: 257

Men: 58%	Women: 42%
African-American: 1.9%	American Indian: 0.8%
Asian-American: 56.4%	Mexican-American: 0.4%
Puerto Rican: 0.8%	Other Hisp-Amer: 1.9%
White: 21.4%	International: 2.3%
Unknown: 14.0%	

Fall 2007 part-time enrollment: 15

Men: 40%	Women: 60%
African-American: 6.7%	American Indian: 6.7%
Asian-American: 53.3%	Mexican-American: 6.7%
Puerto Rican: 0.0%	Other Hisp-Amer: 0.0%
White: 0.0%	International: 0.0%
Unknown: 26.7%	

Attrition rates for 2006-2007 full-time students
Percent of students discontinuing law school:

Men: 2%	Women: 1%
First-year students: 2%	Second-year students: 3%
Third-year students: N/A	

LIBRARY RESOURCES

Total volumes: 353,969
Total seats available for library users: 419

INFORMATION TECHNOLOGY

Number of wired network connections available to students: 280 total (in the law library, excluding computer labs: 254; in classrooms: 11; in computer labs: 5; elsewhere in the law school: 10)
Law school has a wireless network.
Students are required to own a computer.

EMPLOYMENT AND SALARIES

Proportion of 2006 graduates employed at graduation: 64%

Employed 9 months later, as of February 15, 2007: 94%
Salaries in the private sector (law firms, business, industry): $63,500–$74,500 (25th-75th percentile)
Median salary in the private sector: $72,500
Percentage in the private sector who reported salary information: 32%
Median salary in public service (government, judicial clerkships, academic posts, non-profits): $47,052

Percentage of 2006 graduates in:

Law firms: 36%	Government: 15%
Bus./industry: 10%	Judicial clerkship: 24%
Public interest: 11%	Unknown: 1%
Academia: 3%	

2006 graduates employed in-state: 82%
2006 graduates employed in foreign countries: 2%
Number of states where graduates are employed: 9
Percentage of 2006 graduates working in: New England: 2%, Middle Atlantic: N/A, East North Central: N/A, West North Central: N/A, South Atlantic: 8%, East South Central: 1%, West South Central: 1%, Mountain: N/A, Pacific: 85%, Unknown: 1%

BAR PASSAGE RATES

Based on 2006 graduates taking Summer 2006 or Winter 2007 exams. Most of the school's first-time test takers took the bar in Hawaii.

82%
School's bar passage rate for first-time test takers

77%
Statewide bar passage rate for first-time test takers

University of Houston

- 100 Law Center, Houston, TX, 77204-6060
- http://www.law.uh.edu
- Public
- **Year founded:** 1947
- **2007-2008 tuition:** In-state: full-time: $17,192; part-time: $8,901; Out-of-state: full-time: $24,632
- **Enrollment 2007-08 academic year:** full-time: 785; part-time: 170
- **U.S. News 2009 law specialty ranking:** healthcare law: 2, intellectual property law: 7

3.30-3.79 GPA, 25TH-75TH PERCENTILE

158-163 LSAT, 25TH-75TH PERCENTILE

29% ACCEPTANCE RATE

55 2009 U.S. NEWS LAW SCHOOL RANKING

ADMISSIONS

Admissions phone number: **(713) 743-2280**
Admissions email address: **lawadmissions@uh.edu**
Application website: **http://www.law.uh.edu/admissions/**
Application deadline for Fall 2009 admission: 02/15

Admissions statistics:
Number of applicants for Fall 2007: 3,002
Number of acceptances: 880
Number enrolled: 244
Acceptance rate: 29%
GPA, 25th-75th percentile, entering class Fall 2007: 3.30-3.79
LSAT, 25th-75th percentile, entering class Fall 2007: 158-163

Part-time program:
Number of applicants for Fall 2007: 318
Number of acceptances: 79
Number enrolled: 53
Acceptance rate: 25%
GPA, 25th-75th percentile, entering class Fall 2007: 3.10-3.68
LSAT, 25th-75th percentile, entering class Fall 2007: 152-161

FINANCIAL AID

Financial aid phone number: **(713) 743-2269**
Financial aid application deadline: 04/01
Tuition 2007-2008 academic year: In-state: full-time: **$17,192**; part-time: **$8,901**; Out-of-state: full-time: **$24,632**
Room and board: **$8,964**; books: **$1,100**; miscellaneous expenses: **$5,472**
Total of room/board/books/miscellaneous expenses: **$15,536**
University does not offer graduate student housing for which law students are eligible.

Financial aid profile
Percent of students that received grants for the 2006-2007

academic year: full-time: 75%
Median grant amount: full-time: $3,000
The average law-school debt of those in the Class of 2007 who borrowed: $62,584. Proportion who borrowed: 80%

ACADEMIC PROGRAMS

Calendar: **semester**
Joint degrees awarded: **J.D./M.B.A.; J.D./M.P.H.; J.D./Ph.D. Criminal Justice; J.D./M.A. History; J.D./M.S.W.; J.D./Ph.D. Medical Humanities**
Typical first-year section size: Full-time: **80**; Part-time: **60**
Is there typically a "small section" of the first year class, other than Legal Writing, taught by full-time faculty?: Full-time: **yes**; Part-time: **yes**
Number of course titles, beyond the first year curriculum, offered last year: **215**
Percentages of upper division course sections, excluding seminars, with an enrollment of:

Under 25: **58%**		25 to 49: **23%**
50 to 74: **8%**		75 to 99: **11%**
100+: **0%**		

Areas of specialization: appellate advocacy, clinical training, dispute resolution, environmental law, healthcare law, intellectual property law, international law, tax law, trial advocacy

Fall 2007 faculty profile
Total teaching faculty: **202**. Full-time: **53%**; 69% men, 31% women, 14% minorities. Part-time: **47%**; 81% men, 19% women, 7% minorities
Student-to-faculty ratio: **13.9**

SPECIAL PROGRAMS *(as provided by law school)*:
Nationally ranked programs include the Health Law and Policy Institute and the nation's most comprehensive health law curriculum, as well as the Institute for Intellectual Property and Information Law. Other top programs include the Blakely Advocacy Institute (15 mock trial and moot court titles since 2004) and the Center for Consumer Law, which administers the Texas Consumer Complaint Center.

STUDENT BODY

Fall 2007 full-time enrollment: 785

Men: 58%	Women: 42%
African-American: 5.7%	American Indian: 0.6%
Asian-American: 11.3%	Mexican-American: 4.5%
Puerto Rican: 0.0%	Other Hisp-Amer: 4.8%
White: 73.0%	International: 0.0%
Unknown: 0.0%	

Fall 2007 part-time enrollment: 170

Men: 59%	Women: 41%
African-American: 8.8%	American Indian: 1.2%
Asian-American: 10.0%	Mexican-American: 4.7%
Puerto Rican: 0.0%	Other Hisp-Amer: 5.3%
White: 70.0%	International: 0.0%
Unknown: 0.0%	

Attrition rates for 2006-2007 full-time students
Percent of students discontinuing law school:

Men: 1%	Women: 1%
First-year students: N/A	Second-year students: 3%
Third-year students: N/A	

LIBRARY RESOURCES

Total volumes: 523,928
Total seats available for library users: 546

INFORMATION TECHNOLOGY

Number of wired network connections available to students: 0 total (in the law library, excluding computer labs: 0; in classrooms: 0; in computer labs: 0; elsewhere in the law school: 0)
Law school has a wireless network.
Students are required to own a computer.

EMPLOYMENT AND SALARIES

Proportion of 2006 graduates employed at graduation: 77%

Employed 9 months later, as of February 15, 2007: 96%
Salaries in the private sector (law firms, business, industry): $60,000–$135,000 (25th-75th percentile)
Median salary in the private sector: $80,000
Percentage in the private sector who reported salary information: 79%
Median salary in public service (government, judicial clerkships, academic posts, non-profits): $45,000

Percentage of 2006 graduates in:

Law firms: 57%	Government: 8%
Bus./industry: 26%	Judicial clerkship: 5%
Public interest: 3%	Unknown: 0%
Academia: 1%	

2006 graduates employed in-state: 89%
2006 graduates employed in foreign countries: 1%
Number of states where graduates are employed: 13
Percentage of 2006 graduates working in: New England: 1%, Middle Atlantic: 2%, East North Central: 0%, West North Central: 0%, South Atlantic: 2%, East South Central: 1%, West South Central: 89%, Mountain: 2%, Pacific: 4%, Unknown: 0%

BAR PASSAGE RATES

Based on 2006 graduates taking Summer 2006 or Winter 2007 exams. Most of the school's first-time test takers took the bar in Texas.

89%
School's bar passage rate for first-time test takers

82%
Statewide bar passage rate for first-time test takers

University of Idaho

■ PO Box 442321, Moscow, ID, 83844-2321
■ http://www.law.uidaho.edu
■ Public
■ Year founded: 1909
■ 2007-2008 tuition: In-state: full-time: $10,200; part-time: N/A; Out-of-state: full-time: $20,280
■ Enrollment 2007-08 academic year: full-time: 308
■ U.S. News 2009 law specialty ranking: N/A

3.03-3.64 GPA, 25TH-75TH PERCENTILE

151-159 LSAT, 25TH-75TH PERCENTILE

44% ACCEPTANCE RATE

Tier 3 2009 U.S. NEWS LAW SCHOOL RANKING

ADMISSIONS
Admissions phone number: **(208) 885-6423**
Admissions email address: **lawadmit@uidaho.edu**
Application website:
http://www.law.uidaho.edu/admissions/applynow
Application deadline for Fall 2009 admission: **02/15**

Admissions statistics:
Number of applicants for Fall 2007: **675**
Number of acceptances: **295**
Number enrolled: **105**
Acceptance rate: **44%**
GPA, 25th-75th percentile, entering class Fall 2007: **3.03-3.64**
LSAT, 25th-75th percentile, entering class Fall 2007: **151-159**

FINANCIAL AID
Financial aid phone number: **(208) 885-6312**
Financial aid application deadline: **02/02**
Tuition 2007-2008 academic year: In-state: full-time: **$10,200**; part-time: **N/A**; Out-of-state: full-time: **$20,280**
Room and board: **$8,486**; books: **$1,430**; miscellaneous expenses: **$3,666**
Total of room/board/books/miscellaneous expenses: **$13,582**
University offers graduate student housing for which law students are eligible.

Financial aid profile
Percent of students that received grants for the 2006-2007 academic year: full-time: **46%**
Median grant amount: full-time: **$6,030**
The average law-school debt of those in the Class of 2007 who borrowed: **$55,326**. Proportion who borrowed: **95%**

ACADEMIC PROGRAMS
Calendar: **semester**
Joint degrees awarded: **J.D./M.S. Environmental Science; J.D./M.A. Accounting; J.D./M.B.A.; J.D./M.S. Water Resource Management; J.D./Ph.D. Water Resource Management**

Typical first-year section size: Full-time: **52**
Is there typically a "small section" of the first year class, other than Legal Writing, taught by full-time faculty?: Full-time: **no**
Number of course titles, beyond the first year curriculum, offered last year: **65**
Percentages of upper division course sections, excluding seminars, with an enrollment of:
Under 25: **63%**   25 to 49: **16%**
50 to 74: **8%**   75 to 99: **13%**
100+: **2%**
Areas of specialization: appellate advocacy, clinical training, dispute resolution, environmental law, healthcare law, intellectual property law, international law, tax law, trial advocacy

Fall 2007 faculty profile
Total teaching faculty: **36**. Full-time: **44%**; **75%** men, **25%** women, **6%** minorities. Part-time: **56%**; **75%** men, **25%** women, **0%** minorities
Student-to-faculty ratio: **16.0**

SPECIAL PROGRAMS *(as provided by law school):*
Students may focus on natural resources law, entrepreneurialism, or advocacy/dispute resolution. There are also classes in international law, technology, and ethics. Students must perform at least 40 hours of pro bono legal work in order to graduate, the only such program in the Northwest. The College of Law is also home to the renowned Northwest Institute for Dispute Resolution.

STUDENT BODY
Fall 2007 full-time enrollment: **308**
Men: **55%**   Women: **45%**
African-American: **0.6%**   American Indian: **1.3%**
Asian-American: **5.8%**   Mexican-American: **2.6%**
Puerto Rican: **0.0%**   Other Hisp-Amer: **3.9%**
White: **78.9%**   International: **1.9%**
Unknown: **4.9%**

Attrition rates for 2006-2007 full-time students

Percent of students discontinuing law school:

Men: 2%　　　　　　　Women: 4%

First-year students: 8%　　Second-year students: N/A

Third-year students: N/A

LIBRARY RESOURCES

Total volumes: 244,235

Total seats available for library users: 365

INFORMATION TECHNOLOGY

Number of wired network connections available to students: 323 total (in the law library, excluding computer labs: 225; in classrooms: 39; in computer labs: 6; elsewhere in the law school: 53)

Law school has a wireless network.

Students are not required to own a computer.

EMPLOYMENT AND SALARIES

Proportion of 2006 graduates employed at graduation: N/A

Employed 9 months later, as of February 15, 2007: 93%

Salaries in the private sector (law firms, business, industry): $40,000–$50,000 (25th-75th percentile)

Median salary in the private sector: $44,000

Percentage in the private sector who reported salary information: 26%

Median salary in public service (government, judicial clerkships, academic posts, non-profits): N/A

Percentage of 2006 graduates in:

Law firms: 47%　　　　　Government: 9%

Bus./industry: 9%　　　　Judicial clerkship: 24%

Public interest: 8%　　　 Unknown: 0%

Academia: 3%

2006 graduates employed in-state: 61%

2006 graduates employed in foreign countries: 1%

Number of states where graduates are employed: 13

Percentage of 2006 graduates working in: New England: 1%, Middle Atlantic: 1%, East North Central: 0%, West North Central: 0%, South Atlantic: 1%, East South Central: 0%, West South Central: 1%, Mountain: 75%, Pacific: 19%, Unknown: 0%

BAR PASSAGE RATES

Based on 2006 graduates taking Summer 2006 or Winter 2007 exams. Most of the school's first-time test takers took the bar in Idaho.

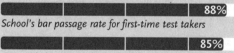

| 88% |
School's bar passage rate for first-time test takers

| 85% |
Statewide bar passage rate for first-time test takers

Univ. of Illinois–Urbana-Champaign

- 504 E. Pennsylvania Avenue, Champaign, IL, 61820
- http://www.law.uiuc.edu/
- Public
- Year founded: 1897
- 2007-2008 tuition: In-state: full-time: $26,056; part-time: N/A; Out-of-state: full-time: $36,056
- Enrollment 2007-08 academic year: full-time: 587
- U.S. News 2009 law specialty ranking: N/A

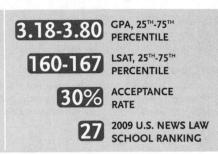

3.18-3.80 GPA, 25TH-75TH PERCENTILE

160-167 LSAT, 25TH-75TH PERCENTILE

30% ACCEPTANCE RATE

27 2009 U.S. NEWS LAW SCHOOL RANKING

ADMISSIONS

Admissions phone number: **(217) 244-6415**
Admissions email address: **admissions@law.uiuc.edu**
Application website:
http://www.law.uiuc.edu/admissions/apply.asp
Application deadline for Fall 2009 admission: **03/15**

Admissions statistics:
Number of applicants for Fall 2007: **2,520**
Number of acceptances: **761**
Number enrolled: **173**
Acceptance rate: **30%**
GPA, 25th-75th percentile, entering class Fall 2007: **3.18-3.80**
LSAT, 25th-75th percentile, entering class Fall 2007: **160-167**

FINANCIAL AID

Financial aid phone number: **(217) 244-6415**
Financial aid application deadline: **04/01**
Tuition 2007-2008 academic year: In-state: full-time: **$26,056**; part-time: N/A; Out-of-state: full-time: **$36,056**
Room and board: **$10,412**; books: **$1,750**; miscellaneous expenses: **$2,740**
Total of room/board/books/miscellaneous expenses: **$14,902**
University offers graduate student housing for which law students are eligible.

Financial aid profile
Percent of students that received grants for the 2006-2007 academic year: full-time: **68%**
Median grant amount: full-time: **$10,000**
The average law-school debt of those in the Class of 2007 who borrowed: **$68,688**. Proportion who borrowed: **80%**

ACADEMIC PROGRAMS

Calendar: **semester**
Joint degrees awarded: **J.D./M.B.A.; J.D./M.H.R.I.R.; J.D./M.Ed.; J.D./Ph.D.Ed.; J.D./M.D.; J.D./M.U.P.;** J.D./D.V.M.; J.D./M.C.S.; J.D./M.S. Journalism; J.D./M.S.N.Res.; J.D./M.S. Chemistry
Typical first-year section size: Full-time: **66**
Is there typically a "small section" of the first year class, other than Legal Writing, taught by full-time faculty?: Full-time: **yes**
Number of course titles, beyond the first year curriculum, offered last year: **145**
Percentages of upper division course sections, excluding seminars, with an enrollment of:
Under 25: **63%**   25 to 49: **22%**
50 to 74: **10%**   75 to 99: **5%**
100+: **0%**
Areas of specialization: appellate advocacy, clinical training, dispute resolution, environmental law, healthcare law, intellectual property law, international law, tax law, trial advocacy

Fall 2007 faculty profile
Total teaching faculty: **113**. Full-time: **53%**; **68%** men, **32%** women, **15%** minorities. Part-time: **47%**; **72%** men, **28%** women, **9%** minorities
Student-to-faculty ratio: **12.4**

SPECIAL PROGRAMS *(as provided by law school):*

The College of Law offers multiple courses in topics ranging from traditional to practical with clinics and very robust externship, trial advocacy, and experiential programs. Over 100 of the upper-level courses had an enrollment of fewer than 25 students. There are also study-abroad options. Finally, students may pursue multidisciplinary study with cross-listed courses and joint-degree programs.

STUDENT BODY

Fall 2007 full-time enrollment: **587**

Men: **60%**	Women: **40%**
African-American: **8.0%**	American Indian: **0.3%**
Asian-American: **11.8%**	Mexican-American: **0.0%**
Puerto Rican: **0.0%**	Other Hisp-Amer: **5.8%**
White: **64.1%**	International: **6.0%**
Unknown: **4.1%**	

Attrition rates for 2006-2007 full-time students
Percent of students discontinuing law school:
Men: 3%   Women: 1%
First-year students: 6%   Second-year students: 1%
Third-year students: 0%

LIBRARY RESOURCES

Total volumes: 770,530
Total seats available for library users: 366

INFORMATION TECHNOLOGY

Number of wired network connections available to students: **802** total (in the law library, excluding computer labs: **80**; in classrooms: **574**; in computer labs: **48**; elsewhere in the law school: **100**)
Law school has a wireless network.
Students are required to own a computer.

EMPLOYMENT AND SALARIES

Proportion of 2006 graduates employed at graduation: **78%**
Employed 9 months later, as of February 15, 2007: **93%**
Salaries in the private sector (law firms, business, industry): **$77,500–$135,000** (25th-75th percentile)
Median salary in the private sector: **$125,000**
Percentage in the private sector who reported salary information: **71%**
Median salary in public service (government, judicial clerkships, academic posts, non-profits): **$50,000**

Percentage of 2006 graduates in:

Law firms: **64%**   Government: **10%**
Bus./industry: **13%**   Judicial clerkship: **7%**
Public interest: **2%**   Unknown: **1%**
Academia: **3%**

2006 graduates employed in-state: **70%**
2006 graduates employed in foreign countries: **0%**
Number of states where graduates are employed: **20**
Percentage of 2006 graduates working in: New England: **1%**, Middle Atlantic: **2%**, East North Central: **74%**, West North Central: **2%**, South Atlantic: **9%**, East South Central: **0%**, West South Central: **1%**, Mountain: **2%**, Pacific: **6%**, Unknown: **4%**

BAR PASSAGE RATES

Based on 2006 graduates taking Summer 2006 or Winter 2007 exams. Most of the school's first-time test takers took the bar in Illinois.

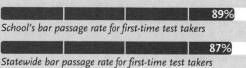

89%

School's bar passage rate for first-time test takers

87%

Statewide bar passage rate for first-time test takers

University of Iowa

■ 320 Melrose Avenue, Iowa City, IA, 52242
■ http://www.law.uiowa.edu
■ Public
■ Year founded: 1865
■ 2007-2008 tuition: In-state: full-time: $16,341; part-time: N/A; Out-of-state: full-time: $32,589
■ Enrollment 2007-08 academic year: full-time: 633
■ U.S. News 2009 law specialty ranking: international law: 13

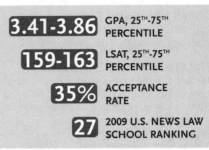

3.41-3.86 GPA, 25TH-75TH PERCENTILE

159-163 LSAT, 25TH-75TH PERCENTILE

35% ACCEPTANCE RATE

27 2009 U.S. NEWS LAW SCHOOL RANKING

ADMISSIONS

Admissions phone number: **(319) 335-9133**
Admissions email address: **law-admissions@uiowa.edu**
Application website:
http://www.uiowa.edu/admissions/graduate/programs/program-details/jd-main.html
Application deadline for Fall 2009 admission: **03/01**

Admissions statistics:

Number of applicants for Fall 2007: **1,778**
Number of acceptances: **616**
Number enrolled: **212**
Acceptance rate: **35%**
GPA, 25th-75th percentile, entering class Fall 2007: **3.41-3.86**
LSAT, 25th-75th percentile, entering class Fall 2007: **159-163**

FINANCIAL AID

Financial aid phone number: **(319) 335-9142**
Financial aid application deadline: **01/01**
Tuition 2007-2008 academic year: In-state: full-time: **$16,341**; part-time: N/A; Out-of-state: full-time: **$32,589**
Room and board: **$9,270**; books: **$2,300**; miscellaneous expenses: **$4,120**
Total of room/board/books/miscellaneous expenses: **$15,690**
University does not offer graduate student housing for which law students are eligible.

Financial aid profile

Percent of students that received grants for the 2006-2007 academic year: full-time: **36%**
Median grant amount: full-time: **$13,374**
The average law-school debt of those in the Class of 2007 who borrowed: **$69,375**. Proportion who borrowed: **86%**

ACADEMIC PROGRAMS

Calendar: **semester**
Joint degrees awarded: **J.D./M.B.A.; J.D./M.A. Sociology; J.D./M.A. Philosophy; J.D./M.A. English;** J.D./M.A.Journalism; J.D./M.A. Higher Ed; J.D./M.Acc.; J.D./M.P.H.; J.D./M.S. Physics; J.D./M.D.; J.D./M.A. Religious Studies; J.D./M.URP.
Typical first-year section size: Full-time: **80**
Is there typically a "small section" of the first year class, other than Legal Writing, taught by full-time faculty?: Full-time: **yes**
Number of course titles, beyond the first year curriculum, offered last year: **73**
Percentages of upper division course sections, excluding seminars, with an enrollment of:
Under 25: **56%**   25 to 49: **25%**
50 to 74: **12%**   75 to 99: **6%**
100+: **0%**
Areas of specialization: appellate advocacy, clinical training, dispute resolution, environmental law, healthcare law, intellectual property law, international law, tax law, trial advocacy

Fall 2007 faculty profile

Total teaching faculty: **N/A**. Full-time: **N/A**; N/A men, N/A women, N/A minorities. Part-time: **N/A**; N/A men, N/A women, N/A minorities
Student-to-faculty ratio: **13.0**

SPECIAL PROGRAMS *(as provided by law school):*

The University of Iowa College of Law offers the following special programs to students: the innovation, business, and law program; the international and comparative law program; the Writing Resource Center; the clinical law program; the Iowa/Bordeaux summer program; the London Law Consortium; and the summer entrant program.

STUDENT BODY

Fall 2007 full-time enrollment: 633

Men: **55%**	Women: **45%**
African-American: **4.1%**	American Indian: **0.8%**
Asian-American: **7.7%**	Mexican-American: **5.1%**
Puerto Rican: **0.0%**	Other Hisp-Amer: **0.0%**
White: **80.7%**	International: **1.6%**
Unknown: **0.0%**	

Attrition rates for 2006-2007 full-time students
Percent of students discontinuing law school:
Men: 3%   Women: 2%
First-year students: 3%   Second-year students: 4%
Third-year students: 1%

LIBRARY RESOURCES
Total volumes: 1,204,116
Total seats available for library users: 679

INFORMATION TECHNOLOGY
Number of wired network connections available to students: **488** total (in the law library, excluding computer labs: 424; in classrooms: 20; in computer labs: 24; elsewhere in the law school: 20)
Law school has a wireless network.
Students are not required to own a computer.

EMPLOYMENT AND SALARIES
Proportion of 2006 graduates employed at graduation: 80%
Employed 9 months later, as of February 15, 2007: 93%
Salaries in the private sector (law firms, business, industry): $60,000–$115,000 (25th-75th percentile)
Median salary in the private sector: $95,000
Percentage in the private sector who reported salary information: 71%
Median salary in public service (government, judicial clerkships, academic posts, non-profits): $39,500

Percentage of 2006 graduates in:
Law firms: 58%   Government: 10%
Bus./industry: 14%   Judicial clerkship: 5%
Public interest: 9%   Unknown: 1%
Academia: 5%

2006 graduates employed in-state: 29%
2006 graduates employed in foreign countries: 0%
Number of states where graduates are employed: 27
Percentage of 2006 graduates working in: New England: 1%, Middle Atlantic: 2%, East North Central: 17%, West North Central: 43%, South Atlantic: 9%, East South Central: 1%, West South Central: 2%, Mountain: 11%, Pacific: 6%, Unknown: 8%

BAR PASSAGE RATES
Based on 2006 graduates taking Summer 2006 or Winter 2007 exams. Most of the school's first-time test takers took the bar in Iowa.

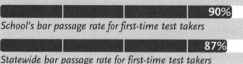

90%
School's bar passage rate for first-time test takers

87%
Statewide bar passage rate for first-time test takers

University of Kansas

- Green Hall, 1535 W. 15th Street, Lawrence, KS, 66045-7577
- http://www.law.ku.edu
- Public
- Year founded: 1878
- 2007-2008 tuition: In-state: full-time: $13,384; part-time: N/A; Out-of-state: full-time: $24,085
- Enrollment 2007-08 academic year: full-time: 491
- U.S. News 2009 law specialty ranking: N/A

3.09-3.77 GPA, 25ᵀᴴ-75ᵀᴴ PERCENTILE

155-160 LSAT, 25ᵀᴴ-75ᵀᴴ PERCENTILE

37% ACCEPTANCE RATE

73 2009 U.S. NEWS LAW SCHOOL RANKING

ADMISSIONS

Admissions phone number: (866) 220-3654
Admissions email address: **admitlaw@ku.edu**
Application website: **http://www.law.ku.edu/apply.shtml**
Application deadline for Fall 2009 admission: 03/15

Admissions statistics:

Number of applicants for Fall 2007: **1,067**
Number of acceptances: **392**
Number enrolled: **159**
Acceptance rate: **37%**
GPA, 25th-75th percentile, entering class Fall 2007: **3.09-3.77**
LSAT, 25th-75th percentile, entering class Fall 2007: **155-160**

FINANCIAL AID

Financial aid phone number: (785) 864-4700
Financial aid application deadline: 03/01
Tuition 2007-2008 academic year: In-state: full-time: **$13,384**; part-time: **N/A**; Out-of-state: full-time: **$24,085**
Room and board: **$9,088**; books: **$900**; miscellaneous expenses: **$4,698**
Total of room/board/books/miscellaneous expenses: **$14,686**
University offers graduate student housing for which law students are eligible.

Financial aid profile

Percent of students that received grants for the 2006-2007 academic year: full-time: **73%**
Median grant amount: full-time: **$1,700**
The average law-school debt of those in the Class of 2007 who borrowed: **$40,690.** Proportion who borrowed: **78%**

ACADEMIC PROGRAMS

Calendar: **semester**
Joint degrees awarded: **J.D./M.B.A.; J.D./Economics; J.D./Heath Services Administration; J.D./Philosophy; J.D./Public Administration; J.D./Social Welfare;**
J.D./Urban Planning; J.D./Indigenous Nations Studies; J.D./Journalism; J.D./East Asian Studies
Typical first-year section size: Full-time: **61**
Is there typically a "small section" of the first year class, other than Legal Writing, taught by full-time faculty?: Full-time: **yes**
Number of course titles, beyond the first year curriculum, offered last year: **99**
Percentages of upper division course sections, excluding seminars, with an enrollment of:

Under 25: **69%**   25 to 49: **22%**
50 to 74: **8%**   75 to 99: **1%**
100+: **1%**

Areas of specialization: appellate advocacy, clinical training, dispute resolution, environmental law, healthcare law, intellectual property law, international law, tax law, trial advocacy

Fall 2007 faculty profile

Total teaching faculty: **70.** Full-time: **53%**; **57%** men, **43%** women, **22%** minorities. Part-time: **47%**; **73%** men, **27%** women, **0%** minorities
Student-to-faculty ratio: **12.1**

SPECIAL PROGRAMS *(as provided by law school):*

The school offers six Certificates, from Elder and Environmental Law to International Trade and Tax; 10 clinics and externships, from prosecution and defense to legal aid, media, and tribal law; eight joint degrees, from business and health services to social welfare and urban planning; two summer study-abroad programs, in Ireland and Turkey; and a semester-abroad program in London.

STUDENT BODY

Fall 2007 full-time enrollment: 491

Men: **62%**	Women: **38%**
African-American: **2.6%**	American Indian: **3.7%**
Asian-American: **5.7%**	Mexican-American: **0.2%**
Puerto Rican: **0.0%**	Other Hisp-Amer: **3.5%**
White: **75.6%**	International: **4.3%**
Unknown: **4.5%**	

Attrition rates for 2006-2007 full-time students
Percent of students discontinuing law school:
Men: 1%   Women: 1%
First-year students: 2%   Second-year students: N/A
Third-year students: N/A

LIBRARY RESOURCES
Total volumes: 358,291
Total seats available for library users: 385

INFORMATION TECHNOLOGY
Number of wired network connections available to students: 0 total (in the law library, excluding computer labs: 0; in classrooms: 0; in computer labs: 0; elsewhere in the law school: 0)
Law school has a wireless network.
Students are not required to own a computer.

EMPLOYMENT AND SALARIES
Proportion of 2006 graduates employed at graduation: 66%
Employed 9 months later, as of February 15, 2007: 95%
Salaries in the private sector (law firms, business, industry): $48,000–$90,000 (25th-75th percentile)
Median salary in the private sector: $56,500
Percentage in the private sector who reported salary information: 62%
Median salary in public service (government, judicial clerkships, academic posts, non-profits): $48,500

Percentage of 2006 graduates in:
Law firms: 51%   Government: 15%
Bus./industry: 18%   Judicial clerkship: 9%
Public interest: 4%   Unknown: 0%
Academia: 3%

2006 graduates employed in-state: 44%
2006 graduates employed in foreign countries: 1%
Number of states where graduates are employed: 23
Percentage of 2006 graduates working in: New England: 0%, Middle Atlantic: 1%, East North Central: 2%, West North Central: 71%, South Atlantic: 5%, East South Central: 1%, West South Central: 7%, Mountain: 8%, Pacific: 4%, Unknown: 0%

BAR PASSAGE RATES
Based on 2006 graduates taking Summer 2006 or Winter 2007 exams. Most of the school's first-time test takers took the bar in Kansas.

92%
School's bar passage rate for first-time test takers

90%
Statewide bar passage rate for first-time test takers

University of Kentucky

- 209 Law Building, Lexington, KY, 40506-0048
- http://www.uky.edu/law
- Public
- **Year founded:** 1908
- **2007-2008 tuition:** In-state: full-time: $13,998; part-time: N/A; Out-of-state: full-time: $24,804
- **Enrollment 2007-08 academic year:** full-time: 426
- **U.S. News 2009 law specialty ranking:** N/A

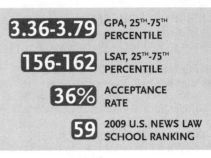

3.36-3.79 GPA, 25TH-75TH PERCENTILE

156-162 LSAT, 25TH-75TH PERCENTILE

36% ACCEPTANCE RATE

59 2009 U.S. NEWS LAW SCHOOL RANKING

ADMISSIONS

Admissions phone number: **(859) 257-6770**
Admissions email address: **lawadmissions@email.uky.edu**
Application website:
  http://www.uky.edu/law/prospective_students
Application deadline for Fall 2009 admission: **03/01**

Admissions statistics:

Number of applicants for Fall 2007: **1,080**
Number of acceptances: **392**
Number enrolled: **127**
Acceptance rate: **36%**
GPA, 25th-75th percentile, entering class Fall 2007: **3.36-3.79**
LSAT, 25th-75th percentile, entering class Fall 2007: **156-162**

FINANCIAL AID

Financial aid phone number: **(859) 257-3172**
Financial aid application deadline: **04/01**
Tuition 2007-2008 academic year: In-state: full-time: **$13,998**; part-time: **N/A**; Out-of-state: full-time: **$24,804**
Room and board: **$10,500**; books: **$900**; miscellaneous expenses: **$3,102**
Total of room/board/books/miscellaneous expenses: **$14,502**
University offers graduate student housing for which law students are eligible.

Financial aid profile

Percent of students that received grants for the 2006-2007 academic year: full-time: **56%**
Median grant amount: full-time: **$5,000**
The average law-school debt of those in the Class of 2007 who borrowed: **$57,400**. Proportion who borrowed: **74%**

ACADEMIC PROGRAMS

Calendar: **semester**
Joint degrees awarded: **J.D./M.B.A.; J.D./M.P.A.; J.D./M.A.**

Typical first-year section size: Full-time: **62**
Is there typically a "small section" of the first year class, other than Legal Writing, taught by full-time faculty?: Full-time: **yes**
Number of course titles, beyond the first year curriculum, offered last year: **50**
Percentages of upper division course sections, excluding seminars, with an enrollment of:
  Under 25: **31%**   25 to 49: **40%**
  50 to 74: **26%**   75 to 99: **3%**
  100+: **0%**
Areas of specialization: appellate advocacy, clinical training, dispute resolution, environmental law, healthcare law, intellectual property law, international law, tax law, trial advocacy

Fall 2007 faculty profile

Total teaching faculty: **53**. Full-time: **47%**; **64%** men, **36%** women, **12%** minorities. Part-time: **53%**; **79%** men, **21%** women, **0%** minorities
Student-to-faculty ratio: **15.0**

SPECIAL PROGRAMS *(as provided by law school):*

The UK Law Clinic gives students the opportunity to represent needy clients on a variety of matters. There are also five externships: the Kentucky Innocence Project externship, the judicial clerkship externship; the prison externship; the prosecutorial externship; and a new externship with the appellate division of the U.S. attorney's office in Lexington.

STUDENT BODY

Fall 2007 full-time enrollment: 426

Men: **57%**	Women: **43%**
African-American: **5.9%**	American Indian: **0.2%**
Asian-American: **1.6%**	Mexican-American: **0.7%**
Puerto Rican: **0.0%**	Other Hisp-Amer: **0.7%**
White: **82.9%**	International: **0.7%**
Unknown: **7.3%**	

Attrition rates for 2006-2007 full-time students
Percent of students discontinuing law school:
Men: 1%   Women: 1%
First-year students: 2%   Second-year students: 1%
Third-year students: N/A

LIBRARY RESOURCES
Total volumes: 477,877
Total seats available for library users: 354

INFORMATION TECHNOLOGY
Number of wired network connections available to students: 40 total (in the law library, excluding computer labs: 30; in classrooms: 0; in computer labs: 0; elsewhere in the law school: 10)
Law school has a wireless network.
Students are not required to own a computer.

EMPLOYMENT AND SALARIES
Proportion of 2006 graduates employed at graduation: 78%
Employed 9 months later, as of February 15, 2007: 99%
Salaries in the private sector (law firms, business, industry): $40,000–$83,000 (25th-75th percentile)
Median salary in the private sector: $55,000
Percentage in the private sector who reported salary information: 49%
Median salary in public service (government, judicial clerkships, academic posts, non-profits): $37,250

Percentage of 2006 graduates in:
Law firms: 51%   Government: 10%
Bus./industry: 11%   Judicial clerkship: 18%
Public interest: 9%   Unknown: 0%
Academia: 1%

2006 graduates employed in-state: 81%
2006 graduates employed in foreign countries: 0%
Number of states where graduates are employed: 18
Percentage of 2006 graduates working in: New England: 1%, Middle Atlantic: 1%, East North Central: 3%, West North Central: 1%, South Atlantic: 7%, East South Central: 82%, West South Central: 1%, Mountain: 3%, Pacific: 1%, Unknown: 0%

BAR PASSAGE RATES
Based on 2006 graduates taking Summer 2006 or Winter 2007 exams. Most of the school's first-time test takers took the bar in Kentucky.

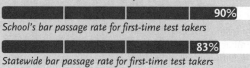

90%
School's bar passage rate for first-time test takers

83%
Statewide bar passage rate for first-time test takers

University of La Verne

■ 32nd E. D Street, Ontario, CA, 91764
■ http://law.ulv.edu
■ Private
■ Year founded: 1970
■ 2007-2008 tuition: full-time: $32,370; part-time: $24,470
■ Enrollment 2007-08 academic year: full-time: 205; part-time: 105
■ U.S. News 2009 law specialty ranking: N/A

2.76-3.31 GPA, 25TH-75TH PERCENTILE

149-155 LSAT, 25TH-75TH PERCENTILE

43% ACCEPTANCE RATE

Unranked 2009 U.S. NEWS LAW SCHOOL RANKING

ADMISSIONS
Admissions phone number: **(909) 460-2001**
Admissions email address: **lawadm@ulv.edu**
Application website: **http://law.ulv.edu**
Application deadline for Fall 2009 admission: **rolling**

Admissions statistics:
Number of applicants for Fall 2007: **867**
Number of acceptances: **377**
Number enrolled: **92**
Acceptance rate: **43%**
GPA, 25th-75th percentile, entering class Fall 2007: **2.76-3.31**
LSAT, 25th-75th percentile, entering class Fall 2007: **149-155**

Part-time program:
Number of applicants for Fall 2007: **282**
Number of acceptances: **119**
Number enrolled: **45**
Acceptance rate: **42%**
GPA, 25th-75th percentile, entering class Fall 2007: **2.65-3.30**
LSAT, 25th-75th percentile, entering class Fall 2007: **148-152**

FINANCIAL AID
Financial aid phone number: **(909) 593-3511**
Financial aid application deadline: **08/01**
Tuition 2007-2008 academic year: full-time: **$32,370**; part-time: **$24,470**
Room and board: **$16,833**; books: **$1,386**; miscellaneous expenses: **$3,618**
Total of room/board/books/miscellaneous expenses: **$21,837**
University does not offer graduate student housing for which law students are eligible.

Financial aid profile
Percent of students that received grants for the 2006-2007 academic year: full-time: **58%**; part-time **73%**

Median grant amount: full-time: **$14,000**; part-time: **$10,500**
The average law-school debt of those in the Class of 2007 who borrowed: **$60,875**. Proportion who borrowed: **85%**

ACADEMIC PROGRAMS
Calendar: **semester**
Joint degrees awarded: **J.D./M.B.A.; J.D./M.P.A.**
Typical first-year section size: Full-time: **50**; Part-time: **30**
Is there typically a "small section" of the first year class, other than Legal Writing, taught by full-time faculty?: Full-time: **no**; Part-time: **no**
Number of course titles, beyond the first year curriculum, offered last year: **43**
Percentages of upper division course sections, excluding seminars, with an enrollment of:
Under 25: **61%**   25 to 49: **30%**
50 to 74: **9%**   75 to 99: **0%**
100+: **0%**
Areas of specialization: appellate advocacy, clinical training, dispute resolution, environmental law, healthcare law, intellectual property law, international law, tax law, trial advocacy

Fall 2007 faculty profile
Total teaching faculty: **36**. Full-time: **44%**; **50%** men, **50%** women, **19%** minorities. Part-time: **56%**; **85%** men, **15%** women, **10%** minorities
Student-to-faculty ratio: **16.8**

SPECIAL PROGRAMS *(as provided by law school):*
A lawyering skills practicum simulates private practice and courtroom settings. A family law practicum provides 30 hours of clinical experience. Students can also participate in immigration and disability rights clinics. Externships are available in governmental agencies and public service organizations in greater Los Angeles. Study abroad and J.D./M.B.A. or J.D./M.P.A. degrees are also offered.

STUDENT BODY

Fall 2007 full-time enrollment: 205

Men: 61%	Women: 39%
African-American: 2.9%	American Indian: 0.5%
Asian-American: 13.7%	Mexican-American: 13.7%
Puerto Rican: 0.0%	Other Hisp-Amer: 0.0%
White: 51.2%	International: 2.0%
Unknown: 16.1%	

Fall 2007 part-time enrollment: 105

Men: 53%	Women: 47%
African-American: 2.9%	American Indian: 0.0%
Asian-American: 13.3%	Mexican-American: 19.0%
Puerto Rican: 0.0%	Other Hisp-Amer: 0.0%
White: 55.2%	International: 0.0%
Unknown: 9.5%	

Attrition rates for 2006-2007 full-time students

Percent of students discontinuing law school:

Men: 8%	Women: 13%
First-year students: 23%	Second-year students: 4%
Third-year students: 2%	

LIBRARY RESOURCES

Total volumes: 306,064

Total seats available for library users: 297

INFORMATION TECHNOLOGY

Number of wired network connections available to students: 134 total (in the law library, excluding computer labs: 41; in classrooms: 8; in computer labs: 35; elsewhere in the law school: 50)

Law school has a wireless network.

Students are not required to own a computer.

EMPLOYMENT AND SALARIES

Proportion of 2006 graduates employed at graduation: N/A

Employed 9 months later, as of February 15, 2007: N/A

Salaries in the private sector (law firms, business, industry): N/A–N/A (25th-75th percentile)

Median salary in the private sector: $62,421

Percentage in the private sector who reported salary information: N/A

Median salary in public service (government, judicial clerkships, academic posts, non-profits): N/A

Percentage of 2006 graduates in:

Law firms: 75%	Government: 11%
Bus./industry: 14%	Judicial clerkship: 0%
Public interest: 0%	Unknown: 0%
Academia: 0%	

2006 graduates employed in-state: 96%

2006 graduates employed in foreign countries: 0%

Number of states where graduates are employed: 2

Percentage of 2006 graduates working in: New England: N/A, Middle Atlantic: 4%, East North Central: N/A, West North Central: N/A, South Atlantic: N/A, East South Central: N/A, West South Central: N/A, Mountain: N/A, Pacific: 96%, Unknown: 0%

BAR PASSAGE RATES

Based on 2006 graduates taking Summer 2006 or Winter 2007 exams. Most of the school's first-time test takers took the bar in California.

N/A

School's bar passage rate for first-time test takers

N/A

Statewide bar passage rate for first-time test takers

University of Louisville (Brandeis)

■ 2301 S. Third Street, Louisville, KY, 40292
■ http://www.louisville.edu/brandeislaw/
■ Public
■ Year founded: 1846
■ 2007-2008 tuition: In-state: full-time: $12,610; part-time: $10,520;
   Out-of-state: full-time: $25,956
■ Enrollment 2007-08 academic year: full-time: 323; part-time: 87
■ U.S. News 2009 law specialty ranking: N/A

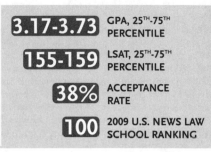

3.17-3.73 GPA, 25TH-75TH PERCENTILE

155-159 LSAT, 25TH-75TH PERCENTILE

38% ACCEPTANCE RATE

100 2009 U.S. NEWS LAW SCHOOL RANKING

ADMISSIONS

Admissions phone number: **(502) 852-6365**
Admissions email address: **lawadmissions@louisville.edu**
Application website: **N/A**
Application deadline for Fall 2009 admission: **05/15**

Admissions statistics:
Number of applicants for Fall 2007: **993**
Number of acceptances: **377**
Number enrolled: **126**
Acceptance rate: **38%**
GPA, 25th-75th percentile, entering class Fall 2007: **3.17-3.73**
LSAT, 25th-75th percentile, entering class Fall 2007: **155-159**

Part-time program:
Number of applicants for Fall 2007: **106**
Number of acceptances: **73**
Number enrolled: **42**
Acceptance rate: **69%**
GPA, 25th-75th percentile, entering class Fall 2007: **2.98-3.61**
LSAT, 25th-75th percentile, entering class Fall 2007: **151-158**

FINANCIAL AID

Financial aid phone number: **(502) 852-6391**
Financial aid application deadline: **03/01**
Tuition 2007-2008 academic year: In-state: full-time: **$12,610**; part-time: **$10,520**; Out-of-state: full-time: **$25,956**
Room and board: **$6,618**; books: **$1,000**; miscellaneous expenses: **$8,780**
Total of room/board/books/miscellaneous expenses: **$16,398**
University offers graduate student housing for which law students are eligible.

Financial aid profile
Percent of students that received grants for the 2006-2007 academic year: full-time: **34%**; part-time **15%**

Median grant amount: full-time: **$5,000**; part-time: **$5,000**
The average law-school debt of those in the Class of 2007 who borrowed: **$57,165**. Proportion who borrowed: **78%**

ACADEMIC PROGRAMS

Calendar: **semester**
Joint degrees awarded: **J.D./M.B.A.; J.D./M.Div.; J.D./M.A. Political Science; J.D./M.S.S.W.; J.D./M.A. Humanities; J.D./M.A. Urban Planning**
Typical first-year section size: Full-time: **51**; Part-time: **40**
Is there typically a "small section" of the first year class, other than Legal Writing, taught by full-time faculty?: Full-time: **no**; Part-time: **no**
Number of course titles, beyond the first year curriculum, offered last year: **64**
Percentages of upper division course sections, excluding seminars, with an enrollment of:
   Under 25: **47%**   25 to 49: **35%**
   50 to 74: **18%**   75 to 99: **0%**
   100+: **0%**
Areas of specialization: appellate advocacy, dispute resolution, environmental law, healthcare law, intellectual property law, international law, tax law, trial advocacy

Fall 2007 faculty profile
Total teaching faculty: **30**. Full-time: **57%**; **59%** men, **41%** women, **6%** minorities. Part-time: **43%**; **77%** men, **23%** women, **15%** minorities
Student-to-faculty ratio: **14.4**

SPECIAL PROGRAMS *(as provided by law school):*
All students take part in a public service program. The school offers faculty-supervised externships (judicial, legal aid, public defender, technology, tax, and domestic violence). It expects to open a clinic by 2008-09. The clinic will represent individuals in areas such as family law, tax, public benefits, and landlord-tenant and will help entrepreneurs open businesses and conduct transactions.

STUDENT BODY

Fall 2007 full-time enrollment: 323

Men: 55%	Women: 45%
African-American: 5.6%	American Indian: 0.0%
Asian-American: 2.5%	Mexican-American: 0.0%
Puerto Rican: 0.0%	Other Hisp-Amer: 1.5%
White: 87.3%	International: 0.3%
Unknown: 2.8%	

Fall 2007 part-time enrollment: 87

Men: 51%	Women: 49%
African-American: 3.4%	American Indian: 0.0%
Asian-American: 2.3%	Mexican-American: 2.3%
Puerto Rican: 0.0%	Other Hisp-Amer: 0.0%
White: 89.7%	International: 0.0%
Unknown: 2.3%	

Attrition rates for 2006-2007 full-time students
Percent of students discontinuing law school:

Men: 5%	Women: 7%
First-year students: 15%	Second-year students: 2%
Third-year students: N/A	

LIBRARY RESOURCES

Total volumes: 423,857
Total seats available for library users: 441

INFORMATION TECHNOLOGY

Number of wired network connections available to students: 5 total (in the law library, excluding computer labs: 5; in classrooms: 0; in computer labs: 0; elsewhere in the law school: 0)
Law school has a wireless network.
Students are not required to own a computer.

EMPLOYMENT AND SALARIES

Proportion of 2006 graduates employed at graduation: 59%
Employed 9 months later, as of February 15, 2007: **94%**

Salaries in the private sector (law firms, business, industry): $45,000–$83,000 (25th-75th percentile)
Median salary in the private sector: $55,000
Percentage in the private sector who reported salary information: 63%
Median salary in public service (government, judicial clerkships, academic posts, non-profits): $36,500

Percentage of 2006 graduates in:

Law firms: 56%	Government: 8%
Bus./industry: 15%	Judicial clerkship: 8%
Public interest: 12%	Unknown: 0%
Academia: 1%	

2006 graduates employed in-state: 83%
2006 graduates employed in foreign countries: 0%
Number of states where graduates are employed: 17
Percentage of 2006 graduates working in: New England: 0%, Middle Atlantic: 1%, East North Central: 3%, West North Central: 1%, South Atlantic: 7%, East South Central: 84%, West South Central: 1%, Mountain: 3%, Pacific: 0%, Unknown: 0%

BAR PASSAGE RATES

Based on 2006 graduates taking Summer 2006 or Winter 2007 exams. Most of the school's first-time test takers took the bar in Kentucky.

85%
School's bar passage rate for first-time test takers

83%
Statewide bar passage rate for first-time test takers

University of Maine

■ 246 Deering Avenue, Portland, ME, 04102
■ http://mainelaw.maine.edu/
■ Public
■ Year founded: 1961
■ 2007-2008 tuition: In-state: full-time: $18,210; part-time: N/A; Out-of-state: full-time: $28,290
■ Enrollment 2007-08 academic year: full-time: 254
■ U.S. News 2009 law specialty ranking: N/A

3.06-3.69 GPA, 25TH-75TH PERCENTILE

154-159 LSAT, 25TH-75TH PERCENTILE

47% ACCEPTANCE RATE

Tier 3 2009 U.S. NEWS LAW SCHOOL RANKING

ADMISSIONS

Admissions phone number: **(207) 780-4341**
Admissions email address: **mainelaw@usm.maine.edu**
Application website:
   http://mainelaw.maine.edu/acrobat/MELawApp.pdf
Application deadline for Fall 2009 admission: **03/01**

Admissions statistics:

Number of applicants for Fall 2007: **761**
Number of acceptances: **357**
Number enrolled: **88**
Acceptance rate: **47%**
GPA, 25th-75th percentile, entering class Fall 2007: **3.06-3.69**
LSAT, 25th-75th percentile, entering class Fall 2007: **154-159**

FINANCIAL AID

Financial aid phone number: **(207) 780-5250**
Financial aid application deadline: **02/15**
Tuition 2007-2008 academic year: In-state: full-time: **$18,210**; part-time: **N/A**; Out-of-state: full-time: **$28,290**
Room and board: **$8,270**; books: **$952**; miscellaneous expenses: **$3,310**
Total of room/board/books/miscellaneous expenses: **$12,532**
University offers graduate student housing for which law students are eligible.

Financial aid profile

Percent of students that received grants for the 2006-2007 academic year: full-time: **50%**
Median grant amount: full-time: **$2,300**
The average law-school debt of those in the Class of 2007 who borrowed: **$48,965**. Proportion who borrowed: **87%**

ACADEMIC PROGRAMS

Calendar: **semester**
Joint degrees awarded: **J.D./M.B.A.; J.D./M.A. Public Policy & Mgmt; J.D/M.C.P.; J.D./M.S. Health Policy**

Typical first-year section size: Full-time: **96**
Is there typically a "small section" of the first year class, other than Legal Writing, taught by full-time faculty?: Full-time: **yes**
Number of course titles, beyond the first year curriculum, offered last year: **74**
Percentages of upper division course sections, excluding seminars, with an enrollment of:
   Under 25: **65%**   25 to 49: **24%**
   50 to 74: **12%**   75 to 99: **0%**
   100+: **0%**
Areas of specialization: appellate advocacy, clinical training, dispute resolution, environmental law, healthcare law, intellectual property law, international law, tax law, trial advocacy

Fall 2007 faculty profile

Total teaching faculty: **57**. Full-time: **33%**; **53%** men, **47%** women, **0%** minorities. Part-time: **67%**; **71%** men, **29%** women, **3%** minorities
Student-to-faculty ratio: **15.3**

SPECIAL PROGRAMS *(as provided by law school):*

Clinic students represent clients in civil, criminal, juvenile, domestic violence, family law, and patent law matters. The Center for Law and Innovation houses the Marine Law Institute and the Maine patent program. The school's coastal location enhances study in environmental, ocean, and coastal law and policy. Externships, bridge courses, and funded fellowships link theory to practice.

STUDENT BODY

Fall 2007 full-time enrollment: 254

Men: **54%**   Women: **46%**
African-American: **0.4%**   American Indian: **0.0%**
Asian-American: **1.2%**   Mexican-American: **0.0%**
Puerto Rican: **0.0%**   Other Hisp-Amer: **0.0%**
White: **97.6%**   International: **0.4%**
Unknown: **0.4%**

Attrition rates for 2006-2007 full-time students
Percent of students discontinuing law school:
Men: **6%**   Women: **6%**
First-year students: **15%**   Second-year students: **N/A**
Third-year students: **N/A**

LIBRARY RESOURCES
Total volumes: **331,316**
Total seats available for library users: **233**

INFORMATION TECHNOLOGY
Number of wired network connections available to students: **0** total (in the law library, excluding computer labs: **0**; in classrooms: **0**; in computer labs: **0**; elsewhere in the law school: **0**)
Law school has a wireless network.
Students are not required to own a computer.

EMPLOYMENT AND SALARIES
Proportion of 2006 graduates employed at graduation: **N/A**
Employed 9 months later, as of February 15, 2007: **92%**
Salaries in the private sector (law firms, business, industry): **$48,000–$68,000** (25th-75th percentile)
Median salary in the private sector: **$60,000**
Percentage in the private sector who reported salary information: **33%**
Median salary in public service (government, judicial clerkships, academic posts, non-profits): **$39,900**

Percentage of 2006 graduates in:
Law firms: **37%**   Government: **12%**
Bus./industry: **25%**   Judicial clerkship: **13%**
Public interest: **8%**   Unknown: **0%**
Academia: **4%**

2006 graduates employed in-state: **64%**
2006 graduates employed in foreign countries: **1%**
Number of states where graduates are employed: **18**
Percentage of 2006 graduates working in: New England: **74%**, Middle Atlantic: **4%**, East North Central: **2%**, West North Central: **0%**, South Atlantic: **10%**, East South Central: **0%**, West South Central: **1%**, Mountain: **1%**, Pacific: **6%**, Unknown: **0%**

BAR PASSAGE RATES
Based on 2006 graduates taking Summer 2006 or Winter 2007 exams. Most of the school's first-time test takers took the bar in Maine.

86%
School's bar passage rate for first-time test takers

83%
Statewide bar passage rate for first-time test takers

University of Maryland

- 500 W. Baltimore Street, Baltimore, MD, 21201-1786
- http://www.law.umaryland.edu
- Public
- **Year founded:** 1870
- **2007-2008 tuition:** In-state: full-time: $20,535; part-time: $15,568; Out-of-state: full-time: $31,814
- **Enrollment 2007-08 academic year:** full-time: 678; part-time: 153
- **U.S. News 2009 law specialty ranking:** clinical training: 8, environmental law: 8, healthcare law: 3

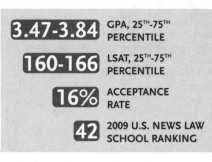

3.47-3.84 GPA, 25TH-75TH PERCENTILE

160-166 LSAT, 25TH-75TH PERCENTILE

16% ACCEPTANCE RATE

42 2009 U.S. NEWS LAW SCHOOL RANKING

ADMISSIONS

Admissions phone number: **(410) 706-3492**
Admissions email address: **admissions@law.umaryland.edu**
Application website:
http://www.law.umaryland.edu/admiss_apply.asp
Application deadline for Fall 2009 admission: **03/01**

Admissions statistics:

Number of applicants for Fall 2007: **3,319**
Number of acceptances: **515**
Number enrolled: **224**
Acceptance rate: **16%**
GPA, 25th-75th percentile, entering class Fall 2007: **3.47-3.84**
LSAT, 25th-75th percentile, entering class Fall 2007: **160-166**

Part-time program:

Number of applicants for Fall 2007: **428**
Number of acceptances: **83**
Number enrolled: **66**
Acceptance rate: **19%**
GPA, 25th-75th percentile, entering class Fall 2007: **3.22-3.66**
LSAT, 25th-75th percentile, entering class Fall 2007: **152-160**

FINANCIAL AID

Financial aid phone number: **(410) 706-0873**
Financial aid application deadline: **03/01**
Tuition 2007-2008 academic year: In-state: full-time: **$20,535**; part-time: **$15,568**; Out-of-state: full-time: **$31,814**
Room and board: **$15,480**; books: **$1,725**; miscellaneous expenses: **$7,193**
Total of room/board/books/miscellaneous expenses: **$24,398**
University offers graduate student housing for which law students are eligible.

Financial aid profile

Percent of students that received grants for the 2006-2007 academic year: full-time: **67%**; part-time **27%**
Median grant amount: full-time: **$5,000**; part-time: **$3,000**
The average law-school debt of those in the Class of 2007 who borrowed: **$63,621**. Proportion who borrowed: **76%**

ACADEMIC PROGRAMS

Calendar: **semester**
Joint degrees awarded: **J.D./Ph.D. Public Policy; J.D./M.A. Public Policy; J.D./M.P.H.; J.D./M.B.A.; J.D./M.A. Criminal Justice; J.D./M.A. Liberal Arts; J.D./M.A. Public Management; J.D./M.S.W.; J.D./Pharm.D.; J.D./M.A. Community Planning; J.D./M.S. Toxicology Risk Assessment; J.D./M.S.N.**
Typical first-year section size: Full-time: **69**; Part-time: **52**
Is there typically a "small section" of the first year class, other than Legal Writing, taught by full-time faculty?: Full-time: **yes**; Part-time: **yes**
Number of course titles, beyond the first year curriculum, offered last year: **193**
Percentages of upper division course sections, excluding seminars, with an enrollment of:

Under 25: **75%**	25 to 49: **17%**
50 to 74: **5%**	75 to 99: **2%**
100+: **0%**	

Areas of specialization: appellate advocacy, clinical training, dispute resolution, environmental law, healthcare law, intellectual property law, international law, tax law, trial advocacy

Fall 2007 faculty profile

Total teaching faculty: **167**. Full-time: **41%**; **54%** men, **46%** women, **22%** minorities. Part-time: **59%**; **61%** men, **39%** women, **7%** minorities
Student-to-faculty ratio: **11.4**

SPECIAL PROGRAMS *(as provided by law school):*

The law school offers specialty programs in business law; clinical law; environmental law; intellectual property law; law and healthcare; women, leadership, and equality. It houses interdisciplinary centers: Health and Homeland Security; Dispute Resolution; Tobacco Regulation, Litigation and Advocacy; Intellectual Property. The school offers a wide range of domestic and international externships.

STUDENT BODY

Fall 2007 full-time enrollment: 678

Men: 45%	Women: 55%
African-American: 11.9%	American Indian: 0.9%
Asian-American: 13.9%	Mexican-American: 0.1%
Puerto Rican: 0.0%	Other Hisp-Amer: 8.7%
White: 59.7%	International: 1.6%
Unknown: 3.1%	

Fall 2007 part-time enrollment: 153

Men: 46%	Women: 54%
African-American: 20.9%	American Indian: 0.7%
Asian-American: 7.8%	Mexican-American: 0.0%
Puerto Rican: 0.0%	Other Hisp-Amer: 4.6%
White: 63.4%	International: 0.0%
Unknown: 2.6%	

Attrition rates for 2006-2007 full-time students
Percent of students discontinuing law school:

Men: 4%	Women: 1%
First-year students: 7%	Second-year students: 0%
Third-year students: N/A	

LIBRARY RESOURCES

Total volumes: 495,538
Total seats available for library users: 522

INFORMATION TECHNOLOGY

Number of wired network connections available to students: 1,208 total (in the law library, excluding computer labs: 385; in classrooms: 718; in computer labs: 15; elsewhere in the law school: 90)
Law school has a wireless network.
Students are required to own a computer.

EMPLOYMENT AND SALARIES

Proportion of 2006 graduates employed at graduation: 80%
Employed 9 months later, as of February 15, 2007: 94%
Salaries in the private sector (law firms, business, industry): $50,000–$110,000 (25th-75th percentile)
Median salary in the private sector: $85,000
Percentage in the private sector who reported salary information: 73%
Median salary in public service (government, judicial clerkships, academic posts, non-profits): $40,000

Percentage of 2006 graduates in:

Law firms: 40%	Government: 15%
Bus./industry: 10%	Judicial clerkship: 25%
Public interest: 5%	Unknown: 0%
Academia: 5%	

2006 graduates employed in-state: 71%
2006 graduates employed in foreign countries: 1%
Number of states where graduates are employed: 17
Percentage of 2006 graduates working in: New England: 1%, Middle Atlantic: 3%, East North Central: 1%, West North Central: 0%, South Atlantic: 90%, East South Central: 0%, West South Central: 0%, Mountain: 1%, Pacific: 3%, Unknown: 0%

BAR PASSAGE RATES

Based on 2006 graduates taking Summer 2006 or Winter 2007 exams. Most of the school's first-time test takers took the bar in Maryland.

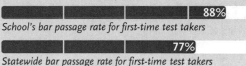

School's bar passage rate for first-time test takers — 88%

Statewide bar passage rate for first-time test takers — 77%

University of Memphis (Humphreys)

- 207 Humphreys Law School, Memphis, TN, 38152-3140
- http://www.law.memphis.edu
- Public
- Year founded: 1962
- 2007-2008 tuition: In-state: full-time: $11,412; part-time: $10,756; Out-of-state: full-time: $30,598
- Enrollment 2007-08 academic year: full-time: 395; part-time: 22
- U.S. News 2009 law specialty ranking: N/A

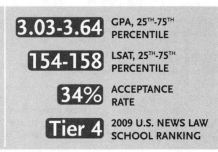

3.03-3.64 GPA, 25TH-75TH PERCENTILE

154-158 LSAT, 25TH-75TH PERCENTILE

34% ACCEPTANCE RATE

Tier 4 2009 U.S. NEWS LAW SCHOOL RANKING

ADMISSIONS
Admissions phone number: (901) 678-5403
Admissions email address:
  lawadmissions@mail.law.memphis.edu
Application website:
  http://www.law.memphis.edu/admissions
Application deadline for Fall 2009 admission: 03/01

Admissions statistics:
Number of applicants for Fall 2007: 906
Number of acceptances: 306
Number enrolled: 144
Acceptance rate: 34%
GPA, 25th-75th percentile, entering class Fall 2007: 3.03-3.64
LSAT, 25th-75th percentile, entering class Fall 2007: 154-158

Part-time program:
Number of applicants for Fall 2007: 35
Number of acceptances: 7
Number enrolled: 5
Acceptance rate: 20%
GPA, 25th-75th percentile, entering class Fall 2007: 2.88-3.19
LSAT, 25th-75th percentile, entering class Fall 2007: 144-155

FINANCIAL AID
Financial aid phone number: (901) 678-3737
Financial aid application deadline: 04/01
Tuition 2007-2008 academic year: In-state: full-time: $11,412; part-time: $10,756; Out-of-state: full-time: $30,598
Room and board: $7,885; books: $1,500; miscellaneous expenses: $4,056
Total of room/board/books/miscellaneous expenses: $13,441
University offers graduate student housing for which law students are eligible.

Financial aid profile
Percent of students that received grants for the 2006-2007 academic year: full-time: 28%; part-time 100%
Median grant amount: full-time: $3,850; part-time: $4,000
The average law-school debt of those in the Class of 2007 who borrowed: $55,250. Proportion who borrowed: 83%

ACADEMIC PROGRAMS
Calendar: semester
Joint degrees awarded: J.D./M.B.A.; J.D./M.A.
Typical first-year section size: Full-time: 75
Is there typically a "small section" of the first year class, other than Legal Writing, taught by full-time faculty?: Full-time: no; Part-time: no
Number of course titles, beyond the first year curriculum, offered last year: 69
Percentages of upper division course sections, excluding seminars, with an enrollment of:

Under 25: 54%	25 to 49: 24%
50 to 74: 16%	75 to 99: 6%
100+: 0%	

Areas of specialization: appellate advocacy, clinical training, dispute resolution, environmental law, healthcare law, intellectual property law, international law, tax law, trial advocacy

Fall 2007 faculty profile
Total teaching faculty: 44. Full-time: 43%; 68% men, 32% women, 5% minorities. Part-time: 57%; 60% men, 40% women, 16% minorities
Student-to-faculty ratio: 17.7

SPECIAL PROGRAMS (as provided by law school):
The Tennessee Institute for Pre-Law is an admission-by-performance summer program for Tennessee residents from underrepresented backgrounds. Child and family advocacy, civil litigation, and elder law clinics provide students with client contact and legal skills training. Externships are available at governmental agencies.

STUDENT BODY

Fall 2007 full-time enrollment: 395

Men: 58%	Women: 42%
African-American: 10.9%	American Indian: 0.5%
Asian-American: 2.0%	Mexican-American: 0.0%
Puerto Rican: 0.0%	Other Hisp-Amer: 1.0%
White: 85.3%	International: 0.3%
Unknown: 0.0%	

Fall 2007 part-time enrollment: 22

Men: 32%	Women: 68%
African-American: 59.1%	American Indian: 0.0%
Asian-American: 4.5%	Mexican-American: 0.0%
Puerto Rican: 0.0%	Other Hisp-Amer: 4.5%
White: 31.8%	International: 0.0%
Unknown: 0.0%	

Attrition rates for 2006-2007 full-time students

Percent of students discontinuing law school:

Men: 7%	Women: 6%
First-year students: 9%	Second-year students: 9%
Third-year students: 2%	

LIBRARY RESOURCES

Total volumes: 275,198
Total seats available for library users: 291

INFORMATION TECHNOLOGY

Number of wired network connections available to students: 30 total (in the law library, excluding computer labs: 30; in classrooms: 0; in computer labs: 0; elsewhere in the law school: 0)
Law school has a wireless network.
Students are not required to own a computer.

EMPLOYMENT AND SALARIES

Proportion of 2006 graduates employed at graduation: 36%
Employed 9 months later, as of February 15, 2007: 89%

Salaries in the private sector (law firms, business, industry): $40,000–$72,000 (25th-75th percentile)
Median salary in the private sector: $55,000
Percentage in the private sector who reported salary information: 38%
Median salary in public service (government, judicial clerkships, academic posts, non-profits): $45,000

Percentage of 2006 graduates in:

Law firms: 56%	Government: 5%
Bus./industry: 21%	Judicial clerkship: 10%
Public interest: 4%	Unknown: N/A
Academia: 4%	

2006 graduates employed in-state: 87%
2006 graduates employed in foreign countries: N/A
Number of states where graduates are employed: 9
Percentage of 2006 graduates working in: New England: 2%, Middle Atlantic: 1%, East North Central: N/A, West North Central: 1%, South Atlantic: 4%, East South Central: 91%, West South Central: 1%, Mountain: N/A, Pacific: 1%, Unknown: N/A

BAR PASSAGE RATES

Based on 2006 graduates taking Summer 2006 or Winter 2007 exams. Most of the school's first-time test takers took the bar in Tennessee.

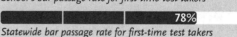

91%
School's bar passage rate for first-time test takers

78%
Statewide bar passage rate for first-time test takers

University of Miami

- PO Box 248087, Coral Gables, FL, 33124-8087
- http://www.law.miami.edu
- Private
- Year founded: 1926
- 2007-2008 tuition: full-time: $34,652; part-time: $25,650
- Enrollment 2007-08 academic year: full-time: 1,252; part-time: 16
- U.S. News 2009 law specialty ranking: tax law: 6

3.21-3.63 GPA, 25TH-75TH PERCENTILE

155-160 LSAT, 25TH-75TH PERCENTILE

51% ACCEPTANCE RATE

82 2009 U.S. NEWS LAW SCHOOL RANKING

ADMISSIONS
Admissions phone number: **(305) 284-2795**
Admissions email address: **admissions@law.miami.edu**
Application website:
   http://www.law.miami.edu/admissions/forms
Application deadline for Fall 2009 admission: **07/31**

Admissions statistics:
Number of applicants for Fall 2007: **4,492**
Number of acceptances: **2,288**
Number enrolled: **489**
Acceptance rate: **51%**
GPA, 25th-75th percentile, entering class Fall 2007: **3.21-3.63**
LSAT, 25th-75th percentile, entering class Fall 2007: **155-160**

FINANCIAL AID
Financial aid phone number: **(305) 284-3115**
Financial aid application deadline: **03/01**
Tuition 2007-2008 academic year: full-time: **$34,652**; part-time: **$25,650**
Room and board: **$10,673**; books: **$1,088**; miscellaneous expenses: **$7,491**
Total of room/board/books/miscellaneous expenses: **$19,252**
University offers graduate student housing for which law students are eligible.

Financial aid profile
Percent of students that received grants for the 2006-2007 academic year: full-time: **35%**
Median grant amount: full-time: **$16,000**
The average law-school debt of those in the Class of 2007 who borrowed: **$90,109**. Proportion who borrowed: **88%**

ACADEMIC PROGRAMS
Calendar: **semester**
Joint degrees awarded: **J.D./M.B.A.; J.D./M.P.H.; J.D./M.A.**

Typical first-year section size: Full-time: **100**
Is there typically a "small section" of the first year class, other than Legal Writing, taught by full-time faculty?:
   Full-time: **yes**; Part-time: **no**
Number of course titles, beyond the first year curriculum, offered last year: **130**
Percentages of upper division course sections, excluding seminars, with an enrollment of:
   Under 25: **41%**   25 to 49: **28%**
   50 to 74: **12%**   75 to 99: **8%**
   100+: **10%**
Areas of specialization: appellate advocacy, clinical training, dispute resolution, environmental law, healthcare law, intellectual property law, international law, tax law, trial advocacy

Fall 2007 faculty profile
Total teaching faculty: **169**. Full-time: **34%**; **71%** men, **29%** women, **17%** minorities. Part-time: **66%**; **70%** men, **30%** women, **19%** minorities
Student-to-faculty ratio: **19.1**

SPECIAL PROGRAMS (as provided by law school):
A small sample of the many programs that enrich UM's first-rate education: skills training, integrating trial, pretrial, and clinical; joint degree and LL.M. programs; clinics devoted to ethics, representation of children, public service, and impact litigation; summer programs abroad; and mock trial and negotiations competitions including international.

STUDENT BODY
Fall 2007 full-time enrollment: 1,252
Men: **56%**   Women: **44%**
African-American: **5.8%**   American Indian: **0.2%**
Asian-American: **4.7%**   Mexican-American: **0.0%**
Puerto Rican: **0.0%**   Other Hisp-Amer: **11.7%**
White: **65.5%**   International: **4.6%**
Unknown: **7.6%**

Fall 2007 part-time enrollment: 16

Men: 75%
Women: 25%
African-American: 12.5%
American Indian: 0.0%
Asian-American: 0.0%
Mexican-American: 0.0%
Puerto Rican: 0.0%
Other Hisp-Amer: 12.5%
White: 56.3%
International: 12.5%
Unknown: 6.3%

Attrition rates for 2006-2007 full-time students

Percent of students discontinuing law school:

Men: 5%
Women: 5%
First-year students: 13%
Second-year students: 1%
Third-year students: 0%

LIBRARY RESOURCES

Total volumes: 626,257
Total seats available for library users: 723

INFORMATION TECHNOLOGY

Number of wired network connections available to students: 111 total (in the law library, excluding computer labs: 97; in classrooms: 14; in computer labs: 0; elsewhere in the law school: 0)

Law school has a wireless network.

Students are not required to own a computer.

EMPLOYMENT AND SALARIES

Proportion of 2006 graduates employed at graduation: 72%

Employed 9 months later, as of February 15, 2007: 91%

Salaries in the private sector (law firms, business, industry): $83,500–$125,000 (25th-75th percentile)

Median salary in the private sector: $103,500

Percentage in the private sector who reported salary information: 40%

Median salary in public service (government, judicial clerkships, academic posts, non-profits): $40,000

Percentage of 2006 graduates in:

Law firms: 70%
Government: 13%
Bus./industry: 7%
Judicial clerkship: 4%
Public interest: 5%
Unknown: 0%
Academia: 1%

2006 graduates employed in-state: 62%
2006 graduates employed in foreign countries: 0%
Number of states where graduates are employed: 19
Percentage of 2006 graduates working in: New England: 2%, Middle Atlantic: 6%, East North Central: 1%, West North Central: 0%, South Atlantic: 69%, East South Central: 1%, West South Central: 2%, Mountain: 3%, Pacific: 5%, Unknown: 11%

BAR PASSAGE RATES

Based on 2006 graduates taking Summer 2006 or Winter 2007 exams. Most of the school's first-time test takers took the bar in Florida.

85%
School's bar passage rate for first-time test takers

74%
Statewide bar passage rate for first-time test takers

University of Michigan–Ann Arbor

- 625 S. State Street, Ann Arbor, MI, 48109-1215
- http://www.law.umich.edu/
- Public
- **Year founded:** 1859
- **2007-2008 tuition:** In-state: full-time: $38,949; part-time: N/A; Out-of-state: full-time: $41,949
- **Enrollment 2007-08 academic year:** full-time: 1,148
- **U.S. News 2009 law specialty ranking:** clinical training: 9, intellectual property law: 11, international law: 7, tax law: 10

3.49-3.79 GPA, 25ᵀᴴ-75ᵀᴴ PERCENTILE

167-170 LSAT, 25ᵀᴴ-75ᵀᴴ PERCENTILE

21% ACCEPTANCE RATE

9 2009 U.S. NEWS LAW SCHOOL RANKING

ADMISSIONS

Admissions phone number: **(734) 764-0537**
Admissions email address: **law.jd.admissions@umich.edu**
Application website:
   http://www.law.umich.edu/ProspectiveStudents/Admissions/applying.htm
Application deadline for Fall 2009 admission: **02/15**

Admissions statistics:
Number of applicants for Fall 2007: **5,675**
Number of acceptances: **1,174**
Number enrolled: **355**
Acceptance rate: **21%**
GPA, 25th-75th percentile, entering class Fall 2007: **3.49-3.79**
LSAT, 25th-75th percentile, entering class Fall 2007: **167-170**

FINANCIAL AID

Financial aid phone number: **(734) 764-5289**
Financial aid application deadline: **N/A**
Tuition 2007-2008 academic year: In-state: full-time: **$38,949**; part-time: N/A; Out-of-state: full-time: **$41,949**
Room and board: **$10,100**; books: **$1,035**; miscellaneous expenses: **$3,865**
Total of room/board/books/miscellaneous expenses: **$15,000**
University offers graduate student housing for which law students are eligible.

Financial aid profile
Percent of students that received grants for the 2006-2007 academic year: full-time: **56%**
Median grant amount: full-time: **$8,800**
The average law-school debt of those in the Class of 2007 who borrowed: **$91,000**. Proportion who borrowed: **95%**

ACADEMIC PROGRAMS

Calendar: **semester**

Joint degrees awarded: **J.D./Ph.D. Economics; J.D./M.S. Information; J.D./M.S. Natural Resources; J.D./M.P.H.; J.D./M.P.P.; J.D./M.S.W.; J.D./M.U.P.; J.D./M.B.A.; J.D./M.A. Kinesiology; J.D./M.A. South Asian Studies; J.D./M.A. South East Asian Studies; J.D./M.A. Asian Studies–Japan; J.D./M.A. Russian/E. European Studies; J.D./M.A. Political Science; J.D./M.A. Chinese Studies; J.D./M.A. Middle East/N. African Studies; J.D./M.A. World Politics**
Typical first-year section size: Full-time: **93**
Is there typically a "small section" of the first year class, other than Legal Writing, taught by full-time faculty?: Full-time: **yes**
Number of course titles, beyond the first year curriculum, offered last year: **135**
Percentages of upper division course sections, excluding seminars, with an enrollment of:

Under 25: **40%**	25 to 49: **27%**
50 to 74: **17%**	75 to 99: **13%**
100+: **4%**	

Areas of specialization: appellate advocacy, clinical training, dispute resolution, environmental law, healthcare law, intellectual property law, international law, tax law, trial advocacy

Fall 2007 faculty profile
Total teaching faculty: **105**. Full-time: **73%**; **70%** men, **30%** women, **12%** minorities. Part-time: **27%**; **64%** men, **36%** women, **4%** minorities
Student-to-faculty ratio: **12.7**

SPECIAL PROGRAMS *(as provided by law school):*
Michigan Law offers extensive clinical, research, scholarly, and practice opportunities including nine clinics, study abroad in one of nine established programs, externships and internships, 14 dual-degree programs, four international centers and programs, and prestigious clerkships in the United States, South Africa, Switzerland, and the European and International Courts of Justice.

STUDENT BODY

Fall 2007 full-time enrollment: 1,148

Men: 56%
African-American: 6.3%
Asian-American: 13.2%
Puerto Rican: 0.0%
White: 57.2%
Unknown: 11.3%

Women: 44%
American Indian: 2.3%
Mexican-American: 0.0%
Other Hisp-Amer: 5.7%
International: 4.0%

Attrition rates for 2006-2007 full-time students
Percent of students discontinuing law school:
Men: N/A
First-year students: N/A
Third-year students: N/A

Women: N/A
Second-year students: N/A

LIBRARY RESOURCES

Total volumes: 976,379
Total seats available for library users: 855

INFORMATION TECHNOLOGY

Number of wired network connections available to students: 332 total (in the law library, excluding computer labs: 8; in classrooms: 280; in computer labs: 24; elsewhere in the law school: 20)
Law school has a wireless network.
Students are not required to own a computer.

EMPLOYMENT AND SALARIES

Proportion of 2006 graduates employed at graduation: 97%
Employed 9 months later, as of February 15, 2007: 99%
Salaries in the private sector (law firms, business, industry): $135,000–$145,000 (25th-75th percentile)
Median salary in the private sector: $135,000

Percentage in the private sector who reported salary information: 78%
Median salary in public service (government, judicial clerkships, academic posts, non-profits): $55,706

Percentage of 2006 graduates in:
Law firms: 73%
Bus./industry: 4%
Public interest: 6%
Academia: 2%

Government: 4%
Judicial clerkship: 13%
Unknown: 0%

2006 graduates employed in-state: 9%
2006 graduates employed in foreign countries: 2%
Number of states where graduates are employed: 32
Percentage of 2006 graduates working in: New England: 2%, Middle Atlantic: 23%, East North Central: 32%, West North Central: 2%, South Atlantic: 15%, East South Central: 1%, West South Central: 2%, Mountain: 3%, Pacific: 17%, Unknown: 2%

BAR PASSAGE RATES

Based on 2006 graduates taking Summer 2006 or Winter 2007 exams. Most of the school's first-time test takers took the bar in New York.

95%
School's bar passage rate for first-time test takers

77%
Statewide bar passage rate for first-time test takers

University of Minnesota–Twin Cities

■ 229 19th Avenue S, Minneapolis, MN, 55455
■ http://www.law.umn.edu
■ Public
■ Year founded: 1888
■ 2007-2008 tuition: In-state: full-time: $22,505; part-time: N/A; Out-of-state: full-time: $32,005
■ Enrollment 2007-08 academic year: full-time: 793
■ U.S. News 2009 law specialty ranking: healthcare law: 11, intellectual property law: 17, international law: 16

3.28-3.78 GPA, 25TH-75TH PERCENTILE

163-167 LSAT, 25TH-75TH PERCENTILE

25% ACCEPTANCE RATE

22 2009 U.S. NEWS LAW SCHOOL RANKING

ADMISSIONS

Admissions phone number: **(612) 625-3487**
Admissions email address: **umnlsadm@umn.edu**
Application website:
https://www.law.umn.edu/admissions/online_application.htm
Application deadline for Fall 2009 admission: **03/01**

Admissions statistics:

Number of applicants for Fall 2007: **2,690**
Number of acceptances: **665**
Number enrolled: **259**
Acceptance rate: **25%**
GPA, 25th-75th percentile, entering class Fall 2007: **3.28-3.78**
LSAT, 25th-75th percentile, entering class Fall 2007: **163-167**

FINANCIAL AID

Financial aid phone number: **(612) 625-3487**
Financial aid application deadline: **03/01**
Tuition 2007-2008 academic year: In-state: full-time: **$22,505**; part-time: **N/A**; Out-of-state: full-time: **$32,005**
Room and board: **N/A**; books: **N/A**; miscellaneous expenses: **N/A**
Total of room/board/books/miscellaneous expenses: **$13,392**
University offers graduate student housing for which law students are eligible.

Financial aid profile

Percent of students that received grants for the 2006-2007 academic year: full-time: **59%**
Median grant amount: full-time: **$8,000**
The average law-school debt of those in the Class of 2007 who borrowed: **$82,981**. Proportion who borrowed: **75%**

ACADEMIC PROGRAMS

Calendar: **semester**
Joint degrees awarded: **J.D./M.U.R.P.; J.D./M.B.S.;**
J.D./M.P.H.; J.D./Ph.D.; J.D./M.D.; J.D./M.B.A.; J.D./M.S.; J.D./M.A.; J.D./M.P.A.; J.D./M.Ed.; J.D./M.B.T.; J.D./M.P.P.
Typical first-year section size: Full-time: **106**
Is there typically a "small section" of the first year class, other than Legal Writing, taught by full-time faculty?: Full-time: **yes**
Number of course titles, beyond the first year curriculum, offered last year: **193**
Percentages of upper division course sections, excluding seminars, with an enrollment of:
Under 25: **60%**   25 to 49: **22%**
50 to 74: **9%**   75 to 99: **7%**
100+: **2%**
Areas of specialization: appellate advocacy, clinical training, dispute resolution, environmental law, healthcare law, intellectual property law, international law, tax law, trial advocacy

Fall 2007 faculty profile

Total teaching faculty: **230**. Full-time: **26%**; **60%** men, **40%** women, **8%** minorities. Part-time: **74%**; **56%** men, **44%** women, **4%** minorities
Student-to-faculty ratio: **12.1**

SPECIAL PROGRAMS *(as provided by law school):*

Clinics: 19, including civil practice clinic and tax clinic. Institutes: 10, including Human Rights Center, Institute on Race and Poverty. Study abroad: eight semester exchange programs. Public service program encourages 50 pro bono hours per student. Judicial externship program with federal and state courts. Joint degrees: 12 programs.

STUDENT BODY

Fall 2007 full-time enrollment: 793

Men: **58%**	Women: **42%**
African-American: **2.3%**	American Indian: **1.1%**
Asian-American: **8.7%**	Mexican-American: **0.3%**
Puerto Rican: **0.0%**	Other Hisp-Amer: **3.2%**
White: **76.5%**	International: **1.9%**
Unknown: **6.1%**	

Attrition rates for 2006-2007 full-time students
Percent of students discontinuing law school:
Men: 2%   Women: 3%
First-year students: 6%   Second-year students: 1%
Third-year students: N/A

LIBRARY RESOURCES
Total volumes: 1,051,968
Total seats available for library users: 773

INFORMATION TECHNOLOGY
Number of wired network connections available to students: 0 total (in the law library, excluding computer labs: 0; in classrooms: 0; in computer labs: 0; elsewhere in the law school: 0)
Law school has a wireless network.
Students are required to own a computer.

EMPLOYMENT AND SALARIES
Proportion of 2006 graduates employed at graduation: 87%
Employed 9 months later, as of February 15, 2007: 98%
Salaries in the private sector (law firms, business, industry): $65,000–$110,000 (25th-75th percentile)
Median salary in the private sector: $100,000
Percentage in the private sector who reported salary information: 83%
Median salary in public service (government, judicial clerkships, academic posts, non-profits): $47,000

Percentage of 2006 graduates in:
Law firms: 51%   Government: 6%
Bus./industry: 15%   Judicial clerkship: 19%
Public interest: 7%   Unknown: 1%
Academia: 2%

2006 graduates employed in-state: 59%
2006 graduates employed in foreign countries: 2%
Number of states where graduates are employed: 30
Percentage of 2006 graduates working in: New England: 3%, Middle Atlantic: 6%, East North Central: 8%, West North Central: 62%, South Atlantic: 7%, East South Central: 0%, West South Central: 1%, Mountain: 3%, Pacific: 10%, Unknown: 1%

BAR PASSAGE RATES
Based on 2006 graduates taking Summer 2006 or Winter 2007 exams. Most of the school's first-time test takers took the bar in Minnesota.

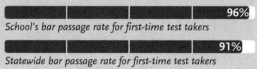

96%
School's bar passage rate for first-time test takers

91%
Statewide bar passage rate for first-time test takers

University of Mississippi

- PO Box 1848, University, MS, 38677
- http://www.olemiss.edu/depts/law_school/
- Public
- Year founded: 1854
- 2007-2008 tuition: In-state: full-time: $8,930; part-time: N/A; Out-of-state: full-time: $18,550
- Enrollment 2007-08 academic year: full-time: 517
- U.S. News 2009 law specialty ranking: N/A

3.28-3.79 GPA, 25TH-75TH PERCENTILE

152-157 LSAT, 25TH-75TH PERCENTILE

31% ACCEPTANCE RATE

Tier 3 2009 U.S. NEWS LAW SCHOOL RANKING

ADMISSIONS
Admissions phone number: **(662) 915-6910**
Admissions email address: **lawmiss@olemiss.edu**
Application website:
**http://www.olemiss.edu/depts/law_school/
admis_APPLICATION.html**
Application deadline for Fall 2009 admission: **02/15**

Admissions statistics:
Number of applicants for Fall 2007: **1,572**
Number of acceptances: **482**
Number enrolled: **173**
Acceptance rate: **31%**
GPA, 25th-75th percentile, entering class Fall 2007: **3.28-3.79**
LSAT, 25th-75th percentile, entering class Fall 2007: **152-157**

FINANCIAL AID
Financial aid phone number: **(800) 891-4569**
Financial aid application deadline: **03/01**
Tuition 2007-2008 academic year: In-state: full-time: **$8,930**; part-time: N/A; Out-of-state: full-time: **$18,550**
Room and board: **$10,218**; books: **$1,300**; miscellaneous expenses: **$3,340**
Total of room/board/books/miscellaneous expenses: **$14,858**
University offers graduate student housing for which law students are eligible.

Financial aid profile
Percent of students that received grants for the 2006-2007 academic year: full-time: **39%**
Median grant amount: full-time: **$4,750**
The average law-school debt of those in the Class of 2007 who borrowed: **$48,400**. Proportion who borrowed: **72%**

ACADEMIC PROGRAMS
Calendar: **semester**
Joint degrees awarded: **N/A**
Typical first-year section size: Full-time: **58**

Is there typically a "small section" of the first year class, other than Legal Writing, taught by full-time faculty?: Full-time: **no**
Number of course titles, beyond the first year curriculum, offered last year: **82**
Percentages of upper division course sections, excluding seminars, with an enrollment of:
Under 25: **49%**   25 to 49: **28%**
50 to 74: **11%**   75 to 99: **7%**
100+: **6%**
Areas of specialization: appellate advocacy, clinical training, dispute resolution, environmental law, healthcare law, intellectual property law, international law, tax law, trial advocacy

Fall 2007 faculty profile
Total teaching faculty: **42**. Full-time: **62%**; **65%** men, **35%** women, **15%** minorities. Part-time: **38%**; **63%** men, **38%** women, **6%** minorities
Student-to-faculty ratio: **15.8**

SPECIAL PROGRAMS *(as provided by law school):*
Public service externship, prosecutorial externship, criminal appeals clinic, civil law clinic, Mississippi Innocence Project, business regulation externship, summer session in Cambridge, England.

STUDENT BODY
Fall 2007 full-time enrollment: 517
Men: **56%**   Women: **44%**
African-American: **11.4%**   American Indian: **0.8%**
Asian-American: **1.5%**   Mexican-American: **0.0%**
Puerto Rican: **0.0%**   Other Hisp-Amer: **0.6%**
White: **84.5%**   International: **0.4%**
Unknown: **0.8%**

Attrition rates for 2006-2007 full-time students
Percent of students discontinuing law school:
Men: **2%**   Women: **2%**
First-year students: **5%**   Second-year students: **N/A**
Third-year students: **1%**

LIBRARY RESOURCES
Total volumes: 336,487
Total seats available for library users: 302

INFORMATION TECHNOLOGY
Number of wired network connections available to students: 735 total (in the law library, excluding computer labs: 121; in classrooms: 458; in computer labs: 4; elsewhere in the law school: 152)
Law school has a wireless network.
Students are not required to own a computer.

EMPLOYMENT AND SALARIES
Proportion of 2006 graduates employed at graduation: 60%
Employed 9 months later, as of February 15, 2007: 88%
Salaries in the private sector (law firms, business, industry): $45,000–$81,000 (25th-75th percentile)
Median salary in the private sector: $66,500
Percentage in the private sector who reported salary information: 76%
Median salary in public service (government, judicial clerkships, academic posts, non-profits): $47,034

Percentage of 2006 graduates in:
Law firms: 58%	Government: 11%
Bus./industry: 6%	Judicial clerkship: 18%
Public interest: 4%	Unknown: 1%
Academia: 2%	

2006 graduates employed in-state: 64%
2006 graduates employed in foreign countries: 1%
Number of states where graduates are employed: 15
Percentage of 2006 graduates working in: New England: 0%, Middle Atlantic: 1%, East North Central: 0%, West North Central: 1%, South Atlantic: 11%, East South Central: 77%, West South Central: 5%, Mountain: 2%, Pacific: 2%, Unknown: 0%

BAR PASSAGE RATES
Based on 2006 graduates taking Summer 2006 or Winter 2007 exams. Most of the school's first-time test takers took the bar in Mississippi.

92%
School's bar passage rate for first-time test takers

88%
Statewide bar passage rate for first-time test takers

University of Missouri—Columbia

■ 203 Hulston Hall, Columbia, MO, 65211-4300
■ http://www.law.missouri.edu
■ Public
■ **Year founded:** 1872
■ **2007-2008 tuition:** In-state: full-time: $14,854; part-time: N/A; Out-of-state: full-time: $28,336
■ **Enrollment 2007-08 academic year:** full-time: 449; part-time: 6
■ **U.S. News 2009 law specialty ranking:** dispute resolution: 2

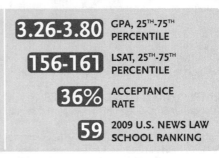

3.26-3.80 GPA, 25TH-75TH PERCENTILE

156-161 LSAT, 25TH-75TH PERCENTILE

36% ACCEPTANCE RATE

59 2009 U.S. NEWS LAW SCHOOL RANKING

ADMISSIONS

Admissions phone number: **(573) 882-6042**
Admissions email address:
umclawadmissions@missouri.edu
Application website:
http://www.law.missouri.edu/admissions.html
Application deadline for Fall 2009 admission: **03/01**

Admissions statistics:

Number of applicants for Fall 2007: **980**
Number of acceptances: **351**
Number enrolled: **145**
Acceptance rate: **36%**
GPA, 25th-75th percentile, entering class Fall 2007: **3.26-3.80**
LSAT, 25th-75th percentile, entering class Fall 2007: **156-161**

FINANCIAL AID

Financial aid phone number: **(573) 882-6643**
Financial aid application deadline: **03/01**
Tuition 2007-2008 academic year: In-state: full-time: **$14,854**; part-time: N/A; Out-of-state: full-time: **$28,336**
Room and board: **$8,100**; books: **$1,460**; miscellaneous expenses: **$5,432**
Total of room/board/books/miscellaneous expenses: **$14,992**
University offers graduate student housing for which law students are eligible.

Financial aid profile

Percent of students that received grants for the 2006-2007 academic year: full-time: **40%**
Median grant amount: full-time: **$4,000**
The average law-school debt of those in the Class of 2007 who borrowed: **$60,858**. Proportion who borrowed: **92%**

ACADEMIC PROGRAMS

Calendar: **semester**

Joint degrees awarded: **J.D./M.B.A.; J.D./M.P.A.; J.D./M.S. Agricultural Economics; J.D./M.H.A.; J.D./M.A. Economics; J.D./M.A. H.D.F.S.; J.D./M.A. E.L.P.A.; J.D./M.A. Journalism; J.D./Ph.D. Journalism; J.D./M.A. Library & Infomation Science; J.D./M.A. Consumer & Family Economics; J.D./M.S. H.D.F.S.**
Typical first-year section size: Full-time: **75**
Is there typically a "small section" of the first year class, other than Legal Writing, taught by full-time faculty?: Full-time: **yes**; Part-time: **no**
Number of course titles, beyond the first year curriculum, offered last year: **111**
Percentages of upper division course sections, excluding seminars, with an enrollment of:
Under 25: **60%**   25 to 49: **19%**
50 to 74: **13%**   75 to 99: **7%**
100+: **0%**
Areas of specialization: appellate advocacy, clinical training, dispute resolution, environmental law, healthcare law, intellectual property law, international law, tax law, trial advocacy

Fall 2007 faculty profile

Total teaching faculty: **52**. Full-time: **60%**; **65%** men, **35%** women, **13%** minorities. Part-time: **40%**; **71%** men, **29%** women, **10%** minorities
Student-to-faculty ratio: **17.2**

SPECIAL PROGRAMS (as provided by law school):

The Center for the Study of Dispute Resolution's LL.M. attracts students worldwide. Students can extern in the Missouri Supreme Court, the state and U.S. attorney's offices, and the Compliance Office of MU Athletics Office, study abroad in South Africa or London, and gain representation and mediation experience in the criminal prosecution, family violence, child protection, and mediation clinics.

STUDENT BODY

Fall 2007 full-time enrollment: 449
Men: 62%   Women: 38%
African-American: 5.1%   American Indian: 1.6%
Asian-American: 4.2%   Mexican-American: 0.0%
Puerto Rican: 0.0%   Other Hisp-Amer: 2.7%
White: 80.6%   International: 0.0%
Unknown: 5.8%

Fall 2007 part-time enrollment: 6
Men: 33%   Women: 67%
African-American: 33.3%   American Indian: 0.0%
Asian-American: 16.7%   Mexican-American: 0.0%
Puerto Rican: 0.0%   Other Hisp-Amer: 16.7%
White: 33.3%   International: 0.0%
Unknown: 0.0%

Attrition rates for 2006-2007 full-time students
Percent of students discontinuing law school:
Men: 2%   Women: 1%
First-year students: 4%   Second-year students: N/A
Third-year students: N/A

LIBRARY RESOURCES

Total volumes: 389,299
Total seats available for library users: 472

INFORMATION TECHNOLOGY

Number of wired network connections available to stu-
    dents: 1 total (in the law library, excluding computer labs:
    0; in classrooms: 0; in computer labs: 1; elsewhere in the
    law school: 0)
Law school has a wireless network.
Students are not required to own a computer.

EMPLOYMENT AND SALARIES

Proportion of 2006 graduates employed at graduation: 55%
Employed 9 months later, as of February 15, 2007: 99%

Salaries in the private sector (law firms, business, indus-
    try): $45,000–$75,000 (25th-75th percentile)
Median salary in the private sector: $55,000
Percentage in the private sector who reported salary
    information: 56%
Median salary in public service (government, judicial clerk-
    ships, academic posts, non-profits): $38,250

Percentage of 2006 graduates in:
Law firms: 52%   Government: 20%
Bus./industry: 5%   Judicial clerkship: 13%
Public interest: 8%   Unknown: 3%
Academia: 0%

2006 graduates employed in-state: 87%
2006 graduates employed in foreign countries: 0%
Number of states where graduates are employed: 14
Percentage of 2006 graduates working in: New England:
    0%, Middle Atlantic: 0%, East North Central: 4%, West
    North Central: 88%, South Atlantic: 2%, East South
    Central: 0%, West South Central: 3%, Mountain: 0%,
    Pacific: 2%, Unknown: 2%

BAR PASSAGE RATES

Based on 2006 graduates taking Summer 2006 or
Winter 2007 exams. Most of the school's first-time test
takers took the bar in Missouri.

91%
School's bar passage rate for first-time test takers

86%
Statewide bar passage rate for first-time test takers

University of Missouri–Kansas City

■ 5100 Rockhill Road, Kansas City, MO, 64110
■ http://www.law.umkc.edu
■ Public
■ Year founded: 1895
■ 2007-2008 tuition: In-state: full-time: $13,681; part-time: $9,844; Out-of-state: full-time: $26,188
■ Enrollment 2007-08 academic year: full-time: 467; part-time: 26
■ U.S. News 2009 law specialty ranking: N/A

3.03-3.64 GPA, 25TH-75TH PERCENTILE

152-156 LSAT, 25TH-75TH PERCENTILE

50% ACCEPTANCE RATE

Tier 3 2009 U.S. NEWS LAW SCHOOL RANKING

ADMISSIONS
Admissions phone number: **(816) 235-1644**
Admissions email address: **law@umkc.edu**
Application website:
  http://www1.law.umkc.edu/admissions/
Application deadline for Fall 2009 admission: **rolling**

Admissions statistics:
Number of applicants for Fall 2007: **967**
Number of acceptances: **487**
Number enrolled: **163**
Acceptance rate: **50%**
GPA, 25th-75th percentile, entering class Fall 2007: **3.03-3.64**
LSAT, 25th-75th percentile, entering class Fall 2007: **152-156**

Part-time program:
Number of applicants for Fall 2007: **37**
Number of acceptances: **18**
Number enrolled: **11**
Acceptance rate: **49%**
GPA, 25th-75th percentile, entering class Fall 2007: **3.03-3.46**
LSAT, 25th-75th percentile, entering class Fall 2007: **149-155**

FINANCIAL AID
Financial aid phone number: **(816) 235-1154**
Financial aid application deadline: N/A
Tuition 2007-2008 academic year: In-state: full-time: **$13,681**; part-time: **$9,844**; Out-of-state: full-time: **$26,188**
Room and board: **$8,630**; books: **$3,900**; miscellaneous expenses: **$7,070**
Total of room/board/books/miscellaneous expenses: **$19,600**
University offers graduate student housing for which law students are eligible.

Financial aid profile
Percent of students that received grants for the 2006-2007 academic year: full-time: **39%**
Median grant amount: full-time: **$5,000**
The average law-school debt of those in the Class of 2007 who borrowed: **$73,343**. Proportion who borrowed: **100%**

ACADEMIC PROGRAMS
Calendar: **semester**
Joint degrees awarded: **N/A**
Typical first-year section size: Full-time: **56**
Is there typically a "small section" of the first year class, other than Legal Writing, taught by full-time faculty?: Full-time: **no**; Part-time: **no**
Number of course titles, beyond the first year curriculum, offered last year: **113**
Percentages of upper division course sections, excluding seminars, with an enrollment of:

Under 25: **67%**	25 to 49: **16%**
50 to 74: **10%**	75 to 99: **7%**
100+: **0%**	

Areas of specialization: appellate advocacy, clinical training, dispute resolution, environmental law, intellectual property law, international law, tax law, trial advocacy

Fall 2007 faculty profile
Total teaching faculty: **71**. Full-time: **44%**; **61%** men, **39%** women, **13%** minorities. Part-time: **56%**; **83%** men, **18%** women, **0%** minorities
Student-to-faculty ratio: **12.8**

SPECIAL PROGRAMS *(as provided by law school):*
The school's location in a metropolitan area provides many opportunities for students to engage in real-life representation of clients in clinical programs that include UMKC's child and family services clinic, guardian ad litem workshop, tax clinic, entrepreneurial law and practice clinic, and the school's Innocence Project. Summer-abroad programs in Ireland, China, and England.

STUDENT BODY

Fall 2007 full-time enrollment: 467

Men: 60%	Women: 40%
African-American: 3.4%	American Indian: 0.6%
Asian-American: 2.6%	Mexican-American: 0.0%
Puerto Rican: 0.0%	Other Hisp-Amer: 2.8%
White: 81.8%	International: 0.6%
Unknown: 8.1%	

Fall 2007 part-time enrollment: 26

Men: 42%	Women: 58%
African-American: 11.5%	American Indian: 0.0%
Asian-American: 3.8%	Mexican-American: 0.0%
Puerto Rican: 0.0%	Other Hisp-Amer: 0.0%
White: 84.6%	International: 0.0%
Unknown: 0.0%	

Attrition rates for 2006-2007 full-time students
Percent of students discontinuing law school:

Men: 2%	Women: 1%
First-year students: 5%	Second-year students: 1%
Third-year students: N/A	

LIBRARY RESOURCES

Total volumes: 333,577
Total seats available for library users: 387

INFORMATION TECHNOLOGY

Number of wired network connections available to students: 24 total (in the law library, excluding computer labs: 0; in classrooms: 0; in computer labs: 0; elsewhere in the law school: 24)
Law school has a wireless network.
Students are not required to own a computer.

EMPLOYMENT AND SALARIES

Proportion of 2006 graduates employed at graduation: N/A

Employed 9 months later, as of February 15, 2007: 91%
Salaries in the private sector (law firms, business, industry): $43,000–$73,000 (25th-75th percentile)
Median salary in the private sector: $50,000
Percentage in the private sector who reported salary information: 81%
Median salary in public service (government, judicial clerkships, academic posts, non-profits): $40,000

Percentage of 2006 graduates in:

Law firms: 57%	Government: 8%
Bus./industry: 25%	Judicial clerkship: 6%
Public interest: 3%	Unknown: 1%
Academia: 1%	

2006 graduates employed in-state: 76%
2006 graduates employed in foreign countries: 1%
Number of states where graduates are employed: 11
Percentage of 2006 graduates working in: New England: N/A, Middle Atlantic: N/A, East North Central: 2%, West North Central: 91%, South Atlantic: 2%, East South Central: N/A, West South Central: 1%, Mountain: 2%, Pacific: 2%, Unknown: 0%

BAR PASSAGE RATES

Based on 2006 graduates taking Summer 2006 or Winter 2007 exams. Most of the school's first-time test takers took the bar in Missouri.

88%
School's bar passage rate for first-time test takers

86%
Statewide bar passage rate for first-time test takers

University of Montana

- 32 Campus Drive, Missoula, MT, 59812
- http://www.umt.edu/law
- Public
- Year founded: 1911
- 2007-2008 tuition: In-state: full-time: $8,973; part-time: N/A; Out-of-state: full-time: $20,239
- Enrollment 2007-08 academic year: full-time: 252
- U.S. News 2009 law specialty ranking: N/A

3.12-3.75 GPA, 25TH-75TH PERCENTILE

151-158 LSAT, 25TH-75TH PERCENTILE

42% ACCEPTANCE RATE

Tier 3 2009 U.S. NEWS LAW SCHOOL RANKING

ADMISSIONS
Admissions phone number: **(406) 243-2698**
Admissions email address: **heidi.fanslow@umontana.edu**
Application website:
   http://www.umt.edu/law/admissions/default.htm
Application deadline for Fall 2009 admission: **03/01**

Admissions statistics:
Number of applicants for Fall 2007: **494**
Number of acceptances: **209**
Number enrolled: **84**
Acceptance rate: **42%**
GPA, 25th-75th percentile, entering class Fall 2007: **3.12-3.75**
LSAT, 25th-75th percentile, entering class Fall 2007: **151-158**

FINANCIAL AID
Financial aid phone number: **(406) 243-5524**
Financial aid application deadline: N/A
Tuition 2007-2008 academic year: In-state: full-time: **$8,973**; part-time: **N/A**; Out-of-state: full-time: **$20,239**
Room and board: **$10,500**; books: **$1,100**; miscellaneous expenses: **$127**
Total of room/board/books/miscellaneous expenses: **$11,727**
University offers graduate student housing for which law students are eligible.

Financial aid profile
Percent of students that received grants for the 2006-2007 academic year: full-time: **N/A**
Median grant amount: full-time: **N/A**
The average law-school debt of those in the Class of 2007 who borrowed: **N/A**. Proportion who borrowed: **N/A**

ACADEMIC PROGRAMS
Calendar: **semester**
Joint degrees awarded: **J.D./M.B.A.; J.D./M.P.A.; J.D./M.S. Environmental Studies**
Typical first-year section size: Full-time: **43**

Is there typically a "small section" of the first year class, other than Legal Writing, taught by full-time faculty?:
   Full-time: **no**
Number of course titles, beyond the first year curriculum, offered last year: **N/A**
Percentages of upper division course sections, excluding seminars, with an enrollment of:
   Under 25: **N/A**   25 to 49: **N/A**
   50 to 74: **N/A**   75 to 99: **N/A**
   100+: **N/A**
Areas of specialization: appellate advocacy, clinical training, dispute resolution, environmental law, healthcare law, intellectual property law, international law, tax law, trial advocacy

Fall 2007 faculty profile
Total teaching faculty: **56**. Full-time: **52%**; **66%** men, **34%** women, **21%** minorities. Part-time: **48%**; **74%** men, **26%** women, **4%** minorities
Student-to-faculty ratio: **14.3**

SPECIAL PROGRAMS (as provided by law school):
All third-year students practice in a public interest setting, either in an in-house clinic at the law school or under the supervision of an attorney in the community. Students apply the skills and knowledge from their first two years of law school to a practice setting where they are challenged to identify and resolve legal, ethical, and professionalism issues like those faced in practice.

STUDENT BODY
Fall 2007 full-time enrollment: 252
Men: **49%**   Women: **51%**
African-American: **0.0%**   American Indian: **6.0%**
Asian-American: **0.4%**   Mexican-American: **0.0%**
Puerto Rican: **0.0%**   Other Hisp-Amer: **0.8%**
White: **92.1%**   International: **0.0%**
Unknown: **0.8%**

Attrition rates for 2006-2007 full-time students
Percent of students discontinuing law school:
Men: **N/A**   Women: **N/A**
First-year students: **N/A**   Second-year students: **N/A**
Third-year students: **N/A**

LIBRARY RESOURCES
Total volumes: **131,684**
Total seats available for library users: **364**

INFORMATION TECHNOLOGY
Number of wired network connections available to students: **190** total (in the law library, excluding computer labs: **56**; in classrooms: **20**; in computer labs: **18**; elsewhere in the law school: **96**)
Law school has a wireless network.
Students are not required to own a computer.

EMPLOYMENT AND SALARIES
Proportion of 2006 graduates employed at graduation: **N/A**
Employed 9 months later, as of February 15, 2007: **94%**
Salaries in the private sector (law firms, business, industry): **$41,500–$50,000** (25th-75th percentile)
Median salary in the private sector: **$45,000**
Percentage in the private sector who reported salary information: **69%**
Median salary in public service (government, judicial clerkships, academic posts, non-profits): **$43,716**

Percentage of 2006 graduates in:
Law firms: **48%**   Government: **6%**
Bus./industry: **5%**   Judicial clerkship: **32%**
Public interest: **9%**   Unknown: **0%**
Academia: **0%**

2006 graduates employed in-state: **76%**
2006 graduates employed in foreign countries: **N/A**
Number of states where graduates are employed: **14**
Percentage of 2006 graduates working in: New England: **N/A**, Middle Atlantic: **N/A**, East North Central: **N/A**, West North Central: **N/A**, South Atlantic: **N/A**, East South Central: **N/A**, West South Central: **N/A**, Mountain: **N/A**, Pacific: **N/A**, Unknown: **N/A**

BAR PASSAGE RATES
Based on 2006 graduates taking Summer 2006 or Winter 2007 exams. Most of the school's first-time test takers took the bar in Montana.

95%
School's bar passage rate for first-time test takers

92%
Statewide bar passage rate for first-time test takers

University of Nebraska–Lincoln

- PO Box 830902, Lincoln, NE, 68583-0902
- http://law.unl.edu
- Public
- Year founded: 1891
- 2007-2008 tuition: In-state: full-time: $9,018; part-time: N/A; Out-of-state: full-time: $20,935
- Enrollment 2007-08 academic year: full-time: 397; part-time: 1
- U.S. News 2009 law specialty ranking: N/A

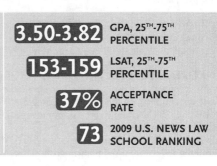

3.50-3.82 GPA, 25TH-75TH PERCENTILE

153-159 LSAT, 25TH-75TH PERCENTILE

37% ACCEPTANCE RATE

73 2009 U.S. NEWS LAW SCHOOL RANKING

ADMISSIONS

Admissions phone number: **(402) 472-2161**
Admissions email address: **lawadm@unl.edu**
Application website: **http://law.unl.edu**
Application deadline for Fall 2009 admission: **03/01**

Admissions statistics:
Number of applicants for Fall 2007: **981**
Number of acceptances: **364**
Number enrolled: **138**
Acceptance rate: **37%**
GPA, 25th-75th percentile, entering class Fall 2007: **3.50-3.82**
LSAT, 25th-75th percentile, entering class Fall 2007: **153-159**

FINANCIAL AID

Financial aid phone number: **(402) 472-2161**
Financial aid application deadline: **05/01**
Tuition 2007-2008 academic year: In-state: full-time: **$9,018**; part-time: **N/A**; Out-of-state: full-time: **$20,935**
Room and board: **$7,454**; books: **$1,286**; miscellaneous expenses: **$3,180**
Total of room/board/books/miscellaneous expenses: **$11,920**
University offers graduate student housing for which law students are eligible.

Financial aid profile
Percent of students that received grants for the 2006-2007 academic year: full-time: **41%**
Median grant amount: full-time: **$8,000**
The average law-school debt of those in the Class of 2007 who borrowed: **$44,985**. Proportion who borrowed: **84%**

ACADEMIC PROGRAMS

Calendar: **semester**
Joint degrees awarded: **J.D./M.A. Economics; J.D./M.P.A.; J.D./M.A. Psychology; J.D./M.B.A.; J.D./Ph.D. Education; J.D./Ph.D. Psychology; J.D./M.A. Political Science; J.D./M.C.R.P.; J.D./M.A. International Affairs**

Typical first-year section size: Full-time: **70**
Is there typically a "small section" of the first year class, other than Legal Writing, taught by full-time faculty?:
Full-time: **no**; Part-time: **no**
Number of course titles, beyond the first year curriculum, offered last year: **75**
Percentages of upper division course sections, excluding seminars, with an enrollment of:
Under 25: **68%**   25 to 49: **20%**
50 to 74: **12%**   75 to 99: **0%**
100+: **0%**
Areas of specialization: appellate advocacy, clinical training, dispute resolution, environmental law, healthcare law, intellectual property law, international law, tax law, trial advocacy

Fall 2007 faculty profile
Total teaching faculty: **60**. Full-time: **48%**; 72% men, 28% women, 7% minorities. Part-time: **52%**; 65% men, 35% women, 0% minorities
Student-to-faculty ratio: **12.5**

SPECIAL PROGRAMS *(as provided by law school):*

Strong interdisciplinary programs, including perhaps the foremost U.S. program in law and psychology. Concentrations in litigation and business transactions; specialized concentration in virtually any substantive area. Practice-oriented experiences, including civil and criminal clinics, externships, and pro bono programs. Summer programs at Cambridge University and the University of Limerick.

STUDENT BODY

Fall 2007 full-time enrollment: **397**
Men: **53%**   Women: **47%**
African-American: **3.0%**   American Indian: **0.8%**
Asian-American: **2.5%**   Mexican-American: **2.5%**
Puerto Rican: **0.0%**   Other Hisp-Amer: **1.3%**
White: **89.7%**   International: **0.3%**
Unknown: **0.0%**

Fall 2007 part-time enrollment: 1

Men: 0%   Women: 100%
African-American: 0.0%   American Indian: 0.0%
Asian-American: 100.0%   Mexican-American: 0.0%
Puerto Rican: 0.0%   Other Hisp-Amer: 0.0%
White: 0.0%   International: 0.0%
Unknown: 0.0%

Attrition rates for 2006-2007 full-time students
Percent of students discontinuing law school:
Men: 4%   Women: 6%
First-year students: 13%   Second-year students: N/A
Third-year students: 1%

LIBRARY RESOURCES
Total volumes: 413,489
Total seats available for library users: 372

INFORMATION TECHNOLOGY
Number of wired network connections available to students: 0 total (in the law library, excluding computer labs: 0; in classrooms: 0; in computer labs: 0; elsewhere in the law school: 0)
Law school has a wireless network.
Students are not required to own a computer.

EMPLOYMENT AND SALARIES
Proportion of 2006 graduates employed at graduation: 79%
Employed 9 months later, as of February 15, 2007: 94%
Salaries in the private sector (law firms, business, industry): $43,125–$76,250 (25th-75th percentile)
Median salary in the private sector: $57,900

Percentage in the private sector who reported salary information: 55%
Median salary in public service (government, judicial clerkships, academic posts, non-profits): $40,000

Percentage of 2006 graduates in:
Law firms: 53%   Government: 13%
Bus./industry: 16%   Judicial clerkship: 6%
Public interest: 8%   Unknown: 0%
Academia: 4%

2006 graduates employed in-state: 65%
2006 graduates employed in foreign countries: 3%
Number of states where graduates are employed: 18
Percentage of 2006 graduates working in: New England: 0%, Middle Atlantic: 2%, East North Central: 2%, West North Central: 76%, South Atlantic: 3%, East South Central: 0%, West South Central: 2%, Mountain: 8%, Pacific: 3%, Unknown: 1%

BAR PASSAGE RATES
Based on 2006 graduates taking Summer 2006 or Winter 2007 exams. Most of the school's first-time test takers took the bar in Nebraska.

87%
School's bar passage rate for first-time test takers

83%
Statewide bar passage rate for first-time test takers

Univ. of Nevada–Las Vegas (Boyd)

■ 4505 S. Maryland Parkway, PO Box 451003, Las Vegas, NV, 89154-1003
■ http://www.law.unlv.edu/
■ Public
■ Year founded: 1997
■ 2007-2008 tuition: In-state: full-time: $10,502; part-time: $6,946; Out-of-state: full-time: $20,302
■ Enrollment 2007-08 academic year: full-time: 341; part-time: 122
■ U.S. News 2009 law specialty ranking: clinical training: 12, dispute resolution: 9

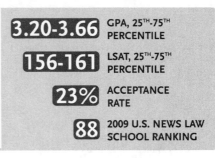

3.20-3.66 GPA, 25ᵀᴴ-75ᵀᴴ PERCENTILE

156-161 LSAT, 25ᵀᴴ-75ᵀᴴ PERCENTILE

23% ACCEPTANCE RATE

88 2009 U.S. NEWS LAW SCHOOL RANKING

ADMISSIONS
Admissions phone number: **(702) 895-2440**
Admissions email address: **request@law.unlv.edu**
Application website:
   http://www.law.unlv.edu/admissions_application.html
Application deadline for Fall 2009 admission: **03/15**

Admissions statistics:
Number of applicants for Fall 2007: **1,430**
Number of acceptances: **329**
Number enrolled: **106**
Acceptance rate: **23%**
GPA, 25th-75th percentile, entering class Fall 2007: **3.20-3.66**
LSAT, 25th-75th percentile, entering class Fall 2007: **156-161**

Part-time program:
Number of applicants for Fall 2007: **283**
Number of acceptances: **66**
Number enrolled: **47**
Acceptance rate: **23%**
GPA, 25th-75th percentile, entering class Fall 2007: **2.81-3.62**
LSAT, 25th-75th percentile, entering class Fall 2007: **154-158**

FINANCIAL AID
Financial aid phone number: **(702) 895-0630**
Financial aid application deadline: **02/01**
Tuition 2007-2008 academic year: In-state: full-time: **$10,502**; part-time: **$6,946**; Out-of-state: full-time: **$20,302**
Room and board: **$13,110**; books: **$900**; miscellaneous expenses: **$250**
Total of room/board/books/miscellaneous expenses: **$14,260**
University does not offer graduate student housing for which law students are eligible.

Financial aid profile
Percent of students that received grants for the 2006-2007 academic year: full-time: **49%**; part-time **14%**
Median grant amount: full-time: **$5,000**; part-time: **$3,170**
The average law-school debt of those in the Class of 2007 who borrowed: **$49,186**. Proportion who borrowed: **78%**

ACADEMIC PROGRAMS
Calendar: **semester**
Joint degrees awarded: **J.D./M.B.A.; J.D./M.S.W.; J.D./Ph.D.**
Typical first-year section size: Full-time: **55**; Part-time: **42**
Is there typically a "small section" of the first year class, other than Legal Writing, taught by full-time faculty?: Full-time: **no**; Part-time: **no**
Number of course titles, beyond the first year curriculum, offered last year: **82**
Percentages of upper division course sections, excluding seminars, with an enrollment of:
   Under 25: **76%**   25 to 49: **17%**
   50 to 74: **6%**   75 to 99: **1%**
   100+: **0%**
Areas of specialization: appellate advocacy, clinical training, dispute resolution, environmental law, intellectual property law, international law, tax law, trial advocacy

Fall 2007 faculty profile
Total teaching faculty: **34**. Full-time: **62%**; **52%** men, **48%** women, **38%** minorities. Part-time: **38%**; **100%** men, **0%** women, **0%** minorities
Student-to-faculty ratio: **14.0**

SPECIAL PROGRAMS *(as provided by law school):*
Students have a variety of opportunities for "learning by doing." Through clinical programs, externships, the Saltman Center for Conflict Resolution, and service learning courses, all students are ensured to have at least one service learning experience.

STUDENT BODY

Fall 2007 full-time enrollment: 341

Men: 53%	Women: 47%
African-American: 4.4%	American Indian: 2.3%
Asian-American: 12.0%	Mexican-American: 4.4%
Puerto Rican: 1.2%	Other Hisp-Amer: 3.5%
White: 62.8%	International: 0.3%
Unknown: 9.1%	

Fall 2007 part-time enrollment: 122

Men: 51%	Women: 49%
African-American: 7.4%	American Indian: 1.6%
Asian-American: 11.5%	Mexican-American: 3.3%
Puerto Rican: 0.8%	Other Hisp-Amer: 6.6%
White: 62.3%	International: 0.8%
Unknown: 5.7%	

Attrition rates for 2006-2007 full-time students
Percent of students discontinuing law school:

Men: 6%	Women: 4%
First-year students: 12%	Second-year students: 3%
Third-year students: 1%	

LIBRARY RESOURCES

Total volumes: 309,759
Total seats available for library users: 313

INFORMATION TECHNOLOGY

Number of wired network connections available to students: 1,104 total (in the law library, excluding computer labs: 475; in classrooms: 410; in computer labs: 50; elsewhere in the law school: 169)
Law school has a wireless network.
Students are not required to own a computer.

EMPLOYMENT AND SALARIES

Proportion of 2006 graduates employed at graduation:
N/A

Employed 9 months later, as of February 15, 2007: 92%
Salaries in the private sector (law firms, business, industry): $60,000–$90,000 (25th-75th percentile)
Median salary in the private sector: $75,000
Percentage in the private sector who reported salary information: 99%
Median salary in public service (government, judicial clerkships, academic posts, non-profits): $55,000

Percentage of 2006 graduates in:

Law firms: 48%	Government: 13%
Bus./industry: 8%	Judicial clerkship: 21%
Public interest: 5%	Unknown: 0%
Academia: 5%	

2006 graduates employed in-state: 84%
2006 graduates employed in foreign countries: 0%
Number of states where graduates are employed: 13
Percentage of 2006 graduates working in: New England: 0%, Middle Atlantic: 0%, East North Central: 1%, West North Central: 1%, South Atlantic: 2%, East South Central: 0%, West South Central: 0%, Mountain: 94%, Pacific: 2%, Unknown: 0%

BAR PASSAGE RATES

Based on 2006 graduates taking Summer 2006 or Winter 2007 exams. Most of the school's first-time test takers took the bar in Nevada.

77%
School's bar passage rate for first-time test takers

72%
Statewide bar passage rate for first-time test takers

University of New Mexico

- 1117 Stanford Drive NE, Albuquerque, NM, 87131-1431
- http://lawschool.unm.edu
- Public
- Year founded: 1947
- 2007-2008 tuition: In-state: full-time: $10,561; part-time: N/A; Out-of-state: full-time: $24,467
- Enrollment 2007-08 academic year: full-time: 347
- U.S. News 2009 law specialty ranking: clinical training: 5

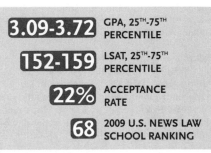

3.09-3.72 GPA, 25ᵀᴴ-75ᵀᴴ PERCENTILE

152-159 LSAT, 25ᵀᴴ-75ᵀᴴ PERCENTILE

22% ACCEPTANCE RATE

68 2009 U.S. NEWS LAW SCHOOL RANKING

ADMISSIONS
Admissions phone number: **(505) 277-0572**
Admissions email address: **admissions@law.unm.edu**
Application website: **http://lawschool.unm.edu**
Application deadline for Fall 2009 admission: **02/15**

Admissions statistics:
Number of applicants for Fall 2007: **1,175**
Number of acceptances: **264**
Number enrolled: **111**
Acceptance rate: **22%**
GPA, 25th-75th percentile, entering class Fall 2007: **3.09-3.72**
LSAT, 25th-75th percentile, entering class Fall 2007: **152-159**

FINANCIAL AID
Financial aid phone number: **(505) 277-0572**
Financial aid application deadline: **03/01**
Tuition 2007-2008 academic year: In-state: full-time: **$10,561**; part-time: N/A; Out-of-state: full-time: **$24,467**
Room and board: **$7,858**; books: **$1,040**; miscellaneous expenses: **$4,702**
Total of room/board/books/miscellaneous expenses: **$13,600**
University does not offer graduate student housing for which law students are eligible.

Financial aid profile
Percent of students that received grants for the 2006-2007 academic year: full-time: **24%**
Median grant amount: full-time: **$9,565**
The average law-school debt of those in the Class of 2007 who borrowed: **$34,558**. Proportion who borrowed: **91%**

ACADEMIC PROGRAMS
Calendar: **semester**
Joint degrees awarded: **J.D./M.B.A.; J.D./M.P.A.; J.D./M.L.A.S.; J.D./Ph.D.; J.D./M.S. Engineering**
Typical first-year section size: Full-time: **57**

Is there typically a "small section" of the first year class, other than Legal Writing, taught by full-time faculty?: Full-time: **yes**
Number of course titles, beyond the first year curriculum, offered last year: **110**
Percentages of upper division course sections, excluding seminars, with an enrollment of:

Under 25: **71%**   25 to 49: **18%**
50 to 74: **11%**   75 to 99: **0%**
100+: **0%**

Areas of specialization: appellate advocacy, clinical training, dispute resolution, environmental law, healthcare law, intellectual property law, international law, tax law, trial advocacy

Fall 2007 faculty profile
Total teaching faculty: **48**. Full-time: **69%**; **55%** men, **45%** women, **45%** minorities. Part-time: **31%**; **73%** men, **27%** women, **20%** minorities
Student-to-faculty ratio: **10.0**

SPECIAL PROGRAMS *(as provided by law school)*:
UNM Law School's curriculum stands out for its clinical, Indian, international, and natural resources law programs. The clinical program is nationally recognized as one of the country's best; the Indian law program offers the Indian law certificate; UNM offers summer law study in Guanajuato, Mexico; and the school is known for its faculty strength in natural resources and environmental law.

STUDENT BODY
Fall 2007 full-time enrollment: 347
Men: **49%**   Women: **51%**
African-American: **3.2%**   American Indian: **9.8%**
Asian-American: **2.3%**   Mexican-American: **29.4%**
Puerto Rican: **0.0%**   Other Hisp-Amer: **0.0%**
White: **46.4%**   International: **0.0%**
Unknown: **8.9%**

Attrition rates for 2006-2007 full-time students
Percent of students discontinuing law school:
Men: 3%   Women: 1%
First-year students: 5%   Second-year students: N/A
Third-year students: 1%

LIBRARY RESOURCES
Total volumes: 433,064
Total seats available for library users: 359

INFORMATION TECHNOLOGY
Number of wired network connections available to students: 331 total (in the law library, excluding computer labs: 143; in classrooms: 156; in computer labs: 12; elsewhere in the law school: 20)
Law school has a wireless network.
Students are required to own a computer.

EMPLOYMENT AND SALARIES
Proportion of 2006 graduates employed at graduation: 61%
Employed 9 months later, as of February 15, 2007: 99%
Salaries in the private sector (law firms, business, industry): $36,000–$72,000 (25th-75th percentile)
Median salary in the private sector: $53,000
Percentage in the private sector who reported salary information: 94%
Median salary in public service (government, judicial clerkships, academic posts, non-profits): $40,000

Percentage of 2006 graduates in:
Law firms: 50%   Government: 17%
Bus./industry: 6%   Judicial clerkship: 9%
Public interest: 12%   Unknown: 1%
Academia: 5%

2006 graduates employed in-state: 79%
2006 graduates employed in foreign countries: 1%
Number of states where graduates are employed: 13
Percentage of 2006 graduates working in: New England: 0%, Middle Atlantic: 1%, East North Central: 1%, West North Central: 1%, South Atlantic: 2%, East South Central: 1%, West South Central: 0%, Mountain: 87%, Pacific: 6%, Unknown: 0%

BAR PASSAGE RATES
Based on 2006 graduates taking Summer 2006 or Winter 2007 exams. Most of the school's first-time test takers took the bar in New Mexico.

92%
School's bar passage rate for first-time test takers

88%
Statewide bar passage rate for first-time test takers

Univ. of North Carolina–Chapel Hill

- Van Hecke-Wettach Hall, CB No. 3380, Chapel Hill, NC, 27599-3380
- http://www.law.unc.edu
- Public
- Year founded: 1843
- **2007-2008 tuition:** In-state: full-time: $13,004; part-time: N/A; Out-of-state: full-time: $25,422
- **Enrollment 2007-08 academic year:** full-time: 699
- **U.S. News 2009 law specialty ranking:** N/A

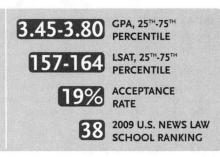

3.45-3.80 GPA, 25TH-75TH PERCENTILE

157-164 LSAT, 25TH-75TH PERCENTILE

19% ACCEPTANCE RATE

38 2009 U.S. NEWS LAW SCHOOL RANKING

ADMISSIONS

Admissions phone number: **(919) 962-5109**
Admissions email address: **law_admission@unc.edu**
Application website:
   http://www.law.unc.edu/PDFs/lawapplicationfinal.pdf
Application deadline for Fall 2009 admission: **02/01**

Admissions statistics:
Number of applicants for Fall 2007: **3,286**
Number of acceptances: **609**
Number enrolled: **241**
Acceptance rate: **19%**
GPA, 25th-75th percentile, entering class Fall 2007: **3.45-3.80**
LSAT, 25th-75th percentile, entering class Fall 2007: **157-164**

FINANCIAL AID

Financial aid phone number: **(919) 962-8396**
Financial aid application deadline: **03/01**
Tuition 2007-2008 academic year: In-state: full-time: **$13,004**; part-time: N/A; Out-of-state: full-time: **$25,422**
Room and board: **$12,330**; books: **$1,000**; miscellaneous expenses: **$3,970**
Total of room/board/books/miscellaneous expenses: **$17,300**
University offers graduate student housing for which law students are eligible.

Financial aid profile
Percent of students that received grants for the 2006-2007 academic year: full-time: **82%**
Median grant amount: full-time: **$2,200**
The average law-school debt of those in the Class of 2007 who borrowed: **$56,740**. Proportion who borrowed: **80%**

ACADEMIC PROGRAMS

Calendar: **semester**
Joint degrees awarded: **J.D./M.B.A.; J.D./M.P.A.; J.D./M.P.P.; J.D./M.P.H.; J.D./M.R.P.; J.D./M.S.W.; J.D./M.L.S.; J.D./M.I.S.; J.D./M.S.A.; J.D./M.M.C.**

Typical first-year section size: Full-time: **77**
Is there typically a "small section" of the first year class, other than Legal Writing, taught by full-time faculty?: Full-time: **yes**
Number of course titles, beyond the first year curriculum, offered last year: **110**
Percentages of upper division course sections, excluding seminars, with an enrollment of:

Under 25: **43%**	25 to 49: **39%**
50 to 74: **9%**	75 to 99: **5%**
100+: **3%**	

Areas of specialization: appellate advocacy, clinical training, dispute resolution, environmental law, healthcare law, intellectual property law, international law, tax law, trial advocacy

Fall 2007 faculty profile
Total teaching faculty: **101**. Full-time: **40%**; **58%** men, **43%** women, **18%** minorities. Part-time: **60%**; **64%** men, **36%** women, **18%** minorities
Student-to-faculty ratio: **15.7**

SPECIAL PROGRAMS *(as provided by law school):*

UNC offers externship placement to over 120 students. It has four clinical programs: civil litigation; community development law; immigration/human-rights policy; juvenile justice; and four centers: Banking and Finance; Civil Rights; Law and Government; Poverty, Work and Opportunity. UNC offers a summer program in Sydney, Australia, and has exchange programs with four European law schools.

STUDENT BODY
Fall 2007 full-time enrollment: 699

Men: **48%**	Women: **52%**
African-American: **7.2%**	American Indian: **2.0%**
Asian-American: **6.6%**	Mexican-American: **1.1%**
Puerto Rican: **0.0%**	Other Hisp-Amer: **4.1%**
White: **66.2%**	International: **0.0%**
Unknown: **12.7%**	

Attrition rates for 2006-2007 full-time students
Percent of students discontinuing law school:
Men: 2%   Women: 2%
First-year students: 4%   Second-year students: 0%
Third-year students: 0%

LIBRARY RESOURCES
Total volumes: 527,954
Total seats available for library users: 481

INFORMATION TECHNOLOGY
Number of wired network connections available to students: 563 total (in the law library, excluding computer labs: 175; in classrooms: 164; in computer labs: 0; elsewhere in the law school: 224)
Law school has a wireless network.
Students are not required to own a computer.

EMPLOYMENT AND SALARIES
Proportion of 2006 graduates employed at graduation: 63%
Employed 9 months later, as of February 15, 2007: 89%
Salaries in the private sector (law firms, business, industry): $70,000–$115,000 (25th-75th percentile)
Median salary in the private sector: $100,000
Percentage in the private sector who reported salary information: 63%
Median salary in public service (government, judicial clerkships, academic posts, non-profits): $45,218

Percentage of 2006 graduates in:
Law firms: 58%   Government: 11%
Bus./industry: 5%   Judicial clerkship: 13%
Public interest: 9%   Unknown: 2%
Academia: 2%

2006 graduates employed in-state: 58%
2006 graduates employed in foreign countries: 1%
Number of states where graduates are employed: 23
Percentage of 2006 graduates working in: New England: 1%, Middle Atlantic: 8%, East North Central: 2%, West North Central: 2%, South Atlantic: 77%, East South Central: 0%, West South Central: 1%, Mountain: 1%, Pacific: 6%, Unknown: 1%

BAR PASSAGE RATES
Based on 2006 graduates taking Summer 2006 or Winter 2007 exams. Most of the school's first-time test takers took the bar in North Carolina.

87%
School's bar passage rate for first-time test takers

74%
Statewide bar passage rate for first-time test takers

University of North Dakota

- 215 Centennial Drive, Stop 9003, Grand Forks, ND, 58202
- http://www.law.und.nodak.edu
- Public
- Year founded: 1899
- 2007-2008 tuition: In-state: full-time: $8,774; part-time: N/A; Out-of-state: full-time: $18,909
- Enrollment 2007-08 academic year: full-time: 249
- U.S. News 2009 law specialty ranking: N/A

3.02-3.73 GPA, 25TH-75TH PERCENTILE

147-154 LSAT, 25TH-75TH PERCENTILE

28% ACCEPTANCE RATE

Tier 4 2009 U.S. NEWS LAW SCHOOL RANKING

ADMISSIONS

Admissions phone number: (701) 777-2260
Admissions email address: hoffman@law.und.edu
Application website:
  http://www.law.und.nodak.edu/prostudents/index.php
Application deadline for Fall 2009 admission: 04/01

Admissions statistics:
Number of applicants for Fall 2007: 699
Number of acceptances: 199
Number enrolled: 79
Acceptance rate: 28%
GPA, 25th-75th percentile, entering class Fall 2007: 3.02-3.73
LSAT, 25th-75th percentile, entering class Fall 2007: 147-154

FINANCIAL AID

Financial aid phone number: (701) 777-6265
Financial aid application deadline: 04/15
Tuition 2007-2008 academic year: In-state: full-time: $8,774; part-time: N/A; Out-of-state: full-time: $18,909
Room and board: $8,250; books: $900; miscellaneous expenses: $4,500
Total of room/board/books/miscellaneous expenses: $13,650
University offers graduate student housing for which law students are eligible.

Financial aid profile
Percent of students that received grants for the 2006-2007 academic year: full-time: 34%
Median grant amount: full-time: $5,780
The average law-school debt of those in the Class of 2007 who borrowed: $53,367. Proportion who borrowed: 93%

ACADEMIC PROGRAMS

Calendar: semester
Joint degrees awarded: J.D./M.P.A.; J.D./M.B.A.
Typical first-year section size: Full-time: 78
Is there typically a "small section" of the first year class,
other than Legal Writing, taught by full-time faculty?:
  Full-time: no
Number of course titles, beyond the first year curriculum, offered last year: 58
Percentages of upper division course sections, excluding seminars, with an enrollment of:
  Under 25: 69%   25 to 49: 24%
  50 to 74: 6%   75 to 99: 2%
  100+: 0%
Areas of specialization: appellate advocacy, clinical training, dispute resolution, environmental law, intellectual property law, international law, tax law, trial advocacy

Fall 2007 faculty profile
Total teaching faculty: 25. Full-time: 56%; 57% men, 43% women, 21% minorities. Part-time: 44%; 73% men, 27% women, 9% minorities
Student-to-faculty ratio: 17.7

SPECIAL PROGRAMS (as provided by law school):

Law school clinic; externship program, including summer federal externships; legislative internships; summer classes; summer program with the University of Oslo, Norway; Tribal Judicial Institute; Tribal Gaming Institute; Tribal Environmental Law Project; Northern Plains Indian Law Center; Tribal Advocacy Training Program.

STUDENT BODY

Fall 2007 full-time enrollment: 249
Men: 53%   Women: 47%
African-American: 1.2%   American Indian: 4.4%
Asian-American: 3.6%   Mexican-American: 0.4%
Puerto Rican: 0.0%   Other Hisp-Amer: 2.8%
White: 65.1%   International: 1.6%
Unknown: 20.9%

Attrition rates for 2006-2007 full-time students
Percent of students discontinuing law school:
Men: 5%   Women: 3%
First-year students: 5%   Second-year students: 5%
Third-year students: N/A

LIBRARY RESOURCES

Total volumes: 326,463
Total seats available for library users: 210

INFORMATION TECHNOLOGY

Number of wired network connections available to students: 123 total (in the law library, excluding computer labs: 81; in classrooms: 2; in computer labs: 0; elsewhere in the law school: 40)
Law school has a wireless network.
Students are not required to own a computer.

EMPLOYMENT AND SALARIES

Proportion of 2006 graduates employed at graduation: N/A
Employed 9 months later, as of February 15, 2007: 92%
Salaries in the private sector (law firms, business, industry): $37,000–$45,000 (25th-75th percentile)
Median salary in the private sector: $42,500
Percentage in the private sector who reported salary information: 64%
Median salary in public service (government, judicial clerkships, academic posts, non-profits): $43,000

Percentage of 2006 graduates in:

Law firms: 44%	Government: 13%
Bus./industry: 4%	Judicial clerkship: 31%
Public interest: 8%	Unknown: 0%
Academia: 0%	

2006 graduates employed in-state: 50%
2006 graduates employed in foreign countries: 0%
Number of states where graduates are employed: 10
Percentage of 2006 graduates working in: New England: N/A, Middle Atlantic: N/A, East North Central: N/A, West North Central: 85%, South Atlantic: 6%, East South Central: N/A, West South Central: N/A, Mountain: 7%, Pacific: 2%, Unknown: 0%

BAR PASSAGE RATES

Based on 2006 graduates taking Summer 2006 or Winter 2007 exams. Most of the school's first-time test takers took the bar in North Dakota.

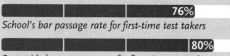

76%
School's bar passage rate for first-time test takers

80%
Statewide bar passage rate for first-time test takers

University of Notre Dame

■ PO Box 780, Notre Dame, IN, 46556-0780
■ http://www.lawadmissions.nd.edu
■ Private
■ Year founded: 1869
■ 2007-2008 tuition: full-time: $35,950; part-time: N/A
■ Enrollment 2007-08 academic year: full-time: 563; part-time: 1
■ U.S. News 2009 law specialty ranking: trial advocacy: 12

3.40-3.76 GPA, 25ᵀᴴ-75ᵀᴴ PERCENTILE

164-167 LSAT, 25ᵀᴴ-75ᵀᴴ PERCENTILE

19% ACCEPTANCE RATE

22 2009 U.S. NEWS LAW SCHOOL RANKING

ADMISSIONS
Admissions phone number: **(574) 631-6626**
Admissions email address: **lawadmit@nd.edu**
Application website:
   http://www.lawadmissions.nd.edu/admissions/
   methods.html
Application deadline for Fall 2009 admission: **03/01**

Admissions statistics:
Number of applicants for Fall 2007: **3,499**
Number of acceptances: **651**
Number enrolled: **176**
Acceptance rate: **19%**
GPA, 25th-75th percentile, entering class Fall 2007: **3.40-3.76**
LSAT, 25th-75th percentile, entering class Fall 2007: **164-167**

FINANCIAL AID
Financial aid phone number: **(574) 631-6626**
Financial aid application deadline: **02/15**
Tuition 2007-2008 academic year: full-time: **$35,950**; part-time: **N/A**
Room and board: **$7,650**; books: **$1,300**; miscellaneous expenses: **$6,450**
Total of room/board/books/miscellaneous expenses: **$15,400**
University offers graduate student housing for which law students are eligible.

Financial aid profile
Percent of students that received grants for the 2006-2007 academic year: full-time: **67%**
Median grant amount: full-time: **$13,000**
The average law-school debt of those in the Class of 2007 who borrowed: **$87,849**. Proportion who borrowed: **85%**

ACADEMIC PROGRAMS
Calendar: **semester**

Joint degrees awarded: **J.D./M.B.A.; J.D./M.A.; J.D./M.S.; J.D./Ph.D.**
Typical first-year section size: Full-time: **99**
Is there typically a "small section" of the first year class, other than Legal Writing, taught by full-time faculty?: Full-time: **no**
Number of course titles, beyond the first year curriculum, offered last year: **113**
Percentages of upper division course sections, excluding seminars, with an enrollment of:
   Under 25: **58%**   25 to 49: **26%**
   50 to 74: **10%**   75 to 99: **5%**
   100+: **1%**
Areas of specialization: appellate advocacy, clinical training, dispute resolution, environmental law, healthcare law, intellectual property law, international law, tax law, trial advocacy

Fall 2007 faculty profile
Total teaching faculty: **92**. Full-time: **40%**; **70%** men, **30%** women, **16%** minorities. Part-time: **60%**; **56%** men, **44%** women, **4%** minorities
Student-to-faculty ratio: **14.7**

SPECIAL PROGRAMS *(as provided by law school):*
Second year in London; trial advocacy; Center for Civil and Human Rights; legal aid clinic; summer London program; public defender externship.

STUDENT BODY
Fall 2007 full-time enrollment: **563**
Men: **63%**   Women: **37%**
African-American: **4.3%**   American Indian: **1.4%**
Asian-American: **7.1%**   Mexican-American: **1.8%**
Puerto Rican: **0.0%**   Other Hisp-Amer: **7.5%**
White: **63.2%**   International: **0.7%**
Unknown: **14.0%**

Fall 2007 part-time enrollment: 1

Men: **0%**
African-American: **0.0%**
Asian-American: **0.0%**
Puerto Rican: **0.0%**
White: **100.0%**
Unknown: **0.0%**

Women: **100%**
American Indian: **0.0%**
Mexican-American: **0.0%**
Other Hisp-Amer: **0.0%**
International: **0.0%**

Attrition rates for 2006-2007 full-time students

Percent of students discontinuing law school:

Men: **2%**
First-year students: **5%**
Third-year students: **1%**

Women: **1%**
Second-year students: **N/A**

LIBRARY RESOURCES

Total volumes: **650,225**
Total seats available for library users: **416**

INFORMATION TECHNOLOGY

Number of wired network connections available to students: **118** total (in the law library, excluding computer labs: **100**; in classrooms: **8**; in computer labs: **0**; elsewhere in the law school: **10**)
Law school has a wireless network.
Students are not required to own a computer.

EMPLOYMENT AND SALARIES

Proportion of 2006 graduates employed at graduation: **84%**
Employed 9 months later, as of February 15, 2007: **97%**
Salaries in the private sector (law firms, business, industry): **$90,000–$125,000** (25th-75th percentile)
Median salary in the private sector: **$110,000**

Percentage in the private sector who reported salary information: **69%**
Median salary in public service (government, judicial clerkships, academic posts, non-profits): **$51,972**

Percentage of 2006 graduates in:

Law firms: **65%**
Bus./industry: **6%**
Public interest: **6%**
Academia: **2%**

Government: **13%**
Judicial clerkship: **10%**
Unknown: **0%**

2006 graduates employed in-state: **10%**
2006 graduates employed in foreign countries: **1%**
Number of states where graduates are employed: **27**
Percentage of 2006 graduates working in: New England: **4%**, Middle Atlantic: **16%**, East North Central: **36%**, West North Central: **4%**, South Atlantic: **22%**, East South Central: **1%**, West South Central: **4%**, Mountain: **4%**, Pacific: **9%**, Unknown: **0%**

BAR PASSAGE RATES

Based on 2006 graduates taking Summer 2006 or Winter 2007 exams. Most of the school's first-time test takers took the bar in Illinois.

90%
School's bar passage rate for first-time test takers

87%
Statewide bar passage rate for first-time test takers

University of Oklahoma

■ Andrew M. Coats Hall, 300 Timberdell Road, Norman, OK, 73019-5081
■ http://www.law.ou.edu
■ Public
■ Year founded: 1909
■ 2007-2008 tuition: In-state: full-time: $15,025; part-time: N/A; Out-of-state: full-time: $24,953
■ Enrollment 2007-08 academic year: full-time: 510
■ U.S. News 2009 law specialty ranking: N/A

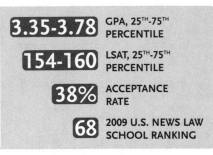

3.35-3.78 GPA, 25TH-75TH PERCENTILE

154-160 LSAT, 25TH-75TH PERCENTILE

38% ACCEPTANCE RATE

68 2009 U.S. NEWS LAW SCHOOL RANKING

ADMISSIONS
Admissions phone number: **(405) 325-4728**
Admissions email address: **admissions@ou.edu**
Application website:
  http://www.law.ou.edu/prospective/admissions
Application deadline for Fall 2009 admission: **03/15**

Admissions statistics:
Number of applicants for Fall 2007: **1,130**
Number of acceptances: **434**
Number enrolled: **174**
Acceptance rate: **38%**
GPA, 25th-75th percentile, entering class Fall 2007: **3.35-3.78**
LSAT, 25th-75th percentile, entering class Fall 2007: **154-160**

FINANCIAL AID
Financial aid phone number: **(405) 325-4521**
Financial aid application deadline: **03/01**
Tuition 2007-2008 academic year: In-state: full-time: **$15,025**; part-time: N/A; Out-of-state: full-time: **$24,953**
Room and board: **$9,906**; books: **$1,110**; miscellaneous expenses: **$4,538**
Total of room/board/books/miscellaneous expenses: **$15,554**
University offers graduate student housing for which law students are eligible.

Financial aid profile
Percent of students that received grants for the 2006-2007 academic year: full-time: **63%**
Median grant amount: full-time: **$2,500**
The average law-school debt of those in the Class of 2007 who borrowed: **$68,208**. Proportion who borrowed: **69%**

ACADEMIC PROGRAMS
Calendar: **semester**
Joint degrees awarded: **J.D./M.B.A.; J.D./M.P.H.**

Typical first-year section size: Full-time: **38**
Is there typically a "small section" of the first year class, other than Legal Writing, taught by full-time faculty?: Full-time: **yes**
Number of course titles, beyond the first year curriculum, offered last year: **99**
Percentages of upper division course sections, excluding seminars, with an enrollment of:
  Under 25: **43%**   25 to 49: **34%**
  50 to 74: **17%**   75 to 99: **5%**
  100+: **0%**
Areas of specialization: appellate advocacy, clinical training, dispute resolution, environmental law, healthcare law, intellectual property law, international law, tax law, trial advocacy

Fall 2007 faculty profile
Total teaching faculty: **49**. Full-time: **65%; 69%** men, **31%** women, **19%** minorities. Part-time: **35%; 88%** men, **12%** women, **12%** minorities
Student-to-faculty ratio: **11.9**

SPECIAL PROGRAMS *(as provided by law school):*
The College of Law offers students the opportunity to participate in live-client civil and criminal clinics, judicial externships, and internships with the United States Department of Justice and the United States Department of the Interior in Washington, D.C. Also, the school offers a study-abroad program with Brasenose College in Oxford, England.

STUDENT BODY
Fall 2007 full-time enrollment: **510**
Men: **56%**   Women: **44%**
African-American: **5.7%**   American Indian: **9.8%**
Asian-American: **3.3%**   Mexican-American: **3.7%**
Puerto Rican: **0.0%**   Other Hisp-Amer: **0.0%**
White: **72.5%**   International: **0.4%**
Unknown: **4.5%**

Attrition rates for 2006-2007 full-time students
Percent of students discontinuing law school:
Men: 3% Women: 2%
First-year students: 7% Second-year students: 1%
Third-year students: N/A

LIBRARY RESOURCES
Total volumes: 355,598
Total seats available for library users: 410

INFORMATION TECHNOLOGY
Number of wired network connections available to students: 106 total (in the law library, excluding computer labs: 92; in classrooms: 14; in computer labs: 0; elsewhere in the law school: 0)
Law school has a wireless network.
Students are not required to own a computer.

EMPLOYMENT AND SALARIES
Proportion of 2006 graduates employed at graduation: 82%
Employed 9 months later, as of February 15, 2007: 96%
Salaries in the private sector (law firms, business, industry): $52,000–$88,000 (25th-75th percentile)
Median salary in the private sector: $65,000
Percentage in the private sector who reported salary information: 47%
Median salary in public service (government, judicial clerkships, academic posts, non-profits): $40,000

Percentage of 2006 graduates in:
Law firms: 58% Government: 16%
Bus./industry: 18% Judicial clerkship: 3%
Public interest: 5% Unknown: 0%
Academia: 0%

2006 graduates employed in-state: 73%
2006 graduates employed in foreign countries: 0%
Number of states where graduates are employed: 12
Percentage of 2006 graduates working in: New England: 1%, Middle Atlantic: 0%, East North Central: 1%, West North Central: 1%, South Atlantic: 3%, East South Central: 0%, West South Central: 92%, Mountain: 1%, Pacific: 1%, Unknown: 0%

BAR PASSAGE RATES
Based on 2006 graduates taking Summer 2006 or Winter 2007 exams. Most of the school's first-time test takers took the bar in Oklahoma.

| 96% |

School's bar passage rate for first-time test takers

| 92% |

Statewide bar passage rate for first-time test takers

University of Oregon

- 1221 University of Oregon, Eugene, OR, 97403-1221
- http://www.law.uoregon.edu
- Public
- **Year founded:** 1884
- **2007-2008 tuition:** In-state: full-time: $19,596; part-time: N/A; Out-of-state: full-time: $24,396
- **Enrollment 2007-08 academic year:** full-time: 528
- **U.S. News 2009 law specialty ranking:** dispute resolution: 7, environmental law: 9

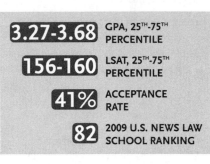

3.27-3.68 GPA, 25ᵀᴴ-75ᵀᴴ PERCENTILE

156-160 LSAT, 25ᵀᴴ-75ᵀᴴ PERCENTILE

41% ACCEPTANCE RATE

82 2009 U.S. NEWS LAW SCHOOL RANKING

ADMISSIONS

Admissions phone number: **(541) 346-3846**
Admissions email address: **admissions@law.uoregon.edu**
Application website:
  http://www.law.uoregon.edu/admissions
Application deadline for Fall 2009 admission: **03/01**

Admissions statistics:

Number of applicants for Fall 2007: **2,026**
Number of acceptances: **826**
Number enrolled: **178**
Acceptance rate: **41%**
GPA, 25th-75th percentile, entering class Fall 2007: **3.27-3.68**
LSAT, 25th-75th percentile, entering class Fall 2007: **156-160**

FINANCIAL AID

Financial aid phone number: **(800) 760-6953**
Financial aid application deadline: **03/01**
Tuition 2007-2008 academic year: In-state: full-time: **$19,596**; part-time: **N/A**; Out-of-state: full-time: **$24,396**
Room and board: **$7,848**; books: **$1,050**; miscellaneous expenses: **$2,556**
Total of room/board/books/miscellaneous expenses: **$11,454**
University offers graduate student housing for which law students are eligible.

Financial aid profile

Percent of students that received grants for the 2006-2007 academic year: full-time: **63%**
Median grant amount: full-time: **$4,000**
The average law-school debt of those in the Class of 2007 who borrowed: **$71,136**. Proportion who borrowed: **91%**

ACADEMIC PROGRAMS

Calendar: **semester**
Joint degrees awarded: **J.D./M.B.A.; J.D./M.A./M.S. Environmental Studies; J.D./M.P.A.; J.D./M.A. International Studies; J.D./M.C.R.P.**

Typical first-year section size: Full-time: **61**
Is there typically a "small section" of the first year class, other than Legal Writing, taught by full-time faculty?: Full-time: **no**
Number of course titles, beyond the first year curriculum, offered last year: **124**
Percentages of upper division course sections, excluding seminars, with an enrollment of:

Under 25: **58%**	25 to 49: **17%**
50 to 74: **14%**	75 to 99: **10%**
100+: **2%**	

Areas of specialization: appellate advocacy, clinical training, dispute resolution, environmental law, healthcare law, intellectual property law, international law, tax law, trial advocacy

Fall 2007 faculty profile

Total teaching faculty: **67**. Full-time: **45%**; 60% men, 40% women, 23% minorities. Part-time: **55%**; 68% men, 32% women, 3% minorities
Student-to-faculty ratio: **17.6**

SPECIAL PROGRAMS *(as provided by law school):*

Certificates in Environmental, Criminal, Intellectual Property, Business, Tax, Public Interest, and Animal Law. Seven clinics; externships around the world; internships in several practice areas. Summer: environmental law, Indian law, summer-abroad partnerships. Law centers: International Environmental Law, National Crime Victims Law Institute, National Animal Law, National Environmental Defense.

STUDENT BODY

Fall 2007 full-time enrollment: 528

Men: **58%**	Women: **42%**
African-American: **2.8%**	American Indian: **1.7%**
Asian-American: **9.3%**	Mexican-American: **0.9%**
Puerto Rican: **0.0%**	Other Hisp-Amer: **3.0%**
White: **81.1%**	International: **1.1%**
Unknown: **0.0%**	

Attrition rates for 2006-2007 full-time students
Percent of students discontinuing law school:
Men: **4%**   Women: **2%**
First-year students: **6%**   Second-year students: **3%**
Third-year students: **1%**

LIBRARY RESOURCES
Total volumes: **375,791**
Total seats available for library users: **296**

INFORMATION TECHNOLOGY
Number of wired network connections available to students: **1,370** total (in the law library, excluding computer labs: **288**; in classrooms: **632**; in computer labs: **16**; elsewhere in the law school: **434**)
Law school has a wireless network.
Students are required to own a computer.

EMPLOYMENT AND SALARIES
Proportion of 2006 graduates employed at graduation: **63%**
Employed 9 months later, as of February 15, 2007: **90%**
Salaries in the private sector (law firms, business, industry): **$48,000–$89,000** (25th-75th percentile)
Median salary in the private sector: **$62,000**
Percentage in the private sector who reported salary information: **90%**
Median salary in public service (government, judicial clerkships, academic posts, non-profits): **$46,000**

Percentage of 2006 graduates in:

Law firms: **47%**	Government: **15%**
Bus./industry: **11%**	Judicial clerkship: **12%**
Public interest: **13%**	Unknown: **1%**
Academia: **1%**	

2006 graduates employed in-state: **56%**
2006 graduates employed in foreign countries: **0%**
Number of states where graduates are employed: **20**
Percentage of 2006 graduates working in: New England: **1%**, Middle Atlantic: **1%**, East North Central: **1%**, West North Central: **0%**, South Atlantic: **3%**, East South Central: **0%**, West South Central: **1%**, Mountain: **12%**, Pacific: **81%**, Unknown: **0%**

BAR PASSAGE RATES
Based on 2006 graduates taking Summer 2006 or Winter 2007 exams. Most of the school's first-time test takers took the bar in Oregon.

85%
School's bar passage rate for first-time test takers

82%
Statewide bar passage rate for first-time test takers

University of Pennsylvania

- 3400 Chestnut Street, Philadelphia, PA, 19104-6204
- http://www.law.upenn.edu
- Private
- Year founded: 1790
- 2007-2008 tuition: full-time: $41,960; part-time: N/A
- Enrollment 2007-08 academic year: full-time: 782
- U.S. News 2009 law specialty ranking: intellectual property law: 26, tax law: 19

3.52-3.86 GPA, 25TH-75TH PERCENTILE

166-171 LSAT, 25TH-75TH PERCENTILE

16% ACCEPTANCE RATE

7 2009 U.S. NEWS LAW SCHOOL RANKING

ADMISSIONS

Admissions phone number: **(215) 898-7400**
Admissions email address: **admissions@law.upenn.edu**
Application website: **http://www.law.upenn.edu/ prospective/jd/apply/index.html**
Application deadline for Fall 2009 admission: **02/15**

Admissions statistics:
Number of applicants for Fall 2007: **5,604**
Number of acceptances: **913**
Number enrolled: **260**
Acceptance rate: **16%**
GPA, 25th-75th percentile, entering class Fall 2007: **3.52-3.86**
LSAT, 25th-75th percentile, entering class Fall 2007: **166-171**

FINANCIAL AID

Financial aid phone number: **(215) 898-7400**
Financial aid application deadline: **03/01**
Tuition 2007-2008 academic year: full-time: **$41,960**; part-time: N/A
Room and board: **$11,695**; books: **$1,150**; miscellaneous expenses: **$4,855**
Total of room/board/books/miscellaneous expenses: **$17,700**
University offers graduate student housing for which law students are eligible.

Financial aid profile
Percent of students that received grants for the 2006-2007 academic year: full-time: **33%**
Median grant amount: full-time: **$14,080**
The average law-school debt of those in the Class of 2007 who borrowed: **$100,701**. Proportion who borrowed: **89%**

ACADEMIC PROGRAMS

Calendar: **semester**
Joint degrees awarded: **J.D./M. Bioethics; J.D./M.B.A.; J.D./M.C.P. City Planning; J.D./M.A./M.S. Criminology; J.D./M.A./M.S.Ed.; J.D./M.E.S.; J.D./M.G.A.; J.D./A.M.**
Islamic Studies; **J.D./M.A. Philosophy; J.D./Ph.D. Communications; J.D./Ph.D. Economics; J.D./M.P.H.; J.D./M.S.W.; J.D./Ph.D. American Legal History; J.D./BSE Engineering; J.D./Ph.D. Philosophy; J.D./M.A. Global Business Law; J.D./M.D.; J.D./M.A. History**
Typical first-year section size: Full-time: **83**
Is there typically a "small section" of the first year class, other than Legal Writing, taught by full-time faculty?: Full-time: **no**
Number of course titles, beyond the first year curriculum, offered last year: **157**
Percentages of upper division course sections, excluding seminars, with an enrollment of:
Under 25: **45%** 25 to 49: **34%**
50 to 74: **10%** 75 to 99: **6%**
100+: **5%**
Areas of specialization: appellate advocacy, clinical training, dispute resolution, environmental law, healthcare law, intellectual property law, international law, tax law, trial advocacy

Fall 2007 faculty profile
Total teaching faculty: **133**. Full-time: **49%**; **74%** men, **26%** women, **11%** minorities. Part-time: **51%**; **74%** men, **26%** women, **15%** minorities
Student-to-faculty ratio: **12.1**

SPECIAL PROGRAMS (as provided by law school):
Special program: cross-disciplinary study. Faculty: Over 75 percent hold nonlaw advanced degrees. Programs: joint degrees and Certificates with nation's finest graduate and professional schools (e.g., Wharton, Annenberg). Public interest and clinics; institutes and programs include economics, health, international, philosophy, criminal, intellectual property/technology, legal history, and tax.

STUDENT BODY
Fall 2007 full-time enrollment: 782
Men: **54%** Women: **46%**
African-American: **7.4%** American Indian: **0.4%**
Asian-American: **9.1%** Mexican-American: **1.0%**

Puerto Rican: **1.3%**
White: **67.5%**
Unknown: **4.1%**

Other Hisp-Amer: **5.6%**
International: **3.6%**

Attrition rates for 2006-2007 full-time students
Percent of students discontinuing law school:
Men: **N/A**
First-year students: **N/A**
Third-year students: **N/A**

Women: **N/A**
Second-year students: **N/A**

LIBRARY RESOURCES
Total volumes: **850,471**
Total seats available for library users: **519**

INFORMATION TECHNOLOGY
Number of wired network connections available to students: **108** total (in the law library, excluding computer labs: **18**; in classrooms: **50**; in computer labs: **0**; elsewhere in the law school: **40**)
Law school has a wireless network.
Students are not required to own a computer.

EMPLOYMENT AND SALARIES
Proportion of 2006 graduates employed at graduation: **95%**
Employed 9 months later, as of February 15, 2007: **98%**
Salaries in the private sector (law firms, business, industry): **$135,000–$145,000** (25th-75th percentile)
Median salary in the private sector: **$145,000**
Percentage in the private sector who reported salary information: **96%**
Median salary in public service (government, judicial clerkships, academic posts, non-profits): **$50,000**

Percentage of 2006 graduates in:
Law firms: **80%**
Bus./industry: **5%**
Public interest: **2%**
Academia: **0%**

Government: **1%**
Judicial clerkship: **13%**
Unknown: **0%**

2006 graduates employed in-state: **21%**
2006 graduates employed in foreign countries: **1%**
Number of states where graduates are employed: **19**
Percentage of 2006 graduates working in: New England: **4%**, Middle Atlantic: **65%**, East North Central: **3%**, West North Central: **2%**, South Atlantic: **13%**, East South Central: **0%**, West South Central: **2%**, Mountain: **1%**, Pacific: **10%**, Unknown: **0%**

BAR PASSAGE RATES
Based on 2006 graduates taking Summer 2006 or Winter 2007 exams. Most of the school's first-time test takers took the bar in New York.

94%
School's bar passage rate for first-time test takers

77%
Statewide bar passage rate for first-time test takers

University of Pittsburgh

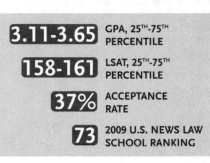

■ 3900 Forbes Avenue, Pittsburgh, PA, 15260
■ http://www.law.pitt.edu
■ Public
■ Year founded: 1895
■ 2007-2008 tuition: In-state: full-time: $22,106; part-time: N/A; Out-of-state: full-time: $30,362
■ Enrollment 2007-08 academic year: full-time: 714
■ U.S. News 2009 law specialty ranking: intellectual property law: 28

3.11-3.65 GPA, 25TH-75TH PERCENTILE

158-161 LSAT, 25TH-75TH PERCENTILE

37% ACCEPTANCE RATE

73 2009 U.S. NEWS LAW SCHOOL RANKING

ADMISSIONS

Admissions phone number: **(412) 648-1415**
Admissions email address: **admissions@law.pitt.edu**
Application website: **N/A**
Application deadline for Fall 2009 admission: **03/01**

Admissions statistics:
Number of applicants for Fall 2007: **2,095**
Number of acceptances: **773**
Number enrolled: **242**
Acceptance rate: **37%**
GPA, 25th-75th percentile, entering class Fall 2007: **3.11-3.65**
LSAT, 25th-75th percentile, entering class Fall 2007: **158-161**

FINANCIAL AID

Financial aid phone number: **(412) 648-1415**
Financial aid application deadline: **03/01**
Tuition 2007-2008 academic year: In-state: full-time: **$22,106**; part-time: **N/A**; Out-of-state: full-time: **$30,362**
Room and board: **$14,910**; books: **$1,500**; miscellaneous expenses: **$690**
Total of room/board/books/miscellaneous expenses: **$17,100**
University does not offer graduate student housing for which law students are eligible.

Financial aid profile
Percent of students that received grants for the 2006-2007 academic year: full-time: **53%**
Median grant amount: full-time: **$10,000**
The average law-school debt of those in the Class of 2007 who borrowed: **$71,787**. Proportion who borrowed: **79%**

ACADEMIC PROGRAMS

Calendar: **semester**
Joint degrees awarded: **J.D./M.B.A.; J.D./M.P.I.A.; J.D./M.P.H.; J.D./M.I.D.; J.D./M.A.; J.D./M.S. (CMU); J.D./M.P.A.; J.D./M.S.W; J.D./M.B.A. (CMU)**

Typical first-year section size: Full-time: **82**
Is there typically a "small section" of the first year class, other than Legal Writing, taught by full-time faculty?: Full-time: **yes**
Number of course titles, beyond the first year curriculum, offered last year: **189**
Percentages of upper division course sections, excluding seminars, with an enrollment of:
Under 25: **62%**   25 to 49: **21%**
50 to 74: **10%**   75 to 99: **5%**
100+: **2%**
Areas of specialization: appellate advocacy, clinical training, dispute resolution, environmental law, healthcare law, intellectual property law, international law, tax law, trial advocacy

Fall 2007 faculty profile
Total teaching faculty: **134**. Full-time: **34%**; **67%** men, **33%** women, **13%** minorities. Part-time: **66%**; **72%** men, **28%** women, **5%** minorities
Student-to-faculty ratio: **15.3**

SPECIAL PROGRAMS *(as provided by law school):*
The school has five Certificate programs and six clinics. A majority of students enroll in the externship program. The languages for lawyers program is a unique curricular offering, and students can serve as editors for JURIST, an award-winning website. The Mellon program has been key to the school's success in graduating its students.

STUDENT BODY
Fall 2007 full-time enrollment: **714**
Men: **57%**   Women: **43%**
African-American: **5.0%**   American Indian: **0.0%**
Asian-American: **7.1%**   Mexican-American: **0.3%**
Puerto Rican: **0.6%**   Other Hisp-Amer: **1.7%**
White: **61.5%**   International: **0.0%**
Unknown: **23.8%**

Attrition rates for 2006-2007 full-time students
Percent of students discontinuing law school:
Men: 2%   Women: 2%
First-year students: 6%   Second-year students: N/A
Third-year students: N/A

LIBRARY RESOURCES
Total volumes: 456,066
Total seats available for library users: 438

INFORMATION TECHNOLOGY
Number of wired network connections available to students: 282 total (in the law library, excluding computer labs: 55; in classrooms: 196; in computer labs: 31; elsewhere in the law school: 0)
Law school has a wireless network.
Students are not required to own a computer.

EMPLOYMENT AND SALARIES
Proportion of 2006 graduates employed at graduation: 74%
Employed 9 months later, as of February 15, 2007: 94%
Salaries in the private sector (law firms, business, industry): $53,500–$120,000 (25th-75th percentile)
Median salary in the private sector: $75,000
Percentage in the private sector who reported salary information: 60%
Median salary in public service (government, judicial clerkships, academic posts, non-profits): $40,000

Percentage of 2006 graduates in:
Law firms: 57%   Government: 7%
Bus./industry: 17%   Judicial clerkship: 11%
Public interest: 6%   Unknown: 2%
Academia: 2%

2006 graduates employed in-state: 63%
2006 graduates employed in foreign countries: 1%
Number of states where graduates are employed: 24
Percentage of 2006 graduates working in: New England: 1%, Middle Atlantic: 70%, East North Central: 6%, West North Central: 1%, South Atlantic: 14%, East South Central: 1%, West South Central: 1%, Mountain: 4%, Pacific: 3%, Unknown: 0%

BAR PASSAGE RATES
Based on 2006 graduates taking Summer 2006 or Winter 2007 exams. Most of the school's first-time test takers took the bar in Pennsylvania.

90%
School's bar passage rate for first-time test takers

83%
Statewide bar passage rate for first-time test takers

University of Richmond (Williams)

■ 28 Westhampton Way, Richmond, VA, 23173
■ http://law.richmond.edu
■ Private
■ Year founded: 1870
■ 2007-2008 tuition: full-time: $30,010; part-time: $1,500/credit hour
■ Enrollment 2007-08 academic year: full-time: 486; part-time: 1
■ U.S. News 2009 law specialty ranking: N/A

3.23-3.66 GPA, 25TH-75TH PERCENTILE

158-162 LSAT, 25TH-75TH PERCENTILE

35% ACCEPTANCE RATE

68 2009 U.S. NEWS LAW SCHOOL RANKING

ADMISSIONS

Admissions phone number: **(804) 289-8189**
Admissions email address: **mrahman@richmond.edu**
Application website:
   http://law.richmond.edu/application/application.htm
Application deadline for Fall 2009 admission: **03/01**

Admissions statistics:
Number of applicants for Fall 2007: **1,886**
Number of acceptances: **655**
Number enrolled: **159**
Acceptance rate: **35%**
GPA, 25th-75th percentile, entering class Fall 2007: **3.23-3.66**
LSAT, 25th-75th percentile, entering class Fall 2007: **158-162**

FINANCIAL AID

Financial aid phone number: **(804) 289-8438**
Financial aid application deadline: **02/25**
Tuition 2007-2008 academic year: full-time: **$30,010**; part-time: **$1,500/credit hour**
Room and board: **$9,360**; books: **$1,200**; miscellaneous expenses: **$3,710**
Total of room/board/books/miscellaneous expenses: **$14,270**
University offers graduate student housing for which law students are eligible.

Financial aid profile
Percent of students that received grants for the 2006-2007 academic year: full-time: **51%**
Median grant amount: full-time: **$7,500**
The average law-school debt of those in the Class of 2007 who borrowed: **$84,714**. Proportion who borrowed: **88%**

ACADEMIC PROGRAMS
Calendar: **semester**
Joint degrees awarded: **J.D./M.B.A.; J.D./M.S.W.; J.D./M.P.A.; J.D./M.H.A.; J.D./M.U.P.**

Typical first-year section size: Full-time: **55**
Is there typically a "small section" of the first year class, other than Legal Writing, taught by full-time faculty?: Full-time: **yes**
Number of course titles, beyond the first year curriculum, offered last year: **90**
Percentages of upper division course sections, excluding seminars, with an enrollment of:
   Under 25: **69%**   25 to 49: **13%**
   50 to 74: **7%**   75 to 99: **10%**
   100+: **0%**
Areas of specialization: appellate advocacy, clinical training, dispute resolution, environmental law, healthcare law, intellectual property law, international law, tax law, trial advocacy

Fall 2007 faculty profile
Total teaching faculty: **135**. Full-time: **19%**; **65%** men, **35%** women, **12%** minorities. Part-time: **81%**; **72%** men, **28%** women, **6%** minorities
Student-to-faculty ratio: **15.6**

SPECIAL PROGRAMS *(as provided by law school):*
Juvenile delinquency clinic, mental disabilities clinic, juvenile law and policy clinic, wrongful conviction clinic, clinical placement program, Merhige Center for Environmental Studies, Intellectual Property Center, National Family Law Center. Summer study abroad in Cambridge, England. John Marshall Scholars Program.

STUDENT BODY
Fall 2007 full-time enrollment: 486
Men: **51%**   Women: **49%**
African-American: **8.0%**   American Indian: **0.6%**
Asian-American: **4.7%**   Mexican-American: **0.0%**
Puerto Rican: **0.0%**   Other Hisp-Amer: **0.4%**
White: **86.2%**   International: **0.0%**
Unknown: **0.0%**

Fall 2007 part-time enrollment: 1

Men: 100%	Women: 0%
African-American: 0.0%	American Indian: 0.0%
Asian-American: 0.0%	Mexican-American: 0.0%
Puerto Rican: 0.0%	Other Hisp-Amer: 0.0%
White: 100.0%	International: 0.0%
Unknown: 0.0%	

Attrition rates for 2006-2007 full-time students
Percent of students discontinuing law school:

Men: 1%	Women: 3%
First-year students: 6%	Second-year students: N/A
Third-year students: N/A	

LIBRARY RESOURCES
Total volumes: 391,009
Total seats available for library users: 640

INFORMATION TECHNOLOGY
Number of wired network connections available to students: 890 total (in the law library, excluding computer labs: 480; in classrooms: 380; in computer labs: 5; elsewhere in the law school: 25)
Law school has a wireless network.
Students are required to own a computer.

EMPLOYMENT AND SALARIES
Proportion of 2006 graduates employed at graduation: 73%
Employed 9 months later, as of February 15, 2007: 95%
Salaries in the private sector (law firms, business, industry): $55,000–$95,000 (25th-75th percentile)

Median salary in the private sector: $70,000
Percentage in the private sector who reported salary information: 50%
Median salary in public service (government, judicial clerkships, academic posts, non-profits): $49,000

Percentage of 2006 graduates in:

Law firms: 38%	Government: 22%
Bus./industry: 13%	Judicial clerkship: 22%
Public interest: 4%	Unknown: 1%
Academia: 1%	

2006 graduates employed in-state: 62%
2006 graduates employed in foreign countries: 1%
Number of states where graduates are employed: 15
Percentage of 2006 graduates working in: New England: 1%, Middle Atlantic: 8%, East North Central: 1%, West North Central: 1%, South Atlantic: 83%, East South Central: 0%, West South Central: 3%, Mountain: 0%, Pacific: 1%, Unknown: 1%

BAR PASSAGE RATES
Based on 2006 graduates taking Summer 2006 or Winter 2007 exams. Most of the school's first-time test takers took the bar in Virginia.

85%
School's bar passage rate for first-time test takers

74%
Statewide bar passage rate for first-time test takers

University of San Diego

■ 5998 Alcala Park, San Diego, CA, 92110-2492
■ http://www.law.sandiego.edu
■ Private
■ Year founded: 1954
■ 2007-2008 tuition: full-time: $37,704; part-time: $26,804
■ Enrollment 2007-08 academic year: full-time: 768; part-time: 280
■ U.S. News 2009 law specialty ranking: tax law: 16

3.10-3.53 GPA, 25TH-75TH PERCENTILE

160-164 LSAT, 25TH-75TH PERCENTILE

32% ACCEPTANCE RATE

82 2009 U.S. NEWS LAW SCHOOL RANKING

ADMISSIONS
Admissions phone number: **(619) 260-4528**
Admissions email address: **jdinfo@SanDiego.edu**
Application website: **http://www.law.sandiego.edu**
Application deadline for Fall 2009 admission: **02/01**

Admissions statistics:
Number of applicants for Fall 2007: **4,210**
Number of acceptances: **1,327**
Number enrolled: **255**
Acceptance rate: **32%**
GPA, 25th-75th percentile, entering class Fall 2007: **3.10-3.53**
LSAT, 25th-75th percentile, entering class Fall 2007: **160-164**

Part-time program:
Number of applicants for Fall 2007: **484**
Number of acceptances: **221**
Number enrolled: **104**
Acceptance rate: **46%**
GPA, 25th-75th percentile, entering class Fall 2007: **2.88-3.43**
LSAT, 25th-75th percentile, entering class Fall 2007: **156-160**

FINANCIAL AID
Financial aid phone number: **(619) 260-4570**
Financial aid application deadline: **03/01**
Tuition 2007-2008 academic year: full-time: **$37,704**; part-time: **$26,804**
Room and board: **$11,268**; books: **$956**; miscellaneous expenses: **$6,372**
Total of room/board/books/miscellaneous expenses: **$18,596**
University offers graduate student housing for which law students are eligible.

Financial aid profile
Percent of students that received grants for the 2006-2007 academic year: full-time: **44%**; part-time **22%**

Median grant amount: full-time: **$18,000**; part-time: **$13,000**
The average law-school debt of those in the Class of 2007 who borrowed: **$93,403**. Proportion who borrowed: **98%**

ACADEMIC PROGRAMS
Calendar: **semester**
Joint degrees awarded: **N/A**
Typical first-year section size: Full-time: **90**; Part-time: **90**
Is there typically a "small section" of the first year class, other than Legal Writing, taught by full-time faculty?: Full-time: **yes**; Part-time: **yes**
Number of course titles, beyond the first year curriculum, offered last year: **136**
Percentages of upper division course sections, excluding seminars, with an enrollment of:
Under 25: **65%**   25 to 49: **18%**
50 to 74: **7%**   75 to 99: **8%**
100+: **1%**
Areas of specialization: appellate advocacy, clinical training, dispute resolution, environmental law, healthcare law, intellectual property law, international law, tax law, trial advocacy

Fall 2007 faculty profile
Total teaching faculty: **117**. Full-time: **53%**; **77%** men, **23%** women, **11%** minorities. Part-time: **47%**; **78%** men, **22%** women, **7%** minorities
Student-to-faculty ratio: **14.0**

SPECIAL PROGRAMS *(as provided by law school)*:
The clinical program is among the most extensive and successful in the nation. Students interview, counsel, and represent clients under faculty supervision. The Center for Public Interest Law, the Children's Advocacy Institute, and the Energy Policy and Initiatives Center offer research and training opportunities. Summer sessions are offered in England, Ireland, France, Spain, Italy, and Russia.

STUDENT BODY

Fall 2007 full-time enrollment: 768

Men: 57%	Women: 43%
African-American: 3.4%	American Indian: 0.8%
Asian-American: 16.9%	Mexican-American: 4.7%
Puerto Rican: 0.4%	Other Hisp-Amer: 3.1%
White: 70.3%	International: 0.4%
Unknown: 0.0%	

Fall 2007 part-time enrollment: 280

Men: 57%	Women: 43%
African-American: 2.9%	American Indian: 0.7%
Asian-American: 17.1%	Mexican-American: 4.3%
Puerto Rican: 1.1%	Other Hisp-Amer: 2.9%
White: 70.7%	International: 0.4%
Unknown: 0.0%	

Attrition rates for 2006-2007 full-time students
Percent of students discontinuing law school:

Men: 5%	Women: 4%
First-year students: 11%	Second-year students: 2%
Third-year students: 1%	

LIBRARY RESOURCES

Total volumes: 529,802
Total seats available for library users: 588

INFORMATION TECHNOLOGY

Number of wired network connections available to students: 240 total (in the law library, excluding computer labs: 202; in classrooms: 17; in computer labs: 0; elsewhere in the law school: 21)
Law school has a wireless network.
Students are not required to own a computer.

EMPLOYMENT AND SALARIES

Proportion of 2006 graduates employed at graduation:
N/A

Employed 9 months later, as of February 15, 2007: **88%**
Salaries in the private sector (law firms, business, industry): **$57,000–$91,000** (25th-75th percentile)
Median salary in the private sector: **$70,000**
Percentage in the private sector who reported salary information: **77%**
Median salary in public service (government, judicial clerkships, academic posts, non-profits): **$55,000**

Percentage of 2006 graduates in:

Law firms: 60%	Government: 13%
Bus./industry: 17%	Judicial clerkship: 2%
Public interest: 5%	Unknown: 1%
Academia: 2%	

2006 graduates employed in-state: **81%**
2006 graduates employed in foreign countries: **0%**
Number of states where graduates are employed: **19**
Percentage of 2006 graduates working in: New England: **1%**, Middle Atlantic: **2%**, East North Central: **1%**, West North Central: **1%**, South Atlantic: **2%**, East South Central: **1%**, West South Central: **2%**, Mountain: **6%**, Pacific: **82%**, Unknown: **3%**

BAR PASSAGE RATES

Based on 2006 graduates taking Summer 2006 or Winter 2007 exams. Most of the school's first-time test takers took the bar in California.

76%
School's bar passage rate for first-time test takers

65%
Statewide bar passage rate for first-time test takers

University of San Francisco

■ 2130 Fulton Street, San Francisco, CA, 94117-1080
■ http://www.usfca.edu/law
■ Private
■ Year founded: 1912
■ 2007-2008 tuition: full-time: $33,870; part-time: $24,245
■ Enrollment 2007-08 academic year: full-time: 556; part-time: 156
■ U.S. News 2009 law specialty ranking: N/A

3.02-3.56 GPA, 25TH-75TH PERCENTILE

156-161 LSAT, 25TH-75TH PERCENTILE

38% ACCEPTANCE RATE

Tier 3 2009 U.S. NEWS LAW SCHOOL RANKING

ADMISSIONS
Admissions phone number: **(415) 422-6586**
Admissions email address: **lawadmissions@usfca.edu**
Application website: **http://www.usfca.edu/law**
Application deadline for Fall 2009 admission: **02/01**

Admissions statistics:
Number of applicants for Fall 2007: **3,114**
Number of acceptances: **1,173**
Number enrolled: **180**
Acceptance rate: **38%**
GPA, 25th-75th percentile, entering class Fall 2007: **3.02-3.56**
LSAT, 25th-75th percentile, entering class Fall 2007: **156-161**

Part-time program:
Number of applicants for Fall 2007: **438**
Number of acceptances: **127**
Number enrolled: **70**
Acceptance rate: **29%**
GPA, 25th-75th percentile, entering class Fall 2007: **2.85-3.45**
LSAT, 25th-75th percentile, entering class Fall 2007: **152-160**

FINANCIAL AID
Financial aid phone number: **(415) 422-6210**
Financial aid application deadline: **02/15**
Tuition 2007-2008 academic year: full-time: **$33,870**; part-time: **$24,245**
Room and board: **$13,500**; books: **$950**; miscellaneous expenses: **$4,660**
Total of room/board/books/miscellaneous expenses: **$19,110**
University offers graduate student housing for which law students are eligible.

Financial aid profile
Percent of students that received grants for the 2006-2007 academic year: full-time: **30%**; part-time **33%**

Median grant amount: full-time: **$9,633**; part-time: **$3,500**
The average law-school debt of those in the Class of 2007 who borrowed: **$100,140**. Proportion who borrowed: **91%**

ACADEMIC PROGRAMS
Calendar: **semester**
Joint degrees awarded: **J.D./M.B.A.**
Typical first-year section size: Full-time: **92**; Part-time: **57**
Is there typically a "small section" of the first year class, other than Legal Writing, taught by full-time faculty?: Full-time: **yes**; Part-time: **no**
Number of course titles, beyond the first year curriculum, offered last year: **93**
Percentages of upper division course sections, excluding seminars, with an enrollment of:

Under 25: **59%**	25 to 49: **22%**
50 to 74: **14%**	75 to 99: **5%**
100+: **0%**	

Areas of specialization: appellate advocacy, clinical training, dispute resolution, environmental law, intellectual property law, international law, tax law, trial advocacy

Fall 2007 faculty profile
Total teaching faculty: **140**. Full-time: **40%**; **63%** men, **38%** women, **34%** minorities. Part-time: **60%**; **69%** men, **31%** women, **19%** minorities
Student-to-faculty ratio: **19.1**

SPECIAL PROGRAMS *(as provided by law school):*
Seven in-house clinics, off-site clinicals, and judicial externships enrich law study at USF. Over 25 international and domestic justice internships were funded in Summer 2007. Summer study is offered in Europe and Asia; clinicals in Spain and Cambodia. The McCarthy Institute promotes intellectual property and cyberlaw development. A two-week intensive advocacy program builds litigation skills.

STUDENT BODY
Fall 2007 full-time enrollment: **556**

Men: **47%**	Women: **53%**
African-American: **4.7%**	American Indian: **0.7%**

Asian-American: 19.2% Mexican-American: 5.4%
Puerto Rican: 0.4% Other Hisp-Amer: 4.0%
White: 46.0% International: 1.4%
Unknown: 18.2%

Fall 2007 part-time enrollment: 156
Men: 53% Women: 47%
African-American: 14.1% American Indian: 1.9%
Asian-American: 19.9% Mexican-American: 3.2%
Puerto Rican: 0.6% Other Hisp-Amer: 8.3%
White: 41.0% International: 1.3%
Unknown: 9.6%

Attrition rates for 2006-2007 full-time students
Percent of students discontinuing law school:
Men: 5% Women: 7%
First-year students: 16% Second-year students: 1%
Third-year students: 1%

LIBRARY RESOURCES
Total volumes: 353,361
Total seats available for library users: 419

INFORMATION TECHNOLOGY
Number of wired network connections available to students: 951 total (in the law library, excluding computer labs: 357; in classrooms: 565; in computer labs: 4; elsewhere in the law school: 25)
Law school has a wireless network.
Students are not required to own a computer.

EMPLOYMENT AND SALARIES
Proportion of 2006 graduates employed at graduation: N/A
Employed 9 months later, as of February 15, 2007: 93%

Salaries in the private sector (law firms, business, industry): $70,000–$135,000 (25th-75th percentile)
Median salary in the private sector: $95,000
Percentage in the private sector who reported salary information: 57%
Median salary in public service (government, judicial clerkships, academic posts, non-profits): $45,000

Percentage of 2006 graduates in:
Law firms: 65% Government: 13%
Bus./industry: 11% Judicial clerkship: 1%
Public interest: 8% Unknown: 2%
Academia: 0%

2006 graduates employed in-state: 97%
2006 graduates employed in foreign countries: 0%
Number of states where graduates are employed: 8
Percentage of 2006 graduates working in: New England: N/A, Middle Atlantic: 1%, East North Central: N/A, West North Central: N/A, South Atlantic: 0%, East South Central: N/A, West South Central: 1%, Mountain: 1%, Pacific: 97%, Unknown: 0%

BAR PASSAGE RATES
Based on 2006 graduates taking Summer 2006 or Winter 2007 exams. Most of the school's first-time test takers took the bar in California.

| 73% |
School's bar passage rate for first-time test takers

| 65% |
Statewide bar passage rate for first-time test takers

University of South Carolina

■ 701 S. Main Street, Columbia, SC, 29208
■ http://www.law.sc.edu
■ Public
■ Year founded: 1867
■ 2007-2008 tuition: In-state: full-time: $16,936; part-time: N/A; Out-of-state: full-time: $33,622
■ Enrollment 2007-08 academic year: full-time: 665; part-time: 2
■ U.S. News 2009 law specialty ranking: N/A

3.04-3.69 GPA, 25TH-75TH PERCENTILE

156-161 LSAT, 25TH-75TH PERCENTILE

31% ACCEPTANCE RATE

95 2009 U.S. NEWS LAW SCHOOL RANKING

ADMISSIONS
Admissions phone number: **(803) 777-6605**
Admissions email address: **usclaw@law.law.sc.edu**
Application website: **N/A**
Application deadline for Fall 2009 admission: **04/01**

Admissions statistics:
Number of applicants for Fall 2007: **1,995**
Number of acceptances: **616**
Number enrolled: **216**
Acceptance rate: **31%**
GPA, 25th-75th percentile, entering class Fall 2007: **3.04-3.69**
LSAT, 25th-75th percentile, entering class Fall 2007: **156-161**

FINANCIAL AID
Financial aid phone number: **(803) 777-6605**
Financial aid application deadline: **02/01**
Tuition 2007-2008 academic year: In-state: full-time: **$16,936**; part-time: **N/A**; Out-of-state: full-time: **$33,622**
Room and board: **$10,985**; books: **$900**; miscellaneous expenses: **$3,875**
Total of room/board/books/miscellaneous expenses: **$15,760**
University offers graduate student housing for which law students are eligible.

Financial aid profile
Percent of students that received grants for the 2006-2007 academic year: full-time: **32%**
Median grant amount: full-time: **$7,992**
The average law-school debt of those in the Class of 2007 who borrowed: **$65,585**. Proportion who borrowed: **85%**

ACADEMIC PROGRAMS
Calendar: **semester**
Joint degrees awarded: **J.D./I.M.B.A.; J.D./M.Acc.; J.D./M.C.J.; J.D./M.E.E.R.M.; J.D./M.H.A.; J.D./M.H.R.; J.D./M.P.A.; J.D./MSB; J.D./M.S.E.L.; J.D./M.S.W.**

Typical first-year section size: Full-time: **75**
Is there typically a "small section" of the first year class, other than Legal Writing, taught by full-time faculty?: Full-time: **no**; Part-time: **no**
Number of course titles, beyond the first year curriculum, offered last year: **118**
Percentages of upper division course sections, excluding seminars, with an enrollment of:
Under 25: **51%**   25 to 49: **25%**
50 to 74: **10%**   75 to 99: **13%**
100+: **1%**
Areas of specialization: appellate advocacy, clinical training, dispute resolution, environmental law, healthcare law, intellectual property law, international law, tax law, trial advocacy

Fall 2007 faculty profile
Total teaching faculty: **82**. Full-time: **55%**; **67%** men, **33%** women, **11%** minorities. Part-time: **45%**; **76%** men, **24%** women, **5%** minorities
Student-to-faculty ratio: **14.3**

SPECIAL PROGRAMS *(as provided by law school):*
Third-year students may represent clients in one of six clinics, developing practical lawyering skills such as trial advocacy, interviewing, counseling, negotiation, alternative dispute resolution, and legal drafting. Judicial internships place students with trial and appellate judges. The School of Law offers a summer-abroad program on transnational dispute resolution at Gray's Inn in London.

STUDENT BODY
Fall 2007 full-time enrollment: **665**
Men: **57%**   Women: **43%**
African-American: **8.3%**   American Indian: **0.3%**
Asian-American: **2.1%**   Mexican-American: **0.0%**
Puerto Rican: **0.0%**   Other Hisp-Amer: **2.7%**
White: **81.7%**   International: **1.1%**
Unknown: **3.9%**

Fall 2007 part-time enrollment: 2

Men: 100%	Women: 0%
African-American: 50.0%	American Indian: 0.0%
Asian-American: 0.0%	Mexican-American: 0.0%
Puerto Rican: 0.0%	Other Hisp-Amer: 0.0%
White: 50.0%	International: 0.0%
Unknown: 0.0%	

Attrition rates for 2006-2007 full-time students
Percent of students discontinuing law school:

Men: 1%	Women: 1%
First-year students: 0%	Second-year students: 1%
Third-year students: 1%	

LIBRARY RESOURCES

Total volumes: 536,022
Total seats available for library users: 504

INFORMATION TECHNOLOGY

Number of wired network connections available to students: 63 total (in the law library, excluding computer labs: 12; in classrooms: 8; in computer labs: 43; elsewhere in the law school: 0)
Law school has a wireless network.
Students are required to own a computer.

EMPLOYMENT AND SALARIES

Proportion of 2006 graduates employed at graduation: 64%
Employed 9 months later, as of February 15, 2007: 94%
Salaries in the private sector (law firms, business, industry): $52,000–$80,000 (25th-75th percentile)
Median salary in the private sector: $68,000

Percentage in the private sector who reported salary information: 79%
Median salary in public service (government, judicial clerkships, academic posts, non-profits): $40,000

Percentage of 2006 graduates in:

Law firms: 52%	Government: 10%
Bus./industry: 5%	Judicial clerkship: 25%
Public interest: 6%	Unknown: 0%
Academia: 2%	

2006 graduates employed in-state: 79%
2006 graduates employed in foreign countries: 0%
Number of states where graduates are employed: 15
Percentage of 2006 graduates working in: New England: 0%, Middle Atlantic: 3%, East North Central: 1%, West North Central: 1%, South Atlantic: 94%, East South Central: 1%, West South Central: 0%, Mountain: 1%, Pacific: 1%, Unknown: 0%

BAR PASSAGE RATES

Based on 2006 graduates taking Summer 2006 or Winter 2007 exams. Most of the school's first-time test takers took the bar in South Carolina.

88%
School's bar passage rate for first-time test takers

81%
Statewide bar passage rate for first-time test takers

University of South Dakota

■ 414 E. Clark Street, Vermillion, SD, 57069-2390
■ http://www.usd.edu/law/
■ Public
■ Year founded: 1901
■ 2007-2008 tuition: In-state: full-time: $8,991; part-time: $4,496; Out-of-state: full-time: $17,606
■ Enrollment 2007-08 academic year: full-time: 222
■ U.S. News 2009 law specialty ranking: N/A

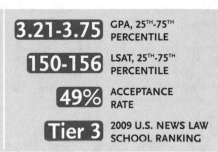

3.21-3.75 GPA, 25TH-75TH PERCENTILE

150-156 LSAT, 25TH-75TH PERCENTILE

49% ACCEPTANCE RATE

Tier 3 2009 U.S. NEWS LAW SCHOOL RANKING

ADMISSIONS
Admissions phone number: **(605) 677-5443**
Admissions email address: **lawreq@usd.edu**
Application website:
  http://www.usd.edu/law/prospective_students/admission.cfm
Application deadline for Fall 2009 admission: **03/01**

Admissions statistics:
Number of applicants for Fall 2007: **420**
Number of acceptances: **207**
Number enrolled: **64**
Acceptance rate: **49%**
GPA, 25th-75th percentile, entering class Fall 2007: **3.21-3.75**
LSAT, 25th-75th percentile, entering class Fall 2007: **150-156**

FINANCIAL AID
Financial aid phone number: **(605) 677-5446**
Financial aid application deadline: **03/15**
Tuition 2007-2008 academic year: In-state: full-time: **$8,991**; part-time: **$4,496**; Out-of-state: full-time: **$17,606**
Room and board: **$6,526**; books: **$1,400**; miscellaneous expenses: **$4,530**
Total of room/board/books/miscellaneous expenses: **$12,456**
University offers graduate student housing for which law students are eligible.

Financial aid profile
Percent of students that received grants for the 2006-2007 academic year: full-time: **33%**
Median grant amount: full-time: **$1,196**
The average law-school debt of those in the Class of 2007 who borrowed: **$46,014**. Proportion who borrowed: **99%**

ACADEMIC PROGRAMS
Calendar: **semester**
Joint degrees awarded: **J.D./M.B.A.; J.D./M.P.A.;**
J.D./M.Acc.; J.D./M.A. Education Administration; J.D./M.A. History; J.D./M.A. Political Science
Typical first-year section size: Full-time: **72**
Is there typically a "small section" of the first year class, other than Legal Writing, taught by full-time faculty?: Full-time: **yes**
Number of course titles, beyond the first year curriculum, offered last year: **46**
Percentages of upper division course sections, excluding seminars, with an enrollment of:
  Under 25: **55%**   25 to 49: **24%**
  50 to 74: **14%**   75 to 99: **6%**
  100+: **N/A**
Areas of specialization: appellate advocacy, dispute resolution, environmental law, healthcare law, intellectual property law, international law, tax law, trial advocacy

Fall 2007 faculty profile
Total teaching faculty: **N/A**. Full-time: **N/A; N/A** men, **N/A** women, **N/A** minorities. Part-time: **N/A; N/A** men, **N/A** women, **N/A** minorities
Student-to-faculty ratio: **16.2**

SPECIAL PROGRAMS *(as provided by law school):*
Joint-degree programs allow students to earn both J.D. and master's degrees in one of nine disciplines in three years. Students may also broaden their education and earn six credit hours toward the J.D. through interdisciplinary study. The extern education program offers students direct personal experience working in a public or private law office while earning six credit hours in the summer.

STUDENT BODY
Fall 2007 full-time enrollment: **222**
Men: **55%**   Women: **45%**
African-American: **0.5%**   American Indian: **1.8%**
Asian-American: **0.0%**   Mexican-American: **0.0%**
Puerto Rican: **0.5%**   Other Hisp-Amer: **0.9%**
White: **96.4%**   International: **0.0%**
Unknown: **0.0%**

Attrition rates for 2006-2007 full-time students
Percent of students discontinuing law school:
Men: **1%** Women: **N/A**
First-year students: **1%** Second-year students: **N/A**
Third-year students: **1%**

LIBRARY RESOURCES
Total volumes: **209,585**
Total seats available for library users: **227**

INFORMATION TECHNOLOGY
Number of wired network connections available to students: **227** total (in the law library, excluding computer labs: **188**; in classrooms: **N/A**; in computer labs: **N/A**; elsewhere in the law school: **39**)
Law school has a wireless network.
Students are not required to own a computer.

EMPLOYMENT AND SALARIES
Proportion of 2006 graduates employed at graduation: **59%**
Employed 9 months later, as of February 15, 2007: **93%**
Salaries in the private sector (law firms, business, industry): **$38,700–$50,000** (25th-75th percentile)
Median salary in the private sector: **$44,500**
Percentage in the private sector who reported salary information: **24%**
Median salary in public service (government, judicial clerkships, academic posts, non-profits): **$39,450**

Percentage of 2006 graduates in:
Law firms: **28%** Government: **16%**
Bus./industry: **17%** Judicial clerkship: **21%**
Public interest: **14%** Unknown: **0%**
Academia: **4%**

2006 graduates employed in-state: **46%**
2006 graduates employed in foreign countries: **1%**
Number of states where graduates are employed: **16**
Percentage of 2006 graduates working in: New England: **0%**, Middle Atlantic: **1%**, East North Central: **3%**, West North Central: **80%**, South Atlantic: **1%**, East South Central: **1%**, West South Central: **0%**, Mountain: **7%**, Pacific: **5%**, Unknown: **0%**

BAR PASSAGE RATES
Based on 2006 graduates taking Summer 2006 or Winter 2007 exams. Most of the school's first-time test takers took the bar in South Dakota.

84%
School's bar passage rate for first-time test takers

87%
Statewide bar passage rate for first-time test takers

Univ. of Southern California (Gould)

■ 699 Exposition Boulevard, Los Angeles, CA, 90089-0071
■ http://lawweb.usc.edu
■ Private
■ Year founded: 1900
■ 2007-2008 tuition: full-time: $42,640; part-time: N/A
■ Enrollment 2007-08 academic year: full-time: 598
■ U.S. News 2009 law specialty ranking: tax law: 22

3.46-3.72 GPA, 25ᵀᴴ-75ᵀᴴ PERCENTILE

165-167 LSAT, 25ᵀᴴ-75ᵀᴴ PERCENTILE

19% ACCEPTANCE RATE

18 2009 U.S. NEWS LAW SCHOOL RANKING

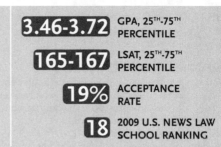

ADMISSIONS
Admissions phone number: **(213) 740-2523**
Admissions email address: **admissions@law.usc.edu**
Application website: **http://lawweb.usc.edu/admissions**
Application deadline for Fall 2009 admission: **02/01**

Admissions statistics:
Number of applicants for Fall 2007: **5,229**
Number of acceptances: **978**
Number enrolled: **196**
Acceptance rate: **19%**
GPA, 25th-75th percentile, entering class Fall 2007: **3.46-3.72**
LSAT, 25th-75th percentile, entering class Fall 2007: **165-167**

FINANCIAL AID
Financial aid phone number: **(213) 740-6314**
Financial aid application deadline: **03/03**
Tuition 2007-2008 academic year: full-time: **$42,640**; part-time: **N/A**
Room and board: **$13,146**; books: **$1,664**; miscellaneous expenses: **$3,856**
Total of room/board/books/miscellaneous expenses: **$18,666**
University offers graduate student housing for which law students are eligible.

Financial aid profile
Percent of students that received grants for the 2006-2007 academic year: full-time: **58%**
Median grant amount: full-time: **$10,000**
The average law-school debt of those in the Class of 2007 who borrowed: **$107,609**. Proportion who borrowed: **83%**

ACADEMIC PROGRAMS
Calendar: **semester**
Joint degrees awarded: **J.D./M.A. Economics; J.D./M.A. International Relations; J.D./M.P.A.; J.D./M.S.W.; J.D./M.B.A.; J.D./M.B.T.; J.D./M.A. Communications Management; J.D./M.R.E.D.; J.D./M.A. Philosophy;**
J.D./M.S. Gerontology; J.D./M.P.P.; J.D./Ph.D.; J.D./Pharm.D.
Typical first-year section size: Full-time: **70**
Is there typically a "small section" of the first year class, other than Legal Writing, taught by full-time faculty?: Full-time: **no**
Number of course titles, beyond the first year curriculum, offered last year: **93**
Percentages of upper division course sections, excluding seminars, with an enrollment of:
Under 25: **58%**   25 to 49: **20%**
50 to 74: **9%**   75 to 99: **4%**
100+: **8%**
Areas of specialization: appellate advocacy, clinical training, dispute resolution, environmental law, healthcare law, intellectual property law, international law, tax law, trial advocacy

Fall 2007 faculty profile
Total teaching faculty: **152**. Full-time: **31%**; **66%** men, **34%** women, **26%** minorities. Part-time: **69%**; **63%** men, **37%** women, **20%** minorities
Student-to-faculty ratio: **12.7**

SPECIAL PROGRAMS *(as provided by law school):*
Clinics: intellectual property, immigration, employment, non-profit business, children's issues, post-conviction matters. Research centers in law and: economics, philosophy, politics, humanities, health, communication, direct democracy. Broad internship/externship program including entertainment law and public interest. Joint degree programs with USC schools, Caltech, London School of Economics.

STUDENT BODY
Fall 2007 full-time enrollment: **598**
Men: **53%**   Women: **47%**
African-American: **9.0%**   American Indian: **0.7%**
Asian-American: **16.9%**   Mexican-American: **7.0%**
Puerto Rican: **0.5%**   Other Hisp-Amer: **3.8%**
White: **50.2%**   International: **2.5%**
Unknown: **9.4%**

Attrition rates for 2006-2007 full-time students
Percent of students discontinuing law school:
Men: 2%   Women: 1%
First-year students: 4%   Second-year students: N/A
Third-year students: 1%

LIBRARY RESOURCES
Total volumes: 429,267
Total seats available for library users: 230

INFORMATION TECHNOLOGY
Number of wired network connections available to students: 42 total (in the law library, excluding computer labs: 30; in classrooms: 12; in computer labs: 0; elsewhere in the law school: 0)
Law school has a wireless network.
Students are not required to own a computer.

EMPLOYMENT AND SALARIES
Proportion of 2006 graduates employed at graduation: 90%
Employed 9 months later, as of February 15, 2007: 96%
Salaries in the private sector (law firms, business, industry): $135,000–$135,000 (25th-75th percentile)
Median salary in the private sector: $135,000
Percentage in the private sector who reported salary information: 79%
Median salary in public service (government, judicial clerkships, academic posts, non-profits): $55,000

Percentage of 2006 graduates in:
Law firms: 68%   Government: 8%
Bus./industry: 10%   Judicial clerkship: 8%
Public interest: 4%   Unknown: 1%
Academia: 3%

2006 graduates employed in-state: 87%
2006 graduates employed in foreign countries: 0%
Number of states where graduates are employed: 16
Percentage of 2006 graduates working in: New England: 0%, Middle Atlantic: 2%, East North Central: 2%, West North Central: 0%, South Atlantic: 3%, East South Central: 0%, West South Central: 1%, Mountain: 2%, Pacific: 91%, Unknown: 0%

BAR PASSAGE RATES
Based on 2006 graduates taking Summer 2006 or Winter 2007 exams. Most of the school's first-time test takers took the bar in California.

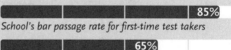

85%
School's bar passage rate for first-time test takers

65%
Statewide bar passage rate for first-time test takers

University of St. Thomas

- MSL 411, 1000 LaSalle Avenue, Minneapolis, MN, 55403-2015
- http://www.stthomas.edu/law
- Private
- Year founded: 2001
- 2007-2008 tuition: full-time: $28,832; part-time: N/A
- Enrollment 2007-08 academic year: full-time: 467
- U.S. News 2009 law specialty ranking: N/A

3.16-3.63 GPA, 25TH-75TH PERCENTILE

154-161 LSAT, 25TH-75TH PERCENTILE

49% ACCEPTANCE RATE

Tier 3 2009 U.S. NEWS LAW SCHOOL RANKING

ADMISSIONS

Admissions phone number: **(651) 962-4895**
Admissions email address: **lawschool@stthomas.edu**
Application website:
http://www.stthomas.edu/law/admissions/applicationinf ormation.asp
Application deadline for Fall 2009 admission: **07/01**

Admissions statistics:
Number of applicants for Fall 2007: **1,555**
Number of acceptances: **755**
Number enrolled: **164**
Acceptance rate: **49%**
GPA, 25th-75th percentile, entering class Fall 2007: **3.16-3.63**
LSAT, 25th-75th percentile, entering class Fall 2007: **154-161**

FINANCIAL AID

Financial aid phone number: **(651) 962-4895**
Financial aid application deadline: **06/01**
Tuition 2007-2008 academic year: full-time: **$28,832**; part-time: **N/A**
Room and board: **N/A**; books: **N/A**; miscellaneous expenses: **N/A**
Total of room/board/books/miscellaneous expenses: **$16,440**
University does not offer graduate student housing for which law students are eligible.

Financial aid profile
Percent of students that received grants for the 2006-2007 academic year: full-time: **70%**
Median grant amount: full-time: **$10,000**
The average law-school debt of those in the Class of 2007 who borrowed: **$75,312**. Proportion who borrowed: **86%**

ACADEMIC PROGRAMS

Calendar: **semester**
Joint degrees awarded: **J.D./M.A. Catholic Studies; J.D./M.A. Educational Leadership; J.D./M.B.A.;**
J.D./M.S.W.; J.D./M.A. Professional Psychology
Typical first-year section size: Full-time: **83**
Is there typically a "small section" of the first year class, other than Legal Writing, taught by full-time faculty?: Full-time: **yes**
Number of course titles, beyond the first year curriculum, offered last year: **71**
Percentages of upper division course sections, excluding seminars, with an enrollment of:

Under 25: **73%**	25 to 49: **13%**
50 to 74: **10%**	75 to 99: **4%**
100+: **0%**	

Areas of specialization: appellate advocacy, clinical training, dispute resolution, environmental law, healthcare law, intellectual property law, international law, tax law, trial advocacy

Fall 2007 faculty profile
Total teaching faculty: **65**. Full-time: **37%**; **58%** men, **42%** women, **13%** minorities. Part-time: **63%**; **63%** men, **37%** women, **7%** minorities
Student-to-faculty ratio: **16.8**

SPECIAL PROGRAMS (as provided by law school):
UST Law students participate in the nationally recognized mentor externship program. They also serve in the innovative legal services clinic of the Interprofessional Center for Counseling and Legal Services, a supervised setting where law students work side by side with graduate students in professional psychology and social work. UST Law offers five joint-degree programs.

STUDENT BODY
Fall 2007 full-time enrollment: 467

Men: **55%**	Women: **45%**
African-American: **4.7%**	American Indian: **0.6%**
Asian-American: **5.6%**	Mexican-American: **1.1%**
Puerto Rican: **0.2%**	Other Hisp-Amer: **2.8%**
White: **71.1%**	International: **0.0%**
Unknown: **13.9%**	

Attrition rates for 2006-2007 full-time students
Percent of students discontinuing law school:
Men: 3%   Women: 2%
First-year students: 6%   Second-year students: 1%
Third-year students: N/A

LIBRARY RESOURCES
Total volumes: 187,413
Total seats available for library users: 374

INFORMATION TECHNOLOGY
Number of wired network connections available to students: 595 total (in the law library, excluding computer labs: 335; in classrooms: 165; in computer labs: 0; elsewhere in the law school: 95)
Law school has a wireless network.
Students are not required to own a computer.

EMPLOYMENT AND SALARIES
Proportion of 2006 graduates employed at graduation: N/A
Employed 9 months later, as of February 15, 2007: 95%
Salaries in the private sector (law firms, business, industry): $48,000–$61,000 (25th-75th percentile)
Median salary in the private sector: $52,000
Percentage in the private sector who reported salary information: 57%
Median salary in public service (government, judicial clerkships, academic posts, non-profits): $42,000

Percentage of 2006 graduates in:
Law firms: 36%   Government: 9%
Bus./industry: 23%   Judicial clerkship: 16%
Public interest: 14%   Unknown: 0%
Academia: 2%

2006 graduates employed in-state: 83%
2006 graduates employed in foreign countries: 1%
Number of states where graduates are employed: 13
Percentage of 2006 graduates working in: New England: 0%, Middle Atlantic: 0%, East North Central: 2%, West North Central: 85%, South Atlantic: 4%, East South Central: 0%, West South Central: 1%, Mountain: 4%, Pacific: 2%, Unknown: 1%

BAR PASSAGE RATES
Based on 2006 graduates taking Summer 2006 or Winter 2007 exams. Most of the school's first-time test takers took the bar in Minnesota.

91%
School's bar passage rate for first-time test takers

91%
Statewide bar passage rate for first-time test takers

University of Tennessee–Knoxville

■ 1505 W. Cumberland Avenue, Knoxville, TN, 37996-1810
■ http://www.law.utk.edu
■ Public
■ **Year founded:** 1890
■ **2007-2008 tuition:** In-state: full-time: $11,502; part-time: N/A; Out-of-state: full-time: $27,762
■ **Enrollment 2007-08 academic year:** full-time: 469
■ **U.S. News 2009 law specialty ranking:** clinical training: 16

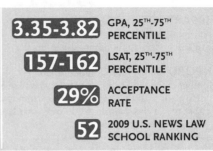

3.35-3.82 GPA, 25TH-75TH PERCENTILE

157-162 LSAT, 25TH-75TH PERCENTILE

29% ACCEPTANCE RATE

52 2009 U.S. NEWS LAW SCHOOL RANKING

ADMISSIONS

Admissions phone number: **(865) 974-4131**
Admissions email address: **lawadmit@utk.edu**
Application website: **http://www.law.utk.edu/departments/admiss/prospecstuhome.htm**
Application deadline for Fall 2009 admission: **03/01**

Admissions statistics:
Number of applicants for Fall 2007: **1,408**
Number of acceptances: **411**
Number enrolled: **171**
Acceptance rate: **29%**
GPA, 25th-75th percentile, entering class Fall 2007: **3.35-3.82**
LSAT, 25th-75th percentile, entering class Fall 2007: **157-162**

FINANCIAL AID

Financial aid phone number: **(865) 974-4131**
Financial aid application deadline: **03/01**
Tuition 2007-2008 academic year: In-state: full-time: **$11,502**; part-time: N/A; Out-of-state: full-time: **$27,762**
Room and board: **$8,996**; books: **$1,514**; miscellaneous expenses: **$3,334**
Total of room/board/books/miscellaneous expenses: **$13,844**
University offers graduate student housing for which law students are eligible.

Financial aid profile
Percent of students that received grants for the 2006-2007 academic year: full-time: **46%**
Median grant amount: full-time: **$5,000**
The average law-school debt of those in the Class of 2007 who borrowed: **$53,767**. Proportion who borrowed: **87%**

ACADEMIC PROGRAMS

Calendar: **semester**
Joint degrees awarded: **J.D./M.B.A.; J.D./M.P.A.**
Typical first-year section size: Full-time: **55**

Is there typically a "small section" of the first year class, other than Legal Writing, taught by full-time faculty?: Full-time: **no**
Number of course titles, beyond the first year curriculum, offered last year: **126**
Percentages of upper division course sections, excluding seminars, with an enrollment of:
Under 25: **72%**   25 to 49: **20%**
50 to 74: **8%**   75 to 99: **0%**
100+: **0%**
Areas of specialization: appellate advocacy, clinical training, dispute resolution, environmental law, healthcare law, intellectual property law, international law, tax law, trial advocacy

Fall 2007 faculty profile
Total teaching faculty: **63**. Full-time: **46%**; **66%** men, **34%** women, **14%** minorities. Part-time: **54%**; **62%** men, **38%** women, **0%** minorities
Student-to-faculty ratio: **13.1**

SPECIAL PROGRAMS *(as provided by law school):*
The advocacy and dispute resolution track and the business transactions track and joint J.D./M.B.A. and J.D./M.P.A. programs are offered. The legal clinic allows third-year students to learn by doing; a mediation clinic is also available. In conjunction with other schools, the College of Law offers two summer programs, one in England and one in Brazil, featuring internationally recognized faculty.

STUDENT BODY
Fall 2007 full-time enrollment: **469**
Men: **52%**   Women: **48%**
African-American: **11.5%**   American Indian: **0.6%**
Asian-American: **2.1%**   Mexican-American: **0.6%**
Puerto Rican: **0.2%**   Other Hisp-Amer: **0.9%**
White: **81.9%**   International: **0.2%**
Unknown: **1.9%**

Attrition rates for 2006-2007 full-time students
Percent of students discontinuing law school:
Men: 2%   Women: 2%
First-year students: 6%   Second-year students: N/A
Third-year students: N/A

LIBRARY RESOURCES
Total volumes: 586,086
Total seats available for library users: 437

INFORMATION TECHNOLOGY
Number of wired network connections available to students: 205 total (in the law library, excluding computer labs: 105; in classrooms: 0; in computer labs: 59; elsewhere in the law school: 41)
Law school has a wireless network.
Students are not required to own a computer.

EMPLOYMENT AND SALARIES
Proportion of 2006 graduates employed at graduation: 74%
Employed 9 months later, as of February 15, 2007: 95%
Salaries in the private sector (law firms, business, industry): $55,000–$85,000 (25th-75th percentile)
Median salary in the private sector: $61,500
Percentage in the private sector who reported salary information: 67%
Median salary in public service (government, judicial clerkships, academic posts, non-profits): $42,750

Percentage of 2006 graduates in:
Law firms: 65%   Government: 12%
Bus./industry: 7%   Judicial clerkship: 11%
Public interest: 4%   Unknown: 0%
Academia: 1%

2006 graduates employed in-state: 72%
2006 graduates employed in foreign countries: 0%
Number of states where graduates are employed: 16
Percentage of 2006 graduates working in: New England: 0%, Middle Atlantic: 2%, East North Central: 1%, West North Central: 1%, South Atlantic: 20%, East South Central: 73%, West South Central: 3%, Mountain: 0%, Pacific: 0%, Unknown: 0%

BAR PASSAGE RATES
Based on 2006 graduates taking Summer 2006 or Winter 2007 exams. Most of the school's first-time test takers took the bar in Tennessee.

92%
School's bar passage rate for first-time test takers

78%
Statewide bar passage rate for first-time test takers

University of Texas—Austin

- 727 E. Dean Keeton Street, Austin, TX, 78705-3299
- http://www.utexas.edu/law
- Public
- Year founded: 1883
- **2007-2008 tuition:** In-state: full-time: $20,632; part-time: N/A; Out-of-state: full-time: $35,130
- **Enrollment 2007-08 academic year:** full-time: 1,291
- **U.S. News 2009 law specialty ranking:** environmental law: 20, intellectual property law: 25, international law: 15, tax law: 10, trial advocacy: 9

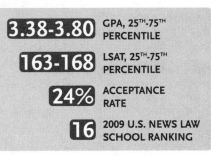

3.38-3.80 GPA, 25TH-75TH PERCENTILE

163-168 LSAT, 25TH-75TH PERCENTILE

24% ACCEPTANCE RATE

16 2009 U.S. NEWS LAW SCHOOL RANKING

ADMISSIONS

Admissions phone number: **(512) 232-1200**
Admissions email address: **admissions@law.utexas.edu**
Application website:
   http://www.utexas.edu/law/depts/admissions/
Application deadline for Fall 2009 admission: **02/01**

Admissions statistics:

Number of applicants for Fall 2007: **4,879**
Number of acceptances: **1,172**
Number enrolled: **401**
Acceptance rate: **24%**
GPA, 25th-75th percentile, entering class Fall 2007: **3.38-3.80**
LSAT, 25th-75th percentile, entering class Fall 2007: **163-168**

FINANCIAL AID

Financial aid phone number: **(512) 232-1130**
Financial aid application deadline: **03/31**
Tuition 2007-2008 academic year: In-state: full-time: **$20,632**; part-time: N/A; Out-of-state: full-time: **$35,130**
Room and board: **$8,896**; books: **$1,000**; miscellaneous expenses: **$3,740**
Total of room/board/books/miscellaneous expenses: **$13,636**
University offers graduate student housing for which law students are eligible.

Financial aid profile

Percent of students that received grants for the 2006-2007 academic year: full-time: **90%**
Median grant amount: full-time: **$6,416**
The average law-school debt of those in the Class of 2007 who borrowed: **$62,399**. Proportion who borrowed: **84%**

ACADEMIC PROGRAMS

Calendar: **semester**
Joint degrees awarded: **J.D./M.B.A.; J.D./M.P.A.; J.D./M.A.; J.D./M.S.C.R.P.**

Typical first-year section size: Full-time: **109**
Is there typically a "small section" of the first year class, other than Legal Writing, taught by full-time faculty?: Full-time: **yes**
Number of course titles, beyond the first year curriculum, offered last year: **160**
Percentages of upper division course sections, excluding seminars, with an enrollment of:

Under 25: **66%**	25 to 49: **19%**
50 to 74: **8%**	75 to 99: **3%**
100+: **5%**	

Areas of specialization: appellate advocacy, clinical training, dispute resolution, environmental law, healthcare law, intellectual property law, international law, tax law, trial advocacy

Fall 2007 faculty profile

Total teaching faculty: **180**. Full-time: **49%**; **66%** men, **34%** women, **9%** minorities. Part-time: **51%**; **77%** men, **23%** women, **10%** minorities
Student-to-faculty ratio: **14.2**

SPECIAL PROGRAMS (as provided by law school):

UT Law provides an extensive clinical education program to help students incorporate law, theory, strategy, and skills in client settings. Internships let students obtain academic credit working with nonprofits, the government, or the courts. UT operates centers, institutes, and scholar programs and offers a summer academic program and study-abroad programs.

STUDENT BODY

Fall 2007 full-time enrollment: 1,291

Men: **60%**	Women: **40%**
African-American: **6.3%**	American Indian: **0.5%**
Asian-American: **6.7%**	Mexican-American: **14.6%**
Puerto Rican: **0.0%**	Other Hisp-Amer: **1.8%**
White: **57.3%**	International: **0.0%**
Unknown: **12.8%**	

Attrition rates for 2006-2007 full-time students

Percent of students discontinuing law school:

Men: 2%   Women: 2%

First-year students: 2%   Second-year students: 3%

Third-year students: 1%

LIBRARY RESOURCES

Total volumes: 1,046,921

Total seats available for library users: 1,317

INFORMATION TECHNOLOGY

Number of wired network connections available to students: 310 total (in the law library, excluding computer labs: 24; in classrooms: 98; in computer labs: 38; elsewhere in the law school: 150)

Law school has a wireless network.

Students are not required to own a computer.

EMPLOYMENT AND SALARIES

Proportion of 2006 graduates employed at graduation: 92%

Employed 9 months later, as of February 15, 2007: 97%

Salaries in the private sector (law firms, business, industry): $100,000–$135,000 (25th-75th percentile)

Median salary in the private sector: $135,000

Percentage in the private sector who reported salary information: 87%

Median salary in public service (government, judicial clerkships, academic posts, non-profits): $50,000

Percentage of 2006 graduates in:

Law firms: 67%   Government: 9%

Bus./industry: 9%   Judicial clerkship: 11%

Public interest: 1%   Unknown: 2%

Academia: 2%

2006 graduates employed in-state: 72%

2006 graduates employed in foreign countries: 1%

Number of states where graduates are employed: 30

Percentage of 2006 graduates working in: New England: 1%, Middle Atlantic: 5%, East North Central: 4%, West North Central: 1%, South Atlantic: 6%, East South Central: 1%, West South Central: 72%, Mountain: 2%, Pacific: 5%, Unknown: 2%

BAR PASSAGE RATES

Based on 2006 graduates taking Summer 2006 or Winter 2007 exams. Most of the school's first-time test takers took the bar in Texas.

89%

School's bar passage rate for first-time test takers

82%

Statewide bar passage rate for first-time test takers

Univ. of the Dist. of Columbia (Clarke)

■ **4200 Connecticut Avenue NW, Building 38 & 39, Washington, DC, 20008**
■ **http://www.law.udc.edu**
■ **Public**
■ **Year founded:** 1988
■ **2007-2008 tuition:** In-state: full-time: $7,350; part-time: N/A; Out-of-state: full-time: $14,700
■ **Enrollment 2007-08 academic year:** full-time: 237
■ **U.S. News 2009 law specialty ranking:** clinical training: 13

2.70-3.40 GPA, 25TH-75TH PERCENTILE

148-153 LSAT, 25TH-75TH PERCENTILE

19% ACCEPTANCE RATE

Tier 4 2009 U.S. NEWS LAW SCHOOL RANKING

ADMISSIONS
Admissions phone number: **(202) 274-7341**
Admissions email address: **vcanty@udc.edu**
Application website:
http://www.law.edu/prospective/apply/html
Application deadline for Fall 2009 admission: **03/15**

Admissions statistics:
Number of applicants for Fall 2007: **1,290**
Number of acceptances: **241**
Number enrolled: **93**
Acceptance rate: **19%**
GPA, 25th-75th percentile, entering class Fall 2007: **2.70-3.40**
LSAT, 25th-75th percentile, entering class Fall 2007: **148-153**

FINANCIAL AID
Financial aid phone number: **(202) 274-7337**
Financial aid application deadline: **04/15**
Tuition 2007-2008 academic year: In-state: full-time: **$7,350**; part-time: **N/A**; Out-of-state: full-time: **$14,700**
Room and board: **N/A**; books: **N/A**; miscellaneous expenses: **N/A**
Total of room/board/books/miscellaneous expenses: **$25,435**
University does not offer graduate student housing for which law students are eligible.

Financial aid profile
Percent of students that received grants for the 2006-2007 academic year: full-time: **70%**
Median grant amount: full-time: **$4,000**
The average law-school debt of those in the Class of 2007 who borrowed: **$74,536**. Proportion who borrowed: **89%**

ACADEMIC PROGRAMS
Calendar: **semester**
Joint degrees awarded: **N/A**
Typical first-year section size: Full-time: **95**

Is there typically a "small section" of the first year class, other than Legal Writing, taught by full-time faculty?:
Full-time: **yes**
Number of course titles, beyond the first year curriculum, offered last year: **38**
Percentages of upper division course sections, excluding seminars, with an enrollment of:
Under 25: **48%**   25 to 49: **35%**
50 to 74: **16%**   75 to 99: **0%**
100+: **0%**
Areas of specialization: appellate advocacy, clinical training, healthcare law, intellectual property law, international law, tax law, trial advocacy

Fall 2007 faculty profile
Total teaching faculty: **33**. Full-time: **55%**; 50% men, 50% women, 50% minorities. Part-time: **45%**; 60% men, 40% women, 67% minorities
Student-to-faculty ratio: **10.5**

SPECIAL PROGRAMS *(as provided by law school):*
The David A. Clarke School of Law is committed to training attorneys with the knowledge, skills, and experience to practice law upon graduation. It fills a unique niche in legal education as a publicly funded urban land-grant member of the historically black colleges and universities committed to public service and clinical legal education. Graduates have at least 700 hours of hands-on experience.

STUDENT BODY
Fall 2007 full-time enrollment: **237**
Men: **40%**   Women: **60%**
African-American: **27.4%**   American Indian: **1.3%**
Asian-American: **4.2%**   Mexican-American: **5.5%**
Puerto Rican: **0.8%**   Other Hisp-Amer: **3.0%**
White: **50.6%**   International: **3.0%**
Unknown: **4.2%**

Attrition rates for 2006-2007 full-time students
Percent of students discontinuing law school:
Men: 15%   Women: 11%
First-year students: 25%   Second-year students: 9%
Third-year students: N/A

LIBRARY RESOURCES
Total volumes: 253,338
Total seats available for library users: 230

INFORMATION TECHNOLOGY
Number of wired network connections available to students: 5 total (in the law library, excluding computer labs: 3; in classrooms: N/A; in computer labs: N/A; elsewhere in the law school: 2)
Law school has a wireless network.
Students are required to own a computer.

EMPLOYMENT AND SALARIES
Proportion of 2006 graduates employed at graduation: N/A
Employed 9 months later, as of February 15, 2007: 67%
Salaries in the private sector (law firms, business, industry): $41,600–$70,000 (25th-75th percentile)
Median salary in the private sector: $61,876
Percentage in the private sector who reported salary information: 36%
Median salary in public service (government, judicial clerkships, academic posts, non-profits): $47,174

Percentage of 2006 graduates in:
Law firms: 9%   Government: 25%
Bus./industry: 27%   Judicial clerkship: 14%
Public interest: 18%   Unknown: 2%
Academia: 5%

2006 graduates employed in-state: 62%
2006 graduates employed in foreign countries: 0%
Number of states where graduates are employed: 10
Percentage of 2006 graduates working in: New England: N/A, Middle Atlantic: N/A, East North Central: N/A, West North Central: N/A, South Atlantic: N/A, East South Central: N/A, West South Central: N/A, Mountain: N/A, Pacific: N/A, Unknown: 2%

BAR PASSAGE RATES
Based on 2006 graduates taking Summer 2006 or Winter 2007 exams. Most of the school's first-time test takers took the bar in Maryland.

| 54% |
School's bar passage rate for first-time test takers

| 77% |
Statewide bar passage rate for first-time test takers

University of the Pacific (McGeorge)

- 3200 Fifth Avenue, Sacramento, CA, 95817
- http://www.mcgeorge.edu
- Private
- Year founded: 1924
- 2007-2008 tuition: full-time: $34,474; part-time: $22,920
- Enrollment 2007-08 academic year: full-time: 615; part-time: 399
- U.S. News 2009 law specialty ranking: international law: 16

3.13-3.60 GPA, 25TH-75TH PERCENTILE

155-159 LSAT, 25TH-75TH PERCENTILE

40% ACCEPTANCE RATE

95 2009 U.S. NEWS LAW SCHOOL RANKING

ADMISSIONS
Admissions phone number: (916) 739-7105
Admissions email address: **admissionsmcge-orge@pacific.edu**
Application website:
 http://www.mcgeorge.edu/admissions/apply/index.htm
Application deadline for Fall 2009 admission: **rolling**

Admissions statistics:
Number of applicants for Fall 2007: 2,881
Number of acceptances: 1,145
Number enrolled: 236
Acceptance rate: 40%
GPA, 25th-75th percentile, entering class Fall 2007: 3.13-3.60
LSAT, 25th-75th percentile, entering class Fall 2007: 155-159

Part-time program:
Number of applicants for Fall 2007: 373
Number of acceptances: 164
Number enrolled: 104
Acceptance rate: 44%
GPA, 25th-75th percentile, entering class Fall 2007: 2.92-3.49
LSAT, 25th-75th percentile, entering class Fall 2007: 151-156

FINANCIAL AID
Financial aid phone number: (916) 739-7158
Financial aid application deadline: N/A
Tuition 2007-2008 academic year: full-time: **$34,474**; part-time: **$22,920**
Room and board: **$12,062**; books: **$950**; miscellaneous expenses: **$6,359**
Total of room/board/books/miscellaneous expenses: **$19,371**
University offers graduate student housing for which law students are eligible.

Financial aid profile
Percent of students that received grants for the 2006-2007

academic year: full-time: **45%**; part-time **32%**
Median grant amount: full-time: **$10,500**; part-time: **$5,000**
The average law-school debt of those in the Class of 2007 who borrowed: **$106,729**. Proportion who borrowed: **90%**

ACADEMIC PROGRAMS
Calendar: **semester**
Joint degrees awarded: **J.D./M.B.A.; J.D./M.S. M.I.S.; J.D./M.P.P.A.; J.D./M.Acc.**
Typical first-year section size: Full-time: **74**; Part-time: **97**
Is there typically a "small section" of the first year class, other than Legal Writing, taught by full-time faculty?: Full-time: **yes**; Part-time: **yes**
Number of course titles, beyond the first year curriculum, offered last year: 133
Percentages of upper division course sections, excluding seminars, with an enrollment of:
 Under 25: **51%**   25 to 49: **21%**
 50 to 74: **16%**   75 to 99: **11%**
 100+: **1%**
Areas of specialization: appellate advocacy, clinical training, dispute resolution, environmental law, healthcare law, intellectual property law, international law, tax law, trial advocacy

Fall 2007 faculty profile
Total teaching faculty: 110. Full-time: **48%**; 60% men, 40% women, 21% minorities. Part-time: **52%**; 74% men, 26% women, 16% minorities
Student-to-faculty ratio: 13.5

SPECIAL PROGRAMS *(as provided by law school)*:
Students can concentrate in advocacy, criminal justice, governmental law and policy, intellectual property, international law, or taxation. Students can also create individualized programs from extensive elective offerings, including clinics, internships, and study abroad. The unique LL.M. programs in international law attract foreign graduate students, giving the campus an international flavor.

STUDENT BODY

Fall 2007 full-time enrollment: 615

Men: 54%	Women: 46%
African-American: 2.6%	American Indian: 1.5%
Asian-American: 14.0%	Mexican-American: 5.0%
Puerto Rican: 0.5%	Other Hisp-Amer: 3.1%
White: 73.3%	International: 0.0%
Unknown: 0.0%	

Fall 2007 part-time enrollment: 399

Men: 50%	Women: 50%
African-American: 4.5%	American Indian: 0.5%
Asian-American: 10.8%	Mexican-American: 5.0%
Puerto Rican: 0.5%	Other Hisp-Amer: 3.3%
White: 75.4%	International: 0.0%
Unknown: 0.0%	

Attrition rates for 2006-2007 full-time students
Percent of students discontinuing law school:

Men: 6%	Women: 5%
First-year students: 9%	Second-year students: 9%
Third-year students: 1%	

LIBRARY RESOURCES

Total volumes: 498,199
Total seats available for library users: 529

INFORMATION TECHNOLOGY

Number of wired network connections available to students: 271 total (in the law library, excluding computer labs: 265; in classrooms: 0; in computer labs: 6; elsewhere in the law school: 0)
Law school has a wireless network.
Students are not required to own a computer.

EMPLOYMENT AND SALARIES

Proportion of 2006 graduates employed at graduation: N/A
Employed 9 months later, as of February 15, 2007: 94%

Salaries in the private sector (law firms, business, industry): $60,000–$80,000 (25th-75th percentile)
Median salary in the private sector: $70,000
Percentage in the private sector who reported salary information: 52%
Median salary in public service (government, judicial clerkships, academic posts, non-profits): $52,000

Percentage of 2006 graduates in:

Law firms: 48%	Government: 18%
Bus./industry: 15%	Judicial clerkship: 3%
Public interest: 9%	Unknown: 1%
Academia: 6%	

2006 graduates employed in-state: 91%
2006 graduates employed in foreign countries: 1%
Number of states where graduates are employed: 11
Percentage of 2006 graduates working in: New England: 0%, Middle Atlantic: 0%, East North Central: 1%, West North Central: 0%, South Atlantic: 1%, East South Central: 0%, West South Central: 0%, Mountain: 5%, Pacific: 92%, Unknown: 0%

BAR PASSAGE RATES

Based on 2006 graduates taking Summer 2006 or Winter 2007 exams. Most of the school's first-time test takers took the bar in California.

73%
School's bar passage rate for first-time test takers

65%
Statewide bar passage rate for first-time test takers

University of Toledo

■ 2801 W. Bancroft, Toledo, OH, 43606
■ http://www.utlaw.edu
■ Public
■ Year founded: 1906
■ 2007-2008 tuition: In-state: full-time: $15,666; part-time: $12,409; Out-of-state: full-time: $25,910
■ Enrollment 2007-08 academic year: full-time: 348; part-time: 195
■ U.S. News 2009 law specialty ranking: N/A

3.10-3.74 GPA, 25TH-75TH PERCENTILE

156-161 LSAT, 25TH-75TH PERCENTILE

27% ACCEPTANCE RATE

Tier 3 2009 U.S. NEWS LAW SCHOOL RANKING

ADMISSIONS
Admissions phone number: (419) 530-4131
Admissions email address: law.admissions@utoledo.edu
Application website: http://www.utlaw.edu/admissions
Application deadline for Fall 2009 admission: 08/01

Admissions statistics:
Number of applicants for Fall 2007: 832
Number of acceptances: 224
Number enrolled: 76
Acceptance rate: 27%
GPA, 25th-75th percentile, entering class Fall 2007: 3.10-3.74
LSAT, 25th-75th percentile, entering class Fall 2007: 156-161

Part-time program:
Number of applicants for Fall 2007: 264
Number of acceptances: 149
Number enrolled: 121
Acceptance rate: 56%
GPA, 25th-75th percentile, entering class Fall 2007: 2.90-3.49
LSAT, 25th-75th percentile, entering class Fall 2007: 151-155

FINANCIAL AID
Financial aid phone number: (419) 530-7929
Financial aid application deadline: 08/01
Tuition 2007-2008 academic year: In-state: full-time: $15,666; part-time: $12,409; Out-of-state: full-time: $25,910
Room and board: $7,859; books: $1,750; miscellaneous expenses: $4,321
Total of room/board/books/miscellaneous expenses: $13,930
University offers graduate student housing for which law students are eligible.

Financial aid profile
Percent of students that received grants for the 2006-2007 academic year: full-time: 59%; part-time 9%

Median grant amount: full-time: $13,426; part-time: $7,800
The average law-school debt of those in the Class of 2007 who borrowed: $65,654. Proportion who borrowed: 89%

ACADEMIC PROGRAMS
Calendar: semester
Joint degrees awarded: J.D./M.B.A.; J.D./M.S.E.; J.D./M.P.A.; J.D./M.C.J.
Typical first-year section size: Full-time: 64; Part-time: 36
Is there typically a "small section" of the first year class, other than Legal Writing, taught by full-time faculty?: Full-time: no; Part-time: no
Number of course titles, beyond the first year curriculum, offered last year: 87
Percentages of upper division course sections, excluding seminars, with an enrollment of:

Under 25: 71%	25 to 49: 19%
50 to 74: 9%	75 to 99: 1%
100+: 0%	

Areas of specialization: appellate advocacy, clinical training, dispute resolution, environmental law, healthcare law, intellectual property law, international law, tax law, trial advocacy

Fall 2007 faculty profile
Total teaching faculty: 61. Full-time: 52%; 53% men, 47% women, 6% minorities. Part-time: 48%; 83% men, 17% women, 0% minorities
Student-to-faculty ratio: 15.1

SPECIAL PROGRAMS (as provided by law school):
Students are offered actual legal experience with a practicing attorney through clinics and externships. Five Certificates are offered: Environmental, International, Intellectual Property, Labor, and Homeland Security Law. The school's lecture series greatly enriches the intellectual atmosphere of the college and provides students with timely discussion of legal and policy issues.

STUDENT BODY

Fall 2007 full-time enrollment: 348

Men: 63%	Women: 37%
African-American: 1.4%	American Indian: 0.6%
Asian-American: 2.3%	Mexican-American: 0.0%
Puerto Rican: 0.0%	Other Hisp-Amer: 2.9%
White: 63.2%	International: 0.9%
Unknown: 28.7%	

Fall 2007 part-time enrollment: 195

Men: 58%	Women: 42%
African-American: 3.1%	American Indian: 0.0%
Asian-American: 4.6%	Mexican-American: 0.0%
Puerto Rican: 0.0%	Other Hisp-Amer: 3.6%
White: 62.1%	International: 1.0%
Unknown: 25.6%	

Attrition rates for 2006-2007 full-time students

Percent of students discontinuing law school:

Men: 6%	Women: 9%
First-year students: 14%	Second-year students: 3%
Third-year students: 2%	

LIBRARY RESOURCES

Total volumes: 352,839

Total seats available for library users: 426

INFORMATION TECHNOLOGY

Number of wired network connections available to students: 28 total (in the law library, excluding computer labs: 12; in classrooms: 0; in computer labs: 0; elsewhere in the law school: 16)

Law school has a wireless network.

Students are not required to own a computer.

EMPLOYMENT AND SALARIES

Proportion of 2006 graduates employed at graduation: 72%

Employed 9 months later, as of February 15, 2007: 92%

Salaries in the private sector (law firms, business, industry): **$40,000–$60,000** (25th-75th percentile)

Median salary in the private sector: **$50,000**

Percentage in the private sector who reported salary information: 60%

Median salary in public service (government, judicial clerkships, academic posts, non-profits): **$47,500**

Percentage of 2006 graduates in:

Law firms: 52%	Government: 15%
Bus./industry: 15%	Judicial clerkship: 4%
Public interest: 6%	Unknown: 5%
Academia: 3%	

2006 graduates employed in-state: 66%

2006 graduates employed in foreign countries: 1%

Number of states where graduates are employed: 14

Percentage of 2006 graduates working in: New England: 0%, Middle Atlantic: 2%, East North Central: 78%, West North Central: 0%, South Atlantic: 8%, East South Central: 0%, West South Central: 3%, Mountain: 6%, Pacific: 0%, Unknown: 2%

BAR PASSAGE RATES

Based on 2006 graduates taking Summer 2006 or Winter 2007 exams. Most of the school's first-time test takers took the bar in Ohio.

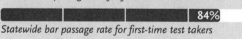

91%

School's bar passage rate for first-time test takers

84%

Statewide bar passage rate for first-time test takers

University of Tulsa

- 3120 E. Fourth Place, Tulsa, OK, 74104
- http://www.law.utulsa.edu
- Private
- Year founded: 1923
- 2007-2008 tuition: full-time: $26,528; part-time: $18,572
- Enrollment 2007-08 academic year: full-time: 452; part-time: 59
- U.S. News 2009 law specialty ranking: N/A

2.95-3.50 GPA, 25TH-75TH PERCENTILE

151-155 LSAT, 25TH-75TH PERCENTILE

51% ACCEPTANCE RATE

Tier 4 2009 U.S. NEWS LAW SCHOOL RANKING

ADMISSIONS

Admissions phone number: **(918) 631-2709**
Admissions email address: **lawadmissions@utulsa.edu**
Application website: **http://www.law.utulsa.edu/admissions**
Application deadline for Fall 2009 admission: **07/31**

Admissions statistics:
Number of applicants for Fall 2007: **1,101**
Number of acceptances: **562**
Number enrolled: **144**
Acceptance rate: **51%**
GPA, 25th-75th percentile, entering class Fall 2007: **2.95-3.50**
LSAT, 25th-75th percentile, entering class Fall 2007: **151-155**

Part-time program:
Number of applicants for Fall 2007: **56**
Number of acceptances: **24**
Number enrolled: **16**
Acceptance rate: **43%**
GPA, 25th-75th percentile, entering class Fall 2007: **3.13-3.59**
LSAT, 25th-75th percentile, entering class Fall 2007: **151-155**

FINANCIAL AID

Financial aid phone number: **(918) 631-2526**
Financial aid application deadline: **07/31**
Tuition 2007-2008 academic year: full-time: **$26,528**; part-time: **$18,572**
Room and board: **$5,850**; books: **$1,500**; miscellaneous expenses: **$5,869**
Total of room/board/books/miscellaneous expenses: **$13,219**
University offers graduate student housing for which law students are eligible.

Financial aid profile
Percent of students that received grants for the 2006-2007 academic year: full-time: **35%**; part-time **39%**
Median grant amount: full-time: **$8,000**; part-time: **$8,000**

The average law-school debt of those in the Class of 2007 who borrowed: **$84,115**. Proportion who borrowed: **65%**

ACADEMIC PROGRAMS

Calendar: **semester**
Joint degrees awarded: **J.D./M.A. Anthropology; J.D./M.Acc.; J.D./M.S. Biosciences; J.D./M.A. English; J.D./M.A. History; J.D./M.B.A.; J.D./M.A. Clinical Psychology; J.D./M.Taxation; J.D./M.S. Geosciences; J.D./M.A. Industrial/Org. Psychology**
Typical first-year section size: Full-time: **50**
Is there typically a "small section" of the first year class, other than Legal Writing, taught by full-time faculty?: Full-time: **yes**; Part-time: **yes**
Number of course titles, beyond the first year curriculum, offered last year: **146**
Percentages of upper division course sections, excluding seminars, with an enrollment of:

Under 25: **71%**   25 to 49: **21%**
50 to 74: **7%**   75 to 99: **1%**
100+: **0%**

Areas of specialization: appellate advocacy, clinical training, dispute resolution, environmental law, healthcare law, intellectual property law, international law, tax law, trial advocacy

Fall 2007 faculty profile
Total teaching faculty: **71**. Full-time: **41%**; **59%** men, **41%** women, **17%** minorities. Part-time: **59%**; **64%** men, **36%** women, **5%** minorities
Student-to-faculty ratio: **13.5**

SPECIAL PROGRAMS *(as provided by law school):*
Programs include the Comparative International Law Center, Native American Law Center, and National Energy-Environment Law and Policy Institute. Summer programs are offered in Dublin; Geneva; Buenos Aires; and Tianjin, China. The Boesche Legal Clinic offers the Immigrant Rights Project and the Social Enterprise and Economic Development Law Project. Internships are offered through career services.

STUDENT BODY

Fall 2007 full-time enrollment: 452

Men: 65%	Women: 35%
African-American: 2.0%	American Indian: 6.0%
Asian-American: 1.3%	Mexican-American: 2.4%
Puerto Rican: 0.0%	Other Hisp-Amer: 0.0%
White: 72.6%	International: 0.7%
Unknown: 15.0%	

Fall 2007 part-time enrollment: 59

Men: 44%	Women: 56%
African-American: 3.4%	American Indian: 10.2%
Asian-American: 0.0%	Mexican-American: 5.1%
Puerto Rican: 0.0%	Other Hisp-Amer: 0.0%
White: 69.5%	International: 0.0%
Unknown: 11.9%	

Attrition rates for 2006-2007 full-time students
Percent of students discontinuing law school:

Men: 8%	Women: 4%
First-year students: 5%	Second-year students: 11%
Third-year students: 4%	

LIBRARY RESOURCES

Total volumes: 402,338
Total seats available for library users: 736

INFORMATION TECHNOLOGY

Number of wired network connections available to students: 376 total (in the law library, excluding computer labs: 276; in classrooms: 100; in computer labs: 0; elsewhere in the law school: 0)
Law school has a wireless network.
Students are not required to own a computer.

EMPLOYMENT AND SALARIES

Proportion of 2006 graduates employed at graduation: 56%
Employed 9 months later, as of February 15, 2007: 91%

Salaries in the private sector (law firms, business, industry): $40,000–$54,000 (25th-75th percentile)
Median salary in the private sector: $46,500
Percentage in the private sector who reported salary information: 29%
Median salary in public service (government, judicial clerkships, academic posts, non-profits): $46,900

Percentage of 2006 graduates in:

Law firms: 64%	Government: 12%
Bus./industry: 17%	Judicial clerkship: 1%
Public interest: 3%	Unknown: 1%
Academia: 2%	

2006 graduates employed in-state: 51%
2006 graduates employed in foreign countries: 0%
Number of states where graduates are employed: 24
Percentage of 2006 graduates working in: New England: 0%, Middle Atlantic: 1%, East North Central: 4%, West North Central: 12%, South Atlantic: 6%, East South Central: 1%, West South Central: 64%, Mountain: 11%, Pacific: 2%, Unknown: 0%

BAR PASSAGE RATES

Based on 2006 graduates taking Summer 2006 or Winter 2007 exams. Most of the school's first-time test takers took the bar in Oklahoma.

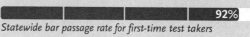

88%
School's bar passage rate for first-time test takers

92%
Statewide bar passage rate for first-time test takers

University of Utah (Quinney)

- 332 S 1400 E, Room 101, Salt Lake City, UT, 84112
- http://www.law.utah.edu
- Public
- Year founded: 1913
- 2007-2008 tuition: In-state: full-time: $11,896; part-time: N/A; Out-of-state: full-time: $26,256
- Enrollment 2007-08 academic year: full-time: 397
- U.S. News 2009 law specialty ranking: environmental law: 17

3.31-3.77 GPA, 25TH-75TH PERCENTILE

156-162 LSAT, 25TH-75TH PERCENTILE

37% ACCEPTANCE RATE

51 2009 U.S. NEWS LAW SCHOOL RANKING

ADMISSIONS
Admissions phone number: **(801) 581-7479**
Admissions email address: **admissions@law.utah.edu**
Application website:
  http://www.law.utah.edu/prospective/admissions.html
Application deadline for Fall 2009 admission: **02/01**

Admissions statistics:
Number of applicants for Fall 2007: **937**
Number of acceptances: **346**
Number enrolled: **122**
Acceptance rate: **37%**
GPA, 25th-75th percentile, entering class Fall 2007: **3.31-3.77**
LSAT, 25th-75th percentile, entering class Fall 2007: **156-162**

FINANCIAL AID
Financial aid phone number: **(801) 581-6211**
Financial aid application deadline: **03/15**
Tuition 2007-2008 academic year: In-state: full-time: **$11,896**; part-time: N/A; Out-of-state: full-time: **$26,256**
Room and board: **$8,964**; books: **$1,916**; miscellaneous expenses: **$4,432**
Total of room/board/books/miscellaneous expenses: **$15,312**
University offers graduate student housing for which law students are eligible.

Financial aid profile
Percent of students that received grants for the 2006-2007 academic year: full-time: **40%**
Median grant amount: full-time: **$2,000**
The average law-school debt of those in the Class of 2007 who borrowed: **$53,839**. Proportion who borrowed: **87%**

ACADEMIC PROGRAMS
Calendar: **semester**
Joint degrees awarded: **J.D./M.B.A.; J.D./M.P.A.**
Typical first-year section size: Full-time: **37**

Is there typically a "small section" of the first year class, other than Legal Writing, taught by full-time faculty?:
  Full-time: **yes**
Number of course titles, beyond the first year curriculum, offered last year: **114**
Percentages of upper division course sections, excluding seminars, with an enrollment of:
  Under 25: **67%**   25 to 49: **24%**
  50 to 74: **5%**   75 to 99: **3%**
  100+: **0%**
Areas of specialization: appellate advocacy, clinical training, dispute resolution, environmental law, healthcare law, intellectual property law, international law, tax law, trial advocacy

Fall 2007 faculty profile
Total teaching faculty: **50**. Full-time: **38%**; **68%** men, **32%** women, **26%** minorities. Part-time: **62%**; **61%** men, **39%** women, **6%** minorities
Student-to-faculty ratio: **9.9**

SPECIAL PROGRAMS *(as provided by law school)*:
The law school collaborates in support of the Utah Criminal Justice Center. The Wallace Stegner Center for Land, Resources and the Environment supports the study of natural resources law. Clinics include: civil, criminal, environmental, and death penalty. LL.M. in energy, environmental, and natural resources law. Joint degrees: J.D./M.B.A. and J.D./M.P.A. Two summer sessions.

STUDENT BODY
Fall 2007 full-time enrollment: **397**
Men: **60%**   Women: **40%**
African-American: **1.0%**   American Indian: **0.5%**
Asian-American: **4.0%**   Mexican-American: **0.0%**
Puerto Rican: **0.0%**   Other Hisp-Amer: **4.5%**
White: **73.0%**   International: **0.5%**
Unknown: **16.4%**

Attrition rates for 2006-2007 full-time students
Percent of students discontinuing law school:
Men: 0%   Women: 1%
First-year students: 2%   Second-year students: N/A
Third-year students: N/A

LIBRARY RESOURCES
Total volumes: 343,979
Total seats available for library users: 356

INFORMATION TECHNOLOGY
Number of wired network connections available to students: 626 total (in the law library, excluding computer labs: 216; in classrooms: 230; in computer labs: 20; elsewhere in the law school: 160)
Law school has a wireless network.
Students are required to own a computer.

EMPLOYMENT AND SALARIES
Proportion of 2006 graduates employed at graduation: 96%
Employed 9 months later, as of February 15, 2007: 99%
Salaries in the private sector (law firms, business, industry): $50,750–$108,500 (25th-75th percentile)
Median salary in the private sector: $68,000
Percentage in the private sector who reported salary information: 100%
Median salary in public service (government, judicial clerkships, academic posts, non-profits): $43,000

Percentage of 2006 graduates in:
Law firms: 58%   Government: 13%
Bus./industry: 11%   Judicial clerkship: 14%
Public interest: 3%   Unknown: 0%
Academia: 0%

2006 graduates employed in-state: 75%
2006 graduates employed in foreign countries: 1%
Number of states where graduates are employed: 16
Percentage of 2006 graduates working in: New England: 1%, Middle Atlantic: 2%, East North Central: 2%, West North Central: 0%, South Atlantic: 2%, East South Central: 0%, West South Central: 0%, Mountain: 85%, Pacific: 8%, Unknown: 0%

BAR PASSAGE RATES
Based on 2006 graduates taking Summer 2006 or Winter 2007 exams. Most of the school's first-time test takers took the bar in Utah.

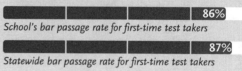

86%

School's bar passage rate for first-time test takers

87%

Statewide bar passage rate for first-time test takers

University of Virginia

- 580 Massie Road, Charlottesville, VA, 22903-1738
- http://www.law.virginia.edu
- Public
- Year founded: 1819
- 2007-2008 tuition: In-state: full-time: $33,500; part-time: N/A; Out-of-state: full-time: $38,500
- Enrollment 2007-08 academic year: full-time: 1,175
- U.S. News 2009 law specialty ranking: international law: 10, tax law: 9

3.51-3.87 GPA, 25TH-75TH PERCENTILE

167-171 LSAT, 25TH-75TH PERCENTILE

24% ACCEPTANCE RATE

9 2009 U.S. NEWS LAW SCHOOL RANKING

ADMISSIONS

Admissions phone number: **(434) 924-7351**
Admissions email address: **lawadmit@virginia.edu**
Application website:
  http://www.law.virginia.edu/admissions
Application deadline for Fall 2009 admission: **03/01**

Admissions statistics:

Number of applicants for Fall 2007: **5,438**
Number of acceptances: **1,304**
Number enrolled: **361**
Acceptance rate: **24%**
GPA, 25th-75th percentile, entering class Fall 2007: **3.51-3.87**
LSAT, 25th-75th percentile, entering class Fall 2007: **167-171**

FINANCIAL AID

Financial aid phone number: **(434) 924-7805**
Financial aid application deadline: **03/01**
Tuition 2007-2008 academic year: In-state: full-time: **$33,500**; part-time: **N/A**; Out-of-state: full-time: **$38,500**
Room and board: **$15,309**; books: **$1,800**; miscellaneous expenses: **$591**
Total of room/board/books/miscellaneous expenses: **$17,700**
University offers graduate student housing for which law students are eligible.

Financial aid profile

Percent of students that received grants for the 2006-2007 academic year: full-time: **60%**
Median grant amount: full-time: **$14,000**
The average law-school debt of those in the Class of 2007 who borrowed: **$86,600**. Proportion who borrowed: **83%**

ACADEMIC PROGRAMS

Calendar: **semester**
Joint degrees awarded: J.D./M.A. History; J.D./M.B.A.; J.D./M.A. Government/Foreign Affairs; J.D./M.S.

Accounting; J.D./M.A. Bioethics; J.D./M.A. Economics; J.D./M.A. English; J.D./M.A. Philosophy; J.D./M.P.H.; J.D./M.A. Sociology; J.D./M.U.E.P.; J.D./M.A. Int'l Relations (Johns Hopk.); J.D./M.A.L.D. (Tufts); J.D./M.P.A. (Princeton)
Typical first-year section size: Full-time: **69**
Is there typically a "small section" of the first year class, other than Legal Writing, taught by full-time faculty?: Full-time: **yes**
Number of course titles, beyond the first year curriculum, offered last year: **230**
Percentages of upper division course sections, excluding seminars, with an enrollment of:

Under 25: **56%**	25 to 49: **15%**
50 to 74: **14%**	75 to 99: **9%**
100+: **6%**	

Areas of specialization: appellate advocacy, clinical training, dispute resolution, environmental law, healthcare law, intellectual property law, international law, tax law, trial advocacy

Fall 2007 faculty profile

Total teaching faculty: **151**. Full-time: **48%**; **74%** men, **26%** women, **10%** minorities. Part-time: **52%**; **85%** men, **15%** women, **3%** minorities
Student-to-faculty ratio: **13.3**

SPECIAL PROGRAMS (as provided by law school):

Virginia offers special curricular programs in law and business, international law, legal history, criminal justice, human rights, race and law, environmental law, intellectual property, health law, and law and humanities. Virginia faculty members run institutes and centers in the areas of law and psychiatry, law and economics, oceans law, national security law, and family law.

STUDENT BODY

Fall 2007 full-time enrollment: 1,175

Men: **61%**	Women: **39%**
African-American: **6.8%**	American Indian: **0.9%**
Asian-American: **6.6%**	Mexican-American: **0.0%**

Puerto Rican: 0.0% Other Hisp-Amer: 2.1%
White: 57.5% International: 0.8%
Unknown: 25.3%

Attrition rates for 2006-2007 full-time students
Percent of students discontinuing law school:
Men: 2% Women: 1%
First-year students: 1% Second-year students: 2%
Third-year students: 1%

LIBRARY RESOURCES
Total volumes: 891,320
Total seats available for library users: 836

INFORMATION TECHNOLOGY
Number of wired network connections available to students: 84 total (in the law library, excluding computer labs: 84; in classrooms: 0; in computer labs: 0; elsewhere in the law school: 0)
Law school has a wireless network.
Students are required to own a computer.

EMPLOYMENT AND SALARIES
Proportion of 2006 graduates employed at graduation: 97%
Employed 9 months later, as of February 15, 2007: 100%
Salaries in the private sector (law firms, business, industry): $115,000–$160,000 (25th-75th percentile)
Median salary in the private sector: $145,000
Percentage in the private sector who reported salary information: 75%
Median salary in public service (government, judicial clerkships, academic posts, non-profits): $55,000

Percentage of 2006 graduates in:
Law firms: 71% Government: 5%
Bus./industry: 4% Judicial clerkship: 16%
Public interest: 4% Unknown: 0%
Academia: 1%

2006 graduates employed in-state: 13%
2006 graduates employed in foreign countries: 2%
Number of states where graduates are employed: 32
Percentage of 2006 graduates working in: New England: 3%, Middle Atlantic: 21%, East North Central: 5%, West North Central: 2%, South Atlantic: 51%, East South Central: 3%, West South Central: 4%, Mountain: 3%, Pacific: 7%, Unknown: 1%

BAR PASSAGE RATES
Based on 2006 graduates taking Summer 2006 or Winter 2007 exams. Most of the school's first-time test takers took the bar in Virginia.

91%
School's bar passage rate for first-time test takers

74%
Statewide bar passage rate for first-time test takers

University of Washington

- Campus Box 353020, Seattle, WA, 98195-3020
- http://www.law.washington.edu
- Public
- Year founded: 1899
- 2007-2008 tuition: In-state: full-time: $17,847; part-time: N/A; Out-of-state: full-time: $26,231
- Enrollment 2007-08 academic year: full-time: 528
- U.S. News 2009 law specialty ranking: clinical training: 28, environmental law: 17, intellectual property law: 20, international law: 16, tax law: 15

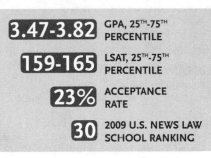

3.47-3.82 GPA, 25TH-75TH PERCENTILE

159-165 LSAT, 25TH-75TH PERCENTILE

23% ACCEPTANCE RATE

30 2009 U.S. NEWS LAW SCHOOL RANKING

ADMISSIONS

Admissions phone number: **(206) 543-4078**
Admissions email address: **lawadm@u.washington.edu**
Application website: **N/A**
Application deadline for Fall 2009 admission: **01/15**

Admissions statistics:
Number of applicants for Fall 2007: **2,585**
Number of acceptances: **587**
Number enrolled: **183**
Acceptance rate: **23%**
GPA, 25th-75th percentile, entering class Fall 2007: **3.47-3.82**
LSAT, 25th-75th percentile, entering class Fall 2007: **159-165**

FINANCIAL AID

Financial aid phone number: **(206) 543-4552**
Financial aid application deadline: **02/27**
Tuition 2007-2008 academic year: In-state: full-time: **$17,847**; part-time: **N/A**; Out-of-state: full-time: **$26,231**
Room and board: **$11,742**; books: **$1,176**; miscellaneous expenses: **$3,708**
Total of room/board/books/miscellaneous expenses: **$16,626**
University offers graduate student housing for which law students are eligible.

Financial aid profile
Percent of students that received grants for the 2006-2007 academic year: full-time: **45%**
Median grant amount: full-time: **$6,000**
The average law-school debt of those in the Class of 2007 who borrowed: **$65,507**. Proportion who borrowed: **79%**

ACADEMIC PROGRAMS

Calendar: **quarter**
Joint degrees awarded: **J.D./M.A. International Studies; J.D./LL.M. Intellectual Property Law; J.D./M.P.A.; J.D./M.P.H.; J.D./M.U.P.**

Typical first-year section size: Full-time: **60**
Is there typically a "small section" of the first year class, other than Legal Writing, taught by full-time faculty?: Full-time: **yes**
Number of course titles, beyond the first year curriculum, offered last year: **122**
Percentages of upper division course sections, excluding seminars, with an enrollment of:
Under 25: **62%**　　25 to 49: **23%**
50 to 74: **13%**　　75 to 99: **1%**
100+: **0%**
Areas of specialization: appellate advocacy, clinical training, dispute resolution, environmental law, healthcare law, intellectual property law, international law, tax law, trial advocacy

Fall 2007 faculty profile
Total teaching faculty: **65**. Full-time: **66%**; **56%** men, **44%** women, **14%** minorities. Part-time: **34%**; **50%** men, **50%** women, **5%** minorities
Student-to-faculty ratio: **10.2**

SPECIAL PROGRAMS *(as provided by law school):*
Current clinics: Innocence Project Northwest, unemployment compensation law, mediation, immigration law, refugee advocacy, child advocacy, tribal court criminal defense, and low-income taxpayer. Centers: Asian Law, Intellectual Property, Native American Law, Rural Development Institute, Shidler Center for Law, Commerce and Technology. Externships: public interest law, courts, government agencies.

STUDENT BODY
Fall 2007 full-time enrollment: 528
Men: **41%**　　　　　　　Women: **59%**
African-American: **2.5%**　American Indian: **2.3%**
Asian-American: **12.1%**　Mexican-American: **0.0%**
Puerto Rican: **0.0%**　　Other Hisp-Amer: **4.2%**
White: **75.0%**　　　　International: **2.5%**
Unknown: **1.5%**

Percent of students discontinuing law school:

Men: 1%   Women: 1%

First-year students: 3%   Second-year students: N/A

Third-year students: 1%

LIBRARY RESOURCES

Total volumes: 617,260

Total seats available for library users: 398

INFORMATION TECHNOLOGY

Number of wired network connections available to students: 0 total (in the law library, excluding computer labs: 0; in classrooms: 0; in computer labs: 0; elsewhere in the law school: 0)

Law school has a wireless network.

Students are not required to own a computer.

EMPLOYMENT AND SALARIES

Proportion of 2006 graduates employed at graduation: 88%

Employed 9 months later, as of February 15, 2007: 97%

Salaries in the private sector (law firms, business, industry): $65,000–$101,000 (25th-75th percentile)

Median salary in the private sector: $90,000

Percentage in the private sector who reported salary information: 62%

Median salary in public service (government, judicial clerkships, academic posts, non-profits): $44,500

Percentage of 2006 graduates in:

Law firms: 54%	Government: 14%
Bus./industry: 7%	Judicial clerkship: 16%
Public interest: 6%	Unknown: 0%
Academia: 2%	

2006 graduates employed in-state: 72%

2006 graduates employed in foreign countries: 4%

Number of states where graduates are employed: 11

Percentage of 2006 graduates working in: New England: 0%, Middle Atlantic: 6%, East North Central: 1%, West North Central: 1%, South Atlantic: 2%, East South Central: 0%, West South Central: 0%, Mountain: 0%, Pacific: 88%, Unknown: 0%

BAR PASSAGE RATES

Based on 2006 graduates taking Summer 2006 or Winter 2007 exams. Most of the school's first-time test takers took the bar in Washington.

88%

School's bar passage rate for first-time test takers

82%

Statewide bar passage rate for first-time test takers

University of Wisconsin–Madison

- 975 Bascom Mall, Madison, WI, 53706-1399
- http://www.law.wisc.edu
- Public
- Year founded: 1868
- 2007-2008 tuition: In-state: full-time: $13,708; part-time: $1,146/credit hour; Out-of-state: full-time: $32,774
- Enrollment 2007-08 academic year: full-time: 807; part-time: 35
- U.S. News 2009 law specialty ranking: N/A

3.32-3.74 GPA, 25TH-75TH PERCENTILE

157-163 LSAT, 25TH-75TH PERCENTILE

30% ACCEPTANCE RATE

36 2009 U.S. NEWS LAW SCHOOL RANKING

ADMISSIONS

Admissions phone number: **(608) 262-5914**
Admissions email address: **admissions@law.wisc.edu**
Application website:
http://www.law.wisc.edu/admissions/reqform.htm
Application deadline for Fall 2009 admission: **02/01**

Admissions statistics:
Number of applicants for Fall 2007: **2,610**
Number of acceptances: **770**
Number enrolled: **264**
Acceptance rate: **30%**
GPA, 25th-75th percentile, entering class Fall 2007: **3.32-3.74**
LSAT, 25th-75th percentile, entering class Fall 2007: **157-163**

FINANCIAL AID

Financial aid phone number: **(608) 262-5914**
Financial aid application deadline: **03/01**
Tuition 2007-2008 academic year: In-state: full-time: **$13,708**; part-time: **$1,146/credit hour**; Out-of-state: full-time: **$32,774**
Room and board: **$7,910**; books: **$2,100**; miscellaneous expenses: **$4,510**
Total of room/board/books/miscellaneous expenses: **$14,520**
University offers graduate student housing for which law students are eligible.

Financial aid profile
Percent of students that received grants for the 2006-2007 academic year: full-time: **24%**
Median grant amount: full-time: **$13,000**
The average law-school debt of those in the Class of 2007 who borrowed: **$65,082**. Proportion who borrowed: **85%**

ACADEMIC PROGRAMS

Calendar: **semester**

Joint degrees awarded: J.D./M.B.A.; J.D./M.A. Education Administration; J.D./M.A. Latin American Studies; J.D./M.S. Environmental Studies; J.D./M.S. Library Information Science; J.D./M.A. Philosophy; J.D./M.A. Sociology; J.D./M.A. Urban and Regional Planning; J.D./M.A. Journalism/Mass Communications; J.D./M.A. Public Affairs; J.D./M.A. Political Science; J.D./M.A. Social Work; J.D./M.S. Medicine; J.D./Ph.D. English; J.D./M.S. Agriculture; J.D./M.S. Biology
Typical first-year section size: Full-time: **71**
Is there typically a "small section" of the first year class, other than Legal Writing, taught by full-time faculty?: Full-time: **yes**
Number of course titles, beyond the first year curriculum, offered last year: **154**
Percentages of upper division course sections, excluding seminars, with an enrollment of:

Under 25: **61%**	25 to 49: **23%**
50 to 74: **12%**	75 to 99: **3%**
100+: **2%**	

Areas of specialization: appellate advocacy, clinical training, dispute resolution, environmental law, healthcare law, intellectual property law, international law, tax law, trial advocacy

Fall 2007 faculty profile
Total teaching faculty: **105**. Full-time: **52%**; **56%** men, **44%** women, **20%** minorities. Part-time: **48%**; **50%** men, **50%** women, **18%** minorities
Student-to-faculty ratio: **13.4**

SPECIAL PROGRAMS *(as provided by law school):*

Marquette students have the opportunity to develop legal skills in one of the school's clinical programs. Students participate in internships with a variety of governmental and legal services agencies, as well as in internships with trial and appellate judges. Students may focus their studies in specific doctrinal areas including dispute resolution, intellectual property, and sports law.

STUDENT BODY

Fall 2007 full-time enrollment: 807

Men: 53%	Women: 47%
African-American: 7.6%	American Indian: 2.6%
Asian-American: 7.3%	Mexican-American: 3.0%
Puerto Rican: 1.4%	Other Hisp-Amer: 3.6%
White: 69.4%	International: 1.0%
Unknown: 4.2%	

Fall 2007 part-time enrollment: 35

Men: 57%	Women: 43%
African-American: 2.9%	American Indian: 2.9%
Asian-American: 5.7%	Mexican-American: 2.9%
Puerto Rican: 0.0%	Other Hisp-Amer: 2.9%
White: 80.0%	International: 0.0%
Unknown: 2.9%	

Attrition rates for 2006-2007 full-time students
Percent of students discontinuing law school:

Men: 1%	Women: 1%
First-year students: 0%	Second-year students: 4%
Third-year students: N/A	

LIBRARY RESOURCES
Total volumes: 567,417
Total seats available for library users: 614

INFORMATION TECHNOLOGY
Number of wired network connections available to students: 526 total (in the law library, excluding computer labs: 333; in classrooms: 184; in computer labs: 0; elsewhere in the law school: 9)
Law school has a wireless network.
Students are required to own a computer.

EMPLOYMENT AND SALARIES
Proportion of 2006 graduates employed at graduation: 73%
Employed 9 months later, as of February 15, 2007: 97%

Salaries in the private sector (law firms, business, industry): $72,000–$125,000 (25th-75th percentile)
Median salary in the private sector: $105,000
Percentage in the private sector who reported salary information: 54%
Median salary in public service (government, judicial clerkships, academic posts, non-profits): $46,000

Percentage of 2006 graduates in:

Law firms: 55%	Government: 17%
Bus./industry: 12%	Judicial clerkship: 7%
Public interest: 7%	Unknown: 0%
Academia: 2%	

2006 graduates employed in-state: 47%
2006 graduates employed in foreign countries: 1%
Number of states where graduates are employed: 27
Percentage of 2006 graduates working in: New England: 2%, Middle Atlantic: 4%, East North Central: 64%, West North Central: 7%, South Atlantic: 7%, East South Central: 1%, West South Central: 3%, Mountain: 2%, Pacific: 9%, Unknown: 0%

BAR PASSAGE RATES
Based on 2006 graduates taking Summer 2006 or Winter 2007 exams. Most of the school's first-time test takers took the bar in Wisconsin.

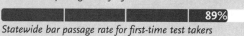

100%
School's bar passage rate for first-time test takers

89%
Statewide bar passage rate for first-time test takers

University of Wyoming

- **Department 3035, 1000 E. University Avenue, Laramie, WY, 82071**
- **http://www.uwyo.edu/law**
- **Public**
- **Year founded:** 1920
- **2007-2008 tuition:** In-state: full-time: $8,491; part-time: N/A; Out-of-state: full-time: $17,977
- **Enrollment 2007-08 academic year:** full-time: 228
- **U.S. News 2009 law specialty ranking:** N/A

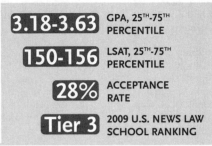

3.18-3.63 GPA, 25ᵀᴴ-75ᵀᴴ PERCENTILE

150-156 LSAT, 25ᵀᴴ-75ᵀᴴ PERCENTILE

28% ACCEPTANCE RATE

Tier 3 2009 U.S. NEWS LAW SCHOOL RANKING

ADMISSIONS
Admissions phone number: **(307) 766-6416**
Admissions email address: **lawadmis@uwyo.edu**
Application website: **N/A**
Application deadline for Fall 2009 admission: **03/02**

Admissions statistics:
Number of applicants for Fall 2007: **807**
Number of acceptances: **223**
Number enrolled: **76**
Acceptance rate: **28%**
GPA, 25th-75th percentile, entering class Fall 2007: **3.18-3.63**
LSAT, 25th-75th percentile, entering class Fall 2007: **150-156**

FINANCIAL AID
Financial aid phone number: **(307) 766-2116**
Financial aid application deadline: **03/01**
Tuition 2007-2008 academic year: In-state: full-time: **$8,491**; part-time: N/A; Out-of-state: full-time: **$17,977**
Room and board: **$9,237**; books: **$1,200**; miscellaneous expenses: **$2,200**
Total of room/board/books/miscellaneous expenses: **$12,637**
University offers graduate student housing for which law students are eligible.

Financial aid profile
Percent of students that received grants for the 2006-2007 academic year: full-time: **75%**
Median grant amount: full-time: **$1,500**
The average law-school debt of those in the Class of 2007 who borrowed: **$39,033**. Proportion who borrowed: **85%**

ACADEMIC PROGRAMS
Calendar: **semester**
Joint degrees awarded: **J.D./M.P.A.; J.D./M.B.A.**
Typical first-year section size: Full-time: **75**

Is there typically a "small section" of the first year class, other than Legal Writing, taught by full-time faculty?: Full-time: **no**
Number of course titles, beyond the first year curriculum, offered last year: **58**
Percentages of upper division course sections, excluding seminars, with an enrollment of:
Under 25: **73%**   25 to 49: **8%**
50 to 74: **19%**   75 to 99: **N/A**
100+: **N/A**
Areas of specialization: appellate advocacy, clinical training, dispute resolution, environmental law, healthcare law, intellectual property law, international law, tax law, trial advocacy

Fall 2007 faculty profile
Total teaching faculty: **24**. Full-time: **71%**; **71%** men, **29%** women, **18%** minorities. Part-time: **29%**; **43%** men, **57%** women, **0%** minorities
Student-to-faculty ratio: **11.4**

SPECIAL PROGRAMS *(as provided by law school):*
The college offers practical experience for academic credit in five clinical programs: defender aid, prosecution assistance, legal services, domestic violence, and the university's student government. Students have a wide range of externships from which to choose, including placement with the U.S. attorney, various levels of the judiciary, Wyoming attorney general, and other governmental agencies.

STUDENT BODY
Fall 2007 full-time enrollment: **228**
Men: **53%**   Women: **47%**
African-American: **1.3%**   American Indian: **0.4%**
Asian-American: **3.5%**   Mexican-American: **0.4%**
Puerto Rican: **0.4%**   Other Hisp-Amer: **2.2%**
White: **79.4%**   International: **1.8%**
Unknown: **10.5%**

Attrition rates for 2006-2007 full-time students
Percent of students discontinuing law school:
Men: **2%**   Women: **3%**
First-year students: **5%**   Second-year students: **N/A**
Third-year students: **1%**

LIBRARY RESOURCES

Total volumes: **283,464**
Total seats available for library users: **282**

INFORMATION TECHNOLOGY

Number of wired network connections available to students: **326** total (in the law library, excluding computer labs: **98**; in classrooms: **178**; in computer labs: **20**; elsewhere in the law school: **30**)
Law school has a wireless network.
Students are not required to own a computer.

EMPLOYMENT AND SALARIES

Proportion of 2006 graduates employed at graduation: **N/A**
Employed 9 months later, as of February 15, 2007: **87%**
Salaries in the private sector (law firms, business, industry): **$43,250–$57,000** (25th-75th percentile)
Median salary in the private sector: **$47,250**
Percentage in the private sector who reported salary information: **80%**
Median salary in public service (government, judicial clerkships, academic posts, non-profits): **$46,000**

Percentage of 2006 graduates in:

Law firms: **53%**	Government: **15%**
Bus./industry: **5%**	Judicial clerkship: **20%**
Public interest: **3%**	Unknown: **0%**
Academia: **3%**	

2006 graduates employed in-state: **58%**
2006 graduates employed in foreign countries: **0%**
Number of states where graduates are employed: **14**
Percentage of 2006 graduates working in: New England: **0%**, Middle Atlantic: **3%**, East North Central: **0%**, West North Central: **2%**, South Atlantic: **3%**, East South Central: **0%**, West South Central: **2%**, Mountain: **87%**, Pacific: **3%**, Unknown: **0%**

BAR PASSAGE RATES

Based on 2006 graduates taking Summer 2006 or Winter 2007 exams. Most of the school's first-time test takers took the bar in Wyoming.

78%
School's bar passage rate for first-time test takers

62%
Statewide bar passage rate for first-time test takers

Valparaiso University

- 656 S. Greenwich Street, Wesemann Hall, Valparaiso, IN, 46383
- http://www.valpo.edu/law
- Private
- Year founded: 1879
- 2007-2008 tuition: full-time: $31,208; part-time: $1,220/credit hour
- Enrollment 2007-08 academic year: full-time: 486; part-time: 56
- U.S. News 2009 law specialty ranking: N/A

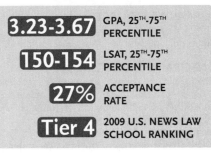

3.23-3.67 GPA, 25TH-75TH PERCENTILE

150-154 LSAT, 25TH-75TH PERCENTILE

27% ACCEPTANCE RATE

Tier 4 2009 U.S. NEWS LAW SCHOOL RANKING

ADMISSIONS
Admissions phone number: **(219) 548-7703**
Admissions email address: **valpolaw@valpo.edu**
Application website:
https://www.valpo.edu/law/admissions/apply
Application deadline for Fall 2009 admission: **06/01**

Admissions statistics:
Number of applicants for Fall 2007: **2,885**
Number of acceptances: **766**
Number enrolled: **187**
Acceptance rate: **27%**
GPA, 25th-75th percentile, entering class Fall 2007: **3.23-3.67**
LSAT, 25th-75th percentile, entering class Fall 2007: **150-154**

Part-time program:
Number of applicants for Fall 2007: **187**
Number of acceptances: **44**
Number enrolled: **27**
Acceptance rate: **24%**
GPA, 25th-75th percentile, entering class Fall 2007: **2.81-3.47**
LSAT, 25th-75th percentile, entering class Fall 2007: **144-148**

FINANCIAL AID
Financial aid phone number: **(219) 465-7818**
Financial aid application deadline: **03/01**
Tuition 2007-2008 academic year: full-time: **$31,208**; part-time: **$1,220/credit hour**
Room and board: **$7,300**; books: **$1,200**; miscellaneous expenses: **$2,610**
Total of room/board/books/miscellaneous expenses: **$11,110**
University does not offer graduate student housing for which law students are eligible.

Financial aid profile
Percent of students that received grants for the 2006-2007

academic year: full-time: **21%**
Median grant amount: full-time: **$14,125**
The average law-school debt of those in the Class of 2007 who borrowed: **$80,424**. Proportion who borrowed: **100%**

ACADEMIC PROGRAMS
Calendar: **semester**
Joint degrees awarded: **J.D./M.A. Psychology; J.D./M.A. C.M.H.C.; J.D./M.B.A.; J.D./M.A.L.S.; J.D./M.S.I.C.P.; J.D./M.S. Sports Administration**
Typical first-year section size: Full-time: **65**
Is there typically a "small section" of the first year class, other than Legal Writing, taught by full-time faculty?: Full-time: **no**; Part-time: **no**
Number of course titles, beyond the first year curriculum, offered last year: **110**
Percentages of upper division course sections, excluding seminars, with an enrollment of:
Under 25: **67%**   25 to 49: **21%**
50 to 74: **7%**   75 to 99: **5%**
100+: **1%**
Areas of specialization: appellate advocacy, clinical training, dispute resolution, environmental law, healthcare law, intellectual property law, international law, tax law, trial advocacy

Fall 2007 faculty profile
Total teaching faculty: **54**. Full-time: **50%**; **56%** men, **44%** women, **11%** minorities. Part-time: **50%**; **59%** men, **41%** women, **7%** minorities
Student-to-faculty ratio: **15.8**

SPECIAL PROGRAMS *(as provided by law school):*
The law school is home to seven clinics (criminal, civil, low-income taxpayer, mediation, juvenile justice, guardianship ad litem, and the nation's only sports law clinic), has summer study programs in England and in Chile/Argentina, houses the Tabor Institute on Law and Ethics, and offers a wealth of judicial, governmental, law practice, nonprofit, and business-related externships.

STUDENT BODY

Fall 2007 full-time enrollment: 486

Men: 54%	Women: 46%
African-American: 4.7%	American Indian: 0.0%
Asian-American: 2.1%	Mexican-American: 2.3%
Puerto Rican: 0.2%	Other Hisp-Amer: 2.3%
White: 82.3%	International: 0.6%
Unknown: 5.6%	

Fall 2007 part-time enrollment: 56

Men: 55%	Women: 45%
African-American: 14.3%	American Indian: 1.8%
Asian-American: 0.0%	Mexican-American: 0.0%
Puerto Rican: 0.0%	Other Hisp-Amer: 7.1%
White: 69.6%	International: 0.0%
Unknown: 7.1%	

Attrition rates for 2006-2007 full-time students
Percent of students discontinuing law school:

Men: 10%	Women: 6%
First-year students: 19%	Second-year students: 1%
Third-year students: N/A	

LIBRARY RESOURCES

Total volumes: 332,337
Total seats available for library users: 231

INFORMATION TECHNOLOGY

Number of wired network connections available to students: 46 total (in the law library, excluding computer labs: 33; in classrooms: 3; in computer labs: 0; elsewhere in the law school: 10)
Law school has a wireless network.
Students are not required to own a computer.

EMPLOYMENT AND SALARIES

Proportion of 2006 graduates employed at graduation: 39%
Employed 9 months later, as of February 15, 2007: 88%

Salaries in the private sector (law firms, business, industry): $47,500–$70,000 (25th-75th percentile)
Median salary in the private sector: $57,000
Percentage in the private sector who reported salary information: 65%
Median salary in public service (government, judicial clerkships, academic posts, non-profits): $45,000

Percentage of 2006 graduates in:

Law firms: 56%	Government: 14%
Bus./industry: 20%	Judicial clerkship: 6%
Public interest: 0%	Unknown: 0%
Academia: 4%	

2006 graduates employed in-state: 46%
2006 graduates employed in foreign countries: 0%
Number of states where graduates are employed: 25
Percentage of 2006 graduates working in: New England: 0%, Middle Atlantic: 3%, East North Central: 72%, West North Central: 5%, South Atlantic: 5%, East South Central: 2%, West South Central: 1%, Mountain: 4%, Pacific: 7%, Unknown: 0%

BAR PASSAGE RATES

Based on 2006 graduates taking Summer 2006 or Winter 2007 exams. Most of the school's first-time test takers took the bar in Indiana.

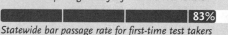

83%
School's bar passage rate for first-time test takers

83%
Statewide bar passage rate for first-time test takers

Vanderbilt University

- 131 21st Avenue S, Nashville, TN, 37203-1181
- http://www.vanderbilt.edu/law/
- Private
- Year founded: 1874
- 2007-2008 tuition: full-time: $39,838; part-time: N/A
- Enrollment 2007-08 academic year: full-time: 601
- U.S. News 2009 law specialty ranking: N/A

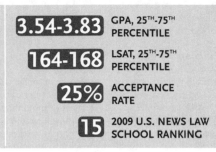

3.54-3.83 GPA, 25TH-75TH PERCENTILE

164-168 LSAT, 25TH-75TH PERCENTILE

25% ACCEPTANCE RATE

15 2009 U.S. NEWS LAW SCHOOL RANKING

ADMISSIONS

Admissions phone number: **(615) 322-6452**
Admissions email address: **admissions@law.vanderbilt.edu**
Application website:
   http://law.vanderbilt.edu/admiss/forms.html
Application deadline for Fall 2009 admission: **03/15**

Admissions statistics:
Number of applicants for Fall 2007: **3,985**
Number of acceptances: **998**
Number enrolled: **193**
Acceptance rate: **25%**
GPA, 25th-75th percentile, entering class Fall 2007: **3.54-3.83**
LSAT, 25th-75th percentile, entering class Fall 2007: **164-168**

FINANCIAL AID

Financial aid phone number: **(615) 322-6452**
Financial aid application deadline: **02/15**
Tuition 2007-2008 academic year: full-time: **$39,838**; part-time: **N/A**
Room and board: **$12,056**; books: **$1,574**; miscellaneous expenses: **$6,988**
Total of room/board/books/miscellaneous expenses: **$20,618**
University offers graduate student housing for which law students are eligible.

Financial aid profile
Percent of students that received grants for the 2006-2007 academic year: full-time: **69%**
Median grant amount: full-time: **$15,000**
The average law-school debt of those in the Class of 2007 who borrowed: **$100,891**. Proportion who borrowed: **84%**

ACADEMIC PROGRAMS

Calendar: **semester**
Joint degrees awarded: **J.D./M.B.A.; J.D./M.T.S.; J.D./M.Div; J.D./M.A.; J.D./Ph.D.; J.D./M.D.; J.D./M.P.P.**

Typical first-year section size: Full-time: **95**
Is there typically a "small section" of the first year class, other than Legal Writing, taught by full-time faculty?: Full-time: **yes**
Number of course titles, beyond the first year curriculum, offered last year: **133**
Percentages of upper division course sections, excluding seminars, with an enrollment of:

Under 25: **51%**	25 to 49: **31%**
50 to 74: **9%**	75 to 99: **6%**
100+: **3%**	

Areas of specialization: appellate advocacy, clinical training, dispute resolution, environmental law, healthcare law, intellectual property law, international law, tax law, trial advocacy

Fall 2007 faculty profile
Total teaching faculty: **132**. Full-time: **31%**; **61%** men, **39%** women, **22%** minorities. Part-time: **69%**; **60%** men, **40%** women, **11%** minorities
Student-to-faculty ratio: **12.9**

SPECIAL PROGRAMS *(as provided by law school):*

Vanderbilt offers specialized programs in law and business; litigation and dispute resolution; constitutional law; regulatory law; intellectual property; and international law. Multiple joint-degree programs are offered, including an innovative J.D./Ph.D. program in law and economics. Students can participate in a number of live-client clinics, externships, and other experiential learning courses.

STUDENT BODY

Fall 2007 full-time enrollment: **601**

Men: **54%**	Women: **46%**
African-American: **8.3%**	American Indian: **0.8%**
Asian-American: **4.7%**	Mexican-American: **0.0%**
Puerto Rican: **0.0%**	Other Hisp-Amer: **2.7%**
White: **61.4%**	International: **2.3%**
Unknown: **19.8%**	

Attrition rates for 2006-2007 full-time students
Percent of students discontinuing law school:

Men: 1%   Women: 2%
First-year students: 4%   Second-year students: 1%
Third-year students: 0%

LIBRARY RESOURCES

Total volumes: 607,105
Total seats available for library users: 252

INFORMATION TECHNOLOGY

Number of wired network connections available to students: 415 total (in the law library, excluding computer labs: 185; in classrooms: 150; in computer labs: 10; elsewhere in the law school: 70)
Law school has a wireless network.
Students are not required to own a computer.

EMPLOYMENT AND SALARIES

Proportion of 2006 graduates employed at graduation: 91%
Employed 9 months later, as of February 15, 2007: 98%
Salaries in the private sector (law firms, business, industry): $100,000–$135,000 (25th-75th percentile)
Median salary in the private sector: $115,000
Percentage in the private sector who reported salary information: 70%
Median salary in public service (government, judicial clerkships, academic posts, non-profits): $43,115

Percentage of 2006 graduates in:

Law firms: 71%   Government: 7%
Bus./industry: 8%   Judicial clerkship: 10%
Public interest: 3%   Unknown: 1%
Academia: 0%

2006 graduates employed in-state: 23%
2006 graduates employed in foreign countries: 1%
Number of states where graduates are employed: 29
Percentage of 2006 graduates working in: New England: 1%, Middle Atlantic: 13%, East North Central: 7%, West North Central: 2%, South Atlantic: 25%, East South Central: 29%, West South Central: 7%, Mountain: 4%, Pacific: 10%, Unknown: 1%

BAR PASSAGE RATES

Based on 2006 graduates taking Summer 2006 or Winter 2007 exams. Most of the school's first-time test takers took the bar in Tennessee.

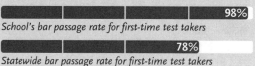

98%

School's bar passage rate for first-time test takers

78%

Statewide bar passage rate for first-time test takers

Vermont Law School

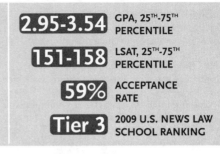

- Chelsea Street, South Royalton, VT, 05068-0096
- http://www.vermontlaw.edu
- Private
- Year founded: 1972
- 2007-2008 tuition: full-time: $31,514; part-time: N/A
- Enrollment 2007-08 academic year: full-time: 555
- U.S. News 2009 law specialty ranking: environmental law: 2

2.95-3.54 GPA, 25TH-75TH PERCENTILE

151-158 LSAT, 25TH-75TH PERCENTILE

59% ACCEPTANCE RATE

Tier 3 2009 U.S. NEWS LAW SCHOOL RANKING

ADMISSIONS
Admissions phone number: **(888) 277-5985**
Admissions email address: **admiss@vermontlaw.edu**
Application website: **N/A**
Application deadline for Fall 2009 admission: **03/01**

Admissions statistics:
Number of applicants for Fall 2007: **989**
Number of acceptances: **580**
Number enrolled: **193**
Acceptance rate: **59%**
GPA, 25th-75th percentile, entering class Fall 2007: **2.95-3.54**
LSAT, 25th-75th percentile, entering class Fall 2007: **151-158**

FINANCIAL AID
Financial aid phone number: **(888) 277-5985**
Financial aid application deadline: **02/15**
Tuition 2007-2008 academic year: full-time: **$31,514**; part-time: **N/A**
Room and board: **$9,720**; books: **$1,000**; miscellaneous expenses: **$7,568**
Total of room/board/books/miscellaneous expenses: **$18,288**
University does not offer graduate student housing for which law students are eligible.

Financial aid profile
Percent of students that received grants for the 2006-2007 academic year: full-time: **52%**
Median grant amount: full-time: **$6,000**
The average law-school debt of those in the Class of 2007 who borrowed: **$108,666**. Proportion who borrowed: **88%**

ACADEMIC PROGRAMS
Calendar: **semester**
Joint degrees awarded: **J.D./M.S.E.L.**
Typical first-year section size: Full-time: **70**
Is there typically a "small section" of the first year class, other than Legal Writing, taught by full-time faculty?:

Full-time: **yes**
Number of course titles, beyond the first year curriculum, offered last year: **123**
Percentages of upper division course sections, excluding seminars, with an enrollment of:
Under 25: **59%**   25 to 49: **27%**
50 to 74: **13%**   75 to 99: **1%**
100+: **0%**
Areas of specialization: appellate advocacy, clinical training, dispute resolution, environmental law, intellectual property law, international law, tax law, trial advocacy

Fall 2007 faculty profile
Total teaching faculty: **55**. Full-time: **73%**; **65%** men, **35%** women, **10%** minorities. Part-time: **27%**; **60%** men, **40%** women, **0%** minorities
Student-to-faculty ratio: **11.6**

SPECIAL PROGRAMS *(as provided by law school):*
Clinics offered. Semester in practice; legislation clinic; environmental semester in Washington, D.C.; environmental and natural resources law clinic; South Royalton legal clinic; general practice program; judicial externships; mediation clinic; M.S.E.L. and LL.M. Environmental Law internships; J.D. internships.

STUDENT BODY
Fall 2007 full-time enrollment: **555**
Men: **50%**   Women: **50%**
African-American: **5.0%**   American Indian: **1.3%**
Asian-American: **2.7%**   Mexican-American: **0.9%**
Puerto Rican: **0.4%**   Other Hisp-Amer: **1.4%**
White: **77.7%**   International: **1.1%**
Unknown: **9.5%**

Attrition rates for 2006-2007 full-time students
Percent of students discontinuing law school:
Men: **3%**   Women: **2%**
First-year students: **7%**   Second-year students: **1%**
Third-year students: **N/A**

LIBRARY RESOURCES

Total volumes: 247,002
Total seats available for library users: 382

INFORMATION TECHNOLOGY

Number of wired network connections available to students: 110 total (in the law library, excluding computer labs: 54; in classrooms: 45; in computer labs: 1; elsewhere in the law school: 10)
Law school has a wireless network.
Students are not required to own a computer.

EMPLOYMENT AND SALARIES

Proportion of 2006 graduates employed at graduation: N/A
Employed 9 months later, as of February 15, 2007: 91%
Salaries in the private sector (law firms, business, industry): $39,500–$70,000 (25th-75th percentile)
Median salary in the private sector: $50,000
Percentage in the private sector who reported salary information: 59%
Median salary in public service (government, judicial clerkships, academic posts, non-profits): $40,000

Percentage of 2006 graduates in:

Law firms: 33%	Government: 13%
Bus./industry: 17%	Judicial clerkship: 16%
Public interest: 18%	Unknown: 0%
Academia: 3%	

2006 graduates employed in-state: 20%
2006 graduates employed in foreign countries: 1%
Number of states where graduates are employed: 35
Percentage of 2006 graduates working in: New England: 40%, Middle Atlantic: 11%, East North Central: 6%, West North Central: 1%, South Atlantic: 22%, East South Central: 1%, West South Central: 0%, Mountain: 3%, Pacific: 14%, Unknown: 0%

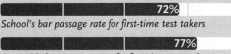

Villanova University

■ 299 N. Spring Mill Road, Villanova, PA, 19085
■ http://www.law.villanova.edu/
■ Private
■ Year founded: 1953
■ 2007-2008 tuition: full-time: $30,890; part-time: N/A
■ Enrollment 2007-08 academic year: full-time: 727
■ U.S. News 2009 law specialty ranking: tax law: 22

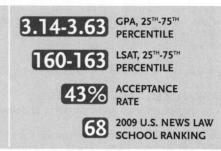

3.14-3.63 GPA, 25TH-75TH PERCENTILE

160-163 LSAT, 25TH-75TH PERCENTILE

43% ACCEPTANCE RATE

68 2009 U.S. NEWS LAW SCHOOL RANKING

ADMISSIONS

Admissions phone number: **(610) 519-7010**
Admissions email address: **admissions@law.villanova.edu**
Application website: **N/A**
Application deadline for Fall 2009 admission: **07/01**

Admissions statistics:
Number of applicants for Fall 2007: **2,557**
Number of acceptances: **1,111**
Number enrolled: **254**
Acceptance rate: **43%**
GPA, 25th-75th percentile, entering class Fall 2007: **3.14-3.63**
LSAT, 25th-75th percentile, entering class Fall 2007: **160-163**

FINANCIAL AID

Financial aid phone number: **(610) 519-7015**
Financial aid application deadline: **N/A**
Tuition 2007-2008 academic year: full-time: **$30,890**; part-time: **N/A**
Room and board: **$14,400**; books: **$1,200**; miscellaneous expenses: **$3,674**
Total of room/board/books/miscellaneous expenses: **$19,274**
University does not offer graduate student housing for which law students are eligible.

Financial aid profile
Percent of students that received grants for the 2006-2007 academic year: full-time: **20%**
Median grant amount: full-time: **$10,000**
The average law-school debt of those in the Class of 2007 who borrowed: **$108,084**. Proportion who borrowed: **81%**

ACADEMIC PROGRAMS

Calendar: **semester**
Joint degrees awarded: **J.D./Ph.D.; J.D./M.B.A.; J.D./LL.M.**
Typical first-year section size: Full-time: **101**

Is there typically a "small section" of the first year class, other than Legal Writing, taught by full-time faculty?: Full-time: **yes**
Number of course titles, beyond the first year curriculum, offered last year: **118**
Percentages of upper division course sections, excluding seminars, with an enrollment of:

Under 25: **63%**   25 to 49: **19%**
50 to 74: **8%**   75 to 99: **8%**
100+: **2%**

Areas of specialization: appellate advocacy, clinical training, dispute resolution, environmental law, healthcare law, intellectual property law, international law, tax law, trial advocacy

Fall 2007 faculty profile
Total teaching faculty: **75**. Full-time: **49%**; **62%** men, **38%** women, **11%** minorities. Part-time: **51%**; **74%** men, **26%** women, **11%** minorities
Student-to-faculty ratio: **16.0**

SPECIAL PROGRAMS (as provided by law school):
Villanova offers five clinics supervised by full-time faculty, capital defense and federal defenders practicums, and 25 externships. It hosts the Pennsylvania Institute on Criminal Sentencing and a sentencing workshop with students, judges, and lawyers. It has joint J.D./M.B.A. and J.D./LL.M. degrees and summer study in Rome. Students participate in national moot court and trial competitions.

STUDENT BODY
Fall 2007 full-time enrollment: 727
Men: **55%**   Women: **45%**
African-American: **4.0%**   American Indian: **0.6%**
Asian-American: **8.3%**   Mexican-American: **0.0%**
Puerto Rican: **0.0%**   Other Hisp-Amer: **3.6%**
White: **82.7%**   International: **1.0%**
Unknown: **0.0%**

Attrition rates for 2006-2007 full-time students
Percent of students discontinuing law school:
Men: 2%   Women: 3%
First-year students: 6%   Second-year students: 1%
Third-year students: N/A

LIBRARY RESOURCES
Total volumes: 539,526
Total seats available for library users: 368

INFORMATION TECHNOLOGY
Number of wired network connections available to students: 318 total (in the law library, excluding computer labs: 106; in classrooms: 60; in computer labs: 130; elsewhere in the law school: 22)
Law school has a wireless network.
Students are not required to own a computer.

EMPLOYMENT AND SALARIES
Proportion of 2006 graduates employed at graduation: 64%
Employed 9 months later, as of February 15, 2007: 94%
Salaries in the private sector (law firms, business, industry): $65,000–$120,000 (25th-75th percentile)
Median salary in the private sector: $100,000
Percentage in the private sector who reported salary information: 66%
Median salary in public service (government, judicial clerkships, academic posts, non-profits): $47,000

Percentage of 2006 graduates in:
Law firms: 59%   Government: 8%
Bus./industry: 14%   Judicial clerkship: 13%
Public interest: 4%   Unknown: 0%
Academia: 2%

2006 graduates employed in-state: 59%
2006 graduates employed in foreign countries: 1%
Number of states where graduates are employed: 19
Percentage of 2006 graduates working in: New England: 3%, Middle Atlantic: 78%, East North Central: 1%, West North Central: 1%, South Atlantic: 15%, East South Central: 1%, West South Central: 1%, Mountain: 1%, Pacific: 2%, Unknown: 0%

BAR PASSAGE RATES
Based on 2006 graduates taking Summer 2006 or Winter 2007 exams. Most of the school's first-time test takers took the bar in Pennsylvania.

86%
School's bar passage rate for first-time test takers

83%
Statewide bar passage rate for first-time test takers

Wake Forest University

- Reynolda Station, PO Box 7206, Winston-Salem, NC, 27109
- http://www.law.wfu.edu
- Private
- Year founded: 1894
- 2007-2008 tuition: full-time: $31,500; part-time: N/A
- Enrollment 2007-08 academic year: full-time: 452; part-time: 10
- U.S. News 2009 law specialty ranking: N/A

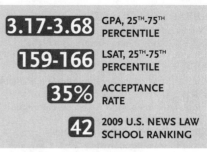

3.17-3.68 GPA, 25ᵀᴴ-75ᵀᴴ PERCENTILE

159-166 LSAT, 25ᵀᴴ-75ᵀᴴ PERCENTILE

35% ACCEPTANCE RATE

42 2009 U.S. NEWS LAW SCHOOL RANKING

ADMISSIONS

Admissions phone number: (336) 758-5437
Admissions email address: **lawadmissions@wfu.edu**
Application website:
  https://www4.lsac.org/school/wakeforest.htm
Application deadline for Fall 2009 admission: 03/15

Admissions statistics:

Number of applicants for Fall 2007: **1,967**
Number of acceptances: **696**
Number enrolled: **160**
Acceptance rate: **35%**
GPA, 25th-75th percentile, entering class Fall 2007: **3.17-3.68**
LSAT, 25th-75th percentile, entering class Fall 2007: **159-166**

FINANCIAL AID

Financial aid phone number: (336) 758-5437
Financial aid application deadline: 04/01
Tuition 2007-2008 academic year: full-time: **$31,500**; part-time: N/A
Room and board: **$8,810**; books: **$800**; miscellaneous expenses: **$6,440**
Total of room/board/books/miscellaneous expenses: **$16,050**
University does not offer graduate student housing for which law students are eligible.

Financial aid profile

Percent of students that received grants for the 2006-2007 academic year: full-time: **40%**
Median grant amount: full-time: **$22,125**
The average law-school debt of those in the Class of 2007 who borrowed: **$83,265**. Proportion who borrowed: **82%**

ACADEMIC PROGRAMS

Calendar: **semester**
Joint degrees awarded: **J.D./M.B.A.**

Typical first-year section size: Full-time: **40**
Is there typically a "small section" of the first year class, other than Legal Writing, taught by full-time faculty?: Full-time: **yes**
Number of course titles, beyond the first year curriculum, offered last year: **96**
Percentages of upper division course sections, excluding seminars, with an enrollment of:
  Under 25: **50%**   25 to 49: **40%**
  50 to 74: **9%**   75 to 99: **1%**
  100+: **0%**
Areas of specialization: appellate advocacy, clinical training, dispute resolution, environmental law, healthcare law, intellectual property law, international law, tax law, trial advocacy

Fall 2007 faculty profile

Total teaching faculty: **65**. Full-time: **62%**; **60%** men, **40%** women, **10%** minorities. Part-time: **38%**; **76%** men, **24%** women, **0%** minorities
Student-to-faculty ratio: **10.3**

SPECIAL PROGRAMS (as provided by law school):

Wake Forest offers two clinical programs: the litigation clinic and the elder law clinic. It also offers three summer-abroad programs in England, Italy, and Austria. Its litigation education program has been hailed as one of the top programs in the country, receiving both the Emil Gumpert Award from the American College of Trial Lawyers and the Roscoe Pound Foundation Award.

STUDENT BODY

Fall 2007 full-time enrollment: 452

Men: **59%**   Women: **41%**
African-American: **7.7%**   American Indian: **0.0%**
Asian-American: **2.9%**   Mexican-American: **0.0%**
Puerto Rican: **0.0%**   Other Hisp-Amer: **1.8%**
White: **81.6%**   International: **0.2%**
Unknown: **5.8%**

Fall 2007 part-time enrollment: 10

Men: 50%	Women: 50%
African-American: 0.0%	American Indian: 0.0%
Asian-American: 0.0%	Mexican-American: 0.0%
Puerto Rican: 0.0%	Other Hisp-Amer: 0.0%
White: 100.0%	International: 0.0%
Unknown: 0.0%	

Attrition rates for 2006-2007 full-time students
Percent of students discontinuing law school:

Men: 0%	Women: 1%
First-year students: 1%	Second-year students: 1%
Third-year students: N/A	

LIBRARY RESOURCES

Total volumes: 418,676
Total seats available for library users: 587

INFORMATION TECHNOLOGY

Number of wired network connections available to students: 123 total (in the law library, excluding computer labs: 64; in classrooms: 0; in computer labs: 30; elsewhere in the law school: 29)
Law school has a wireless network.
Students are required to own a computer.

EMPLOYMENT AND SALARIES

Proportion of 2006 graduates employed at graduation: 71%
Employed 9 months later, as of February 15, 2007: 95%
Salaries in the private sector (law firms, business, industry): $58,000–$115,000 (25th-75th percentile)

Median salary in the private sector: $77,000
Percentage in the private sector who reported salary information: 73%
Median salary in public service (government, judicial clerkships, academic posts, non-profits): $40,000

Percentage of 2006 graduates in:

Law firms: 69%	Government: 11%
Bus./industry: 4%	Judicial clerkship: 11%
Public interest: 3%	Unknown: 2%
Academia: 0%	

2006 graduates employed in-state: 52%
2006 graduates employed in foreign countries: 0%
Number of states where graduates are employed: 25
Percentage of 2006 graduates working in: New England: 3%, Middle Atlantic: 12%, East North Central: 2%, West North Central: 0%, South Atlantic: 69%, East South Central: 6%, West South Central: 1%, Mountain: 3%, Pacific: 3%, Unknown: 0%

BAR PASSAGE RATES

Based on 2006 graduates taking Summer 2006 or Winter 2007 exams. Most of the school's first-time test takers took the bar in North Carolina.

88%
School's bar passage rate for first-time test takers

74%
Statewide bar passage rate for first-time test takers

Washburn University

- 1700 S.W. College Avenue, Topeka, KS, 66621
- http://washburnlaw.edu
- Public
- **Year founded:** 1903
- **2007-2008 tuition:** In-state: full-time: $480/credit hour; part-time: N/A; Out-of-state: full-time: $750/credit hour
- **Enrollment 2007-08 academic year:** full-time: 445
- **U.S. News 2009 law specialty ranking:** N/A

3.06-3.69 GPA, 25TH-75TH PERCENTILE

150-156 LSAT, 25TH-75TH PERCENTILE

52% ACCEPTANCE RATE

Tier 3 2009 U.S. NEWS LAW SCHOOL RANKING

ADMISSIONS

Admissions phone number: **(785) 670-1185**
Admissions email address: **admissions@washburnlaw.edu**
Application website: **http://washburnlaw.edu/applyonline/**
Application deadline for Fall 2009 admission: **04/01**

Admissions statistics:
Number of applicants for Fall 2007: **888**
Number of acceptances: **464**
Number enrolled: **157**
Acceptance rate: **52%**
GPA, 25th-75th percentile, entering class Fall 2007: **3.06-3.69**
LSAT, 25th-75th percentile, entering class Fall 2007: **150-156**

FINANCIAL AID

Financial aid phone number: **(785) 670-1151**
Financial aid application deadline: **07/01**
Tuition 2007-2008 academic year: In-state: full-time: **$480/credit hour**; part-time: **N/A**; Out-of-state: full-time: **$750/credit hour**
Room and board: **$8,381**; books: **$1,772**; miscellaneous expenses: **$4,433**
Total of room/board/books/miscellaneous expenses: **$14,586**
University offers graduate student housing for which law students are eligible.

Financial aid profile
Percent of students that received grants for the 2006-2007 academic year: full-time: **39%**
Median grant amount: full-time: **$5,000**
The average law-school debt of those in the Class of 2007 who borrowed: **$61,200**. Proportion who borrowed: **99%**

ACADEMIC PROGRAMS

Calendar: **semester**
Joint degrees awarded: **J.D./M.S.W.; J.D./M.B.A.**

Typical first-year section size: Full-time: **71**
Is there typically a "small section" of the first year class, other than Legal Writing, taught by full-time faculty?: Full-time: **yes**
Number of course titles, beyond the first year curriculum, offered last year: **92**
Percentages of upper division course sections, excluding seminars, with an enrollment of:

Under 25: **55%**	25 to 49: **31%**
50 to 74: **11%**	75 to 99: **3%**
100+: **0%**	

Areas of specialization: appellate advocacy, clinical training, dispute resolution, environmental law, healthcare law, intellectual property law, international law, tax law, trial advocacy

Fall 2007 faculty profile
Total teaching faculty: **79**. Full-time: **39%**; **61%** men, **39%** women, **23%** minorities. Part-time: **61%**; **75%** men, **25%** women, **4%** minorities
Student-to-faculty ratio: **13.8**

SPECIAL PROGRAMS (as provided by law school):
Law clinics (criminal defense, family law, civil matters, Native American law, transactional law); centers (Excellence in Advocacy, Business and Transactional Law, Children and Family Law); Certificates of specialization (Advocacy; Business and Transactional Law; Estate Planning; Family Law; Natural Resources Law; Tax Law); study abroad (summer and semester programs in the Netherlands).

STUDENT BODY
Fall 2007 full-time enrollment: 445

Men: **60%**	Women: **40%**
African-American: **3.8%**	American Indian: **1.8%**
Asian-American: **2.5%**	Mexican-American: **1.8%**
Puerto Rican: **0.7%**	Other Hisp-Amer: **2.2%**
White: **84.7%**	International: **0.0%**
Unknown: **2.5%**	

Attrition rates for 2006-2007 full-time students
Percent of students discontinuing law school:
Men: 5%   Women: 5%
First-year students: 11%   Second-year students: 1%
Third-year students: 3%

LIBRARY RESOURCES
Total volumes: 385,765
Total seats available for library users: 360

INFORMATION TECHNOLOGY
Number of wired network connections available to students: 27 total (in the law library, excluding computer labs: 27; in classrooms: 0; in computer labs: 0; elsewhere in the law school: 0)
Law school has a wireless network.
Students are not required to own a computer.

EMPLOYMENT AND SALARIES
Proportion of 2006 graduates employed at graduation: N/A
Employed 9 months later, as of February 15, 2007: **94%**
Salaries in the private sector (law firms, business, industry): **$44,000–$65,000** (25th-75th percentile)
Median salary in the private sector: **$51,000**
Percentage in the private sector who reported salary information: 56%
Median salary in public service (government, judicial clerkships, academic posts, non-profits): **$42,036**

Percentage of 2006 graduates in:

Law firms: **49%**	Government: **15%**
Bus./industry: **18%**	Judicial clerkship: **6%**
Public interest: **10%**	Unknown: 0%
Academia: 2%	

2006 graduates employed in-state: **57%**
2006 graduates employed in foreign countries: 0%
Number of states where graduates are employed: **19**
Percentage of 2006 graduates working in: New England: 0%, Middle Atlantic: 1%, East North Central: 2%, West North Central: 76%, South Atlantic: 2%, East South Central: 2%, West South Central: 6%, Mountain: 9%, Pacific: 2%, Unknown: 0%

BAR PASSAGE RATES
Based on 2006 graduates taking Summer 2006 or Winter 2007 exams. Most of the school's first-time test takers took the bar in Kansas.

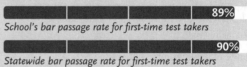

89%
School's bar passage rate for first-time test takers

90%
Statewide bar passage rate for first-time test takers

Washington and Lee University

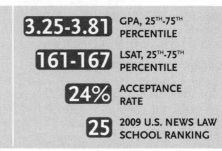

- Sydney Lewis Hall, Lexington, VA, 24450-0303
- http://law.wlu.edu
- Private
- Year founded: 1849
- 2007-2008 tuition: full-time: $33,685; part-time: N/A
- Enrollment 2007-08 academic year: full-time: 395
- U.S. News 2009 law specialty ranking: N/A

3.25-3.81 GPA, 25TH-75TH PERCENTILE

161-167 LSAT, 25TH-75TH PERCENTILE

24% ACCEPTANCE RATE

25 2009 U.S. NEWS LAW SCHOOL RANKING

ADMISSIONS
Admissions phone number: **(540) 458-8504**
Admissions email address: **lawadm@wlu.edu**
Application website:
   http://law.wlu.edu/admissions/application/index.asp
Application deadline for Fall 2009 admission: **02/01**

Admissions statistics:
Number of applicants for Fall 2007: **2,658**
Number of acceptances: **627**
Number enrolled: **116**
Acceptance rate: **24%**
GPA, 25th-75th percentile, entering class Fall 2007: **3.25-3.81**
LSAT, 25th-75th percentile, entering class Fall 2007: **161-167**

FINANCIAL AID
Financial aid phone number: **(540) 458-8729**
Financial aid application deadline: **02/15**
Tuition 2007-2008 academic year: full-time: **$33,685**; part-time: **N/A**
Room and board: **$8,470**; books: **$1,500**; miscellaneous expenses: **$5,725**
Total of room/board/books/miscellaneous expenses: **$15,695**
University offers graduate student housing for which law students are eligible.

Financial aid profile
Percent of students that received grants for the 2006-2007 academic year: full-time: **66%**
Median grant amount: full-time: **$11,500**
The average law-school debt of those in the Class of 2007 who borrowed: **$92,280**. Proportion who borrowed: **82%**

ACADEMIC PROGRAMS
Calendar: **semester**
Joint degrees awarded: **J.D./M.H.A.**

Typical first-year section size: Full-time: **49**
Is there typically a "small section" of the first year class, other than Legal Writing, taught by full-time faculty?:
   Full-time: **yes**
Number of course titles, beyond the first year curriculum, offered last year: **76**
Percentages of upper division course sections, excluding seminars, with an enrollment of:

Under 25: **61%**	25 to 49: **22%**
50 to 74: **14%**	75 to 99: **3%**
100+: **0%**	

Areas of specialization: appellate advocacy, clinical training, dispute resolution, environmental law, healthcare law, intellectual property law, international law, tax law, trial advocacy

Fall 2007 faculty profile
Total teaching faculty: **73**. Full-time: **67%**; 67% men, 33% women, 14% minorities. Part-time: **33%**; 83% men, 17% women, 0% minorities
Student-to-faculty ratio: **10.6**

SPECIAL PROGRAMS *(as provided by law school):*
Community Legal Practice Center, black lung benefits program, Virginia capital case clearinghouse, externships with public interest employers and judges, Shepherd poverty program. Exchange programs with law schools in Germany, Ireland, Denmark, and Canada. Transnational Law Institute, Center for Law and History.

STUDENT BODY
Fall 2007 full-time enrollment: **395**

Men: **62%**	Women: **38%**
African-American: **4.3%**	American Indian: **1.3%**
Asian-American: **7.8%**	Mexican-American: **0.3%**
Puerto Rican: **0.0%**	Other Hisp-Amer: **1.5%**
White: **82.5%**	International: **2.3%**
Unknown: **0.0%**	

Attrition rates for 2006-2007 full-time students
Percent of students discontinuing law school:
Men: **4%**   Women: **4%**
First-year students: **N/A**   Second-year students: **11%**
Third-year students: **N/A**

LIBRARY RESOURCES
Total volumes: **441,228**
Total seats available for library users: **536**

INFORMATION TECHNOLOGY
Number of wired network connections available to students: **345** total (in the law library, excluding computer labs: **0**; in classrooms: **315**; in computer labs: **10**; elsewhere in the law school: **20**)
Law school has a wireless network.
Students are not required to own a computer.

EMPLOYMENT AND SALARIES
Proportion of 2006 graduates employed at graduation: **74%**
Employed 9 months later, as of February 15, 2007: **92%**
Salaries in the private sector (law firms, business, industry): **$70,000–$125,000** (25th-75th percentile)
Median salary in the private sector: **$100,000**
Percentage in the private sector who reported salary information: **99%**
Median salary in public service (government, judicial clerkships, academic posts, non-profits): **$46,725**

Percentage of 2006 graduates in:
Law firms: **56%**   Government: **8%**
Bus./industry: **11%**   Judicial clerkship: **19%**
Public interest: **5%**   Unknown: **1%**
Academia: **0%**

2006 graduates employed in-state: **29%**
2006 graduates employed in foreign countries: **1%**
Number of states where graduates are employed: **23**
Percentage of 2006 graduates working in: New England: **2%**, Middle Atlantic: **11%**, East North Central: **1%**, West North Central: **0%**, South Atlantic: **71%**, East South Central: **3%**, West South Central: **2%**, Mountain: **4%**, Pacific: **4%**, Unknown: **1%**

BAR PASSAGE RATES
Based on 2006 graduates taking Summer 2006 or Winter 2007 exams. Most of the school's first-time test takers took the bar in Virginia.

79%
School's bar passage rate for first-time test takers

74%
Statewide bar passage rate for first-time test takers

Washington University in St. Louis

■ 1 Brookings Drive, Box 1120, St. Louis, MO, 63130
■ http://www.law.wustl.edu/
■ Private
■ Year founded: 1867
■ 2007-2008 tuition: full-time: $38,189; part-time: N/A
■ Enrollment 2007-08 academic year: full-time: 801; part-time: 9
■ U.S. News 2009 law specialty ranking: clinical training: 6, intellectual property law: 22, trial advocacy: 4

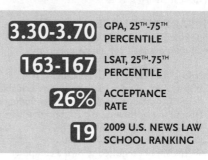

3.30-3.70 GPA, 25ᵀᴴ-75ᵀᴴ PERCENTILE

163-167 LSAT, 25ᵀᴴ-75ᵀᴴ PERCENTILE

26% ACCEPTANCE RATE

19 2009 U.S. NEWS LAW SCHOOL RANKING

ADMISSIONS

Admissions phone number: **(314) 935-4525**
Admissions email address: **admiss@wulaw.wustl.edu**
Application website:
https://www.law.wustl.edu/Admissions/wuforms
Application deadline for Fall 2009 admission: **03/01**

Admissions statistics:

Number of applicants for Fall 2007: **3,644**
Number of acceptances: **936**
Number enrolled: **221**
Acceptance rate: **26%**
GPA, 25th-75th percentile, entering class Fall 2007: **3.30-3.70**
LSAT, 25th-75th percentile, entering class Fall 2007: **163-167**

FINANCIAL AID

Financial aid phone number: **(314) 935-4605**
Financial aid application deadline: **03/01**
Tuition 2007-2008 academic year: full-time: **$38,189**; part-time: **N/A**
Room and board: **$11,000**; books: **$2,000**; miscellaneous expenses: **$6,600**
Total of room/board/books/miscellaneous expenses: **$19,600**
University offers graduate student housing for which law students are eligible.

Financial aid profile

Percent of students that received grants for the 2006-2007 academic year: full-time: **56%**
Median grant amount: full-time: **$15,000**
The average law-school debt of those in the Class of 2007 who borrowed: **$100,220.**
Proportion who borrowed: **78%**

ACADEMIC PROGRAMS

Calendar: **semester**
Joint degrees awarded: **J.D./M.B.A.; J.D./M.A. East Asian Studies; J.D./M.S.W.; J.D./M.A. European Studies; J.D./M.S. Biology; J.D./M.H.A.; J.D./M.S. Engineering and Policy; J.D./M.A. Political Science; J.D./M.A. Islamic Studies; J.D./M.A. International Affairs; J.D./M.A. History; J.D./M.S. Environmental Engineering**
Typical first-year section size: Full-time: **89**
Is there typically a "small section" of the first year class, other than Legal Writing, taught by full-time faculty?: Full-time: **yes**
Number of course titles, beyond the first year curriculum, offered last year: **122**
Percentages of upper division course sections, excluding seminars, with an enrollment of:
Under 25: **64%**   25 to 49: **16%**
50 to 74: **11%**   75 to 99: **5%**
100+: **5%**
Areas of specialization: appellate advocacy, clinical training, dispute resolution, environmental law, healthcare law, intellectual property law, international law, tax law, trial advocacy

Fall 2007 faculty profile

Total teaching faculty: **186.** Full-time: **35%**; **55%** men, **45%** women, **8%** minorities. Part-time: **65%**; **80%** men, **20%** women, **8%** minorities
Student-to-faculty ratio: **11.6**

SPECIAL PROGRAMS *(as provided by law school):*

Students can choose from nine clinics to learn professional skills and values by working in the real world with clients, attorneys, judges, and legislators. Study abroad in the Netherlands at the Summer Institute for Global Justice. Joint degrees: many options for combining law with another master's program, including social work.

STUDENT BODY

Fall 2007 full-time enrollment: 801

Men: 55%   Women: 45%
African-American: 6.5%   American Indian: 0.6%
Asian-American: 8.7%   Mexican-American: 0.2%
Puerto Rican: 0.2%   Other Hisp-Amer: 1.0%
White: 48.9%   International: 6.4%
Unknown: 27.3%

Fall 2007 part-time enrollment: 9

Men: 44%   Women: 56%
African-American: 11.1%   American Indian: 0.0%
Asian-American: 22.2%   Mexican-American: 0.0%
Puerto Rican: 0.0%   Other Hisp-Amer: 0.0%
White: 33.3%   International: 22.2%
Unknown: 11.1%

Attrition rates for 2006-2007 full-time students

Percent of students discontinuing law school:
Men: 2%   Women: 1%
First-year students: 3%   Second-year students: 1%
Third-year students: N/A

LIBRARY RESOURCES

Total volumes: 703,847
Total seats available for library users: 485

INFORMATION TECHNOLOGY

Number of wired network connections available to students: 760 total (in the law library, excluding computer labs: 430; in classrooms: 200; in computer labs: 45; elsewhere in the law school: 85)
Law school has a wireless network.
Students are not required to own a computer.

EMPLOYMENT AND SALARIES

Proportion of 2006 graduates employed at graduation: 84%
Employed 9 months later, as of February 15, 2007: 99%

Salaries in the private sector (law firms, business, industry): $83,000–$130,000 (25th-75th percentile)
Median salary in the private sector: $100,000
Percentage in the private sector who reported salary information: 63%
Median salary in public service (government, judicial clerkships, academic posts, non-profits): $50,000

Percentage of 2006 graduates in:

Law firms: 62%   Government: 17%
Bus./industry: 6%   Judicial clerkship: 10%
Public interest: 5%   Unknown: 0%
Academia: 0%

2006 graduates employed in-state: 26%
2006 graduates employed in foreign countries: 2%
Number of states where graduates are employed: 32
Percentage of 2006 graduates working in: New England: 2%, Middle Atlantic: 13%, East North Central: 21%, West North Central: 28%, South Atlantic: 15%, East South Central: 3%, West South Central: 4%, Mountain: 5%, Pacific: 6%, Unknown: 1%

BAR PASSAGE RATES

Based on 2006 graduates taking Summer 2006 or Winter 2007 exams. Most of the school's first-time test takers took the bar in Illinois.

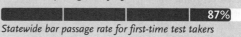

| 93% |

School's bar passage rate for first-time test takers

| 87% |

Statewide bar passage rate for first-time test takers

Wayne State University

- 471 W. Palmer Street, Detroit, MI, 48202
- http://www.law.wayne.edu
- Public
- **Year founded:** 1927
- **2007-2008 tuition:** In-state: full-time: $21,328; part-time: $11,534; Out-of-state: full-time: $23,305
- **Enrollment 2007-08 academic year:** full-time: 481; part-time: 134
- **U.S. News 2009 law specialty ranking:** N/A

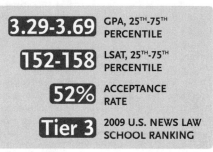

3.29-3.69 GPA, 25ᵀᴴ-75ᵀᴴ PERCENTILE

152-158 LSAT, 25ᵀᴴ-75ᵀᴴ PERCENTILE

52% ACCEPTANCE RATE

Tier 3 2009 U.S. NEWS LAW SCHOOL RANKING

ADMISSIONS

Admissions phone number: **(313) 577-3937**
Admissions email address: **lawinquire@wayne.edu**
Application website: **http://www.law.wayne.edu**
Application deadline for Fall 2009 admission: **03/15**

Admissions statistics:
Number of applicants for Fall 2007: **947**
Number of acceptances: **491**
Number enrolled: **127**
Acceptance rate: **52%**
GPA, 25th-75th percentile, entering class Fall 2007: **3.29-3.69**
LSAT, 25th-75th percentile, entering class Fall 2007: **152-158**

Part-time program:
Number of applicants for Fall 2007: **126**
Number of acceptances: **42**
Number enrolled: **28**
Acceptance rate: **33%**
GPA, 25th-75th percentile, entering class Fall 2007: **3.25-3.67**
LSAT, 25th-75th percentile, entering class Fall 2007: **149-156**

FINANCIAL AID

Financial aid phone number: **(313) 577-5142**
Financial aid application deadline: **N/A**
Tuition 2007-2008 academic year: In-state: full-time: **$21,328**; part-time: **$11,534**; Out-of-state: full-time: **$23,305**
Room and board: **$12,696**; books: **$1,060**; miscellaneous expenses: **$8,424**
Total of room/board/books/miscellaneous expenses: **$22,180**
University offers graduate student housing for which law students are eligible.

Financial aid profile
Percent of students that received grants for the 2006-2007 academic year: full-time: **67%**; part-time **19%**
Median grant amount: full-time: **$4,000**; part-time: **$2,500**
The average law-school debt of those in the Class of 2007 who borrowed: **$60,228**. Proportion who borrowed: **81%**

ACADEMIC PROGRAMS

Calendar: **semester**
Joint degrees awarded: **J.D./M.A. History; J.D./M.A. Political Science; J.D./M.B.A.; J.D./M.A. Dispute Resolution; J.D./M.A. Economics**
Typical first-year section size: Full-time: **86**; Part-time: **38**
Is there typically a "small section" of the first year class, other than Legal Writing, taught by full-time faculty?: Full-time: **no**; Part-time: **no**
Number of course titles, beyond the first year curriculum, offered last year: **80**
Percentages of upper division course sections, excluding seminars, with an enrollment of:

Under 25: **57%**	25 to 49: **29%**
50 to 74: **8%**	75 to 99: **2%**
100+: **4%**	

Areas of specialization: appellate advocacy, clinical training, dispute resolution, environmental law, healthcare law, intellectual property law, international law, tax law, trial advocacy

Fall 2007 faculty profile
Total teaching faculty: **110**. Full-time: **63%**; **68%** men, **32%** women, **9%** minorities. Part-time: **37%**; **73%** men, **27%** women, **2%** minorities
Student-to-faculty ratio: **14.2**

SPECIAL PROGRAMS *(as provided by law school):*
Wayne State offers five live-client clinics (disability, criminal appeals, civil rights, a free legal aid clinic, and a small business clinic), and approximately 70 internship placements with judges, prosecutors, defenders' offices, and organizations. The school has a summer semester with courses offered mostly in the evening and an exchange program with Maastricht University in the Netherlands.

STUDENT BODY

Fall 2007 full-time enrollment: 481

Men: 52%	Women: 48%
African-American: 7.9%	American Indian: 0.2%
Asian-American: 4.2%	Mexican-American: 0.0%
Puerto Rican: 0.0%	Other Hisp-Amer: 4.0%
White: 82.1%	International: 1.7%
Unknown: 0.0%	

Fall 2007 part-time enrollment: 134

Men: 50%	Women: 50%
African-American: 16.4%	American Indian: 0.7%
Asian-American: 5.2%	Mexican-American: 0.7%
Puerto Rican: 0.0%	Other Hisp-Amer: 2.2%
White: 74.6%	International: 0.0%
Unknown: 0.0%	

Attrition rates for 2006-2007 full-time students
Percent of students discontinuing law school:

Men: 3%	Women: 4%
First-year students: 9%	Second-year students: 1%
Third-year students: 1%	

LIBRARY RESOURCES

Total volumes: 615,691
Total seats available for library users: 463

INFORMATION TECHNOLOGY

Number of wired network connections available to students: 173 total (in the law library, excluding computer labs: 68; in classrooms: 50; in computer labs: 25; elsewhere in the law school: 30)
Law school has a wireless network.
Students are not required to own a computer.

EMPLOYMENT AND SALARIES

Proportion of 2006 graduates employed at graduation: N/A
Employed 9 months later, as of February 15, 2007: **88%**

Salaries in the private sector (law firms, business, industry): $50,000–$90,000 (25th-75th percentile)
Median salary in the private sector: **$60,000**
Percentage in the private sector who reported salary information: 43%
Median salary in public service (government, judicial clerkships, academic posts, non-profits): **$48,000**

Percentage of 2006 graduates in:

Law firms: 75%	Government: 4%
Bus./industry: 13%	Judicial clerkship: 3%
Public interest: 3%	Unknown: 0%
Academia: 2%	

2006 graduates employed in-state: 94%
2006 graduates employed in foreign countries: 0%
Number of states where graduates are employed: 9
Percentage of 2006 graduates working in: New England: 0%, Middle Atlantic: 1%, East North Central: 96%, West North Central: 0%, South Atlantic: 2%, East South Central: 0%, West South Central: 0%, Mountain: 1%, Pacific: 1%, Unknown: 0%

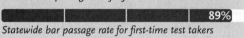

BAR PASSAGE RATES

Based on 2006 graduates taking Summer 2006 or Winter 2007 exams. Most of the school's first-time test takers took the bar in Michigan.

92%	
School's bar passage rate for first-time test takers	
89%	
Statewide bar passage rate for first-time test takers	

West Virginia University

■ PO Box 6130, Morgantown, WV, 26506-6130
■ http://www.wvu.edu/~law
■ Public
■ Year founded: 1878
■ 2007-2008 tuition: In-state: full-time: $9,856; part-time: $551/credit hour; Out-of-state: full-time: $22,432
■ Enrollment 2007-08 academic year: full-time: 443
■ U.S. News 2009 law specialty ranking: N/A

3.18-3.75 GPA, 25TH-75TH PERCENTILE

150-156 LSAT, 25TH-75TH PERCENTILE

37% ACCEPTANCE RATE

Tier 3 2009 U.S. NEWS LAW SCHOOL RANKING

ADMISSIONS

Admissions phone number: **(304) 293-5304**
Admissions email address: **wvu-law.admissions@mail.wvu.edu**
Application website: **https://wvulaw.wvu.edu/Apps/**
Application deadline for Fall 2009 admission: **02/01**

Admissions statistics:

Number of applicants for Fall 2007: **846**
Number of acceptances: **315**
Number enrolled: **141**
Acceptance rate: **37%**
GPA, 25th-75th percentile, entering class Fall 2007: **3.18-3.75**
LSAT, 25th-75th percentile, entering class Fall 2007: **150-156**

FINANCIAL AID

Financial aid phone number: **(304) 293-5302**
Financial aid application deadline: **04/01**
Tuition 2007-2008 academic year: In-state: full-time: **$9,856**; part-time: **$551/credit hour**; Out-of-state: full-time: **$22,432**
Room and board: **$8,700**; books: **$1,225**; miscellaneous expenses: **$2,790**
Total of room/board/books/miscellaneous expenses: **$12,715**
University offers graduate student housing for which law students are eligible.

Financial aid profile

Percent of students that received grants for the 2006-2007 academic year: full-time: **36%**
Median grant amount: full-time: **$1,600**
The average law-school debt of those in the Class of 2007 who borrowed: **$46,094.** Proportion who borrowed: **84%**

ACADEMIC PROGRAMS

Calendar: **semester**
Joint degrees awarded: **J.D./M.B.A.; J.D./M.P.A.**
Typical first-year section size: Full-time: **70**

Is there typically a "small section" of the first year class, other than Legal Writing, taught by full-time faculty?: Full-time: **no**
Number of course titles, beyond the first year curriculum, offered last year: **66**
Percentages of upper division course sections, excluding seminars, with an enrollment of:
Under 25: **49%**   25 to 49: **31%**
50 to 74: **14%**   75 to 99: **5%**
100+: **1%**
Areas of specialization: appellate advocacy, clinical training, dispute resolution, environmental law, healthcare law, intellectual property law, international law, tax law, trial advocacy

Fall 2007 faculty profile

Total teaching faculty: **44.** Full-time: **50%**; **73%** men, **27%** women, **9%** minorities. Part-time: **50%**; **59%** men, **41%** women, **0%** minorities
Student-to-faculty ratio: **13.8**

SPECIAL PROGRAMS *(as provided by law school):*

Live client clinical program (civil, tax, innocence project, mediation, and immigration cases); federal judicial externship program.

STUDENT BODY

Fall 2007 full-time enrollment: 443

Men: **56%**	Women: **44%**
African-American: **7.9%**	American Indian: **0.2%**
Asian-American: **2.9%**	Mexican-American: **0.0%**
Puerto Rican: **0.0%**	Other Hisp-Amer: **0.7%**
White: **87.8%**	International: **0.5%**
Unknown: **0.0%**	

Attrition rates for 2006-2007 full-time students

Percent of students discontinuing law school:
Men: **4%**	Women: **4%**
First-year students: **10%**	Second-year students: **1%**
Third-year students: **N/A**	

LIBRARY RESOURCES

Total volumes: 348,423
Total seats available for library users: 274

INFORMATION TECHNOLOGY

Number of wired network connections available to students: 140 total (in the law library, excluding computer labs: 130; in classrooms: 0; in computer labs: 0; elsewhere in the law school: 10)
Law school has a wireless network.
Students are not required to own a computer.

EMPLOYMENT AND SALARIES

Proportion of 2006 graduates employed at graduation: 68%
Employed 9 months later, as of February 15, 2007: 95%
Salaries in the private sector (law firms, business, industry): $35,400–$106,000 (25th-75th percentile)
Median salary in the private sector: $52,500
Percentage in the private sector who reported salary information: 67%
Median salary in public service (government, judicial clerkships, academic posts, non-profits): $39,000

Percentage of 2006 graduates in:

Law firms: 51%	Government: 7%
Bus./industry: 14%	Judicial clerkship: 19%
Public interest: 5%	Unknown: 0%
Academia: 5%	

2006 graduates employed in-state: 69%
2006 graduates employed in foreign countries: 0%
Number of states where graduates are employed: 15
Percentage of 2006 graduates working in: New England: 1%, Middle Atlantic: 4%, East North Central: 2%, West North Central: 0%, South Atlantic: 91%, East South Central: 1%, West South Central: 1%, Mountain: 2%, Pacific: 0%, Unknown: 0%

BAR PASSAGE RATES

Based on 2006 graduates taking Summer 2006 or Winter 2007 exams. Most of the school's first-time test takers took the bar in West Virginia.

66%

School's bar passage rate for first-time test takers

66%

Statewide bar passage rate for first-time test takers

Western New England College

■ 1215 Wilbraham Road, Springfield, MA, 01119-2684
■ http://www.law.wnec.edu
■ Private
■ Year founded: 1919
■ 2007-2008 tuition: full-time: $31,048; part-time: $23,286
■ Enrollment 2007-08 academic year: full-time: 397; part-time: 182
■ U.S. News 2009 law specialty ranking: N/A

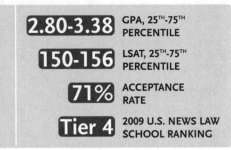

2.80-3.38 GPA, 25TH-75TH PERCENTILE

150-156 LSAT, 25TH-75TH PERCENTILE

71% ACCEPTANCE RATE

Tier 4 2009 U.S. NEWS LAW SCHOOL RANKING

ADMISSIONS

Admissions phone number: **(413) 782-1406**
Admissions email address: **admissions@law.wnec.edu**
Application website:
  http://wneclaw.wnec.edu/inquiries.html
Application deadline for Fall 2009 admission: **rolling**

Admissions statistics:
Number of applicants for Fall 2007: **1,788**
Number of acceptances: **1,270**
Number enrolled: **151**
Acceptance rate: **71%**
GPA, 25th-75th percentile, entering class Fall 2007: **2.80-3.38**
LSAT, 25th-75th percentile, entering class Fall 2007: **150-156**

Part-time program:
Number of applicants for Fall 2007: **276**
Number of acceptances: **140**
Number enrolled: **54**
Acceptance rate: **51%**
GPA, 25th-75th percentile, entering class Fall 2007: **2.77-3.40**
LSAT, 25th-75th percentile, entering class Fall 2007: **148-152**

FINANCIAL AID

Financial aid phone number: **(413) 796-2080**
Financial aid application deadline: **N/A**
Tuition 2007-2008 academic year: full-time: **$31,048**; part-time: **$23,286**
Room and board: **$12,456**; books: **$1,386**; miscellaneous expenses: **$5,867**
Total of room/board/books/miscellaneous expenses: **$19,709**
University offers graduate student housing for which law students are eligible.

Financial aid profile
Percent of students that received grants for the 2006-2007 academic year: full-time: **54%**; part-time **24%**
Median grant amount: full-time: **$17,000**; part-time: **$5,000**
The average law-school debt of those in the Class of 2007 who borrowed: **$82,793**. Proportion who borrowed: **75%**

ACADEMIC PROGRAMS

Calendar: **semester**
Joint degrees awarded: **J.D./M.S.W.; J.D./M.R.P.; J.D./M.B.A.**
Typical first-year section size: Full-time: **50**; Part-time: **50**
Is there typically a "small section" of the first year class, other than Legal Writing, taught by full-time faculty?: Full-time: **no**; Part-time: **no**
Number of course titles, beyond the first year curriculum, offered last year: **90**
Percentages of upper division course sections, excluding seminars, with an enrollment of:

Under 25: **60%**   25 to 49: **35%**
50 to 74: **4%**   75 to 99: **1%**
100+: **0%**

Areas of specialization: appellate advocacy, clinical training, dispute resolution, environmental law, healthcare law, intellectual property law, international law, tax law, trial advocacy

Fall 2007 faculty profile
Total teaching faculty: **65**. Full-time: **46%**; 50% men, 50% women, 7% minorities. Part-time: **54%**; 77% men, 23% women, 3% minorities
Student-to-faculty ratio: **13.8**

SPECIAL PROGRAMS *(as provided by law school):*
All first-year law classes are 50 students or less. Clinics: criminal, consumer protection, legal services, small business, real estate. Externship program with judges or government agencies. Centers: Law and Business Center for Advancing Entrepreneurship; the Legislative and Governmental Affairs Institute. Skills training with simulation courses. Foreign summer study encouraged.

STUDENT BODY

Fall 2007 full-time enrollment: 397

Men: 58%	Women: 42%
African-American: 2.5%	American Indian: 0.5%
Asian-American: 3.8%	Mexican-American: 0.0%
Puerto Rican: 0.0%	Other Hisp-Amer: 3.5%
White: 69.3%	International: 2.5%
Unknown: 17.9%	

Fall 2007 part-time enrollment: 182

Men: 52%	Women: 48%
African-American: 4.4%	American Indian: 0.0%
Asian-American: 1.6%	Mexican-American: 0.0%
Puerto Rican: 0.0%	Other Hisp-Amer: 2.7%
White: 67.6%	International: 0.5%
Unknown: 23.1%	

Attrition rates for 2006-2007 full-time students
Percent of students discontinuing law school:

Men: 6%	Women: 6%
First-year students: 14%	Second-year students: 3%
Third-year students: N/A	

LIBRARY RESOURCES

Total volumes: 349,823
Total seats available for library users: 281

INFORMATION TECHNOLOGY

Number of wired network connections available to students: 32 total (in the law library, excluding computer labs: 20; in classrooms: 6; in computer labs: 6; elsewhere in the law school: 0)
Law school has a wireless network.
Students are not required to own a computer.

EMPLOYMENT AND SALARIES

Proportion of 2006 graduates employed at graduation: N/A
Employed 9 months later, as of February 15, 2007: 76%

Salaries in the private sector (law firms, business, industry): $40,000–$60,000 (25th-75th percentile)
Median salary in the private sector: $50,000
Percentage in the private sector who reported salary information: 69%
Median salary in public service (government, judicial clerkships, academic posts, non-profits): $38,250

Percentage of 2006 graduates in:

Law firms: 43%	Government: 18%
Bus./industry: 26%	Judicial clerkship: 7%
Public interest: 4%	Unknown: 0%
Academia: 2%	

2006 graduates employed in-state: 39%
2006 graduates employed in foreign countries: 2%
Number of states where graduates are employed: 20
Percentage of 2006 graduates working in: New England: 68%, Middle Atlantic: 16%, East North Central: 0%, West North Central: 1%, South Atlantic: 7%, East South Central: 0%, West South Central: 0%, Mountain: 2%, Pacific: 5%, Unknown: 0%

Western State University

■ 1111 N. State College Boulevard, Fullerton, CA, 92831
■ http://www.wsulaw.edu
■ Private
■ Year founded: 1966
■ 2007-2008 tuition: full-time: $29,770; part-time: $20,070
■ Enrollment 2007-08 academic year: full-time: 259; part-time: 129
■ U.S. News 2009 law specialty ranking: N/A

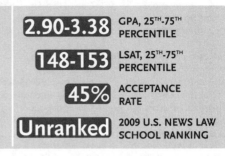

2.90-3.38 GPA, 25TH-75TH PERCENTILE

148-153 LSAT, 25TH-75TH PERCENTILE

45% ACCEPTANCE RATE

Unranked 2009 U.S. NEWS LAW SCHOOL RANKING

ADMISSIONS
Admissions phone number: **(714) 459-1101**
Admissions email address: **adm@wsulaw.edu**
Application website:
   https://www.applyweb.com/aw?wsulaw
Application deadline for Fall 2009 admission: **rolling**

Admissions statistics:
Number of applicants for Fall 2007: **1,418**
Number of acceptances: **640**
Number enrolled: **106**
Acceptance rate: **45%**
GPA, 25th-75th percentile, entering class Fall 2007: **2.90-3.38**
LSAT, 25th-75th percentile, entering class Fall 2007: **148-153**

Part-time program:
Number of applicants for Fall 2007: **398**
Number of acceptances: **145**
Number enrolled: **50**
Acceptance rate: **36%**
GPA, 25th-75th percentile, entering class Fall 2007: **2.90-3.39**
LSAT, 25th-75th percentile, entering class Fall 2007: **148-154**

FINANCIAL AID
Financial aid phone number: **(714) 459-1120**
Financial aid application deadline: **N/A**
Tuition 2007-2008 academic year: full-time: **$29,770**; part-time: **$20,070**
Room and board: **$14,018**; books: **$1,500**; miscellaneous expenses: **$7,299**
Total of room/board/books/miscellaneous expenses: **$22,817**
University does not offer graduate student housing for which law students are eligible.

Financial aid profile
Percent of students that received grants for the 2006-2007 academic year: full-time: **53%**; part-time **47%**
Median grant amount: full-time: **$10,000**; part-time: **$7,300**
The average law-school debt of those in the Class of 2007 who borrowed: **$89,151**. Proportion who borrowed: **92%**

ACADEMIC PROGRAMS
Calendar: **semester**
Joint degrees awarded: **J.D./M.B.A.**
Typical first-year section size: Full-time: **65**; Part-time: **32**
Is there typically a "small section" of the first year class, other than Legal Writing, taught by full-time faculty?: Full-time: **no**; Part-time: **no**
Number of course titles, beyond the first year curriculum, offered last year: **50**
Percentages of upper division course sections, excluding seminars, with an enrollment of:
   Under 25: **61%**   25 to 49: **24%**
   50 to 74: **14%**   75 to 99: **1%**
   100+: **0%**
Areas of specialization: appellate advocacy, clinical training, dispute resolution, environmental law, healthcare law, intellectual property law, international law, tax law, trial advocacy

Fall 2007 faculty profile
Total teaching faculty: **34**. Full-time: **38%**; **69%** men, **31%** women, **31%** minorities. Part-time: **62%**; **57%** men, **43%** women, **19%** minorities
Student-to-faculty ratio: **15.6**

SPECIAL PROGRAMS *(as provided by law school)*:
Civil and family law clinic on-site; Business Law Center offers a Certificate in Business Law; Criminal Law Practice Center offers a Certificate in Criminal Law; civil and criminal internships and externships.

STUDENT BODY

Fall 2007 full-time enrollment: 259
Men: 52%   Women: 48%
African-American: 5.0%   American Indian: 0.4%
Asian-American: 15.4%   Mexican-American: 5.4%
Puerto Rican: 0.4%   Other Hisp-Amer: 4.2%
White: 58.3%   International: 1.5%
Unknown: 9.3%

Fall 2007 part-time enrollment: 129
Men: 50%   Women: 50%
African-American: 2.3%   American Indian: 0.8%
Asian-American: 19.4%   Mexican-American: 5.4%
Puerto Rican: 0.0%   Other Hisp-Amer: 3.9%
White: 56.6%   International: 1.6%
Unknown: 10.1%

Attrition rates for 2006-2007 full-time students
Percent of students discontinuing law school:
Men: 20%   Women: 23%
First-year students: 39%   Second-year students: 18%
Third-year students: 4%

LIBRARY RESOURCES

Total volumes: 203,268
Total seats available for library users: 336

INFORMATION TECHNOLOGY

Number of wired network connections available to students: 249 total (in the law library, excluding computer labs: 148; in classrooms: 68; in computer labs: 21; elsewhere in the law school: 12)
Law school has a wireless network.
Students are not required to own a computer.

EMPLOYMENT AND SALARIES

Proportion of 2006 graduates employed at graduation: N/A
Employed 9 months later, as of February 15, 2007: N/A

Salaries in the private sector (law firms, business, industry): $40,000–$75,000 (25th-75th percentile)
Median salary in the private sector: $54,000
Percentage in the private sector who reported salary information: 82%
Median salary in public service (government, judicial clerkships, academic posts, non-profits): $68,000

Percentage of 2006 graduates in:
Law firms: 55%   Government: 13%
Bus./industry: 21%   Judicial clerkship: 0%
Public interest: 2%   Unknown: 4%
Academia: 5%

2006 graduates employed in-state: 95%
2006 graduates employed in foreign countries: N/A
Number of states where graduates are employed: 3
Percentage of 2006 graduates working in: New England: N/A, Middle Atlantic: N/A, East North Central: N/A, West North Central: N/A, South Atlantic: N/A, East South Central: N/A, West South Central: N/A, Mountain: N/A, Pacific: N/A, Unknown: N/A

BAR PASSAGE RATES

Based on 2006 graduates taking Summer 2006 or Winter 2007 exams. Most of the school's first-time test takers took the bar in California.

N/A			

School's bar passage rate for first-time test takers

N/A			

Statewide bar passage rate for first-time test takers

Whittier Law School

■ 3333 Harbor Boulevard, Costa Mesa, CA, 92626-1501
■ http://www.law.whittier.edu
■ Private
■ Year founded: 1975
■ 2007-2008 tuition: full-time: $31,750; part-time: $21,180
■ Enrollment 2007-08 academic year: full-time: 372; part-time: 220
■ U.S. News 2009 law specialty ranking: N/A

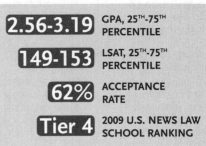

2.56-3.19 GPA, 25TH-75TH PERCENTILE

149-153 LSAT, 25TH-75TH PERCENTILE

62% ACCEPTANCE RATE

Tier 4 2009 U.S. NEWS LAW SCHOOL RANKING

ADMISSIONS
Admissions phone number: **(800) 808-8188**
Admissions email address: **info@law.whittier.edu**
Application website:
http://www4.lsac.org/LSACD_on_the_web/ login/open.aspx
Application deadline for Fall 2009 admission: **03/15**

Admissions statistics:
Number of applicants for Fall 2007: **1,214**
Number of acceptances: **748**
Number enrolled: **183**
Acceptance rate: **62%**
GPA, 25th-75th percentile, entering class Fall 2007: **2.56-3.19**
LSAT, 25th-75th percentile, entering class Fall 2007: **149-153**

Part-time program:
Number of applicants for Fall 2007: **227**
Number of acceptances: **121**
Number enrolled: **54**
Acceptance rate: **53%**
GPA, 25th-75th percentile, entering class Fall 2007: **2.62-3.22**
LSAT, 25th-75th percentile, entering class Fall 2007: **149-154**

FINANCIAL AID
Financial aid phone number: **(714) 444-4141**
Financial aid application deadline: **10/29**
Tuition 2007-2008 academic year: full-time: **$31,750**; part-time: **$21,180**
Room and board: **$10,800**; books: **$1,158**; miscellaneous expenses: **$5,756**
Total of room/board/books/miscellaneous expenses: **$17,714**
University does not offer graduate student housing for which law students are eligible.

Financial aid profile
Percent of students that received grants for the 2006-2007 academic year: full-time: **53%**; part-time **30%**
Median grant amount: full-time: **$12,000**; part-time: **$8,275**
The average law-school debt of those in the Class of 2007 who borrowed: **$98,385**. Proportion who borrowed: **78%**

ACADEMIC PROGRAMS
Calendar: **semester**
Joint degrees awarded: **N/A**
Typical first-year section size: Full-time: **82**; Part-time: **44**
Is there typically a "small section" of the first year class, other than Legal Writing, taught by full-time faculty?: Full-time: **no**; Part-time: **no**
Number of course titles, beyond the first year curriculum, offered last year: **123**
Percentages of upper division course sections, excluding seminars, with an enrollment of:

Under 25: **75%**	25 to 49: **15%**
50 to 74: **6%**	75 to 99: **3%**
100+: **0%**	

Areas of specialization: appellate advocacy, clinical training, dispute resolution, environmental law, healthcare law, intellectual property law, international law, tax law, trial advocacy

Fall 2007 faculty profile
Total teaching faculty: **124**. Full-time: **49%**; N/A men, N/A women, **N/A** minorities. Part-time: **51%**; N/A men, N/A women, **N/A** minorities
Student-to-faculty ratio: **13.9**

SPECIAL PROGRAMS (as provided by law school):
Center for Children's Rights; Center for Intellectual Property Law; Center for International and Comparative Law; exchange programs in France and Spain; five summer-abroad programs in Spain, France, the Netherlands, China, and Israel; Institute for Student and Graduate Academic Support; Institute for Legal Writing and Professional Skills; LL.M. Degree in U.S. Legal Studies for Foreign Lawyers.

STUDENT BODY

Fall 2007 full-time enrollment: 372

Men: 47%	Women: 53%
African-American: 1.1%	American Indian: 0.0%
Asian-American: 22.8%	Mexican-American: 5.6%
Puerto Rican: 0.5%	Other Hisp-Amer: 5.1%
White: 45.7%	International: 0.3%
Unknown: 18.8%	

Fall 2007 part-time enrollment: 220

Men: 49%	Women: 51%
African-American: 4.5%	American Indian: 1.4%
Asian-American: 15.0%	Mexican-American: 4.1%
Puerto Rican: 0.5%	Other Hisp-Amer: 4.1%
White: 53.6%	International: 1.4%
Unknown: 15.5%	

Attrition rates for 2006-2007 full-time students
Percent of students discontinuing law school:

Men: 6%	Women: 4%
First-year students: 16%	Second-year students: 3%
Third-year students: N/A	

LIBRARY RESOURCES

Total volumes: 434,760
Total seats available for library users: 386

INFORMATION TECHNOLOGY

Number of wired network connections available to students: 223 total (in the law library, excluding computer labs: 110; in classrooms: 0; in computer labs: 48; elsewhere in the law school: 65)
Law school doesn't have a wireless network.
Students are not required to own a computer.

EMPLOYMENT AND SALARIES

Proportion of 2006 graduates employed at graduation: N/A
Employed 9 months later, as of February 15, 2007: 92%

Salaries in the private sector (law firms, business, industry): **$65,000–$83,000** (25th-75th percentile)
Median salary in the private sector: **$70,000**
Percentage in the private sector who reported salary information: **49%**
Median salary in public service (government, judicial clerkships, academic posts, non-profits): **$59,000**

Percentage of 2006 graduates in:

Law firms: 49%	Government: 9%
Bus./industry: 30%	Judicial clerkship: 1%
Public interest: 8%	Unknown: 0%
Academia: 2%	

2006 graduates employed in-state: 90%
2006 graduates employed in foreign countries: 3%
Number of states where graduates are employed: 12
Percentage of 2006 graduates working in: New England: 0%, Middle Atlantic: 1%, East North Central: N/A, West North Central: N/A, South Atlantic: 2%, East South Central: N/A, West South Central: 1%, Mountain: 1%, Pacific: 92%, Unknown: 0%

BAR PASSAGE RATES

Based on 2006 graduates taking Summer 2006 or Winter 2007 exams. Most of the school's first-time test takers took the bar in California.

56%
School's bar passage rate for first-time test takers

65%
Statewide bar passage rate for first-time test takers

Widener University

■ PO Box 7474, Wilmington, DE, 19803-0474
■ http://www.law.widener.edu
■ Private
■ Year founded: 1971
■ 2007-2008 tuition: full-time: $30,870; part-time: $23,130
■ Enrollment 2007-08 academic year: full-time: 879; part-time: 497
■ U.S. News 2009 law specialty ranking: healthcare law: 9

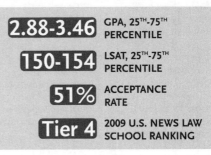

2.88-3.46 GPA, 25TH-75TH PERCENTILE

150-154 LSAT, 25TH-75TH PERCENTILE

51% ACCEPTANCE RATE

Tier 4 2009 U.S. NEWS LAW SCHOOL RANKING

ADMISSIONS

Admissions phone number: (302) 477-2162
Admissions email address:
   law.admissions@law.widener.edu
Application website: http://www.law.widener.edu
Application deadline for Fall 2009 admission: 05/15

Admissions statistics:

Number of applicants for Fall 2007: 2,471
Number of acceptances: 1,259
Number enrolled: 367
Acceptance rate: 51%
GPA, 25th-75th percentile, entering class Fall 2007: 2.88-3.46
LSAT, 25th-75th percentile, entering class Fall 2007: 150-154

Part-time program:

Number of applicants for Fall 2007: 616
Number of acceptances: 315
Number enrolled: 168
Acceptance rate: 51%
GPA, 25th-75th percentile, entering class Fall 2007: 2.84-3.43
LSAT, 25th-75th percentile, entering class Fall 2007: 149-153

FINANCIAL AID

Financial aid phone number: (302) 477-2272
Financial aid application deadline: 04/01
Tuition 2007-2008 academic year: full-time: $30,870; part-time: $23,130
Room and board: $8,930; books: $1,200; miscellaneous expenses: $5,185
Total of room/board/books/miscellaneous expenses: $15,315
University offers graduate student housing for which law students are eligible.

Financial aid profile

Percent of students that received grants for the 2006-2007

academic year: full-time: 32%; part-time 21%
Median grant amount: full-time: $7,170; part-time: $2,875
The average law-school debt of those in the Class of 2007 who borrowed: $87,629. Proportion who borrowed: 82%

ACADEMIC PROGRAMS

Calendar: **semester**
Joint degrees awarded: **J.D./Psy.D; J.D./M.B.A.; J.D./M.S.L.S.; J.D./M.M.P.; J.D/M.P.H.**
Typical first-year section size: Full-time: **62**; Part-time: **46**
Is there typically a "small section" of the first year class, other than Legal Writing, taught by full-time faculty?: Full-time: **yes**; Part-time: **no**
Number of course titles, beyond the first year curriculum, offered last year: **216**
Percentages of upper division course sections, excluding seminars, with an enrollment of:
   Under 25: **75%**   25 to 49: **16%**
   50 to 74: **7%**   75 to 99: **2%**
   100+: **0%**
Areas of specialization: appellate advocacy, clinical training, dispute resolution, environmental law, healthcare law, intellectual property law, international law, tax law, trial advocacy

Fall 2007 faculty profile

Total teaching faculty: **145**. Full-time: **52%**; **57%** men, **43%** women, **9%** minorities. Part-time: **48%**; **67%** men, **33%** women, **4%** minorities
Student-to-faculty ratio: **13.7**

SPECIAL PROGRAMS *(as provided by law school):*

Clinics: environmental, criminal, three civil clinics, veterans assistance. Extensive pro bono opportunities. Judicial externships with state/federal courts in DE, PA, NJ, MD, VA, and DC. Specialized institutes offer Certificates in Health Law; Corporate Law; Trial Advocacy; Law and Government. LL.M., M.L., and S.J.D. in Health Law. Summer-abroad programs: Sydney, Nairobi, Geneva, Venice.

STUDENT BODY

Fall 2007 full-time enrollment: 879

Men: 57%	Women: 43%
African-American: 3.2%	American Indian: 0.3%
Asian-American: 6.1%	Mexican-American: 0.0%
Puerto Rican: 0.5%	Other Hisp-Amer: 1.9%
White: 70.9%	International: 0.6%
Unknown: 16.5%	

Fall 2007 part-time enrollment: 497

Men: 55%	Women: 45%
African-American: 6.8%	American Indian: 0.8%
Asian-American: 5.4%	Mexican-American: 0.0%
Puerto Rican: 0.4%	Other Hisp-Amer: 1.6%
White: 69.2%	International: 0.4%
Unknown: 15.3%	

Attrition rates for 2006-2007 full-time students
Percent of students discontinuing law school:

Men: 7%	Women: 5%
First-year students: 16%	Second-year students: 1%
Third-year students: 0%	

LIBRARY RESOURCES

Total volumes: 617,670
Total seats available for library users: 759

INFORMATION TECHNOLOGY

Number of wired network connections available to students: 85 total (in the law library, excluding computer labs: 60; in classrooms: 25; in computer labs: 0; elsewhere in the law school: 0)
Law school has a wireless network.
Students are not required to own a computer.

EMPLOYMENT AND SALARIES

Proportion of 2006 graduates employed at graduation: 53%
Employed 9 months later, as of February 15, 2007: 83%

Salaries in the private sector (law firms, business, industry): $50,000–$68,600 (25th-75th percentile)
Median salary in the private sector: $60,000
Percentage in the private sector who reported salary information: 36%
Median salary in public service (government, judicial clerkships, academic posts, non-profits): $38,750

Percentage of 2006 graduates in:

Law firms: 38%	Government: 16%
Bus./industry: 22%	Judicial clerkship: 19%
Public interest: 3%	Unknown: 1%
Academia: 1%	

2006 graduates employed in-state: 14%
2006 graduates employed in foreign countries: 0%
Number of states where graduates are employed: 19
Percentage of 2006 graduates working in: New England: 1%, Middle Atlantic: 75%, East North Central: 0%, West North Central: 0%, South Atlantic: 22%, East South Central: 0%, West South Central: 1%, Mountain: 1%, Pacific: 0%, Unknown: 0%

BAR PASSAGE RATES

Based on 2006 graduates taking Summer 2006 or Winter 2007 exams. Most of the school's first-time test takers took the bar in Pennsylvania.

77%
School's bar passage rate for first-time test takers

83%
Statewide bar passage rate for first-time test takers

Willamette University (Collins)

■ 245 Winter Street SE, Salem, OR, 97301
■ http://www.willamette.edu/wucl
■ Private
■ Year founded: 1883
■ 2007-2008 tuition: full-time: $27,495; part-time: N/A
■ Enrollment 2007-08 academic year: full-time: 395
■ U.S. News 2009 law specialty ranking: N/A

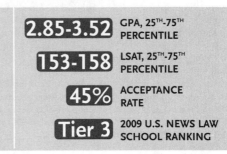

2.85-3.52 GPA, 25TH-75TH PERCENTILE

153-158 LSAT, 25TH-75TH PERCENTILE

45% ACCEPTANCE RATE

Tier 3 2009 U.S. NEWS LAW SCHOOL RANKING

ADMISSIONS

Admissions phone number: **(503) 370-6282**
Admissions email address: **law-admission@willamette.edu**
Application website:
   **http://www.willamette.edu/wucl/admission/
   information/process.htm**
Application deadline for Fall 2009 admission: **04/01**

Admissions statistics:
Number of applicants for Fall 2007: **1,218**
Number of acceptances: **548**
Number enrolled: **158**
Acceptance rate: **45%**
GPA, 25th-75th percentile, entering class Fall 2007: **2.85-3.52**
LSAT, 25th-75th percentile, entering class Fall 2007: **153-158**

FINANCIAL AID

Financial aid phone number: **(503) 370-6273**
Financial aid application deadline: **02/01**
Tuition 2007-2008 academic year: full-time: **$27,495**; part-time: **N/A**
Room and board: **$15,986**; books: **$0**; miscellaneous expenses: **$0**
Total of room/board/books/miscellaneous expenses: **$15,986**
University offers graduate student housing for which law students are eligible.

Financial aid profile
Percent of students that received grants for the 2006-2007 academic year: full-time: **54%**
Median grant amount: full-time: **$12,000**
The average law-school debt of those in the Class of 2007 who borrowed: **$90,196**. Proportion who borrowed: **95%**

ACADEMIC PROGRAMS

Calendar: **semester**
Joint degrees awarded: **J.D./M.B.A.**

Typical first-year section size: Full-time: **79**
Is there typically a "small section" of the first year class, other than Legal Writing, taught by full-time faculty?: Full-time: **yes**
Number of course titles, beyond the first year curriculum, offered last year: **102**
Percentages of upper division course sections, excluding seminars, with an enrollment of:
   Under 25: **62%**   25 to 49: **20%**
   50 to 74: **15%**   75 to 99: **2%**
   100+: **0%**
Areas of specialization: appellate advocacy, clinical training, dispute resolution, environmental law, healthcare law, intellectual property law, international law, tax law, trial advocacy

Fall 2007 faculty profile
Total teaching faculty: **67**. Full-time: **70%**; **70%** men, **30%** women, **13%** minorities. Part-time: **30%**; **75%** men, **25%** women, **5%** minorities
Student-to-faculty ratio: **14.1**

SPECIAL PROGRAMS *(as provided by law school):*

The law school offers Certificates in Business Law; International and Comparative Law; Sustainability; Dispute Resolution; and Law and Government. Students may also enroll in a joint-degree program that offers an M.B.A. in addition to the J.D. The law school offers programs in foreign study enabling students to study in China, Ecuador, and Germany and has an LL.M. program in Transnational Law.

STUDENT BODY

Fall 2007 full-time enrollment: 395
Men: **54%**   Women: **46%**
African-American: **1.5%**   American Indian: **1.0%**
Asian-American: **7.1%**   Mexican-American: **1.3%**
Puerto Rican: **0.3%**   Other Hisp-Amer: **1.8%**
White: **77.0%**   International: **0.0%**
Unknown: **10.1%**

Attrition rates for 2006-2007 full-time students
Percent of students discontinuing law school:
Men: **10%**   Women: **14%**
First-year students: **23%** Second-year students: **11%**
Third-year students: **N/A**

LIBRARY RESOURCES
Total volumes: **294,612**
Total seats available for library users: **492**

INFORMATION TECHNOLOGY
Number of wired network connections available to students: **104** total (in the law library, excluding computer labs: **80**; in classrooms: **13**; in computer labs: **9**; elsewhere in the law school: **2**)
Law school has a wireless network.
Students are not required to own a computer.

EMPLOYMENT AND SALARIES
Proportion of 2006 graduates employed at graduation: **N/A**
Employed 9 months later, as of February 15, 2007: **88%**
Salaries in the private sector (law firms, business, industry): **$43,200–$60,000** (25th-75th percentile)
Median salary in the private sector: **$50,000**
Percentage in the private sector who reported salary information: **70%**
Median salary in public service (government, judicial clerkships, academic posts, non-profits): **$40,000**

Percentage of 2006 graduates in:
Law firms: **56%**   Government: **13%**
Bus./industry: **11%**   Judicial clerkship: **10%**
Public interest: **7%**   Unknown: **3%**
Academia: **0%**

2006 graduates employed in-state: **62%**
2006 graduates employed in foreign countries: **1%**
Number of states where graduates are employed: **14**
Percentage of 2006 graduates working in: New England: **0%**, Middle Atlantic: **1%**, East North Central: **1%**, West North Central: **1%**, South Atlantic: **3%**, East South Central: **1%**, West South Central: **1%**, Mountain: **9%**, Pacific: **82%**, Unknown: **0%**

BAR PASSAGE RATES
Based on 2006 graduates taking Summer 2006 or Winter 2007 exams. Most of the school's first-time test takers took the bar in Oregon.

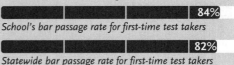

84%
School's bar passage rate for first-time test takers

82%
Statewide bar passage rate for first-time test takers

William Mitchell College of Law

- 875 Summit Avenue, St. Paul, MN, 55105-3076
- http://www.wmitchell.edu
- Private
- Year founded: 1900
- 2007-2008 tuition: full-time: $29,020; part-time: $21,002
- Enrollment 2007-08 academic year: full-time: 233; part-time: 103
- U.S. News 2009 law specialty ranking: clinical training: 23

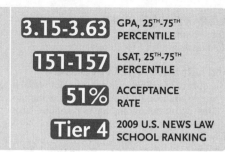

3.15-3.63 GPA, 25TH-75TH PERCENTILE

151-157 LSAT, 25TH-75TH PERCENTILE

51% ACCEPTANCE RATE

Tier 4 2009 U.S. NEWS LAW SCHOOL RANKING

ADMISSIONS

Admissions phone number: **(651) 290-6476**
Admissions email address: **admissions@wmitchell.edu**
Application website: **http://www.wmitchell.edu/ admissions/apply/online.html**
Application deadline for Fall 2009 admission: **05/01**

Admissions statistics:

Number of applicants for Fall 2007: **1,307**
Number of acceptances: **671**
Number enrolled: **233**
Acceptance rate: **51%**
GPA, 25th-75th percentile, entering class Fall 2007: **3.15-3.63**
LSAT, 25th-75th percentile, entering class Fall 2007: **151-157**

Part-time program:

Number of applicants for Fall 2007: **446**
Number of acceptances: **175**
Number enrolled: **103**
Acceptance rate: **39%**
GPA, 25th-75th percentile, entering class Fall 2007: **2.90-3.46**
LSAT, 25th-75th percentile, entering class Fall 2007: **147-154**

FINANCIAL AID

Financial aid phone number: **(651) 290-6403**
Financial aid application deadline: **03/15**
Tuition 2007-2008 academic year: full-time: **$29,020**; part-time: **$21,002**
Room and board: **$13,550**; books: **$1,550**; miscellaneous expenses: **$800**
Total of room/board/books/miscellaneous expenses: **$15,900**
University does not offer graduate student housing for which law students are eligible.

Financial aid profile

Percent of students that received grants for the 2006-2007 academic year: full-time: **43%**; part-time **13%**

Median grant amount: full-time: **$5,000**; part-time: **$3,500**
The average law-school debt of those in the Class of 2007 who borrowed: **$74,555**. Proportion who borrowed: **92%**

ACADEMIC PROGRAMS

Calendar: **semester**
Joint degrees awarded: **J.D./M.S. Women's Studies; J.D./M.A. Public Administration; J.D./M.S. Community Health**
Typical first-year section size: Full-time: **80**; Part-time: **50**
Is there typically a "small section" of the first year class, other than Legal Writing, taught by full-time faculty?: Full-time: **no**; Part-time: **no**
Number of course titles, beyond the first year curriculum, offered last year: **127**
Percentages of upper division course sections, excluding seminars, with an enrollment of:

Under 25: **51%**	25 to 49: **30%**
50 to 74: **15%**	75 to 99: **5%**
100+: **0%**	

Areas of specialization: appellate advocacy, clinical training, dispute resolution, environmental law, healthcare law, intellectual property law, international law, tax law, trial advocacy

Fall 2007 faculty profile

Total teaching faculty: **227**. Full-time: **12%**; **56%** men, **44%** women, **11%** minorities. Part-time: **88%**; **61%** men, **40%** women, **23%** minorities
Student-to-faculty ratio: **22.5**

SPECIAL PROGRAMS *(as provided by law school):*

William Mitchell's distinctive educational approach develops practical wisdom in students by simultaneously embracing scholarship and practice. It has over 100 intellectually rigorous courses, top-ranked clinical and legal writing programs, and externships that put students to work as clerks or researchers with judges or advocacy organizations. Students can choose from nine study-abroad programs.

STUDENT BODY

Fall 2007 full-time enrollment: 233

Men: 54%	Women: 46%
African-American: 0.9%	American Indian: 0.4%
Asian-American: 2.1%	Mexican-American: 0.4%
Puerto Rican: 0.0%	Other Hisp-Amer: 0.4%
White: 70.4%	International: 0.9%
Unknown: 24.5%	

Fall 2007 part-time enrollment: 103

Men: 48%	Women: 52%
African-American: 7.8%	American Indian: 1.9%
Asian-American: 4.9%	Mexican-American: 0.0%
Puerto Rican: 0.0%	Other Hisp-Amer: 0.0%
White: 49.5%	International: 0.0%
Unknown: 35.9%	

Attrition rates for 2006-2007 full-time students
Percent of students discontinuing law school:

Men: 1%	Women: 1%
First-year students: 2%	Second-year students: 0%
Third-year students: 0%	

LIBRARY RESOURCES

Total volumes: 345,527
Total seats available for library users: 671

INFORMATION TECHNOLOGY

Number of wired network connections available to students: 240 total (in the law library, excluding computer labs: 20; in classrooms: 140; in computer labs: 60; elsewhere in the law school: 20)
Law school has a wireless network.
Students are required to own a computer.

EMPLOYMENT AND SALARIES

Proportion of 2006 graduates employed at graduation: N/A
Employed 9 months later, as of February 15, 2007: 90%

Salaries in the private sector (law firms, business, industry): $50,000–$100,000 (25th-75th percentile)
Median salary in the private sector: $63,611
Percentage in the private sector who reported salary information: 75%
Median salary in public service (government, judicial clerkships, academic posts, non-profits): $51,000

Percentage of 2006 graduates in:

Law firms: 45%	Government: 10%
Bus./industry: 25%	Judicial clerkship: 11%
Public interest: 5%	Unknown: 3%
Academia: 1%	

2006 graduates employed in-state: 86%
2006 graduates employed in foreign countries: 0%
Number of states where graduates are employed: 18
Percentage of 2006 graduates working in: New England: 0%, Middle Atlantic: 1%, East North Central: 4%, West North Central: 88%, South Atlantic: 2%, East South Central: 0%, West South Central: 1%, Mountain: 2%, Pacific: 1%, Unknown: 1%

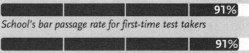

BAR PASSAGE RATES

Based on 2006 graduates taking Summer 2006 or Winter 2007 exams. Most of the school's first-time test takers took the bar in Minnesota.

91%
School's bar passage rate for first-time test takers

91%
Statewide bar passage rate for first-time test takers

Yale University

■ PO Box 208215, New Haven, CT, 06520-8215
■ http://www.law.yale.edu
■ Private
■ Year founded: 1824
■ 2007-2008 tuition: full-time: $43,750; part-time: $22,750
■ Enrollment 2007-08 academic year: full-time: 586; part-time: 1
■ U.S. News 2009 law specialty ranking: clinical training: 7, intellectual property law: 26, international law: 5, tax law: 10

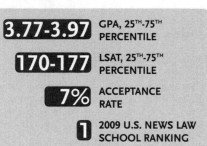

3.77-3.97 GPA, 25TH-75TH PERCENTILE

170-177 LSAT, 25TH-75TH PERCENTILE

7% ACCEPTANCE RATE

1 2009 U.S. NEWS LAW SCHOOL RANKING

ADMISSIONS

Admissions phone number: **(203) 432-4995**
Admissions email address: **admissions.law@yale.edu**
Application website: **http://www.law.yale.edu/admissions**
Application deadline for Fall 2009 admission: **02/16**

Admissions statistics:

Number of applicants for Fall 2007: **3,312**
Number of acceptances: **241**
Number enrolled: **189**
Acceptance rate: **7%**
GPA, 25th-75th percentile, entering class Fall 2007: **3.77-3.97**
LSAT, 25th-75th percentile, entering class Fall 2007: **170-177**

FINANCIAL AID

Financial aid phone number: **(203) 432-1688**
Financial aid application deadline: **04/03**
Tuition 2007-2008 academic year: full-time: **$43,750**; part-time: **$22,750**
Room and board: **$15,100**; books: **$1,000**; miscellaneous expenses: **N/A**
Total of room/board/books/miscellaneous expenses: **$16,100**
University offers graduate student housing for which law students are eligible.

Financial aid profile

Percent of students that received grants for the 2006-2007 academic year: full-time: **50%**
Median grant amount: full-time: **$19,850**
The average law-school debt of those in the Class of 2007 who borrowed: **$85,789**. Proportion who borrowed: **93%**

ACADEMIC PROGRAMS

Calendar: **semester**
Joint degrees awarded: **J.D./Ph.D. Philosophy; J.D./Ph.D. History; J.D./Ph.D. American Studies; J.D./Ph.D. Political Science; J.D./M.E.S. Forestry; J.D./M.A. Arts & Sciences; J.D./M.D.; J.D./M.A. Statistics; J.D./Ph.D.**
Sociology; J.D./M.A. International Relations; J.D./M.A.R. Ethics; J.D./Ph.D. Economics; J.D./M.F.S. Forestry; J.D./M.B.A.; J.D./M.A. East Asian Studies; J.D./M.P.H.; J.D./M.E.M. Forestry; J.D./M.P.P.; J.D./M.A. Economics; J.D./Ph.D. German Language/Literature; J.D./Ph.D. Anthropology; J.D./Ph.D. English; J.D./M.A. Political Science; J.D./M.P.A.
Typical first-year section size: Full-time: **60**
Is there typically a "small section" of the first year class, other than Legal Writing, taught by full-time faculty?: Full-time: **yes**
Number of course titles, beyond the first year curriculum, offered last year: **145**
Percentages of upper division course sections, excluding seminars, with an enrollment of:

Under 25: **50%**	25 to 49: **32%**
50 to 74: **6%**	75 to 99: **7%**
100+: **5%**	

Areas of specialization: appellate advocacy, clinical training, dispute resolution, environmental law, healthcare law, intellectual property law, international law, tax law, trial advocacy

Fall 2007 faculty profile

Total teaching faculty: **142**. Full-time: **53%**; **80%** men, **20%** women, **12%** minorities. Part-time: **47%**; **70%** men, **30%** women, **7%** minorities
Student-to-faculty ratio: **7.4**

SPECIAL PROGRAMS *(as provided by law school):*

Please see the school's bulletin and/or website for information.

STUDENT BODY

Fall 2007 full-time enrollment: 586

Men: **52%**	Women: **48%**
African-American: **7.7%**	American Indian: **0.3%**
Asian-American: **13.3%**	Mexican-American: **1.4%**
Puerto Rican: **0.9%**	Other Hisp-Amer: **4.8%**
White: **61.6%**	International: **3.9%**
Unknown: **6.1%**	

Fall 2007 part-time enrollment: 1

Men: N/A   Women: 100%
African-American: 0.0%   American Indian: 0.0%
Asian-American: 0.0%   Mexican-American: 100.0%
Puerto Rican: 0.0%   Other Hisp-Amer: 0.0%
White: 0.0%   International: 0.0%
Unknown: 0.0%

Attrition rates for 2006-2007 full-time students
Percent of students discontinuing law school:
Men: 1%   Women: 1%
First-year students: 2%   Second-year students: 1%
Third-year students: 1%

LIBRARY RESOURCES
Total volumes: 1,180,379
Total seats available for library users: 414

INFORMATION TECHNOLOGY
Number of wired network connections available to students: **1,009** total (in the law library, excluding computer
  labs: 414; in classrooms: 581; in computer labs: 4; elsewhere in the law school: 10)
Law school has a wireless network.
Students are not required to own a computer.

EMPLOYMENT AND SALARIES
Proportion of 2006 graduates employed at graduation:
  96%
Employed 9 months later, as of February 15, 2007: **100%**
Salaries in the private sector (law firms, business, indus-
  try): **$135,000–$145,000** (25th-75th percentile)
Median salary in the private sector: **$145,000**
Percentage in the private sector who reported salary
  information: 88%
Median salary in public service (government, judicial clerk-
  ships, academic posts, non-profits): **$52,737**

Percentage of 2006 graduates in:
Law firms: 43%   Government: 2%
Bus./industry: 4%   Judicial clerkship: 43%
Public interest: 7%   Unknown: 0%
Academia: 3%

2006 graduates employed in-state: 9%
2006 graduates employed in foreign countries: 3%
Number of states where graduates are employed: 29
Percentage of 2006 graduates working in: New England:
  12%, Middle Atlantic: 35%, East North Central: 3%, West
  North Central: 3%, South Atlantic: 20%, East South
  Central: 2%, West South Central: 5%, Mountain: 2%,
  Pacific: 16%, Unknown: 0%

BAR PASSAGE RATES
Based on 2006 graduates taking Summer 2006 or
Winter 2007 exams. Most of the school's first-time test
takers took the bar in New York.

	91%

School's bar passage rate for first-time test takers

	77%

Statewide bar passage rate for first-time test takers

Yeshiva University (Cardozo)

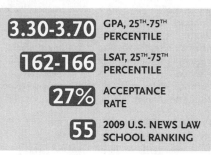

- 55 Fifth Avenue, 10th Floor, New York, NY, 10003
- http://www.cardozo.yu.edu
- Private
- Year founded: 1976
- 2007-2008 tuition: full-time: $39,470; part-time: $39,470
- Enrollment 2007-08 academic year: full-time: 948; part-time: 127
- U.S. News 2009 law specialty ranking: dispute resolution: 8, intellectual property law: 14

3.30-3.70 GPA, 25TH-75TH PERCENTILE

162-166 LSAT, 25TH-75TH PERCENTILE

27% ACCEPTANCE RATE

55 2009 U.S. NEWS LAW SCHOOL RANKING

ADMISSIONS

Admissions phone number: **(212) 790-0274**
Admissions email address: **lawinfo@yu.edu**
Application website:
  http://www.cardozo.yu.edu/admissions/how_to.asp
Application deadline for Fall 2009 admission: **04/01**

Admissions statistics:

Number of applicants for Fall 2007: **4,209**
Number of acceptances: **1,156**
Number enrolled: **245**
Acceptance rate: **27%**
GPA, 25th-75th percentile, entering class Fall 2007: **3.30-3.70**
LSAT, 25th-75th percentile, entering class Fall 2007: **162-166**

Part-time program:

Number of applicants for Fall 2007: **606**
Number of acceptances: **192**
Number enrolled: **126**
Acceptance rate: **32%**
GPA, 25th-75th percentile, entering class Fall 2007: **3.32-3.68**
LSAT, 25th-75th percentile, entering class Fall 2007: **157-160**

FINANCIAL AID

Financial aid phone number: **(212) 790-0392**
Financial aid application deadline: **04/15**
Tuition 2007-2008 academic year: full-time: **$39,470**; part-time: **$39,470**
Room and board: **$18,900**; books: **$1,200**; miscellaneous expenses: **$5,580**
Total of room/board/books/miscellaneous expenses: **$25,680**
University does not offer graduate student housing for which law students are eligible.

Financial aid profile

Percent of students that received grants for the 2006-2007 academic year: full-time: **60%**; part-time **18%**
Median grant amount: full-time: **$12,500**; part-time: **$6,000**
The average law-school debt of those in the Class of 2007 who borrowed: **$100,298**. Proportion who borrowed: **81%**

ACADEMIC PROGRAMS

Calendar: **semester**
Joint degrees awarded: **J.D./M.S.W.**
Typical first-year section size: Full-time: **49**
Is there typically a "small section" of the first year class, other than Legal Writing, taught by full-time faculty?:
  Full-time: **no**; Part-time: **no**
Number of course titles, beyond the first year curriculum, offered last year: **137**
Percentages of upper division course sections, excluding seminars, with an enrollment of:

Under 25: **40%**	25 to 49: **28%**
50 to 74: **13%**	75 to 99: **10%**
100+: **9%**	

Areas of specialization: appellate advocacy, clinical training, dispute resolution, environmental law, healthcare law, intellectual property law, international law, tax law, trial advocacy

Fall 2007 faculty profile

Total teaching faculty: **126**. Full-time: **41%**; **63%** men, **37%** women, **10%** minorities. Part-time: **59%**; **72%** men, **28%** women, **3%** minorities
Student-to-faculty ratio: **16.2**

SPECIAL PROGRAMS (as provided by law school):

Cardozo is especially known for its intellectual property and dispute resolution programs and for the Innocence Project, founded by Prof. Barry Scheck and Peter Neufeld. Cardozo's clinics are entirely client based. Additional programs range from human-rights studies to constitutional democracy and corporate governance.

STUDENT BODY

Fall 2007 full-time enrollment: 948

Men: 52%	Women: 48%
African-American: 3.6%	American Indian: 0.3%
Asian-American: 9.3%	Mexican-American: 1.1%
Puerto Rican: 1.5%	Other Hisp-Amer: 3.5%
White: 37.8%	International: 3.0%
Unknown: 40.1%	

Fall 2007 part-time enrollment: 127

Men: 46%	Women: 54%
African-American: 2.4%	American Indian: 0.0%
Asian-American: 11.8%	Mexican-American: 1.6%
Puerto Rican: 0.0%	Other Hisp-Amer: 6.3%
White: 37.0%	International: 0.8%
Unknown: 40.2%	

Attrition rates for 2006-2007 full-time students
Percent of students discontinuing law school:

Men: 3%	Women: 4%
First-year students: 8%	Second-year students: 2%
Third-year students: 0%	

LIBRARY RESOURCES

Total volumes: 539,391
Total seats available for library users: 483

INFORMATION TECHNOLOGY

Number of wired network connections available to students: 104 total (in the law library, excluding computer labs: 104; in classrooms: 0; in computer labs: 0; elsewhere in the law school: 0)
Law school has a wireless network.
Students are not required to own a computer.

EMPLOYMENT AND SALARIES

Proportion of 2006 graduates employed at graduation: 75%
Employed 9 months later, as of February 15, 2007: 95%

Salaries in the private sector (law firms, business, industry): $65,000–$145,000 (25th-75th percentile)
Median salary in the private sector: $90,000
Percentage in the private sector who reported salary information: 73%
Median salary in public service (government, judicial clerkships, academic posts, non-profits): $50,000

Percentage of 2006 graduates in:

Law firms: 60%	Government: 14%
Bus./industry: 17%	Judicial clerkship: 3%
Public interest: 5%	Unknown: 0%
Academia: 1%	

2006 graduates employed in-state: 82%
2006 graduates employed in foreign countries: 1%
Number of states where graduates are employed: 21
Percentage of 2006 graduates working in: New England: 1%, Middle Atlantic: 89%, East North Central: 1%, West North Central: 1%, South Atlantic: 3%, East South Central: 0%, West South Central: 1%, Mountain: 2%, Pacific: 3%, Unknown: 0%

BAR PASSAGE RATES

Based on 2006 graduates taking Summer 2006 or Winter 2007 exams. Most of the school's first-time test takers took the bar in New York.

89%
School's bar passage rate for first-time test takers

77%
Statewide bar passage rate for first-time test takers

Non-responding Schools

CATHOLIC UNIVERSITY
- 2250 Avenida Las Americas, Suite 584, Ponce, PR, 00717-0777
- http://www.pucpr.edu
- Private
- Admissions phone number: (787) 841-2000
- Admissions email address: admisiones@pucpr.edu
- 2009 U.S.News Law School Ranking: Unranked

INTER-AMERICAN UNIVERSITY
- PO Box 70351, San Juan, PR, 00936-8351
- http://www.metro.inter.edu
- Private
- Admissions phone number: (787) 765-1270
- Admissions email address: edmendez@inter.edu
- 2009 U.S.News Law School Ranking: Unranked

UNIVERSITY OF PUERTO RICO
- PO Box 23303 Estacion Universidad, Rio Piedras, PR, 00931-3302
- http://www.upr.edu
- Public
- Admissions phone number: (787) 764-0000
- Admissions email address: admisiones@upr.edu
- 2009 U.S.News Law School Ranking: Unranked

LIBERTY UNIVERSITY
- 1971 University Boulevard, Lynchburg, VA, 24502
- http://law.liberty.edu
- Private
- Admissions phone number: (434) 592-5300
- Admissions email address: law@liberty.edu
- 2009 U.S.News Law School Ranking: Unranked

Alphabetical Index of Schools

Index of Schools by State

Kansas
University of Kansas, 384
Washburn University, 478

Kentucky
Northern Kentucky University (Chase), 254
University of Kentucky, 386
University of Louisville (Brandeis), 390

Louisiana
Louisiana State University–Baton Rouge, 226
Loyola University New Orleans, 232
Southern University, 298
Tulane University, 332

Massachusetts
Boston College, 138
Boston University, 140
Harvard University, 210
New England School of Law, 242
Northeastern University, 250
Suffolk University, 314
Western New England College, 488

Maryland
University of Baltimore, 346
University of Maryland, 394

Maine
University of Maine, 392

Michigan
Ave Maria School of Law, 132
Michigan State University, 238
Thomas M. Cooley Law School, 328
University of Detroit Mercy, 368
University of Michigan–Ann Arbor, 400
Wayne State University, 484

Minnesota
Hamline University, 208
University of Minnesota–Twin Cities, 402
University of St. Thomas, 444
William Mitchell College of Law, 498

Missouri
St. Louis University, 304
University of Missouri–Columbia, 406
University of Missouri–Kansas City, 408
Washington University in St. Louis, 482

Mississippi
Mississippi College, 240
University of Mississippi, 404

Montana
University of Montana, 410

North Carolina
Campbell University (Wiggins), 148
Duke University, 176
North Carolina Central University, 248
University of North Carolina–Chapel Hill, 418
Wake Forest University, 476

North Dakota
University of North Dakota, 420

Nebraska
Creighton University, 168
University of Nebraska–Lincoln, 412

New Hampshire
Franklin Pierce Law Center, 194

New Jersey
Rutgers State University–Camden, 280
Rutgers State University–Newark, 282
Seton Hall University, 290

New Mexico
University of New Mexico, 416

Nevada
University of Law Vegas (Boyd), 414

New York
Albany Law School–Union University, 122
Brooklyn Law School, 144
Columbia University, 164
Cornell University, 166
CUNY–Queens College, 170
Fordham University, 192
Hofstra University, 212
New York Law School, 244
New York University, 246
Pace University, 266
St. John's University, 302
Syracuse University, 316
Touro College (Fuchsberg), 330
University at Buffalo–SUNY, 334
Yeshiva University (Cardozo), 502

Ohio
Capital University, 150
Case Western Reserve University, 152
Cleveland State University (Marshall), 160
Ohio Northern University (Pettit), 260
Ohio State University (Moritz), 262

University of Akron, 336
University of Cincinnati, 358
University of Dayton, 364
University of Toledo, 454

Oklahoma
Oklahoma City University, 264
University of Oklahoma, 424
University of Tulsa, 456

Oregon
Lewis and Clark College (Northwestern), 224
University of Oregon, 426
Willamette University (Collins), 496

Pennsylvania
Duquesne University, 178
Pennsylvania State University (Dickinson), 268
Temple University (Beasley), 318
University of Pennsylvania, 428
University of Pittsburgh, 430
Villanova University, 474

Rhode Island
Roger Williams University, 278

South Carolina
Charleston School of Law, 158
University of South Carolina, 438

South Dakota
University of South Dakota, 440

Tennessee
University of Memphis (Humphreys), 396
University of Tennessee–Knoxville, 446
Vanderbilt University, 470

Texas
Baylor University, 136
South Texas College of Law, 292
Southern Methodist University, 296
St. Mary's University, 306
Texas Southern University (Marshall), 320
Texas Tech University, 322
Texas Wesleyan University, 324
University of Houston, 376
University of Texas–Austin, 448

Utah
Brigham Young University (Clark), 142
University of Utah (Quinney), 458

Virginia
Appalachian School of Law, 126
College of William and Mary, 162
George Mason University, 196
Regent University, 276
University of Richmond (Williams), 432
University of Virginia, 460
Washington and Lee University, 480

Vermont
Vermont Law School, 472

Washington
Gonzaga University, 206
Seattle University, 288
University of Washington, 462

Wisconsin
Marquette University, 234
University of Wisconsin–Madison, 464

West Virginia
West Virginia University, 486

Wyoming
University of Wyoming, 466

About the Authors & Editors

Founded in 1933, Washington, D.C.-based *U.S.News & World Report* delivers a unique brand of weekly magazine journalism to its 12.2 million readers. In 1983, *U.S. News* began its exclusive annual rankings of American colleges and universities. The *U.S. News* education franchise is second to none, with its annual college and graduate school rankings among the most eagerly anticipated magazine issues in the country.

Anne McGrath, the book's lead writer, is an assistant managing editor at *U.S.News & World Report*. She has written about higher education and previously was managing editor of "America's Best Colleges" and "America's Best Graduate Schools," the two *U.S. News* annual publications featuring rankings of the country's colleges and universities.

Robert Morse is the director of data research at *U.S.News & World Report*. He is in charge of the research, data collection, methodologies, and survey design for the annual "America's Best Colleges" rankings and the "America's Best Graduate Schools" rankings.

Brian Kelly is the editor of *U.S.News & World Report*. As the magazine's chief editor, he oversees the weekly magazine, the website, and a series of newsstand books. He is a former editor at the *Washington Post* and the author of three books.

Other writers who contributed chapters or passages to the book are Carolyn Kleiner Butler, Kristin Davis, Anna Mulrine, Dan Gilgoff, Betsy Streisand, Jill Rachlin Marbaix, and Samantha Stainburn. The work involved in producing the directory and *U.S. News* Insider's Index was handled by deputy director of data research Sam Flanigan.

Notes

Notes

Notes

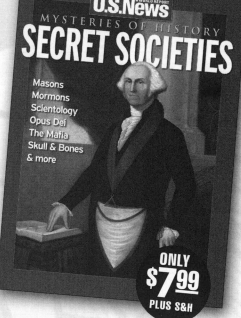